Reading into Writing

A Rhetoric, Reader, and Handbook

Reading into Writing

A Rhetoric, Reader, and Handbook

Eric Gould

University of Denver

Houghton Mifflin Company   Boston

Dallas   Geneva, Ill.   Hopewell, N.J.
Palo Alto   London

Acknowledgments

ALEXANDER, SHANA   Excerpt from the book *Talking Woman* by Shana Alexander. Copyright © 1976 by Shana Alexander. Reprinted by permission of Delacorte Press.

BALDWIN, JAMES   From James Baldwin, *Notes of a Native Son*. Copyright © 1955 by James Baldwin. Reprinted by permission of Beacon Press.

BARTHELME, DONALD   "The King of Jazz" from *Great Days* by Donald Barthelme. Copyright © 1977, 1979 by Donald Barthelme. "The King of Jazz" originally appeared in *The New Yorker*. Reprinted by permission of Farrar, Straus and Giroux, Inc.

BASHO   "The Stillness" by Basho from *An Introduction to Haiku* translated by Harold G. Henderson. Copyright © 1958 by Harold C. Henderson. Reprinted by permission of Doubleday & Company, Inc.

BENCHLEY, ROBERT   "Why I Am Pale" (pp. 319–321) by Robert C. Benchley in *The Benchley Roundup* compiled by Nathaniel Benchley. Copyright © 1933 by Robert C. Benchley. Reprinted by permission of Harper & Row, Publishers, Inc.

BETTELHEIM, BRUNO   "The Art of Moving Pictures" copyright © 1981 by *Harper's Magazine*. All rights reserved. Reprinted from the October 1981 issue by special permission. "The Ignored Lesson of Anne Frank" reprinted by permission of the author from the November 1960 issue of *Harper's Magazine*. Copyright © 1960 by Bruno Bettelheim.

BISHOP, ELIZABETH   "The Fish" from *Elizabeth Bishop: The Complete Poems*. Copyright © 1940, 1969 by Elizabeth Bishop. Reprinted by permission of Farrar, Straus and Giroux, Inc.

BOULDING, KENNETH   "After Civilization, What?" *Bulletin of the Atomic Scientists*, October 1962 reprinted by permission of the *Bulletin of the Atomic Scientists*, a magazine of science and public affairs. Copyright © 1962 by the Educational Foundation for Nuclear Science, Chicago, Ill. 60637

BRANDT, ANTHONY   "Rite of Passage" from the February 1981 issue of the *Atlantic Monthly* and extract from *Reality Police* (New York: William Morrow, 1977) reprinted by permission of the author. Copyright © 1981, 1977 by Anthony Brandt.

Acknowledgments are continued on page 675.

Cover art: Jean-Michel Folon, "Ecrire"; by permission of John Locke Studios, Inc.

Printed in the U.S.A.

Library of Congress Catalog Card Number: 82-83171

ISBN: 0-395-32607-9

Contents

3 The Writing Process I: From Subject to Outline 103

Readings 131

4 The Writing Process II: The First Draft 151

Readings 175

Preface

Reading into Writing aims to do what its title suggests: turn reading skills into writing skills. It describes the way reading and writing are unified as aspects of interpretation, of understanding events and explaining them coherently to others. The text works out its aim in a comprehensive way. It is a rhetoric, a reader, and a handbook that covers reading, writing about reading, the writing process in general (in all its stages from choosing a topic, to interpreting it through generating ideas and organizing them, to drafting and revising an essay), sentence and paragraph structure, description, narration, argument, logic, and persuasion. A final chapter on reading and writing about literature can be incorporated into a writing class to encourage more imaginative reading and writing and serve as a bridge to introduction to literature courses. Included in the text, at the ends of chapters, are about 45 lively essays and long extracts, written mainly by major contemporary writers. A number of the essays are especially challenging and significant; many are topical and humorous commentaries. All should provoke good reading, conversation, and writing on important themes. Each chapter contains additional exercises and writing assignments, most with short readings. In addition there are appendices on writing the research paper and manuscript format, a handbook of grammar and usage, and an editing checklist.

The scope of the text may seem broad, but its thesis can be concisely stated as a practical combination of two main ideas: first, that good writing is intimately linked to good reading, and second, that grammar and rhetoric can be carefully integrated in the teaching of reading and writing. The text opens with an explanation of what happens when one reads (taking note of current interpretation theory, but without the critical jargon). It then moves to writing about reading, that is, to interpretive writing. The emphasis, again, is on close reading skills that can be developed directly into writing-as-interpretation. Many people have trouble writing because they have trouble reading and comprehending. Those problems are treated together in this text. Students begin with reading, proceed to writing about their reading, and then adapt those skills to writing papers that stress the link between interpretation, analysis, explanation, and persuasion. All the chapters in the book are concerned with the similar ways in which both readers and writers create meaning.

The other main informing idea of this text is that grammar and rhetoric can be learned together as part of the interpretation process. We bring certain skills in analysis and understanding to reading and writing, but those skills are to a large extent conditioned by the nature of writing itself and by the ways in which writing is absorbed by readers. At the heart of good reading and writing, then, must lie an understanding, however basic, of what words can do: how they convey meaning through the combination of free and bound elements in sentences and paragraphs.

This text, however, is not theoretical and does not merely categorize the principles of grammar and rhetoric. The combination of words in sentences has a grammar and the inventiveness of sentences has a rhetoric, but neither one can exist on its own. Nor does it make much sense to study one without the other or both in theory alone. Grammar inevitably implies rhetoric, and rhetoric implies interpretation, and interpretation demands explanation and expression. The art of effective writing, then, depends on discovering how meaning is conveyed in the interaction of reader and text, and how the conventions of grammatical combination affect this interaction through the art of rhetoric. It is the art of rhetoric that takes basic grammatical structures and turns them into pleasing, efficient, and diversified communication. Again, the prerequisites to learning this art, it cannot be overemphasized, depend on acquiring close reading skills.

So all the chapters on the writing process use methods that parallel the reading process: interpreting ideas in a text is similar to interpreting ideas in essay preparation, developing an interpretation is analogous to developing a thesis in an essay. Careful attention is given to the difficulties of ambiguity and irony, to sentence and paragraph structure that demonstrate rhetorical variety, and to the development of a personal style. The whole interpretation process takes into account the need for finding and creating emphasis, coherence, unity, and significance in reading and writing.

I assume that students will write mainly interpretive and expository/persuasive essays while at college and later in the word of business and the professions. So this text offers a comprehensive invention and writing process that concentrates on the basic explanatory position paper. The chapters devoted to the process are then supplemented by a chapter on narration and description and three chapters that develop a special focus on arguing logically and persuasively. Persuasion is treated first from the point of view of how readers (and listeners) are influenced by discourse, and then how writers can be persuasive themselves using both traditional (deductive and inductive) argument and a knowledge of how to establish credibility and be tactful with an audience. So the interplay between the reader and the writer is sustained throughout this text, and this I believe is essential to making the business of learning to write well a practical and enjoyable enterprise.

Preparation of this manuscript was made especially pleasant by the care and strong support of my wife, Diane, who also made useful suggestions. The following individuals gave the developing manuscript thoughtful readings, for which I am grateful: Kimberly S. Davis, University of California at Berkeley; Kris D. Gutierrez, University of Colorado; John P. Bodnar, Prince George's Community College; and Mary Pamela Besser, University of Louisville. I want to thank Huntley Dent for valuable criticism of the text and good advice about the selection of readings. Joseph Carroll, of Denver University, read all the chapters and suggested a number of changes that I was happy to make. Burton Feldman, also of Denver University, suggested some reading selections with his usual wit and insight. I am indebted to Joyce Tally, who not only typed the manuscript with great care but provided valuable commentary. Lastly, my thanks go to the staff at Houghton Mifflin, who were there every step of the way with the best support any textbook writer could want.

Eric Gould
University of Denver

Reading into Writing

A Rhetoric, Reader, and Handbook

Reading

Reading and Writing

This text deals with reading and writing together in the belief that there is no good writing without good reading. There are several reasons for this:

- *All writing depends on readers.* If you want to be heard and understood as a writer, you write for a reader; you take account of an audience. So if you know something about what reading is like, it is easier for you to know how to write effectively. Writing is a process of bringing experience into understanding for an audience.

- *When you write, you become your own reader.* You go back over your work as you write, rereading in order to develop a continuous thought on a page. There is no writing without revision, but in order to rewrite well, you have to be a close, objective reader of your own work. Writing is a process of bringing experience into understanding for yourself as well as for an audience.

- *Reading and writing both depend on interpretation.* When you say you have interpreted something—and it can be anything that has significance, like a movie or an art work, as well as a text—you can offer an explanation of it. You have reached understanding. Your imagination has been stimulated; you have collected information about the object being interpreted; you have analyzed that information; you have organized your ideas about it; and you have reached an opinion. So reading and writing are both processes of interpretation in that they are ways of *reaching* and *revealing* your understanding. The art of reading, as we shall discuss it, is intent on developing that understanding; the art of writing is intent on expressing your interpretation so that it in turn can be understood.

- *Writing imitates reading.* That is, it imitates the writing you read. You develop a writing style largely from what you read. You imitate sentence and paragraph structures; you learn to use words and phrases that have caught your attention. Writing is not the only source of what you imitate, of course, for you are surrounded by spoken language too. But it is the main source. You not only absorb what a writer has to say, but you enjoy how the writer has said it. There is much to be learned from the styles and techniques of good writing, as we shall see. You will not learn, however, if you are an inefficient reader. Bad habits in reading (which usually result in poor understanding) relate to bad habits in writing, for the way you read has much to do with your sensitivity to the expressiveness of language.

2

Throughout this text, then, you will explore the relationship between reading and writing with two very practical ends in mind: first, to improve your reading and interpretation skills; second, to develop writing skills that are based on a knowledge of what reading does. We'll begin with the basic activity of reading for understanding.

Getting Involved With a Text

Read the following passage from *Huckleberry Finn.*

The sun was up so high when I waked, that I judged it was after eight o'clock. I laid there in the grass and the cool shade, thinking about things and feeling rested and ruther comfortable and satisfied. I could see the sun out at one or two holes, but mostly it was big trees all about, and gloomy in there amongst them. There was freckled places on the ground where the light sifted down through the leaves, and the freckled places swapped about a little, showing there was a little breeze up there. A couple of squirrels set on a limb and jabbered at me very friendly.

I was powerful lazy and comfortable—didn't want to get up and cook breakfast. Well, I was dozing off again, when I thinks I hears a deep sound of "boom!" away up the river. I rouses up and rests on my elbow and listens; pretty soon I hears it again. I hopped up and went and looked out at a hole in the leaves, and I see a bunch of smoke laying on the water a long ways up—about abreast the ferry. And there was the ferry-boat full of people, floating along down. I knowed what was the matter, now. "Boom!" I see the white smoke squirt out of the ferry-boat's side. You see, they was firing cannon over the water, trying to make my carcass come to the top.

I was pretty hungry, but it warn't going to do for me to start a fire, because they might see the smoke. So I set there and watched the cannon-smoke and listened to the boom. The river was a mile wide, there, and it always looks pretty on a summer morning—so I was having a good enough time seeing them hunt for my remainders, if I only had a bit to eat. Well, then I happened to think how they always put quicksilver in loaves of bread and float them off because they always go right to the drownded carcass and stop there. So says I, I'll keep a look-out, and if any of them's floating around after me, I'll give them a show. I changed to the Illinois edge of the island to see what luck I could have, and I warn't disappointed. A big double loaf come along, and I most got it, with a long stick, but my foot slipped and she floated out further. Of course I was where the current set in the closest to the shore—I knowed enough for that. But by and by along comes another one, and this time I won. I took out the plug and shook out the little dab of quicksilver, and set my teeth in. It was "baker's bread"— what the quality eat—none of your low-down corn-pone.

I got a good place amongst the leaves, and set there on a log, munching the bread and watching the ferry-boat, and very well satisfied. And then something struck me. I says, now I reckon the widow or the parson or somebody prayed that this bread would find me, and here it has gone and done it. So there ain't no doubt but there is something in that thing. That is, there's something in it when a body like the widow or the parson prays, but it don't work for me, and I reckon it don't work for only just the right kind.

Mark Twain, from **HUCKLEBERRY FINN**

If someone were to ask you to describe what you think is most important about this extract from *Huckleberry Finn*, you might say that it relates the incident in which Huck watches the townsfolk trying to raise his sup-posedly dead body from the river. Or perhaps you would say, Huck gets breakfast by eating the quicksilvered loaves the superstitious people think will float to the carcass of a drowned person. Or you might focus on Huck's feeling that prayer brought him the loaves, but praying doesn't work for him because he isn't good enough. No one can predict exactly what you will choose to discuss, and why. There are as many readings of a piece of writing as there are readers, and a reader may read a text differently the second or third time. We each find our own special em-phases, and they can be added to or changed as we reread. Why?

The Reader Makes Meaning

When you read, you help make meaning yourself. You're not reading through someone else's eyes, nor with someone else's experience or consciousness. No matter what you read, you can read only in your own idiosyncratic way, bringing all your general knowledge and experience to the task. For you the text comes alive only in your imagination. Of course, the writer has suggested a meaning, but there is no assurance that you will agree with it, or that the writer's version of the meaning is all that can be said. You aim to find out what the writer has to say, but you may have other motives for reading apart from gaining information. You may be reading selectively in order to substantiate your own point of view. You may be reading for the pleasures of daydreaming or living through books in a way that you cannot in real life, as when you read literature. Or you may be reading to stimulate your powers of deduction. There are many motives that affect reading and many states of mind that can either interfere with interpretation or enrich it and make it your own.

It is true that a group of readers will often produce roughly similar readings of the same text when it contains some unmistakable reference. There had better be some agreement on what the Constitution and the law mean, for example, or we are all in trouble. Explanatory writing especially conveys information that is intended to be shared by an audience. But even in the case of the law, there is always room for interpretation and original readings.

This is true too of fictional writing. Returning to the extract from Twain's novel, we know that the basic facts of the piece are that a boy called Huck is sitting by the riverbank at eight o'clock in the morning, comfortable but hungry, watching the search for his own "remainders," and feeling superstitious about the loaves and the prayers he thinks guided them to him. Few readers are going to argue about that, even if they are not going to agree that these are all important facts. But what an insufficient description of the text that would be. It conveys nothing of the subtleties of meaning a reader can derive from a text, nothing either of the value of the text or of how or why we like it.

Facts are important—and we shall concentrate in this chapter on techniques for locating them in a text—but fact-finding is not the only activity or pleasure of reading. The facts, as you will see, have to be understood and interpreted for their significance.

The Reader Interacts with the Text

No one knows exactly how it happens or in what order the events necessarily occur, but when we become involved with a text, we are responding to what is in it and adapting it to our own particular experience. We picture scenes and fantasize about them. We tend to absorb writing into our storehouse of knowledge and into our private desires and needs. We react when we recognize experiences in books.

As readers we become imaginatively and emotionally involved. Our curiosity is aroused or diminished. For example, when you read the extract from *Huckleberry Finn*, did you perhaps picture the scene, playing it through the leaves of the trees? Did you imagine the way he looks, the expression on his face? Did you fantasize about the scene, maybe identifying with Huck or relating his feelings to your own experience in some way? Perhaps you recognized the pleasurable sensations of nature or the strange desires of childhood. Have you ever been fascinated by "freckled" light on the ground? Have you ever wondered how people would act about you if you were dead and wished you could be at your own funeral? Have you ever dreamed about getting away from civilization altogether?

This storehouse of personal experience and the special ways in which we view the world and ourselves and measure experience comprise our *identity themes*. They are an essential part of our personality, the habitual reactions by which we know ourselves and others know us. Identity themes are not fixed. They are subject to change and rejection. They are aspects of ourselves that we like or dislike, that we are proud or ashamed of. Some are so private that we will share them with no one. Some are immediately available to others because of the way we present ourselves to the public. We can be fully or partly conscious of them. An identity theme is an aspect of our imaginative life that we would rather not do without, in fact, that we cannot do without. So every time we read, we find our identity themes emerging. We may react negatively to certain writings because they touch a raw nerve, a personal reference we haven't yet learned to handle. Or we may find our identity themes in desires and wishes that tell us what we really want to be like.

You may still have secret fantasies of wanting to be a great sportsperson, so you turn to sports writing, games, televised sports, and so on, to satisfy that desire, to live through the lives of sports people. This is not to say, however, that all people who are fond of sports have secret fantasies of wanting to be great players. You may have a strong feeling of bored alienation from a world that strikes you as absurd, so you greatly enjoy the portrayal of the inmates in *One Flew over the Cuckoo's Nest*; or you may wish you could "light out" for the territory with Huck Finn. As an adolescent, you may have wanted to read novels about growing up. Now that you are older, you may still be fascinated by those aspects of adolescence that never quite disappear, so you read *Huckleberry Finn* happily for the seriousness of Huck's criticism of "civilized" society. He may be a nineteenth-century boy, but he still speaks to adults.

Little meaning is available to us as we read until we can relate what we find in a text to our identity themes. Remember, these images of ourselves never just lie on the surface. Good reading is self-discovery. It can happen as we read, or we may have to wait until later for an insight to strike home. Understand, though, that reading, however much it depends on how we view things, is not *just* a matter of turning all the events in a text into what we want them to be. Reading is interaction. Our experiences can be adjusted. Reading begins with experience, but it reveals what we are not as well as what we are, what we don't know as well as what we do. A text is not merely a mirror for us as readers. It has ideas of its own that have to be assimilated and that should be allowed to influence our perspectives. So we will be discussing in the next chapter some techniques for assuring ourselves that we have not lost a text in the delights of our own company. In other words, we shall be looking at the art of interpretation not only as reading imaginatively through our identity themes, but as an objective exercise.

*The Reader Fills in
Gaps*

Reading always comes with a challenge. You discover patterns of information and relationships between events and locate the connections clearly. But you also find contradictions and uncertain meanings. What is the connection between the loaves and the prayers in the *Huckleberry Finn* passage? Why does Huck want to remain hidden? You are especially aware of having to make meaning as you reread difficult and suggestive passages whose significance is never entirely clear. You may find yourself wondering why Huck says, "I was powerful lazy and comfortable—didn't want to get up and cook breakfast," when he doesn't have anything to cook. "If I only had a bit to eat," he says later on. You admire Huck's cleverness at knowing about the loaves with quicksilver and at capitalizing on the town's ritual. But what about *Huck's* "superstition" as he thinks the loaves are propelled to him by prayer?

So you consider the *contradictory appearances* of the text until you think you can at least partially resolve the differences. Perhaps Huck himself is no less superstitious, no less a part of a ritualistic world than the townsfolk? When you try to resolve contradictions, you are conscious of the gap between events in the text: things relate without apparent reason. You are also aware of the gap between *you* and the text when you don't understand what is going on. When the reader's experience of the text seems unified, then the experience is somehow richer. You have an explanation that appears justified. When it is fragmented—that is, when you don't understand why someone says something or why an event takes place—then you have to make the effort to overcome the problem and close the gap by reading the passage over again, experimenting imaginatively with possible meanings.

The example we have been referring to is from a novel, but what of nonfictional writing, which is probably what you will read most during your college years and beyond? No less than fiction, this too most often demands that you read imaginatively. Writing that aims to explain or persuade may seem to keep you at a greater distance than fictional writing and require more of an intellectual response. But that generalization will not hold fast, for there are plenty of novels that are full of ideas, and much nonfiction that makes every effort to arouse your emotions and implicate you in making decisions. Whether you are reading about young boys alienated from civilization or about the relationship of time concepts to the Sioux Indians, you still must be responsible for actively making meaning by closing the gaps in your experience of reading and imaginatively entering the world of the text:

The Sioux Indians provide us with another interesting example of the differing views toward time. Not so long ago a man who was introduced as the superintendent of the Sioux came to my office. I learned that he had been born on the reservation and was a product of both Indian and white cultures, having earned his A.B. at one of the Ivy League colleges.

During a long and fascinating account of the many problems which his tribe was having in adjusting to our way of life, he suddenly remarked: "What would you think of a people who had no word for time? My people have no word for 'late' or for 'waiting,' for that matter. They don't know what it is to wait or to be late." He then continued, "I decided that until they could tell time and knew what time was they could never adjust themselves to white culture. So I set about to teach them time. There wasn't a clock that was running in any of the reservation classrooms. So I first bought some decent clocks. Then I made the school buses start on time, and if an Indian was two minutes late that was just too bad. The bus started at eight forty-two and he had to be there."

He was right, of course. The Sioux could not adjust to European ways until they had learned the meaning of time. The superintendent's methods may have sounded a bit extreme, but they were about the only ones that would work. The idea of starting the buses off and making the drivers hold to a rigid schedule was a stroke of genius, much kinder to the Indian, who could better afford to miss a bus on the reservation than lose a job in town because he was late.

There is, in fact, no other way to teach time to people who handle it as differently from us as the Sioux. The quickest way is to get very technical about it and to make it mean something. Later on these people can learn the informal variations, but until they have experienced and then mastered our type of time they will never adjust to our culture.

Edward Hall, from **THE VOICES OF TIME**

Reading this passage is similar to reading the *Huckleberry Finn* passage. You try to absorb the text into your experience, even if it contains ideas that are hard to comprehend, like that of nontime. You try to picture the scene: the Sioux superintendent entering an office; an Indian arriving two minutes late for the school bus. You tend to fantasize, whether the writing deals with incidents *or* ideas. For example, you may wonder what it is like to live with no sense of time as we know it. You look for the main points and try to unify the text, this time finding relationships between concepts rather than events. You may question whether the author is right: does the Sioux *need* the anxiety that comes with our culture's consciousness of time? What will the short- and long-term effects be for the Indian who is introduced to this new world view? There is still no predicting which ideas you will single out for special interpretation.

No matter what you read, you cannot keep your imagination still. You will always try to make meaning by interacting with a text and filling in gaps. But if that is a general description of reading, what actually takes place? And how can you work through the process of reading efficiently?

The Activities of Reading

Reading is the business of making meaning out of writing by imaginatively interacting with a text, absorbing its information into our own experience, and trying to fill in the gaps created by difficult passages. Reading, then, is an activity. It is easy, though, to think of reading as a kind of *passive* listening: we wait for meaning to unfold from the text as we cast our eyes along the lines on the page and listen to the words spoken in our mind's ear. This kind of reading is not unusual, and it can be fun if the text requires a minimum of concentration—like a good thriller—and we want to lapse into a pleasant state of daydreaming through our reading. But it would be wrong to assume that even this reading is entirely passive, or that reading should at its "best" take little effort. You don't have to cling to the old theory that something has to be difficult to be good, yet it is a fact that not very much writing is written to daydream over. Remember that if a meaning does not immediately unfold from a text, it is wise not to assume immediately that there is something wrong with the writing.

Most reading takes effort. It is a *learned activity* or, rather, a collection of *related activities*. The main ones are outlined below, and they will be referred to frequently in these opening chapters. Later, in the chapters on writing, you will notice that they will be used again as part of the process of writing expository, narrative, descriptive, or persuasive prose.

Reading Is Careful Listening

This is the most basic and often the most ignored reading activity. We have to wait for people to say things to us before we can draw any conclusions. We let them finish. We have to read a text carefully, all of it, allowing it to present its case in its own way, rereading it as often as necessary, before we can claim to know what it is saying. Furthermore, the good reader is an *active* listener who tries to think along with the writer, following the development of a narration or argument. If we skip through the second paragraph of the *Huck Finn* extract, we may miss the humorous aside about breakfast that contradicts but relates to "if I only had a bit to eat." That tells us that Huck is perhaps not quite so "comfortable" as he says he is.

What do we listen to in reading? Plainly, the *voices* of the text. Voices belong to people speaking in the writing; they offer information and a point of view. They belong either to the author of the text or to people that the author lets speak in the text. So we hear Huck speaking in the extract above, but we also hear Mark Twain who is writing the piece. Are they the same voice? You have probably realized by now that they are not always the same, that Twain lets Huck speak in his own way and

9

dominate the narration. But Twain can comment on what Huck is like by allowing Huck's view of reality to be subtly adjusted. In the passage by Hall, we hear Hall's voice mainly, but the Sioux superintendent appears too, adding a perspective Hall cannot provide.

The first thing the reader does, then, is listen to the voices, identifying them and trying to understand what they are saying.

Reading Is the Process of Accumulating Information

We understand what is happening in a text when we can make connections between events. These relationships develop basically from the sequential flow of the writing, from the fact that words come together in place and time. Words form sentences, and sentences paragraphs, and paragraphs flow into each other to form chapters, and chapters make up books. The information in a piece of writing always has a beginning, a middle, and an end. Every text has a history of its own events, even when it cuts back and forth with flashbacks. Huck is on the riverbank, *and then* he hears the cannon, *and then* he catches a loaf of bread, *and then ...* Even information tends to unfold in sequences. We follow words in order as our eyes dart over the page. When we anticipate what will happen, we are still creating meaning within a sequence of information. "If this happens, then this will follow," we say.

But our awareness of what happens in a text does not only work in sequences. We accumulate evidence quite spontaneously from any number of sources. Information unfolds in a sequence—one thing must follow another—but it most often begins to make sense in *clusters* of related ideas or emotions.

■ *We find related and unrelated facts and try to make connections.* Everything exists in networks of similarities and dissimilarities. We ourselves are alike to the extent that we all have bodies, yet we are different in our personalities. We need differences as well as connections to understand anything. A car can be defined as similar to a bus and a truck but different from a train or a bicycle. When we read, events in the text occur to us as being different from each other.

We naturally try to keep the necessary distinctions alive, but we also try to *unify* the text, to make as many connections as we can. It is an interesting fact that the most common assumption in reading is that the text is somehow whole, unified, and understandable, no matter how suggestive it is. So when we find oppositions, we try to break them down, to locate common factors.

Most of the time, explanatory writing tries to avoid contradictions. Hall has unified his paragraphs on the Sioux and time around the story of the Sioux superintendent. But even this passage is suggestive, for when we get to the words "The superintendent's methods may have

sounded a bit extreme,'' we do in fact wonder if they are extreme,
or maybe if his actions are right at all. An issue has presented itself.
This occurs often, of course, in imaginative and interpretive writing,
whether it's fictional or not. The Twain passage offers a good example
of this.

When Huck says that prayer works "for only just the right kind," we
might remember that he is also eating " 'baker's bread'—what the
quality eat—none of your low-down corn-pone." Perhaps in Huck's
mind the "quality people" and the "right kind"—the rich and the
good—are somehow related. We do not know that for sure yet, but
we do know that he does not think of himself as either "quality"
or "right." They're the people back there, in civilization. But is Huck
really neither "quality" nor "right"? How can anyone be so simply
described? It is society that has taught Huck that people can be thought
of this way, and as he repeats this convention, he parodies it. He is
unconsciously making fun of it. At least that is the way Twain seems to
be thinking. The fact that it is the poor boy, the alienated Huck, who
is making the judgment is significant. Civilization, we might feel, is
under fire from Twain. But there is a further problem because we are
not so sure that Huck really prefers being on the outside of civilization.
So you see that the simple statement that Huck is different from the
"quality" and the "right kind" is not as clear as it might at first appear.

■ *We try to solve problem passages.* Don't ignore the difficulties and
apparent contradictions of the text, for, as we have just seen, that is
where special meanings can reside. Again, what exactly does Huck
think about prayer? Perhaps he really believes in it, even though he is
amused watching the body-raising ritual, and says he thinks prayer will
not work for him. But then he believes prayer brought him breakfast.
So Huck may think, or at least say, that he is not the "right kind," but
do you think that deep down he really believes that or that he *wants*
to stay "wrong"?

■ *We question the text.* The most important thing to do when you
read a text—even when it seems to be flowing smoothly, in fact,
especially when it does—is to always ask yourself, *why?* Why is
something happening? Why is the writer arguing this way? Why does
someone make a particular statement? Why did the Sioux not have the
concept of time? Why does Huck not want to be found? Why is Huck
on the run? Search for the characters' and writer's motives. Query
whether events are moral or immoral in their implication, for all writing
is a social act and has social implications. Wonder whether things are
true or false. There are dozens of possible questions that can provoke
you to find relationships and differences and to make judgments.

■ *We experiment with various points of view in the text.* In spite of the fact that we relate most closely to the reinforcement of our identity themes, we must put ourselves inside the minds of different characters and follow different sides of an argument through. We pursue different themes. We experiment with what a writer wants us to think. For example, you can read the Huck Finn extract from the point of view that you are overseeing the action: Huck lies on the grass; he contemplates breakfast; he hears the cannon; and so on. Then on rereading, you can try to see things from Huck's perspective, which is when you start wondering exactly what he means about breakfast, quality folk, and prayer. Or you might concentrate on a theme or idea that emerges from the text, such as the concern with the ritual of raising the body: superstition or myth? Or you can ask what Twain himself is saying about Huck and decide that he paints an affectionate portrait of a likable boy who is comfortable in nature, not really beyond civilized morality, rather vulnerable, and prone to self-deception (about breakfast, anyway). Huck has perhaps a secret longing at this time to return to the domestic virtues. Again, is he really not the "right" kind? Twain seems to be asking, knowing that we must find Huck sympathetic.

Reading Raises Expectations

As you read the Hall extract on time, you may have been conscious of having your interest aroused by the description of the events. Will the Indians adapt easily to time? Or in the *Huckleberry Finn* extract, the " 'boom!' " of the cannon may have caught your attention. You were curious at first as to what it could be and why, as Huck is too. Other questions arise in this passage. Will Huck escape being noticed? What will Huck do next? Literary plots and any other kind of writing will try to arouse our interest and to hold it. The clearest way writing does this is by raising our expectations. We read in part by anticipating what might happen next and by following signals in the text—like " 'boom!' " Much of the pleasure of reading comes from having those expectations satisfied or at least further provoked. If a plot does not thicken, we want to know why. If a writer simply trots out a list of comments without involving the reader, then the reader will surely lose interest.

Reading Is Rereading

Reading depends not only on responding to stimuli but on going back over the writing, either when memory fails you, or when you have not made a meaning, or when the meaning you have made seems to contradict that of other parts of the text, or when you want to check a reading and add to it. There is little reading without rereading for the obvious reason that you rarely see everything whole the first time. You build meaning by accumulating information, by letting facts work on each other to create a density and richness of suggestion. Rereading, then, is not simply a remedial task, but an important way of building on what you have already found. The imagination works in mysterious but persistently repetitive ways in order to find things out for the first time *and* to recapture past pleasures.

Handling Irony

One of the most powerful functions of language is *irony: to suggest more than is actually said.* A reader has to be on the lookout for irony constantly, or else the point can very easily be missed. If any one aspect of language can complicate the act of reading and yet provide it with so much challenge and pleasure, it is irony.

■ *Irony can be found in a tone of voice* in any kind of writing. Irony is relatively easy to catch in conversation: "How good of you to come," says a hostess to an uninvited guest whom she would rather have stayed away. It is a little harder to understand irony in writing. Often a writer's style will suggest it, usually through some kind of exaggeration or deliberate contradiction. An author may make a simple point in a very complicated or overstated way, or may say something so contra-dictory that the reader has to invent another meaning: "Ghenghis Khan continued his travels through the Far East, spreading cheer and good will wherever he went." The ironic tone of voice in speech or writing occurs *when a person says one thing and means another.* Irony reveals how a reader is necessary to make meaning. Note that irony is not sarcasm. Sarcasm is a taunt, a comment that mocks—"So you think you're a clever writer, do you?"—that is more aggressive than irony and has no subtlety in its intent.

■ *Irony can be a world view.* Some people are plainly more ironic than others; that is, they can see contradictions between the way things appear and what they really represent that the rest of us often miss. This occasionally borders on *cynicism.* A cynic is someone who sees little or no good in anything and always suspects an ulterior motive. When greeted by "Good morning! How are you today?" the cynic will usually reply defensively, "What's good about it?" A cynic sneers and believes that most people act for purely selfish motives. Of course, many of us are cynical at times—in response to political campaign promises, for example—and to be cynical is often a necessary attack on what we believe to be a naive acceptance of something that is plainly morally wrong, or most likely not true. Cynics are ironists to the extent that they believe that there are some states of affairs not motivated by good intentions even when they are told the opposite.

But the truly ironic world view is not without good will. The world is not necessarily rotten to the core, and the ironist is intelligently awake to contradictory motives and conditions, skeptical without being cynical. The ironist can experience pleasure but *investigates* appearances.

It is an old saying that things are rarely what they seem, and it is the reader and writer with ironic dispositions who remind us of that frequently. Many newspaper columnists, for example—writers like Ellen Goodman, Erma Bombeck, Art Buchwald, and Shana Alexander—are obviously ironists, as are cartoonists like Feiffer and Trudeau. In almost every column or cartoon, they point out the contradictions between appearance and reality.

Irony may be revealed only for a moment to make a specific point, or a writer with a talent for seriously and wittily revealing contradictions may use it regularly because the world itself appears ironic. Irony takes distinct forms in writing:

■ *Verbal irony* exists when a statement makes an assertion that seems to contradict itself. We know it cannot be true, that the writer or speaker is saying one thing and meaning another. When someone says that it is a gorgeous day in the midst of sleet and rain, that is an example of verbal irony.

■ *Dramatic irony* occurs when a eader or an audience knows something about a character that the character does not seem aware of. This frequently happens in plays and movies, but it can happen in prose narratives, too. The audience shares some knowledge with the author, as we do when we read Huck's words "I reckon it don't work for only just the right kind." Huck makes his comment in a confusing double negative, which, as we have noted, Twain seems to disagree with.

■ *Satirical irony* occurs when irony is sustained in order to make fun of and seriously attack some person or state of affairs. This is the kind of irony we find in novels and films like *One Flew over the Cuckoo's Nest,* or in the pages of magazines like the *New Yorker.* Shana Alexander's article on the next page is satirical.

■ *Cosmic irony* is a kind of irony that may border on perpetual cynicism. It sometimes suggests that we are nothing more than the playthings of destiny, or God, or some other fate, so we remain perpetually frustrated. But cosmic irony has perhaps an even more important use:

14

it can reveal the complexity of things. A writer may talk about a subject so complex that no simple explanation will do.

People who satirize the human condition or specific social problems frequently use cosmic irony. Joseph Heller in *Catch-22* shows his hero constantly frustrated by fate, by the fact that life will apparently always create conditions he can never meet. He satirizes specifically the bureaucracy of the armed services and the horrible waste of war, but lying behind that is the feeling that catch-22—the ideal we can never meet—is part of the complexity of life in general and is demanded by our social institutions. (An extract from *Catch-22* is included at the end of Chapter 12.) Cosmic irony is often associated with *black humor:* the "humor" of situations that can raise only grim laughter or no laughter at all.

Be on the lookout for irony in its many forms when you read. Watch for exaggeration and sweeping statements (though these are not always ironic), or perhaps a bizarre topic being treated in a low-keyed way. Most of the irony you will encounter in persuasive and explanatory writing will be either verbal or satiric. These will occur in literature, too, but there you will commonly find dramatic irony and cosmic irony. Remember that in any context, *irony can be a weapon used to attack something,* and *irony can be found in the complex nature of reality.* Often these two conditions appear together. Consider this short essay by Shana Alexander:

A man in the remote jungles of New Guinea not long ago murdered another man with an ax. Tribal justice ensued. First the murderer was shot and killed with an arrow, and then seven other members of the tribe cut him up and ate him.

When word of the feast reached civilization, the authorities concluded that on this occasion justice had literally been served, and perhaps a bit too swiftly, so they hauled the seven cannibals into court, where a wise Australian judge dismissed all the charges, and acquitted the seven men. "The funerary customs of the people of Papua and New Guinea," he explained, "have been, and in many cases remain, bizarre in the extreme."

What, I wonder, would the judge have to say about the new, high-rise mausoleum now under construction in Nashville, Tennessee? When completed, this model of modern funerary design will be twenty stories high, fully air-conditioned, and capable of holding 65,000 bodies. A second slightly less deluxe tower on an adjoining site will have facilities to entomb 63,500 more. Nashville's enterprising mortician-entrepreneur points out that his high-rise mortuary will be self-contained on only 14 acres, whereas it would require 129 acres to contain all these caskets in the, uh, conventional manner.

Well, not exactly caskets. In the new-style funeral, you will be laid out—after embalming, of course—on something called a "repose," described as "a bedlike structure," complete with white sheets, pillow, and blanket. When the ceremonies are ended, bed, pillow, sheet, and blanket are all whisked away; a fiberglass lid snaps down over what remains; and—zap—it's into the wall, stacked seven-high, with a neat bronze marker attached to the face of the crypt.

The forward-looking undertaker who thought all this up is already respected, in the trade, for bringing to Nashville the one-stop funeral.

But the most important advantage of the high-rise mausoleum is that by putting everything but everything under one roof you cut down on the high cost of dying. Maybe so, maybe so. But I can't help thinking it would be even cheaper to die in New Guinea, where the funerary customs are certainly no less bizarre, and a lot more practical.

Shana Alexander, **THE FASHION IN FUNERALS**

This is a hard-hitting article, which derives its strength largely from its satirical irony. Alexander has a target: the Nashville mortician. She sharply contrasts two styles of burial with her tongue very much in cheek. Note particularly the last line: "But I can't help thinking it would be even cheaper to die in New Guinea, where the funerary customs are certainly no less bizarre, and a lot more practical." You can readily agree with "bizarre," but you should be disturbed by "practical." It seems so out of place. It is as though the whole article boils down to the question, "Are funerals merely practical?"

But before you decide that Alexander is being crude by comparing New Guinea cannibalism with American funeral technology, or that she is being grotesque and sensational, and is dealing flippantly with a very solemn subject, stop and check her language. She deliberately does not make her point immediately clear. Before you feel your sensitivities threatened, you are asked to consider a suggestion: one thing has not changed in funeral fashions from the primitive to the civilized, and that is the need for "practicality." The high-rise, air-conditioned towers seem no less monuments to practical burial than the New Guinea custom. The practical ideal in each seems to be the same. But is it?

There's a certain horrible mystery about the tribal custom, but there is no mystery, Alexander suggests, about our modern technological funerals. They are sanitized and deodorized. Death becomes " 'repose' " on " 'a bedlike structure,' " a commercial enterprise, a monument to our undying narcissism, as anyone knows who has read Evelyn Waugh's *The Loved One* or Jessica Mitford's *The American Way of Death*. Dying is also very expensive and prone to the dictates of fashion. In New Guinea, ironically, the tribal custom is far less elaborate.

Alexander is not attacking simply the funeral industry, for it would not be in business if people did not want its wares. She is also talking to us about *our* responsibilities: shouldn't we want to be buried gracefully and cheaply, as well as practically? The contemporary funeral tower makes a fetish out of practicality, but is it graceful, tactful, inexpensive? Is it any less bizarre than cannibalism? Of course, that's an overstatement: the contemporary funeral *is* less bizarre than cannibalism, but perhaps only a little, and Alexander has made her point by the heavily ironic comparison. There is no difference between the outcome of our rituals and those of the primitive tribesmen, and ours are much more expensive. The point is that decorum and tact, not just practicality, are all at issue, and we have offended the former with our funeral towers.

Out of the black humor of this kind of writing comes a very serious point. We may laugh, but Alexander has lured us into an argument in which we have to be very careful before we reach conclusions. The art of irony is the art of contrast. It is one of the most powerful weapons in language: economical, practical, bizarre, ritualistic, and quick, rather like a New Guinea funeral! Make sure you're not misled by it.

Critical Reading

In the act of reading, you are performing in a way that is peculiarly yours. One can list the activities entailed by reading, but no one can tell you exactly how to read. There are styles of reading just as there are styles of writing. Your style becomes especially apparent when you explain why you do or do not like a piece of writing, a task to be covered in the next chapter. But if you are aiming for understanding, your style will have some aspects in common with the styles of other readers intent on the same thing. Before we get to the business of developing your reading into *writing-about-reading,* here are a few suggestions about the kind of reading that can lead you to critical understanding.

■ *Do not take anything in a text for granted* or expect meaning to be created easily. Sometimes that happens, and when it does, an experienced reader will often be suspicious and will ask, "Have I missed something?" This is not to suggest you be paranoid about your readings, only that you check them. For example, read these opening sentences to I. F. Stone's essay, "A New Solution for the CIA":

Stalin did establish one useful precedent. He made it a practice to bump off whoever served as head of his secret police. He never let anyone stay in the job too long. As a successful dictator, Stalin seems to have felt that anybody who has collected so many secrets would be a No. 1 menace to security if ever he went sour. Stalin thought it safer not to wait.

I think we ought to take Stalin's example one step further. I think we ought to get rid of the CIA altogether, lock, stock, and burglar's kit.

It seems that the writer does not like the CIA, and yet he is asking us to side with Stalin, who is not exactly everyone's favorite democratic leader. So how do we reconcile the two opinions? Either I. F. Stone is supporting Stalin (which the rest of the essay shows he is not), or else he is being ironic. We have to give Stone time to develop his meaning. All is not what it appears to be, and we will miss the point if we read too rapidly and jump to conclusions. Be especially wary of irony. Reading critically means watching the text closely for subtle implications and being prepared to develop an opinion about the text carefully.

■ *Treat each text as unique.* Reading is not often a routine matter. The good reader learns to resist the temptation to scamper through an essay, an article, or a piece of literature in five minutes in preparation for a class or an exercise, for that may produce embarrassing results, and the reader will derive little pleasure from the text. Reading is not to be taken lightly, if for no other reason than our reading habits reveal our habits of making sense of the world. We have to interpret carefully before we can choose wisely and evaluate our options, whether the context be love and marriage, politics, business, writing, or simply, as someone once said, a very good dinner.

■ *Be critically aware of your own reading style.* In these early chapters, you are trying to locate your style of reading, to evaluate it, and to improve it by learning about the way reading works. Everyone's reading can stand a little self-conscious questioning. So what do you bring to your reading? Three characteristics, basically:

Your experience of life outside books as well as your experience of books

Certain physical habits of reading

Identity themes: emotional and psychological habits, ways of reacting to issues

■ In the case of the first—your experience—there is little to say about that except that everything you know and have experienced is relevant. But do not assume that you have too little experience to cope with a text. To begin with, you concentrate on the text itself. The actual experience you have had can be built upon, so a lively imagination is important. Books make available whole worlds in which you could never hope to live in real life.

Everyone's experience, both in life and in reading, differs dramatically, so consider the second characteristic of your personal style of reading:

your physical reading habits about which it is easier to generalize. Physiologically, reading is a matter of perception and thought working together. Your eye scans the lines on a page, and your mind tries to decipher the words, reacting to what is said and looking for a focus and a coherence among possible meanings. We will discuss the reading process in more technical detail in the next chapter, but note here that we know what makes for good and bad habits in reading. The good habits we covered earlier. Here, then, are the problems we all share as readers:

We can read too fast, blurring the text, judging too hastily, letting the eye outstrip comprehension, and even sometimes thinking too rapidly as we read, making the text say what we want it to say.

We can read too selectively, failing to find all the writer's emphases, taking words and ideas out of context, skipping transitions that may very well change the meaning, missing irony, and generally concentrating on an arbitrary selection of facts.

We can read too distractedly and not concern ourselves with coherence, our eyes moving along the lines but our ears listening to something else—usually music or noise from the rooms around us.

All these problems are easily cured by obvious means: reading only as fast as your comprehension allows and rereading when necessary; following carefully the transitions from the beginning through the middle to the end of a text; and concentrating on the page in a quiet place without distractions. If you are not prepared to arrange these conditions for yourself—and remember that every library provides the peace and quiet necessary for good reading—then it is unlikely that you will be giving yourself much of a chance to work imaginatively and intelligently with any kind of writing.

Just as important as the physical conditions of reading, though, are the emotional and psychological habits you bring to reading, the third characteristic of your personal reading style. We all bring presuppositions to a text: our identity themes, our likes and dislikes, our opinions on any number of subjects, and our openness (or not) to experience. Whether a writer is being rational or emotional in an appeal, we as readers have our own world views that become involved in our interpretation of the text. Whether we are aggressive readers, sure that our view of reality is more right than wrong, or passive readers, feeling we have everything to learn, we still have to acknowledge that all reading requires us to be as conscious as possible of our own motives and identity themes. Reading plays off one world view against another: the reader's against the writer's. Some people, sensing this, read very defensively, treating every text with skepticism, feeling themselves attacked. Others can change their opinions by the moment. There are as many styles of reading and as many defenses that readers throw up as there are readers. The sooner you know your own styles and your own defenses, the sooner you will be able to improve your reading skills. It is neither necessary nor possible to categorize all reading styles, but all have in common some version of the reading process outlined in this and the next chapter.

You should not read simply to justify your opinions or your personality, as though they are static and beyond change. You should read to learn and to develop your pleasures. So be wary when you overreact to a text in agreement or disagreement. However powerful your personal needs, don't read simply for agreement, but for information and pleasure, open-mindedly and critically, as if you always have room to grow. That might sound rather moralistic, but it is meant to be a plea for tolerance. Closed-mindedness and a failure to be thorough in interpretation are the most obvious reasons for a reader's failure to understand a text.

Checklist

1. The reader helps make the meaning of a text by getting involved with the writing, by fantasizing and identifying with it, and by recognizing experiences and creating patterns of information.
2. Reading comes with a challenge. We have to close the gap between ourselves and the often alien experiences in a text, and we have to resolve contradictions.
3. The act of reading is made up of a number of learned activities: carefully listening to the voices of the text; interacting with them and adapting the experiences to our identity themes; raising expectations; rereading; and accumulating information through sequences and clusters of related facts, differentiating the facts, reworking problem passages, questioning the text, and experimenting with the text's points of view.
4. Many problems of reading stem from irony in the text. Irony is a tone of voice that can be used to attack satirically or to reveal a subject's complexity. Irony can be verbal, dramatic, satirical, or cosmic.
5. The art of reading depends on developing a personal style. For college and the professions, especially, develop the talent of reading critically with an awareness of irony. Treat each text as a new beginning. Be critically aware of your own reading habits: the experience you bring to books and the physical and emotional habits of your reading.

Exercises

1. Here are three short passages. Read each one carefully, allowing your imagination to work on it. Then with each:

a. Write down your reactions to the piece as they come to you and in the order in which they come. Don't be concerned with grammatical precision; just write. What do you find yourself thinking about as you read each piece? What specific fantasies or mental pictures does it conjure up? Can you identify with the statements or with the people? Do you find any problems or contradictions in what is being said? What "positive" or "negative" feelings insinuate themselves?

b. Choose the extract you like best, and explain why, comparing it with the others.

The sea which lies before me as I write glows rather than sparkles in the bland May sunshine. With the tide turning, it leans quietly against the land, almost unflecked by ripples or by foam. Near to the horizon it is a luxurious purple, spotted with regular lines of emerald green. At the horizon it is indigo. Near to the shore, where my view is framed by rising heaps of humpy yellow rock, there is a band of lighter green, icy and pure, less radiant, opaque however, not transparent. We are in the north, and the bright sunshine cannot penetrate the sea. Where the gentle water taps the rocks there is still a surface skin of colour. The cloudless sky is very pale at the indigo horizon which it lightly pencils in with silver. Its blue gains towards the zenith and vibrates there. But the sky looks cold, even the sun looks cold.

Iris Murdoch, from THE SEA, THE SEA

The fact is, we none of us enough appreciate the nobleness and sacredness of colour. Nothing is more common than to hear it spoken of as a subordinate beauty,—nay, even as the mere source of a sensual pleasure. . . . But it is not so. Such expressions are used for the most part in thoughtlessness; and if the speakers would only take the pains to imagine what the world and their own existence would become, if the blue were taken from the sky, and the gold from the sunshine, and the verdure from the leaves, and the crimson from the blood which is the life of man, the flush from the cheek, the darkness from the eye, the radiance from the hair,—if they could but see, for an instant, white human creatures living in a white world,—they would soon feel what they owe to colour. The fact is, that, of all God's gifts to the sight of man, colour is the holiest, the most divine, the most solemn. We speak rashly of gay colour and sad colour, for colour cannot at once be good and gay. All good colour is in some degree pensive, the loveliest is melancholy, and the purest and most thoughtful minds are those which love colour the most.

John Ruskin, from THE STONES OF VENICE

I was born in a tall apricot-colored house with green shutters overlooking the sea. When I think of my childhood I remember the bright colors, the sounds, the smells and tastes of Nice. We were constantly sent to the seashore, the garden, or the hills to find ingredients for the kitchen. Along the coast we searched for sea urchins and mussels; in our garden we picked zucchini flowers, tiny eggplants, the tenderest lima beans. In the fields we gathered thyme and oregano; in the woods we searched for blackberries, chestnuts, mushrooms, and pine cones full of pignon nuts. And after a rainfall we would collect snails, wild pink cloves, and genista, whose stems we could suck like candy.

There were lazy afternoons when we would sip orange wine under the fig tree, where all around us would be the scent of lavender, jasmine, and honeysuckle—mingling with the fragrance of fruits that would later be made into preserves—and the endless buzzing of cicadas and bees.

On festive days—a carnival, a visit from a relative, a saint's day—our house was filled with special excitement. Feathers of hens and ducks would fly in all directions; large fish filled with stalks of dried fennel would rest under a layer of lettuce leaves; large platters of seaweed and crushed ice would be piled high with mussels, clams, sea urchins; fruits would be left to marinate in large bowls of rum and sugar; and fresh pasta would be drying on sheets of linen spread on beds, chairs, and tables.

Mireille Johnston, from **THE CUISINE OF THE SUN**

2. For each of the following three short extracts, you are again going to describe your "experience of reading," but this time more formally than for Question 1. The questions are based on the activities of reading outlined in this chapter. Answer each of the questions for each extract.

  a. What do the voices in the text tell you?

  b. What do you find yourself thinking as you get further into each text? What fantasies are awakened? Identifications made?

  c. What expectations or questions do you find aroused by the piece?

  d. Do you have any difficulty thinking along with the writer? Are there stubborn passages?

  e. What do you think of the writer?

  f. What do you think the writer thinks of the reader?

His exacting consciousness spared him nothing. He knew only too well that the city in which he lived was without trees, without national monuments, without ponds or flower gardens, without even a single building to attract visitors from other parts of the world. It was a small bleak city consisting almost entirely of cheaply built concrete dwellings and unfinished apartment houses. It was a city without interest, without pride, without efficiency. Sacks of concrete lined the streets; the low-hung electrical wires fed only the barest energy to the tin trolley cars and the precious unshaded light bulbs; in the single park the play equipment for children resembled a collection of devices for inflicting torture. As for shape or plan or boundaries: to the east was the school, to the west the railway station, to the north La Violaine, to the south a hospital that bore on its roof an enormous cross the color of blood washed in the rain. The cemetery, not far from the park for children, more or less marked the center. And always the dust, the dry air, the sound of iron against iron, the visibility of systems (for trains, traffic, school, prison, playground, cemetery), the signs and posters displayed in shopwindows or pasted to bare walls in order to fix for the eye a steam-pressing mechanism, a suit of clothes, a wrench, a bowl of food. Here was the outcome of the centuries of death and agony; the paths of the great minds ended here; dreamers of palaces and holocausts had invented nothing. And what was this city, denying in its daily life the validity of recorded history, if not the very domain of the human psyche? The irony of order existing only in desolation and discomfort was a satisfaction beyond imagining.

John Hawkes, from **THE PASSION ARTIST**

The Beatles' music is said to belong to the young, but if it does that's only because the young have the right motive for caring about it—they enjoy themselves. They also know what produces the fun they have, by phrase and instrument, or sometimes by sheer volume, and they're very quick, as I've discovered, to shoot down inflated interpretations. They should indeed exercise proprietary rights. This is the first time that people of school age have been tuned in to sounds invented not by composers approved by adults but in to sounds invented by their own near contemporaries, sounds associated with lyrics, manners, and dress that they also identify as their own. David Amram, the New York Philharmonic's first resident composer, is understandably optimistic that this kind of identification will develop an avidity of attention to music that could be the salvation of American musical composition and performance.

Perhaps in some such way the popular arts can help restore all the arts to their status as entertainment and performance. To help this process along it isn't necessary that literary and academic grown-ups go to school to their children. Rather, they must begin to ask some childlike and therefore some extremely difficult questions about particular works: Is this any fun? How and where is it any fun? And if it isn't, why bother? While listening together to recordings of popular music, people of any age tend naturally to ask these questions, and I've heard them asked by young people with an eager precision which they almost never exhibit, for want of academic encouragement, when they talk about a poem or a story. If, as I've suggested, their writing about music isn't nearly so good as their talk can be, this may only mean that the conventions of written criticism serve rock even less well than they do the other arts.

Richard Poirier, from THE PERFORMING SELF

There is not a single feature of her youthful face that I do not vividly recall. Everything in it bespoke childishness, roguishness, and the propensity to laughter. Impossible to find anywhere in that face, from the fair hair to the sweet dimple of the weak little chin, any line that was not a line of laughter, any sign of the hidden tragic melancholy that throbs in the poetry of Renée Vivien. I never saw Renée sad. She would exclaim, in her lisping English accent, "Oh, my dear little Colette, how disgusting this life is!" Then she would burst into laughter. In all too many of her notes, I find that same exclamation repeated, often spelled out frankly in the coarsest words: "Isn't this life sheer muck? Well, I hope it will soon be over!" This impatience of hers amused her friends, but her hope was not dashed, for she died in her thirtieth year.

Our friendship was in no way literary, it goes without saying—or rather, I should say, thanks to my respect for literature. I am sparing of words on that subject, except for occasional exclamations of admiration, and in Renée Vivien I found the same diffidence and well-bred restraint. She, too, refused to "talk shop." Whenever she gave me any of her books, she always hid them under a bouquet of violets or a basket of fruit or a length of Oriental silk. She was secretive with me on the two literary aspects of her brief existence: the cause of her sadness, and her method of work. Where did she work? And at what hours? The vast, dark, sumptuous, and ever changing flat in the avenue du Bois gave no hint of work. That ground-floor flat in the avenue du Bois has never been well described, by the way. Except for some gigantic Buddhas, all the furnishings moved mysteriously: after provoking surprise and admiration for a time, they had a way of disappearing . . .

Among the unstable marvels, Renée wandered, not so much clad as veiled in black or purple, almost invisible in the scented darkness of the immense rooms barricaded with leaded windows, the air heavy with curtains and incense. Three or four times I caught her curled up in a corner of a divan, scribbling with a pencil on a writing pad propped on her knees. On these occasions she always sprang up guiltily, excusing herself, murmuring, "It's nothing, I've finished now . . ." Her lithe body devoid of density languidly drooped, as if beneath the weight of her poppy-flower head with its pale golden hair, surmounted by immense and unsteady hats. She held her long and slender hands in front of her, gropingly. The dresses she wore were always long, covering her feet, and she was afflicted with an angelic clumsiness, was always losing as she went her gloves, handkerchief, sunshade, scarf . . .

Colette, from THE PURE AND THE IMPURE

3. This question is concerned with *ironic* writing. Each of the following extracts is clearly ironic. With each, answer the following questions:

a. What do you think the writer *really* means? Explain the evidence that leads you to your conclusion.

b. Discuss how the writer achieves his or her ironic effect.

c. Discuss how the writing had an impact on you and how effective you think it is.

My family couldn't brush their teeth after every meal, but we had something more precious together. I guess you could call it "togetherness."

My mother and father did everything together, and so did we. I can't remember a single moment when there wasn't a family-size bottle of Coke on the indoor barbecue pit.

So many scenes flash through my mind as I think of those years in Crest-wood: my father, laughing through his smoke rings as he chortled, "Winston tastes good!"; Aunt Birdie, who came from Mobile, chirping roguishly "Lahk a cigarette should!"; my mother seeing my teen-age sister Shirley off to a dance with the heart-warming whisper: "Don't be half-safe!"

My mother was the most unforgettable character I had ever met. I see her now, rubbing her freshly ironed wash against her cheek and murmuring of its whiteness; or rushing to my father as he came home from work and crying, "Darling, have you heard the wonderful news? Professional laundries use *soap*, not detergents!" My mother had that kind of mind.

We children spent many childhood hours browsing through old *Reader's Digests*. "It's the small things that count," my father always used to say. Years later, in the isolation booths of jackpot shows, we used to thank our stars for the rich background of knowledge those little old *Digests* gave us. Everyone said we sparkled.

Every Sunday we had Norman Vincent Peale for dinner, and Mother used to make Kraft pizzas for him. He often remarked on her sealed-in goodness and creamy richness. Some people said it was Geritol, but we knew that it was her moral and spiritual values that made her like that.

"Never forget," she used to say when she sipped her calorie-free beer. "This is a friendly, freedom-loving nation."

The only sad note in those unforgettable years concerned my nearest brother, Prelvis. He lived in a dream world of his own. "I wonder," he would say, vacantly, "where the yellow went!" But he had great sweetness in him, and my mother was infinitely patient. Even when he ice-skated over the kitchen floor, she would merely run a mop over the wax and the tracks would disappear. "No rub, no wipe!" she would quip merrily as she rubbed and wiped.

The most unforgettable character I ever knew (next to Mother) was our family doctor, whom we called "Doc." Whenever any of us were sick, no matter what from, "Doc" would draw little pictures of our intestines and show us how fast Bufferin brought relief. (He was the fifth out of four doctors.)

Yet we were not without romance. I will never forget when Shirley married Bob and he gave her a set of flat silver. As she looked up into his eyes, fingering a salad fork, he said, with infinite tenderness, "This Regency pattern is another way of saying 'I love you.' " Putting on my Playtex "living gloves" to help Mother with the dishes, I yearned for a love like that. "With Joy," she comforted me, instinctively, "dishwashing is *almost* nice!"

Part of our "togetherness" in those days was the sharing of minds as well as hands, and, of course, the spirit. Each of us prayed before our respective tasks: Father before his board meeting, Mother before cooking, us children before exams. Every morning Mother read aloud from Mr. Peale's column in *Look*, and once a week Father read us the *Life* editorial, to set us straight. And on Christmas Eve, we joined our voices to Bing Crosby's as he sang carols from Hollywood.

I will never forget when our world fell apart. It was the year when four out of five doctors said "Anxiety is Good for You." This marked the end of an era.

My mother no longer rubs her cheek against her wash or lets something golden happen with Fluffo. She plays a bull fiddle and reads Ionesco.

My father wears hair shirts and corresponds with Françoise Sagan; my sister Shirley and Bob got divorced after she put his Ike buttons in the Disposall, and Prelvis is waiting for Godot in a degraded Southern town.

Miltown Place, the Temple of Togetherness, has been sold to the Society for the Propagation of the Failure.

And I? As I write, I am lying in a stupor from Wolfschmidt, sucking my thumb.

Marya Mannes, **MILTOWN PLACE, OR LIFE WITH SPONSORS**

Just before she left the house the other morning, said Letitia Baldridge, who has revised and expanded "The Amy Vanderbilt Complete Book of Etiquette," to a roomful of tableware manufacturers and merchandisers, her husband said to her, "My God! Who would want to hear you at this hour?" Miss Baldridge, a large, pink-faced woman, said this with such comic skill that the whole roomful of tableware manufacturers and merchandisers laughed extremely hard. Miss Baldridge told them that she went to Vassar, and received a B.A., but the funny thing about going to college was that when she graduated she couldn't type, she couldn't take shorthand, and she couldn't file. The roomful of tableware manufacturers and merchandisers let that pass. Then, said Miss Baldridge, she went to work for Ambassador David Bruce and his wife, Evangeline, at the United States Embassy in Paris. Evangeline Bruce, she said, was an incredible woman, who could speak seven languages by the time she was seventeen, cared very much about how a table looked, and would always take care of the table setting herself. But then once, for some reason or other,

Miss Baldridge had to take care of the table setting all by herself. At this particular dinner, there were more men than women, so some of the men had to be seated next to each other. Well, when they all sat down, it turned out that Miss Baldridge had seated one of the top ambassadors next to his wife's lover, and, because the ambassador and his wife and his wife's lover were an open secret, everybody at the dinner almost passed out. And so did the roomful of tableware manufacturers and merchandisers; again they laughed extremely hard. When something like this happens, she said, you don't cry about it, because then it only gets worse. After that, she told about working for Ambassadress Clare Boothe Luce, in Italy. This was soon after the Second World War, and what an experience *that* was! The Italians were so baroque, the dollar was tops, and the Luces were wonderful. Miss Baldridge, on the other hand, had her problems. There was the time she introduced the Pakistani Ambassador to a party of Italians as the Indian Ambassador. That didn't go down too well with the Pakistani Ambassador, naturally, but it got a big laugh from the roomful of tableware manufacturers and merchandisers. And the time when, for the first dinner she organized, everything was white—everything: the dishes, the soup, the wine. It wasn't funny then, but it got a big laugh now. And the time she served some Mormons a dinner they couldn't eat: the soup had sherry in it, and the fish had been cooked in white wine, the meat in red wine, the dessert in cognac. It wasn't funny then, but it was sidesplitting now. Winding up, Miss Baldridge told about working for Tiffany's, and how once, for a display, she ordered some exotic birds, and how they escaped from their cage, causing near-havoc on the third floor, which was filled with fine crystal and china. For that, the roomful of tableware manufacturers and merchandisers had lots of sharp intakes of breath. Miss Baldridge told about working in the White House for Mrs. Jacqueline Kennedy, and what a great decorator and restorer Mrs. Kennedy was, and how conscious of the tableware she was. The roomful of tableware manufacturers and merchandisers emitted some "Ah!"'s. Then Miss Baldridge said that it was a wonderful world and an affirmative world, and the roomful of tableware manufacturers and merchandisers applauded wildly, as if they were surprised and grateful that someone could feel that way after a life filled with table settings.

"The Talk of the Town," from **THE NEW YORKER**

"O Lord our Father, our young patriots, idols of our hearts, go forth to battle— be Thou near them! With them, in spirit, we also go forth from the sweet peace of our beloved firesides to smite the foe. O Lord our God, help us to tear their soldiers to bloody shreds with our shells; help us to cover their smiling fields with the pale forms of their patriot dead; help us to drown the thunder of the guns with the shrieks of their wounded, writhing in pain; help us to lay waste their humble homes with a hurricane of fire; help us to wring the hearts of their unoffending widows with unavailing grief; help us to turn them out roofless with their little children to wander unfriended the wastes of their desolated land in rags and hunger and thirst, sports of the sun flames of summer and the icy winds of winter, broken in spirit, worn with travail, imploring Thee for the refuge of the grave and denied it—for our sakes who adore Thee, Lord, blast their hopes, blight their lives, protract their bitter pilgrimage, make heavy their steps, water their way with their tears, stain the white snow with the blood of their wounded feet! We ask it, in the spirit of love, of Him Who is the Source of Love, and Who is the ever-faithful refuge and friend of all that are sore beset and seek His aid with humble and contrite hearts. Amen."

(After a pause) "Ye have prayed it; if ye still desire it, speak! The messenger of the Most High waits."

It was believed afterward that the man was a lunatic, because there was no sense in what he said.

Mark Twain, **THE WAR PRAYER**

Writing Assignment

Keep a reading journal. A reading journal is simply a record of your reading, a diary of your thoughts and reactions to what you read. Write down your reactions to anything you read: newspapers, magazines, novels, poetry, plays, and so on. Don't worry about grammar or stylistic niceties. Simply take off from the text and write down your reactions. You can also note particularly fine sayings or short quotes that appeal to you. Give your teacher the journal at the end of the course, with a short account of what you think of yourself as a reader. The account should be based on a careful examination of your journal. Read it as a record of your reading habits, your special identity themes, your range as a reader, your strengths and weaknesses. Be honest with yourself.

Readings

Edmund Wilson **INDIAN CORN DANCE**

"And as they watch, they imagine the dancers experiencing some profound satisfaction, renewing themselves with some draft of ecstasy of religion or poetry which they themselves do not know."

Helen Keller **THREE DAYS TO SEE**

"I who am blind can give one hint to those who see—one admonition to those who would make full use of the gift of sight: Use your eyes as if tomorrow you would be stricken blind."

William Golding **THINKING AS A HOBBY**

"I would dust Venus and set her aside, for I have come to love her and know her for the fair thing she is. But I would put the Thinker, sunk in desperate thought, where there were shadows before him—and at his back, I would put the Leopard, crouched and ready to spring."

Bruno Bettelheim **THE IGNORED LESSON OF ANNE FRANK**

"The desire of Anne Frank's parents not to interrupt their intimate family living, and their inability to plan more effectively for their survival, reflect the failure of all too many others faced with the threat of Nazi terror. It is a failure that deserves close examination because of the inherent warnings it contains for us, the living."

INDIAN CORN DANCE

Edmund Wilson

Cal Clay, the Crooning Cowboy, rides in a purple roadster with his signature in gold on both doors. People say that he has never been on a horse—that he used to work in a Denver hotel. But he always wears enormous chaps and a silver-studded sombrero. He has appeared in movies, vaudeville and night clubs all over the country, and he has made popular phonograph records. He whines to a guitar about the prairie, the coyotes and the old Chisholm Trail. Lately, however, his General Motors stock has shrunk to almost nothing, and it is harder for him to get engagements, so he has thought seriously of putting on a tent-show at the Indian ritual dances, and he has come to take it up with the Indians.

Muna Gibbs has had some losses, too, but is still in a very sound financial condition, since her father was a Morgan partner. The great passion of her life has been the Indians. She spent years persuading Navahos and Hopis to make sacred sand-paintings in her patio so that she could frame them under glass, and she ended by going to live in a pueblo, where she tried to look as dumpy as a squaw. The Indians, however, who, though they do not prize chastity, disapprove of wanton promiscuity, decreed at last that Muna must leave. She still dresses like a squaw and continually smokes cigarettes.

Dirk Macdougal, from Albuquerque, is an old real-estate man, who set out a few years ago to run a dude ranch de luxe—$150 a week, with a bathroom and radio in every cabin, a guide on every ride and all you wanted to drink. For a while he was fairly successful, and the Santa Teresa Valley was full of bellowing millionaires. But the overhead turned out to be high—especially for liquor and crippled horses—and there were no longer so many millionaires. Dirk has had to cut down his rates and now charges his patrons for drinks and for taking them to the Indian dances. The party he has brought over today are behaving very sourly, because they don't think they are getting their money's worth.

Gus Fay and Luella Lamb have just arrived from Hollywood. Mr. Fay is going to direct Miss Lamb in a picture which will show the struggle between a white man and a Navaho Indian for the love of a covered-wagon girl, so they have come in a big blue Pierce-Arrow to get the spirit of a pueblo dance. Mr. Fay has bone-rimmed spectacles, marcelled hair and a green whipcord riding-suit with polished puttees, and he has brought the little one-legged portable stool that he carries around on the lot. He watches the dance through field-glasses. Miss Lamb is also dressed in riding-costume; she is a doughy-looking blonde. When they first arrived in the pueblo, the Indians were engaged in their cruel sport of snatching a rooster from horseback, and Miss Lamb assumed that the antics and yells were a demonstration in her honor.

Bill Peck is a well-meaning fellow. He started to go to Yale, but was always having awful hangovers and not showing up at his classes, and on trains he would get into card games with people who won all his money. So his father, a wealthy drug-manufacturer, sent him out West to a ranch. At the ranch, Bill read books about lost gold mines and the buried treasures of the Spanish; his allowance had by that time been cut down, and he decided to go out and search for them. He wears a pistol slung under his arm and an old hat slouched over his eyes, and he goes for long walks in the woods with a pickaxe over his shoulder. One day he came back much excited and said that he had got into a cave which was all frozen full of ice and that in the ice were two American soldiers in a perfect state of preservation. But when people went out with him to look for the cave, he couldn't find the way again, and he never succeeded in getting back there.

Jo Romero runs the peanut-and-pop stand and shortchanges the women and children. He has even mastered a trick which makes it possible for him to let people see that he has the right amount of money in his hand and then hold part of it back in his palm. He always overcharges for the pop, making everybody return the bottles and then not giving them their nickel rebate.

Lobo Baily is an old Roosevelt Rough Rider, who draws a small pension and has been drunk ever since the Spanish War. He used to live in Texas, but was recently convicted of killing a man who had said to him, "You think you're tough, don't you?" Lobo shot the man full of holes, and when he came out of jail after serving his sentence, he was met by a group of his townsmen, who ran him out of the state. Nobody likes him in New Mexico either, but people take a certain satisfaction in hearing him swear at Jo Romero. Lobo has been refusing to give the pop-bottles back, and as Jo keeps on demanding them, he slings one of them into Jo's stand with a parting high-pitched spew of bad language, and knocks over all the Crackerjack boxes.

Ella Davis and Sam Furstman are married, though Miss Davis keeps her maiden name. She comes from Kansas and paints flat lengths of landscape, diversified only by sagebrush or cactus, and with darkish mountains rising in the background. Today she is wearing neat boots, a fancy pink sombrero and a green silk scarf at the neck of her blouse; she has spectacles with yellow rims, because, with her feeling for color, she wants them to harmonize with her hair. Sam Furstman is a writer, and they live mostly on what he makes: he has been quite successful in a moderate way with an Indian-lore series for boys and is now doing a set of magazine articles for grownups called *The Golden Legend of the Rio Grande*. In conversation, he has psychoanalytic theories about Geronimo, Kit Carson, Archbishop Lamy, Montezuma and Billy the Kid.

Father Rafaele is the priest and, unlike most of the priests in the country parishes, he is serious and even fanatical. The Indians are nominally Catholics, having been baptized centuries ago by the Spaniards—so their dances are always inaugurated by a ceremony in honor of the local saint, after which the rain-invocation proceeds as in the days before the Christian medicine had been added to the native ones. Father Rafaele is a Spanish-speaking New Mexican, and he has been profoundly disturbed by the news of the Spanish revolution. Just outside the pueblo stands a little white adobe church, which has been decorated partly by the Indians; for reasons never quite understood, they painted on the façade, many years ago, not only two brightly colored angels, but some butterflies and two horses, one spotted and one red, and both with saddles on—perhaps to carry the saved to Heaven. The day after Father Rafaele had read about the burning of the convents in Madrid, he went around to the pueblo and had the butterflies and horses painted out.

Clifford Leadgood comes from Rockport, Massachusetts, and did postgraduate work at Harvard in the Italian lyric before Dante. Then he came down with t.b. and was sent out to Santa Fe. He is cured now, but still stays on—he has a very small income from an interest in the Lawrence textile mills. Ever since he came to New Mexico, Clifford has been fascinated by the Penitentes, the Franciscan sect of flagellants which has survived in old Mexico and here. On Good Fridays, the Penitentes go out at night and flagellate themselves in the hills. They also, on this occasion, have a rite of crucifixion; one of their number is fastened to a cross, and the others first whip him fiercely, then, with cactus-spikes clasped in their armpits, kneel down before him and worship him. Clifford has been cultivating the Penitentes, and they have admitted him to their windowless chapels. He will not tell you what he has seen there, but he will assert with quiet casual Harvard assurance that the Penitentes are one of the only really great things left in the world today. He has long thought of trying to join them, and the dream which he nurses in secret, and which he has intimated to a very few friends, is of offering himself as the crucified. The government some years ago put a stop to their nailing people up the way they used to do; they are only supposed to tie them up now, and Clifford is by no means certain that this isn't a degradation of the cult. Yet they tie you terribly tight and leave you a long time and lay it onto you with whips and cactus; three years ago a man died. Clifford wonders whether they really do have a doctor—as the government has tried to require —to check up on your pulse at intervals and be sure you're taken down in time.

It is thus that the white race is represented at such of the Indian dances as the public are allowed to see. In the case of the Hopi snake dance—which Lawrence has done so much to advertise—the Indians are said to feel that the attendance of curious whites has caused it to lose its virtue, with the result they now have two dances, one to deceive the whites and one in a sacred place. Some of the dances have always been secret; but people have done their best to get into them. It is as if they felt that the Indians were in possession of some sacred key, some integrity, some harmony with nature, which they, the white Americans, lacked. And as they watch, they imagine the dancers experiencing some profound satisfaction, renewing themselves with some draft of the ecstasy of religion or poetry which they themselves do not know.

1. Why do you think Wilson gives us a list of descriptions of people at the Indian Corn Dance?
2. Briefly summarize in one sentence for each the relationship between the onlookers and the Indians.
3. What gives coherence to this list of onlookers?
4. Do you see any interesting comparisons between the religion of the Penitentes and the Indians? Why do you think Wilson mentions the Penitentes?
5. Reread Wilson's last paragraph.
   a. What does it contribute to the overall unity of the essay?
   b. How is it related to the list of onlookers?
   c. Do you think Wilson reaches a conclusion?

THREE DAYS TO SEE

Helen Keller

All of us have read thrilling stories in which the hero had only a limited and specified time to live. Sometimes it was as long as a year; sometimes as short as twenty-four hours. But always we were interested in discovering just how the doomed man chose to spend his last days or his last hours. I speak, of course, of free men who have a choice, not condemned criminals whose sphere of activities is strictly delimited.

Such stories set us thinking, wondering what we should do under similar circumstances. What events, what experiences, what associations should we crowd into those last hours as mortal beings? What happiness should we find in reviewing the past, what regrets?

Sometimes I have thought it would be an excellent rule to live each day as if we should die tomorrow. Such an attitude would emphasize sharply the values of life. We should live each day with a gentleness, a vigor, and a keenness of appreciation which are often lost when time stretches before us in the constant panorama of more days and months and years to come. There are those, of course, who would adopt the epicurean motto of "Eat, drink, and be merry," but most people would be chastened by the certainty of impending death.

In stories, the doomed hero is usually saved at the last minute by some stroke of fortune, but almost always his sense of values is changed. He becomes more appreciative of the meaning of life and its permanent spiritual values. It has often been noted that those who live, or have lived, in the shadow of death bring a mellow sweetness to everything they do.

Most of us, however, take life for granted. We know that one day we must die, but usually we picture that day as far in the future. When we are in buoyant health, death is all but unimaginable. We seldom think of it. The days stretch out in an endless vista. So we go about our petty tasks, hardly aware of our listless attitude toward life.

The same lethargy, I am afraid, characterizes the use of all our faculties and senses. Only the deaf appreciate hearing, only the blind realize the manifold blessings that lie in sight. Particularly does this observation apply to those who have lost sight and hearing in adult life. But those who have never suffered impairment of sight or hearing seldom make the fullest use of these blessed faculties. Their eyes and ears take in all sights and sounds hazily, without concentration and with little appreciation. It is the same old story of not being grateful for what we have until we lose it, of not being conscious of health until we are ill.

I have often thought it would be a blessing if each human being were stricken blind and deaf for a few days at some time during his early adult life. Darkness would make him more appreciative of sight; silence would teach him the joys of sound.

Now and then I have tested my seeing friends to discover what they see. Recently I was visited by a very good friend who had just returned from a long walk in the woods, and I asked her what she had observed. "Nothing in particular," she replied. I might have been incredulous had I not been accustomed to such responses, for long ago I became convinced that the seeing see little.

How was it possible, I asked myself, to walk for an hour through the woods and see nothing worthy of note? I who cannot see find hundreds of things to interest me through mere touch. I feel the delicate symmetry of a leaf. I pass my hands lovingly about the smooth skin of a silver birch, or the rough shaggy bark of a pine. In spring I touch the branches of trees hopefully in search of a bud, the first sign of awakening Nature after her winter's sleep. I feel the delightful, velvety texture of a flower, and discover its remarkable convolutions, and something of the miracle of Nature is revealed to me. Occasionally, if I am fortunate, I place my hand gently on a small tree and feel the happy quiver of a bird in full song. I am delighted to have the cool waters of a brook rush through my open fingers. To me a lush carpet of pine needles or spongy grass is more welcome than the most luxurious Persian rug. To me the pageant of seasons is a thrilling and unending drama, the action of which streams through my finger tips.

At times my heart cries out with longing to see all these things. If I can get so much pleasure from mere touch, how much more beauty must be revealed by sight. Yet, those who have eyes apparently see little. The panorama of color and action which fills the world is taken for granted. It is human, perhaps, to appreciate little that which we have and to long for that which we have not, but it is a great pity that in the world of light the gift of sight is used only as a mere convenience rather than as a means of adding fullness to life.

If I were the president of a university I should establish a compulsory course in "How to Use Your Eyes." The professor would try to show his pupils how they could add joy to their lives by really seeing what passes unnoticed before them. He would try to awake their dormant and sluggish faculties.

Perhaps I can best illustrate by imagining what I should most like to see if I were given the use of my eyes, say, for just three days. And while I am imagining, suppose you, too, set your mind to work on the problem of how you would use your own eyes if you had only three more days to see. If with the oncoming darkness of the third night you knew that the sun would never rise for you again, how would you spend those three precious intervening days? What would you most want to let your gaze rest upon?

I, naturally, should want most to see the things which have become dear to me through my years of darkness. You, too, would want to let your eyes rest long on the things that have become dear to you so that you could take the memory of them with you into the night that loomed before you.

If, by some miracle I were granted three seeing days, to be followed by a relapse into darkness, I should divide the period into three parts.

On the first day, I should want to see the people whose kindness and gentleness have made my life worth living. First I should like to gaze long upon the face of my dear teacher, Mrs. Anne Sullivan Macy, who came to me when I was a child and opened the outer world to me. I should want not merely to see the outline of her face, so that I could cherish it in my memory, but to study that face and find in it the living evidence of the sympathetic tenderness and patience with which she accomplished the difficult task of my education. I should like to see in her eyes that strength of character which has enabled her to stand firm in the face of difficulties, and that compassion for all humanity which she has revealed to me so often.

I do not know what it is to see into the heart of a friend through that "window of the soul," the eye. I can only "see" through my finger tips the outline of a face. I can detect laughter, sorrow, and many other obvious emotions. I know my friends from the feel of their faces. But I cannot really picture their personalities by touch. I know their personalities, of course, through other means, through the thoughts they express to me, through whatever of their actions are revealed to me. But I am denied that deeper understanding of them which I am sure would come through sight of them, through watching their reactions to various expressed thoughts and circumstances, through noting the immediate and fleeting reactions of their eyes and countenance.

Friends who are near to me I know well, because through the months and years they reveal themselves to me in all their phases; but of casual friends I have only an incomplete impression, an impression gained from a handclasp, from spoken words which I take from their lips with my finger tips, or which they tap into the palm of my hand.

How much easier, how much more satisfying it is for you who can see to grasp quickly the essential qualities of another person by watching the subtleties of expression, the quiver of a muscle, the flutter of a hand. But does it ever occur to you to use your sight to see into the inner nature of a friend or acquaintance? Do not most of you seeing people grasp casually the outward features of a face and let it go at that?

For instance, can you describe accurately the faces of five good friends? Some of you can, but many cannot. As an experiment, I have questioned husbands of long standing about the color of their wives' eyes, and often they express embarrassed confusion and admit they do not know. And, incidentally, it is a chronic complaint of wives that their husbands do not notice new dresses, new hats, and changes in household arrangements.

The eyes of seeing persons soon become accustomed to the routine of their surroundings, and they actually see only the startling and spectacular. But even in viewing the most spectacular sights the eyes are lazy. Court records reveal every day how inaccurately "eyewitnesses" see. A given event will be "seen" in several different ways by as many witnesses. Some see more than others, but few see everything that is within the range of their vision.

Oh, the things that I should see if I had the power of sight for just three days!

The first day would be a busy one. I should call to me all my dear friends and look long into their faces, imprinting upon my mind the outward evidences of the beauty that is within them. I should let my eyes rest, too, on the face of a baby, so that I could catch a vision of the eager, innocent beauty which precedes the individual's consciousness of the conflicts which life develops.

And I should like to look into the loyal, trusting eyes of my dogs—the grave, canny little Scottie, Darkie, and the stalwart, understanding Great Dane, Helga, whose warm, tender, and playful friendships are so comforting to me.

On that busy first day I should also view the small simple things of my home. I want to see the warm colors in the rugs under my feet, the pictures on the walls, the intimate trifles that transform a house into home. My eyes would rest respectfully on the books in raised type which I have read, but they would be more eagerly interested in the printed books which seeing people can read, for during the long night of my life the books I have read and those which have been read to me have built themselves into a great shining lighthouse, revealing to me the deepest channels of human life and the human spirit.

In the afternoon of that first seeing day, I should take a long walk in the woods and intoxicate my eyes on the beauties of the world of Nature, trying desperately to absorb in a few hours the vast splendor which is constantly unfolding itself to those who can see. On the way home from my woodland jaunt my path would lie near a farm so that I might see the patient horses plowing in the field (perhaps I should see only a tractor!) and the serene content of men living close to the soil. And I should pray for the glory of a colorful sunset.

When dusk had fallen, I should experience the double delight of being able to see by artificial light, which the genius of man has created to extend the power of his sight when Nature decrees darkness.

In the night of that first day of sight, I should not be able to sleep, so full would be my mind of the memories of the day.

The next day—the second day of sight—I should arise with the dawn and see the thrilling miracle by which night is transformed into day. I should behold with awe the magnificent panorama of light with which the sun awakens the sleeping earth.

This day I should devote to a hasty glimpse of the world, past and present. I should want to see the pageant of man's progress, the kaleidoscope of the ages. How can so much be compressed into one day? Through the museums, of course. Often I have visited the New York Museum of Natural History to touch with my hands many of the objects there exhibited, but I have longed to see with my eyes the condensed history of the earth and its inhabitants displayed there—animals and the races of men pictured in their native environment; gigantic carcasses of dinosaurs and mastodons which roamed the earth long before man appeared, with his tiny stature and powerful brain, to conquer the animal kingdom; realistic presentations of the processes of evolution in animals, in man, and in the implements which man has used to fashion for himself a secure home on this planet; and a thousand and one other aspects of natural history.

I wonder how many readers of this article have viewed this panorama of the face of living things as pictured in that inspiring museum. Many, of course, have not had the opportunity, but I am sure that many who have had the opportunity have not made use of it. There, indeed, is a place to use your eyes. You who see can spend many fruitful days there, but I, with my imaginary three days of sight, could only take a hasty glimpse, and pass on.

My next stop would be the Metropolitan Museum of Art, for just as the Museum of Natural History reveals the material aspects of the world, so does the Metropolitan show the myriad facets of the human spirit. Throughout the history of humanity the urge to artistic expression has been almost as powerful as the urge for food, shelter, and procreation. And here, in the vast chambers of the Metropolitan Museum, is unfolded before me the spirit of Egypt, Greece, and Rome, as expressed in their art. I know well through my hands the sculptured gods and goddesses of the ancient Nile-land. I have felt copies of Parthenon friezes, and I have sensed the rhythmic beauty of charging Athenian warriors. Apollos and Venuses and the Wingèd Victory of Samothrace are friends of my finger tips. The gnarled, bearded features of Homer are dear to me, for he, too, knew blindness.

My hands have lingered upon the living marble of Roman sculpture as well as that of later generations. I have passed my hands over a plaster cast of Michelangelo's inspiring and heroic Moses; I have sensed the power of Rodin; I have been awed by the devoted spirit of Gothic wood carving. These arts which can be touched have meaning for me, but even they were meant to be seen rather than felt, and I can only guess at the beauty which remains hidden from me. I can admire the simple lines of a Greek vase, but its figured decorations are lost to me.

So on this, my second day of sight, I should try to probe into the soul of man through his art. The things I knew through touch I should now see. More splendid still, the whole magnificent world of painting would be opened to me, from the Italian Primitives, with their serene religious devotion, to the Moderns, with their feverish visions. I should look deep into the canvases of Raphael, Leonardo da Vinci, Titian, Rembrandt. I should want to feast my eyes upon the warm colors of Veronese, study the mysteries of El Greco, catch a new vision of Nature from Corot. Oh, there is so much rich meaning and beauty in the art of the ages for you who have eyes to see!

Upon my short visit to this temple of art I should not be able to review a fraction of that great world of art which is open to you. I should be able to get only a superficial impression. Artists tell me that for a deep and true appreciation of art one must educate the eye. One must learn through experience to weigh the merits of line, of composition, of form and color. If I had eyes, how happily would I embark upon so fascinating a study! Yet I am told that, to many of you who have eyes to see, the world of art is a dark night, unexplored and unilluminated.

It would be with extreme reluctance that I should leave the Metropolitan Museum, which contains the key to beauty—a beauty so neglected. Seeing persons, however, do not need a Metropolitan to find this key to beauty. The same key lies waiting in smaller museums, and in books on the shelves of even small libraries. But naturally, in my limited time of imaginary sight, I should choose the place where the key unlocks the greatest treasures in the shortest time.

The evening of my second day of sight I should spend at a theater or at the movies. Even now I often attend theatrical performances of all sorts, but the action of the play must be spelled into my hand by a companion. But how I should like to see with my own eyes the fascinating figure of Hamlet, or the gusty Falstaff amid colorful Elizabethan trappings! How I should like to follow each movement of the graceful Hamlet, each strut of the hearty Falstaff! And since I could see only one play, I should be confronted by a many-horned dilemma, for there are scores of plays I should want to see. You who have eyes can see any you like. How many of you, I wonder, when you gaze at a play, a movie, or any spectacle, realize and give thanks for the miracle of sight which enables you to enjoy its color, grace, and movement?

I cannot enjoy the beauty of rhythmic movement except in a sphere restricted to the touch of my hands. I can vision only dimly the grace of a Pavlova, although I know something of the delight of rhythm, for often I can sense the beat of music as it vibrates through the floor. I can well imagine that cadenced motion must be one of the most pleasing sights in the world. I have been able to gather something of this by tracing with my fingers the lines in sculptured marble; if this static grace can be so lovely, how much more acute must be the thrill of seeing grace in motion.

One of my dearest memories is of the time when Joseph Jefferson allowed me to touch his face and hands as he went through some of the gestures and speeches of his beloved Rip Van Winkle. I was able to catch thus a meager glimpse of the world of drama, and I shall never forget the delight of that moment. But, oh, how much I must miss, and how much pleasure you seeing ones can derive from watching and hearing the interplay of speech and movement in the unfolding of a dramatic performance! If I could see only one play, I should know how to picture in my mind the action of a hundred plays which I have read or had transferred to me through the medium of the manual alphabet.

So, through the evening of my second imaginary day of sight, the great figures of dramatic literature would crowd sleep from my eyes.

The following morning, I should again greet the dawn, anxious to discover new delights, for I am sure that, for those who have eyes which really see, the dawn of each day must be a perpetually new revelation of beauty.

This, according to the terms of my imagined miracle, is to be my third and last day of sight. I shall have no time to waste in regrets or longings; there is too much to see. The first day I devoted to my friends, animate and inanimate. The second revealed to me the history of man and Nature. Today I shall spend in the workaday world of the present, amid the haunts of men going about the business of life. And where can one find so many activities and conditions of men as in New York? So the city becomes my destination.

I start from my home in the quiet little suburb of Forest Hills, Long Island. Here, surrounded by green lawns, trees, and flowers, are neat little houses, happy with the voices and movements of wives and children, havens of peaceful rest for men who toil in the city. I drive across the lacy structure of steel which spans the East River, and I get a new and startling vision of the power and ingenuity of the mind of man. Busy boats chug and scurry about the river—racy speed boats, stolid, snorting tugs. If I had long days of sight ahead, I should spend many of them watching the delightful activity upon the river.

I look ahead, and before me rise the fantastic towers of New York, a city that seems to have stepped from the pages of a fairy story. What an awe-inspiring sight, these glittering spires, these vast banks of stone and steel—structures such as the gods might build for themselves! This animated picture is a part of the lives of millions of people every day. How many, I wonder, give it so much as a second glance? Very few, I fear. Their eyes are blind to this magnificent sight because it is so familiar to them.

I hurry to the top of one of those gigantic structures, the Empire State Building, for there, a short time ago, I "saw" the city below through the eyes of my secretary. I am anxious to compare my fancy with reality. I am sure I should not be disappointed in the panorama spread out before me, for to me it would be a vision of another world.

Now I begin my rounds of the city. First, I stand at a busy corner, merely looking at people, trying by sight of them to understand something of their lives. I see smiles, and I am happy. I see serious determination, and I am proud. I see suffering, and I am compassionate.

I stroll down Fifth Avenue. I throw my eyes out of focus so that I see no particular object but only a seething kaleidoscope of color. I am certain that the colors of women's dresses moving in a throng must be a gorgeous spectacle of which I should never tire. But perhaps if I had sight I should be like most other women—too interested in styles and the cut of individual dresses to give much attention to the splendor of color in the mass. And I am convinced, too, that I should become an inveterate window shopper, for it must be a delight to the eye to view the myriad articles of beauty on display.

From Fifth Avenue I make a tour of the city—to Park Avenue, to the slums, to factories, to parks where children play. I take a stay-at-home trip abroad by visiting the foreign quarters. Always my eyes are open wide to all the sights of both happiness and misery so that I may probe deep and add to my understanding of how people work and live. My heart is full of the images of people and things. My eye passes lightly over no single trifle; it strives to touch and hold closely each thing its gaze rests upon. Some sights are pleasant, filling the heart with happiness; but some are miserably pathetic. To these latter I do not shut my eyes, for they, too, are part of life. To close the eye on them is to close the heart and mind.

My third day of sight is drawing to an end. Perhaps there are many serious pursuits to which I should devote the few remaining hours, but I am afraid that on the evening of that last day I should again run away to the theater, to a hilariously funny play, so that I might appreciate the overtones of comedy in the human spirit.

At midnight my temporary respite from blindness would cease, and permanent night would close in on me again. Naturally in those three short days I should not have seen all I wanted to see. Only when darkness had again descended upon me should I realize how much I had left unseen. But my mind would be so crowded with glorious memories that I should have little time for regrets. Thereafter the touch of every object would bring a flowing memory of how that object looked.

Perhaps this short outline of how I should spend three days of sight does not agree with the program you would set for yourself if you knew that you were about to be stricken blind. I am, however, sure that if you actually faced that fate your eyes would open to things you had never seen before, storing up memories for the long night ahead. You would use your eyes as never before. Everything you saw would become dear to you. Your eyes would touch and embrace every object that came within your range of vision. Then, at last, you would really see, and a new world of beauty would open itself before you.

I who am blind can give one hint to those who see—one admonition to those who would make full use of the gift of sight: Use your eyes as if tomorrow you would be stricken blind. And the same method can be applied to the other senses. Hear the music of voices, the song of a bird, the mighty strains of an orchestra, as if you would be stricken deaf tomorrow. Touch each object you want to touch as if tomorrow your tactile sense would fail. Smell the perfume of flowers, taste with relish each morsel, as if tomorrow you could never smell and taste again. Make the most of every sense; glory in all the facets of pleasure and beauty which the world reveals to you through the several means of contact which Nature provides. But of all the senses, I am sure that sight must be the most delightful.

1. Listen carefully to Helen Keller's voice and describe its variations. What emotions does she convey? Can you find more than one voice? What is her attitude to life? And her audience?

2. This is an essay about *not* taking the senses for granted, written by a woman who was both deaf and blind. Do you think this essay indicates that she managed to overcome a sense of the tragedy of her own life?

3. "... suppose you, too, set your mind to work on the problem of how you would use your own eyes if you had only three more days to see." Write a short account of how you would remedy your own deficiencies in using your sight.

4. In this essay, you find yourself confronted by a writer whose primary topic is herself. Describe the personality of the writer as carefully as you can. How does she avoid appearing self-centered?

5. Does Keller rouse your expectations and keep your interest sustained? Explain with examples from the text.

THINKING AS A HOBBY

William Golding

While I was still a boy, I came to the conclusion that there were three grades of thinking; and since I was later to claim thinking as my hobby, I came to an even stranger conclusion—namely, that I myself could not think at all.

I must have been an unsatisfactory child for grownups to deal with. I remember how incomprehensible they appeared to me at first, but not, of course, how I appeared to them. It was the headmaster of my grammar school who first brought the subject of thinking before me—though neither in the way, nor with the result he intended. He had some statuettes in his study. They stood on a high cupboard behind this desk. One was a lady wearing nothing but a bath towel. She seemed frozen in an eternal panic lest the bath towel slip down any farther; and since she had no arms, she was in an unfortunate position to pull the towel up again. Next to her, crouched the statuette of a leopard, ready to spring down at the top drawer of a filing cabinet labeled A-AH. My innocence interpreted this as the victim's last, despairing cry. Beyond the leopard was a naked, muscular gentleman, who sat, looking down, with his chin on his fist and his elbow on his knee. He seemed utterly miserable.

Some time later, I learned about these statuettes. The headmaster had placed them where they would face delinquent children, because they symbolized to him the whole of life. The naked lady was the Venus of Milo. She was Love. She was not worried about the towel. She was just busy being beautiful. The leopard was Nature, and he was being natural. The naked, muscular gentleman was not miserable. He was Rodin's Thinker, an image of pure thought. It is easy to buy small plaster models of what you think life is like.

I had better explain that I was a frequent visitor to the headmaster's study, because of the latest thing I had done or left undone. As we now say, I was not integrated. I was, if anything, disintegrated; and I was puzzled. Grownups never made sense. Whenever I found myself in a penal position before the headmaster's desk, with the statuettes glimmering whitely above him, I would sink my head, clasp my hands behind my back and writhe one shoe over the other.

The headmaster would look opaquely at me, through flashing spectacles.

"What are we going to do with you?"

Well, what *were* they going to do with me? I would writhe my shoe some more and stare down at the worn rug.

"Look up, boy! Can't you look up?"

Then I would look up at the cupboard, where the naked lady was frozen in her panic and the muscular gentleman contemplated the hindquarters of the leopard in endless gloom. I had nothing to say to the headmaster. His spectacles caught the light so that you could see nothing human behind them. There was no possibility of communication.

"Don't you ever think at all?"

No, I didn't think, wasn't thinking, couldn't think—I was simply waiting in anguish for the interview to stop.

"Then you'd better learn—hadn't you?"

On one occasion the headmaster leaped to his feet, reached up and plonked Rodin's masterpiece on the desk before me.

"That's what a man looks like when he's really thinking."

I surveyed the gentleman without interest or comprehension.

"Go back to your class."

Clearly there was something missing in me. Nature had endowed the rest of the human race with a sixth sense and left me out. This must be so, I mused, on my way back to the class, since whether I had broken a window, or failed to remember Boyle's Law, or been late for school, my teachers produced me one, adult answer: "Why can't you think?"

As I saw the case, I had broken the window because I had tried to hit Jack

Arney with a cricket ball and missed him; I could not remember Boyle's Law because I had never bothered to learn it; and I was late for school because I preferred looking over the bridge into the river. In fact, I was wicked. Were my teachers, perhaps, so good that they could not understand the depths of my depravity? Were they clear, untormented people who could direct their every action by this mysterious business of thinking? The whole thing was incomprehensible. In my earlier years, I found even the statuette of the Thinker confusing. I did not believe any of my teachers were naked, ever. Like someone born deaf, but bitterly determined to find out about sound, I watched my teachers to find out about thought.

There was Mr. Houghton. He was always telling me to think. With a modest satisfaction, he would tell me that he had thought a bit himself. Then why did he spend so much time drinking? Or was there more sense in drinking than there appeared to be? But if not, and if drinking were in fact ruinous to health—and Mr. Houghton was ruined, there was no doubt about that—why was he always talking about the clean life and the virtues of fresh air? He would spread his arms wide with the action of a man who habitually spent his time striding along mountain ridges.

"Open air does me good, boys—I know it!"

Sometimes, exalted by his own oratory, he would leap from his desk and hustle us outside into a hideous wind.

"Now, boys! Deep breaths! Feel it right down inside you—huge draughts of God's good air!"

He would stand before us, rejoicing in his perfect health, an open-air man. He would put his hands on his waist and take a tremendous breath. You could hear the wind, trapped in the cavern of his chest and struggling with all the unnatural impediments. His body would reel with shock and his ruined face go white at the unaccustomed visitation. He would stagger back to his desk and collapse there, useless for the rest of the morning.

Mr. Houghton was given to high-minded monologues about the good life, sexless and full of duty. Yet in the middle of one of these monologues, if a girl passed the window, tapping along on her neat little feet, he would interrupt his discourse, his neck would turn of itself and he would watch her out of sight. In this instance, he seemed to me ruled not by thought but by an invisible and irresistible spring in his nape.

His neck was an object of great interest to me. Normally it bulged a bit over his collar. But Mr. Houghton had fought in the First World War alongside both Americans and French, and had come—by who knows what illogic?—to a settled detestation of both countries. If either country happened to be prominent in current affairs, no argument could make Mr. Houghton think well of it. He would bang the desk, his neck would bulge still further and go red. "You can say what you like," he would cry, "but I've thought about this—and I know what I think!"

Mr. Houghton thought with his neck.

There was Miss Parsons. She assured us that her dearest wish was our welfare, but I knew even then, with the mysterious clairvoyance of childhood, that what she wanted most was the husband she never got. There was Mr. Hands—and so on.

I have dealt at length with my teachers because this was my introduction to the nature of what is commonly called thought. Through them I discovered that thought is often full of unconscious prejudice, ignorance and hypocrisy. It will lecture on disinterested purity while its neck is being remorselessly twisted toward a skirt. Technically, it is about as proficient as most businessmen's golf, as honest as most politicians' intentions, or—to come near my own preoccupation—as coherent as most books that get written. It is what I came to call grade-three thinking, though more properly, it is feeling, rather than thought.

True, often there is a kind of innocence in prejudices, but in those days I viewed grade-three thinking with an intolerant contempt and an incautious mockery. I delighted to confront a pious lady who hated the Germans with the proposition that we should love our enemies. She taught me a great truth in dealing with grade-three thinkers; because of her, I no longer dismiss lightly a mental process which for nine-tenths of the population is the nearest they will ever get to thought. They have immense solidarity. We had better respect them, for we are outnumbered and surrounded. A crowd of grade-three thinkers, all shouting the same thing, all warming their hands at the fire of their own prejudices, will not thank you for pointing out the contradictions in their beliefs. Man is a gregarious animal, and enjoys agreement as cows will graze all the same way on the side of a hill.

Grade-two thinking is the detection of contradictions. I reached grade two when I trapped the poor, pious lady. Grade-two thinkers do not stampede easily, though often they fall into the other fault and lag behind. Grade-two thinking is a withdrawal, with eyes and ears open. It became my hobby and brought satisfaction and loneliness in either hand. For grade-two thinking destroys without having the power to create. It set me watching the crowds cheering His Majesty the King and asking myself what all the fuss was about, without giving me anything positive to put in the place of that heady patriotism. But there were compensations. To hear people justify their habit of hunting foxes and tearing them to pieces by claiming that the foxes liked it. To hear our Prime Minister talk about the great benefit we conferred on India by jailing people like Pandit Nehru and Gandhi. To hear American politicians talk about peace in one sentence and refuse to join the League of Nations in the next. Yes, there were moments of delight.

But I was growing toward adolescence and had to admit that Mr. Houghton was not the only one with an irresistible spring in his neck. I, too, felt the compulsive hand of nature and began to find that pointing out contradiction could be costly as well as fun. There was Ruth, for example, a serious and attractive girl.

I was an atheist at the time. Grade-two thinking is a menace to religion and knocks down sects like skittles. I put myself in a position to be converted by her with an hypocrisy worthy of grade three. She was a Methodist—or at least, her parents were, and Ruth had to follow suit. But, alas, instead of relying on the Holy Spirit to convert me, Ruth was foolish enough to open her pretty mouth in argument. She claimed that the Bible (King James Version) was literally inspired. I countered by saying that the Catholics believed in the literal inspiration of Saint Jerome's *Vulgate,* and the two books were different. Argument flagged.

At last she remarked that there were an awful lot of Methodists, and they couldn't be wrong, could they—not all those millions? That was too easy, said I restively (for the nearer you were to Ruth, the nicer she was to be near to) since there were more Roman Catholics than Methodists anyway; and they couldn't be wrong, could they—not all those hundreds of millions? An awful flicker of doubt appeared in her eyes. I slid my arm round her waist and murmured breathlessly that if we were counting heads, the Buddhists were the boys for my money. But Ruth had *really* wanted to do me good, because I was so nice. She fled. The combination of my arm and those countless Buddhists was too much for her.

That night her father visited my father and left, red-cheeked and indignant. I was given the third degree to find out what had happened. It was lucky we were both of us only fourteen. I lost Ruth and gained an undeserved reputation as a potential libertine.

So grade-two thinking could be dangerous. It was in this knowledge, at the age of fifteen, that I remember making a comment from the heights of grade two, on the limitations of grade three. One evening I found myself alone in the school hall, preparing it for a party. The door of the headmaster's study was open. I went in. The headmaster had ceased to thump Rodin's Thinker down on the desk as an example to the young. Perhaps he had not found any more candidates, but the statuettes were still there, glimmering and gathering dust on top of the cupboard. I stood on a chair and rearranged them. I stood Venus in her bath towel on the filing cabinet, so that now the top drawer caught its breath in a gasp of sexy excitement. "A-ah!" The portentous Thinker I placed on the edge of the cupboard so that he looked down at the bath towel and waited for it to slip.

Grade-two thinking, though it filled life with fun and excitement, did not make for content. To find out the deficiencies of our elders bolsters the young ego but does not make for personal security. I found that grade two was not only the power to point out contradictions. It took the swimmer some distance from the shore and left him there, out of his depth. I decided that Pontius Pilate was a typical grade-two thinker. "What is truth?" he said, a very common grade-two thought, but one that is used always as the end of an argument instead of the beginning. There is a still higher grade of thought which says, "What is truth?" and sets out to find it.

But these grade-one thinkers were few and far between. They did not visit my grammar school in the flesh though they were there in books. I aspired to them, partly because I was ambitious and partly because I now saw my hobby as an unsatisfactory thing if it went no further. If you set out to climb a mountain, however high you climb, you have failed if you cannot reach the top.

I *did* meet an undeniably grade-one thinker in my first year at Oxford. I was looking over a small bridge in Magdalen Deer Park, and a tiny mustached and hatted figure came and stood by my side. He was a German who had just fled from the Nazis to Oxford as a temporary refuge. His name was Einstein.

But Professor Einstein knew no English at that time and I knew only two words of German. I beamed at him, trying wordlessly to convey by my bearing all the affection and respect that the English felt for him. It is possible—and I have to make the admission—that I felt here were two grade-one thinkers standing side by side; yet I doubt if my face conveyed more than a formless awe. I would have given my Greek and Latin and French and a good slice of my English for enough German to communicate. But we were divided; he was as inscrutable as my headmaster. For perhaps five minutes we stood together on the bridge, undeniable grade-one thinker and breathless aspirant. With true greatness, Professor Einstein realized that any contact was better than none. He pointed to a trout wavering in midstream.

He spoke: "*Fisch.*"

My brain reeled. Here I was, mingling with the great, and yet helpless as the veriest grade-three thinker. Desperately I sought for some sign by which I might convey that I, too, revered pure reason. I nodded vehemently. In a brilliant flash I used up half my German vocabulary.

"*Fisch. Ja. Ja.*"

For perhaps another five minutes we stood side by side. Then Professor Einstein, his whole figure still conveying good will and amiability, drifted away out of sight.

I, too, would be a grade-one thinker. I was irreverent at the best of times. Political and religious systems, social customs, loyalties and traditions, they all came tumbling down like so many rotten apples off a tree. This was a fine hobby and a sensible substitute for cricket, since you could play it all the year round. I came up in the end with what must always remain the justification for grade-one thinking, its sign, seal and charter. I devised a coherent system for living. It was a moral system, which was wholly logical. Of course, as I readily admitted, conversion of the world to my way of thinking might be difficult, since my system did away with a number of trifles, such as big business, centralized government, armies, marriage. . . .

It was Ruth all over again. I had some very good friends who stood by me, and still do. But my acquaintances vanished, taking the girls with them. Young women seemed oddly contented with the world as it was. They valued the meaningless ceremony with a ring. Young men, while willing to concede the chaining sordidness of marriage, were hesitant about abandoning the organizations which they hoped would give them a career. A young man on the first rung of the Royal Navy, while perfectly agreeable to doing away with big business and marriage, got as red-necked as Mr. Houghton when I proposed a world without any battleships in it.

Had the game gone too far? Was it a game any longer? In those prewar days, I stood to lose a great deal, for the sake of a hobby.

Now you are expecting me to describe how I saw the folly of my ways and came back to the warm nest, where prejudices are so often called loyalties, where pointless actions are hallowed into custom by repetition, where we are content to say we think when all we do is feel.

But you would be wrong. I dropped my hobby and turned professional.

If I were to go back to the headmaster's study and find the dusty statuettes still there, I would arrange them differently. I would dust Venus and put her aside, for I have come to love her and know her for the fair thing she is. But I would put the Thinker, sunk in his desperate thought, where there were shadows before him—and at his back, I would put the leopard, crouched and ready to spring.

1. What do you understand Golding thinks of himself as a thinker? Is he in any way ironic about himself?

2. Compare the two scenes in which Golding rearranges the three statues and explain the significance of the changes.

3. Choose what you think is Golding's most emphatic statement about thinking and explain what it means.

4. There are, according to Golding, three grades of thinking. What are they? If reading were to be classified in a similar manner, what would its three grades be?

5. Golding claims he has turned from thinking as a hobby to thinking as a profession. What does that mean?

THE IGNORED LESSON OF ANNE FRANK

Bruno Bettelheim

When the world first learned about the Nazi concentration and death camps, most civilized people felt the horrors committed in them to be so uncanny as to be unbelievable. It came as a severe shock that supposedly civilized nations could stoop to such inhuman acts. The implication that modern man has such inadequate control over his cruel and destructive proclivities was felt as a threat to our views of ourselves and our humanity. Three different psychological mechanisms were most frequently used for dealing with the appalling revelation of what had gone on in the camps:

(1) its applicability to man in general was denied by asserting—contrary to evidence—that the acts of torture and mass murder were committed by a small group of insane or perverted persons;

(2) the truth of the reports was denied by declaring them vastly exaggerated and ascribing them to propaganda (this originated with the German government, which called all reports on terror in the camps "horror propaganda"—*Greuel-propaganda*);

(3) the reports were believed, but the knowledge of the horror repressed as soon as possible.

All three mechanisms could be seen at work after liberation of those prisoners remaining. At first, after the discovery of the camps and their death-dealing, a wave of extreme outrage swept the Allied nations. It was soon followed by a general repression of the discovery in people's minds. Possibly this reaction was due to something more than the blow dealt to modern man's narcissism by the realization that cruelty is still rampant among men. Also present may have been the dim but extremely threatening realization that the modern state now has available the means for changing personality, and for destroying millions it deems undesirable. The ideas that in our day a people's personalities might be changed against their will by the state, and that other populations might be wholly or partially exterminated, are so fearful that one tries to free oneself of them and their impact by defensive denial, or by repression.

The extraordinary world-wide success of the book, play, and movie *The Diary of Anne Frank* suggests the power of the desire to counteract the realization of the personality-destroying and murderous nature of the camps by concentrating all attention on what is experienced as a demonstration that private and intimate life can continue to flourish even under the direct persecution by the most ruthless totalitarian system. And this although Anne Frank's fate demonstrates how efforts at disregarding in private life what goes on around one in society can hasten one's own destruction.

What concerns me here is not what actually happened to the Frank family, how they tried—and failed—to survive their terrible ordeal. It would be very wrong to take apart so humane and moving a story, which aroused so much well-merited compassion for gentle Anne Frank and her tragic fate. What is at issue is the universal and uncritical response to her diary and to the play and movie based on it, and what this reaction tells about our attempts to cope with the feelings her fate—used by us to serve as a symbol of a most human reaction to Nazi terror—arouses in us. I believe that the world-wide acclaim given her story cannot be explained unless we recognize in it our wish to forget the gas chambers, and our effort to do so by glorifying the ability to retreat into an extremely private, gentle, sensitive world, and there to cling as much as possible to what have been one's usual daily attitudes and activities, although surrounded by a maelstrom apt to engulf one at any moment.

The Frank family's attitude that life could be carried on as before may well have been what led to their destruction. By eulogizing how they lived in their hiding place while neglecting to examine first whether it was a reasonable or an effective choice, we are able to ignore the crucial lesson of their story—that such an attitude can be fatal in extreme circumstances.

While the Franks were making their preparations for going passively into hiding, thousands of other Jews in Holland (as elsewhere in Europe) were trying to escape to the free world, in order to survive and/or fight. Others who could not escape went underground—into hiding—each family member with, for example, a different gentile family. We gather from the diary, however, that the chief desire of the Frank family was to continue living as nearly as possible in the same fashion to which they had been accustomed in happier times.

Little Anne, too, wanted only to go on with life as usual, and what else could she have done but fall in with the pattern her parents created for her existence? But hers was not a necessary fate, much less a heroic one; it was a terrible but also a senseless fate. Anne had a good chance to survive, as did many Jewish children in Holland. But she would have had to leave her parents and go to live with a gentile Dutch family, posing as their own child, something her parents would have had to arrange for her.

Everyone who recognized the obvious knew that the hardest way to go underground was to do it as a family; to hide out together made detection by the SS most likely; and when detected, everybody was doomed. By hiding singly, even when one got caught, the others had a chance to survive. The Franks, with their excellent connections among gentile Dutch families, might well have been able to hide out singly, each with a different family. But instead, the main principle of their planning was continuing their beloved family life—an understandable desire, but highly unrealistic in those times. Choosing any other course would have meant not merely giving up living together, but also realizing the full measure of the danger to their lives.

The Franks were unable to accept that going on living as a family as they had done before the Nazi invasion of Holland was no longer a desirable way of life, much as they loved each other; in fact, for them and others like them, it was most dangerous behavior. But even given their wish not to separate, they failed to make appropriate preparations for what was likely to happen.

There is little doubt that the Franks, who were able to provide themselves with so much while arranging for going into hiding, and even while hiding, could have provided themselves with some weapons had they wished. Had they had a gun, Mr. Frank could have shot down at least one or two of the "green police" who came for them. There was no surplus of such police, and the loss of an SS with every Jew arrested would have noticeably hindered the functioning of the police state. Even a butcher knife, which they certainly could have taken with them into hiding, could have been used by them in self-defense. The fate of the Franks wouldn't have been very different, because they all died anyway except for Anne's father. But they could have sold their lives for a high price, instead of walking to their death. Still, although one must assume that Mr. Frank would have fought courageously, as we know he did when a soldier in the first World War, it is not everybody who can plan to kill those who are bent on killing him, although many who would not be ready to contemplate doing so would be willing to kill those who are bent on murdering not only them but also their wives and little daughters.

An entirely different matter would have been planning for escape in case of discovery. The Franks' hiding place had only one entrance; it did not have any other exit. Despite this fact, during their many months of hiding, they did not try to devise one. Nor did they make other plans for escape, such as that one of the family members—as likely as not Mr. Frank—would try to detain the police in the narrow entrance way—maybe even fight them, as suggested above—thus giving other members of the family a chance to escape, either by reaching the roofs of adjacent houses, or down a ladder into the alley behind the house in which they were living.

Any of this would have required recognizing and accepting the desperate straits in which they found themselves, and concentrating on how best to cope with them. This was quite possible to do, even under the terrible conditions in which the Jews found themselves after the Nazi occupation of Holland. It can be seen from many other accounts, for example from the story of Marga Minco, a girl of about Anne Frank's age who lived to tell about it. Her parents had planned that when the police should come for them, the father would try to detain them by arguing and fighting with them, to give the wife and daughter a chance to escape through a rear door. Unfortunately it did not quite work out this way, and both parents got killed. But their short-lived resistance permitted their daughter to make her escape as planned and to reach a Dutch family who saved her.[1]

This is not mentioned as a criticism that the Frank family did not plan or behave along similar lines. A family has every right to arrange their life as they wish or think best, and to take the risks they want to take. My point is not to criticize what the Franks did, but only the universal admiration of their way of coping, or rather of not coping. The story of little Marga who survived, every bit as touching, remains totally neglected by comparison.

Many Jews—unlike the Franks, who through listening to British radio news were better informed than most—had no detailed knowledge of the extermination camps. Thus it was easier for them to make themselves believe that complete compliance with even the most outrageously debilitating and degrading Nazi

1. Marga Minco, *Bitter Herbs* (New York: Oxford University Press), 1960.

orders might offer a chance for survival. But neither tremendous anxiety that inhibits clear thinking and with it well-planned and determined action, nor ignorance about what happened to those who responded with passive waiting for being rounded up for their extermination, can explain the reaction of audiences to the play and movie retelling Anne's story, which are all about such waiting that results finally in destruction.

I think it is the fictitious ending that explains the enormous success of this play and movie. At the conclusion we hear Anne's voice from the beyond, saying, "In spite of everything, I still believe that people are really good at heart." This improbable sentiment is supposedly from a girl who had been starved to death, had watched her sister meet the same fate before she did, knew that her mother had been murdered, and had watched untold thousands of adults and children being killed. This statement is not justified by anything Anne actually told her diary.

Going on with intimate family living, no matter how dangerous it might be to survival, was fatal to all too many during the Nazi regime. And if all men are good, then indeed we can all go on with living our lives as we have been accustomed to in times of undisturbed safety and can afford to forget about Auschwitz. But Anne, her sister, her mother, may well have died because her parents could not get themselves to believe in Auschwitz.

While play and movie are ostensibly about Nazi persecution and destruction, in actuality what we watch is the way that, despite this terror, lovable people manage to continue living their satisfying intimate lives with each other. The heroine grows from a child into a young adult as normally as any other girl would, despite the most abnormal conditions of all other aspects of her existence, and that of her family. Thus the play reassures us that despite the destructiveness of Nazi racism and tyranny in general, it is possible to disregard it in one's private life much of the time, even if one is Jewish.

True, the ending happens just as the Franks and their friends had feared all along: their hiding place is discovered, and they are carried away to their doom. But the fictitious declaration of faith in the goodness of all men which concludes the play falsely reassures us since it impresses on us that in the combat between Nazi terror and continuance of intimate family living the latter wins out, since Anne has the last word. This is simply contrary to fact, because it was she who got killed. Her seeming survival through her moving statement about the goodness of men releases us effectively of the need to cope with the problems Auschwitz presents. That is why we are so relieved by her statement. It explains why millions loved the play and movie, because while it confronts us with the fact that Auschwitz existed it encourages us at the same time to ignore any of its implications. If all men are good at heart, there never really was an Auschwitz; nor is there any possibility that it may recur.

The desire of Anne Frank's parents not to interrupt their intimate family living, and their inability to plan more effectively for their survival, reflect the failure of all too many others faced with the threat of Nazi terror. It is a failure that deserves close examination because of the inherent warnings it contains for us, the living.

Submission to the threatening power of the Nazi state often led both to the disintegration of what had once seemed well-integrated personalities and to a return to an immature disregard for the dangers of reality. Those Jews who submitted passively to Nazi persecution came to depend on primitive and infantile thought processes: wishful thinking and disregard for the possibility of death. Many persuaded themselves that they, out of all the others, would be spared. Many more simply disbelieved in the possibility of their own death. Not believing in it, they did not take what seemed to them desperate precautions, such as giving up everything to hide out singly; or trying to escape even if it meant risking their lives in doing so; or preparing to fight for their lives when no escape was possible and death had become an immediate possibility. It is true that defending their lives in active combat before they were rounded up to be transported into the camps might have hastened their deaths, and so, up to a point, they were protecting themselves by "rolling with the punches" of the enemy.

But the longer one rolls with the punches dealt not by the normal vagaries of life, but by one's eventual executioner, the more likely it becomes that one will no longer have the strength to resist when death becomes imminent. This is particularly true if yielding to the enemy is accompanied not by a commensurate strengthening of the personality, but by an inner disintegration. We can observe such a process among the Franks, who bickered with each other over trifles, instead of supporting each other's ability to resist the demoralizing impact of their living conditions.

Those who faced up to the announced intentions of the Nazis preprared for the worst as a real and imminent possibility. It meant risking one's life for a self-chosen purpose, but in doing so, creating at least a small chance for saving one's own life or those of others, or both. When Jews in Germany were restricted to their homes, those who did not succumb to inertia took the new restrictions as a warning that it was high time to go underground, join the resistance movement, provide themselves with forged papers, and so on, if they had not done so long ago. Many of them survived.

Some distant relatives of mine may furnish an example. Early in the war, a young man living in a small Hungarian town banded together with a number of other Jews to prepare against a German invasion. As soon as the Nazis imposed curfews on the Jews, his group left for Budapest—because the bigger capital city with its greater anonymity offered chances for escaping detection. Similar groups from other towns converged in Budapest and joined forces. From among themselves they selected typically "Aryan" looking men who equipped themselves with false papers and immediately joined the Hungarian SS. These spies were then able to warn of impending persecution and raids.

Many of these groups survived intact. Furthermore, they had also equipped themselves with small arms, so that if they were detected, they could put up enough of a fight for the majority to escape while a few would die fighting to make the escape possible. A few of the Jews who had joined the SS were discovered and immediately shot, probably a death preferable to one in the gas chambers. But most of even these Jews survived, hiding within the SS until liberation.

Compare these arrangements not just to the Franks' selection of a hiding place that was basically a trap without an outlet but with Mr. Frank's teaching typically academic high-school subjects to his children rather than how to make a getaway: a token of his inability to face the seriousness of the threat of death. Teaching high-school subjects had, of course, its constructive aspects. It relieved the ever-present anxiety about their fate to some degree by concentrating on different matters, and by implication it encouraged hope for a future in which such knowledge would be useful. In this sense such teaching was purposeful, but it was erroneous in that it took the place of much more pertinent teaching and planning: how best to try to escape when detected.

Unfortunately the Franks were by no means the only ones who, out of anxiety, became unable to contemplate their true situation and with it to plan accordingly. Anxiety, and the wish to counteract it by clinging to each other, and to reduce its sting by continuing as much as possible with their usual way of life incapacitated many, particularly when survival plans required changing radically old ways of living that they cherished, and which had become their only source of satisfaction.

My young relative, for example, was unable to persuade other members of his family to go with him when he left the small town where he had lived with them. Three times, at tremendous risk to himself, he returned to plead with his relatives, pointing out first the growing persecution of the Jews, and later the fact that transport to the gas chambers had already begun. He could not convince these Jews to leave their homes and break up their families to go singly into hiding.

As their desperation mounted, they clung more determinedly to their old living arrangements and to each other, became less able to consider giving up the possessions they had accumulated through hard work over a lifetime. The more severely their freedom to act was reduced, and what little they were still permitted to do restricted by insensible and degrading regulations imposed by the Nazis, the more did they become unable to contemplate independent action. Their life energies drained out of them, sapped by their ever-greater anxiety. The less they found strength in themselves, the more they held on to the little that was left of what had given them security in the past—their old surroundings, their customary way of life, their possessions—all these seemed to give their lives some permanency, offer some symbols of security. Only what had once been symbols of security now endangered life, since they were excuses for avoiding change. On each successive visit the young man found his relatives more incapacitated, less willing or able to take his advice, more frozen into inactivity, and with it further along the way to the crematoria where, in fact, they all died.

Levin renders a detailed account of the desperate but fruitless efforts made by small Jewish groups determined to survive to try to save the rest. She tells how messengers were "sent into the provinces to warn Jews that deportation meant death, but their warnings were ignored because most Jews refused to contemplate their own annihilation."[2] I believe the reason for such refusal has to be found in their inability to take action. If we are certain that we are helpless to protect ourselves against the danger of destruction, we cannot contemplate it. We can consider the danger only as long as we believe there are ways to protect ourselves, to fight back, to escape. If we are convinced none of this is possible for us, then there is no point in thinking about the danger; on the contrary, it is best to refuse to do so.

As a prisoner in Buchenwald, I talked to hundreds of German Jewish prisoners who were brought there as part of the huge pogrom in the wake of the murder of vom Rath in the fall of 1938. I asked them why they had not left Germany, given the utterly degrading conditions they had been subjected to. Their answer was: How could we leave? It would have meant giving up our homes, our work, our sources of income. Having been deprived by Nazi persecution and degradation of much of their self-respect, they had become unable to give up what still gave them a semblance of it: their earthly belongings. But instead of using possessions, they became captivated by them, and this possession by earthly goods became the fatal mask for their possession by anxiety, fear, and denial.

How the investment of personal property with one's life energy could make people die bit by bit was illustrated throughout the Nazi persecution of the Jews. At the time of the first boycott of Jewish stores, the chief external goal of the Nazis was to acquire the possessions of the Jews. They even let Jews take some things out of the country at that time if they would leave the bulk of their property behind. For a long time the intention of the Nazis, and the goal of their first discriminatory laws, was to force undesirable minorities, including Jews, into emigration.

Although the extermination policy was in line with the inner logic of Nazi racial ideology, one may wonder whether the idea that millions of Jews (and other foreign nationals) could be submitted to extermination did not partially result from seeing the degree of degradation Jews accepted without fighting back. When no violent resistance occurred, persecution of the Jews worsened, slow step by slow step.

Many Jews who on the invasion of Poland were able to survey their situation and draw the right conclusions survived the Second World War. As the Germans approached, they left everything behind and fled to Russia, much as they distrusted and disliked the Soviet system. But there, while badly treated, they could at least

2. Nora Levin, *The Holocaust* (New York: Thomas Y. Crowell, 1968).

survive. Those who stayed on in Poland believing they could go on with life-as-before sealed their fate. Thus in the deepest sense the walk to the gas chamber was only the last consequence of these Jews' inability to comprehend what was in store; it was the final step of surrender to the death instinct, which might also be called the principle of inertia. The first step was taken long before arrival at the death camp.

We can find a dramatic demonstration of how far the surrender to inertia can be carried, and the wish not to know because knowing would create unbearable anxiety, in an experience of Olga Lengyel.[3] She reports that although she and her fellow prisoners lived just a few hundred yards from the crematoria and the gas chambers and knew what they were for, most prisoners denied knowledge of them for months. If they had grasped their true situation, it might have helped them save either the lives they themselves were fated to lose, or the lives of others.

When Mrs. Lengyel's fellow prisoners were selected to be sent to the gas chambers, they did not try to break away from the group, as she successfully did. Worse, the first time she tried to escape the gas chambers, some of the other selected prisoners told the supervisors that she was trying to get away. Mrs. Lengyel desperately asks the question: How was it possible that people denied the existence of the gas chamber when all day long they saw the crematoria burning and smelled the odor of burning flesh? Why did they prefer ignoring the exterminations to fighting for their very own lives? She can offer no explanation, only the observation that they resented anyone who tried to save himself from the common fate, because they lacked enough courage to risk action themselves. I believe they did it because they had given up their will to live and permitted their death tendencies to engulf them. As a result, such prisoners were in the thrall of the murdering SS not only physically but also psychologically, while this was not true for those prisoners who still had a grip on life.

Some prisoners even began to serve their executioners, to help speed the death of their own kind. Then things had progressed beyond simple inertia to the death instinct running rampant. Those who tried to serve their executioners in what were once their civilian capacities were merely continuing life as usual and thereby opening the door to their death.

For example, Mrs. Lengyel speaks of Dr. Mengele, SS physician at Auschwitz, as a typical example of the "business as usual" attitude that enabled some prisoners, and certainly the SS, to retain whatever balance they could despite what they were doing. She describes how Dr. Mengele took all correct medical precautions during childbirth, rigorously observing all aseptic principles, cutting the umbilical cord with greatest care, etc. But only half an hour later he sent mother and infant to be burned in the crematorium.

Having made his choice, Dr. Mengele and others like him had to delude them-

3. Olga Lengyel, *Five Chimneys: The Story of Auschwitz* (Chicago: Ziff-Davis, 1947).

selves to be able to live with themselves and their experience. Only one personal document on the subject has come to my attention, that of Dr. Nyiszli, a prisoner serving as "research physician" at Auschwitz.[4] How Dr. Nyiszli deluded himself can be seen, for example, in the way he repeatedly refers to himself as working in Auschwitz as a physician, although he worked as the assistant of a criminal murderer. He speaks of the Institute for Race, Biological, and Anthropological Investigation as "one of the most qualified medical centers of the Third Reich," although it was devoted to proving falsehoods. That Nyiszli was a doctor didn't alter the fact that he—like any of the prisoner foremen who served the SS better than some SS were willing to serve it—was a participant in the crimes of the SS. How could he do it and live with himself?

The answer is: by taking pride in his professional skills, irrespective of the purpose they served. Dr. Nyiszli and Dr. Mengele were only two among hundreds of other—and far more prominent—physicians who participated in the Nazis' murderous pseudo-scientific human experiments. It was the peculiar pride of these men in their professional skill and knowledge, without regard for moral implications, that made them so dangerous. Although the concentration camps and crematoria are no longer here, this kind of pride still remains with us; it is characteristic of a modern society in which fascination with technical competence has dulled concern for human feelings. Auschwitz is gone, but so long as this attitude persists, we shall not be safe from cruel indifference to life at the core.

I have met many Jews as well as gentile anti-Nazis, similar to the activist group in Hungary described earlier, who survived in Nazi Germany and in the occupied countries. These people realized that when a world goes to pieces and inhumanity reigns supreme, man cannot go on living his private life as he was wont to do, and would like to do; he cannot, as the loving head of a family, keep the family living together peacefully, undisturbed by the surrounding world; nor can he continue to take pride in his profession or possessions, when either will deprive him of his humanity, if not also of his life. In such times, one must radically reevaluate all of what one has done, believed in, and stood for in order to know how to act. In short, one has to take a stand on the new reality—a firm stand, not one of retirement into an even more private world.

If today, Negroes in Africa march against the guns of a police that defends *apartheid*—even if hundreds of dissenters are shot down and tens of thousands rounded up in camps—their fight will sooner or later assure them of a chance for liberty and equality. Millions of the Jews of Europe who did not or could not escape in time or go underground as many thousands did, could at least have died fighting as some did in the Warsaw ghetto at the end, instead of passively waiting to be rounded up for their own extermination.

4. Miklos Nyiszli, *Auschwitz: A Doctor's Eyewitness Account* (New York: Frederick Fell, 1960).

1. What exactly is the ignored lesson of Anne Frank?
2. This is a provocative essay that tries to change public opinion from mere pity for murdered Jews to a new awareness of the tragedy. How did you find yourself reacting to Bettelheim's argument?
3. What is the lesson of Mengele and Nyiszli in the extermination camps? How does it relate to us now?
4. How does Bettelheim try to counter a sense of cosmic irony in this essay?
5. Bettelheim writes: ''... when a world goes to pieces and inhumanity reigns supreme, man cannot go on living his private life as he was wont to do, and would like to do; ... In short, one has to take a stand on the new reality—a firm stand, not one of retirement into an even more private world.'' Read Helen Keller's essay in this chapter, and see if you can reconcile her message with Bettelheim's. If so, how? If not, why not?

Interpretation

An interpretation is an explanation. Almost any kind of writing you will do about your reading in any course—from book reviews to applications of a textbook theory—will require you to show that you understand what you have read. You will need to be able to describe and explain the information in it. Interpretation starts with reading with a purpose: you should direct your reading toward understanding the text so that you may evaluate it or adapt the information in it.

When you write an interpretation, you are expected not only to account for the information in the text—information you select and organize—but to judge the text's emphasis, coherence, unity, and significance. You may also explore the implications of what you found, how the information may be applied and developed. If you are writing an essay about an imaginative piece of writing, an interpretation goes further than merely discussing information. It also describes—as you will see in Chapter 12—the *experience of reading*, the way in which you find yourself making meaning, your successes and difficulties in understanding.

The usual aims of interpretation, then, are as follows:

To clearly explain the information in the text, summarizing it when necessary

To describe the experience of reading the text, dealing with questions the text raises and any difficulties

To make judgments and to evaluate the text, referring to its emphasis, coherence, unity, and significance

These aims are part of writing any essay no matter what its purpose. Whether you are trying to persuade, describe, narrate, or explain, at some point you will have to reveal your interpretive powers. These in turn, of course, depend on your ability to read closely, as we learned in Chapter 1. In this chapter, we will concentrate on directed reading and on writing a basic interpretive paper. The writing process itself will be explained in more detail in the next five chapters.

Getting Your Reading into Words

In the process of reading closely and getting your ideas into words, you will be asking yourself a number of questions, such as: What does the text say? How does it say it? What does the writing suggest to me? Why am I absorbed in it, repelled by it, or indifferent to it? What can I say about the text that I think is important? Why do I find it easy or hard to understand? These questions may be difficult to answer coherently the first time you confront them. Understanding what the text means often takes some time and several readings. But you can interpret a text more efficiently if you begin writing notes as soon as you start reading.

A good way to begin is to jot down marginal comments, called annotations, as you read a text the first time. In the later stages, you will move to fuller separate note taking. This act of writing something down helps clarify your reading. Remember, this is not a formal exercise at this point, even though you are passing through specific stages. Grammar, syntax, and spelling are not your real concern now. You are only trying to increase your chances of developing a close, critical reading. Your note-taking, if you follow the stages outlined below, will fulfill this purpose.

Let's assume that you have been asked to write an interpretation of John Updike's essay "Beer Can" for your English class. You should pass through the following stages when preparing the interpretation:

Annotating the text, noting emphatic statements and paraphrasing them in the margins

Summarizing the text

Questioning the text by carefully reviewing the voices heard in the writing

Judging the emphasis, coherence, unity, and significance of the text, thus arriving at a conclusion about it

Each of these stages will be described in turn. They do not contradict each other but are part of the sequence of making an interpretation. It is not always necessary to pass through every stage to develop a close reading; you can decide to employ certain questions and judgments, for example, given the kind of writing you are reading. The more difficult the piece of writing, though, the better it is to use all the stages.

Annotating the Text

Here is an unusually short essay, the famous "Beer Can" by the well-known contemporary writer John Updike.

This seems to be an era of gratuitous inventions and negative improvements. Consider the beer can. It was beautiful—as beautiful as the clothespin, as inevitable as the wine bottle, as dignified and reassuring as the fire hydrant. A tranquil cylinder of delightfully resonant metal, it could be opened in an instant, requiring only the application of a handy gadget freely dispensed by every grocer. Who can forget the small, symmetrical thrill of those two triangular punctures, the dainty *pffff,* the little crest of suds that foamed eagerly in the exultation of release? Now we are given, instead, a top beetling with an ugly, shmoo-shaped "tab," which, after fiercely resisting the tugging, bleeding fingers of the thirsty man, threatens his lips with a dangerous and hideous hole. However, we have discovered a way to thwart Progress, usually so unthwartable. *Turn the beer can upside down and open the bottom.* The bottom is still the way the top used to be. True, this operation gives the beer an unsettling jolt, and the sight of a consistently inverted beer can might make people edgy, not to say queasy. But the latter difficulty could be eliminated if manufacturers would design cans that looked the same whichever end was up, like playing cards. What we need is Progress with an escape hatch.

How would you annotate this? *Annotation* is a kind of running commentary down the margins of a page that aims to highlight the message and anything else that is important in terms of style or meaning. It is especially useful to annotate when you are dealing with a complex explanation, such as you might find in a research source for a project.

> *Read the text right through.* Do not decide on the main statement immediately even though you will be developing a sense of what the piece is about as you read.
>
> *Use a dictionary* to check any words you do not understand.
>
> *Reread and annotate.* As you reread, mark the important points in the text by underlining them. Underline only emphatic statements and key words. Place a question mark next to passages you do not understand.

Here is what happens to "Beer Can" when it is annotated:

Modern inventions are not always a good thing

This seems to be an era of gratuitous inventions and negative improvements. Consider the beer can. [*Theme Statement*] It was beautiful—as beautiful as the clothespin, as [*Example*] inevitable as the wine bottle, as dignified and reassuring as the fire hydrant. A tranquil cylinder of delightfully resonant metal, it could be opened in an instant, requiring only the application of a handy gadget freely dispensed by every grocer. Who can forget the small, symmetrical thrill of those two triangular punctures, the dainty pffff, the little crest of suds that foamed eagerly in the exultation of release? Now we are given, instead, a top beetling [*problem*] with an ugly, shmoo-shaped "tab," which, after fiercely resisting the tugging, bleeding fingers of the thirsty man, threatens his lips with a dangerous and hideous hole. However, we have discovered

for example, once the beer can was easily opened with an opener

now with a tab, it is not

but we can turn progress on its head by opening the bottom of the can

a way to thwart Progress, usually so unthwartable. <u>Turn the beer can upside down and open the bottom.</u> The bottom is still the way the top used to be. True, this operation gives the beer an unsettling jolt, and the sight of a consistently inverted beer can might make people edgy, not to say queasy. But the latter difficulty could be eliminated if manufacturers would design cans that looked the same whichever end was up, like playing cards. <u>What we need is Progress with an escape hatch.</u>

[solution]

[conclusion]

so we can have an escape from progress

There are two main ways of annotating. Some readers merely put in the margin single words or phrases that remind them of the content of the passage. Others paraphrase the content of key sentences, as was done in the "Beer Can" annotation. For beginners, the latter is the best policy. A *paraphrase* is a restatement of a passage in your own words. When you paraphrase, you should try to clarify an author's meaning. This may seem like a lot of work, but the paraphrase can be a very useful method of making sure you understand what is being said. By paraphrasing in the margins, not only are you making clear and simple something that is complex, but you are *reinforcing* your reading, with one note building on the last, again, as you can see in the annotation of the Updike essay. You can then read your marginal notes in sequence and see clearly the way the argument of an essay has been built up.

In addition to summarizing the development of a text, your annotation marks problem passages that you can come back to: places where the argument or the style's relevance, or the tone, is not clear. The annotation may also include your own ideas and comments on what the writer is saying. And it may indicate places where you agree or disagree, or are not sure of your response. The value of annotating—not merely underlining or using a highlighting pen—is that you are *actively* interpreting as you move through a text. The discipline of keeping your mind working on what you read is an important one if you want to acquire information quickly and efficiently, and become a close reader.

It is useful to remember, too, that you do not write a summary or consider your annotations complete until you have answered the important question of *whether a writer means what is said,* a point we took up in considering irony in the last chapter. The question is: is there anything in the writer's style and tone that affects the argument and the message that is coming across to the reader? As far as "Beer Can" is concerned, the author's message, which is annotated in the margins, does not appear to be contradicted by anything we can say about the writer's style and tone. We can probably take the topic sentence to mean what the author says—that progress is not always progress—for Updike does not deny that statement anywhere in the essay, either by irony or by a change of argument.

Summarizing the Text

The information content of any piece of writing can be summarized in a few sentences. This is a more formal undertaking than annotation. You may not have to write a summary of your reading for your own purposes if you have clear annotations, but it is always a useful exercise that enables you to focus on what you are interpreting, especially if the text is full of information. The summary enables you to establish the text's coherence. It is likely, if you are writing about your reading or applying the knowledge from it, that you will need a summary anyhow.

A *summary*, like the annotation, is based upon simplified or condensed statements about a text. Actually, if you have paraphrased well, your summary is usually available to you in the margins of your text. But as you can see from the annotations of ''Beer Can,'' you may need to tidy up the marginal expressions, building a little on some of the major points you have isolated in order to write clear, complete sentences.

A summary contains the reader's choice of the most important details in a text and the way they are linked in argument or explanation. It does not go into much detail. Only the crucial points are mentioned. Usually, a summary generalizes about the subject, the argument, and the conclusion of the text. It does not attempt to offer a critical interpretation or evaluation, but relies only on selecting the most important of the writer's emphases and on condensing the writer's conclusion.

The key to writing a summary is to build on your annotations and paraphrases. Note, especially, the main statements in the text. After you have annotated ''Beer Can,'' for example, look for the sentence or sentences that seem to sum up the argument. Look for strong value judgments or sentences that point a direction in the argument or state a conclusion. You have to be careful to keep the integrity of the writer's argument, whether you agree with it or not, so it is especially important for you to note the *writer's* statement of the problem and the solution. But if a writer says one thing and means another, your summary must say what you think the writer really means. It pays, then, to identify your annotations before you begin the summary, as ''main statement,'' ''example,'' ''problem,'' ''solution,'' and ''conclusion,'' as was done in the ''Beer Can'' annotation above.

But what if you cannot find a clear subject and message? And if you can, how do you know if your summary is adequate? Let's take the second question first. It is wise to reread the text and check your annotations. If you are sure you have identified all the main points of the writer's argument and they fit together, that you have not missed any irony, and that you have discovered the writer's meaning, then you can say you have understood the text. If you cannot adequately summarize a text because you don't know how to arrange the material or because you have not understood a part of it, then there are three strategies for organizing your ideas into a summary and finding a subject and a message for problem passages. For each of these methods, you take notes:

■ *Ask Who? What? When? Where? How? and Why?* This famous list of journalists' questions can help you retrieve essential facts from your reading, or from any event that you are reporting on. Simply ask these questions of the text in any order. We'll follow the order listed above:

(Who?) John Updike . . . (What?) "Beer Can": an essay on the problem of unnecessary inventions . . . (When?) the problem is a present one . . . (Where?) in America and other countries with high technology . . . (How? That is, how does Updike make his point?) through comic exaggeration . . . (Why?) because he is satirizing progress.

This particular line of questioning is most appropriate for sorting out complicated material. For essays that are short and concise, like Updike's, these questions will yield only basic information.

■ *Develop any major statement or idea in the text.* Simply take any major statement or idea and pursue it through the text, clustering ideas around it as you find them:

An age of useless inventions . . . beer can a good example of a negative improvement . . . tab is dangerous . . . old can opener is better . . . how do we turn progress on its head? . . . open the bottom of the can.

We shall discuss clustering of ideas in more detail in the next chapter. For now, just remember that with this strategy what you are doing is collecting together related ideas (or ideas that develop from other ideas) as they come to mind to see where they lead you. Then go back over your notes and decide which ones are the most important and use them in your summary.

■ *Find the subject and the message.* In Updike's case, we have a problem: is the essay about beer cans, or progress, or thwarting progress? It could be any one, and in order to choose, we have to find the theme that seems to cover the most information, or that is the most interesting and provocative in its application. This is where clustering is useful. Try out "beer cans" first since, as the title, that is the likely subject. What would be its message? That beer can tabs are a symbol of progress and that they are a useless invention. Is the passage mainly about that? The subject seems too specific. What then of "thwarting progress"? Updike's punch line leads us to believe that this may be his main theme. The message then would be: "We must thwart progress by standing it on its head for there are too many useless inventions." That certainly is better than "beer cans," but it has an aggressive ring to it that Updike seems to be trying to avoid by his playfulness. To say that his motive in writing the essay is to be directive would be an exaggeration.

So we are left with "progress" as a subject, and its message might be "progress is a contradiction: it is not always as useful as it seems." Here we have a subject that attracts attention and a message that is relatively suggestive. By dealing with the *possible* subjects and their messages first, as you try out your options based on the text, you focus your reading and give yourself a subject to think about and later to write on.

Here, then, is a summary of "Beer Can":

In "Beer Can," Updike declares, with tongue in cheek, that modern technological progress has not always brought genuine advances, that progress itself is a contradiction. He uses the example of changes in the style of beer can openings, from the plain top and separate opener to the pull-tab. This change, he says, is not an improvement. However, we can always turn the beer can upside-down and open the bottom with an old-fashioned opener. So, claims Updike, we can escape Progress.

Whether you summarize or simply annotate, this initial stage of reading should show you the extent to which you have actually understood the main features of a writer's explanation or argument. This is not a stage to be rushed through, nor one in which you should fool yourself as a reader by proceeding without understanding.

Questioning the Voices in the Text

The Writing Environment

You will recall from Chapter 1 that the reader has to be a good listener. You hear voices in the text, that of the writer and sometimes of others too, and your understanding of what goes on in the text depends on what you think these voices are saying and how they are saying it. Try to get clear who the speaker is. What is the voice like? Calm, troubled, informative, muddled, aggressive, indifferent, ironic, sarcastic, cynical, comfortable, witty? There are many possible voices to be heard in speech and in writing. Be on the lookout for conflicting voices even from a single speaker, that is, for contradictions in what is being said; they may be deliberate, subtle, or mistaken. You have to be especially careful of this when you interpret writing as opposed to speech.

The environment of the writer, the reader, and the text seems similar to the familiar environment of speech, but there are important differences. A speaker can be substituted for a writer and a listener for a reader, but when we talk to each other, our intended meanings are conveyed and received as much by bodily gestures as by the words we use. We have more direct access to our audience when we are speaking than we do in writing. The context of the speech act, too, is wider than that of writing. It includes the setting where the conversation takes place and its memory associations, our bodily movements, our clothing, and so on. Dressing up for an interview with a prospective employer is part of the message we wish to convey. Everything that accompanies the words we use and hear is part of our meaning.

Writing, though, is unique among the communication acts in that *its context is words alone and the way they appear in print or handwriting.* The medium is visual to the extent that different kinds of type, for example, are used to achieve different effects, or illustrations are provided to complement a text. But writing is its own environment. In spite of its apparent indirectness, it offers wider possibilities because it can refer *out* to the real world or *in* to the world of the text, to things implied by the writing. Writing alone is capable of carrying a high level of complexity, abstraction, and imaginative suggestion. In this way, voices are as subtle in their expression in writing as they are in speech.

Voice and the Parts of a Text

We can ask of every text: Who is speaking? What is being said? How is it being said? Why is it being said? Who is the writer talking to? For each of these questions, we have to pay attention to some particular aspect of the writing of the text: the writer; the subject and message; the diction, tone, and style; the aim and implications; and the implied reader.

If you ask yourself these questions seriously, you can broaden the scope of your interpretation. Perhaps you will turn up only material you have already found, but at least you will have covered the basic range of ways in which you and the text *interact* in order to create meaning. Again, you should write notes in response to each question.

Who Is Speaking?

It is not essential to find out everything you can about a writer or even to conduct any research at all into the writer in order to interpret a text.

The writer's voice should be evident from the text itself. In most expository and persuasive writing, you will find only one voice but, again, be careful how you react to it on first hearing. Too often, you may decide the value of what is being said on the basis of your knowledge of who is saying it. But you should not assume that you know what a writer is going to say because you know who he or she is. Some writers are deliberately devious in their writing and take on attitudes or stances or even personalities that are not their own in order to make a point, especially in ironic writing. Here are some brief notes about "who is speaking?" in "Beer Can":

Updike is well-informed, urbane, and witty . . . he seems facetious and playful, but is his voice too melodramatic, too prone to exaggeration?

What Is Being Said?

Here you are looking for the message of the text: the way its information is arranged and the ambiguities it presents. You know what the subject and basic message are from your summary. But finding the subject and the message is only part of the problem of interpreting what is being said. The message can be complicated, as it is even in the short essay by Updike. Ask yourself the following questions:

What are the most significant details of the message?

Are they presented in a significant order?

What connections exist between facts?

Which facts are unrelated or even contradictory?

In other words, center on the emphasis and coherence of the message. For the Updike essay, you might respond to this question as follows:

Updike argues from the idea that progress is not necessarily progress . . . the beer can tab is a good example of this . . . But isn't the example overstated? Is Updike exaggerating for the fun of it? . . . the argument that Updike offers is witty and consistent: turn beer can upside-down if the tab is dangerous to open—turning progress on its head.

How Is the Message Presented?

■ *Diction.* When you read, you are engaging the particular use of language a writer chooses to emphasize. This is called diction: the selection of words every writer makes. Apart from the fact that a writer may call on a special vocabulary—a group of words that have specific

meanings in specific contexts, such as we find in scientific writing—
all writers must use language either referentially or suggestively. The
usual terms used to describe these functions of language are *denotation*
and *connotation.* Words by their very nature carry not only explicit
references (denotation), but also suggestive, symbolic, or associated
references (connotation). We all know that a *saucer* is an item of
crockery (which is its strict denotation, its first dictionary definition), but
it takes on a connotative role when it is a *flying saucer,* when the
saucer imaginatively lends its shape to an alien flying object.

So you have to decide when you read a text whether the writer is
using language with a denotative or a connotative emphasis. Does the
writer want to be explicit or suggestive? Clearly most scientific writing
aims for explicit reference and denotation, but the suggestive use of
language turns up there too and almost everywhere else, from news
reporting to literature, which is primarily connotative. Updike, you
might say, is using a mixture of denotation (references to the beer can
explicitly) and connotation (references to progress as associated with
the can's tab) with the emphasis on the latter. Knowing what kind of
language is being used may not seem of great consequence, but it is
important that you be aware of the possibility of suggestive language
so that you can be on the lookout for what it is suggesting.

■ *Tone.* The tone of a piece of writing refers to the writer's relationship or attitude to the subject. The emphasis here is not simply on
the subject itself but on the *way* the writer talks about it. Tone, that is,
is reflected in the voice you hear. A writer may decide to take a low-
keyed approach and let the topic speak for itself, but other times a
writer takes on a tone of voice that reveals a more complex relationship
to the subject. There are as many tones of voice as there are moods
generated by the relationships between people, or between people
and things. You may be solemn or flippant, sarcastic or warmly approving, playful or serious, intimate or formal, ironic or straightforward,
and so on. The reader can often tell where emphasis lies in a piece of
writing by the way a writer adopts a sharply dominating tone. Irony,
especially, is one of the most emphatic of tones, even though its tongue-
in-cheek performance is sometimes hard to catch. Updike, however, is
not really being ironic—rather he is facetious, playful, and critical.

■ *Style.* Style is not merely ornamentation; it is the writer's expression.
Style conveys the tone of voice a writer wishes to use. It also reflects
the writer's motives. So we look again at a writer's diction, or choice of

words, and also at the *syntax,* or structure, of the sentences (the effects of their patterns, length, and variety). We look especially at the *uses* of connotation and the colorfulness of language.

Every good writer has a personal style, which we can come to recognize. The art of writing involves learning something about strategies of style, as we shall see especially in the chapters on paragraphs and sentences. Whatever the style, it must above all be appropriate to the subject and the writer's message. It is useful to remember the old division between "high," or formal, and "low," or popular, styles with "informal," or everyday, in between. A *high style* is deliberately complex and literary, a *low style* involves the use of language often referred to as vulgar, and an *informal style* is the language of everyday speech. So Hamlet's "Alas, poor Yorick!—I knew him, Horatio; a fellow of infinite jest, of most excellent fancy" (Shakespeare, *Hamlet,* 5, i) is now distinctly high style, whereas "Gimme the salt, fathead" is low, and "Updike is a clever writer with a good sense of humor" is informal. A statement like "Would you have the goodness, pardon the intrusion, to hold my little doggy" (Samuel Beckett, *Murphy*) we would call *mixed,* that is, a mixture of formal and informal.

As far as "Beer Can" is concerned, your notes might say that Updike is writing in a comic high style about a subject that he believes needs satirical treatment. Here is a summary of the presentation of the message in "Beer Can":

Updike emphasizes his message with highly connotative language which is at the same time facetious, playful, and critical . . . a satirically comic high style

What Is the Aim of the Text?

Writing usually carries a motive: to explain, to persuade, to narrate, or to describe. These are frequently referred to as the four basic *rhetorical modes: exposition* (or explanation), *persuasion, narration,* and *description.* Most writing is a *mixture* of these modes, and we will discuss all of them more fully in later chapters in the book. However, it is safe to say that in every piece of writing, however mixed the modes, one of them is probably dominant. Updike, for example, primarily wants to *persuade* us of a point, no matter that he does it entertainingly, and he uses description and exposition to bring about that end. Knowing the writer's aim is, of course, essential in making an interpretation of a text.

Ask yourself the following questions:

What is the writer really getting at?

What do the message, diction, style, and tone add up to?

What are the implications of the message?

Here are some summary notes:

Updike seems to suggest that his subject is greater than a beer can, that it is progress itself . . . he aims to persuade us that the can is an adequate symbol of nonprogress . . . his attack on technological progress could be extended to any number of apparently useless inventions, or at least inventions that don't seem very necessary, like electric toothbrushes, computerized car dashboards, electronic home dental plaque detectors.

Who is the Writer Talking to?

■ *The implied reader.* Because every writer has an audience in mind, there is always an implied reader. Writers know how intelligent an audience must be in order to understand an explanation or be persuaded or entertained. So a reader is *created* by the text, and we often like or dislike a piece of writing depending on what we think the writer thinks about the reader. In the Updike essay, we discover certain assumptions: the reader is presumably someone with a sense of humor, who can follow the cleverness of Updike's attack. The reader is also likely to be someone who can be persuaded by the "liberal" notion that technology does not always mean progress. Updike is not exactly stereotyping his reader, but he is indicating by his exaggeration that his reader must be somewhat playful and have some affection for the good old days. How else can Updike hope to persuade us, since he is not using a fully worked out argument? It would seem clear that Updike is not talking to serious-minded heavy beer drinkers who (another unfortunate stereotype) are delighted with labor-saving inventions that make their access to beer as uncomplicated as possible.

■ *The reader's personal reactions.* What fantasies, identifications, recognitions, agreements, fears, and associated ideas do you find or conjure up on reading a text? In short, how do you directly react to the text? Do you go along with the version of the implied reader you find in the text? Here are some notes based on the implied reader and a personal reaction:

Updike's overstatement is suggestive and amusing, directed to an audience of liberal skeptics, but the problem is that it is an overstatement . . . how dangerous really is the can tab?!... Updike has a tendency to be "cute," unless of course he means to back progress and produce an ironic statement ... seems to be no evidence for that ... it is difficult to do anything but admire the wit but feel the writer has missed out on a satirical purpose.

Arriving at a Conclusion

Let's briefly review what you have done so far in developing an interpretation. You have annotated the text, made a summary of it, and asked five crucial questions about the speaker, the message, the presentation, the aim, and the audience of the text. You have almost all the information you need on which to base an interpretation. All that is missing is a final judgment about the text and an organization of all the materials. An interpretation is always more than simply a summary or a translation of what the writer is saying or a statement of what the reader feels. An interpretation should always reveal an interaction between a text and a reader, as we discussed the process in Chapter 1. That is, a reader of an interpretation expects to find an original reading *and* a sense of the text being read.

How can you go about ensuring that your interpretation is tactful and makes a point? By summarizing carefully and following the questions outlined so far, you are not imposing yourself on the text. Rather, you are giving the text a chance and allowing your opinions to develop out of an interaction with it. Now you have finally *to organize your material, selecting the most important points from it, and come to a conclusion* that will form the thesis of your interpretation. This is how to go about it:

Select for Emphasis

Consider the writer's focus. Go through your notes and make a list of the writer's emphatic points. You are rewriting your notes at this point, rearranging them so that you can work directly from this new summary as you write the first draft of your interpretation. For your emphasis notes, you will need your summary and your notes in response to "what are the aims of the message?"

Updike's "Beer Can" is about progress that does not bring genuine advances ... it emphasizes the beer can tab as a symbol of nonprogress ... but we can turn the can upside-down to open it and turn progress on its head ... Updike aims to persuade us that the subject is not the beer can but progress itself, and that the can is an adequate symbol of nonprogress ... this could be extended, presumably, to any other apparently useless invention.

Judge the Coherence of the Text

Now you focus on the coherence of the writer's message and its presentation. Does the explanation follow logically? Are there any unresolved issues? Is the explanation integrated; that is, does the information fit together, like parts of a whole? Your personal reactions are now slowly moving to center stage. When you judge emphasis and coherence, you tend to let the text speak for itself, but you realize now that *you* are selecting the emphasis and *you* are judging the coherence. This demands care. Turn to your notes in response to ''who is speaking?'' ''what is being said?'' ''how is the message presented?'' and ''who is the writer talking to?''. You are looking through your notes for ideas that are related and those that are not. Write a short summary of what you find:

Updike's voice is witty and critical . . . he expects his audience to consist of liberal skeptics . . . but he makes large generalizations . . . troublesome problem of over-statement . . . tendency to be cute . . . a comical high style intending to be satirical which inflates the importance of the beer can . . . but coherence is threatened by a tendency to melodrama . . . seems to be some ambiguity in Updike's aim.

Judge the Unity of the Text

You are concerned now with the overall impression the piece of writing gives. Does it strike you as being unified? Does it give an impression of treating its subject consistently? If an essay's coherence depends on its parts making a whole, then the characteristic to look for when deciding on unity is *consistent* emphasis. So turn to all your notes: Do you hear a single dominant voice? If not, is the use of more than one voice deliberate? Do they all lead to a dominant impression? Is the message clear? Are your reactions consistent? Do you have any unsatisfied expectations? Are the implications of the essay as a whole consistent with the message? Do the diction, tone, and style all enhance and confirm the conclusion? Does the writer keep a consistent focus on the thoughts of the piece, on what the reader is expected to find? Summarize.

The essay's dominant impression is that Updike is trying to be satirical . . . but the reader is unsure of the overstatement . . . ambiguity over usefulness of beer tab for the writer's aim although logically connected to the theme.

Note that if there is any problem with the coherence of a text, then it is likely that there will be some problem with its unity.

Judge Significance

This is the most personal of all the judgments you make about a piece of writing. Here you say whether you think the text is good or bad: what you liked and what you didn't like. But you will notice that your opinion—if you have followed the above sequence—has developed slowly, not impetuously. It will depend on your previous arguments (in fact, you are summarizing their significance), and will not simply be tacked on to the end of a piece. No one is really interested in any one else's opinion unless it appears to be justified. So it is wise for you to evaluate on the basis of your earlier judgments unless you have changed your mind for good reason. Thus you look for the good and bad points you found earlier and weigh them off against each other in order to reach a conclusion. This conclusion becomes the thesis, or main message, of your interpretation:

The reader is left in the position of laughing along with Updike and feeling that he has indeed turned progress on its head, or of sensing that the whole satirical attack has failed because of the overstatement . . . the reader is left with a distinct ambivalence about the piece: clever, but consequential?

You will notice that this process of writing down reactions on a piece of paper and organizing them into judgments about emphasis, coherence, unity, and significance deals over and over again with the same ideas. Your reactions are constantly being reviewed and developed, and that is perhaps the most important part of the reading process. You have arrived at a conclusion and an interpretation after reworking an opinion. When you come to write the interpretation, you can do so with a pretty good idea of what your major theme will be. But of course it can change from your notes. *The notes are not your last thoughts.* Some point may trouble you, and on going back to the text, you discover that you have a new and important interpretation. Change your opinions then, but make sure they do not contradict any other aspects of your interpretation. If they do, then you must review all your judgments.

Writing the Interpretation

You can base your interpretation directly on the notes you have just written:

You have a summary of the emphatic points in the text.

You have judged how the explanation works or how the narrative fits together.

You have an overall impression of what the text is trying to say, and you have considered its consistency in saying it.

You have made a personal judgment about the significance of the text based on a close reading and have arrived at a conclusion.

You may write your interpretive essay following the order of your notes about emphasis, coherence, unity, and significance. There is a logical progression implied by this sequence. But it is important to note that you do not have to keep to it. Many interpretive essays begin forcefully with the reader's judgment as to significance, and then work through the material on emphasis, coherence, and unity in such a way that the judgments may overlap. Remember, though, that your writing will be judged by a reader in the same way that you have been judging your chosen text. You too must aim for emphasis, coherence, unity, and significance in your own essay, and the sequence above or an alternative sequence (beginning with significance) will help you do that.

Here is an interpretation of "Beer Can" based on an outline that follows this sequence: emphasis→coherence→unity→significance. The outline notes are beside it. Understand that the essay is not as rough as a first draft would probably be. We shall discuss in detail in the next few chapters the preparation of an essay from subject to outline, to first draft, to revision, to final draft.

BEER CAN

Emphasis

Updike's "Beer Can" is about progress that does not bring genuine advances ... it emphasizes the beer can tab as a symbol of nonprogress ... but we can turn the can upside-down to open it and turn progress on its head ... Updike aims to persuade us that the subject is not the beer can but progress itself, and that the can is an adequate symbol of nonprogress ... this could be extended, presumably, to any other apparently useless invention.

The emphasis of Updike's essay falls on a familiar object, the beer can, which is treated by the author as if it is not all that it appears to be. The familiar object takes on suggestive, even symbolic qualities. It is both a can and a symbol of progress. That plainly is what the writer wants us to believe. His argument depends, therefore, on persuading us that the beer can is indeed an appropriate representative of progress. His conclusion is that progress can be bad for our health, and not always an improvement. So we should turn progress on its head, a plea that is linked to the literal advice: "Turn the beer can upside-down and open the bottom." We must use technology to subvert technology.

Coherence

Updike's voice is witty and critical . . . he expects his audience to consist of liberal skeptics . . . but he makes large generalizations . . . troublesome problem of overstatement . . . tendency to be cute . . . a comical high style intending to be satirical which inflates the importance of the beer can . . . but coherence is threatened by a tendency to melodrama . . . seems to be some ambiguity in Updike's aim.

Updike does not leave himself a lot of room to room to argue in—one paragraph only—and he is relying as much on his wit as he is on his reason. But is the wit integrated with the reason? Are the tone and style related to the argument?

The essay begins with a large generalization, which is always risky. In this case, Updike has identified his audience as liberal skeptics, and he thinks he can persuade us with the statement: "This seems to be an era of gratuitous inventions and negative improvements." That is a common statement, but what if we do not believe it to begin with? Updike realizes the risk and avoids being moralistic by comically inflating his language about the beer can as a symbol of progress.

We can accept the basic exaggeration and the playful aim on which the essay hangs, but is Updike's tone and style really consistent with the argument? He opens the paragraph in a high-flying style which has a comic effect: "an era of gratuitous inventions," "as beautiful as the clothespin, as inevitable as the wine bottle, as dignified and reassuring as the fire hydrant," and so on. In the first few lines, Updike is plainly consistent in his comic exaggeration. Opening a beer can is described melodramatically and with overstated sensuousness: a "symmetrical thrill," a "dainty *pffff*," an "exultation of release."

But then the high style takes on perhaps an even

more melodramatic turn when we reach his claim that the new can "fiercely resist(s) the tugging, bleeding fingers of the thirsty man."

This is amusing but it also disturbs the unity of the piece. After all, Updike did choose a beer and not a soft drink can. There's something symbolically tough about the drink of good old boys and comrades. As current advertisements attest, the appeal of beer is not effeminate; it is the macho beverage of construction workers, oil drillers, athletes, and no-nonsense fellows (even when it is low caloric), and they are unlikely to rip their gnarled paws on tiny tabs. They are more likely to have the tab come away in their hands and then have to go at the can with a pointed instrument or even the more conventional opener.

Updike's high style, then, suggests that his proposal about progress needing an escape hatch comes to the reader a little too facetiously. He needs more examples than just a beer can to make a serious point. After all, progress does include trips to the moon and space shuttles, life-saving drugs, and new technologies for television and information gathering. Yet we have only been offered a short, sharp parable of modern life, and the choice of an appropriate symbol can make it or break it.

Updike's beer can becomes an ambiguous symbol, which can even undercut the writer's intentions. We are left with two thoroughly opposed yet legitimate readings of the paragraph, depending on how we

Unity

The essay's dominant impression is that Updike is trying to be satirical ... but the reader is unsure of the overstatement ... ambiguity over usefulness of beer tab for the writer's aim although logically connected to the theme.

Significance

The reader is left in the position of laughing along with Updike and feeling that he has indeed turned progress on its head, *or* of sensing that the whole satirical attack has failed because of the overstate-ment. . . . the reader is left with a distinct ambivalence about the piece: clever, but consequential?

want to look at it. On the one hand, we can approve of the sarcasm and find the overstatement appropriate, humorous, and not exaggerated at all. We can say: Updike is making fun of technology and progress, and he's right. Let's all try to find a way out, a way as simple and ingenious as the one he offers. Let's look for the weak links in technology and take advantage of them in order to return to the good old days. We can add to that: let's not read a short essay like this *too* closely, for its intentions are lighthearted.

But on the other hand, what if we don't like Updike's sentiments? Updike is exaggerating, we say, and being facetious about a serious topic. After all, the development of the tab top removed the bothersome habit of having to carry around can openers which were always getting lost. How can we condemn progress just because of changes in a beer can, which are not all bad anyhow? At least we don't throw tabs about. His example is inappropriate, and he is guilty of a rather reactionary nostalgia. Furthermore, one does not usually cut one's fingers on the tab. The overstatement has been carried too far.

Conclusion

Which interpretation should the reader make? Here is a legitimate stand-off created by a failure to be consistent in tone but not by an inability to emphasize a theme. The issue is that we are allowed to read the essay in two contradictory ways at once and get away with it. The subject and tone do not cohere exactly and form a unified whole. The evidence does not limit the argument to a specific direction, because it is not always appropriate. The style and tone point up the ambiguity of the example of the beer can, and the essay ends up rather more facetious and playful—even bordering on the cute—than sharply satirical.

Do you agree?

Checklist

1. The aims of interpretation are:
   - To clearly explain the information in the text
   - To describe the experience of reading the text
   - To make judgments and evaluate the text
2. Follow these stages in writing an interpretation:
   - Annotation
   - Summary
   - Questioning of the text
     Who is speaking? What is being said? (subject and message) How is the message presented? (diction, tone, and style) What is the aim of the text? Who is the writer talking to? (the implied reader)
   - Arriving at an interpretation
     Select for emphasis. Judge the text for coherence. Judge the text for unity. Judge the text for significance.
3. Follow the sequence of: emphasis→coherence→unity→significance (or begin with significance) when writing the interpretation.

Exercises

1. For each of the passages below:
   a. Provide an annotation
   b. Write a short (one-paragraph) summary
   c. Pursue the development of the key idea in some rough notes

. . . the beauty of the magical vision is the beauty of the deeply sensed, sacramental presence. The perception is not one of order, but of power. Such experience yields no sense of accomplished and rounded-off knowledge, but, on the contrary, it may begin and end in an overwhelming sense of mystery. We are awed, not informed. The closest most of us are apt to come nowadays to recapturing this mode of experience would be in sharing the perception of the poet or painter in the presence of a landscape, of the lover in the presence of the beloved. In the sweep of such experience, we have no interest in finding out about, summing up, or solving. On the contrary, we settle for celebrating the sheer, amazing fact that this wondrous thing is self-sufficiently there before us. We lose ourselves in the splendor or the terror of the moment and ask no more. We leave what we experience—this mountain, this sky, this place filled with forbidding shadows, this remarkable person—to be what it is, for its being alone is enough.

The scientist studies, sums up, and has done with his puzzle; the painter paints the same landscape, the same vase of flowers, the same person over and over again, content to reexperience the inexhaustible power of this presence interminably. The scientist reduces the perception of colored light to a meteorological generalization; the intoxicated poet announces, "My heart leaps up when I behold a rainbow in the sky," and then goes on to find a hundred ways to say the same thing over again without depleting the next poet's capacity to proclaim the same vision still again. What conceivable similarity is there between two such different modes of experience? None whatsoever. One clichéd argument suggests that the work of the scientist *begins* with the poet's sense of wonder (a dubious hypothesis at best) but then goes *beyond* it armed with spectroscope and light meter. The argument misses the key point: the poet's experience is defined precisely by the fact that the poet does *not* go beyond it. He begins and ends with it. Why? Because it is sufficient. Or rather, it is inexhaustible. What he has seen (and what the scientist has *not* seen) is not improved upon by being pressed into the form of knowledge. Or are we to believe it was by failure of intelligence that Wordsworth never graduated into the status of weatherman?

Theodore Roszak, from **THE MAKING OF A COUNTER CULTURE**

One cannot doubt that the study of history makes people wiser. But it is indispensable to understand the limits of historical analogy. Most useful historical generalizations are statements about massive social and intellectual movements over a considerable period of time. They make large-scale, long-term prediction possible. But they do not justify small-scale, short-term prediction. For short-run prediction is the prediction of detail and, given the complex structure of social events, the difficulty of anticipating the intersection or collision of different events and the irreducible mystery, if not invincible freedom, of individual decision, there are simply too many variables to warrant exact forecasts of the immediate future. History, in short, can answer questions, after a fashion, at long range. It cannot answer questions with confidence or certainty at short range. Alas, policy makers are rarely interested in the long run—"in the long run," as Keynes used to say, "we are all dead"—and the questions they put to history are thus most often the questions which history is least qualified to answer.

Far from offering a short cut to clairvoyance, history teaches us that the future is full of surprises and outwits all our certitudes. For the study of history issues not in scientific precision nor in moral finality but in irony. If twenty-five years ago, anyone had predicted that before the end of the decade of the 'forties Germany and Japan would be well on the way to becoming close friends and allies of Britain and the United States, he would have been considered mad. If fifteen years ago, as the Russians and Chinese were signing their thirty-year pact of amity and alliance, anyone predicted that by the end of the fifties they would be at each other's throats, he too would have been considered mad. The chastening fact is that many of the pivotal events of our age were unforeseen: from the Nazi-Soviet pact and the Tito-Stalin quarrel of years ago to such events in today's newspapers as the anti-communist upsurge in Indonesia and the overthrow of Nkrumah in Ghana (and his resurrection in Guinea).

Arthur Schlesinger, from **THE BITTER HERITAGE**

Recently, photography has become almost as widely practiced an amusement as sex and dancing—which means that, like every mass art form, photography is not practiced by most people as an art. It is mainly a social rite, a defense against anxiety, and a tool of power.

Memorializing the achievements of individuals considered as members of families (as well as of other groups) is the earliest popular use of photography. For at least a century, the wedding photograph has been as much a part of the ceremony as the prescribed verbal formulas. Cameras go with family life. According to a sociological study done in France, most households have a camera, but a household with children is twice as likely to have at least one camera as a household in which there are no children. Not to take pictures of one's children, particularly when they are small, is a sign of parental indifference, just as not turning up for one's graduation picture is a gesture of adolescent rebellion.

Through photographs, each family constructs a portrait-chronicle of itself—a portable kit of images that bears witness to its connectedness. It hardly matters what activities are photographed so long as photographs get taken and are cherished. Photography becomes a rite of family life just when, in the industrializing countries of Europe and America, the very institution of the family starts undergoing radical surgery. As the claustrophobic unit, the nuclear family, was being carved out of a much larger family aggregate, photography came along to memorialize, to restate symbolically, the imperiled continuity and vanishing extendedness of family life. Those ghostly traces, photographs, supply the token presence of the dispersed relatives. A family's photograph album is generally about the extended family—and, often, is all that remains of it.

As photographs give people an imaginary possession of a past that is unreal, they also help people to take possession of space in which they are insecure. Thus, photography develops in tandem with one of the most characteristic of modern activities: tourism. For the first time in history, large numbers of people regularly travel out of their habitual environments for short periods of time. It seems positively unnatural to travel for pleasure without taking a camera along. Photographs will offer indisputable evidence that the trip was made, that the program was carried out, that fun was had. Photographs document sequences of consumption carried on outside the view of family, friends, neighbors. But dependence on the camera, as the device that makes real what one is experiencing, doesn't fade when people travel more. Taking photographs fills the same need for the cosmopolitans accumulating photograph-trophies of their boat trip up the Albert Nile or their fourteen days in China as it does for lower-middle-class vacationers taking snapshots of the Eiffel Tower or Niagara Falls.

Susan Sontag, from ON PHOTOGRAPHY

Readings

Annie Dillard from **PILGRIM AT TINKER CREEK**

"Beauty itself is the language to which we have no key; it is the mute cipher, the cryptogram, the uncracked, unbroken code."

Tom Wolfe **THE RINGLEADER**

"As befitted a millionaire celebrity—by now the paperback and motion-picture rights had been sold—Joe Rocks' charge was reduced from first-degree murder to negligent homicide, his remaining term was changed from hard time to 'country-club' time, and he received an early parole."

Gore Vidal **TARZAN REVISITED**

"In its naive way, the Tarzan legend returns us to that Eden where, free of clothes and the inhibitions of an oppressive society, man is able, as William Faulkner put it in his high Confederate style, to prevail as well as endure."

Adam Smith **ZEN AND THE CROSS-COURT BACKHAND**

"It wasn't taking any orders from me, and, in fact, It would go away if I even pretended to notice....It had a much better serve than I did but wouldn't play with any of my friends....It was actually a bit frightening, was It."

Virginia Woolf **PROFESSIONS FOR WOMEN**

"Indeed it will be a long time still, I think, before a woman can sit down to write a book without finding a phantom to be slain, a rock to be dashed against. And if this is so in literature, the freest of all professions for women, how is it in the new professions which you are now for the first time entering?"

from PILGRIM AT TINKER CREEK

Annie Dillard

When I was quite young I fondly imagined that all foreign languages were codes for English. I thought that "hat," say, was the real and actual name of the thing, but that people in other countries, who obstinately persisted in speaking the code of their forefathers, might use the word "ibu," say, to designate not merely the concept "hat," but the English *word* "hat." I knew only one foreign word, "oui," and since it had three letters as did the word for which it was a code, it seemed, touchingly enough, to confirm my theory. Each foreign language was a different code, I figured, and at school I would eventually be given the keys to unlock some of the most important codes' systems. Of course I knew that it might take years before I became so fluent in another language that I could code and decode easily in my head, and make of gibberish a nimble sense. On the first day of my first French course, however, things rapidly took on an entirely unexpected shape. I realized that I was going to have to learn speech all over again, word by word, one word at a time—and my dismay knew no bounds.

The birds have started singing in the valley. Their February squawks and naked chirps are fully fledged now, and long lyrics fly in the air. Birdsong catches in the mountains' rim and pools in the valley; it threads through forests, it slides down creeks. At the house a wonderful thing happens. The mockingbird that nests each year in the front-yard spruce strikes up his chant in high places, and one of those high places is my chimney. When he sings there, the hollow chimney acts as a soundbox, like the careful emptiness inside a cello or violin, and the notes of the song gather fullness and reverberate through the house. He sings a phrase and repeats it exactly; then he sings another and repeats that, then another. The mockingbird's invention is limitless; he strews newness about as casually as a god. He is tireless, too; toward June he will begin his daily marathon at two in the morning and scarcely pause for breath until eleven at night. I don't know when he sleeps.

When I lose interest in a given bird, I try to renew it by looking at the bird in either of two ways. I imagine neutrinos passing through its feathers and into its heart and lungs, or I reverse its evolution and imagine it as a lizard. I see its scaled legs and that naked ring around a shiny eye; I shrink and deplume its feathers to lizard scales, unhorn its lipless mouth, and set it stalking dragonflies, cool-eyed, under a palmetto. Then I reverse the process once again, quickly; its forelegs unfurl, its scales hatch feathers and soften. It takes to the air seeking cool forests; it sings songs. This is what I have on my chimney; it might as well keep me awake out of wonder as rage.

Some reputable scientists, even today, are not wholly satisfied with the notion that the song of birds is strictly and solely a territorial claim. It's an important point. We've been on earth all these years and we still don't know for certain why birds sing. We need someone to unlock the code to this foreign language and give us the key; we need a new Rosetta stone. Or should we learn, as I had to, each new word one by one? It could be that a bird sings I am sparrow, sparrow, sparrow, as Gerald Manley Hopkins suggests: "myself it speaks and spells, Crying *What I do is me: for that I came.*" Sometimes birdsong seems just like the garbled speech of infants. There is a certain age at which a child looks at you in all earnestness and delivers a long, pleased speech in all the true inflections of spoken English, but with not one recognizable syllable. There is no way you can tell the child that if language had been a melody, he had mastered it and done well, but that since it was in fact a sense, he had botched it utterly.

Today I watched and heard a wren, a sparrow, and the mockingbird singing. My brain started to trill why why why, what is the meaning meaning meaning? It's not that they know something we don't; we know much more than they do, and surely they don't even know why they sing. No; we have been as usual asking the wrong question. It does not matter a hoot what the mockingbird on the chimney is singing. If the mockingbird were chirping to give us the long-sought formulae for a unified field theory, the point would be only slightly less irrelevant. The real and proper question is: Why is it beautiful? I hesitate to use the word so baldly, but the question is there. The question is there since I take it as given, as I have said, that beauty is something objectively performed—the tree that falls in the forest—having being externally stumbled across or missed, as real and present as both sides of the moon. This modified lizard's song welling out of the fireplace has a wild, utterly foreign music; it becomes more and more beautiful as it becomes more and more familiar. If the lyric is simply "mine mine mine," then why the extravagance of the score? It has the liquid, intricate sound of every creek's tumble over every configuration of rock creek-bottom in the country. Who, telegraphing a message, would trouble to transmit a five-act play, or Coleridge's "Kubla Khan," and who, receiving the message, could understand it? Beauty itself is the language to which we have no key; it is the mute cipher, the cryptogram, the uncracked, unbroken code. And it could be that for beauty, as it turned out to be for French, that there is no key, that "oui" will never make sense in our language but only in its own, and that we need to start all over again, on a new continent, learning the strange syllables one by one.

1. As you read this piece of writing, you are listening to Annie Dillard, who in turn has been listening to bird songs, wondering what they might mean.
   a. What does Dillard hear?
   b. What do you hear her saying? Pick out two or three statements that you think are the most important to illustrate your response.

c. What is the connection between what you are doing as you read and listen to Dillard, and what Dillard is doing as she listens to the birds?

2. What, according to Dillard, is the relationship between learning a new language and trying to understand bird song?

3. What does Dillard have to say about the nature of beauty?

4. What do you think is the logic of the *sequence* of Dillard's argument? Do you agree with her conclusion?

5. Do you think Dillard's writing is beautiful? Explain your response.

THE RINGLEADER

Tom Wolfe

Joe Rocks' one asset was his face. Since early manhood he had possessed the countenance of a proud, fierce, if rather battered, nobleman. Unfortunately, as Selective Service was to discover, his IQ was 78 and falling. The appellation "Joe Rocks," which he had picked up as a boy, did not refer to his hard face but to his brain, as in the expression, "This guy's got rocks in his head."

His face had served him well at the level of street robbery and petty extortion. When he attempted anything more complicated, however, Joe Rocks seemed to run into bad luck and had spent half of his mature years behind bars.

So it was that during the riot one of the young guards they were holding hostage panicked and bolted, and Joe Rocks, unable, as usual, to think of anything brighter to do, stabbed him; and he died. This was one of the few crimes for which a man could go to the electric chair.

Half the newspapers in the country ran the Associated Press picture of a platoon of National Guardsmen leading Joe Rocks out of the cellblock. He had never looked harder, nobler, more formidable in his life. The captions identified him as the ringleader, which gave everybody in Cellblock C a big laugh. Joe Rocks could barely lead his shoes across a level floor.

No one was more startled than Joe Rocks himself when Leonard Wringer, the famous lawyer and defender of underdogs, turned up at the prison and offered to take on his case. Ever the wary animal, Joe Rocks said: "What's in it for you?" Wringer launched into a goulash of prison slang—half of which Joe Rocks couldn't follow—and Marxist philosophy. There was no way the eminent couselor could bring himself to explain that in fact his real source of income was public lecturing. He gave seventy-five lectures a year at universities at $4,500 a crack, a heady livelihood that depended, however, on his staying in the news. Nothing served the purpose so neatly as great public eruptions reeking of blood, iron, and social conflict.

Two days later Joe Rocks was visited by Loren Miller, author of several best-selling crime books, who said he wanted to write Joe's autobiography for him. Joe Rocks said, "What's in it for you?" "Fifty percent," said Loren Miller.

He asked Joe Rocks a lot of questions about the ring he led. This brought a rare laugh from the noble face. "Ring?" he said. "There ain't nothing in Cellblock C but psychos and f——ups." The writer didn't even blink. He asked Joe Rocks how the ring in one maximum security prison managed to keep in touch with the rings in the others. Gradually Joe Rocks began to get the drift. A book called *The Rocks* began to take shape, a book about the inverse nobility-behind-bars who today control life, death, and destiny in America's prisons, a secret society of super-hard carborundum criminals known as the Rocks.

"Who's gonna believe it?" said Joe Rocks. "Everybody," said Loren Miller, who had already spent a small part of their $600,000 advance to arrange for a correction officer to leak the existence of the dreaded cabal to a young investigative reporter named Bob Siding.

Even young Siding, who still wore his hair over his ears, thought the story smelled a bit high, but he was at a desperate point in his career. Six months ago he had been hired, at a big salary, as an investigative reporter; so far, all he had dug up was an assistant city manager who had charged the city for five consecutive dinners for two in excess of $125 per at an urban renewal conference in Seattle.

His exclusive about the Rocks was immediately picked up by the wire services, and soon all of America knew of the Rocks and the rock of all the Rocks, Joe Rocks. At his many televised news conferences Leonard Wringer told how the American penal system had broken down so completely that it required hard men like Joe Rocks and the other Rocks to bring some semblance of justice, however brutal, into the jungle-inside-the-cage.

As befitted a millionaire celebrity—by now the paperback and motion-picture rights had been sold—Joe Rocks' charge was reduced from first-degree murder to negligent homicide, his remaining term was changed from hard time to "country-club" time, and he received an early parole.

He was tempted to accept some of the many talk-show invitations he received, but for once he used his head and followed the advice Wringer, Miller, and Siding had all given him: "For God's sake, Joe, if anybody asks you *anything* about *anything*—just stare at him like Al Pacino in *Godfather II*, and never mind the dialogue."

1. What do you think is the tone of this piece? List all the major statements that you think carry strong suggestions of tone and discuss their impact on you.

2. How does Wolfe's style contribute to the tone? Describe it and say how effective you think it is.

3. Discuss how Wolfe sets up the sequence of his argument and its effect on the reader. Is he convincing?
4. What is the central issue that Wolfe raises? Describe it carefully.
5. Write an outline showing your judgments of the emphasis, coherence, unity, and significance of Wolfe's narrative.

TARZAN REVISITED

Gore Vidal

There are so many things that people who take polls never get around to asking. Fascinated as we all are to know what our countrymen think of great issues (approving, disapproving, don't-knowing, with that native shrewdness which made a primeval wilderness bloom with Howard Johnson signs), the pollsters never get around to asking the sort of interesting personal questions our new Romans might be able to answer knowledgeably. For instance, how many adults have an adventure serial running in their heads? How many consciously daydream, turning on a story in which the dreamer ceases to be an employee of IBM and becomes a handsome demigod moving through splendid palaces, saving maidens from monsters (or monsters from maidens: this is a jaded time). Most children tell themselves stories in which they figure as powerful figures, enjoying the pleasures not only of the adult world as they conceive it but of a world of wonders unlike dull reality. Although this sort of Mittyesque daydreaming is supposed to cease in maturity, I suggest that more adults than we suspect are dazedly wandering about with a full Technicolor extravaganza going on in their heads. Clad in tights, rapier in hand, the daydreamers drive their Jaguars at fantastic speeds through a glittering world of adoring love objects, mingling anachronistic historic worlds with science fiction. "Captain, the time-warp's been closed! We are now trapped in a parallel world, inhabited entirely by women with three breasts!" Though from what we can gather about these imaginary worlds, they tend to be more Adlerian than Freudian: the motor drive is the desire not for sex (other briefer fantasies take care of that) but for power, for the ability to dominate one's environment through physical strength, best demonstrated in the works of Edgar Rice Burroughs, whose books are enjoying a huge revival.

When I was growing up, I read all twenty-three Tarzan books, as well as the ten Mars books. My own inner storytelling mechanism was vivid. At any one time, I had at least three serials going as well as a number of tried and true reruns. I mined Burroughs largely for source material. When he went to the center of the earth à la Jules Verne (much too fancy a writer for one's taste), I immediately worked up a thirteen-part series, with myself as lead and various friends as guest stars. Sometimes I used the master's material, but more often I adapted it freely to suit myself. One's daydreams tended to be Tarzanish pre-puberty (physical strength and freedom) and Martian post-puberty (exotic worlds and subtle *combinazione* to be worked out). After adolescence, if one's life is sufficiently interesting, the desire to tell oneself stories diminishes. My last serial ran into sponsor trouble when I was in the Second World War, and it was never renewed.

Until recently I assumed that most people were like myself: daydreaming ceases when the real world becomes interesting and reasonably manageable. Now I am not so certain. Pondering the life and success of Burroughs leads one to believe that a good many people find their lives so unsatisfactory that they go right on year after year telling themselves stories in which they are able to dominate their environment in a way that is not possible in the overorganized society.

According to Edgar Rice Burroughs, "Most of the stories I wrote were the stories I told myself just before I went to sleep." He is a fascinating figure to contemplate, an archetypal American dreamer. Born in 1875 in Chicago, he was a drifter until he was thirty-six. He served briefly in the U.S. Cavalry; then he was a gold miner in Oregon, a cowboy in Idaho, a railroad policeman in Salt Lake City; he attempted several businesses that failed. He was perfectly in the old-American grain: the man who could take on almost any job, who liked to keep moving, who tried to get rich quick but could never pull it off. And while he was drifting through the unsatisfactory real world, he consoled himself with an inner world where he was strong and handsome, adored by beautiful women and worshiped by exotic races. His principal source of fantasy was Rider Haggard. But even that rich field was limited, and so, searching for new veins to tap, he took to reading the pulp magazines, only to find that none of the stories could compare for excitement with his own imaginings. Since the magazine writers could not please him, he had no choice but to please himself, and the public. He composed a serial about Mars and sold it to *Munsey's*. The rest was easy, for his fellow daydreamers recognized at once a master dreamer.

In 1914 Burroughs published *Tarzan of the Apes* (Rousseau's noble savage reborn in Africa), and history was made. To date the Tarzan books have sold over twenty-five million copies in fifty-six languages. There is hardly an American male of my generation who has not at one time or another tried to master the victory cry of the great ape as it issued from the androgynous chest of Johnny Weissmuller, to the accompaniment of thousands of arms and legs snapping during attempts to swing from tree to tree in the backyards of the Republic. Between 1914 and his death in 1950, the squire of Tarzana, California (a prophet more than honored in his own land), produced over sixty books, while enjoying the unique status of being the first American writer to be a corporation. Burroughs is said to have been a pleasant, unpretentious man who liked to ride and play golf. Not one to compromise a vivid unconscious with dim reality, he never set foot in Africa.

With a sense of recapturing childhood, I have just reread several Tarzan books. It is fascinating to see how much one recalls after a quarter century. At times the sense of *déjà vu* is overpowering. It is equally interesting to discover that one's memories of Tarzan of the Apes are mostly action scenes. The plot had slipped one's mind . . . and a lot of plot there is. The beginning is worthy of Conrad. "I had this story from one who had no business to tell it to me, or to any other. I may credit the seductive influence of an old vintage upon the narrator for the beginning of it, and my own skeptical incredulity during the days that followed for the balance of the strange tale." It is 1888. The young Lord and Lady Greystoke are involved in a ship mutiny ("there was in the whole atmosphere of the craft that undefinable something which presages disaster"). The peer and peeress are put ashore on the west coast of Africa, where they promptly build a tree house. Here Burroughs is at his best. He tells you the size of the logs, the way to hang a door when you have no hinges, the problems of roofing. One of the best things about his books is the descriptions of making things. The Greystokes have a child and conveniently die. The "man-child" is discovered by Kala, a Great Ape, who brings him up as a member of her tribe. As anthropologist, Burroughs is pleasantly vague. His apes are carnivorous, and they are able, he darkly suspects, to mate with human beings.

Tarzan grows up as an ape, kills his first lion (with a full nelson), teaches himself to read and write English by studying some books found in the cabin. The method he used, sad to say, is the currently fashionable "look-see." Though he can read and write, he cannot speak any language except that of the apes. He also gets on well with other members of the animal kingdom, with Tantor the elephant, Ska the vulture, Numa the lion (Kipling was also grist for the Burroughs dream mill). Then white folks arrive: Professor Archimedes Q. Porter and his daughter Jane. Also, a Frenchman named D'Arnot who teaches Tarzan to speak French, which is confusing. By an extraordinary coincidence, Jane's suitor is the current Lord Greystoke, who thinks the Greystoke baby is dead. Tarzan saves Jane from an ape. Then he puts on clothes and goes to Paris, where he drinks absinthe. Next stop, America. In Wisconsin, he saves Jane Porter from a forest fire: only to give her up nobly to Lord Greystoke, not revealing the fact that *he* is the real Lord Greystoke. Fortunately in the next volume, *The Return of Tarzan*, he marries Jane and they live happily ever after in Africa, raising a son John, who in turn grows up and has a son. Yet even as a grandfather, Tarzan continues to have adventures with people a foot high, with descendants of Atlantis, with the heirs of a Roman legion who think that Rome is still a success. All through these stories one gets the sense that one is daydreaming, too. Episode follows episode with no particular urgency. Tarzan is always knocked on the head and taken captive; he always escapes; there is always a beautiful princess or high priestess who loves him and assists him; there is always a loyal friend who fights beside him, very much in that Queequeg tradition which, Professor Leslie Fiedler assures us, is the urning in the fuel supply of the American psyche. But no matter how difficult the adventure, Tarzan, clad only in a loincloth with no weapon save a knife (the style is comforting to imitate), wins against all odds and returns to his shadowy wife.

Stylistically, Burroughs is—how shall I put it?—uneven. He has moments of ornate pomp, when the darkness is "Cimmerian"; of redundancy, "she was hideous and ugly"; of extraordinary dialogue: "Name of a name," shrieked Rokoff. "Pig, but you shall die for this!" Or Lady Greystoke to Lord G.: "Duty is duty, my husband, and no amount of sophistries may change it. I would be a poor wife for an English lord were I to be responsible for his shirking a plain duty." Or the grandchild: "Muvver," he cried, "Dackie doe? Dackie doe?" "Let him come along," urged Tarzan. "Dare!" exclaimed the boy, turning triumphantly upon the governess, "Dackie do doe yalk!" Burroughs's use of coincidence is shameless even for a pulp writer. In one book he has three sets of characters shipwrecked at exactly the same point on the shore of Africa. Even Burroughs finds this a bit much. "Could it be possible [muses Tarzan] that fate had thrown him up at the very threshold of his own beloved jungle?" It was possible since anything can happen in a daydream.

Though Burroughs is innocent of literature and cannot reproduce human speech, he does have a gift very few writers of any kind possess: he can describe action vividly. I give away no trade secrets when I say that this is as difficult for a Tolstoi as it is for a Burroughs (even William). Because it is so hard, the craftier contemporary novelists usually prefer to tell their stories in the first person, which is simply writing dialogue. In character, as it were, the writer settles for an impression of what happened rather than creating the sense of the thing happening. In action Tarzan is excellent.

There is something basic in the appeal of the 1914 Tarzan which makes me think that he can still hold his own as a daydream figure, despite the sophisticated challenge of his two young competitors, James Bond and Mike Hammer. For most adults, Tarzan (and John Carter of Mars) can hardly compete with the conspicuous consumer consumption of James Bond or the sickly violence of Mike Hammer, but for children and adolescents the old appeal continues. All of us need the idea of a world alternative to this one. From Plato's Republic to Opar to Bondland, at every level, the human imagination has tried to imagine something better for itself than the existing society. Man left Eden when he got up off all fours, endowing his descendants with nostalgia as well as chronic backache. In its naïve way, the Tarzan legend returns us to that Eden where, free of clothes and the inhibitions of an oppressive society, a man is able, as William Faulkner put it in his high Confederate style, to prevail as well as endure. The current fascination with LSD and nonaddictive drugs—not to mention alcohol—is all a result of a general sense of boredom. Since the individual's desire to dominate his environment is not a desirable trait in a society that every day grows more and more confining, the average man must take to daydreaming. James Bond, Mike Hammer, and Tarzan are all dream selves, and the aim of each is to establish personal primacy in a world that, more and more, diminishes the individual. Among adults, the current popularity of these lively fictions strikes me as a most significant and unbearably sad phenomenon.

1. What reasons does Vidal give for the *popularity* of Burroughs' Tarzan books?
2. What reasons does he give for the *need* for Burroughs' Tarzan books?
3. Why does Vidal call Burroughs an ''archetypal American dreamer''?
4. Can you detect any changes of tone in this essay? Where and why?
5. Choose any other popular fiction hero or heroine—or a popular novelist—and write a short essay that parallels what Vidal has written about Burroughs's Tarzan.

ZEN AND THE CROSS-COURT BACKHAND

Adam Smith

I signed up for ''yoga tennis.'' Yoga tennis surfaced at Esalen, and then I pursued it other places. *Sports Illustrated* wanted to know about it, and secretly I hoped to fix my serve while exploring this new frontier. I had one yoga tennis teacher who wore a blue jogging suit and a Sikh beard and a turban; he was a former business-forms salesman who talked a lot about *ki*, energy. And another there was yoga tennis instructor who hoped to have ''a tennis ashram.''

But Tim Gallwey did not wear a beard or a turban. Gallwey had been the captain of the Harvard tennis team, and he had been brooding about tennis while following the Guru Maharaj Ji. He was very articulate, and eventually I took him to see my publisher, and Gallwey wrote *The Inner Game of Tennis*.

''We learn tennis element by element,'' Gallwey said, standing on a tennis court at the California junior college where Esalen was having a sports seminar. ''If we learned it as totality, we could learn it in one-hundredth the time. Our biggest problem is Ego, is trying too hard. We know how to play perfect tennis. Perfect tennis is in us all. Everyone knows how to ride a bicycle, and just before we really ride for the first time, we know we know. The problem with Ego is that it has to achieve; we are not sure who we are until by achieving we become. So we hit the ball out and the Ego says, 'Ugh out.' Then it starts to give commands, 'Do it right.' We shouldn't have a judgment. The ball goes *there*, not out. Ninety percent of the bad things students do are intentional corrections of something else they are doing. We have to let the body experiment and by-pass the mind. The mind acts like a sergeant with the body a private. How can anybody play as a duality?''

I recognized the sergeant's voice right away; in my mind, it says, "Move your feet, dummy," and "Watch the ball." What to do about the sergeant?

"You have to check the mind, to preoccupy it, stop it from fretting. Look at the ball. Look at the *seams* on the ball, watch the pattern, get preoccupied so the mind can't judge. In between points put your mind on your breathing. In, out. In, out. A quiet mind is the secret of yoga tennis. Most people think concentration is fierce effort. Watch your facial muscles after you hit the ball. Are they tensed or relaxed? Concentration is effortless effort, is *not trying*. The body is sophisticated; its computer commands hundreds of muscles instantly; it is wise about itself; the Ego isn't. Higher consciousness is not a mystical term. You see more when all of your energy runs in the same direction. Concentration produces joy, so we look for things that will quiet the mind."

I could see that parking the mind would be essential. I sat next to Jascha Heifetz once at a dinner party and asked him what he thought about when he was giving a concert. He said if the concert was, say, on a Saturday night he thought about the smoked salmon and the marvelous bagel he was going to have on Sunday morning. If he was thinking about the bagel, then who was thinking about the concerto? His hands.

Don't you have to know the right form before you park the mind?

The body seeks out the right form if the mind doesn't get in the way, Gallwey said. No teenager could do a monkey or a locomotive or whatever teenage dance is now rampant from a set of instructions, but he can do it in one night by observing.

Ah, observing. You didn't say observing.

"You have to talk to the body in its native language," said the tennis guru. "Its native language is not English, it is sight and feel, mostly sight. The stream of instructions most students get are verbal and have to be translated by the body before they are understood. If you are taking a tennis lesson, let the pro show you, don't let him tell you. If you want the ball to go to a cross-court corner, get an image of where you want the ball to go and let the body take it over. Say: 'Body, cross-court corner, please.' "

"Let the serve serve itself," Gallwey said. "When I first used this technique my serve got hot. Then I thought, wow, I've mastered the serve and immediately it got cold because it was me, not the serve, serving itself."

This imagining the ball into the corner, was this the power of positive thinking, Norman Vincent Peale?

"Oh, no. Positive thinking is negative thinking in disguise. If you double-fault six times in a row your positive thinking will flip to negative. So I try not to pay compliments because the compliment can always be withheld on the next shot. What we are talking about is *no thinking*."

It seemed a marvelously Rousseauistic philosophy. Man is born with a perfect tennis game and he is everywhere in chains. Rousseau was influenced by the sunny Polynesians brought to Europe by the eighteenth-century sailors; what if they had sailed a little further over, and brought back fierce and aggressive Melanesians? You don't need a tennis pro with negative instructions, you need a movie of each shot and a ball machine to drill with. It was hard for me to see the difference between the instruction "Be aware of your racket head," from the tennis guru, and "Follow through, where is your racket head?" from the ordinary pro.

"The distinction is, the pro says, good shot, bad shot," Gallwey said. "I just want to focus awareness, not make a judgment."

It occurred to me that yoga tennis was a misnomer. Hatha yoga has breathing and movement, but what the "yoga tennis" pros had come up with was a version of the Japanese and Chinese martial arts. *Zen in the Art of Archery* would be closer. The student was a middle-aged German philosophy professor in Japan, Eugen Herrigel, and he suffered through the same agonies as a yoga tennis student. He tried to tell his right hand to release the bowstring properly with his sergeant mind. The Zen master never coached him at all. The master said, "The right shot at the right moment does not come because you do not let go of yourself . . . the right art is purposeless, aimless! What stands in your way is that you have a much too willful will. You think that what you do not do yourself does not happen." The breathing exercises were to detach the student from the world, to increase a concentration that would be comparable to "the jolt that a man who has stayed up all night gives himself when he knows that his life depends on all his senses being alert." Nothing more is required of the student than that he copy the teacher: "The teacher does not harass and the pupil does not overtax himself."

One day the Zen student of archery Herr Professor Doktor Herrigel loosed a shot and the master bowed and said, "Just then It shot," and the Herr Professor Doktor gave a whoop of delight and the Zen master got so mad he wouldn't talk to him, because this wasn't the student's achievement and there he was thinking he had done it and taking the credit.

There are some pros playing, said my Zen tennis teachers, who are well into these forms of concentration without articulating them, just as Jack Nicklaus may never have gone hi-tot-tsu hu-tot-tsu mi-it-tsu. Billie Jean King, it is said, meditates upon a tennis ball. Ken Rosewall gets mentioned all the time, a perfectly balanced, classical game. And Stan Smith—if you asked Stan Smith what he was thinking about during one of those booming serves he would say the bagel he had for breakfast. (Nobody would be foolish enough to ask Jimmy Connors.) A grooved game means you can play without your head.

I told some friends about watching the patterns on the ball. One of them said later: "I tried that. It worked, it really worked. But I got so much into watching the patterns on the ball that I didn't get to play tennis, it was like a lot of work, I'd rather be lousy and not watch the patterns on the ball."

There was no immediate impact on my game, but then, the Zen archery student got restless in his fourth year of instruction, when he still had met with no success. Depressed, he said to the master that he hadn't managed yet to get one single arrow off right—four years, and not one single arrow off right—or It had not appeared to loose the arrow—and his stay in Japan was limited and four years he'd been at it.

The master got cross with him. "The way to the goal is not to be measured!" he said. "Of what importance are weeks, months, years?"

Zen has gotten to be a good word now, the true thing, the thing itself. We have *Zen and the Art of Running,* and *Zen and the Art of Seeing,* and an autobiography, *Zen and the Art of Motorcycle Maintenance.* We still have to go through *Zen and Turning Your Spares into Strikes,* and *Zen Your Way to Higher Earnings;* the Zen books are getting shorter and more flowery, with any luck they will soon be mostly soupy photographs and we can be done with it.

I went back to my tennis guru. My requirements were simple: I wanted a serve, that's all, with the power of a rocket, accurate to within six inches, one that would zing into the corner of the service court and spin away with such a dizzying kick that the opponent would retire nauseated.

We went out to the court with a basket of balls. I hit a couple. The Zen master didn't say anything. Some went in, some went out. The Zen master didn't say anything. I hit some more.

"Okay," he said. "Breathe in with your racket back, and out when it moves."

That was easy.

"Okay, now, where should the ball go over the net? And where should it land?"

I pointed.

"Okay, ask your body to send it there, and get out of the way."

"Please, body, send it there."

A miss.

"It's not listening."

"Slow it down. Visualize the whole shot before you hit it. Listen to the sound the ball makes against the string."

It's amazing, but if you really visualize, and you really listen to the sound, you can't go ratcheta racheta with your mind, which is very uncomfortable, mutiny in the enlisted men's quarters.

We set up an empty tennis ball can in the corner of the service court. I know, those fierce kids in California and Florida who are out hitting three hundred sixty days a year, who hit five hundred serves a day for practice, can knock over the empty can a couple of times a day, but weekend players can't even get the ball in the court.

"Slow it down more. More. Please, body, send the ball—"

"Please, body, send the ball—"

"Slower. Slower. Make time stand still. No time."

"Please, body, send the ball—"

Zank! The empty tennis ball can went up into the air and bounced metallically. "Who did that?" I said.

The tennis guru said nothing. He handed me another ball. It went into the corner of the service court, on roughly the same spot. So did the next one.

I began to giggle wildly. I danced around a little, the scarecrow had a brain, the cowardly lion had courage, I had a serve. "I did it! I did it!" I said.

Immediately it went away.

The next five balls went into the net.

"I shouldn't have said that," I said. "That sonofabitch is sure sensitive."

"Please, body, send the ball—"

"Please, body, send the ball—"

"Visualize. Don't use words. Don't think. Use images. In between shots, count your breath."

Now the afternoon began to take on a very eerie quality indeed, an underwater, slow-motion quality. Who-o-o-ck went the ball to its accustomed place in the service court; I had to consciously fight the exhilaration. It went away. My breathing sounded like the breathing in scuba gear. The ball was going into the service court, into the corner, but I wasn't feeling anything, no joy, no sorrow, and this was so uncomfortable I came up for air. I felt greed.

"It's going in, but it isn't going in very *hard,*" I said. "I want power, more power."

"Power comes from the snap of the wrist. Ask your wrist to snap at the top of the arc, and don't try. Use images: please, wrist, snap at the top—"

The serve began to pick up speed.

"I don't know what this is," I said, "but it isn't tennis and it isn't me."

I didn't feel at all well. The next afternoon I went out alone at a tennis club. A guy came up and asked me if I wanted to hit some. We rallied. He was very strong. He asked me if I wanted to play. I thought: he doesn't even know my name, I can lose six–love, six–love, and no one will ever know. I put on my mental scuba gear. I wasn't very nice to play with, because you can't say "Oh, nice shot" when you are breathing into your scuba mask. I watched the pattern on the ball, the serve went in, and far, far away I could hear my opponent talking to himself: "Oh, watch the ball, stupid! Don't hit it out! Don't double-fault! Move your feet, idiot!" He began to hit the ball harder and harder. Some of his hard shots were winners, but more of them began to go out. He began to get better at the end. Six–love, six–two.

"I don't know what was the matter with me today," said my opponent.

I was afraid to say anything, but I shouldn't have been afraid—the serve packed its bags and went away as soon as I got back to playing with people I knew.

Sometimes it would reappear for a flash, like a tiny acid rerun. Once, on the court, I shouted, sounding like a madman: "I know you're in there, you bastid, come on out!" Please, body, send it there, please, body—and nothing. Nothing. It is on Its vacation. If I wanted It, It wouldn't come, and if I didn't want It, It might, but then who cared? And gradually it began to seem like there was tennis and Something Else, very difficult to do both at the same time even if Something Else has one hell of a serve.

And this was a bit spooky: It was living in there with me; It could bring the music back on with a thumb twitch, without telling me; It could make the bio-feedback machine switch from beep beep to boop boop without letting me know; It wasn't taking any orders from me, and, in fact, It would go away if I even pretended to notice, sensitive bastid. It had a much better serve than I did but wouldn't play with any of my friends. It could take over but only if I would go do some idiot child-task like breath-counting; why does It only like me if I will play idiot? It was actually a bit frightening, was It.

1. Write a one-paragraph summary of the essay.
2. Describe your reactions to this essay as you read it. Summarize your full range of feelings using the questions outlined in Chapter 2 under the headings of voices, sequence of information, and so on.
3. If someone asked you to explain what the Zen "system" is, what would you say?
4. Consider the topic "Zen and the Art of Writing." Write a couple of paragraphs on the possible application of the Zen technique outlined in this essay to the art of writing (of any kind: creative, reporting, interpretation.) You may find some assistance in Virginia Woolf's essay, which follows, as well as in Adam Smith's essay.

PROFESSIONS FOR WOMEN

Virginia Woolf

When your secretary invited me to come here, she told me that your Society is concerned with the employment of women and she suggested that I might tell you something about my own professional experiences. It is true I am a woman; it is true I am employed; but what professional experiences have I had? It is difficult to say. My profession is literature; and in that profession there are fewer experiences for women than in any other, with the exception of the stage—fewer, I mean, that are peculiar to women. For the road was cut many years ago—by Fanny Burney, by Aphra Behn, by Harriet Martineau, by Jane Austen, by George Eliot—many famous women, and many more unknown and forgotten, have been before me, making the path smooth, and regulating my steps. Thus, when I came to write, there were very few material obstacles in my way. Writing was a reputable and harmless occupation. The family peace was not broken by the scratching of a pen. No demand was made upon the family purse. For ten and sixpence one can buy paper enough to write all the plays of Shakespeare—if one has a mind that way. Pianos and models, Paris, Vienna and Berlin, masters and mistresses, are not needed by a writer. The cheapness of writing paper is, of course, the reason why women have succeeded as writers before they have succeeded in the other professions.

But to tell you my story—it is a simple one. You have only got to figure to yourselves a girl in a bedroom with a pen in her hand. She had only to move that pen from left to right—from ten o'clock to one. Then it occurred to her to do what is simple and cheap enough after all—to slip a few of those pages into an envelope, fix a penny stamp in the corner, and drop the envelope into the red box at the corner. It was thus that I became a journalist; and my effort was rewarded on the first day of the following month—a very glorious day it was for me—by a letter from an editor containing a cheque for one pound ten shillings and sixpence. But to show you how little I deserve to be called a professional woman, how little I know of the struggles and difficulties of such lives, I have to admit that instead of spending that sum upon bread and butter, rent, shoes and stockings, or butcher's bills, I went out and bought a cat—a beautiful cat, a Persian cat, which very soon involved me in bitter disputes with my neighbours.

What could be easier than to write articles and to buy Persian cats with the profits? But wait a moment. Articles have to be about something. Mine, I seem to remember, was about a novel by a famous man. And while I was writing this review, I discovered that if I were going to review books I should need to do battle with a certain phantom. And the phantom was a woman, and when I came to know her better I called her after the heroine of a famous poem, The Angel in the House. It was she who used to come between me and my paper when I was writing reviews. It was she who bothered me and wasted my time and so tormented me that at last I killed her. You who come of a younger and happier generation may not have heard of her—you may not know what I mean by the Angel in the House. I will describe her as shortly as I can. She was intensely sympathetic. She was immensely charming. She was utterly unselfish. She excelled in the difficult arts of family life. She sacrificed herself daily. If there was chicken, she took the leg; if there was a draught she sat in it—in short she was so constituted that she never had a mind or a wish of her own, but preferred to sympathize always with the minds and wishes of others. Above all—I need not say it—she was pure. Her purity was supposed to be her chief beauty—her blushes, her great grace. In those days—the last of Queen Victoria—every house had its Angel. And when I came to write I encountered her with the very first words. The shadow of her wings fell on my page; I heard the rustling of her skirts in the room. Directly, that is to say, I took my pen in hand to review that novel by a famous man, she slipped behind me and whispered: "My dear, you are a young woman. You are writing about a book that has been written by a man. Be sympathetic; be tender; flatter; deceive; use all the arts and wiles of our sex. Never let anybody guess that you have a mind of your own. Above all, be pure." And she made as if to guide my pen. I now record the one act for which I take some credit to myself, though the credit rightly belongs to some excellent ancestors of mine who left me a certain sum of money, shall we say five hundred pounds a year?—so that it was not necessary for me to depend solely on charm for my living. I turned upon her and caught her by the throat. I did my best to kill her. My excuse, if I were to be had up in a court of law, would be that I acted in self-defence. Had I not killed her she would have killed me. She would have plucked the heart out of my writing. For, as I found, directly I put pen to paper, you cannot review even a novel without having a mind of your own, without expressing what you think to be the truth about human relations, morality, sex. And all these questions, according to the Angel in the House, cannot be dealt with freely and openly by women; they must charm, they must conciliate, they must—to put it bluntly—tell lies if they are to succeed. Thus, whenever I felt the shadow of her wing or the radiance of her halo upon my page, I took up the inkpot and flung it at her. She died hard. Her fictitious nature was of great assistance to her. It is far harder to kill a phantom than a reality. She was always creeping back when I thought I had despatched her. Though I flatter myself that I killed her in the end, the struggle was severe; it took much time that had better have been spent upon learning Greek grammar; or in roaming the world in search of adventures. But it was a real experience; it was an experience that was bound to befall all women writers at that time. Killing the Angel in the House was part of the occupation of a woman writer.

But to continue my story. The Angel was dead; what then remained? You may say that what remained was a simple and common object—a young woman in a bedroom with an inkpot. In other words, now that she had rid herself of falsehood, that young woman had only to be herself. Ah, but what is "herself"? I mean, what is a woman? I assure you, I do not know. I do not believe that you know. I do not believe that anybody can know until she has expressed herself in all the arts and professions open to human skill. That indeed is one of the reasons why I have come here—out of respect for you, who are in process of showing us by your experiments what a woman is, who are in process of providing us, by your failures and successes, with that extremely important piece of information.

But to continue the story of my professional experiences. I made one pound ten and six by my first review; and I bought a Persian cat with the proceeds. Then I grew ambitious. A Persian cat is all very well, I said; but a Persian cat is not enough. I must have a motor car. And it was thus that I became a novelist—for it is a very strange thing that people will give you a motor car if you will tell them a story. It is a still stranger thing that there is nothing so delightful in the world as telling stories. It is far pleasanter than writing reviews of famous novels. And yet, if I am to obey your secretary and tell you my professional experiences as a novelist, I must tell you about a very strange experience that befell me as a novelist. And to understand it you must try first to imagine a novelist's state of mind. I hope I am not giving away professional secrets if I say that a novelist's chief desire is to be as unconscious as possible. He has to induce in himself a state of perpetual lethargy. He wants life to proceed with the utmost quiet and regularity. He wants to see the same faces, to read the same books, to do the same things day after day, month after month, while he is writing, so that nothing may break the illusion in which he is living—so that nothing may disturb or disquiet the mysterious nosing about, feelings round, darts, dashes and sudden discoveries of that very shy and illusive spirit, the imagination. I suspect that this state is the same both for men and women. Be that as it may, I want you to imagine me writing a novel in a state of trance. I want you to figure to yourselves a girl sitting with a pen in her hand, which for minutes, and indeed for hours, she never dips into the inkpot. The image that comes to my mind when I think of this girl is the image of a fisherman lying sunk in dreams on the verge of a deep lake with a rod held out over the water. She was letting her imagination sweep unchecked round every rock and cranny of the world that lies submerged in the depths of our unconscious being. Now came the experience, the experience that I believe to be far commoner with women writers than with men. The line raced through the girl's fingers. Her imagination had rushed away. It had sought the pools, the depths, the dark places where the largest fish slumber. And then there was a smash. There was an explosion. There was foam and confusion. The imagination had dashed itself against something hard. The girl was roused from her dream. She was indeed in a state of the most acute and difficult distress. To speak without figure she had thought of something, something about the body, about the passions which it was unfitting for her as a woman to say. Men, her reason told her, would be shocked. The consciousness of what men will say of a woman who speaks the truth about her passions had roused her from her artist's state of unconsciousness. She could write no more. The trance was over. Her imagination could work no longer. This I believe to be a very common experience with women writers—they are impeded by the extreme conventionality of the other sex. For though men sensibly allow themselves great freedom in these respects, I doubt that they realize or can control the extreme severity with which they condemn such freedom in women.

These then were two very genuine experiences of my own. These were two of the adventures of my professional life. The first—killing the Angel in the House— I think I solved. She died. But the second, telling the truth about my own experiences as a body, I do not think I solved. I doubt that any woman has solved it yet. The obstacles against her are still immensely powerful—and yet they are very difficult to define. Outwardly, what is simpler than to write books? Outwardly, what obstacles are there for a woman rather than for a man? Inwardly, I think, the case is very different; she has still many ghosts to fight, many prejudices to overcome. Indeed it will be a long time still, I think, before a woman can sit down to write a book without finding a phantom to be slain, a rock to be dashed against. And if this is so in literature, the freest of all professions for women, how is it in the new professions which you are now for the first time entering?

Those are the questions that I should like, had I time, to ask you. And indeed, if I have laid stress upon these professional experiences of mine, it is because I believe that they are, though in different forms, yours also. Even when the path is nominally open—when there is nothing to prevent a woman from being a doctor, a lawyer, a civil servant—there are many phantoms and obstacles, as I believe, looming in her way. To discuss and define them is I think of great value and importance; for thus only can the labour be shared, the difficulties be solved. But besides this, it is necessary also to discuss the ends and the aims for which we are fighting, for which we are doing battle with these formidable obstacles. Those aims cannot be taken for granted; they must be perpetually questioned and examined. The whole position, as I see it—here in this hall surrounded by women practising for the first time in history I know not how many different professions—is one of extraordinary interest and importance. You have won rooms of your own in the house hitherto exclusively owned by men. You are able, though not without great labour and effort, to pay the rent. You are earning your five hundred pounds a year. But this freedom is only a beginning; the room is your own, but it is still bare. It has to be furnished; it has to be decorated; it has to be shared. How are you going to furnish it, how are you going to decorate it? With whom are you going to share it, and upon what terms? These, I think are questions of the utmost importance and interest. For the first time in history you are able to ask them; for the first time you are able to decide for yourselves what the answers should be. Willingly would I stay and discuss those questions and answers—but not tonight. My time is up; and I must cease.

1. As you read this essay, did you find yourself agreeing or disagreeing with Woolf's sentiments? Explain your reaction. Did you find the piece dated?

2. Summarize why Woolf thinks it is difficult to be a woman novelist.

3. "A mind of your own" and "a room of your own"—are these two ideas related for Woolf? If so, how?

4. Discuss the tone of Woolf's statements and how you think it matches the experiences she underwent learning to be a novelist, her motives in giving the talk, and her understanding of her audience.

5. There are, says Woolf, "still many ghosts to fight, many prejudices to overcome." Carefully explain what you think these are now for a woman writer.

The Writing Process I:

From Subject to

Outline

Writing for Readers

As you have seen in the last two chapters, you will have little chance of writing effectively if you do not learn to read effectively, for you will not know how to write *for a reader*. You are more likely to be an efficient writer if you bear in mind the characteristics writing should have in order that a reader may make an interpretation.

Remember that:

■ Reading is the process of discovering emphasis, coherence, unity, and significance in a text.

■ Reading is an active process of helping to make meaning: listening to the voices of the text, interacting with it, imaginatively absorbing it into private experiences and fantasies, accumulating information, trying to find the writer's aim and the writer's view of the reader, solving problems in the text, sensitively reacting to the style and tone, and trying to re-create the text as a unified whole.

■ Reading is a process of rereading: the creation of meaning between a writer and a reader may take several readings in order to build up a coherent interpretation.

All this, of course, has little chance of taking place unless the writing allows it, unless the conditions are created for good reading. What, in general then, must writing do?

■ Writing must create emphasis, carry a coherent and unified argument, explanation, description, or narration that suggests something significant.

■ Writing must carry a clear authorial voice. Writing must help make meaning by conveying information with a purpose, and developing an appropriate style, tone, and view of the audience that invites the reader to gain access to the ideas.

■ Writing must include careful preparation to develop ideas, and then development of a thesis, an outline, preliminary and second drafts, and a revised version, in order to achieve consistency and coherence.

The primary aim of writing you will do at college or in your work is to convey information and the position you take on that information. Your aim will be to write informative, reader-centered prose that both explains and argues. This kind of prose depends on developing a genuine opinion and justifying it. It is not simply a description or telling a story, but rather involves an interpretation that shows you understand the information, know how to use it, and want to persuade a reader of the facts.

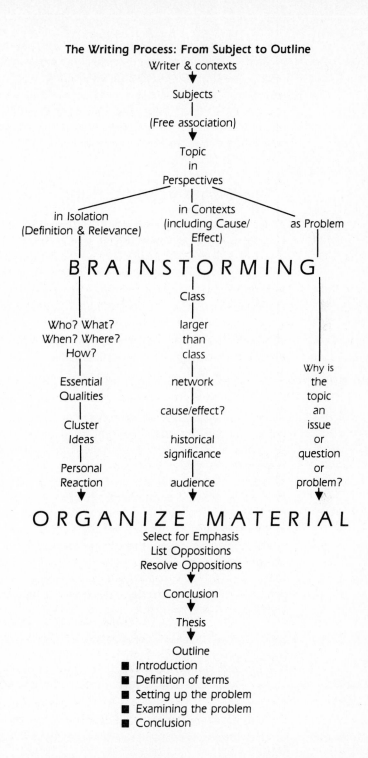

The Writing Process: From Subject to Outline

Writer & contexts

Subjects

(Free association)

Topic
in
Perspectives

in Isolation
(Definition & Relevance)

in Contexts
(including Cause/
Effect)

as Problem

B R A I N S T O R M I N G

Class

Who? What?
When? Where?
How?

larger
than
class

Essential
Qualities

network

cause/effect?

Why is
the
topic
an
issue
or
question
or
problem?

Cluster
Ideas

historical
significance

Personal
Reaction

audience

O R G A N I Z E   M A T E R I A L

Select for Emphasis
List Oppositions
Resolve Oppositions

Conclusion

Thesis

Outline

■ Introduction
■ Definition of terms
■ Setting up the problem
■ Examining the problem
■ Conclusion

In these chapters on writing, we will be concerned with this kind of expository "position" paper, especially emphasizing its usefulness for problem solving. There are other kinds of writing, of course—descriptive, narrative, argumentative, and persuasive—and these will be covered in the last part of this book. But the position paper is the most frequent mode of expository writing and the one that forms the basis of college, business, professional, technical, and much journalistic writing.

The Stages in the Writing Process

Like reading, writing carries you from a subject to a coherent and unified view of that subject. That should be the thrust of every act of writing: you select a strong subject, you accumulate information about it, you organize the information coherently around a thesis, and you try to give the finished product a unity of message, style, and tone. Expository writing, therefore, is basically an interpretive, problem-solving act, which uses strategies that link clear thinking and analysis to persuasive and pleasing effects. The stages in the writing process cover the invention of ideas, their careful organization, and the discovery of a thesis even before you write the first draft.

The stages outlined below are by no means lock step. As you become more adept at focusing, analyzing, and synthesizing, you will see your writing less as a step-by-step procedure and more as a unified act. You will get to the first draft faster and think more easily while writing. The sequence outlined covers steps that can be consciously taken as you adapt the sequence to suit your topic and aim. But events will occur out of sequence, too. As you analyze your subject, for example, you wonder how to persuade your audience. Even as you focus, reactions begin to form, and you develop some idea of what your conclusion will be early in the essay because you are already testing your decisions.

The point of detailing the writing process is not to suggest that you actually control the rate and sequence by which you form ideas. Of course, you cannot. But you can *stimulate* your thinking, logically and emphatically *limit* your topic, and carefully *check* your discussion of it. There is a discipline to writing well that can be learned; it is the process by which you encourage idea-making and evaluate your thoughts on a subject so that you can reach a well-considered opinion and create a persuasive discussion.

Note that during each of the following stages, you are writing: from making notes, no matter how rough, as you generate ideas, through organizing them into a thesis and an outline, to producing a first draft, revising it, and rewriting it as final copy. Note, too, that the process you will follow is much the same as that of writing an interpretation from reading. Any act of writing *is* an act of interpretation, after all, whether you are writing about a text or a concept, a person, a thing, or a state of affairs. Now you are interpreting a topic.

■ *Finding a topic.* The first step involves the selection of a subject and its refinement into a topic.

■ *Opening up the topic.* The writer then considers options with the topic, literally "reading" it from various perspectives and accumulating information about it in note form.

■ *Limiting the topic.* The writer focuses on key ideas and tries to solve any contradictions. This is perhaps the crucial part of preparation as the writer reasons through the information and develops a genuine opinion about it.

■ *Writing an outline.* This involves organizing the information already obtained about the topic in order to develop a sense of its relevance: its nature, why it is an issue, its context, and its significance.

■ *Considering the audience.* The writer decides how the audience should react and plans matters of style and tone accordingly, readjusting the outline where necessary.

■ *Writing the first draft.* Now that the preparations are complete, the writer will develop the first draft, working from an outline.

■ *Revising.* The first draft is never a final draft; it is always necessary to revise and rewrite in order to improve expression and remove errors of judgment, fact, grammar, style, tone, the development of paragraphs, and the conciseness of sentence structure. The writer also checks for any perceptual, emotional, or culturally created blocks.

■ *Writing the final draft* and proofreading it. Only after the first draft has been revised does the writer begin a final draft. Sometimes, more than one "final" draft is needed. The only rule is: revise as many times as necessary, but only to make the argument more cogent and to refine the style.

In this chapter and the next four, we will examine each of these stages in detail, creating an essay as we go along.

Choosing a Subject and a Topic

You are going to write a piece of critical, expository prose: a college paper, a technical or analytic report, a commentary or article for a newspaper, it does not matter what. They all have different formats, but they all proceed by explaining a position you are taking on a subject. How do you begin? Every writer starts from a position of uncertainty. No one simply sits down and writes with perfectly sustained inspiration or coherence. So you always need some early preparation to create a focus. Furthermore, you must allow your ideas to change as you prepare in order to develop your argument.

Many of the problems with writing begin with the focus on a subject. The question is: have you chosen an interesting enough subject, and have you limited it to a workable topic? If you cannot answer yes to this question, then it is unlikely that you will maintain an accurate focus throughout your paper, and you will find it difficult to think continuously about your topic. Of course, there will be other problems you can expect to find as you write: too little or too much information, evidence that contradicts your argument, explanations that are fuzzy or that reach unimportant conclusions, an ineffective style and tone. Every writer has experienced these setbacks. You may also have problems revising and evaluating what you have written because you are not sufficiently objective and are too emotionally attached to your words.

All these problems, you say, so why bother? Apart from the fact that you often have to bother to fulfill assignments, there is a very practical answer. Writing is not a way of creating problems. It is, as we said earlier, a problem-solving act, *a learning process*. Most of the problems that occur in writing *can be eliminated in the planning stages*. So let's begin with the way in which the writer moves from a subject to a topic.

Opening Up a Subject

If a subject has not been given to you as an assignment and few or no guidelines have been offered either, your subject can be literally anything that appeals to you, an inspiration of any kind. It need not be a concept; it can be a person or thing or event. It need not be a coherent sense of a whole event laid out before you; it can be a partial insight into something. Subjects can be general or particular, something you know about or something you can explore. But the main criterion for choosing a subject is that *you feel strongly about it*. Either you have a genuine opinion about it, or you are curious to develop one. The subject stands out in your mind as something that you want and may even need to explore.

You cannot think of anything? Then turn to the various contexts of your experience in school, home, entertainment, sports, social life, public affairs, conversations, reading, television watching, movie going, and so on. What has irritated you? Delighted you? Struck you as abrasive, morally wrong or morally good? In other words, what has struck a deeper than usual response from you, or what, now that you think about it, are you curious about?

Once you have found a subject, you have to open it up, see what your options are, and then from them, pick a topic of manageable size. A topic is an *aspect* of a subject that focuses the subject for you. "Aeronautics" is a subject; "space travel" is a topic within the broad scope of the subject. There are many ways to decide on a topic, including reading up on the subject in the library and talking to friends. You have to be careful, though, not to get involved with other people's interests at the beginning, but to talk about *your* topic and to develop your relationship with it early in the writing process. One good way of opening up a subject on your own is to use the tactic of *free association*.

Say you are interested in and provoked by social issues; by considering your recent reading and television and movie watching, you decide on the general subject of "crime in America." It is a subject that is given a good deal of media space and that seems to pose insuperable problems. But plainly "crime in America" is far too large a subject for a topic in itself. If you tried to write on it, you would have to settle for vast generalizations that would prove nothing, would be frustrating to write, and would bore your reader. So you free associate about the subject to discover what aspect of it you want to write on.

In the process of free association, you *write down* everything that comes to your mind suggested by the subject: questions, related issues, examples, and so on. Each item is a potential topic.

Crime in America ... epidemic ... why so high compared with other countries? ... organized crime ... corruption in government ... easy availability of weapons ... violent society ... lack of respect for human life ... people as commodities ... drug-related crime ... media-induced violence (movies, TV, magazines) ... economic inequality ... street muggings ... prison reform ... insufficient crime control ... result of educational problems? ... need for psychological testing in schools ... gun control ...

And so on and on. Let the ideas flow as they come; do not censor them.

Choosing a Topic

The ideas will begin to suggest their own importance to you as you write them down. You can, for example, see that the ideas begin to fall into categories that are still too large for you to deal with. For example: Why are U.S. crime statistics so high compared with those of other countries? ... organized crime ... violent society. Exclude these topics that are plainly too general, and concentrate on issues *you can discuss.* The criteria for choosing a topic from your list of free associations are as follows:

■ You must be interested in the topic. It attracts your attention in some way even if you cannot at this point fully explain why. Remember that it is valuable to explore even half-formed ideas.

■ You believe you can realistically write about the topic. It is neither too broad nor too narrow. It does not require specialized knowledge nor too much information you cannot provide or find. It is open to interpretation.

■ The topic is not so idiosyncratic that it means something only to you. The topic must to some extent be of general interest. However, it does not have to be so grand or so general that it contains everything (like "how America feels about foreign cars"). Note that in the previous chapter Updike got us into high technology through a beer can.

If you look at the topics you have generated from your free association in the light of these criteria for selection, you will get a good idea of whether you are about to waste a lot of time struggling with something that is unlikely to develop interest, either yours or the audience's. You are trying to make sure at this point that you are interested in the subject and that it is a practical choice that you believe you can make come alive in the mind of a reader.

For the sake of illustration, let's assume you have chosen the topic "gun control." For you it fits the above criteria. It constantly attracts your attention in the press and in other media, and it is probably going to continue to be a hot political issue for some time. It is a topic that does not require a great deal of specialized knowledge; we all have opinions about it. Many of us are faced at some time with the question: should I buy a handgun for the protection of my home? Others have grown up with such weapons readily available. Because it has been discussed so frequently, you must be careful not to merely repeat points you have read in magazines or heard politicians make. Some may even say that the topic has been written about too often; but because it is still an open question, you can justify exploring it yet again.

Opening Up the Topic

Whether you choose "gun control" or it chooses you because it has been assigned, the next stage is to explore your options. You would probably begin here if you were working with an assigned topic; it can be useful to run any subject through the free-association process to see how it develops and what aspect of it you want to concentrate on. You will remember that in the previous section we moved from the subject to the topic by first *opening up* the subject (through free association) and then *limiting* it (through the criteria for a sensible choice). This process of opening and closing, of generalizing and particularizing, runs back and forth throughout the interpretation and writing process.

There will be times during the writing of an essay when you will find that you have defined your topic too narrowly, and you need to develop more ideas. Other times you will find your topic too broad and realize that you must focus more clearly. Be prepared to do either at any time. Remember that books and articles carrying the title "everything you always wanted to know about . . ." *ought* to be ironic, even if they are not. You constantly alternate when writing between opening up options and focusing and selecting among them, in exactly the same way as you do when you read. You could say that the process of developing a plan for your essay is the process of discovering and interpreting your options.

To discover your options, you examine your topic from one of three major *perspectives,* or points of view:

■ You view the topic itself as *isolated:* you want to *define* it and discuss its *relevance.* So with "gun control," you would concentrate on the terms *gun* and *control.*

■ You view the topic in various *contexts,* that is, in relationship to other ideas. You would consider whether "gun control" is a cause or an effect, a social or a legal problem, a national or an international issue.

■ You view the topic as a *problem,* as a controversial issue. Why is "gun control" an issue, and what makes it so controversial?

You can open up a topic by examining it from any or all of these perspectives. What you will do with your topic depends on its *nature,* its *contexts,* and whether or not it has a *problematic* status. To discover your topic's characteristics, you must ask questions about it.

Seeing Your Topic in Perspective

Each of these three general approaches to a topic has its own set of questions and tactics. Not all will be appropriate to ask of every topic, but most are. (Remember that you are taking notes for each relevant heading. Don't worry if information duplicates itself.)

The Topic Isolated

■ *Ask Who? What? When? Where? How?* You want to determine the most important aspects of the topic, or its key ideas. If it is an object, a state of affairs, a person, or an event, then observe it closely and describe what you find. If it is a concept—like "gun control"—then define its terms, using a dictionary or some other reference if necessary, and list any other key ideas. If it is a process (such as the way an

111

organization works or a historical sequence), then briefly detail its key events or parts in order.

■ *What are its essential, changeless qualities?* In other words, if change occurred, which of its characteristics would remain? When does a gun cease to be a legitimate weapon we should all have the right to own, and when does it become a weapon that should be banned because it is lethal and of no social value?

■ *Cluster thoughts around each of the key ideas.* Take the main qualities, key ideas, or defined terms that you have discovered and free associate about each of them. If your topic were the "Middle East Crisis," you would let ideas cluster around its main terms:

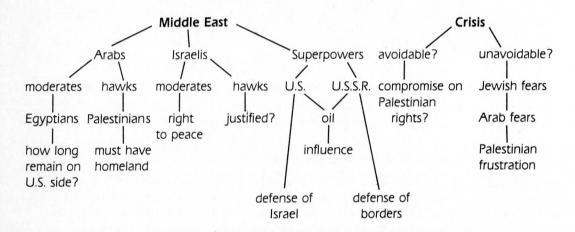

■ *Why are you interested in the topic?* Note your major reactions to the topic, your special likes and dislikes, and any problems you have relating to it. Why did you choose the topic?

The Topic in Its Contexts

■ *Is it part of a class or group?* If so, then note how it differs from others in the group. A household cat is part of the class of animal but it can be differentiated from other animals by various qualities: it is carnivorous and four-legged, has a tail, is covered with fur, is about 1 foot long and 10 inches high, and is domesticated. You can classify emotions, concepts, and events, as well as things.

■ *Is it part of a context larger than a class?* Nothing exists in a vacuum. Knowledge is made up of ideas that relate, and any thing or concept can be placed in increasingly larger contexts. You could consider the social, political, cultural, legal, and psychological aspects of gun control, for example, and never start your essay, let alone finish it. To be realistic, choose only the major contexts: for example, is gun control primarily a social or a legal problem?

■ *Is the topic part of a network of facts?* Does the topic interrelate with other ideas or facts to form a system? Is gun control part of a network of issues concerning crime in society?

■ *Is the topic a cause or an effect?* See Chapter 10 for a discussion of cause and effect in some detail, but for now just ask yourself if the topic is really the heart of the problem, or whether it is simply a symptom or effect of another problem. In other words, is gun control really the problem or is the problem one of reducing crime? Be careful not to mistake a cause for an effect or to assume that there is only one cause or one effect.

■ *Does the topic have a history?* That is, does it have a history that is worth exploring? If it has, then research the topic briefly and in general terms. (See Appendix A for comments on a research paper.) Here you are not being asked to do elaborate research in order to take a position—at least not yet—but it will pay you to survey the field briefly. Checking with pro– and anti–gun control organizations for literature is useful, for example.

■ *Try out the topic in the context of an audience. Discuss the topic with your friends.* See what other people think is important about the topic and if anyone has an original angle. But remember, you should not just be relying on other people's ideas here. You are basically trying out your ideas and reacting to your friends' opinions.

The Topic as a Problem

Is your topic a controversial issue? If so, then ask why and proceed from there. If it doesn't seem to be, try making it a question and see what happens. Gun control is clearly a problem as demonstrated by all the debate. Horse breeding, on the other hand, would not seem at first sight to be a problem at all, but if you posed the hypothetical topic, "The problem (or question) of horse breeding," then maybe investigative possibilities would emerge related to the high cost of stud fees, training practices for race horses, or the like, which you may or may not consider worth discussing. It pays you to ask Why? of all your topics. Why is the topic an issue? Why are people concerned about it?

You probably will not ask all these questions of every topic. Some are clearly more suitable for topics dealing with concepts than with those dealing with events, for example. But at least run through all the possible questions about your topic, and then pursue the relevant ones as far as you can. How do you do this?

■ Answers are developed through a process of *brainstorming.* This is not quite like free association, but is close to it. In brainstorming, the writer allows intuition and associations to flow in a direction dictated by a question. You increase the references while keeping close to the associations suggested by the specific question.

■ Jot your answers down on a piece of paper under the relevant heading or question. There is no need to write full sentences unless you want to, nor should you interrupt the continuous flow of your thinking by worrying about grammar or syntax. Just write.

Brainstorming the Topic

Here is how the process of brainstorming works for the topic of "gun control." Note that you do not answer all questions firmly at this point by choosing only one response. Use all the answers you can think of. You are looking for *options,* remember.

The Topic Isolated

■ *Who? What? When? Where? How?* Define the topic: By "guns," do I mean handguns or all firearms? By "control," do I mean licensing, banning, or some other form of control?

■ *Essential qualities:* Guns are for killing.

■ *Idea cluster:*

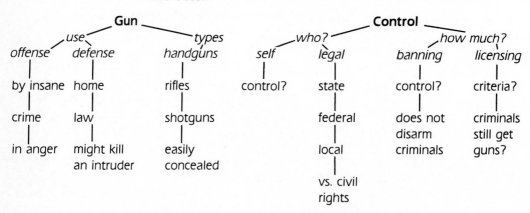

■ *Personal Reaction:* Should probably just ban all weapons, but is that possible or likely, given political facts? . . . topic relevant to all.

The Topic in its Contexts

- *Class:* Part of a class of legal problems associated with violence.

- *Larger context:* Primarily an American problem, since almost all other countries have stricter gun control laws at the federal level ... problem related to constitutional law ... or to frontier mentality (law by gun)?

- *Cause or effect?* Cause of crime or result of social violence? ... do people kill or do guns?

- *Network:* Relates to study of social problem of violence.

- *Historical significance:* Discussed for many years now ... arguments as represented by lobbies for and against at federal and state levels are deadlocked ... supporters make this a political issue concerning rights.

- *Discussion:* Can't find any real agreement ... those who own guns claim it's the people who have them and not the guns themselves that are a problem ... needed for self-defense ... those who don't own them think they're a dangerous weapon too often misused in anger ... an encouragement to crime.

The Topic as a Problem

- *Why is gun control an issue?* Civil rights? Constitutional question? . . . disagreement in the media between lobbies and politicians ... U.S. presidents campaign on opposite sides ... potential problem of opposition between right to bear arms and need to control violence ... vicious circle: we need guns for self-defense versus those who use guns for criminal reasons ... already against the law to carry a concealed weapon but that has not cut down on killings ... even if we did have gun control, could any government really administer it? ... legal problem: constitutional amendment needed?

These, of course, are only some of the possibilities. Continue this part of the writing process for as long as you have ideas and they associate with your topic in your mind. Move back and forth from one heading to another. Make sure you arrange your ideas (which will come in all directions) under the appropriate heading.

Limiting the Topic

Selection and Elimination

When you have opened up the topic and compiled your information from brainstorming, you will have one more stage to go before you decide on your thesis. The topic is open now, but you do not have a firm opinion about it. You need to limit your information, to focus on important emphases, to locate the oppositions and connections among your facts in order to resolve contradictions and refine the information. An essay on "gun control," for example, should not be so broad that it is about the "psycho-socio-political-economic state of the nation today." Of course no subject is ever totally closed; you are not trying to nail the topic down forever. But you do want to define your position, so now you try to arrive at an opinion on the subject.

How do you limit a topic? By two closely related processes: *selection* and *resolving contradictions.*

Selection for Emphasis Read the information you have listed under the three perspectives and decide which are the most emphatic points you have made. Then choose the most important of these. Distinguish between major and minor ideas. This is based on your response to the information as if you were reading for interpretation. Your decision will be very personal: you'll choose themes *you* find interesting, because after all you have to write about them. But be as objective as you can, looking especially for points that are closest to the topic and that give you the most scope with the topic. You do not want to be entirely idiosyncratic and thereby miss any important information. For example, you should try not to avoid issues that you think are unpleasant, at least not before considering them seriously. Always select for emphasis in terms of ideas that are most relevant to an analysis of your topic.

Resolving Contradictions Much of your information will be in the form of questions: questions that you have not yet answered and that may even pose contradictions. For example, do you mean "banning" or "licensing" for "control"? Ask these questions of each of your three areas of information.

■ Which oppositions or differences between points of view have emerged from the questioning?

■ Which comparisons and contrasts are significant?

■ Which problems seem particularly stubborn and resist simplification?

When you have found all the questions, then ask:

■ Which questions can be answered immediately?

■ What relationships, combinations, and unlikely connections can be found between items?

You are going to have to make decisions, but it is good to know that if you find later you have made the wrong decision, you can always change your mind. You systematically analyze and synthesize the information you have.

Hard-to-Answer Questions

What do you do with questions that are not easily answered?

■ *Look for any stubborn oppositions that turn up in your list,* the black and white issues, those stand-offs that look as though they have no solution. Do not be put off by the difficulty of these problems, because whatever headway you make with them will attract a reader's attention. After all, no one is very interested in reading about an issue that has been largely resolved. You may not be able to crack some of the tough questions of life, but a reader values a careful, modest approach to big issues (social, political, legal, or whatever) that asks the right questions even if they're not answered. We all tend to be armchair critics and we all have opinions. Do not leave them out of the process, but develop and test them. The relationships and unlikely connections you find between stubborn opposites may be the key to your argument.

■ *But what do you do when you reach a stand-off?* This is the time for you to get uncompromisingly tough with each position. Take them separately, and turn each argument into one long question. Say you are inclined to think that the constitutional-rights lobby is correct about gun control. You must ask "Why?" over and over again. Why does the anti–gun control position claim to be right? Because, among other things, law-abiding citizens have the right to bear arms under the U.S. Constitution. But why? To protect themselves. Is there no other protection? Yes, there are the police, but they cannot be everywhere, least of all in one's own home and rarely ever at the actual moment of a crime. Well, maybe the real issue is controlling crime? That certainly *is* an issue, but it is far too big and impractical a subject to try to write about. But surely if we got rid of crime, we would not need gun control? The only problem is that we could all be dead by the time crime is controlled. Then maybe there is some other kind of protection? Can you think of one? Bulletproof vests are impractical for everyday wear. Looks like the anti-gun control people have won the argument, and you confidently settle down to write your essay. But you have not finished developing the topic yet.

■ *Check your conclusions.* Consider how opposing arguments build up their main points. Go back to the line of reasoning from the anti-gun control lobby: violent society = need for defense = need for small arms + maintaining constitutional rights = no gun control. The leap from "violent society" to "need for defense" and "small arms" is troublesome, but you have not been able to shake the argument. But consider the leap in reasoning from the "need for small arms" to "no gun control." How are the two points related? They are not, and there is your possible breakthrough. The one does not exclusively imply the need for the other: you can have guns for defense *and* have gun control. So that argument won't do, and now you have to find another if you are determined to take sides. This time you might emphasize that control infringes on your constitutional rights, and you're off again. Is the Constitution automatically right? It is the basis for laws about personal freedom. Yet we have had amendments. The Constitution is the work of men and therefore is fallible. But *why* change it? And so on. By the time you have carried this argument to its conclusion, you may very well feel that perhaps the point of your essay should be *not* to take sides but to pose the problem and dramatize it, showing that both sides have something to say. Perhaps the only sensible position to take is that of wanting gun control but also wanting to preserve the rights of the anti–gun controllers.

Organizing Your Information

So far you have brainstormed your topic from three perspectives: the topic in isolation (definition and relevance), in contexts, and as a problem. You have gone over your brainstorming notes and selected the most important points from them. You have located emphases and oppositions and have tried to resolve them, answering the questions they create. You need now to organize all the material you have because you must come to a conclusion. This need not be done formally; you can either write down whole thoughts or simply underline on your brainstorming list the points you want to emphasize. You can write in further notes to supplement what you have and cross out the pieces of information you do not want to deal with further. On the other hand, there is value in rewriting your outline in more detail now, concentrating on relevant questions. The actual business of writing out material often provokes further thought, and this is the time when you want to explore your options as far as you can. Choose the most important questions to consider in each section.

This is how the comments for the "gun control" essay might look after you have made selections, arranged connections and oppositions, and resolved the contradictions in your brainstorming notes. These new notes will be used later as the main source for the first draft. It is helpful to keep oppositions, connections, and resolutions separate for each point.

The Topic Isolated

DEFINITION

Emphasis: Basically considering all firearms and the problem of whether they should be controlled, for guns are lethal weapons.

Oppositions: Control or no control? Licensing or banning? All guns or some guns? Federal or state control?

Resolution: Must define terms. Deal with handguns and federal control.

RELEVANCE

Emphasis: Every citizen is involved. There are large political, legal, and economic interests at stake. It is a constitutional issue. Everyone wants a solution to the problem of high crime, even anti–gun controllers.

Oppositions: Has the question not been answered because it is intrinsically difficult *or* because of special interests and political considerations?

Resolution: All acknowledge some connection between violence and guns, but which is to blame? Which does one tackle first? The problem is the connection between violence and guns, but political interests have clouded the issue. Will try to avoid lobby issues by saying that the problem is an open one—either control violence or guns—with difficult legal problems. Need to find a meeting point for the two sides.

The Topic in Its Contexts

CONTEXT

Emphasis: An American problem: a question of constitutional rights and the law.

Oppositions: Legal thinking versus psychology and sociology.

Resolution: The law has in common both private and public interests. So we must turn to the possibility of legislation as the rightful context. Sociology and psychology offer support and evidence on which the law bases its rulings, but we are concerned with *control,* so the law is central.

CAUSE/EFFECT

Emphasis: Whether guns are a cause or an effect, the gun control question is concerned with violence *with* guns. That must be our overriding concern.

Oppositions: Is gun violence a cause or an effect? "Control guns and you control violence" versus "control violence and you lessen crime with guns." People kill versus guns kill. If we do not want gun control on grounds that it infringes on personal freedom, then are we ironically creating the freedom to kill more readily?

Resolution: Avoid the question of cause or effect as unanswerable and an unnecessary question. Violence and guns are necessarily linked.

The Topic as a Problem

Emphasis: Why is gun control a problem? Political or legal, or both?

Oppositions: Freedom to bear arms or federal licensing. Constitutional rights or crime control via new laws. Could a gun control law control violence? Unarmed public versus armed criminals.

Resolution: Can synthesize everything under need to control deaths from gun-related crime *and* at the same time to preserve individual rights. Both sides want this. Gun control must be efficient and effective. It must preserve the rights of law-abiding citizens to bear arms, at least for special purposes. Guns and violence are unavoidably tied together. The question is not which is logically the more efficient of the two issues to tackle first: for example, control violence through stiffer legal penalties or guns through specific controls. Instead, one must tackle both issues together by working on the *legal* question of gun control in order to get at violence.

Now this may seem to be a tedious task which is keeping you from writing your first draft, but you are in fact creating your essay as you organize your ideas. You are setting yourself up to do two things:

To come to a considered coherent conclusion

To write a first draft that already largely has a beginning, middle, and end

The Thesis and the Conclusion

Your thesis depends on your arguing to a logical conclusion based on the evidence you have assembled. You may think it odd that a writer should wait so long to actually decide on a thesis, but it is odd only if you insist that a thesis is something you know fully *before* you write. Sometimes it is, but rarely. You may decide to write an essay on U.S. foreign policy and know before you start that you are going to support foreign aid. But on many a topic, you will not have an opinion. The point of the writing process so far is to help you develop an informed opinion.

Most of the time *you will be discovering what you really think in the process of preparing your essay and writing it.* Do not be overconfident about a thesis discovered early. What is the effect, for example, of an antiwar essay that does not take into account that sometimes wars have been fought for very good reasons and for the protection of freedoms? On the other hand, do not despair if you "can't think of what to say" even though you have found something that interests you and you have formed a topic from that interest. The writing process is one of discovery. It is creative thinking in action, and if you even show small signs of thinking imaginatively and carefully about a topic, you will interest your reader.

So far, then, you have opened up a subject and limited it to a topic, then opened up a topic and limited it to the extent that you can now discover the thesis. You have a shape to your essay achieved by dramatizing your topic in isolation, in context, and as a problem. Now you must come to a conclusion. You have in fact reached several "miniconclusions," one for each of the perspectives in your revised brainstorming notes under "resolution." Read the resolutions and write down a couple of main points about each so that they are clearly defined and summed up. Are they all consistent? Or are there contradictions between them? If there are contradictions, then now is the time for you to decide which position makes most sense.

The question is: can you come to a conclusion based on the evidence you have focused on and dramatized? Remember that the conclusion is not just a summary, although it is helpful to the reader if it does recall the main points of your argument. It is also a final interpretation which develops the earlier evidence. It will not say anything radically new, but it will sharpen a perspective, declare a moral position, make a value judgment, or offer a critical decision. A conclusion should appear to be clearly derived from the evidence you have accumulated; it should not be simply a statement of habitual opinion. Let's illustrate how you might reach a conclusion on the gun control question:

■ *Summarize your miniconclusions from the three main perspectives*

Topic isolated: Will deal with federal control of handguns. Political interests have clouded issue; will deal with problem as open question.

Topic in contexts: Will deal with defining the problem as a legal one. Avoid cause-and-effect argument because violence and guns are connected; to split them is to tackle neither the symptom nor the cause.

Topic as problem: A problem because there must be an effective law + control of violence + preservation of individual rights.

■ *Are your conclusions consistent?* Do they allow a consistent perspective? They seem to here. There are no contradictions now.

■ *To what conclusion do your conclusions lead you?* Synthesize and develop your points. You might decide that gun control is part of the question of violence control, and that the two cannot clearly be kept apart. You have discovered that from your outline. You cannot define one aspect of the problem without the other. You have also decided that since the topic is the question of "control," you are not properly discussing the "social causes of violence." You do not want to get sidetracked onto that. So if you center on "control," you are considering the issue as a *legal* one and you need to think about what those controls might be.

■ *Write out your conclusion in note form*

Federal gun control is necessary, but the law must preserve the right to bear arms for purposes of sport or defense.

Control by police permits and the right of refusal on the grounds of a criminal record or mental health problem.

A general amnesty for all gun owners with guns bought back at a fair price with federal money.

Strict penalties for owning a gun without a permit.

All gun owners must attend federally sponsored safety programs through gun associations.

This is a compromise solution, an attempt to get both sides together, with no guarantee that such a licensing law would stop violent crime. But it would at least help preserve our rights to self-defense and remove many guns from circulation.

So much for an amateur's opinion of what the law should do. You may or may not agree with the conclusion above, but that is not the point of this discussion. The point is to show you that a message can be developed by closely focusing on and dramatizing a subject. By asking questions about your topic, you have invented an explanation and argument for it. You have, in effect, created your thesis which is none other than your conclusion.

Preparing an Outline

The most important points about an outline are that it should be broad enough to guide you in the actual process of composition but flexible enough to allow new ideas to emerge as you write. It is most likely that you will at some time change your mind about an emphasis or find that your argument needs adjustment, especially during the revision stage of writing. You may even make more sweeping changes. The kind of outline proposed here will allow you to do that while keeping the main outline of a logical development of your thesis clear.

The outline below is a simple one based on the bare necessities a reader expects to find. You will remember from the chapters on reading that a reader judges a text usually on some variation of the requirements of emphasis, coherence, unity, and significance. Bearing this in mind, it is reasonable to say that a reader expects from explanatory writing:

An introduction to the topic, enticing the reader into the text

A coherent explanation

A unified argument

A significant conclusion

The following outline builds on these expectations:

1. *Introduction.* This explains the relevance of the topic and your thesis and asks the reader to consider them. You draw material for this from your conclusion.

2. *Definition of terms.* This describes the event or states the questions raised by the topic and gives essential general information, such as defining the terms you will use and how you propose to limit the topic. This section of the essay is based on your material from the perspective of "the topic isolated."

3. *Setting up the problem/issue.* You proceed to open up the topic for the reader by using material from "the topic as problem," examining its interest or why it is controversial.

4. *Examining the problem/issue.* Here you use the most important material from your second brainstorming perspective concerning "the topic in its contexts," discussing the topic in relationship to: its class, its larger contexts, cause and effect, a network of facts, its historical significance, and its impact on people.

5. *Conclusion.* Here you restate your thesis, briefly account for what you have been saying, offer solutions to the problem, and end the discussion on a significant note.

Some Variations

■ Sections (3) and (4) of the outline, the problem and the contexts, are very often reversed in essays emphasizing explanation rather than problem solving. If the context appears more important to you than the issues suggested by the topic, then deal with the contexts first.

■ Chapter 7 goes into detail concerning the beginnings and endings of essays. You may at this point want to read the sections on opening and closing paragraphs; they explain some of the variations available to you.

The outline, once again, should contain only brief notes, especially if you have listed your points fully during the last stage when you were organizing your information under the three topic headings. If you did not make full notes then but relied on your earlier brainstorming jottings, now is the best time to collect your thoughts in a fairly complete outline.

Gun Control Essay Outlined

What would an outline for the "gun control" essay look like? The one below is short and refers back to the notes on organization which were more fully written out. The whole outline is shown next to the first draft in the next chapter.

1. *Introduction:*
   Use the material from "Relevance" and "Conclusion." Emphasize constitutional issue.
2. *Definition of terms:*
   Use the material from "Definition." Emphasize federal handgun control.
3. *Setting up the problem:*
   Use material from "Topic as problem." Emphasize common ground between pro– and anti–gun controllers.
4. *Examining the Problem:*
   Use material from "Context." Emphasize defining the problem legally.
5. *Conclusion:*
   Use material from your notes on "Conclusion." Emphasize need for compromise legislation.

Remember that this orderly and sequential process of preparing an outline will help you arrange your thoughts in the proper order for your essay. Of course you will not, as we noted at the outset, receive inspiration in any order at all. Ideas will come from all directions, and that's as it should be. The purpose here is to offer a format by which your ideas can be both *stimulated* (by questioning and outlining) and *organized* so that you can understand their relevance. This process should help you create more ideas, but never hesitate to adjust an outline or move information around when you write your first draft, if it will help you make your point more emphatically.

Checklist

1. If you have not been assigned a subject or topic, choose as a subject a context you know well: family, friends, public affairs, education, social life, studies, sports, the arts, media, special interests, and so on.

2. Free associate with your subject, writing down all it suggests to you. You have then opened it up to a range of possible topics.

3. Choose from these associations a topic that you find interesting and challenging. It should fit the following criteria:

You can realistically write about it.

It is general enough to interest a reader.

It is open to discussion; it creates questions.

4. Open up the topic from the following perspectives:

Consider the topic in isolation, as self-contained: ask Who? What? Where? When? How? What are its essential, changeless qualities? Cluster ideas around its main terms. Note your personal reactions to its relevance.

Place the topic in its contexts, those of class and larger ones. Is it part of a network of facts? Is it a cause or an effect? What is its historical significance? Talk about it with others.

Consider the topic as a problem, issue, or question.

Brainstorm the topic by following each of these questions as far as you can, listing all the main points that occur to you under the appropriate perspective.

5. Limit your topic by selecting the main ideas from each of the perspectives you have placed it in, discovering the oppositions between ideas, and resolving them.

6. Reorganize your main points from the perspectives of topic isolated, topic in contexts, and topic as problem, keep these notes for writing your first draft.

7. Work on your thesis and conclusion by reviewing your miniconclusions under each perspective. Are they consistent? To what conclusion do they lead you? Brainstorm the questions further and synthesize your conclusions to form one conclusion.

8. Write an outline that follows these general contours:

Introduction: using material from "Conclusion" and "Relevance"

Definition of terms: material from "Topic isolated"

Setting up the topic as problem: material from "Topic as problem"

Examining the problem: material from "Topic as context"

Conclusion

Exercises

1. Reconsider the question of "gun control" as it is discussed in this chapter. Say you want to prove either that all handguns should be banned or that there should be no gun control legislation at all. What then would your material under the three perspectives (isolation, context, and problem) look like? List your entries in note form, then write an outline for an essay supporting either position with sufficient data listed under each heading (introduction, definition of terms, and so on).

2. Here are three short prose excerpts. Your instructor will indicate how many or which ones you should choose, but for each one:

a. Annotate the piece and summarize it, including the theme statement and the supporting argument.

b. Take the theme statement and use it as a topic for an outline. Follow the criteria for opening up and limiting the topic as covered in this chapter and develop an essay outline.

c. Summarize your own conclusion, showing how it differs from or resembles the argument you have found in the extract.

In other words, by the time you have completed this exercise you should have written down (a) a summary of the piece you have read, (b) an outline of how you would develop an essay on the subject, and (c) a list of points based on your outline that cover how you would develop the topic in different directions from the writer of the extract/essay.

The illusions by which men have lived seem to be of two kinds. First, there is what one may perhaps call the Great Illusion—I mean the religious illusion that the universe is moral and good, that it follows a wise and noble plan, that it is gradually generating some supreme value, that goodness is bound to triumph in it. Secondly, there is a whole host of minor illusions on which human happiness nourishes itself. How much of human happiness notoriously comes from the illusions of the lover about his beloved? Then again we work and strive because of the illusions connected with fame, glory, power, or money. Banners of all kinds, flags, emblems, insignia, ceremonials, and rituals are invariably symbols of some illusion or other. The British Empire, the connection between mother country and dominions, is partly kept going by illusions surrounding the notion of kingship. Or think of the vast amount of human happiness which is derived from the illusion of supposing that if some nonsense syllable, such as "sir" or "count" or "lord," is pronounced in conjunction with our names, we belong to a superior order of people.

There is plenty of evidence that human happiness is almost wholly based upon illusions of one kind or another. But the scientific spirit, or the spirit of truth, is the enemy of illusions and therefore the enemy of human happiness. That is why it is going to be so difficult to live with the truth.

W. T. Stace, from **MAN AGAINST DARKNESS**

I never could understand the story of Christmas. People used to weep and wail every year over the fact that "there was no room for Mary in the inn." Every Christmas the innkeeper took a beating in my church for the way he treated poor Mary and Joseph. But Mary was pregnant. Suppose Mary and Joseph came back today and walked into the lobby of the Conrad Hilton and said to the desk clerk, "This is Mary and I am Joseph. We're not married, but let me tell you about this dream we had." You know they would be thrown out immediately. The dream might be legitimate, but you don't tell the desk clerk about it and then get mad because he doesn't believe you. You can't go into a hotel today with a pregnant woman to have a baby. Nor can you check into the hospital just to have a place to sleep. It is just the reverse. You go to the hospital to have the baby and go to the hotel to read the Bible—there is one in every room. The government has taken the Bibles out of the schools, but it left them in the hotel rooms. So maybe the government knows which place is more hip.

My momma could never understand how white folks could twist the words of the Bible around to justify racial segregation. Yet she could read the Ten Commandments, which clearly say, "Thou shalt not kill," and still justify eating meat. Momma couldn't read the newspaper very well, but she sure could interpret the Word of God. "God meant you shouldn't kill people," she used to say. But I insisted, "Momma, he didn't say that. He said, 'Thou shalt not kill.' If you leave that statement alone, a whole lot of things would be safe from killing. But if you are going to twist the words about killing to mean what you want them to mean, then let white folks do the same thing with justifying racial segregation."

"You can't live without eating meat," Momma would persist. "You'd starve." I couldn't buy that either. You get milk from a cow without killing it. You do not have to kill an animal to get what you need from it. You get wool from the sheep without killing it. Two of the strongest animals in the jungle are vegetarians—the elephant and the gorilla. The first two years are the most important years of a man's life, and during that period he is not involved with eating meat. If you suddenly become very ill, there is a good chance you will be taken off a meat diet. So it is a myth that killing is necessary for survival. The day I decide that I must have a piece of steak to nourish my body, I will also give the cow the same right to nourish herself on human beings.

There is so little basic difference between animals and humans. The process of reproduction is the same for chickens, cattle, and humans. If suddenly the air stopped circulating on the earth, or the sun collided with the earth, animals and humans would die alike. A nuclear holocaust will wipe out all life. Life in the created order is basically the same and should be respected as such. It seems to me the Bible says it is wrong to kill—period.

If we can justify *any* kind of killing in the name of religion, the door is opened for all kinds of other justifications. The fact of killing animals is not as frightening as our human tendency to justify it—to kill and not even be aware that we are taking life. It is sobering to realize that when you misuse one of the least of Nature's creatures, like the chicken, you are sowing the seed for misusing the highest of Nature's creatures, man.

Dick Gregory, from **THE SHADOW THAT SCARES ME**

"Would you teach me about peyote, don Juan?"

"Why would you like to undertake such learning?"

"I really would like to know about it. Is not just to want to know a good reason?"

"No! You must search in your heart and find out why a young man like you wants to undertake such a task of learning."

"Why did you learn about it yourself, don Juan?"

"Why do you ask that?"

"Maybe we both have the same reasons."

"I doubt that. I am an Indian. We don't have the same paths."

"The only reason I have is that I *want* to learn about it, just to know. But I assure you, don Juan, my intentions are not bad."

"I believe you. I've smoked you."

"I beg your pardon!"

"It doesn't matter now. I know your intentions."

"Do you mean you saw through me?"

"You could put it that way."

"Will you teach me, then?"

"No!"

"Is it because I'm not an Indian?"

"No. It is because you don't know your heart. What is important is that you know exactly why you want to involve yourself. Learning about 'Mescalito' is a most serious act. If you were an Indian your desire alone would be sufficient. Very few Indians have such a desire."

C. Castaneda, from **THE TEACHINGS OF DON JUAN: A YAQUI WAY OF KNOWLEDGE**

Writing Assignment

You will now write an essay, carrying the process through further stages of composition in the next three chapters. In this exercise, you need to:

1. Choose a subject
2. Refine the subject into a topic
3. Open up your options with the topic
4. Limit those options to essentials
5. Arrive at a conclusion and create a thesis

Use the checklist on p. 125 as a reminder of what this chapter has to say about the writing process, and:

1. Choose a subject, writing a paragraph explaining the relevance of your choice.
2. Free associate in writing on your subject.
3. Choose a topic from among those free associations, making sure you check the criteria listed in this chapter for your choice. Write a paragraph justifying your choice.
4. From the perspectives of the topic in *isolation,* in its *contexts,* and as a *problem,* open up your topic, brainstorming in writing under each heading.
5. Limit each perspective to its *oppositions, connections,* and your *resolution,* listing all the information you will need under the headings of *isolation, context,* and *problem.*
6. Write a one-line summary of each of your *resolutions* and check for consistency. Rework any inconsistent perspective.
7. Decide on your overall conclusion based on the evidence of the *resolutions* and write down your theme statement with notes on how you will express your conclusion.

If you do not want to begin from a subject of your own choosing, select one of the following topics or quotations as your starting point, and begin at stage 2 above:

"I can't get no satisfaction . . ."   The Equal Rights Amendment
Overpaid athletes   Welfare is society's responsibility
Politicians' rhetoric   The greatest spectator sport of all
Do we need a core curriculum?   Why *were* we in Vietnam?
Nuclear power

"It is in the ability to deceive oneself that the greatest talent is shown."
"There is nothing good or bad but thinking makes it so."
"Terrible experiences give one cause to speculate whether the one who experiences them may not be something terrible."

Readings

Paul Tillich **THE LOST DIMENSION IN RELIGION**

"If the resurgence of religion would produce a new understanding of the symbols of the past and their relevance for our situation, instead of premature and deceptive answers, it would become a creative factor in our culture and a saving factor for many who live in estrangement, anxiety, and despair."

Lewis Thomas **DEBATING THE UNKNOWABLE**

"It is the admission of ignorance that leads to progress, not so much because the solving of a particular puzzle leads directly to a new piece of understanding but because the puzzle—if it interests enough scientists—leads to *work.*"

Bruno Bettelheim **THE ART OF MOVING PICTURES**

"It might be said that the state of the art of the moving image can be assessed by the degree to which it meets the mythopoetic task of giving us myths suitable to live by in our time—visions that transmit to us the highest and best feelings to which men have risen—and by how well the moving images give us that delight which leads to wisdom."

THE LOST DIMENSION IN RELIGION

Paul Tillich

Every observer of our Western civilization is aware of the fact that something has happened to religion. It especially strikes the observer of the American scene. Everywhere he finds symptoms of what one has called religious revival, or more modestly, the revival of interest in religion. He finds them in the churches with their rapidly increasing membership. He finds them in the mushroomlike growth of sects. He finds them on college campuses and in the theological faculties of universities. Most conspicuously, he finds them in the tremendous success of men like Billy Graham and Norman Vincent Peale, who attract masses of people Sunday after Sunday, meeting after meeting. The facts cannot be denied, but how should they be interpreted? It is my intention to show that these facts must be seen as expressions of the predicament of Western man in the second half of the twentieth century. But I would even go a step further. I believe that the predicament of man in our period gives us also an important insight into the predicament of man generally—at all times and in all parts of the earth.

There are many analyses of man and society in our time. Most of them show important traits in the picture, but few of them succeed in giving a general key to our present situation. Although it is not easy to find such a key, I shall attempt it and, in so doing, will make an assertion which may be somewhat mystifying at first hearing. The decisive element in the predicament of Western man in our period is his loss of the dimension of depth. Of course, "dimension of depth" is a metaphor. It is taken from the spatial realm and applied to man's spiritual life. What does it mean?

It means that man has lost an answer to the question: What is the meaning of life? Where do we come from, where do we go to? What shall we do, what should we become in the short stretch between birth and death? Such questions are not answered or even asked if the "dimension of depth" is lost. And this is precisely what has happened to man in our period of history. He has lost the courage to ask such questions with an infinite seriousness—as former generations did—and he has lost the courage to receive answers to these questions, wherever they may come from.

I suggest that we call the dimension of depth the religious dimension in man's nature. Being religious means asking passionately the question of the meaning of our existence and being willing to receive answers, even if the answers hurt. Such an idea of religion makes religion universally human, but it certainly differs from what is usually called religion. It does not describe religion as the belief in the existence of gods or one God, and as a set of activities and institutions for the sake of relating oneself to these beings in thought, devotion and obedience. No one can deny that the religions which have appeared in history are religions in this sense. Nevertheless, religion in its innermost nature is more than religion in this narrower sense. It is the state of being concerned about one's own being and being universally.

There are many people who are ultimately concerned in this way who feel far removed, however, from religion in the narrower sense, and therefore from every historical religion. It often happens that such people take the question of the meaning of their life infinitely seriously and reject any historical religion just for this reason. They feel that the concrete religions fail to express their profound concern adequately. They are religious while rejecting the religions. It is this experience which forces us to distinguish the meaning of religion as living in the dimension of depth from particular expressions of one's ultimate concern in the symbols and institutions of a concrete religion. If we now turn to the concrete analysis of the religious situation of our time, it is obvious that our key must be the basic meaning of religion and not any particular religion, not even Christianity. What does this key disclose about the predicament of man in our period?

If we define religion as the state of being grasped by an infinite concern we must say: Man in our time has lost such infinite concern. And the resurgence of religion is nothing but a desperate and mostly futile attempt to regain what has been lost.

How did the dimension of depth become lost? Like any important event, it has many causes, but certainly not the one which one hears often mentioned from ministers' pulpits and evangelists' platforms, namely that a widespread impiety of modern man is responsible. Modern man is neither more pious nor more impious than man in any other period. The loss of the dimension of depth is caused by the relation of man to his world and to himself in our period, the period in which nature is being subjected scientifically and technically to the control of man. In this period, life in the dimension of depth is replaced by life in the horizontal dimension. The driving forces of the industrial society of which we are a part go ahead horizontally and not vertically. In popular terms this is expressed in phrases like "better and better," "bigger and bigger," "more and more." One should not disparage the feeling which lies behind such speech. Man is right in feeling that he is able to know and transform the world he encounters without a foreseeable limit. He can go ahead in all directions without a definite boundary.

A most expressive symbol of this attitude of going ahead in the horizontal dimension is the breaking through of the space which is controlled by the gravitational power of the earth into the world-space. It is interesting that one calls this world-space simply "space" and speaks, for instance, of space travel, as if every trip were not travel into space. Perhaps one feels that the true nature of space has been discovered only through our entering into indefinite world-space. In any case, the predominance of the horizontal dimension over the dimension of depth has been immensely increased by the opening up of the space beyond the space of the earth.

If we now ask what does man do and seek if he goes ahead in the horizontal dimension, the answer is difficult. Sometimes one is inclined to say that the mere movement ahead without an end, the intoxication with speeding forward without limits, is what satisfies him. But this answer is by no means sufficient. For on his way into space and time man changes the world he encounters. And the changes made by him change himself. He transforms everything he encounters into a tool; and in doing so he himself becomes a tool. But if he asks, a tool for what, there is no answer.

One does not need to look far beyond everyone's daily experience in order to find examples to describe this predicament. Indeed our daily life in office and home, in cars and airplanes, at parties and conferences, while reading magazines and watching television, while looking at advertisements and hearing radio, are in themselves continuous examples of a life which has lost the dimension of depth. It runs ahead, every moment is filled with something which must be done or seen or said or planned. But no one can experience depth without stopping and becoming aware of himself. Only if he has moments in which he does not care about what comes next can he experience the meaning of this moment here and now and ask himself about the meaning of his life. As long as the preliminary, transitory concerns are not silenced, no matter how interesting and valuable and important they may be, the voice of the ultimate concern cannot be heard. This is the deepest root of the loss of the dimension of depth in our period—the loss of religion in its basic and universal meaning.

If the dimension of depth is lost, the symbols in which life in this dimension has expressed itself must also disappear. I am speaking of the great symbols of the historical religions in our Western world, of Judaism and Christianity. The reason that the religious symbols became lost is not primarily scientific criticism, but it is a complete misunderstanding of their meaning; and only because of this misunderstanding was scientific critique able, and even justified, in attacking them. The first step toward the non-religion of the Western world was made by religion itself. When it defended its great symbols, not as symbols, but as literal stories, it had already lost the battle. In doing so the theologians (and today many religious laymen) helped to transfer the powerful expressions of the dimension of depth into objects or happenings on the horizontal plane. There the symbols lose their power and meaning and become an easy prey to physical, biological and historical attack.

If the symbol of creation which points to the divine ground of everything is transferred to the horizontal plane, it becomes a story of events in a removed past for which there is no evidence, but which contradicts every piece of scientific evidence. If the symbol of the Fall of Man, which points to the tragic estrangement of man and his world from their true being is transferred to the horizontal plane, it becomes a story of a human couple a few thousand years ago in what is now present-day Iraq. One of the most profound psychological descriptions of the

general human predicament becomes an absurdity on the horizontal plane. If the symbols of the Saviour and the salvation through Him which point to the healing power in history and personal life are transferred to the horizontal plane, they become stories of a half-divine being coming from a heavenly place and returning to it. Obviously, in this form, they have no meaning whatsoever for people whose view of the universe is determined by scientific astronomy.

If the idea of God (and the symbols applied to Him) which expresses man's ultimate concern is transferred to the horizontal plane, God becomes a being among others whose existence or nonexistence is a matter of inquiry. Nothing, perhaps, is more symptomatic of the loss of the dimension of depth than the permanent discussion about the existence or nonexistence of God—a discussion in which both sides are equally wrong, because the discussion itself is wrong and possible only after the loss of the dimension of depth.

When in this way man has deprived himself of the dimension of depth and the symbols expressing it, he then becomes a part of the horizontal plane. He loses his self and becomes a thing among things. He becomes an element in the process of manipulated production and manipulated consumption. This is now a matter of public knowledge. We have become aware of the degree to which everyone in our social structure is managed, even if one knows it and even if one belongs himself to the managing group. The influence of the gang mentality on adolescents, of the corporation's demands on the executives, of the conditioning of everyone by public communication, by propaganda and advertising under the guidance of motivation research, et cetera, have all been described in many books and articles.

Under these pressures, man can hardly escape the fate of becoming a thing among the things he produces, a bundle of conditioned reflexes without a free, deciding and responsible self. The immense mechanism, set up by man to produce objects for his use, transforms man himself into an object used by the same mechanism of production and consumption.

But man has not ceased to be man. He resists this fate anxiously, desperately, courageously. He asks the question, for what? And he realizes that there is no answer. He becomes aware of the emptiness which is covered by the continuous movement ahead and the production of means for ends which become means again without an ultimate end. Without knowing what happened to him, he feels that he has lost the meaning of life, the dimension of depth.

Out of this awareness the religious question arises and religious answers are received or rejected. Therefore, in order to describe the contemporary attitude toward religion, we must first point to the places where the awareness of the predicament of Western man in our period is most sharply expressed. These places are the great art, literature and, partly, at least, the philosophy of our time. It is both the subject matter and the style of these creations which show the passionate and often tragic struggle about the meaning of life in a period in which man has lost the dimension of depth. This art, literature, philosophy is not religious in the narrower sense of the word; but it asks the religious question more radically and more profoundly than most directly religious expressions of our time.

It is the religious question which is asked when the novelist describes a man who tries in vain to reach the only place which could solve the problem of his life, or a man who disintegrates under the memory of a guilt which persecutes him, or a man who never had a real self and is pushed by his fate without resistance to death, or a man who experiences a profound disgust of everything he encounters.

It is the religious question which is asked when the poet opens up the horror and the fascination of the demonic regions of his soul, or if he leads us into the deserts and empty places of our being, or if he shows the physical and moral mud under the surface of life, or if he sings the song of transitoriness, giving words to the ever-present anxiety of our hearts.

It is the religious question which is asked when the playwright shows the illusion of a life in a ridiculous symbol, or if he lets the emptiness of a life's work end in self-destruction, or if he confronts us with the inescapable bondage to mutual hate and guilt, or if he leads us into the dark cellar of lost hopes and slow disintegration.

It is the religious question which is asked when the painter breaks the visible surface into pieces, then reunites them into a great picture which has little similarity with the world at which we normally look, but which expresses our anxiety and our courage to face reality.

It is the religious question which is asked when the architect, in creating office buildings or churches, removes the trimmings taken over from past styles because they cannot be considered an honest expression of our own period. He prefers the seeming poverty of a purpose-determined style to the deceptive richness of imitated styles of the past. He knows that he gives no final answer, but he does give an honest answer.

The philosophy of our time shows the same hiddenly religious traits. It is divided into two main schools of thought, the analytic and the existentialist. The former tries to analyze logical and linguistic forms which are always used and which underlie all scientific research. One may compare them with the painters who dissolve the natural forms of bodies into cubes, planes and lines; or with those architects who want the structural "bones" of their buildings to be conspicuously visible and not hidden by covering features. This self-restriction produces the almost monastic poverty and seriousness of this philosophy. It is religious—without any contact with religion in its method—by exercising the humility of "learned ignorance."

In contrast to this school the existentialist philosophers have much to say about the problems of human existence. They bring into rational concepts what the writers and poets, the painters and architects, are expressing in their particular material. What they express is the human predicament in time and space, in anxiety and guilt and the feeling of meaninglessness. From Pascal in the seventeenth century to Heidegger and Sartre in our time, philosophers have emphasized the contrast between human dignity and human misery. And by doing so, they have raised the religious question. Some have tried to answer the question they have asked. But if they did so, they turned back to past traditions and offered to our time that which does not fit our time. Is it possible for our time to receive answers which are born out of our time?

Answers given today are in danger of strengthening the present situation and with it the questions to which they are supposed to be the answers. This refers to some of the previously mentioned major representatives of the so-called resurgence of religion, as for instance the evangelist Billy Graham and the counseling and healing minister, Norman Vincent Peale. Against the validity of the answers given by the former, one must say that, in spite of his personal integrity, his propagandistic methods and his primitive theological fundamentalism fall short of what is needed to give an answer to the religious question of our period. In spite of all his seriousness, he does not take the radical questions of our period seriously.

The effect that Norman Peale has on large groups of people is rooted in the fact that he confirms the situation which he is supposed to help overcome. He heals people with the purpose of making them fit again for the demands of the competitive and conformist society in which we are living. He helps them to become adapted to the situation which is characterized by the loss of the dimension of depth. Therefore, his advice is valid on this level; but it is the validity of this level that is the true religious question of our time. And this question he neither raises nor answers.

In many cases the increase of church membership and interest in religious activities does not mean much more than the religious consecration of a state of things in which the religious dimension has been lost. It is the desire to participate in activities which are socially strongly approved and give internal and a certain amount of external security. This is not necessarily bad, but it certainly is not an answer to the religious question of our period.

Is there an answer? There is always an answer, but the answer may not be available to us. We may be too deeply steeped in the predicament out of which the question arises to be able to answer it. To acknowledge this is certainly a better way toward a real answer than to bar the way to it by deceptive answers. And it may be that in this attitude the real answer (within available limits) is given. The real answer to the question of how to regain the dimension of depth is not given by increased church membership or church attendance, nor by conversion or healing experiences. But it is given by the awareness that we have lost the decisive dimension of life, the dimension of depth, and that there is no easy way of getting it back. Such awareness is in itself a state of being grasped by that which is symbolized in the term, dimension of depth. He who realizes that he is separated from the ultimate source of meaning shows by this realization that he is not only separated but also reunited. And this is just our situation. What we need above all—and partly have—is the radical realization of our predicament, without trying to cover it up by secular or religious ideologies. The revival of religious interest would be a creative power in our culture if it would develop into a movement of search for the lost dimension of depth.

This does not mean that the traditional religious symbols should be dismissed. They certainly have lost their meaning in the literalistic form into which they have been distorted, thus producing the critical reaction against them. But they have not lost their genuine meaning, namely, of answering the question which is implied in man's very existence in powerful, revealing and saving symbols. If the resurgence of religion would produce a new understanding of the symbols of the past and their relevance for our situation, instead of premature and deceptive answers, it would become a creative factor in our culture and a saving factor for many who live in estrangement, anxiety and despair. The religious answer has always the character of "in spite of." In spite of the loss of dimension of depth, its power is present, and most present in those who are aware of the loss and are striving to regain it with ultimate seriousness.

1. What does *dimension of depth* mean? Contrast it to *the horizontal dimension.*
2. How did the dimension of depth become lost, according to Tillich?
3. How has religion misused its symbols?
4. Why are art and philosophy important to Tillich?
5. What is wrong with Billy Graham and Norman Vincent Peale in Tillich's view?
6. This is an essay based on a problem and its solution. Briefly describe how Tillich raises the problem and how he goes about trying to solve it.
7. Provide a short outline of the essay under the headings of *introduction, definition, problem, examining the problems,* and *conclusion* in which you briefly list the main points Tillich covers under each heading. Does Tillich follow this sequence closely? If not, explain what variations to this outline he introduces to develop the argument of his essay.

DEBATING THE UNKNOWABLE

Lewis Thomas

The greatest of all the accomplishments of twentieth-century science has been the discovery of human ignorance. We live, as never before, in puzzlement about nature, the universe, and ourselves most of all. It is a new experience for the species. A century ago, after the turbulence caused by Darwin and Wallace had subsided and the central idea of natural selection had been grasped and accepted, we thought we knew everything essential about evolution. In the eighteenth century there were no huge puzzles; human reason was all you needed in order to figure out the universe. And for most of the earlier centuries, the Church provided both the questions and the answers, neatly packaged. Now, for the first time in human history, we are catching glimpses of our incomprehension. We can still make up stories to explain the world, as we always have, but now the stories have to be confirmed and reconfirmed by experiment. This is the scientific method, and once started on this line we cannot turn back. We are obliged to grow up in skepticism, requiring proofs for every assertion about nature, and there is no way out except to move ahead and plug away, hoping for comprehension in the future but living in a condition of intellectual instability for the long time.

It is the admission of ignorance that leads to progress, not so much because the solving of a particular puzzle leads directly to a new piece of understanding but because the puzzle—if it interests enough scientists—leads to *work*. There is a similar phenomenon in entomology known as stigmergy, a term invented by Grassé, which means "to incite to work." When three or four termites are collected together in a chamber they wander about aimlessly, but when more termites are added, they begin to build. It is the presence of other termites, in sufficient numbers at close quarters, that produces the work: they pick up each other's fecal pellets and stack them in neat columns, and when the columns are precisely the right height, the termites reach across and turn the perfect arches that form the foundation of the termitarium. No single termite knows how to do any of this, but as soon as there are enough termites gathered together they become flawless architects, sensing their distances from each other although blind, building an immensely complicated structure with its own air-conditioning and humidity control. They work their lives away in this ecosystem built by themselves. The nearest thing to a termitarium that I can think of in human behavior is the making of language, which we do by keeping *at* each other all our lives, generation after generation, changing the structure by some sort of instinct.

Very little is understood about this kind of collective behavior. It is out of fashion these days to talk of "superorganisms," but there simply aren't enough reductionist details in hand to explain away the phenomenon of termites and other social insects: some very good guesses can be made about their chemical signaling systems, but the plain fact that they exhibit something like a collective intelligence is a mystery, or anyway an unsolved problem, that might contain important implications for social life in general. This mystery is the best introduction I can think of to biological science in college. It should be taught for its strangeness, and for the ambiguity of its meaning. It should be taught to premedical students, who need lessons early in their careers about the uncertainties in science.

College students, and for that matter high school students, should be exposed very early, perhaps at the outset, to the big arguments currently going on among scientists. Big arguments stimulate their interest, and with luck engage their absorbed attention. Few things in life are as engrossing as a good fight between highly trained and skilled adversaries. But the young students are told very little about the major disagreements of the day; they may be taught something about the arguments between Darwinians and their opponents a century ago, but they do not realize that similar disputes about other matters, many of them touching profound issues for our understanding of nature, are still going on and, indeed, are an essential feature of the scientific process. There is, I fear, a reluctance on the part of science teachers to talk about such things, based on the belief that before students can appreciate what the arguments are about they must learn and master the "fundamentals." I would be willing to see some experiments along this line, and I have in mind several examples of contemporary doctrinal dispute in which the drift of the argument can be readily perceived without deep or elaborate knowledge of the subject.

There is, for one, the problem of animal awareness. One school of ethologists devoted to the study of animal behavior has it that human beings are unique in the possession of consciousness, differing from all other creatures in being able to think things over, capitalize on past experience, and hazard informed guesses at the future. Other, "lower," animals (with possible exceptions made for chimpanzees, whales, and dolphins) cannot do such things with their minds; they live from moment to moment with brains that are programmed to respond, automatically or by conditioning, to contingencies in the environment. Behavioral psychologists believe that this automatic or conditioned response accounts for human mental activity as well, although they dislike that word "mental." On the other side are some ethologists who seem to be more generous-minded, who see no compelling reasons to doubt that animals in general are quite capable of real thinking and do quite a lot of it—thinking that isn't as dense as human thinking, that is sparser because of the lack of language and the resultant lack of metaphors to help the thought along, but thinking nonetheless.

The point about this argument is not that one side or the other is in possession of a more powerful array of convincing facts; quite the opposite. There are not enough facts to sustain a genuine debate of any length; the question of animal awareness is an unsettled one. In the circumstance, I put forward the following notion about a small beetle, the mimosa girdler, which undertakes three pieces of linked, sequential behavior: finding a mimosa tree and climbing up the trunk and out to the end of a branch; cutting a longitudinal slit and laying within it five or six eggs; and crawling back on the limb and girdling it neatly down into the cambium. The third step is an eight-to-ten-hour task of hard labor, from which the beetle gains no food for itself—only the certainty that the branch will promptly die and fall to the ground in the next brisk wind, thus enabling the larvae to hatch and grow in an abundance of dead wood. I propose, in total confidence that even though I am probably wrong nobody today can prove that I am wrong, that the beetle is not doing these three things out of blind instinct, like a little machine, but is thinking its way along, just as we would think. The difference is that we possess enormous brains, crowded all the time with an infinite number of long thoughts, while the beetle's brain is only a few strings of neurons connected in a modest network, capable therefore of only three *tiny* thoughts, coming into consciousness one after the other: find the right tree; get up there and lay eggs in a slit; back up and spend the day killing the branch so the eggs can hatch. End of message. I would not go so far as to anthropomorphize the mimosa tree, for I really do not believe plants have minds, but something has to be said about the tree's role in this arrangement as a beneficiary: mimosas grow for twenty-five to thirty years and then die, unless they are vigorously pruned annually, in which case they can live to be a hundred. The beetle is a piece of good luck for the tree, but nothing more: one example of pure chance working at its best in nature—what you might even wish to call good nature.

This brings me to the second example of unsettlement in biology, currently being rather delicately discussed but not yet argued over, for there is still only one orthodoxy and almost no opposition, yet. This is the matter of chance itself, and the role played by blind chance in the arrangement of living things on the planet. It is, in the orthodox view, pure luck that evolution brought us to our present condition, and things might just as well have turned out any number of other, different ways, and might go in any unpredictable way for the future. There is, of course, nothing chancy about natural selection itself: it is an accepted fact that selection will always favor the advantaged individuals whose genes succeed best in propagating themselves within a changing environment. But the creatures acted upon by natural selection are themselves there as the result of chance: mutations (probably of much more importance during the long period of exclusively microbial life starting nearly 4 billion years ago and continuing until about one billion years ago); the endless sorting and re-sorting of genes within chromosomes during replication; perhaps recombination of genes across species lines at one time or another; and almost certainly the carrying of genes by viruses from one creature to another.

The argument comes when one contemplates the whole biosphere, the conjoined life of the earth. How could it have turned out to possess such stability and coherence, resembling as it does a sort of enormous developing embryo, with nothing but chance events to determine its emergence? Lovelock and Margulis, facing this problem, have proposed the Gaia Hypothesis, which is, in brief, that the earth is itself a form of life, "a complex entity involving the Earth's biosphere, atmosphere, oceans and soil; the totality constituting a feedback or cybernetic system which seeks an optimal physical and chemical environment for life on this planet." Lovelock postulates, in addition, that "the physical and chemical condition of the surface of the Earth, of the atmosphere, and of the oceans has been and is actively made fit and comfortable by the presence of life itself."

This notion is beginning to stir up a few signs of storm, and if it catches on, as I think it will, we will soon find the biological community split into fuming factions, one side saying that the evolved biosphere displays evidences of design and purpose, the other decrying such heresy. I believe that students should learn as much as they can about the argument. In an essay in *Coevolution* (Spring 1981), W.F. Doolittle has recently attacked the Gaia Hypothesis, asking, among other things, "... how does Gaia know if she is too cold or too hot, and how does she instruct the biosphere to behave accordingly?" This is not a deadly criticism in a world where we do not actually understand, in anything like real detail, how even Dr. Doolittle manages the stability and control of his own internal environment, including his body temperature. One thing is certain: none of us can instruct our body's systems to make the needed corrections beyond a very limited number of rather trivial tricks made possible through biofeedback techniques. If something goes wrong with my liver or my kidneys, I have no advice to offer out of my cortex. I rely on the system to fix itself, which it usually does with no help from me beyond crossing my fingers.

Another current battle involving the unknown is between sociobiologists and antisociobiologists, and it is a marvel for students to behold. To observe, in open-mouthed astonishment, one group of highly intelligent, beautifully trained, knowledgeable, and imaginative scientists maintaining that all behavior, animal and human, is governed exclusively by genes, and another group of equally talented scientists asserting that all behavior is set and determined by the environment or by culture, is an educational experience that no college student should be allowed to miss. The essential lesson to be learned has nothing to do with the relative validity of the facts underlying the argument. It is the argument itself that is the education: we do not yet know enough to settle such questions.

One last example. There is an uncomfortable secret in biology, not much talked about yet, but beginning to surface. It is, in a way, linked to the observations that underlie the Gaia Hypothesis. Nature abounds in instances of cooperation and collaboration, partnerships between species. There is a tendency of living things to join up whenever joining is possible: accommodation and compromise are more common results of close contact than combat and destruction. Given the opportunity and the proper circumstances, two cells from totally different species—a mouse cell and a human cell, for example—will fuse to become a single cell, and then the two nuclei will fuse into a single nucleus, and then the hybrid cell will divide to produce generations of new cells containing the combined genomes of both species. Bacteria are indispensable partners in the fixation of atmospheric nitrogen by plants. The oxygen in our atmosphere is put there, almost in its entirety, by the photosynthetic chloroplasts in the cells of green plants, and these organelles are almost certainly the descendants of blue-green algae that joined up when the nucleated cells of higher plants came into existence. The mitochondria in all our own cells, and in all other nucleated cells, which enable us to use oxygen for energy, are the direct descendants of symbiotic bacteria. These are becoming accepted facts, and there is no longer an agitated argument over their probable validity; but there are no satisfactory explanations for how such amiable and useful arrangements came into being in the first place. Axelrod and Hamilton (*Science*, March 27, 1981) have recently reopened the question of cooperation in evolution with a mathematical approach based on game theory (the Prisoner's Dilemma game), which permits the hypothesis that one creature's best strategy for dealing repeatedly with another is to concede and cooperate rather than to defect and go it alone.

This idea can be made to fit with the mathematical justification based on kinship already accepted for explaining altruism in nature—that in a colony of social insects the sacrifice of one individual for another depends on how many of the sacrificed member's genes are matched by others and thus preserved, and that the extent of the colony's altruistic behavior can be mathematically calculated. It is, by the way, an interesting aspect of contemporary biology that true altruism—the giving away of something without return—is incompatible with dogma, even though it goes on all over the place. Nature, in this respect, keeps breaking the rules, and needs correcting by new ways of doing arithmetic.

The social scientists are in the hardest business of all—trying to understand how humanity works. They are caught up in debates all over town; everything they touch turns out to be one of society's nerve endings, eliciting outrage and cries of pain. Wait until they begin coming close to the bone. They surely will some day, provided they can continue to attract enough bright people—fascinated by humanity, unafraid of big numbers, and skeptical of questionnaires—and provided the government does not starve them out of business, as is now being tried in Washington. Politicians do not like pain, not even wincing, and they have some fear of what the social scientists may be thinking about thinking for the future.

The social scientists are themselves too modest about the history of their endeavor, tending to display only the matters under scrutiny today in economics, sociology, and psychology, for example—never boasting, as they might, about one of the greatest of all scientific advances in our comprehension of humanity, for which they could be claiming credit. I refer to the marvelous accomplishments of the nineteenth-century comparative linguists. When the scientific method is working at its best, it succeeds in revealing the connection between things in nature that seem at first totally unrelated to each other. Long before the time when the biologists, led by Darwin and Wallace, were constructing the tree of evolution and the origin of species, the linguists were hard at work on the evolution of language. After beginning in 1786 with Sir William Jones and his inspired hunch that the remarkable similarities among Sanskrit, Greek, and Latin meant, in his words, that these three languages must "have sprung from some common source, which, perhaps, no longer exists," the new science of comparative grammar took off in 1816 with Franz Bopp's classic work "On the conjugational system of the Sanskrit language in comparison with that of the Greek, Latin, Persian and Germanic languages"—a piece of work equivalent, in its scope and in its power to explain, to the best of nineteenth-century biology. The common Indo-European ancestry of English, Germanic, Slavic, Greek, Latin, Baltic, Indic, Iranian, Hittite, and Anatolian tongues, and the meticulous scholarship connecting them was a tour de force for research—science at its best, and social science at that.

It is nice to know that a common language, perhaps 20,000 years ago, had a root word for the earth which turned, much later, into the technical term for the complex polymers that make up the connective tissues of the soil: humus and what are called the humic acids. There is a strangeness, though, in the emergence from the same root of words such as "human" and "humane," and "humble." It comes as something of a shock to realize that the root for words such as "miracle" and "marvel" meant, originally, "to smile," and that from the single root *sa* were constructed, in the descendant tongues, three cognate words, "satisfied," "satiated," and "sadness." How is it possible for a species to show so much wisdom in its most collective of all behaviors—the making and constant changing of language—and at the same time be so habitually folly-prone in the building of nation-states? Modern linguistics has moved into new areas of inquiry as specialized and inaccessible for most laymen (including me) as particle physics; I cannot guess where linguistics will come out, but it is surely aimed at scientific comprehension, and its problem—human language—is as crucial to the species as any other field I can think of, including molecular genetics.

But there are some risks involved in trying to do science in the humanities before its time, and useful lessons can be learned from some of the not-so-distant history of medicine. A century ago it was the common practice to deal with disease by analyzing what seemed to be the underlying mechanism and applying whatever treatment popped into the doctor's head. Getting sick was a hazardous enterprise in those days. The driving force in medicine was the need to *do* something, never mind what. It occurs to me now, reading in incomprehension some of the current reductionist writings in literary criticism, especially poetry criticism, that the new schools are at risk under a similar pressure. A poem is a healthy organism, really in need of no help from science, no treatment except fresh air and exercise. I thought I'd just sneak that in.

1. How does ignorance lead to progress, according to Thomas?
2. How is the story of the termites relevant to Thomas's argument?
3. When will the scientific method not work?
4. What should students be exposed to?
5. What are the risks of science in the humanities?
6. What definitions of his topic does Thomas offer his reader?
7. List all the problems Thomas raises about his topic.
8. What exactly is Thomas's thesis?
9. What conclusion does Thomas come to about dealing with the question of the unknowable?

THE ART OF MOVING PICTURES

Bruno Bettelheim

Whether we like it or not—and many may disagree with my thesis because painting, or music, or some other art is more important to them—the art of the moving image is the only art truly of our time, whether it is in the form of the film or television. The moving picture is our universal art, which comprises all others, literature and acting, stage design and music, dance and the beauty of nature, and, most of all, the use of light and of color.

It is always about us, because the medium is truly part of the message and the medium of the moving image is uniquely modern. Everybody can understand it, as everyone once understood religious art in church. And as people used to go to church on Sundays (and still do), so the majority today go to the movies on weekends. But while in the past most went to church only on some days, now everybody watches moving images every day.

All age groups watch moving pictures, and they watch them for many more hours than people have ever spent in churches. Children and adults watch them separately or together; in many ways and for many people, it is the only experience common to parents and children. It is the only art today that appeals to all social and economic classes, in short, that appeals to everybody, as did religious art in times past. The moving picture is thus by far the most popular art of our time, and it is also the most authentically American of arts.

When I speak here of the moving picture as the authentic American art of our time, I do not think of art with a capital A, nor of "high" art. Putting art on a pedestal robs it of its vitality. When the great medieval and Renaissance cathedrals were erected, and decorated outside and in with art, these were popular works, that meant something to everybody.

Some were great works of art, others not, but every piece was significant and all took pride in each of them. Some gain their spiritual experience from the masterpiece, but many more gain it from the mediocre works that express the same vision as the masterpiece but in a more accessible form. This is as true for church music or the church itself as for paintings and sculptures. This diversity of art objects achieves a unity, and differences in quality are important, provided they all represent, each in its own way, the overarching vision and experience of a larger, important cosmos. Such a vision confers meaning and dignity on our existence, and is what forms the essence of art.

So among the worst detriments to the healthy development of the art of the moving image are efforts by aesthetes and critics to isolate the art of film from popular movies and television. Nothing could be more contrary to the true spirit of art. Whenever art was vital, it was always equally popular with the ordinary man and the most refined person. Had Greek drama and comedy meant nothing to most citizens, the majority of the population would not have sat all day long entranced on hard stone slabs, watching the events on the stage; nor would the entire population have conferred prizes on the winning dramatist. The medieval pageants and mystery plays out of which modern drama grew were popular entertainments, as were the plays of Shakespeare. Michelangelo's David stood at the most public place in Florence, embodying the people's vision that tyranny must be overthrown, while it also related to their religious vision, as it represented the myth of David and Goliath. Everybody admired the statue; it was simultaneously popular and great art, but one did not think of it in such disparate terms. Neither should we. To live well we need both: visions that lift us up, and entertainment that is down to earth provided both art and entertainment, each in its different form and way, are embodiments of the same visions of man. If art does not speak to all of us, common men and elites alike, it fails to address itself to that true humanity that is common to all of us. A different art for the elites and another one for average man tears society apart; it offends what we most need: visions that bind us together in common experiences that make life worth living.

When I speak of an affirmation of man, I do not mean the presentation of fake images of life as wonderfully pleasant. Life is best celebrated in the form of a battle against its inequities, of struggles, of dignity in defeat, of the greatness of discovering oneself and the other.

Quite a few moving pictures have conveyed such visions. In *Kagemusha*, the great beauty of the historical costumes, the cloak-and-dagger story with its beguiling Oriental settings, the stately proceedings, the pageantry of marching and fighting armies, the magnificent rendering of nature, the consummate acting—all these entrance us and convince us of the correctness of the vision here: the greatness of the most ordinary of men. The hero, a petty thief who turns impostor, grows before our eyes into greatness, although it costs him his life. The story takes place in sixteenth-century Japan, but the hero is of all times and places: he accepts a destiny into which he is projected by chance and turns a false existence into a real one. At the end, only because he wants to be true to his new self, he sacrifices his life and thus achieves the acme of suffering and human greatness. Nobody wants him to do so. Nobody but he will ever know that he did it. Nobody but the audience observes it. He does it only for himself; it has no consequences whatsoever for anybody or anything else. He does it out of conviction; this is his greatness. Life that permits the lowest of men to achieve such dignity is life worth living, even if in the end it defeats him, as it will defeat all who are mortal.

Two other films, very different, render parallel visions that celebrate life, a celebration in which we, as viewers, vicariously participate although we are saddened by the hero's defeat. The first was known in the United States by its English name, *The Last Laugh*, although its original title, *The Last Man*, was more appropriate. It is the story of the doorman of a hotel who is demoted to cleaning washrooms. The other movie is *Patton*. In one of these films the hero stands on the lowest rung of society and existence; in the other, he is on society's highest level. In both pictures we are led to admire a man's struggle to discover who he really is, for, in doing so, he achieves tragic greatness. These three films, as do many others, affirm man and life, and so inspire in us visions that can sustain us.

My choice of these three films out of many is arbitrary. What I want to illustrate is their celebration of life in forms appropriate to an age in which self-discovery may exact the highest possible price. Only through incorporating such visions can we achieve satisfaction with our own life, defeat and transcend existential despair.

What our society suffers from most today is the absence of consensus about what it and life in it ought to be. Such consensus cannot be gained from society's present stage, or from fantasies about what it ought to be. For that the present is too close and too diversified, and the future too uncertain, to make believable claims about it. A consensus in the present hence can be achieved only through a shared understanding of the past, as Homer's epics informed those who lived centuries later what it meant to be Greek, and by what images and ideals they were to live their lives and organize their societies.

Most societies derive consensus from a long history, a language all their own, a common religion, common ancestry. The myths by which they live are based on all of these. But the United States is a country of immigrants, coming from a great variety of nations. Lately, it has been emphasized that an asocial, narcissistic personality has become characteristic of Americans, and that it is this type of personality that makes for the malaise, because it prevents us from achieving a consensus that would counteract a tendency to withdraw into private worlds. In his study of narcissism, Christopher Lasch says that modern man, "tortured by self-consciousness, turns to new cults and therapies not to free himself of his personal obsessions but to find meaning and purpose in life, to find something to live for." There is widespread distress because national morale has declined, and we have lost an earlier sense of national vision and purpose.

Contrary to rigid religions or political beliefs, as are found in totalitarian societies, our culture is one of great individual differences, at least in principle and in theory. But this leads to disunity, even chaos. Americans believe in the value of diversity, but just because ours is a society based on individual diversity, it needs consensus about some overarching ideas more than societies based on the uniform origin of their citizens. Hence, if we are to have consensus, it must be based on a myth— a vision—about a common experience, a conquest that made us Americans, as the myth about the conquest of Troy formed the Greeks. Only a common myth can offer relief from the fear that life is without meaning or purpose. Myths permit us to examine our place in the world by comparing it to a shared idea. Myths are shared fantasies that form the tie that binds the individual to other members of his group. Such myths help to ward off feelings of isolation, guilt, anxiety, and purposelessness—in short, they combat isolation and anomie.

We used to have a myth that bound us together; in *The American Adam*, R. W. B. Lewis summarizes the myth by which Americans used to live:

God decided to give man another chance by opening up a new world across the sea. Practically vacant, this glorious land had almost inexhaustible natural resources. Many people came to this new world. They were people of special energy, self-reliance, intuitive intelligence, and purity of heart. . . . This nation's special mission in the world would be to serve as the moral guide for all other nations.

The movies used to transmit this myth, particularly the westerns, which presented the challenge of bringing civilization to places where before there was none. The same movies also suggested the danger of that chaos; the wagon train symbolized the community men must form on such a perilous journey into the untamed wilderness, which in turn became a symbol for all that is untamed within ourselves. Thus the western gave us a vision of the need for cooperation and civilization, because without it man would perish. Another symbol often used in these westerns was the railroad, which formed the link between wilderness and civilization. The railroad was the symbol of man's role as a civilizer.

Robert Warshow delineates in *The Immediate Experience* how the hero of the western—the gunfighter—symbolizes man's potential: to become either an outlaw or a sheriff. In the latter role, the gunfighter was the hero of the past, and his opening of the West was our mythos, our equivalent of the Trojan War. Like all such heroes, the sheriff experienced victories and defeats, but, through these experiences, he grew wiser and learned to accept the limitations that civilization imposes.

This was a wonderful vision of man—or the United States—in the New World; it was a myth by which one could live and grow, and it served as a consensus about what it meant to be an American. But although most of us continue to enjoy this myth, by now it has lost most of its vitality. We have become too aware of the destruction of nature and of the American Indian—part of the reality of opening the West—to be able to savor this myth fully; and, just as important, it is based on an open frontier that no longer exists. But the nostalgic infatuation with the western suggests how much we are in need of a myth about the past that cannot be invalidated by the realities of today. We want to share a vision, one that would enlighten us about what it means to be an American today, so that we can be proud not only of our heritage but also of the world we are building together.

Unfortunately, we have no such myth, nor, by extension, any that reflects what is involved in growing up. The child, like the society, needs such myths to provide him with ideas of what difficulties are involved in maturation. Fairy tales used to fill this need, and they would still do so, if we would take them seriously. But sugar-sweet movies of the Disney variety fail to take seriously the world of the child—the immense problems with which the child has to struggle as he grows up, to make himself free from the bonds that tie him to his parents, and to test his own strength. Instead of helping the child, who wants to understand the difficulties ahead, these shows talk down to him, insult his intelligence, and lower his aspirations.

While most of the popular shows for children fall short of what the child needs most, others at least provide him with some of the fantasies that relieve pressing anxieties, and this is the reason for their popularity. Superman, Wonder Woman, and the Bionic Woman stimulate the child's fantasies about being strong and invulnerable, and this offers some relief from being overwhelmed by the powerful adults who control his existence. The Incredible Hulk affords a confrontation with destructive anger. Watching the Hulk on one of his rampages permits a vicarious experience of anger without having to feel guilty about it or anxious about the consequences, because the Hulk attacks only bad people. As food for fantasies that offer temporary relief, such shows have a certain value, but they do not provide material leading to higher integration, as myths do.

Science-fiction movies can serve as myths about the future and thus give us some assurance about it. Whether the film is *2001* or *Star Wars,* such movies tell about progress that will expand man's powers and his experiences beyond anything now believed possible, while they assure us that all these advances will not obliterate man or life as we now know it. Thus one great anxiety about the future—that it will have no place for us as we now are—is allayed by such myths. They also promise that even in the most distant future, and despite the progress that will have occurred in the material world, man's basic concerns will be the same, and the struggle of good against evil—the central moral problem of our time—will not have lost its importance.

Past and future are the lasting dimensions of our lives; the present is but a fleeting moment. So these visions about the future also contain our past; in *Star Wars,* battles are fought around issues that also motivated man in the past. There is good reason that Yoda appears in George Lucas's film: he is but a reincarnation of the teddy bear of infancy, to which we turn for solace; and the Yedi Knight is the wise old man, or the helpful animal, of the fairy tale, the promise from our distant past that we shall be able to rise to meet the most difficult tasks life can present us with. Thus, any vision about the future is really based on visions of the past, because that is all we can know for certain.

As our religious myths about the future never went beyond Judgment Day, so our modern myths about the future cannot go beyond the search for life's deeper meaning. The reason is that only as long as the choice between good and evil remains man's paramount moral problem does life retain that special dignity that derives from our ability to choose between the two. A world in which this conflict has been permanently resolved eliminates man as we know him. It might be a universe peopled by angels, but it has no place for man.

What Americans need most is a consensus that includes the idea of individual freedom, as well as acceptance of the plurality of ethnic backgrounds and religious beliefs inherent in the population. Such consensus must rest on convictions about moral values and the validity of overarching ideas. Art can do this because a basic ingredient of the aesthetic experience is that it binds together diverse elements. But only the ruling art of a period is apt to provide such unity: for the Greeks, it was classical art; for the British, Elizabethan art; for the many petty German states, it was their classical art. Today, for the United States, it has to be the moving picture, the central art of our time, because no other art experience is so open and accessible to everyone.

The moving picture is a visual art, based on sight. Speaking to our vision, it ought to provide us with the visions enabling us to live the good life; it ought to give us insight into ourselves. About a hundred years ago, Tolstoy wrote, "Art is a human activity having for its purpose the transmission to others of the highest and best feelings to which men have risen." Later, Robert Frost defined poetry as "beginning in delight and ending in wisdom." Thus it might be said that the state of the art of the moving image can be assessed by the degree to which it meets the mythopoetic task of giving us myths suitable to live by in our time—visions that transmit to us the highest and best feelings to which men have risen—and by how well the moving images give us that delight which leads to wisdom. Let us hope that the art of the moving image, this most authentic American art, will soon meet the challenge of becoming truly the great art of our age.

1. Why is the moving picture "always about us"?
2. What does Bettelheim mean by *the affirmation of man?*
3. How do movies "celebrate life" and carry a "vision" of America?
4. What do Americans need most, according to Bettelheim? Do movies fulfill that need? Explain.
5. How would you define the art of the moving picture?
6. Is Bettelheim's conclusion based on earlier facts mentioned in the essay? If so, which ones? If not, is the conclusion weakened?
7. How effective are the introductory paragraphs?
8. How does Bettelheim define his terms?
9. In what contexts does Bettelheim place the movie?
10. What is the problem issue for Bettelheim?

The Writing Process II:

The First Draft

The Writer and the Audience

It is wise not to begin to prepare a first draft of your essay until you have decided who you are writing for, because your audience will affect your message, style, and tone. So far you have been concerned only with the clarity and thoroughness of the argument, and there is good reason for that. It is more important to discover first what you think is the truth about your topic, or what really happened, than it is to concern yourself with persuading an audience by saying what you think someone wants to hear. Once your argument is developed, however, you must take your audience into account. The question now becomes: *Who are your readers, and how will you gain their interest?*

■ *Your reader is you.* You read your own work in order to revise it as you write. You also reread the finished product to see what *you* can learn from your writing. You do not know what you can actually say until you have said it. You cannot expect anyone else to understand what you yourself do not understand in your writing. Moreover, if you are bored with the topic and it shows, then most likely your reader will be bored too.

■ *Your audience has those qualities you value in a reader*: curiosity, clear thought, intelligence, and sensitivity. Assume this, for *a reader loves to be flattered.* But do not overdo the flattery. Aim for an informed neutrality. You do not know your reader's private life, so do not guess at it. Do not assume too much: no cute nudges about how we all know what it is like to sniff cocaine or trudge through the Himalayas. Remember your reader brings very private needs and prejudices to every reading, the same as you do.

■ *Your reader is not someone you know intimately, but someone you would ideally like to know.* A good technique is to think of your reader as a person who, quite simply, wants to be told something interesting and important, and wants to be entertained and involved in your particular interests. Be very careful how you judge your teacher as reader. *You get nowhere by stereotyping your readers, including your teachers.* The reader realizes the stereotype and resents it, even if it happens to be true.

■ *Make some educated guesses about what your reader is like.* You can anticipate a response based on the nature of the subject, your treatment of it, and the kinds of people who might be reading your writing. Here is a list of questions you can ask about any audience:

What values and beliefs does the audience have (about money, morality, civil rights, religion, and so on)?

What experience (professional, educational) does the audience have?

What does your audience think about your topic?

What does your audience think about you and the way you express yourself? How can you avoid any problems of expression and emphasize your strong points?

Do you want to be an authority, an equal, a friend, or a neutral observer?

What role can you ask your audience to play?

These questions fall under three general headings:
1. What do you know about your audience?
2. What do you know about the way you relate to people?
3. How can you help create the reader?

If you are writing about gun control, for example, you should be aware that you can assume only a mixed audience for such a controversial subject. (If you have any doubts whether an audience holds a variety of opinions on this subject or any other, try out the arguments of the essay on your friends.) Second, you should not plan to pose as an authority if you are not an expert on constitutional law. But you can ask a layperson's questions and try to make a complex issue simpler by dramatizing the main points in everyday terms. Finally, you can assume that the reader you are helping to create by your writing will be someone who is willing to be written for, but is not willing to be patronized on the subject of gun control. Such a person may be stubborn about strongly held ideas, but will be ready to react and to argue, and maybe even to give in to a reasonable appeal. *You can assume that your reader is willing to be persuaded reasonably.*

■ *What role can you ask the reader to play?* You can never fully predict your audience, for our feelings about ourselves are often notoriously inaccurate. But to ask how you can help create the reader's role is to seek the grounds for good communication. You want to put your best foot forward with someone you do not know. So try to

Create a climate of shared values

Show you value the reader

Avoid irrelevance, interruptions in the flow of thought, dramatic shifts in tone, and unnecessary ambiguity

Put yourself forward honestly as someone with a considered opinion you feel strongly about

Avoid making your reader defensive by being judgmental, by acting superior, or by showing indifference

Avoid a self-centered focus, trying instead to set up genuine relationships among yourself, the subject, and the reader

It is always helpful to keep these reminders about your audience handy for planning and evaluating the style and tone of your writing, and, of course, for planning the way you will present your thesis.

Setting the Essay's Style and Tone

Chapters 1 and 2 briefly discussed style from the perspective of the reader. Now you must think of style not as something you *find* but as something you *make*. Style is the way you express yourself in writing, the way words are arranged to carry a message and to create sound and images. Style refers to all the physical aspects of writing. Sentence and paragraph structure (which will be covered in the next two chapters) and your choice of words combine to create an effect, reveal your attitude toward a topic, and provoke a reaction from the reader.

The style of a piece of writing, then, is an integral part of the message. If you write in an overly colloquial style, then your message is that the topic is somehow informal or you have not considered it deeply. This does not mean, however, that the most important topics must always be treated with formality. Good explanatory prose tries not to draw too much attention to itself by being either grandiose or jargon-ridden.

A writer's style should be natural to the writer. Style reveals your personality, so make sure *your* voice is heard and is distinct. Do not strain for special effects, however. Beware of overwriting or underwriting. You don't want either to embellish the message or explain it away. On the other hand, beware of *affecting* a breezy style that is more gesture than content.

Consider the following short extract. It is written mainly in an informal style which is characteristic of the essay writing you will do most:

True maleness is never without its vein of femininity. The Greeks understood this and made it the theme of their tales of sexual metamorphosis, the remarkable account of Hercules, of all men, taking on temporarily the character of a woman and wearing women's clothes. Total masculinity is an ideal of the frustrated, not a fact of biology. With the cult of masculinity put aside, maleness might have a better chance to develop in the United States.

Harold Rosenberg, from **DISCOVERING THE PRESENT**

You should not want to write more formally than this by saying things like "donning female attire" or "a fact to be found in investigations within the biological sciences''; that is merely pompous and wordy. Nor should you try for a better effect by dressing down the style and resorting to vague colloquialisms:

Let me fill you in about being a man. Men, I think, are not much good unless they're just a little bit like women. Not too much, just a bit. Even the Greeks put this idea into their stories about sex changes. Like the one about Hercules, a *real* heavyweight, who even became a woman for a while! It's only men who don't act like men who dream about being macho. You certainly won't find that turning up in your biology textbook. In fact, I don't think we're going to develop *men* in this country until we get rid of the whole fad for macho body building.

Remember that your style and tone work together. In the first extract, the writer's tone is quite argumentative. He does have a point to make about "the cult of masculinity," which, it is quite plain, he does not approve of. But he expresses his argument in neutral terms. He does not force any ideas suddenly upon his reader. He does not aim to persuade by acting overly familiar with his reader or by acting overly intellectual, either. His message is carried simply and forcefully. In the rewritten version of the message, though, the writer thinks that he can make a point by being chatty and friendly, and perhaps by appearing to be plainly not an intellectual. The result is foolish, because he assumes that the reader is capable only of understanding banal comments like "let me fill you in about men" or "a *real* heavyweight." In other words, the writer intrudes too much on his material in the second extract and does not let it speak for itself. By using a relatively vulgar style and an overfriendly tone of voice, the writer offers *himself*, not his topic, to the reader.

Bearing in mind that you must be careful about both your style and your tone of voice, consider the following points:

■ *A writer's style is carried by a tone of voice*. But you cannot decide how you want your language to sound until you decide what relationship to form with your topic.

■ *The tone of voice you choose to take—committed but qualified, or ironic, critical, enthusiastic—must be appropriate to your topic and to the conclusion of your argument.* Note that tone is not imposed artificially. It is created by the relationship a writer has to a subject. Tone is a function of how a writer interprets an event, and it should accompany your argument and make it more effective.

■ *A writer's tone should be rational and carefully controlled.* There is no point in writing surreal nonsense or noisy polemics, or you will lose the reader's respect.

■ *A writer's tone and style should be consistent.* Be very careful about shifting attitudes. Any shift you make should be consistent with your perspective about your subject. You might start off humorously and then get seriously involved. But change tone only for clear reasons related to your argument, or you will give the impression that you are not sure what your feelings are about a subject.

Returning to our essay on gun control, the argument there is that an inflexible approach to the anti–gun control lobby is inappropriate, for the lobby has some reason on its side. However, the essay concludes that the opposite view is worth arguing for. You could take an ironic or argumentative tone if you wanted to take sides in the argument, but the conclusion of the outline, even though it is in favor of gun control, depends on the openendedness of the question. So you decide to choose a neutral, informative tone since you want to emphasize the *legal* nature of the question.

Writing with Color

You can bring color to your writing by using a lively vocabulary and by making forceful and unusual connections between events.

Colorful Language

You should use colorful language not merely to decorate but to create emphasis.

■ *Use concrete, not abstract, language whenever you can.* Be specific in your choice of words in order to make your style and tone effective. Concrete language is the language of the senses. It refers to things you can see, hear, touch, taste, and smell, and, of course, the qualities of those objects. These are the qualities a reader engages most readily. Abstract language conveys ideas and concepts, not things. Of course, you cannot avoid abstractions all the time, but you should not use words that are vague and highly abstract when concrete terms will do.

■ *Avoid jargon terms and clichés.* Why? Clichés *are* easily understood and part of everyday conversation. But they are also overused and lack emphasis. Writing is not speech, and you cannot afford the possibility of misinterpretation or of boring a reader. When you write, you do not know exactly whom you are talking to, so you must aim for a general audience, most often using a neutral, informative tone. If you are writing a personal letter, then jargon and cliché do have their place, because the reader knows you and what you are like. If you are being consistently ironic or trying to be humorous in the style of, say, Art Buchwald or Erma Bombeck, then you may also get away with clichés.

156

Otherwise, in expository writing, you should not refer to marriage as "tying the knot," or to love as "a four-letter word" or "never having to say you're sorry." Avoid any expression that is so overused, flattened out, and colorless that it lacks meaning.

Similarly, don't use a highly specialized vocabulary that cannot be shared by a general audience. Such a vocabulary has its place only in professional journals.

You should also be very careful not to use the sociopolitical jargon that is currently fashionable and constantly turns everything into an "experience," a "conduit," or a "situation" at some "point in time." It is amazing how little one learns from such "experience." Remember that by using jargon and clichés, you are stereotyping your reader, and that is one of the worst things you can do to an audience.

■ *Avoid euphemisms.* A *euphemism* is a word, phrase, or sentence that supposedly cleans up or makes nicer a term that is considered either too blunt or not genteel enough. Thus, *sex* becomes *conjugal intimacy,* and *rape* becomes *attack on a woman.* Say what you mean without assuming that your audience is frail, overdelicate, or in need of a censor. The word *sex* is not dirty. The word *rape* should not be prettified and neutralized. Its power lies in its connotation of viciousness, and to say that it amounts only to "an attack on a woman" is to deny that it is vicious and even that the problem exists. Euphemisms are not merely cloyingly cute and evasive; they are often morally thoughtless and undesirable.

■ *Avoid circumlocution. Circumlocution* derives from the Latin words meaning "to talk around." Do not talk around a subject; get to the point and be concise. If you have written a statement like "I should now like to arrive at a conclusion to this paper by saying that some form of gun control is to be highly recommended," refine that to "In conclusion, I strongly support some form of gun control." Be especially careful not to try to sound clever by finding esoteric words in a dictionary or thesaurus. We all know what the following sentence means: "Employees must wash their hands before serving food." If you were trying to find a new way of saying that and did not know any better, you might turn to a dictionary and produce the following: "Persons hired by this company are implored to cleanse with soap and water the terminal parts of their arms below the wrist consisting of the palm and five digits (forming the organ of prehension characteristic of man) at a time closely preceding the moment they prepare and offer all substance taken into and assimilated by persons sitting at table for the purpose of keeping those persons alive and enabling them to grow." Maybe you've seen similar passages in government papers or legal documents or testimony before Senate committee hearings. But this kind of verbose legalese is nonsense and has no place in your writing.

■ *Avoid redundancy. Redundancy* is a form of circumlocution that refers specifically to the repetition of a meaning that has already been expressed, in short, unnecessary words used for padding or effect. To say that you will "battle on and struggle" or that you have made a "new innovation" is to waste words; *to battle* means "to struggle" and all innovations are by definition new.

■ *Beware of superlatives, absolute terms, and comparisons (intensifiers).* Never use the superlative when comparing *two* things: "x is *more* interesting than y; of the two, x is more (*not* most) interesting." Avoid superlative phrases like "by far the most amazing..." Not only does exaggeration quickly wear out its welcome, but multiple superlatives are also redundant. If something is the best, then make sure it is, and say so simply. Be careful with terms like *absolute, pinnacle, completely, infinite, zenith,* and *perfect.* Understatement or plain statement is always more effective than overstatement. (If you say something is more effective, be sure you say more effective than what.)

It is perhaps easier to say what colorful language is *not,* since unsuccessful writing is easily recognized. Colorful language is *not* abstract, clichéd, euphemistic, evasive, or overstated. It *is* concrete and direct, and it is usually carefully chosen as in this description by Benjamin DeMott of a recent book on Elvis Presley's death:

The book opens with a series of chapters describing the hectic onset of awareness in the media that Presley's death was indeed a sensationally big story. (The authors' research persuaded them that it was the fans who, by jamming switchboards with calls for information, shocked the media into action, ultimately dictating continuous "feature feeds" by the wire services, ragged TV specials, convulsive searches of newspaper back files for reports of the performer's local appearances, and on-the-spot coverage by broadcasters and papers unaccustomed to sending staffers out of town, but perfectly prepared to profit from the popular will.) Next comes an account of the pre-funeral spectacle at Graceland, Presley's Memphis home—thousands of mourners and hundreds of reporters keeping an around-the-clock vigil marked by grotesque outbursts of grief and dementia (at one point in the predawn hours, a desperately drunken man drove his car into the crowd, killing two of the bereaved). The narrative interrupts itself, after a report on the funeral, to survey Presley's life, the emphasis being upon class background and musical influences. Then come separate chapters about the White House response to the event, the international reaction, and subsequent efforts—pious, commercial, or both—to keep Presley's flame alive. The book ends with an epilogue discussing the performer's drug usage and the present state of his reputation; the final sentences affirm that Elvis Presley "symbolized the ultimate rebellion of all common folk against all forms of restraint."

Atlantic, January 1981

The topic, of course, lends itself to some sensationalizing, and it is precisely the sensationalism of Presley's death which is DeMott's subject here. But the author does not overindulge his language or overstate the case. Phrases like *the hectic onset of awareness, continuous "feature feeds" by the wire services, ragged TV specials,* and *an around-the-clock vigil marked by grotesque outbursts of grief and dementia* are concrete, direct, catchy, precise, and loaded with feeling.

Of course, color varies enormously in writing. The color of literary—especially poetic—writing is usually more pronounced than that of nonfiction. The kind of writing you will do in college and at work, however, can always be improved by an imaginative use of adjectives and adverbs that refer to tangible qualities. In the next chapter, you will also find advice on how to make your writing more concrete by emphasizing other strong parts of speech, especially verbs.

Metaphor and Simile

An important way of injecting color into your writing is to make appropriate but unusual comparisons and relationships between things. These, again, should not be so abstract that the reader has to struggle to understand what you mean. But you can try to elicit special meanings that are not obvious in order to strengthen an assertion. You can make either *similes* or *metaphors.*

■ A *simile* is a comparison between two things or actions which makes the first item in the comparison more vivid and concrete. Similes say something is like something else. "The eggs look and taste like melted sponge" (Gail Greene).

■ A *metaphor,* on the other hand, does not simply draw a comparison: it says that something *is* something else. "War is hell" and "The flowers begged for water during the drought" are metaphors. In the former, war *is* the place or state of mind we call hell; in the latter, flowers are given human desires. Metaphors are very strong assertions that say that one thing can be substituted for or be given the qualities of something else which it plainly is not. By making a metaphor, you point out the important connections between things and establish interrelationships.

■ *When do you use similes, and when do you use metaphors?*
Plainly to say "war is like hell" (a simile) is weaker than to say "war is

hell." Yet on the other hand, "eggs are melted sponge" is weaker than "eggs look and taste like melted sponge." If a *detailed context* (a listing of specific qualities) is needed, use a simile. "Eggs are melted sponge" is a silly exaggeration which no one will believe, simply because it doesn't say *why* the eggs are melted sponge. The simile makes it plain that the eggs *look* and *taste* that way.

Do not use a simile, though, when a metaphor will do. You don't want to weaken the metaphor, "When people go to war, evolution turns the clock back," by changing it into the cumbersome simile, "When people go to war, it is as if evolution turns the clock back." If the connection you are making between two things is apparent without listing qualities, then make a metaphor.

■ *Beware of mixed metaphors.* These are usually of two kinds and are very obvious to the careful reader. The first kind amounts to an accumulation of clichés: "There he was, happy as a lark, chopping up wood as if he were stoking the fires of hell. No wonder, though, for he was as strong as an ox, with muscles that bulged like the coffers of the Incas, and hairs on his chest as long as an anteater's tongue." This is a mess: a series of overused or highly strained connections. It is a mess because metaphorical language is supposed to make some point clear, not be merely decorative.

The second common kind of mixed metaphor occurs when an extended metaphor is not thought through: "Nursing homes are for those in their twilight years, but why can't the federal government bring a new sunrise into old people's lives and lower the boom on those charging outrageous fees for such a service?" Although the metaphors of "twilight" and "a new sunrise" are at least consistent, "lower the boom" is another metaphor altogether. Use metaphorical language within a given passage consistently and economically. It is better to write with a referential and literal turn of phrase than it is to provide verbal color only to find that the colors have run together.

Maintaining Irony

A word on writing ironically is appropriate here, because irony is a powerful stylistic weapon. We have discussed irony from the reader's perspective, but it is clearly more difficult to carry off an ironic effect when writing than it is to talk about it as a reader. Here is an example of heavily ironic writing by Alexander Cockburn:

Any sensible dictator knows that in terms of unfavorable international publicity it is perfectly safe to kill the social entity known to news editors as "tribesmen" in fairly large numbers—let us say up to 30,000, to be on the safe side. "Peasants"—a noun with affecting pastoral undertones—are a little trickier. Perhaps one "peasant" for every hundred "tribesmen." Ratios vary from area to area. Afghan "tribesmen," for the moment, are at a premium in the news market. By contrast, Indians in Paraguay or peasants in East Timor—discounted by the news desk—may be slaughtered by the thousands without undue commotion.

Working our way up, reckon one urban worker as having a death news value equivalent to ten peasants, with one student for every ten workers, and one professor for every ten students. (Fisherfolk are a separate category, of death news value mainly in the event of tidal waves, hurricanes, etc.) The murder of priests, missionaries, and nuns is an affair of the nicest judgment, as we shall see in the case of El Salvador. It is really a matter of location, race, and religious persuasion. As a rule of thumb, men of the cloth should be spared, although the elimination of Dominicans, particularly those in rural areas, may be practiced in moderation. Count 200 peasants for one priest.

What our Third World dictator should avoid is the murder of journalists, or at least of those who are citizens of the United States. The penalties—denunciation in Congress and in the news media—are obvious. Count 10,000 peasants for one American reporter; 30,000, if the reporter is from one of the networks; 50,000, if the murder takes place on camera. The moment Bill Stewart of ABC was murdered on network news the fate of Anastasio Somoza was sealed. The United States "lost," or at least decided that it could not "save," Nicaragua.

And this is where El Salvador enters the picture. With Nicaragua gone, it became a Domino and thus the object of grave concern to the State Department, Defense Department, and cognate agencies, and of interest (intermittently) to the American press and (even more intermittently) to the American news consumer.

Harpers, February 1981

The tone is ironic, but what controls it? This is primarily a piece of journalistic narrative, describing some events of political importance and obviously conveying an opinion that the writer hopes he will shame his reader into accepting. It contains a marvelous parody of statistics and our apparent concern for things only when they are big enough or when enough people have died in a war or of disease. The places are accurately described, the names correct and appropriately chosen (East Timor peasants, Bill Stewart of ABC, and so on).

But what is the reader really interested in, once it is established that the tone is ironic? The reader is interested in the validity of Cockburn's satire. Is Cockburn justified in writing this way? You have to decide for yourself. Some may say that this piece overexploits our need for statistics, and that our government is not so cynical. Others will say that this is a brilliant, outrageously witty indictment of our foreign policy. And both sides will have missed part of the point. What makes this piece work is not an understanding of whether Cockburn has his facts and figures straight (even hypothetically and in parody), but an understanding of how he is talking about the way we all read the news, whether we are "liberal-minded" or not. Is it not true that we pay attention to and get emotional mileage out of only the big headlines, the threats and acts of war, and the heavy casualty lists? A cynical government is not Cockburn's only subject, but the cynical reader, too: you and me. Another reason why the ironic tone works is that Cockburn has carefully controlled the sarcasm and pained expression of his feelings. Irony becomes sarcastic when it begins to sneer and be caustic; it must be controlled to be effective, and Cockburn does just that.

You could summarize the Cockburn piece by following the list on style and tone on pages 155–156.

■ The author has clearly established his attitude to his subject: he is critical of the value we place on newsworthy events.

■ In spite of his outrage, the tone is rational and controlled, even when he parodies the way we justify our foreign policy through statistics. His own "statistics" are carefully and proportionally contrived (1 peasant = 100 tribesmen; 200 peasants = 1 priest; 10,000 peasants = 1 American reporter; so how many tribesmen = 1 American reporter?) He takes our irrationality to logically "rational" extremes.

■ The tone is consistent. Indeed, it is ruthlessly consistent. Cockburn does not relieve the irony for a moment, and that includes colloquial touches and a downshifting into informal statements like "working our way up," "an affair of the nicest judgment", and "this is where El Salvador enters the picture."

■ The tone is based on providing particular references to places and people. There are no vague generalizations. Explicit feelings need explicit references.

For irony to work well in expository writing, be sure that

> You know what you are being ironic about and have located your target clearly and concisely
>
> You never lapse into mere name calling or give the game away by telling the reader what to think
>
> You argue with reason and consistency, offering clear, particularized details (even "scientific" data)
>
> You say one thing but really mean another

Of course, irony may not be a tone you wish to sustain throughout an essay. Ironic asides can be made at any time.

Translating the Outline to the First Draft

You now have a comprehensive outline. Your preparations so far have taken you through some essential stages of critical thinking. You have decided what your audience might be like and what your major strategy about tone and style will be. If you have prepared well, it will not be too difficult to write your first draft.

■ *Work directly from your final outline,* using and developing the sentences you have already started in your outline notes. You may find that you do not want to use all the information in the outline as you go along. Then don't. You can always include more in revision. Right now you are trying to get a first draft written which follows the *conclusions* you have reached and the specific *emphases, oppositions,* and *relationships* that help create them. Do not try to pad your discussion. In this first draft, write at least one paragraph each for the *introduction,* the *definition* of terms, the *topic as problem,* the *contexts,* and the *conclusion.* It is likely that you will need more than one paragraph for each of these.

■ *Keep your view of your audience and your perspective tone consistent,* but by all means experiment with changes of tone in this first draft if you sense you can improve on your plan as you see what your writing is like.

■ *Treat your outline flexibly.* As you write, you will find that ideas develop in ways you might not have anticipated when you were brainstorming and preparing your outline. Frequently during essay writing, ideas sort themselves out into new relationships as you develop them, and varying degrees of importance among the relationships suggest themselves. So let your writing change your outline if necessary. If, while you are writing the introduction, you think of an important point that is really part of the topic as problem, say, then jot it down under that heading to be dealt with later. Remember that the point of an outline is to develop a shape for the flow of your ideas, not to act as an iron-clad structure. But keep in mind that if you make a point out of sequence or before its time, you will spoil your overall argument unless it is a definite improvement over the outline.

■ *Revise as you write.* We will discuss the process of revision in more detail in Chapter 7, but it is important to realize here that revision begins the moment you have completed your first sentence. As you write, you find ideas taking shape that no amount of preparation can necessarily predict. A flow of ideas and a network of statements develop. This cannot happen coherently unless you constantly review and revise what you have written. If you leave your writing for any length of time, you should read over what you have written in order to restart your thinking. It is equally important *as you write* to read your completed sentences and revise them for continuity of thought and development of ideas as well as for mechanical problems.

Several things happen when you revise as you write. You will find a design for your ideas emerging. You may even find the emphasis and order of your ideas changing. You will, if you revise well, narrow down the topic to essentials and solve new contradictions. This *revision-as-you-write* is not very different from the revision that is done after an essay is completed in first draft, as you will see. Right now, though, you are revising for continuity of thought above all.

Say you have just written the following paragraph:

(1) The forest floor was covered with fall leaves that were dry and crisp from the lack of rain. (2) Each step I took sounded as if I was walking on corn flakes. (3) I worked my way around the point of the ridge I was on, taking several steps at a time and then pausing for a few minutes to listen. (4) Because the leaves were so dry I could not move fast but I knew the deer would also have to make noise as they moved form their early feeding areas to their daytime beds. (5) As I rested on a stump momentarily, I heard a faint sound of hoofs trotting through the dry leaves.

As you read this paragraph, you would justifiedly be happy with the overall effect. Sentences 1 and 2 are especially effective, and you like the simile of walking on corn flakes. Sentence 3 refers to a sufficiently specific action and holds the reader's interest. There are no mechanical problems with the first three sentences, and you don't see any need to change the writing. What about sentence 4, though? *Because the leaves were so dry I could not move fast* seems to state the obvious, merely repeating the previous sentence. You feel your attention slacken as you read this, so you assume the reader's attention will slacken too. It's not a serious problem, but you decide to begin the fourth sentence with *I knew the deer would also have to make noise.* And you correct *form* to *from,* and in sentence 5, *hoofs* to *hooves.*

These are minor changes, but as you will see in Chapter 7, they can be considerably more complicated. The point here, though, is that you should not be concentrating simply on the effectiveness of your language, but on the effective development of ideas.

Here is a first draft of the essay on gun control with an abbreviated outline beside it. The essay at this stage contains organizational, grammatical, and syntactical errors. The final revision appears in Chapter 7.

THE QUESTION OF GUN CONTROL

1. Introduction: Relevance of the Topic

Oppositions

Has the question not been asked because it is genuinely difficult, or because of special interests?

Connections

Every citizen is involved; there are large political, legal, and economic interests. It is a constitutional issue, and everyone wants a solution to the problem of crime, even anti–gun controllers.

Resolution

A connection between violence and guns—but which is to blame? Which problem to be tackled first? The problem is the connection between violence and guns, but political interests have clouded the argument. Will try to avoid lobby issues by saying that the problem is an open one—either control violence or guns—with difficult legal problems. Need to find a meeting point for the two sides.

2. Definition of Terms

Oppositions

Control or no control? Licensing or banning? All guns

The arguments between pro– and anti–gun control groups rage on. Why? Because it is both a genuinely difficult question to answer and one suspects also because there are many special interests involved. Still it is a question we should all try to answer because it has implications for everyone, both you and me. Everyone wants a solution to the problem of high crime, even anti–guncontrollers. Its genuinely a constitutional issue. Everyone anyhow acknowledges that there is some connection between violence and guns, but which one do we tackle first? The problem is that somehow the guns and violence connection has become clouded by political considerations.

So how can we make sense of the problem? We have to begin by saying that there is a real stand-off between the two sides so the important thing to do is to take no sides at all and treat the problem as an open one at least as an experiment. There are difficult legal considerations, so we need to find a meeting point for the two sides.

or some guns? Federal or State control?

Connections

Firearms that can be concealed: seem to be the focus of the argument.

Resolution

Must define terms. Deal with handguns and federal control.

3. *Setting Up the Problem*

Oppositions

Freedom to bear arms or federal licensing? Constitutional rights or crime control via new laws? Could a gun control law control violence? Unarmed public vs. armed criminals.

Connections

Can synthesize everything under need to control deaths from gun-related crime *and* at the same time preserve individual rights. Both sides want this.

Resolution

Gun control must be efficient and effective. It must preserve the rights of law-abiding citizens to bear arms, at least for special purposes.

Whether we are for or against gun control, we have to define our terms. For the sake of argument we will take the phrase "gun control" to refer to the *federal* control of the use of handguns, through licensing or restriction. These are concealed lethal weapons. It doesn't matter what the states do we have to refer to the national context because we are arguing the principle of the issue.

But why is all this an issue at all? The question has boiled down to the main problem of whether the government has the constitutional right to ban handguns in defense. But then what if we do have gun control? Will it control violence effectively? Will it leave an unarmed public against armed criminals? Can it ever be effective in a country as big as the U.S.? And if we don't have gun control what happens then as more and more crimes increase and involve handguns.

These questions seem incredible to answer. They simply don't have much in common when you first look at them and they don't make much sense either in isolation. But people do agree on something and that is that we need to control deaths from gun-related crime somehow. Both sides agree on that. So instead of getting bogged down by unanswerable questions, let's see if we can answer this one: If gun control is a concept which makes any sense at all,

4. *Examining the Problem*

(a) *Context*

Oppositions

U.S. thinking vs. the rest of the world. Legal thinking vs. psychology and sociology.

Connections

The Law has in common both private and public interests. So why not turn to the possibility of legislation as the rightful context? Sociology and psychology offer support and evidence on which the Law bases its rulings but we are concerned with *control* so the Law is central.

Resolution

Concentrate on the U.S. and on the issue of Constitutional rights and the Law. Main context is the legal one, but still a problem of whether to legislate against guns or violence, or both. Whole cause/effect issue to be solved.

(b) *Cause or Effect?*

Oppositions

Is gun violence a cause or an effect? "Control guns

can it control killings and burglaries involving handguns, *and* preserve our civil rights? Let's see if a compromise is possible.

If you look at the question closely, it is not hard to see what the rightful context for the issue is. We have constitutional rights and the law and we have social and psychological theory which tries to explain why we have violence. I don't think it matters much if we know that an assassin is insane. We want a practical conclusion. What is more important: theory or protection? Our paradox now is that an individual is guaranteed the right to bear arms but finds himself needing to be protected by those who do carry guns.

The Law alone offers protection, for only the Law has in common the interests of both the gun carrier and the person who won't carry guns. Whatever psychology and sociology have to say about how violence operates in society and why we need handguns must become part of the legal issue. It doesn't matter if we know why handguns are associated with so much crime all that theorizing is irrelevant besides we don't know whether we need gun control or not. Do we need laws against guns or against violence?

So is gun control a cause or an effect? What an obsessive question. Do people kill or do guns? Are handgun killings an effect of social violence or is the

and you control violence" vs. "control violence and you lessen crime with guns." People kill vs. guns kill. If we do not want gun control on grounds that it infringes on personal freedom, then are we ironically creating the freedom to kill more readily?

Connections

Whether cause or effect, the gun control question is concerned with violence with guns. That's the point. All laws in some way impede freedom but in interests of greater good for all. We can have guns for sport or for defense *and* gun control.

Resolution

Avoid the question of cause or effect as basically unanswerable. Violence and guns are necessarily linked and we have to deal with that.

5. Conclusion

* federal gun control is necessary...but the Law must preserve the right to bear arms for purpose of sport or defense

* control by police permits and the right of refusal on the grounds of criminal record or mental health problems

* a general amnesty for all gun owners with guns

availability of guns a cause of social violence? Do you control guns to control violence or violence to control guns or what? Here's a chicken-and-egg argument. I don't think it matters what the answer is, that is whether violence with guns is a cause or an effect. There is a great network of social disorder out there which no simple analysis can solve. The point is that violence *with* guns is overwhelmingly present and we don't need a sociologist to tell us that. We know it and now we have a legal problem which centers on the protection of all of us in our homes and on the streets. Besides you can't assume that gun control is necessarily bad because it blocks our freedom. Should we then have freedom to kill? Is this what is implied? Is freedom an absolute? Surely all laws interfere with someone's freedoms but for the good of the greater number. What we have to do is to make legislation to protect our right to bear arms for defense and control handgun killings. Is it going to be possible to have one with the other?

I don't think that there is going to be a law which satisfies everyone. But a compromise surely seems possible. There could be a gun control law which tightens up a lot on present restraints and at the same time leaves the Constitution alone. It should involve the compulsory licensing of all handguns when a police permit would be given for each gun if the owner has no criminal record and is mentally

bought back at a fair price with federal money

* strict penalities for owning a gun without a permit

* all gun owners must attend federally sponsored safety programs through gun associations

* this is a compromise solution, an attempt to get both sides together with no guarantee that such a licensing law would stop violent crime. But it would at least preserve our rights to self-defense and remove many guns from circulation.

stable and if the owner could give good reasons for owning such a weapon. These are restricted sporting uses and an exceptional need for defense in areas where there is little police patrolling. No one could buy a firearm without a police permit, and the permit should be regularly renewed. Then there would need to be a general amnesty for all gun owners. Also there would be very strict penalties for owning an unlicensed weapon, concealed or not, and stricter penalties than at present for committing a crime with the aid of a firearm. All sportsmen and gun owners would be required to take federally sponsored training courses in gun safety.

Of course there will be found loopholes in this argument. And we do know that there is no guarantee that this control would stop criminals obtaining black market guns. But we can't go on arguing in circles forever. Nor should we impose a harsher gun control law than the one I have suggested or else it won't get through Congress at all. We shouldn't avoid the legal issue because gun killings grow greater each year. So why not examine this compromise law for a start. Many guns would be taken out of circulation but the sportsmen could go on using them.

You now have a first draft written largely from your outline but with variations that you have introduced in the process of writing. You have taken the plunge and created an essay, but not a completed one. The worst mistake any writer can make is to assume that the first draft is the last. It never is. As the novelist Saul Bellow puts it, "To rewrite ten times is not unusual." That is an arbitrary figure, of course, but many good writers have spoken of the need to turn out at least three or more drafts. The process of preparing your ideas outlined in the last chapter *may* allow you to get away with two. But it is easy to see that no matter how well you think you have written something, you will inevitably find improvements to make if you are an astute reader.

The most important point is that you have generated ideas and committed them to paper. You have something to work with, and much of the anxiety of writing is now over. It remains for you to develop this first draft into a substantial piece of writing, a process that involves repeating some of the activities you have already carried out. It also involves an understanding of how the structure of paragraphs and sentences forms a successful essay. So in the next three chapters you will be learning techniques for reworking and firming up your first draft.

Checklist

1. Decide on the audience you are writing for in the light of the following questions:

   ■ What values and beliefs does the audience have (about money, morality, civil rights, religion, and so on)?

   ■ What experience (professional, educational) does the audience have?

   ■ What does your audience think about your essay's topic?

   ■ What does your audience think about you and the way you express yourself? How can you avoid any problems of expression and emphasize your strong points?

   ■ Do you want to be an authority, an equal, a friend, or a neutral observer?

   ■ What role can you ask your audience to play?

2. Remember, you can help create your audience if you

   ■ Form a climate of shared values

   ■ Obviously respect the reader

   ■ Avoid irrelevance, interruptions in the flow of thought, dramatic shifts in tone, and unnecessary ambiguity

   ■ Put yourself forward honestly as someone with a considered opinion you feel strongly about

- Avoid making your reader defensive by being judgmental, by acting superior, or by showing indifference

- Avoid a self-centered focus, trying instead to set up genuine relationships among yourself, the subject, and the reader.

3. Decide on your essay's tone or manner of expression based on your relationship to your topic. Will it be committed but qualified, or ironic, angry, critically enthusiastic, or accepting? Remember to make your tone as rational as possible in expository writing. If you decide to be ironic, you should

- Locate your target clearly and concisely

- Not lapse into mere name calling

- Argue consistently

- Say one thing but mean another

4. Decide on your essay's style. Unless you have some special purpose, it should be largely informal.

5. Begin writing your first draft directly from your outline, making sure that

- You write at least one paragraph each for the *introduction* (relevance), *definition, problem, contexts,* and *conclusion*

- You keep your view of the audience, and your tone and style consistent

- You do not use your outline as a rigid guide but rather, let your thoughts develop; you should correct misplaced elements or errors of judgment

- You constantly reread what you have written and revise-as-you-write, especially checking the emphasis, coherence, and unity of your ideas

Exercises

Read the following extracts carefully and answer these questions:
1. What does the writer think about the reader? Work from the criteria in the checklist.
2. Does the writer create an audience effectively?

The thinnest watch ever designed for a woman: Concord Delirium III™.
    The Concord Delirium is acknowledged as the thinnest watch in the world. It

has been a scientific feat of Swiss watchmaking genius since its inception in January 1979. But before now, it was designed for a man.

This is a watch for the woman who insists technology be accompanied by refinement and beauty.

Every proportion of Concord Delirium III has been miniaturized. Each part, inside and out, re-designed. (Sacrificing, in no way, however, the accuracy of the electronic quartz movement.)

It contains the smallest patented energy cell ever created. A dial infinitesimal in thickness. A sapphire crystal so razor thin it measures a mere .28 mm.

On your wrist, it is a seeming sliver of warm, rich 18 karat gold. 1.69 mm. thin. And devastatingly feminine.

Strapped in sleek, black satin, it anticipates the fashion mood of the future.

Concord Delirium III. A unique timepiece befitting the woman who has made unique use of her time.

In Limited Edition. Accompanied by a Certificate of Authenticity. $4,900.

Concord Watch Corporation

"What is the nude?" It is an art form invented by the Greeks in the fifth century, just as opera is an art form invented in seventeenth-century Italy. The conclusion is certainly too abrupt, but it has the merit of emphasizing that the nude is not the subject of art, but a form of art.

It is widely supposed that the naked human body is in itself an object upon which the eye dwells with pleasure and which we are glad to see depicted. But anyone who has frequented art schools and seen the shapeless, pitiful model that the students are industriously drawing will know this is an illusion. The body is not one of those subjects which can be made into art by direct transcription—like a tiger or a snowy landscape. Often in looking at the natural and animal world we joyfully identify ourselves with what we see and from this happy union create a work of art. This is the process students of aesthetics call empathy, and it is at the opposite pole of creative activity to the state of mind that has produced the nude. A mass of naked figures does not move us to empathy, but to disillusion and dismay. We do not wish to imitate; we wish to perfect. We become, in the physical sphere, like Diogenes with his lantern looking for an honest man; and, like him, we may never be rewarded. Photographers of the nude are presumably engaged in this search, with every advantage; and having found a model who pleases them, they are free to pose and light her in conformity with their notions of beauty; finally, they can tone down and accentuate by retouching. But in spite of all their taste and skill, the result is hardly ever satisfactory to those whose eyes have grown accustomed to the harmonious simplifications of antiquity. We are immediately disturbed by wrinkles, pouches, and other small imperfections, which, in the classical scheme, are eliminated. By long habit we do not judge it as a living organism, but as a design; and we discover that the transitions are inconclusive, the outline is faltering. We are bothered because the various parts of the body cannot be perceived as simple units and have no clear relationship to one another. In almost every detail the body is not the shape that art had led us to believe it should be. Yet we can look with pleasure at photographs of trees and animals, where the canon of perfection is less strict. Consciously or unconsciously, photographers have usually recognized that in a photograph of the nude their real object is not to reproduce the naked body, but to imitate some artist's view of what the naked body should be.

Kenneth Clark, from **THE NUDE**

Writing Assignments

1. Continue work on the essay you began in question 1 of the exercises for Chapter 3.

a. Write a paragraph explaining who you think your audience will be and how you would describe it according to the criteria in the checklist.

b. Write a paragraph each explaining what your tone and style will be, and why.

c. Write the first draft of your essay:

■ Develop at least one paragraph each (and probably more) for the *introduction* to and the *relevance* of the topic, its *definition, problem, contexts* and *conclusion*.

■ Keep your view of your audience, your tone, and your style consistent.

■ Keep to your outline but allow new thoughts to develop and correct misplaced elements or errors of judgment.

■ Revise as you write.

2. Examine the essay on gun control contained in this chapter. Write a paragraph on each of the following:

a. Does the essay keep to the outline closely enough?

b. How would you describe the style and tone?

c. How would you anticipate improving the essay? You don't have to revise it.

3. Choose two of the following topics and write a paragraph on each *in an ironic tone.* Before you do so, write down what your exact target is going to be (some aspect of the topic) and how you will treat it.

The topics are: oil companies; the arms race; welfare; liberals; conservatives; fresh air in the city.

4. Here are three assignments. Choose one and
a. Indicate the appropriate style and tone and the reasons for your choice.
b. Prepare an outline of what you will say.
c. Write a letter or short article, following the instructions in the description of each situation.

■ You want to write a letter to the chancellor or president of your college because the intramural sports program is about to be dropped by the administration.

■ You are writing a short article for your student newspaper on the university's decision to prosecute a paper-writing service operating out of a university dorm.

■ You are writing a letter to a large city's newspaper to protest too little coverage of international news in comparison to local crime stories and sports.

Readings

James Baldwin **AUTOBIOGRAPHICAL NOTES**

"Any writer, looking back over even so short a span of time as I am here forced to assess, finds that the things which hurt him and the things which helped him cannot be divorced from each other; he could be helped in a certain way only because he was hurt in a certain way...."

Katherine Anne Porter **THE NECESSARY ENEMY**

"It is true that if we say I love you, it may be received with doubt, for there are times when it is hard to believe. Say I hate you, and the one spoken to believes it instantly, once for all."

James Thurber **THERE'S AN OWL IN MY ROOM**

"People who do not understand pigeons—and pigeons can be understood only when you understand that there is nothing to understand about them—should not go around describing pigeons or the effect of pigeons. Pigeons come closer to a zero of impingement than any other birds."

AUTOBIOGRAPHICAL NOTES
from NOTES OF A NATIVE SON

James Baldwin

I was born in Harlem thirty-one years ago. I began plotting novels at about the time I learned to read. The story of my childhood is the usual bleak fantasy, and we can dismiss it with the restrained observation that I certainly would not consider living it again. In those days my mother was given to the exasperating and mysterious habit of having babies. As they were born, I took them over with one hand and held a book with the other. The children probably suffered, though they have since been kind enough to deny it, and in this way I read *Uncle Tom's Cabin* and *A Tale of Two Cities* over and over and over again; in this way, in fact, I read just about everything I could get my hands on—except the Bible, probably because it was the only book I was encouraged to read. I must also confess that I wrote—a great deal—and my first professional triumph, in any case, the first effort of mine to be seen in print, occurred at the age of twelve or thereabouts, when a short story I had written about the Spanish revolution won some sort of prize in an extremely short-lived church newspaper. I remember the story was censored by the lady editor, though I don't remember why, and I was outraged.

Also wrote plays, and songs, for one of which I received a letter of congratulations from Mayor La Guardia, and poetry, about which the less said, the better. My mother was delighted by all these goings-on, but my father wasn't; he wanted me to be a preacher. When I was fourteen I became a preacher, and when I was seventeen I stopped. Very shortly thereafter I left home. For God knows how long I struggled with the world of commerce and industry—I guess they would say they struggled with *me*—and when I was about twenty-one I had enough done of a novel to get a Saxton Fellowship. When I was twenty-two the fellowship was over, the novel turned out to be unsalable, and I started waiting on tables in a Village restaurant and writing book reviews—mostly, as it turned out, about the Negro problem, concerning which the color of my skin made me automatically an expert. Did another book, in company with photographer Theodore Pelatowski, about the store-front churches in Harlem. This book met exactly the same fate as my first—fellowship, but no sale. (It was a Rosenwald Fellowship.) By the time I was twenty-four I had decided to stop reviewing books about the Negro problem—which, by this time, was only slightly less horrible in print than it was in life—and I packed my bags and went to France, where I finished, God knows how, *Go Tell It on the Mountain*.

Any writer, I suppose, feels that the world into which he was born is nothing less than a conspiracy against the cultivation of his talent—which attitude certainly has a great deal to support it. On the other hand, it is only because the world looks on his talent with such a frightening indifference that the artist is compelled to make his talent important. So that any writer, looking back over even so short a span of time as I am here forced to assess, finds that the things which hurt him and the things which helped him cannot be divorced from each other; he could be helped in a certain way only because he was hurt in a certain way; and his help is simply to be enabled to move from one conundrum to the next—one is tempted to say that he moves from one disaster to the next. When one begins looking for influences one finds them by the score. I haven't thought much about my own, not enough anyway; I hazard that the King James Bible, the rhetoric of the store-front church, something ironic and violent and perpetually understated in Negro speech—and something of Dickens' love for bravura—have something to do with me today; but I wouldn't stake my life on it. Likewise, innumerable people have helped me in many ways; but finally, I suppose, the most difficult (and most rewarding) thing in my life has been the fact that I was born a Negro and was forced, therefore, to effect some kind of truce with this reality. (Truce, by the way, is the best one can hope for.)

One of the difficulties about being a Negro writer (and this is not special pleading, since I don't mean to suggest that he has it worse than anybody else) is that the Negro problem is written about so widely. The bookshelves groan under the weight of information, and everyone therefore considers himself informed. And this information, furthermore, operates usually (generally, popularly) to reinforce traditional attitudes. Of traditional attitudes there are only two—For or Against—and I, personally, find it difficult to say which attitude has caused me the most pain. I am speaking as a writer; from a social point of view I am perfectly aware that the change from ill-will to good-will, however motivated, however imperfect, however expressed, is better than no change at all.

But it is part of the business of the writer—as I see it—to examine attitudes, to go beneath the surface, to tap the source. From this point of view the Negro problem is nearly inaccessible. It is not only written about so widely; it is written about so badly. It is quite possible to say that the price a Negro pays for becoming articulate is to find himself, at length, with nothing to be articulate about. ("You taught me language," says Caliban to Prospero, "and my profit on't is I know how to curse.") Consider: the tremendous social activity that this problem generates imposes on whites and Negroes alike the necessity of looking forward, of working to bring about a better day. This is fine, it keeps the waters troubled; it is all, indeed, that has made possible the Negro's progress. Nevertheless, social affairs are not generally speaking the writer's prime concern, whether they ought to be or not; it is absolutely necessary that he establish between himself and these affairs a distance which will allow, at least, for clarity, so that before he can look forward in any meaningful sense, he must first be allowed to take a long look back. In the context of the Negro problem neither whites nor blacks, for excellent reasons of their own, have the faintest desire to look back; but I think that the past is all that makes the present coherent, and further, that the past will remain horrible for exactly as long as we refuse to assess it honestly.

I know, in any case, that the most crucial time in my own development came when I was forced to recognize that I was a kind of bastard of the West; when I followed the line of my past I did not find myself in Europe but in Africa. And this meant that in some subtle way, in a really profound way, I brought to Shakespeare, Bach, Rembrandt, to the stones of Paris, to the cathedral at Chartres, and to the Empire State Building, a special attitude. These were not really my creations, they did not contain my history; I might search in them in vain forever for any reflection of myself. I was an interloper; this was not my heritage. At the same time I had no other heritage which I could possibly hope to use—I had certainly been unfitted for the jungle or the tribe. I would have to appropriate these white centuries, I would have to make them mine—I would have to accept my special attitude, my special place in this scheme—otherwise I would have no place in *any* scheme. What was the most difficult was the fact that I was forced to admit something I had always hidden from myself, which the American Negro has had to hide from himself as the price of his public progress; that I hated and feared white people. This did not mean that I loved black people; on the contrary, I despised them, possibly because they failed to produce Rembrandt. In effect, I hated and feared the world. And this meant, not only that I thus gave the world an altogether murderous power over me, but also that in such a self-destroying limbo I could never hope to write.

One writes out of one thing only—one's own experience. Everything depends on how relentlessly one forces from this experience the last drop, sweet or bitter, it can possibly give. This is the only real concern of the artist, to recreate out of the disorder of life that order which is art. The difficulty then, for me, of being a Negro writer was the fact that I was, in effect, prohibited from examining my own experience too closely by the tremendous demands and the very real dangers of my social situation.

I don't think the dilemma outlined above is uncommon. I do think, since writers work in the disastrously explicit medium of language, that it goes a little way towards explaining why, out of the enormous resources of Negro speech and life, and despite the example of Negro music, prose written by Negroes has been generally speaking so pallid and so harsh. I have not written about being a Negro at such length because I expect that to be my only subject, but only because it was the gate I had to unlock before I could hope to write about anything else. I don't think that the Negro problem in America can be even discussed coherently without bearing in mind its context; its context being the history, traditions, customs, the moral assumptions and preoccupations of the country; in short, the general social fabric. Appearances to the contrary, no one in America escapes its effects and everyone in America bears some responsibility for it. I believe this the more firmly because it is the overwhelming tendency to speak of this problem as though it were a thing apart. But in the work of Faulkner, in the general attitude and certain specific passages in Robert Penn Warren, and, most significantly, in the advent of Ralph Ellison, one sees the beginnings—at least—of a more genuinely penetrating search. Mr. Ellison, by the way, is the first Negro novelist I have ever read to utilize in language, and brilliantly, some of the ambiguity and irony of Negro life.

About my interests: I don't know if I have any, unless the morbid desire to own a sixteen-millimeter camera and make experimental movies can be so classified. Otherwise, I love to eat and drink—it's my melancholy conviction that I've scarcely ever had enough to eat (this is because it's *impossible* to eat enough if you're worried about the next meal)—and I love to argue with people who do not disagree with me too profoundly, and I love to laugh. I do *not* like bohemia, or bohemians, I do not like people whose principal aim is pleasure, and I do not like people who are *earnest* about anything. I don't like people who like me because I'm a Negro; neither do I like people who find in the same accident grounds for contempt. I love America more than any other country in the world, and, exactly for this reason, I insist on the right to criticize her perpetually. I think all theories are suspect, that the finest principles may have to be modified, or may even be pulverized by the demands of life, and that one must find, therefore, one's own moral center and move through the world hoping that this center will guide one aright. I consider that I have many responsibilities, but none greater than this: to last, as Hemingway says, and get my work done.

I want to be an honest man and a good writer.

1. How does Baldwin arrive at a "truce" with the "reality" of being born black?
2. Baldwin says that the writer's business is to examine attitudes below the surface. What does he find there?
3. Apart from his color, what else does Baldwin say makes writing difficult for him?
4. Comment on the style, tone, organization, and implied audience of this essay.
5. Write your own brief autobiographical notes explaining honestly your own best and worst feelings as you grew up, and how your background has led you to act in certain ways.

THE NECESSARY ENEMY

Katherine Anne Porter

She is a frank, charming, fresh-hearted young woman who married for love. She and her husband are one of those gay, good-looking young pairs who ornament this modern scene rather more in profusion perhaps than ever before in our history. They are handsome, with a talent for finding their way in their world, they work at things that interest them, their tastes agree and their hopes. They intend in all good faith to spend their lives together, to have children and do well by them and each other—to be happy, in fact, which for them is the whole point of their marriage. And all in stride, keeping their wits about them. Nothing romantic, mind you; their feet are on the ground.

Unless they were this sort of person, there would be not much point to what I wish to say; for they would seem to be an example of the high-spirited, right-minded young whom the critics are always invoking to come forth and do their duty and practice all those sterling old-fashioned virtues which in every generation seem to be falling into disrepair. As for virtues, these young people are more or less on their own, like most of their kind; they get very little moral or other aid from their society; but after three years of marriage this very contemporary young woman finds herself facing the oldest and ugliest dilemma of marriage.

She is dismayed, horrified, full of guilt and forebodings because she is finding out little by little that she is capable of hating her husband, whom she loves faithfully. She can hate him at times as fiercely and mysteriously, indeed in terribly much the same way, as often she hated her parents, her brothers and sisters, whom she loves, when she was a child. Even then it had seemed to her a kind of black treacherousness in her, her private wickedness that, just the same, gave her her only private life. That was one thing her parents never knew about her, never seemed to suspect. For it was never given a name. They did and said hateful things to her and to each other as if by right, as if in them it was a kind of virtue. But when they said to her, "Control your feelings," it was never when she was amiable and obedient, only in the black times of her hate. So it was her secret, a shameful one. When they punished her, sometimes for the strangest reasons, it was, they said, only because they loved her—it was for her good. She did not believe this, but she thought herself guilty of something worse than ever they had punished her for. None of this really frightened her: the real fright came when she discovered that at times her father and mother hated each other; this was like standing on the doorsill of a familiar room and seeing in a lightning flash that the floor was gone, you were on the edge of a bottomless pit. Sometimes she felt that both of them hated her, but that passed, it was simply not a thing to be thought of, much less believed. She thought she had outgrown all this, but here it was again, an element in her own nature she could not control, or feared she could not. She would have to hide from her husband, if she could, the same spot in her feelings she had hidden from her parents, and for the same no doubt disreputable, selfish reason: she wants to keep his love.

Above all, she wants him to be absolutely confident that she loves him, for that is the real truth, no matter how unreasonable it sounds, and no matter how her own feelings betray them both at times. She depends recklessly on his love; yet while she is hating him, he might very well be hating her as much or even more, and it would serve her right. But she does not want to be served right, she wants to be loved and forgiven—that is, to be sure he would forgive her anything, if he had any notion of what she had done. But best of all she would like not to have anything in her love that should ask for forgiveness. She doesn't mean about their quarrels—they are not so bad. Her feelings are out of proportion, perhaps. She knows it is perfectly natural for people to disagree, have fits of temper, fight it out; they learn quite a lot about each other that way, and not all of it disappointing either. When it passes, her hatred seems quite unreal. It always did.

Love. We are early taught to say it. I love you. We are trained to the thought of it as if there were nothing else, or nothing else worth having without it, or nothing worth having which it could not bring with it. Love is taught, always by precept, sometimes by example. Then hate, which no one meant to teach us, comes of itself. It is true that if we say I love you, it may be received with doubt, for there are times when it is hard to believe. Say I hate you, and the one spoken to believes it instantly, once for all.

Say I love you a thousand times to that person afterward and mean it every time, and still it does not change the fact that once we said I hate you, and meant that too. It leaves a mark on that surface love had worn so smooth with its eternal caresses. Love must be learned, and learned again and again; there is no end to it. Hate needs no instruction, but waits only to be provoked . . . hate, the unspoken word, the unacknowledged presence in the house, that faint smell of brimstone among the roses, that invisible tongue-tripper, that unkempt finger in every pie, that sudden oh-so-curiously *chilling* look—could it be boredom?—on your dear one's features, making them quite ugly. Be careful: love, perfect love, is in danger.

If it is not perfect, it is not love, and if it is not love, it is bound to be hate sooner or later. This is perhaps a not too exaggerated statement of the extreme position of Romantic Love, more especially in America, where we are all brought up on it, whether we know it or not. Romantic Love is changeless, faithful, passionate, and its sole end is to render the two lovers happy. It has no obstacles save those provided by the hazards of fate (that is to say, society), and such sufferings as the lovers may cause each other are only another word for delight: exciting jealousies, thrilling uncertainties, the ritual dance of courtship within the charmed closed circle of their secret alliance; all *real* troubles come from without, they face them unitedly in perfect confidence. Marriage is not the end but only the beginning of true happiness, cloudless, changeless to the end. That the candidates for this blissful condition have never seen an example of it, nor ever knew anyone who had, makes no difference. That is the ideal and they will achieve it.

How did Romantic Love manage to get into marriage at last, where it was most certainly never intended to be? At its highest it was tragic: the love of Héloïse and Abélard. At its most graceful, it was the homage of the trouvère for his lady. In its most popular form, the adulterous strayings of solidly married couples who meant to stray for their own good reasons, but at the same time do nothing to upset the property settlements or the line of legitimacy; at its most trivial, the pretty trifling of shepherd and shepherdess.

This was generally condemned by church and state and a word of fear to honest wives whose mortal enemy it was. Love within the sober, sacred realities of marriage was a matter of personal luck, but in any case, private feelings were strictly a private affair having, at least in theory, no bearing whatever on the fixed practice of the rules of an institution never intended as a recreation ground for either sex. If the couple discharged their religious and social obligations, furnished forth a copious progeny, kept their troubles to themselves, maintained public civility and died under the same roof, even if not always on speaking terms, it was rightly regarded as a successful marriage. Apparently this testing ground was too severe for all but the stoutest spirits; it too was based on an ideal, as impossible in its way as the ideal Romantic Love. One good thing to be said for it is that society took responsibility for the conditions of marriage, and the sufferers within its bonds could always blame the system, not themselves. But Romantic Love crept into the marriage bed, very stealthily, by centuries, bringing its absurd notions about love as eternal springtime and marriage as a personal adventure meant to provide personal happiness. To a Western romantic such as I, though my views have been much modified by painful experience, it still seems to be a charming work of the human imagination, and it is a pity its central notion has been taken too literally and has hardened into a convention as cramping and enslaving as the older one. The refusal to acknowledge the evils in ourselves which therefore are implicit in any human situation is as extreme and unworkable a proposition as the doctrine of total depravity; but somewhere between them, or maybe beyond them, there does exist a possibility for reconciliation between our desires for impossible satisfactions and the simple unalterable fact that we also desire to be unhappy and that we create our own sufferings; and out of these sufferings we salvage our fragments of happiness.

Our young woman who has been taught that an important part of her human nature is not real because it makes trouble and interferes with her peace of mind and shakes her self-love, has been very badly taught; but she has arrived at a most important stage of her re-education. She is afraid her marriage is going to fail because she has not love enough to face its difficulties; and this because at times she feels a painful hostility toward her husband, and cannot admit its reality because such an admission would damage in her own eyes her view of what love should be, an absurd view, based on her vanity of power. Her hatred is real as her love is real, but her hatred has the advantage at present because it works on a blind instinctual level, it is lawless; and her love is subjected to a code of ideal conditions, impossible by their very nature of fulfillment, which prevents its free growth and deprives it of its right to recognize its human limitations and come to grips with them. Hatred is natural in a sense that love, as she conceives it, a young person brought up in the tradition of Romantic Love, is not natural at all. Yet it did not come by hazard, it is the very imperfect expression of the need of the human imagination to create beauty and harmony out of chaos, no matter how mistaken its notion of these things may be, nor how clumsy its methods. It has conjured love out of the air, and seeks to preserve it by incantations; when she spoke a vow to love and honor her husband until death, she did a very reckless thing, for it is not possible by an act of the will to fulfill such an engagement. But it was the necessary act of faith performed in defense of a mode of feeling, the statement of honorable intention to practice as well as she is able the noble, acquired faculty of love, that very mysterious overtone to sex which is the best thing in it. Her hatred is part of it, the necessary enemy and ally.

1. What is wrong with the ideal of Romantic Love in Porter's view? And why is it in danger?

2. Does Porter say we *learn* to hate? Explain carefully.

3. How does Porter argue for the necessity of hatred? That is, how does she redeem hatred and make it the "necessary enemy"?

4. Comment on the style, organization, and implied audience of this essay.

THERE'S AN OWL IN MY ROOM

James Thurber

I saw Gertrude Stein on the screen of a newsreel theater one afternoon and I heard her read that famous passage of hers about pigeons on the grass, alas (the sorrow is, as you know, Miss Stein's). After reading about the pigeons on the grass alas, Miss Stein said, "This is a simple description of a landscape I have seen many times." I don't really believe that that is true. Pigeons on the grass alas may be a simple description of Miss Stein's own consciousness, but it is not a simple description of a plot of grass on which pigeons have alighted, are alighting, or are going to alight. A truly simple description of the pigeons alighting on the grass of the Luxembourg Gardens (which, I believe, is where the pigeons alighted) would say of the pigeons alighting there only that they were pigeons alighting. Pigeons that alight anywhere are neither sad pigeons nor gay pigeons, they are simply pigeons.

It is neither just nor accurate to connect the word alas with pigeons. Pigeons are definitely not alas. They have nothing to do with alas and they have nothing to do with hooray (not even when you tie red, white, and blue ribbons on them and let them loose at band concerts); they have nothing to do with mercy me or isn't that fine, either. White rabbits, yes, and Scotch terriers, and bluejays, and even hippopotamuses, but not pigeons. I happen to have studied pigeons very closely and carefully, and I have studied the effect, or rather the lack of effect, of pigeons very carefully. A number of pigeons alight from time to time on the sill of my hotel window when I am eating breakfast and staring out the window. They never alas me, they never make me feel alas; they never make me feel anything.

Nobody and no animal and no other bird can play a scene so far down as a pigeon can. For instance, when a pigeon on my window ledge becomes aware of me sitting there in a chair in my blue polka-dot dressing-gown, worrying, he pokes his head far out from his shoulders and peers sideways at me, for all the world (Miss Stein might surmise) like a timid man peering around the corner of a building trying to ascertain whether he is being followed by some hoofed fiend or only by the echo of his own footsteps. And yet it is *not* for all the world like a timid man peering around the corner of a building trying to ascertain whether he is being followed by a hoofed fiend or only by the echo of his own footsteps, at all. And that is because there is no emotion in the pigeon and no power to arouse emotion. A pigeon looking is just a pigeon looking. When it comes to emotion, a fish, compared to a pigeon, is practically beside himself.

A pigeon peering at me doesn't make me sad or glad or apprehensive or hopeful. With a horse or a cow or a dog it would be different. It would be especially different with a dog. Some dogs peer at me as if I had just gone completely crazy or as if they had just gone completely crazy. I can go so far as to say that most dogs peer at me that way. This creates in the consciousness of both me and the dog a feeling of alarm or downright terror and legitimately permits me to work into a description of the landscape, in which the dog and myself are figures, a note of emotion. Thus I should not have minded if Miss Stein had written: dogs on the grass, look out, dogs on the grass, look out, look out, dogs on the grass, look out Alice. That would be a simple description of dogs on the grass. But when any writer pretends that a pigeon makes him sad, or makes him anything else, I must instantly protest that this is a highly specialized fantastic impression created in an individual consciousness and that therefore it cannot fairly be presented as a simple description of what actually was to be seen.

People who do not understand pigeons—and pigeons can be understood only when you understand that there is nothing to understand about them—should not go around describing pigeons or the effect of pigeons. Pigeons come closer to a zero of impingement than any other birds. Hens embarrass me the way my old Aunt Hattie used to when I was twelve and she still insisted I wasn't big enough to bathe myself; owls disturb me; if I am with an eagle I always pretend that I am not with an eagle; and so on down to swallows at twilight who scare the hell out of me. But pigeons have absolutely no effect on me. They have absolutely no effect on anybody. They couldn't even startle a child. That is why they are selected from among all birds to be let loose, with colored ribbons attached to them, at band concerts, library dedications, and christenings of new dirigibles. If anybody let loose a lot of owls on such an occasion there would be rioting and catcalls and whistling and fainting spells and throwing of chairs and the Lord only knows what else.

From where I am sitting now I can look out the window and see a pigeon being a pigeon on the roof of the Harvard Club. No other thing can be less what it is not than a pigeon can, and Miss Stein, of all people, should understand that simple fact. Behind the pigeon I am looking at, a blank wall of tired gray bricks is stolidly trying to sleep off oblivion; underneath the pigeon the cloistered windows of the Harvard Club are staring in horrified bewilderment at something they have seen across the street. The pigeon is just there on the roof being a pigeon, having been, and being, a pigeon and, what is more, always going to be, too. Nothing could be simpler than that. If you read that sentence aloud you will instantly see what I mean. It is a simple description of a pigeon on a roof. It is only with an effort that I am conscious of the pigeon, but I am acutely aware of a great sulky red iron pipe that is creeping up the side of the building intent on sneaking up on a slightly tipsy chimney which is shouting its head off.

There is nothing a pigeon can do or be that would make me feel sorry for it or for myself or for the people in the world, just as there is nothing I could do or be that would make a pigeon feel sorry for itself. Even if I plucked his feathers out it would not make him feel sorry for himself and it would not make me feel sorry for myself or for him. But try plucking the quills out of a porcupine or even plucking the fur out of a jackrabbit. There is nothing a pigeon could be, or can be, rather, which could get into my consciousness like a fumbling hand in a bureau drawer and disarrange my mind or pull anything out of it. I bar nothing at all. You could dress up a pigeon in a tiny suit of evening clothes and put a tiny silk hat on his head and a tiny gold-headed cane under his wing and send him walking into my room at night. It would make no impression on me. I would not shout, "Good god almighty, the birds are in charge!" But you could send an owl into my room, dressed only in the feathers it was born with, and no monkey business, and I would pull the covers over my head and scream.

No other thing in the world falls so far short of being able to do what it cannot do as a pigeon does. Of being *unable* to do what it *can* do, too, as far as that goes.

1. "Nobody and no animal and no other bird can play a scene so far down as a pigeon can." What does Thurber mean by this?
2. A pigeon is a pigeon is a pigeon, implies Thurber. Why does he emphasize this?

3. If "a pigeon looking is just a pigeon looking," then why, in paragraph 3, does it become "a timid man"? What is the point of the change?

4. What is the point of the contrast between the pigeon and the owl?

5. Comment on the style, tone, organization, and implied audience of this essay.

Sentences

Main Statements

Nothing reveals the importance of good ideas more powerfully than a well-constructed sentence. Again, think of yourself as reader, and remember that you want to find in writing forceful, accurate statements made economically, so that an opinion is clarified, an argument is developed, a problem is solved, or an event is made memorable.

How do sentences allow a reader to find all this, regardless of the subject matter? Read this final paragraph from George Orwell's famous essay, "Why I Write":

Looking back through the last page or two, I see that I have made it appear as though my motives in writing were wholly public-spirited. I don't want to leave that as the final impression. All writers are vain, selfish and lazy, and at the very bottom of their motives there lies a mystery. Writing a book is a horrible, exhausting struggle, like a long bout of some painful illness. One would never undertake such a thing if one were not driven on by some demon whom one can neither resist nor understand. For all one knows that demon is simply the same instinct that makes a baby squall for attention. And yet it is also true that one can write nothing readable unless one constantly struggles to efface one's own personality. Good prose is like a windowpane. I cannot say with certainty which of my motives are the strongest, but I know which of them deserve to be followed. And looking back through my work, I see that it is invariably where I lacked a *political* purpose that I wrote lifeless books and was betrayed into purple passages, sentences without meaning, decorative adjectives and humbug generally.

Start from the reader's point of view and decide what you think the writer means. You could summarize the passage by saying that Orwell believes that writing a book is a complex experience: it is tiresome and disturbing, even "painful," and one would not write if it were not for an irresistible motive. Orwell says he is not sure what that motive always is, for writers are by nature "vain, selfish, and lazy": they cry out for attention like children. But he knows what produces his best writing. Without a political purpose, Orwell's writing is without life or meaning, mere decoration.

You will remember from the chapters on reading that you instinctively follow sequences and look for emphasis and coherent development when you read. As you do this with the Orwell excerpt, you find that it is a cleverly written suspended paragraph which does not really get to the key point until the final sentence, when Orwell reveals his political motives in writing. But in getting there you follow several clearly signposted statements that lead to that conclusion, even if they do not at first seem to have much to do with it:

1. All writers are vain, selfish, and lazy.
2. Writing a book is a horrible and exhausting struggle.
3. The writer is driven to write by some mysterious motive or demon.
4. Good writers constantly struggle to efface their own personalities.
5. Good prose is like a windowpane. You can see through it directly to the issue, not merely to the presence of a writer.
6. Good writing results from a political motive.

When the final sentence is reached, you realize that the whole point is that only writing for a political purpose redeems the act of writing.

Now apart from the lesson of this piece, which is probably one of the most useful you can learn as a writer, note how you are led to the conclusion through a series of directly expressed, emphatic statements that link together to form an argument. As a writer concerned with producing effective sentences, you can learn a good deal from this arrangement. Orwell's prose exemplifies the first rule of good sentence writing: *make direct assertions whenever it is possible to do so.*

Every aspect of your essay outline, every piece of evidence that you are thinking clearly and logically, is carried by *a network of main statements,* one in each sentence. Sometimes the main statement is called the *core assertion* or, to use a term from the study of logic, the *proposition* carried by the sentence. This main statement, core assertion, or proposition is simply the most important idea in a sentence. It is the part of the sentence that could stand on its own. For example:

Looking back through the last page or two, *I see that I have made it appear as though my motives in writing were wholly public-spirited.*

The italicized portion could be a complete sentence in itself. In sum, if you want to write effectively, you should have something significant to say; you should say it clearly and assertively, liberally sprinkling your prose with strong statements; and you should make sure that every sentence carries a main statement.

Contrast and Variety

Assertiveness cannot be all, though. Obviously, not every sentence can or should suggest an equally weighted focus, for the reader does not want to be bombarded in every line. Orwell's paragraph contains a number of strong main statements because it is the concluding paragraph in his essay. But the statements are not all of the same value. He poses the problems of selfishness, pain, exhaustion, and readability for the writer, but that is superseded by the claim that he can get away from egocentric writing by following his political motives. ''My starting point,'' he says elsewhere in the essay, "is always a feeling of partnership, a sense of injustice." The political motive overrides all others, even though it cannot dismiss the problems attached to writing.

Good writing develops a contrast and variety among main statements:

■ *Main statements are contrasted within the context of the paragraph.* The sentence beginning "And looking back through my work..." is the theme sentence, and the one that starts "And yet it is also true that one can write nothing readable..." is a strong supporting sentence. The paragraph actually pivots and changes direction with this sentence as Orwell moves from the exhausting vanities of writing to the political motive.

■ *Main statements can be highlighted within the sentence itself.* As we shall see in more detail later in this chapter, there are two basic kinds of sentence structure, one that involves only main statements, and one that includes other, less important elements that set off the main statement. *The simple sentence* contains only one main statement (MS):

Good prose is like a windowpane.

The co-ordinated or compound sentence contains two main statements joined together by a conjunction:

MS

All writers are vain, selfish, and lazy, and *at the*

MS

very bottom of their motives there lies a mystery.

The subordinated or complex sentence contains one or more main statements together with a subordinate element (SE):

SE   MS

For all one knows *that demon is simply the same instinct*

SE

that makes a baby squall for attention.

Orwell achieves emphasis through the variety of his sentence structures. A main statement needs subordinating elements to create a contrast, and it is the art of subordinating for contrast that we will explore in a moment. Here, though, is another important rule for developing the assertiveness of your sentences. *Vary the impact of your main statements by contrasting them to subordinate elements within the sentence.* The power of the sentence lies in its assertiveness and its variety. Orwell is plainly an effective writer not merely because he has good ideas but because he has expressed those ideas in *effective sentence structure, using strong grammatical elements.* How can this be achieved?

Strong Parts of Speech

Ideas should be expressed using strong grammatical elements. What is a grammatical element? Grammar describes the way words come together to create meaning. When words link together to create meaning in any sentence, they do so for two reasons:

Every word carries one or more meanings which are part of the storehouse of language usage.

Every word fits into a grammatical "slot" in the sentence which determines its function (it is a noun, a verb, and so on).

Meaning

The conventions of usage are very important in determining meaning. The sentence "Good prose is like a windowpane," however metaphorical, is understandable because we know what each of the words refers to. Prose can be like a windowpane only if we know what a windowpane actually is. Then we can guess that the point has something to do with transparency or a focused viewpoint. Understanding is based on the way words refer to things, events, or ideas. Specifically, our understanding is based on the way words refer to things in our experience, including our experience of ideas and concepts and even of things we find difficult to put into words.

Grammar

Part of that reference is built up each time we use language by the *function* of words in sentences. Grammar describes this function. Words carry meaning, not simply because we have heard them before, but because they have a recognizable function in the structure of all sentences.

Grammar concerns itself with the description of this function based on the conventions of language as it has evolved through centuries of usage. We can describe individual words and their function in each sentence in terms of their *usage and parts of speech,* and in terms of their *relationship to other words in the sentence.* Both are descriptions of function, and both are needed for an accurate description of what makes effective

191

writing. In this section, we will concentrate on the parts of speech, in the next section, on word relationships.

Parts of Speech

The description of words as they refer to events, things, qualities, time, and place covers the *parts of speech* (see Handbook PS).

Nouns are words that name or refer to things (*dog, cat*).

Adjectives are words that describe the qualities of things (*gray, energetic*).

Pronouns are words that stand for nouns (*I, it*).

Verbs are words that convey actions (*to run*).

Adverbs are words that describe actions (*quickly*).

Prepositions are words that connect a noun or pronoun to another word in the sentence (*in, by, with*).

Conjunctions are words that connect things or actions, nouns or verbs (*and, but*).

Interjections are words expressing strong emotion (*Oh, damn*).

Articles are indicator words immediately preceding nouns (*the, a, an*).

It is impossible to rank all the parts of speech in some fixed order, for the meaning of words obviously contributes something to their emphasis. But it is possible to make some generalizations about the strength of various parts of speech based on the role they play in conveying information. Words that convey actions (verbs) tend to be stronger than words that name an object or refer to an idea (nouns). Both nouns and verbs are more powerful than those words that modify them (adjectives and adverbs) and those that stand in for nouns (pronouns). Adverbs, adjectives, and pronouns in turn tend to be more powerful than prepositions, conjunctions, interjections, and articles.

Yet every part of speech is essential to create meaning, for clearly the effectiveness of any assertion depends on

Strong grammatical elements

The relationship between strong and weak elements

There is no mystery to this. Think of a sentence not so much as a coded grammatical system but as a sequence of words that has a logical emphasis dependent on the function of the words.

The rule for effective writing is a simple one: *Focus on an action rather than a thing, an abstraction, or an idea.* That is, *make sure verbs carry the emphasis rather than nouns.* Transform nouns into verbs where at all possible:

> She *made a decision to take a run* to Pueblo.

> She *decided to run* to Pueblo.

The same rule applies to the use of adverbs with verbs. Avoid the use of a verb in combination with an adverb when a single strong action verb is available:

> He *walked intermittently* from room to room.

> He *dawdled* from room to room.

Effective Assertions

Meaning and Sentence Structure

Parts of speech only hint at the power of grammar to determine meaning. The whole structure of a sentence and the function of words in their sequence are also very important. Even when words are nonsensical, we can at least begin to know what they might mean from the way they function, providing they keep some basic inflections—like verb endings (-s, -ed), -ly for adverbs, capitalization for proper names, prepositions preceding nouns, and so on. Consider this piece of nonsense: "Niglegs bandiwacks troggled mavely hem kerplexit." We can compare its structure with that of sentences like "Lovely flowers bloomed profusely this summer" (that is, adjective + noun + verb + adverb + a further adverbial element). We begin to decode the sentence by knowing that *troggled* is probably a past tense of a verb (based on the *-ed* ending) and *mavely* is an adverb following the verb (since it ends in *-ly*). And since every sentence contains a subject and a predicate, *bandiwacks* must be a noun and *niglegs* an adjective. This leaves *hem kerplexit* to fill the role of an additional adverbial element.

Of course, we quickly get to the limit of what grammar can tell us when we deal with nonsense sentences, but it is a limit that actually defines the possibility of meaning. Meaning is not only a matter of words having references and associations, it is also determined by the function of words in a sequence. *Meaning is created by the placement of words.* As codes are broken through the discovery of repetitive determining structures, so sentences reveal meaning through our knowledge of various repetitive sentence patterns. Furthermore, we know how to make more effective assertions through that understanding. Structure in itself would not be important if it were not for the fact that direct statements in English fall into a basic *subject and predicate* pattern.

Subject and Predicate

The *subject* (S) carries out the action of the verb; the *predicate* (P) is the word or group of words that is affected by the verb and either affirms or denies something about the subject (see Handbook SE-1). All sentences contain a subject and a predicate. The simplest kind of sentence is a subject and a predicate that is only a verb (V):

S   P

Orwell   writes.

(S)   P

Watch out! (The implied subject is *you*)

But we can build onto this S-P pattern, adding various *sentence elements:*

■ *Objects* of the verb, which are either direct (DO) or indirect (IO), are nouns or their equivalents that are directly or indirectly affected by the action of the verb (see Handbook SE-2).

S   V   DO

Orwell   writes *a book.*

The subject directly acts on something through the verb.

S   V   IO   DO

Orwell   bought *his friend* *a book.*

The subject affects two objects: one directly (*book*), one indirectly (*friend*). The *indirect object* is one for whom or which or to whom or which something is done.

■ *Complements* of the verb (C) are nouns, pronouns, or adjectives that can be either a subject (SC) or an object (OC). The *subject complement* is either a predicate noun (PN) or a predicate adjective (PA) (see Handbook SE-3). A *complement* is a word or words in the predicate that completes or adds something more to, or complements, the subject or the object.

S   V   SC–PN

Orwell   is a good writer.

Writer is a subject complement and a predicate noun.

      S   V   SC–PA

Orwell   is very political.

Political is a subject complement and a predicate adjective.

      S   V   DO   OC

Orwell   called his novel *1984.*

1984 is an object complement.

      S   V   DO   OC

Critics   call   Orwell   brilliant.

Brilliant is an object complement.

■ *Modifiers* are adjectives, adverbs, articles, and possessive pronouns (*my, your, his, its, their*), any of which can modify the subject, object, or verb (see Handbook SE-4).

    Good critics have *often* called Orwell a *brilliant political* satirist.
Good, brilliant, and *political* are all adjectives. *Often* is an adverb.

■ *Appositives* are nouns or substitutes for nouns standing beside other nouns or their substitutes and identifying or explaining them (see Handbook SE-5).

    Orwell, *the novelist,* is well known.

    Orwell, *the political satirist,* sold many books.

■ *Connectives* are words or phrases—such as *and, but, also, on the one hand, on the other hand, neither, nor*—that link words or groups of words (see Handbook PS-7).

    Orwell is *both* a novelist *and* a satirist.

    Most of the assertive statements you will write will be of the subject-verb-object (or complement) pattern with modifiers, yet it is surprising how easy it is to write ineffectively even with this most basic of sentences. Say you want to convey the following message:

    Philosophy is the art of asking unanswerable questions.

This is a simple subject-verb-complement structure which is stated as directly as it can be here. But without a good deal of imagination, anyone could take the assertiveness out of the sentence in order to gain some misguided ''effect'':

1. Asking unanswerable questions is the art of philosophy.
2. Unanswerable questions are asked artistically by philosophy.
3. Philosophy makes asking unanswerable questions an art.
4. The value of philosophy is that it is the art of asking unanswerable questions.

And so on. Not all these sentences are downright bad, of course, and you can imagine special circumstances in which each may even be appropriate. Most often, though, you are called upon to deliver information simply, clearly, and directly, and none of the rewritten sentences does this as well as the original.

Direct Statements

Here is a set of guidelines for writing cogent, direct statements. Learn them well enough to be able to catch yourself when you find yourself writing in a roundabout way.

■ *Focus on a verb rather than a noun, and on a direct, active form of the verb.* Avoid the passive where possible. So sentence 2 above is unnecessarily weakened by being cast as passive.

X We were appreciated by the teacher.

√ The teacher appreciated us.

■ *Avoid inverting the subject and object unless it really does produce a stronger emphasis than the S-V-O pattern.* In sentence 1 above, it does not.

■ *Avoid using the verb* to be *as a weak linking verb when you are describing an action.*

X I am a player for the Denver Broncos.

√ I play for the Denver Broncos.

■ *Beware of* do, got, have, make, put, feel, give, hold, go, mean, come, *and* take, *which are weak and overworked verbs.* This is the problem with sentence 3.

I *got* out of class early, and decided to *take* a walk in the town in order to *make* my headache *go* away. This soon *put* me in a good mood, and since things were *going* better, I *felt* I could *give* myself the evening off. However, this *meant* that I did not *do* well on the test in biology which was *held* the next day. The professor later *had* a chat with me about it, and said I must *put* everything on the line when it *came* to the final.

Remove almost all these weak verbs and you have:

Class finished early, so I walked in the town to ease my headache. The pain soon disappeared, and in a good mood, I decided not to work that evening. As a result, I did badly on the biology test the next day. The professor later talked to me about it and told me that my only hope was to score highly on the final.

- *Avoid the use of the unemphatic* it is, there are, the thing is, *for these constructions impersonalize the verb and weaken the action.*

X There is a chance for us to survive by cleaning up pollution.

√ We can survive by cleaning up pollution.

X The thing is that he knows he is wrong.

√ He knows he is wrong.

- *Focus on a positive action rather than a negative.*

X I do not agree with your principles.

√ I disagree with your principles.

- *Double negatives* should be avoided when they merely add up to a positive statement.

X I do not think that you are a man of no character.

√ I think you are a man of character.

But some double negatives are effective, such as "Death is nothing more than the negation of life." Beware of compounding words that carry negative connotations, for that can make your meaning unclear.

X It is *unfortunate* that you have *ignored* my *failure* to *avoid* the price increase, and are demanding that I *lose* even more money by selling my house now when there is a *slump* in the market.

√ I have already lost a lot of money by not selling my house when the prices went up. You should understand that and withdraw your demand that I sell now during a slump.

- *Focus on a direct statement about who is carrying out an action.* In other words, make sure that nouns carry the weight of reference rather than awkward constructions like "What this means is that . . . ," "What I want to say is that . . . ," "The result is that . . . ," "The reason is that . . . ," "The value is that . . . ," "The meaning of x is that . . ." This is the problem with sentence 4 on page 196.

X The meaning of the play is that life is hard in the working class.

√ The play tells us that life is hard in the working class.

X What I want to say is that the play is truthful.

√ The play is truthful.

or

√ I think the play is truthful.

■ *Make sure that your adjectives and adverbs are precise, economical, and necessary.* In describing an event, do not overload your sentences with adjectives and adverbs, for this slows the reader's understanding. Keep only essential adjectives, and only those that are strong. Do not overstate your adjectives or adverbs.

X On February 3, 1976, the grossly incompetent adviser to the secretary of HEW made a ludicrously disastrous recommendation that the ailing and almost bankrupt welfare system should be quickly sent to its logical and inevitable end.

√ On February 3, 1976, the incompetent adviser to the secretary of HEW recommended that the welfare system, which was near bankruptcy at the time, be quickly ended.

Phrases

Sentence elements comprise not only single words but groups of words as well: phrases and clauses. We will discuss what they are first, then how to use them.

A *phrase* is a group of words that does not have a subject and a predicate (see Handbook SE-6).

A *clause* is a group of words that does have a subject and a predicate (see Handbook SE-7).

Phrases as Parts of Speech

Phrases function as nouns, adjectives, or adverbs. They are invaluable for accumulating information about a main statement without interfering with the action of the verb. Here are all the varieties of phrases listed according to their possible function:

Phrases Used as Nouns

■ *Noun phrases* are groups of words that include modified nouns:

The green parrots disturbed *the tired monkeys.*

Noun phrases often exist in apposition to a subject or object; that is, they are set off by commas right next to the noun they refer to:

Then came Patton, *the famous general.*

■ *Infinitive phrases* are phrases in which the infinitive or *to* form of the verb becomes a subject or an object (see Handbook V-3).

To love is better than *to work.*

■ *Gerund phrases* comprise a gerund—the *-ing* form of the verb which functions as a noun—and its object (see Handbook V-1).

Running is fun but *walking* is easier. (gerunds)

Running a business can be fun. (gerund phrase)

■ *Prepositional phrases* comprise prepositions together with their objects. These phrases can function as nouns, adjectives, or adverbs:

Before Christmas is the time to come. (adverb function)

Phrases Used as Adjectives

■ *Prepositional phrases.*

She is a woman *of substance.*

■ *Infinitive phrases.*

We had a meal *to end them all.*

■ *Participial phrases.* These should not be confused with gerund phrases. Participles are also *-ing* forms of the verb as well as past participle verb endings. Participial phrases always act only as adjectives (see Handbook V-2).

The dancers *wearing green* are Irish.

Phrases Used as Adverbs

■ *Prepositional phrases.*

Come and see me *by next week.*

■ *Infinitive phrases.*

We are ready *to tell the truth.*

■ *Absolute phrases* modify the action of the *whole* sentence. They exist in a parenthetical relationship to the rest of the sentence unrelated by a conjunction and are sometimes marked off by commas. An absolute phrase is always made up of a noun and a participle.

The battle having been lost, the enemy surrendered.

His face having grown dark red, we stopped joking.

Bound and Free Phrases

The most important facts about phrases, in Francis Christensen's words, are that they are either *bound* or *free, restricted* or *unrestricted,* in their relationship to the main statement or any element of the main statement.[1]

1. Francis Christensen and Bonniejean Christensen, *A New Rhetoric* (New York: Harper & Row, 1976).

Either way they can be used to add information to the main statement, but as bound or free they have different stylistic impacts.

A *bound phrase* is an integral part of a main statement. To separate the phrase from the main statement would be to remove something essential from the meaning. Bound phrases are not set off from the main statement by commas.

There's a new soap opera on TV *at 4:00 P.M. every day.*

"At 4:00 P.M. every day" is a prepositional phrase used as an adverb.

A *free phrase* is added to a statement to give additional information that is considered important. The information is set off by commas from the main statement:

$$\overleftarrow{\qquad 1 \qquad}\overrightarrow{}$$

There is a new soap opera on TV, *"Ryan's University,"* and it shows

$$\overleftarrow{\qquad 2 \qquad}\overrightarrow{}$$

every day at 4:00 P.M., *a good hour for students and*

$$\overleftarrow{\qquad 3 \qquad}\overrightarrow{}$$

teachers returning from work.

In this sentence, 1 and 2 are appositive noun phrases that are free in their relationship to the two main clauses respectively. Phrase 3 is a participial phrase used as an adjective bound to "a good hour for students and teachers." Note, though, that sometimes the only difference between a bound and a free phrase is its placement. This is particularly true of prepositional phrases:

You should leave town *by next week.* (bound)

By next week, you should leave town. (free)

The change from a bound to a free phrase does change the emphasis. The bound version is more emphatic.

Clauses

Types of Clauses

Clauses, again, are groups of words that contain both a subject and a predicate (see Handbook SE-7). They can be either main or subordinate (independent or dependent). A *main clause* (MC) is the part of the sentence that can stand on its own. So a main statement, as we have been discussing it, is a main, or independent, clause. A *subordinate clause* (SC) also contains a subject and a predicate, but it is subordinate to the main clause in its function.

MC   SC

We won the game, although we were three players short.

To discover the main clause, you simply look for the main statement in the sentence, the key idea. You can identify a dependent clause easily because they all begin with some kind of relative pronoun or subordinating conjunction:

Relative pronouns: who, which, that, what, whoever, whom, whose, whomever

Subordinating conjunctions: after, although, as, because, before, if, where, since, once, that, unless, until, when, whenever, where, wherever, while, as if, as soon as, even though, in order that, so that, no matter how

Main clauses are joined by coordinating conjunctions: *and, but, or, nor, for, so, yet.*

Clauses and Sentences

As we have seen, you can write sentences that are just a single independent clause (simple sentence). But most of your sentences will require more variety, and the main statement will be joined either to another main statement (compound sentence) or to a dependent, or subordinate, clause or clauses (complex sentence), or to both (compound-complex sentence) (see Handbook ST).

■ *Compound sentences* are made up of two or more main clauses joined by conjunctions (see Handbook ST-2):

        MC   MC

I run five miles every day of the week, *and* on the weekends I go mountain climbing.

The general rule is to place a comma before the conjunction when it links two main clauses unless its omission makes reading easier:

        MC   MC

I ran five miles and I climbed the mountain in one day.

■ *Complex sentences* contain one or more main clauses with one or more subordinate clauses (see Handbook ST-3):

        MC   SC

Two fried eggs lay by the bacon which was crisp and lean.

■ *Compound-complex sentences* contain at least two main clauses and at least one subordinate clause (see Handbook ST-4):

    MC   SC

You know that there is a stop sign at the corner of Blake Street, but

    MC

you ignored it.

Subordinate Clauses

There are three kinds of subordinate clauses:

■ *Noun clauses* can function

As a *subject:* "*What you say* will be taken down."

As a *direct object:* "I'll tell you *what you will say.*"

As an *indirect object:* "We will give *what you tell us* full consideration."

As an *object of preposition:* "The evidence will be passed on to *whoever needs it.*" (Note that *whoever* is the subject of *needs,* so do not write *to whomever.*)

As an *appositive:* "The fact *that his evidence was untrue* convicted him."

■ *Adjectival clauses,* sometimes called relative clauses, modify a noun or a pronoun. These are introduced by *who, which, when, where,* or *why.*

The Mad Hatter's comments revealed a logic *which was highly questionable.*

The relative clause modifies *logic.*

■ *Adverbial clauses* modify a verb or an adjective, adverb, infinitive, gerund, participle, or the rest of the sentence. This type of clause is usually introduced by subordinating conjunctions (listed on p. 201).

As soon as the Dormouse had spoken, it fell asleep.

Alice would not grow smaller *unless she took the medicine.*

Bound and Free Clauses

Like phrases, clauses are also bound or free, restricted or unrestricted in their relationship to the main clause. They too are used to add information to the main statement.

■ A *bound clause* (BC) is an integral part of a main statement and is not set off from the main statement by commas.

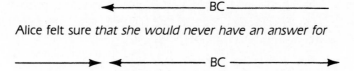

Alice felt sure *that she would never have an answer for*

the Mad Hatter so long as he controlled the conversation.

■ A free clause (FC) can be added to the main clause optionally as a supplement to the main statement. The clause is set off by commas from the main statement.

FC

Although Alice seems quite a normal young girl, she is not overly surprised by the Cheshire Cat.

Creating Emphasis with Bound and Free Elements

Now that you can recognize the basic elements of sentence structure, you will find it easier to absorb some simple guidelines that will help you to develop clarity, economy, and forcefulness in your writing. Remember that in all writing, be it fictional or nonfictional, the main clause in every sentence should be the center of attention. These guidelines refer to ways in which main clauses can be set off clearly in your writing by the use of free and bound elements—both phrases and clauses—and by the use of punctuation.

The Power of Free Elements

Modifying elements are usually more powerful as free rather than bound elements. Use free elements to build up layers of meaning in sentences.

■ The most powerful free elements are the various kinds of phrases and clauses discussed above.

Noun phrases used appositively

Participial phrases used adjectivally

Prepositional, infinitive, and absolute phrases used adverbially

Relative or adjectival clauses

Adverbial clauses

Free elements are *modifying* elements. They *add* information to the subject, object, and verb. But we frequently fall into the trap of using more bound elements than free in our writing. Bound elements also add information, but they do so in a way that restricts the main statement. Remember that the simplest way of recognizing bound and free elements is through punctuation. Free elements—both phrases and clauses—are set off by commas; bound elements are not.

- Bound elements comprise the following:

  Infinitive, gerund, and prepositional phrases which all function as nouns

  Prepositional, infinitive, and participial phrases which function as adjectives

  Prepositional phrases which function as adverbs

Try to keep your bound elements to a minimum, no more than two or three in a sentence. Add free elements to provide more information and to adjust the rhythms of the sentence, mainly to break up the unbroken flow of information coming from bound elements.

Read this sentence:

The Stinkos, a punk rock band from London's East End, made their first American tour in 1980.

The sentence has one main statement, *The Stinkos made their first American tour in 1980,* which includes one bound element, the prepositional phrase *in 1980.* The remainder of the sentence comprises a free element, two phrases bound together, *a punk rock band,* which is a noun phrase in apposition, and *from London's East End,* which is a prepositional phrase modifying *rock band.* The sentence can be diagrammed as follows to show how the layers are built up:

1. The Stinkos
    2. a punk rock band
    2. from London's East End
1. made their first American tour in 1980.

The sentence is well balanced and reads easily for there are pauses within the items of information created by the free elements.

- You can literally play with free elements varying their placement from sentence to sentence, not only to modify nouns, but to build up *layers of action* by using participial and absolute phrases with the main verb:

1. They played in several small clubs in Los Angeles, Chicago, and New York,
    2. tearing the stage apart with their raucous music,
        3. their guitars cranking out discordant notes
            4. never combined before in modern pop music.

Note that this sentence shows a useful mixture of bound and free elements. Element 1 is the main clause containing the bound preposi- tional phrase *in Los Angeles, Chicago, and New York.* Element 2 is a participial phrase modifying *played.* Element 3 is an absolute phrase that further modifies *played.*

■ There is a corollary to the rule that you should use free elements to layer meaning: *make sure you use your free elements in conjunction with bound elements* for the sake of balance and to provide adequate density. You'll note that in the sentence above the free and not the bound elements seem to carry the thrust of the meaning, but the bound elements nonetheless unobtrusively provide some essential information.

Placing Free Elements

■ A free element should be placed adjacent to the item it modifies. If you place it after the noun or pronoun, you run less risk of misinterpre- tation, but sometimes, if the phrase or clause being modified is clearly one item, then you can place the modifying element before it.

The audience loved the Stinkos' act, vulgar as it was.

Here *vulgar as it was* should follow *Stinkos' act,* or else the meaning will be changed. "Vulgar as it was, the audience loved the Stinkos' act" means that the audience and not the Stinkos' act was vulgar. But read the following sentence:

The Stinkos' act, vulgar as it was, played to full houses.

Here we have a free modifying clause, *vulgar as it was,* which could be placed before or after *the Stinkos' act* since there is no chance of ambi- guity.

■ A free element that discusses a precondition or involves an action coming before the main verb or that explains the main statement should be placed first.

Having torn the night club apart, the Stinkos happily left Chicago.

Free Elements as Modifying Words

Modifying words—like *however, nevertheless, furthermore,* and *though*— can be used within a main statement as free elements. This use provides an interruption to a particularly dense main statement, or changes the rhythm from one sentence to the next.

The ethics of punk rock, however, can be a subject of exaggerated concern, for the bands are merely playing out rituals of boredom and harmless narcissism.

Single modifying words should be used sparingly and should indicate a genuine shift in emphasis. Otherwise, they will merely suggest a pause that is little more than an affectation.

Using Subordination

If there is more than one action taking place in a sentence, consider subordination rather than coordination. If you are going to coordinate two main statements in a sentence, make sure that both actions are short, precise, logically related, and of equal importance.

Young people are still interested in education, *but* they will not find much opportunity if the loan programs are cut.

This is adequate coordination. But consider this sentence:

Young people want a vocational education in order to find jobs, *and* this is important for them.

The second statement is a weak accompaniment to the first; in fact, it is redundant and is best left out altogether. Beware of *and* as a conjunction. How often you hear statements like "I went to the movies today and then we had an ice cream sundae and some doughnuts and then we went downtown and looked in shop windows." An endless stream of actions linked together by *and* is very hard to avoid in conversation, and it frequently has a place in literary writing. But in expository writing you are much better off subordinating, layering your actions, setting up a hierarchy of events. It is much easier for a reader to follow events or ideas arranged in some kind of clearly defined relationship rather than as a string of apparently equal happenings. So use subordinating conjunctions for variety.

In order to get jobs, young people need a vocational education.

Reduce your focus to *one* main action or idea where possible, and use free or bound elements to develop your meaning.

X Universities still offer humanities courses and they know this is essential to a general education.

√ Universities still offer humanities courses *because* they know this is essential to a general education.

Sometimes it helps to simply list your main statements and then consider the order in which to assemble them. For example, here is a paragraph from an essay "Kingsfield's Folly" by John Houseman, which deals with the ratings for the television series, "The Paper Chase." Note how Houseman develops carefully modified and subordinated main statements. All the main statements without their modification by clauses or phrases have been underlined:

The first ratings for "The Paper Chase" were predictably low. For our opening show, which was aired on a Friday with considerable promotional fanfare, we received a national rating of 13 with a 27 percent share of viewers. The following

Tuesday, on our first appearance in our regular 8:00 P.M. death slot against "Happy Days" and "Laverne and Shirley," we were down to 11.3 with a share of 19 percent. There we remained with minor fluctuations for the next three months, as compared with ABC's average rating of more than 20 with a 40 to 45 percent share. In other words, "The Paper Chase" was being watched in some 8.5 million households, "Happy Days" and "Laverne and Shirley" in about 15 million.

These figures should have surprised no one, yet a deep gloom enveloped the studio when it was realized that we were being watched by less than 15 million people as against ABC's 30 million. This depression was only slightly relieved by our great reviews, by far the best received by a new series of this or any other recent season. Two dozen of these were reprinted with full-page advertisements that CBS took out in a number of the nation's leading newspapers.

HARPER'S, December 1979

Balancing Ideas

If a sentence contains more than one idea or action and they are equal, then balance the ideas to create emphasis. There are several ways in which actions, things, people, and ideas that belong together can be effectively arranged together. With each of the methods outlined below, you are looking for a *balance* of similar events or a *matching* of similar elements. We call this creating *parallel sentences.* Here are the main ways in which it can be done.

■ You can join two or more grammatical elements—words, phrases, or clauses—using similar grammatical forms.

Neither punk *nor* New Wave will be here in ten years.

Either you play the drums *or* I find a new drummer.

Not only are the songs too loud, *but also* they are too short.

I do not know *whether* to go to the concert *or* to prepare for my class.

Both the audience *and* the band cared little about the critics.

The noise level was *so* high *that* everyone held their ears.

It seemed *more* important to play with style *than* with precision.

Emphasis is achieved in each of these constructions by *repetition* and *balance.* This even suggests a kind of logical relationship between the items. Parallelism also raises our interest by offering us an event together with an anticipatory word (like *not only* or *both*) which we know will be related to another.

■ This same effect can take place even when there is no signposting by matching words. Whole clauses can be balanced against each other and whole sentences, too:

I came without hope and *left without satisfaction.*

Drumming and *strumming* have always been youthful pastimes.

The Stinkos arrived on stage in an armored car, *their hair in rollers* and *their faces painted green.*

The audience wanted blood; the Stinkos wanted money.

A balanced effect is brought about, then, by the repetition of both a grammatical structure and a key word. So "I came without hope and left without satisfaction" repeats the same sentence pattern (S-V-adverbial phrase), contrasts the verbs *to come* and *to leave,* and repeats the word *without.*

■ You can achieve a pleasant balance by matching a series of related items. You must make sure that all the items actually fit into the series: they should all be of the same part of speech or other grammatical element. They should also all have the same kind of reference and importance. Do not mix nouns and adjectives, or vegetables and musical instruments. This sentence is not correctly balanced:

Come to sunny Tonga where the maidens are beautiful, the beaches are enchanting, the food is delicious, and the construction projects are kept to a minimum.

Sometimes sentences like this are written for humorous purposes, but unless that is the effect you are seeking (and they should be funnier than this one), be sure that all the elements are perfectly matched, and do not lead to an anticlimax:

The old think that I am wise to dislike punk rock; the young think that I am foolish; and the middle aged cannot make up their minds.

■ Sometimes parallelism can also be expressed by *inversion* where the order of a phrase or clause is reversed for contrast. This is an effective way of drawing attention to one main statement in opposition to another.

One of our current problems is that we cannot decide *if the end justifies the means* or *the means justifies the end.*

Sentence Variety

As you might realize from what we have said so far, sentence variety is not some arbitrary prettiness which you impose on your writing. Variety grows from two things:

The emphasis you put on the main statements in your sentences through subordination and modification

The relationship of the structure of one sentence to those around it

Sentence variety then is a function of grammar and structure, but to the good writer, it is not a matter of theory. You can develop an *eye,* an *ear,* and even a *feeling* for a good sentence *as you write it.*

Whole Sentences

■ *The visual aspects of sentence variety* have to do with the length of sentences. Plainly, sentences that are too long demand constant flitting back and forth of the eyes as you read. Readers want sentences to be economical, especially in expository writing. They also expect a certain variation between short, long, and middle-sized sentences. So journalists, not wanting to risk losing their readers, rarely carry on for more than a couple of lines.

Yet it is not the actual length of a sentence that is important, for there is no perfect or ideal length. Length is relative to what must be said. All that is desirable is that in the interests of varying the *pace* and *rhythm* of your sentences, you vary the length somewhat. Note how Orwell does this in the paragraph quoted at the opening of this chapter.

■ If you read your sentences aloud and listen to the way they accumulate meaning, *you will develop an ear* for sentence structure. Nothing reveals an overly complex sentence more clearly than such a reading. You get used to the sound of your sentences in your mind's ear as you write them. Unless you jolt yourself into hearing them as they might sound to a reader, *as you go along,* you may be missing some important variations that could be introduced. This need not wait till the revision process, though it will be repeated then. Develop an ear for the *rhythms* of your sentences as you write. Immediately break up any long, ungainly constructions. Stop and reread frequently.

■ Finally, *you develop a feeling* for the way you construct sentences, for the density and texture of your writing. After a while you will know whether your writing tends to have too many, or too few, or just the right number of ideas in it, and whether your explanation is usually adequate. You should think of your own needs in dealing with a subject as well as those of your audience and develop a *typical* style for handling ideas. It is important to *evenly pace* your writing, not to move too fast and too slow alternately, but to let ideas emerge in a varied but thoughtful rhythm. The writer has to create congenial conditions for reading, and few things are more uncongenial than prose that is too dense or too light.

Developing a Style

Clearly, sentence variety does not become an issue until you have passed through all the other stages of the writing process: the preparation of ideas, the decisions about tone and audience, and the development of all this in concise and coherent paragraphs and sentences. Remember that a variety of good ideas makes it easier to develop a variety of sentences about those good ideas. But now let's summarize the ways in which you can develop a style as you write. All these points are worth remembering as you finally check over your essay, but try to be conscious of the need for variety as you write even your first draft. Revising as you write for stylistic traits will not cripple your spontaneity but will allow you to handle ideas more clearly.

■ *Vary the relationship between free and bound elements within the sentence.* You will achieve a greater variety in sentence construction if you allow free elements to develop. Think especially in terms of modifying phrases and clauses that are unrestricted.

■ *Where possible, develop a balance between your ideas in parallel sentences.*

■ *Vary the direction your sentences take.* There are basically four kinds of sentences.

The periodic sentence builds up to its main point at the end:

There is little point in arguing about the good or bad musical qualities of modern rock, for, above all, *rock is an important ritual event.*

The pivoting sentence interrupts the main statement with some parenthetical modification, either a phrase or a clause, which can be placed between dashes:

Many of the local craftsmen—*especially the potters and jewelry makers*—exhibited at the Renaissance Fair.

The cumulative sentence begins with the main statement and builds on it:

Literature has everything to do with life, even if sometimes, in those very personal moments when we see things all too clearly, it is hard to tell each apart.

The balanced sentence contains some kind of coordination, parallelism, or antithesis between two main statements:

Let not your heart be troubled nor *your mind disturbed.*

■ *Vary the length of your sentences,* so that the rhythm has some variety.

■ *Vary the levels of density within your sentences.* You will recall that earlier we discussed the use of modifying phrases or clauses to create a layered effect in your sentences. Here is part of a paragraph from Northrop Frye's *Educated Imagination* which shows you how effective layered expository writing can be. All the main statements and their bound elements have been underlined.

1. In all our literary experience <u>there are two kinds of response</u>.

  2. <u>There is the direct experience of the work itself</u>, while we're reading a book or seeing a play, especially for the first time.
     3. <u>This experience is uncritical</u>, or rather pre-critical, so <u>it's not infallible</u>.
     3. If our experience is limited, <u>we can be roused to enthusiasm or carried away by something that we can later see to have been second-rate or even phony</u>.

  2. <u>Then there is the conscious, critical response</u> we make after we've finished reading or left the theater, where we compare what we've experienced with other things of the same kind, and form a judgment of value and proportion on it.
     3. <u>This critical response</u>, with practice, <u>gradually makes our pre-critical responses more sensitive and accurate, or improves our taste</u>, as we say.
     3. But behind our responses to individual works, <u>there's a bigger response to our literary experience as a whole</u>, as a total possession.

Now this is a paragraph that begins with a theme sentence. Frye then supports the theme sentence with two examples (making it a paragraph that also gives examples or illustrations). Each illustration is supported by two sentences that further modify the examples. Each example is introduced by a *there is* . . . construction and is followed by a sentence directly modifying it, beginning with *This* and a main clause. There is a clear contrast between the two kinds of literary response, and you'll note that Frye is careful to balance his explanations. The first response is perhaps rather easier to explain than the second, but he does not upset the antithesis.

If we move from the structure of the whole paragraph to the structure and variety of the sentences, we can see that Frye is not so predictable. The overall shape of the paragraph is neatly balanced and carefully shaped, but each sentence tends to balance the other with some free modifying elements providing some variety. Compare, for example, each of the sentences carrying Frye's statements about the two responses to literature:

There is the direct experience of the work itself, *[main clause]* while we're reading a book *[adverbial clause]*, or [we are] seeing a play *[adverbial clause]*, especially for the first time *[adverbial phrase]*.

Then there is the conscious, critical response *[main clause]* *[which]* we make *[adjectival clause]* after we've finished reading *[adverbial clause]* or left the theater *[adverbial clause]*, where we compare what we've experienced with other things of the same kind *[adjectival clause containing a noun clause]* and *[where we]* form a judgment of value and proportion on it *[adjectival clause]*.

There is no need to diagram all the remaining sentences. Note that at least half this information-packed, directly expressed paragraph comprises free elements modifying the main statements *and* carefully contrasting each other at the same time. So this is an example of ordered and yet remarkably free-flowing prose which is not only a pleasure to read but which says all it has to say most efficiently.

■ *Make sure you have enough pauses within your sentences.* As Frederick Crews wisely points out, "pauses, not clauses, make for a sense of adequate complexity."[2] That might be a slight overstatement, but the point is a very important one. There is nothing more irritating for the reader than to have to deal with staccato-like sentences that simply list assertions or ramble on with little interest in adequate subordination. It is not enough to have all the information present. You have to express it in an interesting way. *So be kind to your reader,* who must have time to breathe between ideas. Pause and let a point sink in. Notice how Northrop Frye achieves this with his development of multileveled sentences *(especially for the first time* and *as we say)* and his use of the modifying clause.

You can be thoughtful of your reader by allowing for adequate subordination and interruption in the development of your sentences. Pauses are created by the use of single words like *however,* or by free phrases, or even by unrestricted clauses. But note also that if you have prepared your argument well and understand the *relationship between your ideas,* you stand a much better chance of creating easily paced sentences that make their point with elegance as well as strength.

Checklist

1. Every sentence should carry a clear main statement.
2. Make direct assertions wherever possible.
3. Emphasize your main statements by contrasting them with subordinate elements.
4. Focus on verbs rather than nouns.

   Focus on active rather than passive verbs.

   Avoid using the verb *to be* as a weak linking verb.

   Avoid weak, overworked verbs like *do, got, have, make, put, feel, give, hold, go, mean, come,* and *take.*

2. Frederick Crews, *The Random House Handbook,* 3rd ed. (New York: Random House, 1980).

Avoid awkward constructions like *it is, there are, the thing is, what this means is that, what I want to say is that, the result is that, the reason is that, the value is that, the meaning is that.*

Use positive forms of the verb rather than the negative.

Use precise, economical adjectives and adverbs.

5. Create emphasis by using free modifying elements, phrases, and clauses in contrast with bound elements.

6. Place free elements adjacent to the item they modify, carefully avoiding ambiguity.

7. Place free elements first if they set conditions for the main statement.

8. Use modifying words like *however, nevertheless,* and so on (sparingly) to create pauses.

9. If two actions or ideas are equal, balance them in a parallel sentence. If two actions are unequal, subordinate the weaker to the stronger.

10. Create emphasis by

Varying the *length* of sentences

Varying the *density* of sentences through the placement of free and bound elements

Varying the *direction* of sentences, which can be periodic, cumulative, balanced, and pivoting

Creating pauses and breath stops within the sentence

Exercises

1. Rewrite these sentences so that all traces of awkwardness and weak emphasis are removed.

a. Cooking Italian food is the fun activity of many people.

b. He wanted to know if I was a supporter of the Democratic party.

c. You do not like me, so why not come out and say what you think?

d. Do you think that if I got more exercise my legs would feel bet-better?

e. Arriving late means that you will miss the plane that would give you direct passage to New York.

f. I don't know how anyone with even the smallest amount of intelligence could fail to see that the budget won't be balanced properly by 1984 no matter what we do.

g. If you were liked by the talent scout then why didn't you get hired by him?

h. Necessity makes studying grammar an important exercise.

i. We were much disliked by the crowds at our last game.

j. What an absolutely inconceivably imbecilic act of crass incompetence the builder showed by forgetting to insulate the walls.

k. The meaning of this book is that white males are not to be trifled with.

l. I do not agree that you should put this highly desirable car on the market which is plainly in the worst doldrums, when you could wait till the price gets better.

m. Do not say you won't come for we need you badly though perhaps not so badly that we can't do without you.

n. I want to hold a meeting before it comes to popular knowledge that I am getting away with little work as chairman of the board.

o. No fair lady was ever won by a faint heart.

p. You are a student of the humanities, so take more history.

q. It is perfectly clear that you have no intention of cooking me dinner but at least there is one consolation for me in that you will give me a drink.

r. The thing is that he doesn't know how to sail, so what's the point of taking him on the cruise?

s. You can't avoid the criticism that you weren't at practice and the reason is that everyone is fed up with your lack of interest.

t. The advantage of this project is that it will support out-of-work teachers.

2. For each of the following short paragraphs,
   a. Identify all the main clauses
   b. Indicate the phrases and subordinate clauses and identify the first three of each

When Picasso bought ''La Californie,'' though he had seen it only by twilight, he realised that its most precious asset to him, in addition to its nearness to Vallauris, was the light that penetrates into every corner of the house. He was happy at once in the luminous atmosphere of the lofty rooms, and as he had done before, he began to paint pictures inspired by the objects that lay around and the tall windows with their art nouveau tracery, through which a yellow-green light is filtered by the branches of the palm trees. Day after day he saw his studio anew. Sometimes the main feature to be placed in the composition was Jacqueline seated in a rocking-chair in front of stacked canvases on which could be seen former versions of the same studio. In other paintings the pattern of the windows dominated everything, towering high like a cathedral nave; or again cool recesses led the eye deep into the picture, past chairs, sculptures, easels and the Moorish charcoal-burner which looked like another relic of Matisse.

Robert Penrose, from **PICASSO**

It is impossible to escape the impression that people commonly use false standards of measurement—that they seek power, success and wealth for themselves and admire them in others, and that they underestimate what is of true value in life. And yet, in making any general judgement of this sort, we are in danger of forgetting how variegated the human world and its mental life are. There are a few men from whom their contemporaries do not withhold admiration, although their greatness rests on attributes and achievements which are completely foreign to the aims and ideals of the multitude. One might easily be inclined to suppose that it is after all only a minority which appreciates these great men, while the large majority cares nothing for them. But things are probably not as simple as that, thanks to the discrepancies between people's thoughts and their actions, and to the diversity of their wishful impulses.

Sigmund Freud, from **CIVILIZATION AND ITS DISCONTENTS**

What I have most wanted to do throughout the past ten years is to make political writing into an art. My starting point is always a feeling of partisanship, a sense of injustice. When I sit down to write a book, I do not say to myself, "I am going to produce a work of art." I write it because there is some lie that I want to expose, some fact to which I want to draw attention, and my initial concern is to get a hearing. But I could not do the work of writing a book, or even a long magazine article, if it were not also an aesthetic experience. Anyone who cares to examine my work will see that even when it is downright propaganda it contains much that a full-time politician would consider irrelevant. I am not able, and I do not want, completely to abandon the world-view that I acquired in childhood. So long as I remain alive and well I shall continue to feel strongly about prose style, to love the surface of the earth, and to take a pleasure in solid objects and scraps of useless information. It is no use trying to suppress that side of myself. The job is to reconcile my ingrained likes and dislikes with the essentially public, non-individual activities that this age forces on all of us.

George Orwell, from "**WHY I WRITE**" . . .

3. Combine the following statements into groups of sentences—*as few sentences as you can in each*—that are carefully subordinated and contain as many free elements as are needed for variety. That is, some of the statements *can* be shortened into free elements. For example:

There is a very old covered bridge near the town. It has been there for sixty years. The bridge is in a state of bad disrepair. It spans the Onawaga River. It is wide enough for only one car. It is the property of the state. The state historical trust wants to buy it and repair it. The state historical trust wants to get it back to full use.

A sixty-year-old covered bridge, wide enough for only one car and in bad state of disrepair, spans the Onawaga River near the town. The bridge is the property of the state, and the state historical trust wants to buy it and repair it in order to get it back into full use.

a. Thousands of travelers go each year to Europe from America. Most travelers prefer Western Europe. Britain is a popular spot. There are no language problems in Britain. France is a favorite for its good food and wine and marvelous cathedrals. People like Spain for the sun and old castles. The Greek Islands are famous for their beaches and unspoiled terrain. Italian cities are hectic but stimulating. There are many wonderful buildings and museums in Italy. There are fairy-tale castles in Germany. Swiss scenery is charming. The Dutch people are very friendly.

b. John Sullivan is an American journalist. This is a true story. Sullivan is missing in El Salvador. Sullivan disappeared in December 1980. Eight foreign journalists have died covering the civil war in El Salvador. Sullivan is the only American journalist missing. His relatives think that he is probably dead. Two people have said that they saw Sullivan interrogated by the military.

c. There were many large family-owned book publishers in New York and Boston. Many giant corporations have taken over these publishing houses. Many independent booksellers are going out of business. Computers analyze sales and profits and determine what the large chains should carry. Book production costs have risen enormously. First-book authors have little chance of getting published. The IRS will not allow publishers to take a tax write-off for unsold books. Some publishers refuse to allow booksellers to return books. Booksellers must buy fewer books. Few books by an unknown author are bought. The trend is to best-selling mass-market material.

d. We are obsessed with the idea of genius. We want intellectual and artistic heroes. The idea is a Romantic one. The Romantic Movement was a revolt of the individual. Geniuses are those apart from the bland, ordinary masses. Geniuses are indifferent to what the public thinks. Many modern artists would rather be geniuses than craftsmen. Craftsmen just make things. Geniuses blaze new trails. Do we have any real artistic geniuses today? Geniuses are made by their contexts and environments, not by themselves. Geniuses are just super versions of the norm.

4. Here are some main statements. Develop the ideas or describe the qualities of each one so that you write a complete sentence with at least one bound and one free element to create greater emphasis.

Identify each element by using the abbreviations FE (free element) and BE (bound element).

Example

The cat sat on the mat.

FE	BE

Purring softly to itself, the cat *with the long white fur* sat

BE

quietly on the mat.

a. The president flew to the disaster area.
b. You can win a fortune in this sweepstake.
c. Variety is the spice of life.
d. The film lasted for five hours.
e. One good turn deserves another.
f. Let the trumpets sound.
g. Mankind cannot bear very much reality.
h. Would you buy a used car from this man?
i. All good things must come to an end.
j. If the shoe fits, wear it.

5. Develop a balanced, parallel, or subordinated sentence out of these statements, whichever is most appropriate for emphatic effect.

Example:

The snow was powder. The snow was deep. I chose this slope.
I chose this slope because the snow was deep powder.

a. This university will be here in one hundred years. The town will have grown large enough for two universities.
b. You did not arrive in time to catch the first show. I did not arrive in time to catch the first show.
c. Camels. Dates. Oases. Pyramids. Everything is exotic. Visit Egypt.
d. The sunset was beautiful. We stared in awe.
e. It rains. It shines. We will plant the garden tomorrow.
f. The jacket is too long. The sleeves are too short. Return it.
g. The birds sang songs. The songs were about birds. An evening of ornithological music under the stars.
h. The medicine man leads people into a world of jungle animals. Men become boars. They eat manioc root. Realistic behavior?
i. The lights were hot. The music was fast. The grease paint ran.
j. Truth is stranger than fiction. Fiction these days is strange enough.

6. For each of the three paragraphs that follow,
a. Comment on the sentence variety
b. Diagram the paragraph (as shown in this chapter), revealing the layering of main statements and subordinating elements
c. Name the first four kinds of free elements in each paragraph

But the desire signified the victory of his adolescent vigor and sensuality and the first intimation of the mighty forces of life, and the pain signified that the morning peace had been broken, that his soul had left that childhood land which can never be found again. His small fragile ship had barely escaped a near disaster; now it entered a region of new storms and uncharted depths through which even the best-led adolescent cannot find a trust-worthy guide. He must find his own way and be his own savior.

Herman Hesse, from BENEATH THE WHEEL

I have so many plans that I hardly dare to undertake them alone—you would soon enough make out what they are, what they mean. Though I wish it were not so, I am extremely sensitive as to what is said of my work, as to what impression I make personally. If I meet with distrust, if I stand alone, I feel a certain void which cripples my initiative. Now, you would be just the person to understand it—I don't want the least flattery, or that people should say "I like it," if they did not; no, what I want is an intelligent sincerity, which is not vexed by failures. Which, if a thing fails six times, just when I begin to lose courage, would say: now you must try again a seventh time. You see, that's the encouragement I need, and cannot do without. And I think you would understand it, and you would be an enormous help to me.

Vincent van Gogh, from LETTERS

In the harsh world of Attica before the uprising, Dr. Williams in fact had spent most of his time with inmates separated from them by a wire screen. When they lined up for sick call, he and an associate prison doctor, Paul G. Sternberg, were on the other side of a waist-high counter; the screen ran from the counter to the ceiling. No examinations were given, except in rare cases. The patient described his problem. Through the screen the doctor gave him medication, often aspirin, sometimes a placebo, not infrequently a tranquilizer if the complaint was psychological. Sometimes one of the doctors would dismiss the complaining inmate since both believed they could tell by looking at a man whether he was malingering. Cases judged serious enough could be treated in the 26-bed infirmary. If necessary, men could be sent to outside hospitals, usually Meyer Memorial in Buffalo. In the prison, there were no special diet facilities, no rehabilitation or withdrawal programs for drug addicts, and psychiatric help was so limited in comparison to need as to have been virtually useless. Attempts at group therapy programs invariably foundered for lack of time, facilities, and personnel. Only dental care was anywhere near adequate at Attica in September 1971.

Tom Wicker, from **A TIME TO DIE**

Readings

M. F. K. Fisher **LET THE SKY RAIN POTATOES**

"Most important, however, is the potato's function as a gastronomic complement. It is this that should be considered, to rob it of its dangerous monotony, and clothe it with the changing mysterious garment of adaptability."

Anthony Brandt **RITE OF PASSAGE**

"The whole thing had been a subtle act of violence, a violation of the sensibilities, made all the worse by the fact that I knew it wasn't really her fault, that she was a victim of biology, of life itself. Hard knowledge for a boy just turned fourteen. She became the color of all my expectations."

LET THE SKY RAIN POTATOES

M. F. K. Fisher

There are two questions which can easily be asked about a potato: What is it, and Why is it?

Both these questions are irritating to a true amateur. The answers to the first are self-evident: a potato is a food, delicious, nourishing, and so on. The second question is perhaps too impertinent even to be answered, although many a weary housewife has felt like shouting it to the high heavens if her family has chanced to be the kind that takes for granted the daily appearance of this ubiquitous vegetable.

A dictionary will say that a potato is a farinaceous tuber used for food. An encyclopædia will cover eight or nine large pages with a sad analysis of its origins, modes of cultivation, and diseases, some of which are enough in themselves to discourage any potato enthusiast who might read them carefully.

Between these two extremes of definition is a story interesting even to one who is not overly fond of potatoes as a food. There are romance and colour, and the fine sound of brave names in its telling.

In Peru, the Spanish found *papas* growing in the early 1500's, and the monk Hieronymus Cardán took them back with him to his own people. The Italians liked them, and then the Belgians.

About that time, Sir Walter Raleigh found a potato in the American South, and carried it back to his estate near Cork. Some say it was a yam he had, thought strongly aphrodisiac by the Elizabethans. Some say it was a white potato. A German statue thanks Raleigh for bringing it to Europe. On the other hand, the Spanish claim recognition for its European introduction.

No matter what its origin, eat it, eat it, urged the British Royal Society. But for many decades its cultivation made but little progress.

By the time it had become important as a food, especially for poor people, its diseases also had matured, and in 1846 potato blight sent thousands of hungry Irishmen to their graves, or to America.

Warts and scabs and rusts and rots did their work, too, and men worked hard to breed new varieties of potatoes before newer plagues seized them. Great Scott, the Boston Comrade, Magnum Bonum, Rhoderick Dhu and Up-to-Date, Ninetyfold: these and many hundreds more filled pots around the world, and still do.

But no matter the name; a spud's a spud, and by any other name it would still be starchy, and covered with dusty cork for skin, and, what's worse, taken for granted on every blond-head's table.

If the men are darker, it is pastes in slender strings they'll eat, or tubes, always farinaceous, as the dictionary says; but more often on Anglo-Saxon fare the potato takes place before any foreign macaroni or spaghetti.

It is hard sometimes to say why. A potato is good when it is cooked correctly.

Baked slowly, with its skin rubbed first in a buttery hand, or boiled in its jacket and then "shook," it is delicious. Salt and pepper are almost always necessary to its hot moist-dusty flavour. Alone, or with a fat jug of rich cool milk or a chunk of fresh Gruyère, it fills the stomach and the soul with a satisfaction not too easy to attain.

In general, however, a potato is a poor thing, poorly treated. More often than not it is cooked in so unthinking and ignorant a manner as to make one feel that it has never before been encountered in the kitchen, as when avocados were sent to the Cornish Mousehole by a lady who heard months later that their suave thick meat had been thrown away and the stones boiled and boiled to no avail.

"Never have I tasted such a poor, flaccid, grey sad mixture of a mess," says my mother when she tells of the potatoes served in Ireland. And who would contradict her who has ever seen the baked-or-boiled in a London Lyons or an A.B.C.?

The Irish prefer them, evidently, to starvation, and the English, too. And in mid-western Europe, in a part where dumplings grow on every kitchen-range, there are great cannon balls of them, pernicious as any shrapnel to a foreign palate, but swallowed like feathery egg-whites by the natives.

They are served with goose at Christmas, and all around the year. They are the size of a toddling child's round head. They are grey, and exceedingly heavy. They are made painstakingly of grated raw potato, moulded, then boiled, then added to by moulding, then boiled again. Layer after layer is pressed on, cooked, and cooled, and finally the whole sodden pock-marked mass is bounced in bubbling goose broth until time to heave it to the platter.

Forks may bend against its iron-like curves, stomachs may curdle in a hundred gastric revolutions; a potato dumpling is more adamantine. It survives, and is served to ever-renewing decades of hungry yodelling mouths.

In itself, this always fresh desire for starch, for the potato, is important. No matter what its form, nor its national disguise, the appetite for it is there, impervious to the mandates of dictators or any other blight.

Perhaps its most insidious manifestation is that Anglo-Saxons take it for granted. A meal for them includes potatoes in some form; it always has, therefore it always will. And no revolt, no smouldering rebellion of the meal-planner, can change this smug acceptance.

Most important, however, is the potato's function as a gastronomic complement. It is this that should be considered, to rob it of its dangerous monotony, and clothe it with the changing mysterious garment of adaptability.

Although few realize it, to be complementary is in itself a compliment. It is a subtle pleasure, like the small exaltation of a beautiful dark woman who finds herself unexpectedly in the company of an equally beautiful blonde. It is what a great chef meant once when he repulsed a consolation.

He was a Frenchman, summoned to London when King Edward VII found that his subjects resented his dining more in Paris than at home.

This great cook one day prepared a dish of soles in such a manner that the guests at Edward's table waited assuredly for a kingly compliment. He was summoned. Their mouths hung open in sated expectation.

"The Château Yquem," said Edward VII, "was excellent."

Later the master chef shrugged, a nonchalance denied by every muscle in his pleased face.

"How could my dish have had a greater compliment?" he demanded, calmly. "His Majesty knows, as I do, that when a dish is perfect, as was my sole to-night, the wine is good. If the dish is lower than perfection, the wine, lacking its complement, tastes weak and poor. So—you see?"

Although there are few ways of preparing potatoes to make them approach the perfection of a royal plate of fish, and none I know of to make them worth the compliment of a bottle of Château Yquem, they in their own way are superlative complements. And it is thus, as I have said, that they should be treated.

If, French fried, they make a grilled sirloin of beef taste richer; if, mashed and whipped with fresh cream and salty butter, they bridge the deadly gap between a ragôut and a salad; if, baked and pinched open and bulging with mealy snowiness, they offset the fat spiced flavour of a pile of sausages—then and then alone should they be served.

Then they are dignified. Then they are worthy of a high place, not debased to the deadly rank of daily acceptance. Then they are a gastronomic pleasure, not merely "tubers used for food."

1. As Fisher notes, the potato is generally considered to be "a poor thing." Comment on the style with which she writes about so supposedly insignificant an object. Is it appropriate to her subject? Why or why not?

2. Do you still consider the potato a poor thing after you have read this essay? Explain your answer.

3. The next-to-last paragraph of this essay consists of but a single sentence. Reread it; then analyze how Fisher has constructed it. What is the effect?

4. Choose any object that might, like the potato, be considered a poor thing and write a brief essay about it. You need not follow Fisher's style exclusively, but your style should lend humor and flair to your subject.

RITE OF PASSAGE

Anthony Brandt

Some things that happen to us can't be borne, with the paradoxical result that we carry them on our backs the rest of our lives. I have been half obsessed for almost thirty years with the death of my grandmother. I should say with her dying: with the long and terrible changes that came at the worst time for a boy of twelve and thirteen, going through his own difficult changes. It felt like and perhaps was the equivalent of a puberty rite: dark, frightening, aboriginal, an obscure emotional exchange between old and young. It has become part of my character.

I grew up in New Jersey in a suburban town where my brother still lives and practices law. One might best describe it as quiet, protected, and green; it was no preparation for death. Tall, graceful elm trees lined both sides of the street where we lived. My father's brother-in-law, a contractor, built our house; we moved into it a year after I was born. My grandmother and grandfather (my mother's parents; they were the only grandparents who mattered) lived up the street "on the hill"; it wasn't much of a hill, the terrain in that part of New Jersey being what it is, but we could ride our sleds down the street after it snowed, and that was hilly enough.

Our family lived, or seemed to a young boy to live, in very stable, very ordinary patterns. My father commuted to New York every day, taking the Jersey Central Railroad, riding in cars that had windows you could open, getting off the train in Jersey City and taking a ferry to Manhattan. He held the same job in the same company for more than thirty years. The son of Swedish immigrants, he was a funny man who could wiggle his ears without raising his eyebrows and made up the most dreadful puns. When he wasn't being funny he was quiet, the newspaper his shield and companion, or the *Saturday Evening Post,* which he brought home without fail every Wednesday evening, or *Life,* which he brought home Fridays. It was hard to break through the quiet and the humor, and after he died my mother said, as much puzzled as disturbed, that she hardly knew him at all.

She, the backbone of the family, was fierce, stern, the kind of person who can cow you with a glance. My brother and I, and my cousins, were all a little in awe of her. The ruling passion in her life was to protect her family; she lived in a set of concentric circles, sons and husband the closest, then nieces, nephews, brothers, parents, then more distant relatives, and outside that a few friends, very few. No one and nothing else existed for her; she had no interest in politics, art, history, or even the price of eggs. "Fierce" is the best word for her, or single-minded. In those days (I was born in 1936) polio was every parent's bugbear; she, to keep my brother and me away from places where the disease was supposed to be communicated, particularly swimming pools, took us every summer for the entire summer to the Jersey shore, first to her parents' cottage, later to a little cottage she and my father bought. She did that even though it meant being separated from my father for nearly three months, having nobody to talk to, having to handle my brother and me on her own. She hated it, she told us years later, but she did it: fiercely. Or there's the story of one of my cousins who got pregnant when she was sixteen or seventeen; my mother took her into our house, managed somehow to hide her condition from the neighbors, then, after the birth, arranged privately to have the child adopted by a family the doctor recommended, all this being done without consulting the proper authorities, and for the rest of her life never told a single person how she made these arrangements or where she had placed the child. She was a genuine primitive, like some tough old peasant woman. Yet her name was Grace, her nickname Bunny; if you saw through the fierceness, you understood that it was a version of love.

Her mother, my grandmother, seemed anything but fierce. One of our weekly routines was Sunday dinner at their house on the hill, some five or six houses from ours. When I was very young, before World War II, the house had a mansard roof, a barn in the back, lots of yard space, lots of rooms inside, and a cherry tree. I thought it was a palace. Actually it was rather small, and became smaller when my grandmother insisted on tearing down the mansard roof and replacing it with a conventional peaked roof; the house lost three attic rooms in the process. Sunday dinner was invariably roast beef or chicken or leg of lamb with mashed potatoes and vegetables, standard American fare but cooked by my grandparents' Polish maid, Josephine, not by my grandmother. Josephine made wonderful pies in an old cast-iron coal stove and used to let me tie her with string to the kitchen sink. My grandfather was a gentle man who smoked a pipe, had a bristly reddish moustache, and always seemed to wind up paying everybody else's debts in the family; my mother worshipped him. There were usually lots of uncles at these meals, and they were a playful bunch. I have a very early memory of two of them tossing me back and forth between them, and another of the youngest, whose name was Don, carrying me on his shoulders into the surf. I also remember my grandmother presiding at these meals. She was gray-haired and benign.

Later they sold that house. My benign grandmother, I've been told since, was in fact a restless, unsatisfied woman; changing the roof line, moving from house to house, were her ways of expressing that dissatisfaction. In the next house, I think it was, my grandfather died; my grandmother moved again, then again, and then to a house down the street, at the bottom of the hill this time, and there I got to know her better. I was nine or ten years old. She let me throw a tennis ball against the side of the house for hours at a time; the noise must have been terribly aggravating. She cooked lunch for me and used to make pancakes the size of dinner plates, and corn fritters. She also made me a whole set of yarn figures a few inches long, rolling yarn around her hand, taking the roll and tying off arms, legs, and a head, then sewing a face onto the head with black thread. I played with these and an odd assortment of hand-me-down toy soldiers for long afternoons, setting up wars, football games, contests of all kinds, and designating particular yarn figures as customary heroes. Together we played a spelling game: I'd be on the floor playing with the yarn figures, she'd be writing a letter and ask me how to spell "appreciate" (it was always that word), and I'd spell it for her while she pretended to be impressed with my spelling ability and I pretended that she hadn't asked me to spell that same word a dozen times before. I was good, too, at helping her find her glasses.

One scene at this house stands out. My uncle Bob came home from the war and the whole family, his young wife, other uncles, my mother and father and brother and I, gathered at the house to meet him, and he came in wearing his captain's uniform and looking to me, I swear it, like a handsome young god. In fact he was an ordinary man who spent the rest of his life selling insurance. He had been in New Guinea, a ground officer in the Air Corps, and the story I remember is of the native who came into his tent one day and took a great deal of interest in the scissors my uncle was using. The native asked in pidgin English what my uncle would require for the scissors in trade, and he jokingly said, well, how about a tentful of bananas. Sure enough, several days later two or three hundred natives came out of the jungle, huge bunches of bananas on their shoulders, and filled my uncle's tent.

Things went on this way for I don't know how long, maybe two years, maybe three. I don't want to describe it as idyllic. Youth has its problems. But this old woman who could never find her glasses was wonderful to me, a grandmother in the true likeness of one, and I couldn't understand the changes when they came. She moved again, against all advice, this time to a big, bare apartment on the other side of town. She was gradually becoming irritable and difficult, not much fun to be around. There were no more spelling games; she stopped writing letters. Because she moved I saw her less often, and her home could no longer be a haven for me. She neglected it, too; it grew dirtier and dirtier, until my mother eventually had to do her cleaning for her.

Then she began to see things that weren't there. A branch in the back yard became a woman, I remember, who apparently wasn't fully clothed, and a man was doing something to her, something unspeakable. She developed diabetes and my mother learned to give her insulin shots, but she wouldn't stop eating candy, the worst thing for her, and the diabetes got worse. Her face began to change, to slacken, to lose its shape and character. I didn't understand these things; arteriosclerosis, hardening of the arteries, whatever the explanation, it was only words. What I noticed was that her white hair was getting thinner and harder to control, that she herself seemed to be shrinking even as I grew, that when she looked at me I wasn't sure it was me she was seeing anymore.

After a few months of this, we brought her to live with us. My mother was determined to take care of her, and certain family pressures were brought to bear too. That private man my father didn't like the idea at all, but he said nothing, which was his way. And she was put in my brother's bedroom over the garage, my brother moving in with me. It was a small house, six rooms and a basement, much too small for what we had to face.

What we had to face was a rapid deterioration into senile dementia and the rise from beneath the surface of this smiling, kindly, white-haired old lady of something truly ugly. Whenever she was awake she called for attention, calling, calling a hundred times a day. Restless as always, she picked the bedclothes off, tore holes in sheets and pillows, took off her nightclothes and sat naked talking to herself. She hallucinated more and more frequently, addressing her dead husband, a dead brother, scolding, shouting at their apparitions. She became incontinent and smeared feces on herself, the furniture, the walls. And always calling—''Bunny, where are you? Bunny, I want you!''—scolding, demanding; she could seldom remember what she wanted when my mother came. It became an important event when she fell asleep; to make sure she stayed asleep the radio was kept off, the four of us tiptoed around the house, and when I went out to close the garage door, directly under her window (it was an overhead door and had to be pulled down), I did it so slowly and carefully, half an inch at a time, that it sometimes took me a full fifteen minutes to get it down.

That my mother endured this for six months is a testimony to her strength and determination, but it was really beyond her and almost destroyed her health. My grandmother didn't often sleep through the night; she would wake up, yell, cry, a creature of disorder, a living *memento mori,* and my mother would have to tend to her. The house began to smell in spite of all my mother's efforts to keep my grandmother's room clean. My father, his peace gone, brooded in his chair behind his newspaper. My brother and I fought for *Lebensraum,* each of us trying to grow up in his own way. People avoided us. My uncles were living elsewhere— Miami, Cleveland, Delaware. My grandmother's two surviving sisters, who lived about ten blocks away, never came to see her. Everybody seemed to sense that something obscene was happening, and stayed away. Terrified, I stayed away, too. I heard my grandmother constantly, but in the six months she lived with us I think I went into her room only once. That was as my mother wished it. She was a nightmare, naked and filthy without warning.

After six months, at my father's insistence, after a night nurse had been hired and left, after my mother had reached her limits and beyond, my parents started looking for a nursing home, anyplace they could put her. It became a family scandal; the two sisters were outraged that my mother would consider putting her own mother in a home, there were telephone calls back and forth between them and my uncles, but of course the sisters had never come to see her themselves, and my mother never forgave them. One of my uncles finally came from Cleveland, saw what was happening, and that day they put my grandmother in a car and drove her off to the nearest state mental hospital. They brought her back the same day; desperate as they were, they couldn't leave her in hell. At last, when it had come time to go to the shore, they found a nursing home in the middle of the Pine Barrens, miles from anywhere, and kept her there for a while. That, too, proving unsatisfactory, they put her in a small nursing home in western New Jersey, about two hours away by car. We made the drive every Sunday for the next six months, until my grandmother finally died. I always waited in the car while my mother visited her. At the funeral I refused to go into the room for one last look at the body. I was afraid of her still. The whole thing had been a subtle act of violence, a violation of the sensibilities, made all the worse by the fact that I knew it wasn't really her fault, that she was a victim of biology, of life itself. Hard knowledge for a boy just turned fourteen. She became the color of all my expectations.

Life is savage, then, and even character is insecure. Call no man happy until he be dead, said the Greek lawgiver Solon. But what would a wise man say to this? In that same town in New Jersey, that town I have long since abandoned as too flat and too good to be true, my mother, thirty years older now, weighing in at ninety-two pounds, incontinent, her white hair wild about her head, sits strapped into a chair in another nursing home talking incoherently to her fellow patients and working her hands at the figures she thinks she sees moving around on the floor. It's enough to make stones weep to see this fierce, strong woman, who paid her dues, surely, ten times over, reduced to this.

Yet she is *cheerful.* This son comes to see her and she quite literally babbles with delight, introduces him (as her father, her husband—the connections are burnt out) to the aides, tells him endless stories that don't make any sense at all, and *shines,* shines with a clear light that must be her soul. Care and bitterness vanish in her presence. Helpless, the victim of numerous tiny strokes—"shower strokes," the doctors call them—that are gradually destroying her brain, she has somehow achieved a radiant serenity that accepts everything that happens and incorporates and transforms it.

Is there a lesson in this? Is some pattern larger than life working itself out; is this some kind of poetic justice on display, a mother balancing a grandmother, gods demonstrating reasons beyond our comprehension? It was a bitter thing to put her into that place, reeking of disinfectant, full of senile, dying old people, and I used to hate to visit her there, but as she has deteriorated she has also by sheer force of example managed to change my attitude. If she can be reconciled to all this, why can't I? It doesn't last very long, but after I've seen her, talked to her for half an hour, helped feed her, stroked her hair, I walk away amazed, as if I had been witness to a miracle.

1. Why does Brandt say his grandmother's death was a puberty rite for him?

2. Why did Brandt keep away from his grandmother's room when she moved into his house?

3. How did Brandt's own mother become an example to him?

4. At the opening of the essay, Brandt says, "Some things that happen to us can't be borne." Do you think he has managed to bear, or understand, or even explain the process of aging by the end of the essay?

5. How would you describe Brandt's style? Choose any one paragraph and analyze it, showing the layering of sentences and the free and bound elements within the sentences to support your argument.

Paragraphs

Paragraph Coherence

Theme and Variation

Each paragraph should have a clear development. It should accumulate meaning around its main assertion. Make sure, then, that each of your paragraphs has *one theme sentence and some supporting and modifying sentences,* that is, that each paragraph has a theme and variations on the theme. This is the main principle underlying the coherence of the paragraph, and it is created by the effort you put into your outline to make emphatic assertions and then to express support for them.

■ Your theme sentence is an assertion that you consider to be the main statement about your subject. Any other assertion either supports (or coordinates with) the theme assertion or modifies (or limits) it. Every successful paragraph has not only a clearly discernible theme sentence, but also strong supporting and modifying sentences.

■ There is one other kind of sentence you can find in a paragraph: the *transitional sentence,* which either begins or ends the paragraph (or you may have one at each end). It links directly to the last sentence of the previous paragraph or anticipates the first sentence of the next. Consider these paragraphs from the gun control essay (in final draft; see pp. 293–299), and note how the theme, support, modifying, and transitional sentences work together:

Transitional sentences

At first sight, these questions seem impossible to answer and have little in common. If you were to take them in isolation, they would *remain* difficult to answer. No one knows for sure if gun control would reduce

Supporting sentence

violence. But people do agree on something: the need to control deaths from gun-related crime. So instead of getting sidetracked by unanswer-

Theme sentence

able questions, let's consider the following issue: if gun control is a concept that makes any sense at all, can it control killings and burglaries involving handguns, *and* preserve our civil rights, specifically our right

Modifying sentence and transition

to bear arms for defense? It may seem as though we want to have it both ways by posing the question in this way, but let's see if we can make a compromise between the two sides.

Transitional sentence

The rightful context for this issue is not difficult to pin down. On the one hand, we have constitutional rights and the law; on the other, social

232

Modifying sentences

and psychological theory which tries to explain why we have violence. Let's discount the latter at this point in an attempt to reach a practical conclusion. It helps little to know, for example, that an assassin is insane. What is more important, after all, theory or protection? Instead we have a legal crisis: we are guaranteed the right to bear arms but find ourselves needing to be protected from those who do. Only the law can offer that

Supporting sentence

protection, for only the law has in common the interests of both the gun carrier and the person who refuses to bear arms. Psychological and

Theme sentence

sociological explanations of the violence that creates the need for hand-

Supporting sentence

guns must become part of the *legal* issue. For even if we can determine why handguns are associated with so much violence, we still have not solved the problem of whether we need gun control.

Placement of the Theme Sentence

The most important sentence in any paragraph is the theme sentence. Its placement determines what happens to the rest of the sentences in the paragraph, and that in turn affects the texture of your writing. Paragraphs that follow exactly the same pattern of construction (say, theme + modifying + support + transitional sentences) are likely to become very monotonous. No matter how good your ideas and how tight your argument, your reader will either be lulled to sleep by the repetitive rhythms of your writing or simply be irritated by the lack of variety. You may not think this is a problem in a short essay, but it is wise even there to introduce as much variety as you can into your paragraph structure.

Paragraph variety should not mean a loss of coherence, however. The questions you ask yourself about each of the perspectives you are taking on the topic (oppositions? connections? resolution?) are important for developing paragraphs. It seems unlikely that your conclusion will be convincing without some sense of the emphasis, coherence, and unity of your topic. But following this sequence does not necessarily mean that your theme sentence must always turn up at or near the end of the paragraph because resolution follows analysis. The theme sentence is last in the first sample paragraph above. In the first paragraph of the gun control essay, it comes near the beginning: "Yet the question of whether we should *control* the possession of handguns remains an open one." In the third paragraph, the theme sentence falls in the middle under *relationship* ("For the sake of argument, we will take the phrase 'gun control' to refer to the *federal* control...").

Your theme sentence is the sentence that carries the main idea of your paragraph. Its placement should be determined by the emphasis of the argument in each section. Sometimes the emphasis will fall on the *oppositions,* sometimes the *connections,* sometimes the *resolution.* This gives rise to three basic paragraph patterns:

Direct Paragraph Paragraphs may open with a theme sentence or with a transitional sentence. The effect is to get straight to the point. You have something you must say quickly. Usually the writer will want to make suggestions in the opening statement and will follow the main statement with either modifying or supporting sentences. (THEME + SUPPORTING/MODIFYING SENTENCES)

As Clifford Alexander has pointed out, if you are recruiting eighteen-year-olds, you are not going to get a lot of college graduates. The main reason there were more college men in the Army of the 1950s and 1960s was the student deferment program, which permitted them to finish their schooling before being eligible for the draft. Theoretically, today's Army might be getting the same kind of people a few years earlier—before they go to college, instead of after. But talking with soldiers, an outsider learns that many of them joined precisely because they did not have the money or the opportunity to go to college, and because there was no better job in sight.

James Fallows, from THE CIVILIZATION OF THE ARMY

Indirect Paragraph Paragraphs may lead up to a theme sentence located near the middle of the paragraph. This occurs when you have been considering contradictions and find in the relationship a firm emphasis which becomes the main idea. The pattern for this paragraph is the modifying + theme + supporting sentences. Note that you should not further limit the main idea once it is made. You should follow the theme sentence *only* by supporting sentences. (MODIFYING + THEME + SUPPORTING)

In 1980, of the 100,860 men who were serving their first term as enlistees in the "combat arms" of the Army—infantry, armor, artillery: the ones who fight—how many had degrees from any college, of any quality, anywhere in the United States? Twenty-five. Not 25 percent, but twenty-five people. There are nearly twice as many graduates on any forty-five-man team in the National Football League. Of the 340,000 enlisted men in the entire Army who in 1980 were serving their first term, a total of 276 had college degrees.

James Fallows, from THE CIVILIZATION OF THE ARMY

Suspended Paragraph Paragraphs may develop an explanation through oppositions and relationships (modifying and supporting sentences) and leave the theme sentence till the end of the paragraph. By delaying the main idea, the writer creates anticipation, and maybe even suspense, in the reader. The writer also aims to persuade by providing the information and analysis before the conclusion. (SUPPORTING/MODIFYING + THEME)

In 1964, the last year of the pre-Vietnam draft, 17 percent of all draftees had some college education, as did 14 percent of those who enlisted. In 1979, only 3 percent of men who joined the volunteer Army had ever been to college. In 1964, slightly more than one quarter of all draftees were high school dropouts. In 1979, 41 percent of the volunteer Army had not finished high school. Charles Moskos, a sociologist from Northwestern who served in the Army after graduating from Princeton in the 1950s, and who now spends much of his time traveling to bases and interviewing soldiers, points out that over the past fifteen years, a larger and larger percentage of the American young-adult population has managed to complete high school—the percentage increased from 66 in 1965 to 76 in 1977. He says, ''Thus, while the national trend has been toward a higher percentage of high school graduates, the percentage of graduates among Army enlistees has been dropping.''

James Fallows, from **THE CIVILIZATION OF THE ARMY**

The Implied Theme Sentence

There are times when a writer can create emphasis by *implication.* Something can go unsaid either because it is obvious or because its main idea can clearly be inferred from the information given. In the following paragraph, for example, the theme sentence might very well be something like: ''In the Spanish Civil War, the bombing of defenseless Guernica by the Germans with Franco's approval was a vicious, cowardly act which did not break the Basque spirit.'' But the author does not have to say that. His description is enough.

Guernica, with its ancient Basque oak and its traditions as the center of Basque rational spirit, was, in actuality, a small market town situated about twenty-three miles behind the battle lines. On Monday, April 26, 1937—a market day, when the town was crowded with farmers from miles around—the church bells of Guernica rang out at half-past four in the afternoon to announce the approach of enemy planes. A few minutes later Heinkel bombers, followed by Junker bombers, roared in over the town. After bombing it they turned to machine-gun the streets. Those who tried to run from the town were shot down on the roads by the Junkers. Both high explosive and incendiary bombs were dropped. Wave after wave of bombers passed over every twenty minutes for three hours. The entire center of the city was destroyed; over 1,600 people were killed and close to a thousand wounded. Miraculously, the Basque oak escaped damage.

Robert Goldston, from **THE CIVIL WAR IN SPAIN**

The implied theme sentence can be a powerful stylistic device, but be careful how you use it. Remember that even if you do not actually make a theme statement, the reader must be able to infer it from the supporting and modifying sentences. The theme sentence is not exactly absent; it simply goes unspoken because the information is otherwise clear.

Paragraph Variations

The three basic paragraph patterns—direct, indirect, and suspended—do not cover all possibilities. In order to state the relevance of your topic or evidence, for example, you will at times need to write paragraphs that not only *define* but *describe, classify,* and provide *illustration* and *analysis* of component parts, or an outline of the *process* by which something is done. When you examine the context of your topic, you may have to emphasize *classification* and *comparison, contrast* and *analogy.* When you consider the topic from the perspective of *cause-effect,* you may have to write the kind of paragraph that shows how some information moves from cause to effect or from effect to cause.

Definition

Defining a topic means trying to create the most precise, concise, and understandable statement you can about your topic for the purpose of establishing common ground between yourself and your audience. You can do this in three basic ways: by *denotation,* by *connotation,* and by *classification.*

Definition by Denotation This definition occurs when you define an event by its properties or by examples. So a *garden* can be defined as a collection of shrubs, flowers, lawn, trees, and vegetables, which can be either private or public. Some famous examples are the Portland rose gardens, the front garden at the White House, and the Versailles estate.
You may need to refer to a dictionary to make sure you know what your options are when you define denotatively. You look at your topic in isolation and say what its terms mean. Be careful not to make the references too personal, which is why it is useful to refer to a dictionary. This is not to say that you should simply quote a dictionary definition, nor does it mean that you can't invent a special limitation of the meaning. If

you do the latter, however, make sure that your definition is general enough to provide easy access to the topic by your reader.

When you define by denotation, you see an object as an item with distinguishing features, whether it is a concept, a feeling, an event, or a thing. You also see the item as a closed system in which these distinguishing features form a self-contained relationship. So if you were to define *university student,* you would offer a list of distinguishing features (such as male and female, age range, subjects taken, and so on). Then you would look at these characteristics as a closed system forming relationships among themselves (for example, is there a connection between sex and subjects taken? age and interests? financial background and major?). No matter what your topic is, you should ask *who? what?* and *where?* about it. These distinguishing features are indispensable for any definition. Here is an example of a typical paragraph based on a denotative definition:

> Writing, on the other hand, is a kind of premeditated speech. Even in its simplest form, it involves acute self-consciousness. Furthermore, it depends only upon itself. It does not take place in a person-to-person context. It must convey its message clearly and completely to one or more persons. Once edited, written material is inflexible. As we talk we are continually shading, correcting, expanding, bettering (or, it may be, worsening) our fluid statements. But written communication cannot rely on such assistance. To achieve its end, therefore, it uses a different set of tools: the disciplines of composition and the rules of syntax, grammar, spelling, punctuation, and paragraphing.
>
> Clifton Fadiman and James Howard, from **EMPTY PAGES**

Definition by Connotation   This kind of definition, as you might guess, is more imaginative and personal than the denotative definition. A connotative definition refers to synonyms and is usually interpretive, offering a particular perspective on a topic. For example, someone might denotatively (and with the use of annoying jargon) define *love* as "a function of pair-bonding." But a connotative definition of *love* might be "the feeling of mutual pleasure two people share in each other's company."

Definition by Classification   If the object is complex, it can be defined according to its properties, as we saw with the denotative definition. It can also be explained by referring to its class and the differences between the item and others in that class. So a *human* can be defined as belonging to the class of animal, but be considered as different from other animals in the capacity to reason. So a definition by classification of the term *human* might be "the rational animal."

A paragraph developing a denotative definition will usually fit the direct pattern. You begin with the definition and explain its properties. So, too, the definition by classification is usually carefully direct in its explanation. The connotative definition, however, is more flexible and can fit any of the patterns.

Description

One of the most common of all paragraph forms is that based on description of the evidence or topic. Here, for example, is a description of the book *The Double Helix,* which describes one of the most important of all scientific discoveries, the structure of DNA:

Considered as literature, *The Double Helix* will be classified under Memoirs, Scientific. No other book known to me can be so described. It will be an enormous success, and deserves to be so—a classic in the sense that it will go on being read. As with all good memoirs, a fair amount of it consists of trivialities and idle chatter. Like all good memoirs it has not been emasculated by considerations of good taste. Many of the things Watson says about the people in his story will offend them, but his own artless candor excuses him, for he betrays in himself faults graver than those he professes to discern in others. *The Double Helix* is consistent in literary structure. Watson's gaze is always directed outward. There is no philosophizing or psychologizing to obscure our understanding; Watson displays but does not observe himself. Autobiographies, unlike all other works of literature, are part of their own subject matter. Their lies, if any, are lies *of* their authors but not *about* their authors, who (when discovered in falsehood) merely reveal a truth about themselves, namely that they are liars. Although it sounds a bit too well remembered, Watson's scientific narrative strikes me as perfectly convincing. This is not to say that the apportionments of credits or demerits are necessarily accurate: that is something which cannot be decided in abstraction, but only after the people mentioned in the book have had their say, if they choose to have it. Nor will an intelligent reader suppose that Watson's judgments upon the character, motives, and probity of other people (sometimes apparently shrewd, sometimes obviously petty) are "true" simply because he himself believes them to be so.

Peter Medawar, from **LUCKY JIM**

The pattern of a descriptive paragraph can be of any kind, but it is often direct, like the one above. The writer opens with the theme statement and then proceeds to back it up by elaborating on the qualities of the object. Descriptive paragraphs, of course, tend to have a function similar to those that define.

Illustration

These paragraphs are sometimes described as exemplification paragraphs, for they contain examples which illustrate some general statement.

They are very often forms of the direct pattern, opening with a generalization, or law, or authoritative statement, and following that with a series of examples and a conclusion, either in the same paragraph or in the next.

Make sure that your generalization is clearly substantiated, and that you have reached it carefully by means of your outline so that you know it fits in with the rest of your argument. Then support the generalization with carefully chosen examples. The examples you offer are critical parts of the argument. In legal writing, for example, they are the precedents on which the argument is built. In expository writing, the example often makes clear a difficult concept or even provides the proof to a particular statement.

In writing an illustrative paragraph then, make your theme statement as clear and cogent as possible, reinforcing it by as many supporting or modifying sentences as are necessary. You may signal your examples by using such transitional words as *for example,* or *it follows that.* Here is an example of a paragraph aiming to illustrate:

Supporting sentence
Theme sentence

Supporting examples

We are now, of course, at the threshold of that special, eternally hospitable world that has been made in man's image by the so-called fine arts. That the fine arts have been willing to mirror the meanest of truths is well known: Oedipus blinds himself, and Medea murders her own children; Anna Karenina ends beneath the wheels of a train, and obsessed Ahab clings to the back of a monster; though Dante's Hell would seem to be full, Michelangelo continues to rain upon it a storm of stunned sinners; galleries can scarcely contain all the bloodied St. Sebastians; the orchestra must be expanded to accommodate Beethoven's cry.

Walter Kerr, from **The DECLINE OF PLEASURE**

Kerr's examples serve to illustrate the main statement in the paragraph. His examples from the fine arts reveal "the meanest of truths" but they are also examples of artistic order. Note that the list of examples is subtly arranged in pairs, one balancing the other (Oedipus-Medea; Anna Karenina-Ahab; Dante-Michelangelo) until Kerr changes the arrangement for the last two examples. Be careful to arrange your illustrations dramatically, pointing to a conclusion. Do not simply provide lists. In the above example, the reader is led to the climax of "Beethoven's cry."

Analysis

Analytic paragraphs have one direct purpose: to make the problematic simple by dividing a difficult concept or complex object into its component parts. Again, you most often find a direct pattern for analytic paragraphs, although they can be suspended. Concentrate on making a clear statement of what you are going to analyze and then account for the component parts.

The societies that grew up and flourished in Polynesia were all governed by a strict belief in two abstract dynamic forces: *mana* and *tapu*. *Mana* was believed to be an underlying power and vital force which was active in all things and could be controlled and acquired through careful training, contact and ritual. Animate as well as inanimate things were believed to have their own *mana,* but its strength varied greatly from one object to another. The method of judging the quality of a particular *mana* was through evidence of performance. Thus an adze that was particularly well balanced and easy to carve with, an especially seaworthy canoe or an unusually successful fishing lure all had greater *mana* than other things of only average efficiency. *Mana* as a human property was also measured in terms of performance.

Tapu was a closely related negative force which provided a great degree of religious and social control in Polynesian society. Anything which was declared *tapu* by priests, chiefs or ancient tradition was scrupulously avoided under the pain of a severe loss to one's own *mana,* or even death, if the transgression were serious enough. Actions, objects, places and people could all be designated *tapu,* as was contact with a person or object endowed with an especially great amount of *mana*. There were a series of complex rituals of purification throughout all of Polynesia which were directed at nullifying or avoiding a particular *tapu*. Careful education from specialists in the various vocations concerned rules of handling objects or correct approaches to people with strong *tapu,* and was given to all male members of each society.

Allen Wardwell, from **THE SCULPTURE OF POLYNESIA**

Process and Narrative

When you want to describe how to do something or how something is made or what has happened, you are describing the parts of an event that go to make up the whole (*process*). Or you may be describing events that follow a chronological sequence to create a unified action (*narrative*). You should first decide on the most significant parts or events and emphasize those, building up the relationship of the parts to the whole or following the step-by-step sequence of events. A clear description of relationships or sequential order should emerge in process and narrative paragraphs.

Narrative:

The day I left, Eddie, the alcoholic, came over to where I was cleaning out my bureau drawers. Eddie seemed to be living in the 1950's; he sported a crewcut, his slang was out of date. Was I leaving? he asked me. Yes. Could he have those oranges a friend had brought me? Of course. And then he gave me his advice. Move out of state, he said. That way they won't be able to get you in here again. Eddie was a sensitive person, very easily hurt. He would be talking to you and something you would say, you never knew what, would offend him and he would say, "Excuse me," and abruptly walk away. People avoided him because he summed it all up. The place was destroying him and you could see it happening; besides, he was always bumming cigarettes. After he delivered himself of this advice I should have said, "You're right, Eddie. I'll do that," but instead I stupidly told him it was not a problem for me, I was a voluntary patient signing myself out, they couldn't lay a finger on me; and Eddie, who was not on voluntary status, who had no idea when—whether—he would ever get out, said, "Excuse me," and abruptly walked away. Excuse me. Pardon my insignificant life. The words will be on his tombstone, no doubt. I wanted to cry.

Twenty minutes later my wife, Barbara, walked down the long corridor smiling at me and I did start to cry. All I remember clearly about leaving is choking back tears. I choked them back all the way home, trying not to let go. In an attempt to comfort me, Barbara made the only insensitive remark she made through the whole experience. I was out now, she said. Think of the people who can't go out. That was just it. Wasn't I one of them? I *felt* like one of them. I didn't know who I was. I didn't know whether I wanted to cry for them or for myself. I was trying not to think about them, I wanted to get away from them, get back into my own life as quickly as possible; if I thought about them I would break down. Months or years of that bitter life remained to them. You try to harden yourself, you try not to identify with other people's tragedies.

Anthony Brandt, from **REALITY POLICE**

Process:

There is, however, a harmless breathing exercise which may be used to calm the mind and prepare it for concentration. Close the right nostril with the thumb of the right hand and breathe in deeply through the left nostril. Feel, as you do so, that you are inhaling the pure and the sacred prana in the life-breath and sending a current down the ida nerve to the kundalini, situated within its basic triangular lotus at the bottom of the spine. Hold the breath for a moment, repeating the sacred syllable OM. Then as you release the right nostril, close the left nostril with the forefinger. Exhale through the right nostril, feeling, as you do so, that you are expelling all impurities from the body. Then, still keeping the left nostril closed, inhale through the right nostril, sending the current down the pingala nerve, and repeating the process in reverse.

from **HOW TO KNOW GOD: THE YOGA APHORISMS OF PANTANJALI**

Comparison and Contrast

Paragraphs devoted to comparison build up their argument through a discussion of how the qualities of two (or more) things, people, or events can be contrasted. The events themselves must be related for the comparison to make any sense. You can compare anger and guilt as emotions, but you obviously cannot compare anger and stopwatches.

Comparison paragraphs are usually direct or suspended, depending on whether the theme statement refers to the actual comparison stated at the beginning of the paragraph or the theme is the conclusion arrived at after the comparison has been explained. Here, for example, is a direct paragraph in which anger and guilt are compared as forms of anxiety:

Anger in many ways parallels guilt. As another form of anxiety it, too, can be a signal, and has its own dialectic. Just as guilt in its most harmful expressions can lead to different degrees of *self*-destruction, so anger can give way to rage and violence toward targets outside the self, toward people and things in one's environment. And there can be an animating or life-enhancing relationship to anger no less than to guilt. Generally speaking, within our paradigm of death and continuity, anger has to do with a struggle to assert vitality by attacking the other rather than the self.

R. J. Lifton, from **THE BROKEN CONNECTION**

Cause-Effect / Effect-Cause

There are two basic options with a cause-effect paragraph. Either you begin with an event that is the effect and account for the causes, or you begin with a cause and account for the effects. Either way you are writing a direct paragraph, again, though once more it is possible for this kind of paragraph to employ the suspended pattern: your single effect or single cause may be left till last. Either kind of cause-effect paragraph describes a chain of events all intimately related to either a cause or an effect. The following paragraph develops a relationship between the arrival of the European in Polynesia (cause) and the decay of native culture (effect):

The sudden influx of the European into Polynesia which followed Captain Cook's spectacularly successful voyages of discovery from 1768 to 1780 brought with it the familiar pattern of destruction and decay to the native cultures and the people themselves. In the case of Polynesia, the disappearance of the old cultures was hastened by the belief that each generation had more *mana* and was therefore better than the last. The Polynesians were thus extremely adaptable to change. They were easily impressed by the great *mana* evident in the white man's iron tools, his huge ships, the various machines, the firearms, and, in fact, all of his possessions. Accordingly, the slightest pressure from the missionaries who arrived in force during the first quarter of the 19th century was enough to induce the natives to give up their old religions and destroy the objects connected with them.

Allen Wardwell, from **THE SCULPTURE OF POLYNESIA**

Linking Sentences within the Paragraph

There can be no coherence to your paragraphs if your sentences do not link up with each other in obvious ways through transitions. However, when the connection is clear because the argument follows from one sentence to the next, there is no need to use transitions. In this example, the second sentence supports the argument of the first clearly:

I have often thought of it as one of the most barbarous customs in the world, considering us as a civilized and Christian country, that we deny the advantages of learning to women. We reproach the sex every day with folly and impertinence, while I am confident, had they the advantages of education equal to us, they would be guilty of less than ourselves.

Daniel Defoe, from AN ESSAY ON PROJECTS (1698)

However, there are many occasions when you need to signal a development in your argument. Here are a number of ways in which this can be done.

Transitional Words

Theme sentence
Supporting sentence
Transition word
Modifying sentence

Supporting sentence

You can use transitional words in supporting or modifying sentences, even when the modifying sentence does not dramatically alter the theme but intensifies it, as we see below:

Miss America stands in a long line of queens going back to Isis, Ceres, and Aphrodite. Everything from the elaborate sexual taboos surrounding her person to the symbolic gifts at her coronation hints at her ancient ancestry. *But* the real proof comes when we find that the function served by The Girl in our culture is just as much a "religious" one as that served by Cybele in hers. The functions are identical—to provide a secure personal "identity" for initiates and to sanctify a particular value structure.

Harvey Cox, from SEX AND SECULARIZATION

The transition word here is the familiar *but* which implies *contrast.* Here are some other familiar transition words and phrases you will use to link sentences:

Contrast: but, however, nevertheless, although, on the contrary, on the other hand, by contrast

Concession: still, granted that, of course, admittedly, it is true that

Likeness: similarly, likewise

Amplification: and, also, second, in addition, furthermore, moreover, too

Consequence: so, then, thus, as a result, hence, accordingly, therefore, it follows that

Emphasis: in fact, indeed, chiefly, even more important, equally

Example: for example, that is, for instance

Time: next, then, afterward, as soon as, later, earlier, formerly, subsequently, at the same time, so far, until now, finally, last

Place: here, there, in the foreground, in the background

Sequence: first, second, finally

Restatement: that is, in effect, in other words, in simpler terms, to put it differently, in short

Conclusion: to sum up, in sum, thus, therefore, finally, in conclusion

Be careful not to use transitional terms vaguely. *However* really should refer to some kind of contrast, and material prefaced by *in simpler terms* should indeed be simpler. Beware also of too liberally sprinkling transitional words and phrases in every sentence. Especially in supporting sentences linked to a theme sentence, you should let the flow of ideas carry the weight of the connection. Your signaling should be clear but not overstated. Beware of beginning sentences too regularly with *and* or *but* or *yet*. The following paragraph, for example, exaggerates the need for transitional words.

Miss America stands in a long line of queens going back to Isis, Ceres, and Aphrodite. <u>And</u> everything from the elaborate sexual taboos surrounding her person to the symbolic gifts at her coronation hints at her ancient ancestry. <u>But</u> the real proof comes when we find that the function served by The Girl in our culture is just as much a "religious" one as that served by Cybele in hers. <u>Furthermore</u>, the functions are identical—to provide a secure personal "identity" for initiates and to sanctify a particular value structure.

As you can see from the original paragraph, *and, but,* and *furthermore* are unnecessary, for the sentences they begin naturally follow from their predecessors. There are occasions to begin sentences with *and* or *but,* but they should not be used when thematic transitions are clear.

Repeating Key Words

You can make very effective transitions by repeating key words. In this paragraph, for example, you see a simple but most effective use of *it is* repeated over and over again to drive home a broad and disturbing description of contrasting qualities in an urban ghetto:

The ghetto is ferment, paradox, conflict, and dilemma. Yet within its pervasive pathology exists a surprising human resilience. The ghetto is hope, it is despair, it is churches and bars. It is aspiration for change, it is apathy. It is vibrancy, it is stagnation. It is courage, and it is defeatism. It is cooperation and concern, and it is suspicion, competitiveness, and rejection. It is the surge toward assimilation, and it is alienation and withdrawal within the protective walls of the ghetto.

Kenneth Clark, from DARK GHETTO: DILEMMAS OF SOCIAL POWER

The Series

In *process* paragraphs, or paragraphs that involve any kind of narrative sequence (whether it is historical or the description of an event), you can frequently link sentences as if they were parts of series. That is, each incident in a sentence follows from another in a chronological sequence, usually with the sentences introduced by such key words as *first, second,* and *third.*

Have you ever thought about how to introduce an Englishman brought up on cricket to the fine art of baseball? *First,* you explain that the two games have a lot in common. Someone throws a ball at someone else who tries to hit it with a bat. *Second,* scores are built up by runs as the batter tries to cover a distance before he is run out. *Third,* much of the finesse of the game is the result of what the pitcher (or bowler) can do with a leather-covered ball: how he moves it through the air, for one thing.

From the Part to the Whole

One important transition depends on a shift in the argument or description from an aspect of the argument (or the part of an event or thing) to the whole argument (or the whole event or thing). The reverse is quite common too. The reader can catch the natural transition without necessarily needing any transition words.

Love is as primary a phenomenon as sex. Normally, sex is a mode of expression for love. Sex is justified, even sanctified, as soon as, but only as long as, it is a vehicle of love. This love is not understood as a mere side effect of sex but sex as a way of expressing the experience of that ultimate togetherness that is called love.

Viktor Frankl, from MAN'S SEARCH FOR MEANING

Pronoun Reference

Perhaps the most common of all transitions is the reference to the subject or object of the previous sentence by means of a pronoun like *this, that, these, those, he, she, it, they, you,* and so on. It is important that your reference be unambiguous and clear.

We travelled thirty miles down river in a dug-out canoe beating off numerous crocodiles. These creatures would snap at the oars, and on several occasions broke them off. One of the crocodiles almost got on board but fortunately Kramer hit it on the snout. He nearly broke his gun stock doing that.

245

Parallel Structures If you are contrasting two events, concepts, or things, and you need more than one sentence to do so, signal the contrast by using the same grammatical structure in each sentence. You can set up two parallel questions or commands, or simply repeat any distinctive sentence form, or use contrasting phrases, like *in the daytime/in the nighttime, on the one hand/on the other.*

If you want happiness, *be kind. If you want* power, *be kinder* still.

Springtime brings the first signs of life; *summertime* dries them up.

Paragraph Transitions

Again, careful preparation will help you solve most of the problems of creating unity in your essay before you actually settle down to write. For example, it should be clear in your outline of the essay that you expect those paragraphs, say, under *context* to genuinely refer to the context of the topic. Each perspective we have outlined does relate to the earlier one and allows for a logical sequence to develop:

relevance of topic → definition of topic → issues → the contexts of the issues → causes and effects of those issues → conclusion and redefined relevance

The aim of a good outline is not only to make progress and develop a theme but to come full circle and enlarge upon your starting point.

So your paragraphs should relate to each other according to the development of ideas. Your whole essay is tied to one main idea, but it develops in blocks of paragraphs, each clinging to the specific emphasis of each of your major perspectives (*relevance, definition,* and so on). A paragraph block is simply a group of paragraphs related to the same theme. In a short essay, there may be only one block of related paragraphs; in a long one, there may be several.

How should you signpost the transition of ideas between paragraphs? You will notice that the transitions between several of the paragraphs in the essay on gun control take the form of a question at the end of a paragraph and its answer at the beginning of the next; or a statement ends one paragraph and is then questioned in the next. Other common transitions involve developing paragraphs either in contrast to one another or in a series in exactly the same way as we linked sentences earlier. However you make your transition, a paragraph must always directly link to the preceding one.

Thus, *paragraphs, like sentences, support or modify the paragraphs they follow.* All the transitional words and phrases used for linking sentences within paragraphs are used to link paragraphs too. Here, in sum, is a list of ways in which you can make transitions between paragraphs:

By asking a question at the end of one paragraph and answering it at the beginning of the next

By ending a paragraph with a statement that is then referred to immediately at the beginning of the next

By repeating a key word from an earlier paragraph

By developing an emphasis in one paragraph that either supports or modifies an emphasis in the preceding paragraph.

Support is most often expressed by the following transitional words:

Likeness: similarly, likewise

Amplification: and, also, again, in addition, furthermore, moreover, too

Example: for example, that is, for instance

Restatement: that is, in effect, in other words, in simpler terms, to put it differently, in short

Conclusion: to sum up, in sum, thus, therefore, finally, in conclusion

Modification of some kind is often expressed by the following transitional words:

Contrast: but, however, nevertheless, although, on the contrary, on the other hand, by contrast

Concession: still, granted that, of course, admittedly, it is true that

Consequence: so, then, thus, as a result, hence, accordingly, therefore, it follows that

Emphasis: in fact, indeed, chiefly, even more important, equally

Time: next, then, afterward, as soon as, later, earlier, formerly, subsequently, at the same time, so far, until now, finally, last

Place: here, there, in the foreground, in the background

Sequence: first, second, finally

A clue to the smooth transition of paragraphs is that they must always be seen to relate in terms of theme, above all. Transitional words alone are of little use unless there is genuine support or modification of ideas from one paragraph to the next. The transitional words then signpost the development, letting a reader know immediately the kind of relationship that is being proposed.

Opening Paragraphs

We all know how difficult it is to begin an essay, since it is most important that the opening paragraph encourage the reader to read on. Very often we try too hard to be appealing; sometimes we give up altogether and start with one of the traditional weak openings—such as a dictionary definition—because we think that the meat of the essay will justify the reading. There is no simple formula for an effective opening, but there are some important clues as to how you can create a strong opening as well as signs that indicate a weak opening.

Your opening paragraph establishes the relevance of your topic to the perspective you will take. If you have plotted your outline well, you have your emphatic opening lined up when you start writing.

■ The opening paragraph is a statement of information or facts about your topic. *It expresses your thesis* or sets the scene clearly for a discussion of the thesis in the next paragraph, providing some early relevant information. That is, the opening either states the thesis or delays it for a very good reason (such as enticing your reader to read on).

■ The opening paragraph *provides an emphasis,* a focus on your topic that highlights it.

In short, your opening should provide fact and emphasis.

How is this done? Techniques vary enormously, but basically anything that provides or leads directly to emphasis will work well. You could begin the gun control essay with the lukewarm statement, "Gun control has become a real issue in the United States." But it is better to try to attract the reader's attention with a sharply defined statement that you know you can prove. Here is a list of possibilities, by no means exhaustive, for making your opening sentence eye-catching:

■ *The dramatic statement*: "The clash of political ideas that burst into civil war in Spain very quickly made that country the principal theater in which a worldwide tragedy was unfolding" (Robert Goldston, *The Civil War in Spain*). Beware of hyperbole or overstatement, but take your point as far as you can in terms of your real opinion about your topic, without distorting the facts.

■ *The anecdotal opening*: "On July 11, 1936—just one day before Lieutenant Castillo's murder in Madrid—a French airplane of the type known as *Dragon Rapide* taxied down the long runway of Croyden Airport outside London" (Goldston). Start with an enticing fact, the beginning of a story that the reader will want to know more about. Set the scene with one or two bold details.

- *The enigmatic opening*: "At first it was hard to find a battle line in Spain" (Goldston). The reader reads on because such a statement is enigmatic and enticing. The question is "why?" And a reader who is forced to ask "why?" early in an essay is hooked. Here's another one: "Within a few weeks of the rebellion two very different yet similar Spains emerged behind the fighting lines" (Goldston).

- *The one-liner*: "Autobiography is only to be trusted when it reveals something disgraceful" (George Orwell, "Benefit of Clergy"). One-liners are usually aphorisms, short pithy sayings that uniquely sum things up. They can be witty, scathing, or droll, but they are never bland or neutral. Be sure that the one-liner is effective. Never begin with a clichéd saying like "Variety is the spice of life."

- *The question:* "Did you ever try to compare the different ways in which artists, living at different times or in different countries, handle the same subject? It is well worth doing. Usually it tells us something new about each of the artists, and the ages they lived in—something we might have suspected, but never realized with such vividness" (Gilbert Highet, "Pictures of War"). The question is always an immediate challenge, but of course, it has to be a question interesting enough to require an affirmative answer.

- *The description*: This is usually of something dramatic and eye-catching: "As the corpse went past, the flies left the restaurant table in a cloud and rushed after it, but they came back a few minutes later" (George Orwell, "Marrakech").

- *The contrast or paradox:* This immediately opens up an opposition that you will try to resolve: "One striking fact about English literature during the present century is the extent to which it has been dominated by foreigners—for example, Conrad, Henry James, Shaw, Joyce, Yeats, Pound, and Eliot" (George Orwell, "Arthur Koestler").

There are several ways you should *never* open an essay. You should not apologize for your lack of knowledge or experience. You should not quote a dictionary definition, or any authority for that matter, *unless* the quotation is particularly relevant and intelligent. You should at all costs avoid the cosmic emptiness of statements that fail to provide a focus: "There are many people in America who love the movies," or "The price of gas has gone up again." Also be careful not to repeat the title of the essay or to paraphrase it in the opening sentence. Instead, turn your attention always to *facts and emphasis* expressed with drama, clarity, and, if you can carry it off and it is appropriate, maybe even with wit.

However you begin the opening paragraph, your troubles are not over until the paragraph is complete. The principles that draw you to certain openings and not to others should be consistently carried through. You will rarely *begin* the opening paragraph with your thesis—that is, as the first sentence—unless perhaps it is a particularly dramatic one. Instead you will *build up to* your thesis. This can be done either by gradually refining general statements till you get to your precise thesis or by setting up examples or contrasts that will be converted into the generalization that is your thesis, that is, by a *suspended paragraph*.

The first kind of opening is called the *funnel paragraph*, because it begins with a wide opening (generalizations) and narrows down to the spout out of which your key ideas will flow (thesis).

All my early life lies open to my eye within five city blocks. When I passed the school, I went sick with all my old fear of it. With its standard New York public-school brown brick courtyard shut in on three sides of the square and the pretentious battlements overlooking that cockpit in which I can still smell the fiery sheen of the rubber ball, it looks like a factory over which has been imposed the façade of a castle. It gave me the shivers to stand up in that courtyard again; I felt as if I had been mustered back into the service of those Friday morning "tests" that were the terror of my childhood.

Alfred Kazin, from **A WALKER IN THE CITY**

In this paragraph, you will notice that Kazin begins with an area of five city blocks, then narrows that down to his old school, then to the courtyard, and finally to the real cause of his fear: those "Friday morning 'tests'" which the next paragraph goes on to describe.

If the funnel paragraph is the most usual opening, it need not be the only one. Instead of starting with broad generalizations which you progressively narrow down, you might want to start with a dramatic example or anecdote which will lead directly to a suspended thesis statement or perhaps to a question you will answer.

In this opening paragraph, for example, you will see that the writer moves from a specific example, Humphrey Bogart, to a generalization about some of our modern stars: their "mask of romantic introspection."

Humphrey Bogart sits at a table behind a drink, moodily staring into the middle distance, a glint of heroic self-pity in his eyes. We are looking at a shot from *Casablanca* (1943) which has come to represent for many people the essence not only of that film but of Bogart's whole screen personality. Blown up into a poster, and scattered through the clubs, cafés, foyers, flats, dens, and dormitories of the

Western world, it offers a maudlin echo to an equally famous poster of Ché Guevara: the mask of romantic introspection answers the mask of romantic action.

Michael Wood, from **AMERICA IN THE MOVIES**

It is plain to see, then, that your opening paragraph can either move from the general to the specific, or from the specific to the general, but always it must tantalize the reader and not give the whole story away. Your opening paragraph provides the fact and the emphasis; your middle paragraphs develop, with close reference to the logic of your outline, the significance of your topic.

The Final Paragraph

Ending an essay poses as big a challenge as opening one. A reader certainly expects the final paragraph or two to take the argument or explanation to some kind of conclusion. We all like to see a discussion neatly tied together, with all the possibilities raised by the writer accounted for, all the questions answered, and all the major points developed. So concluding paragraphs will refer to your thesis, but they are not mere repetitions of your thesis. It is wise to remember that you should not end your essay with "In conclusion, I have proved what I set out to show . . ." or something like that. Conclusions are not simple paraphrases, even though some recall of the previous argument is necessary, especially if that argument has been complex.

On the other hand, *conclusions should never break new ground.* The end is not an anticipation, unless it is the ending of a chapter in a book. The ending refers only to what has gone before, and you should be careful not to contradict anything you have said earlier nor to make too grand a claim for your achievement in the essay. Too often, concluding paragraphs make heroic leaps beyond the scope of an essay and suggest conclusions too inflated for the discussion.

This is only to say what a final paragraph is not. What can you do to ensure that your essay ends with tact but also with the right kind of emphasis?

■ *Your concluding paragraph(s) should be governed by the logical development of your argument,* but they are most effective when they shift into a slightly wider view than you have been taking throughout each section of your essay. Your conclusion should offer a perspective on your perspectives. You want to suggest a broad context of significance. In the essay on gun control, the conclusion that a gun control

251

law would be appropriate might begin by developing a summary of what that law could look like; that is, it would build on what has gone before. It would then try to justify that law by pointing out its general problems and its more important advantages. In other words, keep your critical thinking alive right to the end of the essay. Do not let your conclusion be a yell of triumph *or* a mere sigh and a laying down of arms.

■ *You may want to make your final paragraph link closely to your opening paragraph.* This does not mean repeating the wording of your first paragraph but rather showing the progress you have made from your opening. Avoid forecasting this with "You will notice that my argument has developed from . . . to . . ." But you can show that an argument has come full circle. Your beginning emphasis has not changed, but it has necessarily been modified. Here is the final paragraph of Michael Wood's chapter "America First" in *America in the Movies,* and you can guess how he has developed his initial insight about Bogart and "romantic introspection" into an evocation of the American West as being simply too big a space for anything but a "final silence." This is a poetic last paragraph which fulfills the need to broaden the writer's perspective and to ensure a link with the opening paragraph.

But the West has one last, glowing card up its sleeve: all that space (especially in technicolor and on a wide screen), those vast, empty landscapes—all invitations to loneliness. In the attraction of those images, in the lure of that invitation, a great deal of what I have been trying to discuss in this chapter comes together and is cancelled: hankerings for a lost innocence and for a forfeited individualism combined with a sense of the inevitable encroachments of civilization; dreams of a justified, glorified, sanctified selfishness paired with extravagantly selfless gestures; fears of entanglement matched by a clear need of others. For loneliness here is not just one of the poles of these arguments, it is the argument's end, its lapse into silence. In these solitary spaces neither self nor society has any claims on you. The plain and the prairie and the mountain, enlarged and depopulated by the movie camera, offer a life without others, a life with no one, a pacified life in which even your own ego scarcely lifts its voice above a whisper.

■ *The conclusion can make a special appeal to the reader to become involved,* to accept responsibility for continuing the search for the right explanation, or to consider the growing significance of what has been said. Such a plea may even be ironic. Edgar Friedenberg ends his essay on "The Modern High School: A Profile" with these highly ironic words which clearly imply that *we* are the subject of the essay—though he has avoided preaching to us. Have we merely gone along with the crowd or been original in some way following our high school education?

> Thus the high school is permitted to infantilize adolescence; in fact, it is encouraged to by the widespread hostility to "teen-agers" and the anxiety about their conduct found throughout our society. It does not allow much maturation to occur during the years when most maturation would naturally occur. Maturity, to be sure, is not conspicuously characteristic of American adult life, and would almost certainly be a threat to the economy. So perhaps in this, as in much else, the high school is simply the faithful servant of the community.

> There are two important ways in which it can render such service. The first of these is through its impact on individuals: on their values, their conception of their personal worth, their patterns of anxiety, and on their mastery and ease in the world—which determine so much of what they think of as their fate. The second function of the school is Darwinian; its biases, though their impact is always on individual youngsters, operate systematically to mold entire social groups. These biases endorse and support the values and patterns of behavior of certain segments of the population, providing their members with the credentials and shibboleths needed for the next stages of their journey, while they instill in others a sense of inferiority and warn the rest of society against them as troublesome and untrustworthy. In this way the school contributes simultaneously to social mobility and to social stratification. It helps see to it that the kind of people who get ahead are the kind who will support the social system it represents, while those who might, through intent or merely by their being, subvert it, are left behind as a salutary moral lesson.

■ *An effective way of ending an essay is to offer a quotation or make a historical reference.* Be sure to choose a particularly relevant and cogent quotation, though, not one that is too general or else means something to you only. Robert Goldston ends his book *The Civil War in Spain* movingly with a quotation that sums up what we can only hope is the lesson learned from that tragedy:

> But these signs of a rebirth of political consciousness must not be interpreted as a widespread will to revolution. The disillusionments of the Civil War are still too familiar to most Spaniards to permit their enthusiastic engagement on behalf of any political party, slogan, or battle cry whatsoever. And with the passage of the years the old political solutions have come to seem irrelevant to Spanish needs. The rising class of leaders in Spain are today more interested in economic and social realities than political theories. Above all, they are determined to avoid the dreadful blood bath of another civil war. In this

determination they are fulfilling a prophecy and a hope made during the fiercest days of the Civil War by Manuel Azaña, President of the Republic:

"When the torch passes to other hands, to other men, to other generations, let them remember, if they ever feel their blood boil and the Spanish temper is once more infuriated with intolerance, hatred, and destruction, let them think of the dead, and listen to their lesson: the lesson of those who have bravely fallen in battle, generously fighting for a great ideal, and who now, protected by their maternal soil, feel no hate or rancor, and who send us with the sparkling of their light, tranquil and remote as that of a star, the message of the eternal Fatherland which says to all its sons: Peace, Pity, and Pardon."

■ *The last paragraph may not be a final paragraph at all.* It may not summarize because you feel that that has already been adequately done. Instead it ends with more of what has gone before, only this time the final anecdote or explanation is particularly dramatic and suggestive, and of course, entirely consistent with the earlier discussion. We can see this at the end of one of the most powerful of modern speeches, Martin Luther King's "I Have a Dream."

I have a dream today.

I have a dream that one day every valley shall be exalted and every hill and mountain shall be made low, the rough places will be made plains and the crooked places will be made straight, and the glory of the Lord shall be revealed, and all flesh shall see it together.

This is our hope. This is the faith with which I return to the South. With this faith we will be able to hew out of the mountain of despair a stone of hope. With this faith we will be able to transform the jangling discords of our nation into a beautiful symphony of brotherhood. With this faith we will be able to work together, to pray together, to struggle together, to go to jail together, to stand up for freedom together, knowing that we will be free one day.

This will be the day when all of God's children will be able to sing with new meaning

My country, 'tis of thee
Sweet land of liberty,
Of thee I sing:
Land where my fathers died,
Land of the pilgrims' pride
From every mountain-side
Let freedom ring.

And if America is to be a great nation this must become true. So let freedom ring from the prodigious hilltops of New Hampshire. Let freedom ring from the mighty mountains of New York. Let freedom ring from the heightening Alleghenies of Pennsylvania!

Let freedom ring from the snowcapped Rockies of Colorado!

Let freedom ring from the curvacious peaks of California!

But not only that; let freedom ring from Stone Mountain of Georgia!

Let freedom ring from Lookout Mountain of Tennessee!

Let freedom ring from every hill and molehill of Mississippi. From every mountainside, let freedom ring.

When we let freedom ring, when we let it ring from every village and every hamlet, from every state and every city, we will be able to speed up that day when all of God's children, black men and white men, Jews and Gentiles, Protestants and Catholics, will be able to join hands and sing in the words of the old Negro spiritual, "Free at last! Free at last! thank God almighty, we are free at last!"

Checklist

1. Each paragraph should have one theme sentence—clear or implied—with supporting and modifying sentences.

2. Varying the placement of the theme sentence leads to Direct Paragraphs (theme + supporting/modifying), Indirect Paragraphs (modifying + theme + supporting), and Suspended Paragraphs (supporting/modifying + theme).

3. Paragraphs can be varied to define, describe, illustrate, analyze, reveal process or narrative, compare and contrast, or explain cause or effect.

4. Sentences are linked within paragraphs by using transitional words, repeating key words, developing a series, shifting from part to whole (or vice-versa), or by using pronoun references or parallel structures.

5. Paragraphs are linked to other paragraphs using the same techniques as the linking of sentences.

6. Opening paragraphs establish the relevance of a topic by providing fact and emphasis. Openings can be dramatic, anecdotal, enigmatic, aphoristic (one-liners), questioning, descriptive, or paradoxical.

7. The final paragraph should not break new ground but offer a perspective on the essay's perspectives, link to the opening, make a special appeal, or carry a special quotation or reference.

Exercises

1. Here are three extracts which have been printed without their original paragraph breaks. For each extract,

  a. Indicate where the paragraph breaks should occur and explain why

b. Back up your choice by indicating the theme, supporting, and modifying sentences for each paragraph

Whether they arrive early or late during the 70-day pilgrimage season (which begins annually with the start of the tenth month of the Muslim lunar calendar), pilgrims spend the eve of the ninth day of the twelfth month in the village of Mina, four miles east of Mecca. Following the practice of the Prophet, they rest there before the day of the "standing." During this high point of all hajj rituals, pilgrims stand on the Plain of Arafat and pray from noon until sundown. By the time of our arrival Mina had become a crowded tent city. After dawn prayers, we joined the rush of one-way traffic flowing to the Plain of Arafat, eight miles farther east, greeted by the bright colors of sunrise. Pilgrims crammed cars, buses, and trucks and rode on the backs of camels and donkeys. Often those on foot seemed to make the fastest passage. By noon all would make it to the hot desert plain, all clad in the same simple attire, rulers and subjects, rich and poor, men and women, black and white. It was a scene to last in memory: a million and a half people assembled for the day on this barren, rocky plain, leaving all wealth and fame behind, praying for salvation and for our brethren's deliverance. Thus we reinforced the sense of equality before the Lord and reminded ourselves of the day to come when all will be raised and gathered for accountability, leading to eternal bliss or affliction.

Muhammad Abdul-Rauf, from **PILGRIMAGE TO MECCA**

One of the reasons (in case you give a darn) for that unreasonable pallor of mine in mid-Summer, is that I can seem to find no comfortable position in which to lie in the sun. A couple of minutes on my elbows, a couple of minutes on my back, and then the cramping sets in and I have to scramble to my feet. And you can't get very tanned in four minutes. I see other people, especially women (who must be made of rubber), taking books to the beach or up on the roof for a whole day of lolling about in the sun in various attitudes of relaxation, hardly moving from one position over a period of hours. I have even tried it myself. But after arranging myself in what I take, for the moment, to be a comfortable posture, with vast areas of my skin exposed to the actinic rays and the book in a shadow so that I do not blind myself, I find that my elbows are beginning to dig their way into the sand, or that they are acquiring "sheet-burns" from the mattress; that the small of my back is sinking in as far as my abdomen will allow, and that both knees are bending backward, with considerable tugging at the ligaments. This is obviously not the way for me to lie. So I roll over on my back, holding the book up in the air between my eyes and the sun. I am not even deluding myself by this maneuver. I know that it won't work for long. So, as soon as paralysis of the arms sets in, I drop the book on my chest (without having read more than three consecutive words), thinking that perhaps I may catch a little doze. But sun shining on closed eyelids (on *my* closed eyelids) soon induces large purple azaleas whirling against a yellow background, and the sand at the back of my neck starts crawling. (I can be stark naked and still have something at the back of my neck for sand to get in under.) So it is a matter of perhaps a minute and a half before I am over on my stomach again with a grunt, this time with the sand in my lips. There are several positions in which I may arrange my arms, all of them wrong. Under my head, to keep the sand or mattress out of my mouth; down straight at my sides, or stretched out like a cross; no matter which, they soon develop unmistakable symptoms of arthritis and have to be shifted, also with grunting. Lying on one hip, with one elbow supporting the head, is no better, as both joints soon start swelling and aching, with every indication of becoming infected, and often I have to be assisted to my feet from this position. Once on my feet, I try to bask standing up in various postures, but this results only in a sunburn on the top of my forehead and the entire surface of my nose, with occasional painful blisters on the tops of my shoulders. So gradually, trying to look as if I were just ambling aimlessly about, I edge my way toward the clubhouse, where a good comfortable chair and a long, cooling drink soon put an end to all this monkey-business. I am afraid that I am more the pale type, and should definitely give up trying to look rugged.

Robert Benchley, **WHY I AM PALE**

Soviet Union

The Soviet Union will supply natural gas for the pipeline from its Urengoi field, perhaps the largest natural gas field in the world. The field is in Siberia, where temperatures drop as low as 50 degrees below zero Fahrenheit, making construction difficult.

The Russians are providing tens of thousands of construction workers. Labor costs are expected to be relatively small because of lower wages than in the West, conscripted labor, and use of the military.

Large amounts of 56-inch diameter steel pipe will be made in the Soviet Union. Some might be diverted from other pipeline projects within the U.S.S.R. if necessary, because the natural gas line to Western Europe is the top priority. It would be a propaganda victory over the U.S. and would bring badly needed foreign exchange. The natural gas could bring as much as $8 billion a year in foreign earnings, replacing oil as Russia's biggest exchange earner.

Natural gas production is one of the few parts of the Soviet economy that is performing well. It is scheduled to rise by 40% or 50% during the current five-year plan. The pipeline will increase Soviet capacity to export natural gas by 160% to 2.3 trillion cubic feet a year.

The Soviets also will provide some of the turbines and compressor stations needed to keep the gas flowing through the pipeline. Some of the compressors are as powerful as the General Electric Co. components embargoed by the U.S. government, but they are still in the prototype stage of development. It isn't clear yet whether they can be used.

The entire project will demand unusual cooperation between the U.S.S.R's many bureaucracies. The Ministry of Foreign Trade is negotiating all contracts with foreign companies, although different divisions negotiate gas sales and equipment purchases. "We have approximately 60 ministries and maybe one third or one half are involved," says Michael Lysenko, an official at the Soviet embassy in Washington.

West Germany

West Germany has taken the lead role in pipeline talks. It will buy about 30% of the gas and has the largest contracts to provide equipment.

Ruhrgas is the West German gas distributor, owned 67% by international oil companies, 26% by U.S. oil companies Exxon Corp., Texaco Inc. and Mobil Corp. It has agreed to buy about 370 billion cubic feet a year of natural gas to market to its residential and commerical customers.

Ruhrgas will pay about $4.60 to $4.90 a thousand cubic feet at the Czech border. The price is tied to competitive fuels, mainly home heating oil and gasoil.

The Soviets must fulfill the 25-year contract even if the pipeline isn't finished. About three quarters of the gas is to go to West Berlin. The provision of power to West Berlin has been a long-standing controversy between West Germany and the Soviet Union.

Steve Mufson, "Anatomy of continuing Soviet Pipeline Controversy,"
Wall Street Journal

2. Here is a paragraph with jumbled sentences.
   a. Rearrange the sentences in what you think is the correct order.
   b. Indicate which are the theme, supporting, and/or modifying sentences.
   c. Describe the structure of the paragraph (direct, indirect, or suspended).

We press our technological imperialism forward against the natural environment until we reach the point at which it comes as startling and not entirely credible news to our urban masses to be told by anxious ecologists that their survival has anything whatever to do with air, water, soil, plant, or animal. Like Narcissus, modern men and women take pride in seeing themselves—their products, their planning—reflected in all that they behold. That is the lesson in vanity the city teaches us every moment of every day. Already in the western world and Japan millions of city-dwellers and suburbanites have grown accustomed to an almost hermetically sealed and sanitized pattern of living in which very little of their experience ever impinges on non-human phenomena. For on all sides we see, hear, and smell the evidence of human supremacy over nature—right down to the noise and odor and irritants that foul the air around us. For those of us born to such an existence, it is all but impossible to believe that anything is any longer beyond human adjustment, domination, and improvement. The more artifice, the more progress; the more progress, the more security.

Theodore Roszak, from **WHERE THE WASTELAND ENDS**

3. Using each of the following theme sentences, write a paragraph with supporting and modifying sentences:

a. When a young woman graduates from college and starts looking for a job, one question every interviewer is sure to ask her is ''Can you type?'' (Shirley Chisholm).

b. I wish Karl Marx were alive to watch *The Newlywed Game* (John Leonard).

c. Teachers are more than any other class the guardians of civilization (Bertrand Russell).

d. If men could get pregnant, abortion would be a sacrament (Florynce R. Kennedy).

e. In the past four or five years, millions of middle Americans (I call them that for convenience) suddenly found out that marijuana was something with which their own children were experimenting (William F. Buckley).

4. Here are a series of numbered jumbled paragraphs that make a sequence.

a. Write down the numbers of the paragraphs in their right order.

b. Explain your choice with reference to the kinds of transitions made between the paragraphs.

i. This optimism which marks every aspect of American life is expressed in the confidence in universal suffrage for direct election of the President. We find the same confidence in the authority delegated to local government to administer everyday aspects of life and to make decisions in the fields of city planning, health, and education—decision-making powers our central government would be terrified to put into the hands of elected officials. We see it again in the catalytic role of research, where ideas are not ornaments but tools to change the world. And nothing is more *profitable* than a good idea. In the United States adult education is considered an investment, not a form of humanitarianism.

ii. A century ago Tocqueville saw this as an essential, indeed the fundamental, characteristic of the New World. ''Each individual, whoever he may be, possesses the degree of intelligence necessary to manage those affairs which concern him exclusively—this is the great principle on which civil and political society rests. The father applies it to his children, the master to his servants, the community to its citizens, the county to its communities, the state to its counties, and the federal union to the states. Taken as a whole, it becomes the dogma of popular sovereignty. . . . From this comes the belief that the individual is the best judge of his own particular interests."

iii. All clichés to the contrary, American society wagers much more on human intelligence than it wastes on gadgets. As we have seen, scientific studies are beginning to confirm what intuition led us to suspect: *this wager on man is the origin of America's new dynamism.* Despite important changes over the past 20 years, European society presents a very different picture.

iv. In a small committee of the productivity department, French business men discuss the advantages of "periodic recycling" for their executives. But how many of them would dare make a bet on intelligence by losing a few engineer-hours—even if they won them back again many times over in increased productivity?

v. In 1968 Soviet agriculture remains petrified in the kolkhoz system and commerce in the state-owned stores. The "great leap forward" took place in the United States, whose production increases every two years by an amount equal to Britain's total annual output, and whose capacity for innovation astonishes foreign managers and scholars alike.

vi. Americans are not more intelligent than other people. Yet human factors—the ability to adapt easily, flexibility of organizations, the creative power of teamwork—are the key to their success. Beyond any single explanation, each of which has an element of truth, the secret lies in the confidence of the society in its citizens. This confidence often seems rather naive to Europeans, but America places it both in the ability of its citizens to decide for themselves, and in the capacity of their intelligence.

vii. By contrast, the French subsidiary of IBM spends 10 percent of its total payroll on the continual training of its personnel. Visitors from Europe have observed that American universities have been invaded by adults wanting to learn new skills. This same American determination and optimism explain the introduction of scientific methods into areas which until now have been marked by routine.

J. J. Servan-Schreiber, from THE AMERICAN CHALLENGE

5. Explain what is wrong with the following opening paragraphs and revise them so that they are more effective;

a. Looking back over my life—a short life so far, admittedly—I can remember those times when I was forced to cope with stress. Lots of us feel anxious all the time, and some of us feel anxious part of the time, but all of us surely know what anxiety is. It's very hard to know how to cope with it at the time, however, and lots of people turn to all those psychological methods available, those me-generation encounter groups and so on, which help somewhat but don't always get to the heart of the matter. It's not enough to know that you can relieve anxiety by being a "me" person. You've got to grab the psychological bull by the horns and pull its tail. This means that you need psychological help, friend, if you've got a problem.

b. Think of all the everyday occurrences people take for granted. For instance, no one ever gives a second thought to the simple task of climbing a few stairs, or the ability to view the beauties of nature, or the pleasure derived from listening to fine music. Yet millions of people, because of various handicaps, are unable to experience these basic events. For them life is completely different because they cannot enjoy the simple things most people never even think about. (student essay)

6. Here are two concluding paragraphs. For each one,
a. Explain the function
b. If necessary, revise the paragraph so that it is more effective

To try to be free of self-deception, to try to see with clear eyes oneself and others and the world, does not necessarily bring an undiluted kind of happiness. Yet it is something I would not exchange for any happiness built on any other foundation. There is only one way in which one can endure man's inhumanity to man and that is to try, in one's own life, to exemplify man's humanity to man. "Teach me, oh Lord, to seek not so much to be consoled as to console."

Alan Paton, from **THE CHALLENGE OF FEAR**

The pants have become a tradition, and along the way have acquired a history of their own—so much so that the company has opened a museum in San Francisco. There was, for example, the turn-of-the-century trainman who replaced a faulty coupling with a pair of jeans; the Wyoming man who used his jeans as a towrope to haul his car out of a ditch; the Californian who found several pairs in an abandoned mine, wore them, then discovered they were sixty-three years old and still as good as new and turned them over to the Smithsonian as a tribute to their toughness. And then there is the particularly terrifying story of the careless construction worker who dangled fifty-two stories above the street until rescued, his sole support the Levi's belt loop through which his rope was hooked.

Carin C. Quinn, from **THE JEANING OF AMERICA—AND THE WORLD**

7. Here is a short essay without its final paragraph. Write the most effective substitute for the final paragraph that you can, and explain in some detail why you have written it the way you have with reference to the argument of the rest of the essay.

Why should any words be called obscene? Don't they all describe natural human functions? Am I trying to tell them, my students demand, that the "strong, earthy, gut-honest"—or, if they are fans of Norman Mailer, the "rich, liberating, existential"—language they use to describe sexual activity isn't preferable to "phony-sounding, middle-class words like 'intercourse' and 'copulate'?" "Cop You Late!" they say with fancy inflections and gagging grimaces. "Now, what is *that* supposed to mean?"

Well, what is it supposed to mean? And why indeed should one group of words describing human functions and human organs be acceptable in ordinary conversation and another, describing presumably the same organs and functions, be tabooed—so much so, in fact, that some of these words still cannot appear in print in many parts of the English-speaking world?

The argument that these taboos exist only because of "sexual hangups" (middle-class, middle-age, feminist), or even that they are a result of class oppression (the contempt of the Norman conquerors for the language of their Anglo-Saxon serfs), ignores a much more likely explanation, it seems to me, and that is the sources and functions of the words themselves.

The best known of the tabooed sexual verbs, for example, comes from the German *ficken,* meaning "to strike"; combined, according to Partridge's etymological dictionary *Origins,* with the Latin sexual verb *futuere;* associated in turn with the Latin *fustis,* "a staff or cudgel"; the Celtic *buc,* "a point, hence to pierce"; the Irish *bot,* "the male member"; the Latin *battuere,* "to beat"; the Gaelic *batair,* "a cudgeller"; the Early Irish *bualaim,* "I strike"; and so forth. It is one of what etymologists sometimes call "the sadistic group of words for the man's part in copulation."

The brutality of this word, then, and its equivalents ("screw," "bang," etc.), is not an illusion of the middle class or a crotchet of Women's Liberation. In their origins and imagery these words carry undeniably painful, if not sadistic, implications, the object of which is almost always female. Consider, for example, what a "screw" actually does to the wood it penetrates; what a painful, even mutilating, activity this kind of analogy suggests. "Screw" is particularly interesting in this context, since the noun, according to Partridge, comes from words meaning "groove," "nut," "ditch," "breeding sow," "scrofula" and "swelling," while the verb, besides its explicit imagery, has antecedent associations to "write on," "scratch," "scarify," and so forth—a revealing fusion of a mechanical or painful action with an obviously denigrated object.

Not all obscene words, of course, are as implicitly sadistic or denigrating to women as these, but all that I know seem to serve a similar purpose: to reduce the human organism (especially the female organism) and human functions (especially sexual and procreative) to their least organic, most mechanical dimension; to substitute a trivializing or deforming resemblance for the complex human reality of what is being described.

Tabooed male descriptives, when they are not openly denigrating to women, often serve to divorce a male organ or function from any significant interaction with the female. Take the word "testes," for example, suggesting "witnesses" (from the Latin *testis*) to the sexual and procreative strengths of the male organ; and the obscene counterpart of this word, which suggests little more than a mechanical shape. Or compare almost any of the "rich," "liberating" sexual verbs, so fashionable today among male writers, with that much-derided Latin word "copulate" ("to bind or join together") or even that Anglo-Saxon phrase (which seems to have had no trouble surviving the Norman Conquest) "make love."

How arrogantly self-involved the tabooed words seem in comparison to either of the other terms, and how contemptuous of the female partner. Understandably so, of course, if she is only a "skirt," a "broad," a "chick," a "pussycat" or a "piece." If she is, in other words, no more than her skirt, or what her skirt conceals; no more than a breeder, or the broadest part of her; no more than a piece of a human being or a "piece of tail."

The most severely tabooed of all the female descriptives, incidentally, are those like a "piece of tail," which suggest (either explicitly or through antecedents) that there is no significant difference between the female channel through which we are all conceived and born and the anal outlet common to both sexes—a distinction that pornographers have always enjoyed obscuring.

This effort to deny women their biological identity, their individuality, their humanness, is such an important aspect of obscene language that one can only marvel at how seldom, in an era preoccupied with definitions of obscenity, this fact is brought to our attention. One problem, of course, is that many of the people in the best position to do this (critics, teachers, writers) are so reluctant today to admit that they are angered or shocked by obscenity. Bored, maybe, unimpressed, aesthetically displeased, but—no matter how brutal or denigrating the material—never angered, never shocked.

And yet how eloquently angered, how iously shocked many of these same people become if denigrating language is used about any minority group other than women; if the obscenities are racial or ethnic, that is, rather than sexual. Words like ''coon,'' ''kike,'' ''spic,'' ''wop,'' after all, deform identity, deny individuality and humanness in almost exactly the same way that sexual vulgarisms and obscenities do.

Barbara Lawrence, ''——— **ISN'T A DIRTY WORD**''

Readings

Loren Eiseley **THE BROWN WASPS**

"It is as though all living creatures, and particularly the more intelligent, can survive only by fixing or transforming a bit of time into space or by securing a bit of space with its objects immortalized and made permanent in time."

Virginia Woolf **THE DEATH OF THE MOTH**

"When there was nobody to care or know, this gigantic effort on the part of an insignificant little moth, against a power of such magnitude, to retain what no one else valued or desired to keep, moved one strangely."

THE BROWN WASPS

Loren Eiseley

There is a corner in the waiting room of one of the great Eastern stations where women never sit. It is always in the shadow and overhung by rows of lockers. It is, however, always frequented—not so much by genuine travelers as by the dying. It is here that a certain element of the abandoned poor seeks a refuge out of the weather, clinging for a few hours longer to the city that has fathered them. In a precisely similar manner I have seen, on a sunny day in midwinter, a few old brown wasps creep slowly over an abandoned wasp nest in a thicket. Numbed and forgetful and frost-blackened, the hum of the spring hive still resounded faintly in their sodden tissues. Then the temperature would fall and they would drop away into the white oblivion of the snow. Here in the station it is in no way different save that the city is busy in its snows. But the old ones cling to their seats as though these were symbolic and could not be given up. Now and then they sleep, their gray old heads resting with painful awkwardness on the backs of the benches.

Also they are not at rest. For an hour they may sleep in the gasping exhaustion of the ill-nourished and aged who have to walk in the night. Then a policeman comes by on his round and nudges them upright.

"You can't sleep here," he growls.

A strange ritual then begins. An old man is difficult to waken. After a muttered conversation the policeman presses a coin into his hand and passes fiercely along the benches prodding and gesturing toward the door. In his wake, like birds rising and settling behind the passage of a farmer through a cornfield, the men totter up, move a few paces, and subside once more upon the benches.

One man, after a slight, apologetic lurch, does not move at all. Tubercularly thin, he sleeps on steadily. The policeman does not look back. To him, too, this has become a ritual. He will not have to notice it again officially for another hour.

Once in a while one of the sleepers will not awake. Like the brown wasps, he will have had his wish to die in the great droning center of the hive rather than in some lonely room. It is not so bad here with the shuffle of footsteps and the knowledge that there are others who share the bad luck of the world. There are also the whistles and the sounds of everyone, everyone in the world, starting on journeys. Amidst so many journeys somebody is bound to come out all right. Somebody.

Maybe it was on a like thought that the brown wasps fell away from the old paper nest in the thicket. You hold till the last, even if it is only to a public seat in a railroad station. You want your place in the hive more than you want a room or a place where the aged can be eased gently out of the way. It is the place that matters, the place at the heart of things. It is life that you want, that bruises your gray old head with the hard chairs; a man has a right to his place.

But sometimes the place is lost in the years behind us. Or sometimes it is a thing of air, a kind of vaporous distortion above a heap of rubble. We cling to a time and a place because without them man is lost, not only man but life. This is why the voices, real or unreal, which speak from the floating trumpets at spiritualist seances are so unnerving. They are voices out of nowhere whose only reality lies in their ability to stir the memory of a living person with some fragment of the past. Before the medium's cabinet both the dead and the living revolve endlessly about an episode, a place, an event that has already been engulfed by time.

This feeling runs deep in life; it brings stray cats running over endless miles, and birds homing from the ends of the earth. It is as though all living creatures, and particularly the more intelligent, can survive only by fixing or transforming a bit of time into space or by securing a bit of space with its objects immortalized and made permanent in time. For example, I once saw, on a flower pot in my own living room, the efforts of a field mouse to build a remembered field. I have lived to see this episode repeated in a thousand guises, and since I have spent a large portion of my life in the shade of a nonexistent tree I think I am entitled to speak for the field mouse.

One day as I cut across the field which at that time extended on one side of our suburban shopping center, I found a giant slug feeding from a runnel of pink ice cream in an abandoned Dixie cup. I could see his eyes telescope and protrude in a kind of dim uncertain ecstasy as his dark body bunched and elongated in the curve of the cup. Then, as I stood there at the edge of the concrete, contemplating the slug, I began to realize it was like standing on a shore where a different type of life creeps up and fumbles tentatively among the rocks and sea wrack. It knows its place and will only creep so far until something changes. Little by little as I stood there I began to see more of this shore that surrounds the place of man. I looked with sudden care and attention at things I had been running over thoughtlessly for years. I even waded out a short way into the grass and the wild-rose thickets to see more. A huge black-belted bee went droning by and there were some indistinct scurryings in the underbrush.

Then I came to a sign which informed me that this field was to be the site of a new Wanamaker suburban store. Thousands of obscure lives were about to perish, the spores of puffballs would go smoking off to new fields, and the bodies of little white-footed mice would be crunched under the inexorable wheels of the bulldozers. Life disappears or modifies its appearances so fast that everything takes on an aspect of illusion—a momentary fizzing and boiling with smoke rings, like pouring dissident chemicals into a retort. Here man was advancing, but in a few years his plaster and bricks would be disappearing once more into the insatiable maw of the clover. Being of an archaeological cast of mind, I thought of this fact with an obscure sense of satisfaction and waded back through the rose thickets to the concrete parking lot. As I did so, a mouse scurried ahead of me, frightened of my steps if not of that ominous Wanamaker sign. I saw him vanish in the general direction of my apartment house, his little body quivering with fear in the great open sun on the blazing concrete. Blinded and confused, he was running straight away from his field. In another week scores would follow him.

I forgot the episode then and went home to the quiet of my living room. It was not until a week later, letting myself into the apartment, that I realized I had a visitor. I am fond of plants and had several ferns standing on the floor in pots to avoid the noon glare by the south window.

As I snapped on the light and glanced carelessly around the room, I saw a little heap of earth on the carpet and a scrabble of pebbles that had been kicked merrily over the edge of one of the flower pots. To my astonishment I discovered a full-fledged burrow delving downward among the fern roots. I waited silently. The creature who had made the burrow did not appear. I remembered the wild field then, and the flight of the mice. No house mouse, no *Mus domesticus*, had kicked up this little heap of earth or sought refuge under a fern root in a flower pot. I thought of the desperate little creature I had seen fleeing from the wild-rose thicket. Through intricacies of pipes and attics, he, or one of his fellows, had climbed to this high green solitary room. I could visualize what had occurred. He had an image in his head, a world of seed pods and quiet, of green sheltering leaves in the dim light among the weed stems. It was the only world he knew and it was gone.

Somehow in his flight he had found his way to this room with drawn shades where no one would come till nightfall. And here he had smelled green leaves and run quickly up the flower pot to dabble his paws in common earth. He had even struggled half the afternoon to carry his burrow deeper and had failed. I examined the hole, but no whiskered twitching face appeared. He was gone. I gathered up the earth and refilled the burrow. I did not expect to find traces of him again.

Yet for three nights thereafter I came home to the darkened room and my ferns to find the dirt kicked gaily about the rug and the burrow reopened, though I was never able to catch the field mouse within it. I dropped a little food about the mouth of the burrow, but it was never touched. I looked under beds or sat reading with one ear cocked for rustlings in the ferns. It was all in vain; I never saw him. Probably he ended in a trap in some other tenant's room.

But before he disappeared I had come to look hopefully for his evening burrow. About my ferns there had begun to linger the insubstantial vapor of an autumn field, the distilled essence, as it were, of a mouse brain in exile from its home. It was a small dream, like our dreams, carried a long and weary journey along pipes and through spider webs, past holes over which loomed the shadows of waiting cats, and finally, desperately, into this room where he had played in the shuttered daylight for an hour among the green ferns on the floor. Every day these invisible dreams pass us on the street, or rise from beneath our feet, or look out upon us from beneath a bush.

Some years ago the old elevated railway in Philadelphia was torn down and replaced by a subway system. This ancient El with its barnlike stations containing nut-vending machines and scattered food scraps had, for generations, been the favorite feeding ground of flocks of pigeons, generally one flock to a station along the route of the El. Hundreds of pigeons were dependent upon the system. They flapped in and out of its stanchions and steel work or gathered in watchful little audiences about the feet of anyone who rattled the peanut-vending machines. They even watched people who jingled change in their hands, and prospected for food under the feet of the crowds who gathered between trains. Probably very few among the waiting people who tossed a crumb to an eager pigeon realized that this El was like a food-bearing river, and that the life which haunted its banks was dependent upon the running of the trains with their human freight.

I saw the river stop.

The time came when the underground tubes were ready; the traffic was transferred to a realm unreachable by pigeons. It was like a great river subsiding suddenly into desert sands. For a day, for two days, pigeons continued to circle over the El or stand close to the red vending machines. They were patient birds, and surely this great river which had flowed through the lives of unnumbered generations was merely suffering from some momentary drought.

They listened for the familiar vibrations that had always heralded an approaching train; they flapped hopefully about the head of an occasional workman walking along the steel runways. They passed from one empty station to another, all the while growing hungrier. Finally they flew away.

I thought I had seen the last of them about the El, but there was a revival and it provided a curious instance of the memory of living things for a way of life or a locality that has long been cherished. Some weeks after the El was abandoned workmen began to tear it down. I went to work every morning by one particular station, and the time came when the demolition crews reached this spot. Acetylene torches showered passers-by with sparks, pneumatic drills hammered at the base of the structure, and a blind man who, like the pigeons, had clung with his cup to a stairway leading to the change booth, was forced to give up his place.

It was then, strangely, momentarily, one morning that I witnessed the return of a little band of the familiar pigeons. I even recognized one or two members of the flock that had lived around this particular station before they were dispersed into the streets. They flew bravely in and out among the sparks and the hammers and the shouting workmen. They had returned—and they had returned because the hubbub of the wreckers had convinced them that the river was about to flow once more. For several hours they flapped in and out through the empty windows, nodding their heads and watching the fall of girders with attentive little eyes. By the following morning the station was reduced to some burned-off stanchions in the street. My bird friends had gone. It was plain, however, that they retained a memory for an insubstantial structure now compounded of air and time. Even

269

the blind man clung to it. Someone had provided him with a chair, and he sat at the same corner staring sightlessly at an invisible stairway where, so far as he was concerned, the crowds were still ascending to the trains.

I have said my life has been passed in the shade of a nonexistent tree, so that such sights do not offend me. Prematurely I am one of the brown wasps and I often sit with them in the great droning hive of the station, dreaming sometimes of a certain tree. It was planted sixty years ago by a boy with a bucket and a toy spade in a little Nebraska town. That boy was myself. It was a cottonwood sapling and the boy remembered it because of some words spoken by his father and because everyone died or moved away who was supposed to wait and grow old under its shade. The boy was passed from hand to hand, but the tree for some intangible reason had taken root in his mind. It was under its branches that he sheltered; it was from this tree that his memories, which are my memories, led away into the world.

After sixty years the mood of the brown wasps grows heavier upon one. During a long inward struggle I thought it would do me good to go and look upon that actual tree. I found a rational excuse in which to clothe this madness. I purchased a ticket and at the end of two thousand miles I walked another mile to an address that was still the same. The house had not been altered.

I came close to the white picket fence and reluctantly, with great effort, looked down the long vista of the yard. There was nothing there to see. For sixty years that cottonwood had been growing in my mind. Season by season its seeds had been floating farther on the hot prairie winds. We had planted it lovingly there, my father and I, because he had a great hunger for soil and live things growing, and because none of these things had long been ours to protect. We had planted the little sapling and watered it faithfully, and I remembered that I had run out with my small bucket to drench its roots the day we moved away. And all the years since it had been growing in my mind, a huge tree that somehow stood for my father and the love I bore him. I took a grasp on the picket fence and forced myself to look again.

A boy with the hard bird eye of youth pedaled a tricycle slowly up beside me.

"What'cha lookin' at?" he asked curiously.

"A tree," I said.

"What for?" he said.

"It isn't there," I said, to myself mostly, and began to walk away at a pace just slow enough not to seem to be running.

"What isn't there?" the boy asked. I didn't answer. It was obvious I was attached by a thread to a thing that had never been there, or certainly not for long. Something that had to be held in the air, or sustained in the mind, because it was part of my orientation in the universe and I could not survive without it. There was more than an animal's attachment to a place. There was something else, the attachment of the spirit to a grouping of events in time; it was part of our mortality.

So I had come home at last, driven by a memory in the brain as surely as the field mouse who had delved long ago into my flower pot or the pigeons flying forever amidst the rattle of nut-vending machines. These, the burrow under the greenery in my living room and the red-bellied bowls of peanuts now hovering in midair in the minds of pigeons, were all part of an elusive world that existed nowhere and yet everywhere. I looked once at the real world about me while the persistent boy pedaled at my heels.

It was without meaning, though my feet took a remembered path. In sixty years the house and street had rotted out of my mind. But the tree, the tree that no longer was, that had perished in its first season, bloomed on in my individual mind, unblemished as my father's words. "We'll plant a tree here, son, and we're not going to move any more. And when you're an old, old man you can sit under it and think how we planted it here, you and me, together."

I began to outpace the boy on the tricycle.

"Do you live here, Mister?" he shouted after me suspiciously. I took a firm grasp on airy nothing—to be precise, on the bole of a great tree. "I do," I said. I spoke for myself, one field mouse, and several pigeons. We were all out of touch but somehow permanent. It was the world that had changed.

1. "We cling to a time and a place because without them man is lost, not only man but life." Discuss this theme as it runs through Eiseley's essay.

2. "Life disappears or modifies its appearances so fast that everything takes on an aspect of illusion."

   a. What events in the story point to this?

   b. What has this fact got to do with the writer?

3. Explain how Eiseley arrives at an explanation of the tree-planting scene in relationship to the events that have gone before.

4. a. Comment on the effectiveness of Eiseley's opening and closing paragraphs.

   b. Discuss whether you think Eiseley develops his theme with sufficient variety in the middle paragraphs.

THE DEATH OF THE MOTH

Virginia Woolf

Moths that fly by day are not properly to be called moths; they do not excite that pleasant sense of dark autumn nights and ivy-blossom which the commonest yellow-underwing asleep in the shadow of the curtain never fails to rouse in us. They are hybrid creatures, neither gay like butterflies nor sombre like their own species. Nevertheless the present specimen, with his narrow hay-coloured wings, fringed with a tassel of the same colour, seemed to be content with life. It was a pleasant morning, mid-September, mild, benignant, yet with a keener breath than that of the summer months. The plough was already scoring the field opposite the window, and where the share had been, the earth was pressed flat and gleamed with moisture. Such vigour came rolling in from the fields and the down beyond that it was difficult to keep the eyes strictly turned upon the book. The rooks too were keeping one of their annual festivities; soaring round the tree tops until it looked as if a vast net with thousands of black knots in it had been cast up into the air; which, after a few moments sank slowly down upon the trees until every twig seemed to have a knot at the end of it. Then, suddenly, the net would be thrown into the air again in a wider circle this time, with the utmost clamour and vociferation, as though to be thrown into the air and settle slowly down upon the tree tops were a tremendously exciting experience.

The same energy which inspired the rooks, the ploughmen, the horses, and even, it seemed, the lean bare-backed downs, sent the moth fluttering from side to side of his square of the window-pane. One could not help watching him. One was, indeed, conscious of a queer feeling of pity for him. The possibilities of pleasure seemed that morning so enormous and so various that to have only a moth's part in life, and a day moth's at that, appeared a hard fate, and his zest in enjoying his meagre opportunities to the full, pathetic. He flew vigorously to one corner of his compartment, and, after waiting there a second, flew across to the other. What remained for him but to fly to a third corner and then to a fourth? That was all he could do, in spite of the size of the downs, the width of the sky, the far-off smoke of houses, and the romantic voice, now and then, of a steamer out at sea. What he could do he did. Watching him, it seemed as if a fibre, very thin but pure, of the enormous energy of the world had been thrust into his frail and diminutive body. As often as he crossed the pane, I could fancy that a thread of vital light became visible. He was little or nothing but life.

Yet, because he was so small, and so simple a form of the energy that was rolling in at the open window and driving its way through so many narrow and intricate corridors in my own brain and in those of other human beings, there was something marvellous as well as pathetic about him. It was as if someone had taken a tiny bead of pure life and decking it as lightly as possible with down and feathers, had set it dancing and zigzagging to show us the true nature of life. Thus displayed one could not get over the strangeness of it. One is apt to forget all about life, seeing it humped and bossed and garnished and cumbered so that it has to move with the greatest circumspection and dignity. Again, the thought of all that life might have been had he been born in any other shape caused one to view his simple activities with a kind of pity.

After a time, tired by his dancing apparently, he settled on the window ledge in the sun, and, the queer spectacle being at an end, I forgot about him. Then, looking up, my eye was caught by him. He was trying to resume his dancing, but seemed either so stiff or so awkward that he could only flutter to the bottom of the window-pane; and when he tried to fly across it he failed. Being intent on other matters I watched these futile attempts for a time without thinking, unconsciously waiting for him to resume his flight, as one waits for a machine, that has stopped momentarily, to start again without considering the reason of its failure. After perhaps a seventh attempt he slipped from the wooden ledge and fell, fluttering his wings, on to his back on the window sill. The helplessness of his attitude roused me. It flashed upon me that he was in difficulties; he could no longer raise himself; his legs struggled vainly. But, as I stretched out a pencil, meaning to help him to right himself, it came over me that the failure and awkwardness were the approach of death. I laid the pencil down again.

The legs agitated themselves once more. I looked as if for the enemy against which he struggled. I looked out of doors. What had happened there? Presumably it was mid-day, and work in the fields had stopped. Stillness and quiet had replaced the previous animation. The birds had taken themselves off to feed in the brooks. The horses stood still. Yet the power was there all the same, massed outside indifferent, impersonal, not attending to anything in particular. Somehow it was opposed to the little hay-coloured moth. It was useless to try to do anything. One could only watch the extraordinary efforts made by those tiny legs against an oncoming doom which could, had it chosen, have submerged an entire city, not merely a city, but masses of human beings; nothing, I knew, had any chance against death. Nevertheless after a pause of exhaustion the legs fluttered again. It was superb this last protest, and so frantic that he succeeded at last in righting himself. One's sympathies, of course, were all on the side of life. Also, when there was nobody to care or to know, this gigantic effort on the part of an insignificant little moth, against a power of such magnitude, to retain what no one else valued or desired to keep, moved one strangely. Again, somehow, one saw life, a pure bead. I lifted the pencil again, useless though I knew it to be. But even as I did so, the unmistakable tokens of death showed themselves. The body relaxed, and instantly grew stiff. The struggle was over. The insignificant little creature now knew death. As I looked at the dead moth, this minute wayside triumph of so great a force over so mean an antagonist filled me with wonder. Just as life had been strange a few minutes before, so death was now as strange. The moth having righted himself now lay most decently and uncomplainingly composed. O yes, he seemed to say, death is stronger than I am.

1. Woolf watches the moth on a windowpane and looks beyond it to the expanses of the downs, the sea, and the sky. What contrast does she develop from this perspective?
2. What is the significance of the death of the moth?
3. Discuss the effectiveness of Woolf's opening and closing paragraphs.
4. What paragraph patterns does Woolf develop? Describe them carefully and comment on whether you think they are effective enough and provide variety.

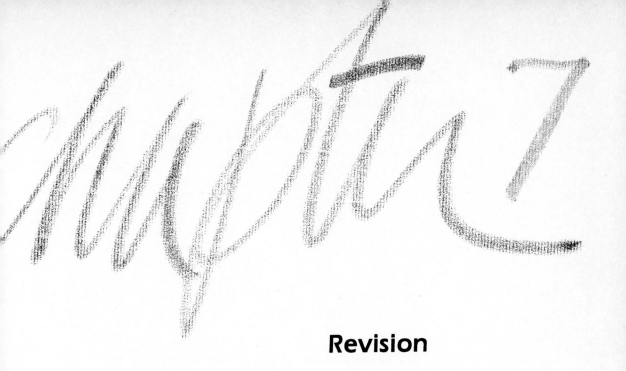

Revision

Re-envisioning

The revision process begins, you will recall, from the moment you start writing. In Chapter 4 we briefly discussed *revision-as-you-write:* the writer's need to constantly reread during the act of writing, adjusting both ideas and sentence forms in order to develop a continuous and coherent explanation, argument, or narration. Revision, in other words, is always part of the process of writing and making meaning, and if you begin revising at once, you will find it brings about improvements in your writing quite readily.

There are two practical reasons for thinking of revision as a process that is part of writing from the start. First, writing is not a single completed act. Writing is developed bit by bit as you reread and supplement, reorder or change what you are saying. Writing is *incremental:* it moves through stages, and revision is part of every stage of the process as we have covered it so far. Texts, however short, are not made in one sitting but over a period of time that can vary enormously from writer to writer. The writing process outlined in this book encourages you to take the time to try out your ideas and your writing before you finally commit yourself. You do not know what you want to say until you have said it, and then not until you have rehearsed saying it, arriving at a way that satisfies you fully.

Second, if you refine your writing as you write, you will encourage writing to shape your ideas carefully, and this makes the final process of revision less confusing. If you write a whole essay without rereading what you have written and without adjusting your thinking, you will find that any necessary revisions at the end will create large disruptions and make writing more painful than it need be. Some disruption is inevitable, but the degree of annoyance and the heavy work of revision can be reduced by revising-as-you-write.

So you have completed your essay and are faced now with the final review. Think of this as an extension of the revision process that has been going on all along. Now, however, you have the advantage of being able to see the essay as a whole, and that does introduce some new practical necessities to the art of revision.

■ *A final revision follows time off from writing.* Nothing will reveal the need for revision more clearly than staying away from an essay you have written for at least a day or two. A fresh perspective uncovers problems you were not able to see while in the throes of writing. In fact, it is not at all unusual to be self-deprecating after reading something you have written and to wonder how you could have said it that way at all. Show a healthy distrust of your writing, but try to stop short of the self-disgust that can make writing difficult. If you plan your writing so that there is time for a leisurely final revision, gaining a fresh perspective will seem less dramatic. No one but you, anyhow, need ever know what mistakes you almost made.

■ *Revision is re-envisioning.* Revision is not simply a matter of correcting the wording of an essay as well as a few mechanical errors. Think of revision as that time when you reconsider the project from the point of view of your whole statement. Re-envisioning does not mean that you try to find a new perspective and then rewrite the essay accordingly. It means that you see your original perspective now more fully because you have the whole essay in front of you. Revision is not a new stage or a separate process; at this point it is a more complete envisioning of your intentions in writing than was possible before you had written them out.

■ *Revision must not disturb an original freshness.* Every piece of writing should be a fresh dramatization of yourself in a new context, not just the trotting out of habitual or repetitive opinions. Be sure, then, that revision does not disturb the freshness of the original perception. On the other hand, if the original vision is tired or incoherent, you may need more than ever a change of perspective.

■ *Revision depends on close reading.* As you will see, revision comprises strategies that above all reinforce the close link between reading and writing. Review the process of reading for interpretation outlined in Chapters 1 and 2, for when you make a final revision, you are becoming your own closest reader. Read your writing for emphasis, coherence, and unity, evaluating it exactly as you would any other text.

There follows, then, a series of appropriate questions you can ask yourself about your first draft. These are worth remembering, no matter how experienced an editor you think you have become. It is very difficult to discover every mistake, incomplete idea, and misjudgment you make as a writer. It is also difficult to know how you can improve your writing unless you ask yourself some pertinent questions about what you are trying to achieve, and unless you know something about what you can do with sentences and paragraphs.

Furthermore, you must confront the doubts that build up in your mind as to whether you have said all you can as effectively as possible, or whether your audience will like and understand what you have to say. Revision corrects, but it also *confirms,* and it is sometimes hard to do both at once. Writers become emotionally attached to their sentences. They like the way the words sound together; they feel they have hit upon especially appropriate images. So you can invest a lot of work in your sentences only to find that they cannot remain in their present form or may have to be deleted altogether. You change your mind often, perhaps, about an approach or intended meaning. All this is quite normal, although that realization hardly lessens the hard work of rewriting and revision. Let's move now from general words of advice to the specific, practical details of the task.

Reading for Emphasis, Coherence, and Unity

Reading the Text

Read your text aloud either to yourself or to a friend. Your first aim is to re-engage what you have written, to re-enter the text, to renew your relationship to the topic, and to reawaken your opinions. By reading your writing aloud, you can gain an important distance on your work. This is also that stage of the writing process when you must be scrupulously honest with yourself. *Trust your initial reactions.* If something doesn't seem right or doesn't make sense, underline the words, phrases, clauses, sentences, or paragraphs. As you read,

■ *Mark passages that do not sound right.* It does not matter what your reason is; you may have no reason at all, just a hunch. Sound and rhythm are important indicators of whether your writing is moving continuously and harmoniously, or whether you have a problem of development. Reading aloud will reveal to your ear all sorts of writing errors that your eye may not catch: errors of sentence and paragraph structure and matters of style. Doesn't this passage *sound* odd to you if you read it aloud?

(1) High school students, who are football oriented, look upon college football as a step in the right direction toward their future life. (2) And what is a university for? (3) It's an institution based upon the young learning and being accepted into society's play. (4) For those who plan on playing football, no matter how much they've been persuaded against it, their minds are made up, and should a school disregard these people, for they are people. (5) We all have a choice, and there's no reason why a choice should be denied.

■ *Mark those places in the text where transitions are not made properly,* where information has not been accumulated in logical sequences, where it is not clear why one idea leads to the next (for example, see the lack of transition between sentences 1 and 2, between 3 and 4, and within sentence 4 in the passage above).

278

■ *Mark passages you have to reread because the meaning is not clear.* You may hear inconsistent voices or find ambiguity. You may simply not understand what you were getting at because the sentences are too dense, or explanations are not made. You might mark the whole of the paragraph on the opposite page.

■ *Mark passages that bore you and show little life,* places where ideas seem not to appear at all or where you have just been stating the obvious, so that your expectations have not been raised.

■ *Mark passages that are wordy and overstated.*

What are some of the common errors you might find?

Lack of a thesis

Incoherent argument

Poor transitions

Oblique or ambiguous explanations: talking around a subject

Inconsistencies in viewpoint

Stale, overly abstract, vague, repetitious, and weak language

Failure to take an audience into account

Poor sentence and paragraph construction

Grammatical, spelling, and punctuation errors

Rather a daunting list, isn't it? But we all make these mistakes at some time or other. You will find *all* these problems in the football paragraph. Right now, you are not concentrating on grammatical errors, however. Your first run through the text is made to detect major errors in the handling of ideas. You are concentrating on the thesis and its development, and any large-scale problems with them can lead to rather drastic revision. After your first reading aloud and the initial marking of the text, go over it again, still listening carefully in your mind's ear, but now reading closely for emphasis, coherence, and unity.

Emphasis and the Writer's Intention

The reader wants to find emphasis, and that begins with a focus on a subject or a problem. The subject leads to a thesis statement, and you will remember, if you followed the focusing stages, that your subject should emerge in statements that are *emphatic and defined, of general interest,* and *open to interpretation.* If, as you read, you find there is a gap between what you think you ought to be saying and what you are actually saying, then maybe you need to run through the focusing stages again, to brainstorm some more, to play out some new oppositions, or perhaps to reconsider your audience. Don't compromise on this, however much it appears to be sheer drudgery. Without a clear thesis or a clear statement of the problem, you have no hope of writing a good paper.

Here are some questions you should ask yourself about handling emphasis in an essay:

Does the title relate to the thesis or problem?

Is the topic clearly described and defined early in the essay?

Is the thesis clear?

Are there accurate and forceful main statements about the topic?

Does the topic have a realistic focus? Is it neither too large nor too small?

Is the topic interesting?

Is there a clear conclusion related to the problem or the thesis?

Reread the football paragraph on page 278. Clearly there is no focus on a theme. In fact, it is very difficult to tell exactly what the thesis or problem might be, though you might suspect that it has something to do with the need for a football program at a particular college. Regardless of the problems with the argument, the shifting perspective and lack of transitions make it difficult for the reader to find continuity. Without continuity, it is unlikely that an emphasis can be developed. How, then, would you correct the problem of not having a clear emphasis?

■ *If the problem occurs throughout an entire essay*—that is, if you cannot find a clear thesis or problem statement anywhere—then it is likely that the essay will have to be rewritten. This means that you need to return to the stage of the writing process where you brainstormed, organized your material, and formed a conclusion. If you have no thesis statement, you have no conclusion, and you have merely been writing the essay *impressionistically,* that is, you have simply been listing your impressions without examining their significance and relationships. Brainstorm again, reorganize your ideas, and form a conclusion and a new outline.

Where do you especially look for emphasis in an essay? In the opening and closing paragraphs. Ask yourself the following questions:

Does the first paragraph arouse interest and provide a focus?
Does the closing paragraph show the progress of the argument and keep critical thinking alive until the last moment? Does it form a real conclusion?

Chapter 6 provided considerable detail about how to write effective opening and closing paragraphs. Review that material and remember that your opening paragraph should state your emphasis, or at least arouse the reader's interest in it if the main statement is delayed until the next paragraph. You should never keep a reader waiting too long to find out what you are talking about. If you have followed the recommended position paper plan presented in Chapter 3, you have dealt first with the relevance of your topic. So does your opening paragraph express this? The opening paragraph of our gun control essay, for example, might raise some of the special problems of discussing the question, especially the problem of whether one tackles the question of violence control or gun control.

The second point to consider, as again Chapter 6 pointed out, is that concluding paragraphs should effectively summarize your discussion without merely repeating what you have said before. In other words, there should be a genuine conclusion. As the gun control essay proposes, the question of control is not easily answered, but some efficient compromise has to be reached as soon as possible. This is a possible method of justifying the suggestion for a gun control law.

What do you do if you do not find emphasis in some specific paragraph?

■ *If the problem occurs in isolated paragraphs only,* then the following procedure is useful: Find the clear or implied thesis statement in the paragraph and start from there, recasting sentences after it. In the example above, the statement is made that "high school students . . . look upon college football as a step in the right direction toward their future life." This is exaggerated and so broad a generalization as to make no sense at all. In fact, there is no clear thesis statement in the paragraph. However, if you read the whole paragraph, you can see an argument developing, however obliquely. The writer wants to say that students who have played or watched football in high school may want to play or watch it in college and often expect to find football available. Clearly the whole paragraph needs recasting, and a thesis statement needs to be added. It might be something like "High school students who have either played or enjoyed watching football will think of college football as an important part of the curriculum." From there the argument can develop. In other words, go over your writing until you find the seeds of your argument and rewrite the paragraph around a new thesis statement that allows an argument, not just a collection of unrelated thoughts, to develop.

> High school students who have either played or enjoy watching football will think of college football as an important part of the college curriculum. They may choose a university on the basis of whether it has a football team

or not. Therefore, a university can attract students by offering football and giving a broad range of students the choice of watching and playing it.

■ *If the problem occurs within a sentence,* then you must recast your sentence(s) to provide clear, direct main statements. Chapter 5 explained this in detail, and you should remember that regardless of how you construct your main statements, they must be capable of being understood directly. This final sentence from the paragraph on college football is clumsy to say the least: "We all have a choice, and there's no reason why a choice should be denied." It does not matter what the grammatical and other errors are in this sentence. The point is that it *sounds* convoluted and barely literate. No one is going to be convinced by such sentiments. Don't waste time with sentences that seem to you muddled and roundabout. Simply decide what you really mean to say, and recast the sentence as a clear statement: "It would be good if we were all given a chance to choose whether we want football or not."

As Chapter 5 explains, emphasis is carried by direct statements adequately modified. Ask yourself these questions about your sentences:

Do the sentences make clear statements?

Are the sentences adequately varied?

Are there any awkward constructions or roundabout statements?

Are there any unnecessary repetitions or overqualifications?

Are there concrete rather than overly abstract references?

These kinds of problems are easy to catch if you read your essay aloud. What is wrong with the following paragraph, for example?

The content of this soliloquy by Hamlet sets the emotional stage for the subsequent events in the play. It outlines the range and extent of Hamlet's feelings. He is grief-stricken and angered by the undesirable happenings in his life. Generally, this soliloquy becomes crucial to the overall understanding and empathy toward events which will take place later in the play.

When you read this aloud, do you find yourself listening to the sound of your own voice and not registering the meanings of the words? The sentences are not clear. They make overly abstract references that fade into no meaning at all. How can the content of a soliloquy set an emotional stage? Why say *range* and *extent* of feelings without saying what the range is? The writer speaks only of grief and anger. The word *undesirable* is weak and *happenings* is vague. *Generally* is just that: too general. Yet we learn that the soliloquy becomes *crucial* to an *overall understanding and empathy,* whatever that means. Not only are the sentences too abstract, but the abstractness is overqualified: too much has been said about the soliloquy without any direct statement.

Again, in order to correct sentences like these, stand back from your writing and ask yourself: What am I trying to say? What kernel of meaning can I find in the writing? When you have decided, say it simply, directly, and with feeling:

> Hamlet's soliloquy tells us all we need to know about his grief and anger over his father's death and his mother's marriage to his uncle. Without this soliloquy the events which follow in the play have little meaning.

■ *If the problem occurs mainly in the language you use,* consider the following possibilities: that you are using jargon, clichés, euphemisms, commonly confused words, abstract rather than concrete language, circumlocution, redundancy, inappropriate intensifiers, or mixed metaphors.

If your writing sounds like overcolloquial speech, and clumsy speech at that, you know something is wrong. Usually language that sounds too roundabout, abstract, evasive, unnecessary, overstated, or inappropriate (as do certain words we noted in the paragraph above) should simply be replaced. (Review the discussion of colorful language in Chapter 4.)

When you revise your essay, try to inject some color, feeling, and personality into your writing if it is not already there. There is something very wrong with this paragraph from a freshman essay, for example:

> Napoleon Bonaparte once said (this is not a direct quote): Man will always repeat his mistakes, trying to win wars that should not have taken place. Mankind has already made two mistakes, World War I and World War II. Some of my high school friends that are now attending other colleges, have already registered for the draft. If there is ever another conflict over a key point or country, we the 18 through 20 year olds hope the indifference doesn't lead to war.

Now, apart from the muddled logic of this piece, what is wrong with the language?

The "quotation" from Bonaparte is not memorable and merely states the obvious.

Referring to two world wars as *mistakes* is an ineffective understatement here.

The reference to high school friends *at other colleges* is vague and inconsequential.

The words *conflict over a key point or country* are flat and evasive. Wars are not fought over key points.

What does *indifference* refer to, especially since the writer has just referred to war as a *mistake?*

How do you correct writing as vague and uncommitted as this? Before you even think about the problems of the language, you must rethink the main statement you want to make and the tone you want to convey. Decide whether *indifference* or some stronger version of *mistake* is really your focus. Assume the thesis statement will be that "we never seem to learn from the horrors of war." Then express your feelings directly and concretely.

> We never seem to learn from the horrors of war. Two major conflicts this century have made no difference. When people go to war, evolution turns the clock back. Yet even though we know how primitive and irrational war can be, the young must sign up for the draft, perpetuating the need for more necessary mistakes.

This may not be a brilliant paragraph, but it contains more color:

It locates an idea clearly: the frustrating fact that we easily revert to irrational behavior.

The language is more concrete.

It attempts to use some figurative language with the statement "When people go to war, evolution turns the clock back."

It injects a note of irony with "necessary mistakes."

Coherence and the Message

Revising for coherence is very closely related to revising for emphasis. In fact, once you establish an emphasis and develop it clearly, you are on your way to creating a coherent message, as you saw in Chapter 3. But emphasis alone is not enough. Coherence depends on how you develop your discussion.

Is the discussion developed from the thesis statement or problem?

Are there clearly defined relationships and oppositions between facts?

Has a network of accurately established facts been presented?

Does the argument, explanation, or solution hold together?

If the message involves value judgments, have they been justified?

Coherence should be present in every paragraph. Here is a case where it is not:

(1) The 1980 Olympics in Moscow were boycotted by the U.S. and several other countries. (2) They were protesting Soviet intervention in Afghanistan. (3) Early in 1979, Russian military forces invaded Afghanistan and set up a puppet government. (4) The Soviets met with stiff opposition from strong and determined desert nomads who tried as hard as they could to rout the Russians.

There is a thesis sentence in this paragraph, presumably the first one, and sentence 2 develops the thesis by offering an explanation of the boycott. But from there on, the argument drifts into a theme not directly related to the U.S. boycott, namely, the situation in Afghanistan.

■ *Lack of coherence in individual paragraphs is caused by a change of direction in the argument.* This can be remedied by locating the theme sentence and those that clearly support it, and then deleting the sentences that do not. Sentences 3 and 4 above should be cut out altogether, and new sentences developing the nature and problems of the boycott should be substituted.

Similarly, if there is a problem of coherence in the structure of the essay as a whole—and the middle paragraphs are the place to look for this—be firm about which paragraphs and which sentences contribute to the main argument or explanation. Remove all the others and replace them. An incoherent message is one that has not been thought through or is one in which statements have been complicated by inappropriate information or ideas. Beware of digressions.

■ *Review your middle paragraphs carefully,* for it is the paragraphing of the middle of the essay that holds the key to success. Ask yourself the following questions:

Does each paragraph have just one clear theme?

Is each paragraph made up of coherently related sentences?

Do the paragraphs flow into each other?

Consider the following paragraphs from the essay "The Question of Gun Control" from the point of view of these questions. As you check the paragraphs for coherence, take each one on its own in turn and look first for the relationship between the sentences. Do you find any changes of direction or difficult transitions as there are in the paragraph above on the 1980 Olympics?

These questions seem incredible to answer. They simply don't have much in common when you first look at them, and they don't make much sense either in isolation. But people do agree on something and that is that we need to control deaths from gun-related crime somehow. Both sides agree on that. So instead of getting bogged down by unanswerable questions, let's see if we can answer this one: If gun control is a concept which makes any sense at all, can it control killings and burglaries involving handguns, and preserve our civil rights? Let's see if a compromise is possible.

If you look at the question closely, it is not hard to see what the rightful context for the issue is. We have constitutional rights and the law and we have social and psychological theory which tries to explain why we have violence. I don't think it matters much if we know that an assasin is insane. We want a practical conclusion. What is more important: theory or protection? Our paradox now is that an individual is guaranteed the right to bear arms but finds herself needing to be protected by those who do carry guns.

The Law alone offers protection, for only the Law has in common the interests of both the gun carrier and the person who won't carry guns. Whatever psychology and sociology have to say about how violence operates in society and why we need handguns must become part of the legal issue. It doesn't matter if we know why handguns are associated with so much crime all that theorizing is irrelevant besides we don't know whether we need gun control or not. Do we need laws against guns or against violence?

There are a number of problematic transitions *within* the paragraphs. In paragraph 1, we move from the general agreement that there should be some gun control to the need for a law to preserve our civil rights. In paragraph 2, the question of a context and the need for a practical conclusion are placed side by side with no direct relationship. The second to last sentence of paragraph 3 raises two issues—the irrelevance of theorizing and the doubts we may have about gun control—and neither one seems to be taken up coherently by the question at the end of the paragraph. In each paragraph, then, there are faulty transitions between sentences.

What about the transition between *paragraphs* in the gun control essay? This is a little better than the transition within paragraphs. There is, however, some difficulty between paragraphs 1 and 2. You will remember than one of the simplest of transitions is that of the first sentence of a paragraph connecting thematically with the last sentence of the preceding one. So the opening of paragraph 2 should refer to the compromise mentioned at the end of paragraph 1. You would rewrite the opening sentence thus: "Such a compromise could exist within the context of the law."

Unity and the Whole Essay

If you have achieved emphasis and coherence, it is unlikely that you will have to rewrite for unity, though some stylistic revisions may be needed. The unity of an essay, you will recall, depends on the overall development of the argument and the consistency of the emphasis, viewpoint, and tone of voice. Here are a few questions you should ask when checking for unity in your essay:

Are there any passages that stop the flow of the argument?

Is there a consistent point of view?

Is there a consistent and authentic tone of voice?

Does the tone develop from your relationship to the topic?

Is the tone rational and carefully controlled?

Is the style consistent with the tone and appropriate to the topic?

It is a good idea to read for unity *after* you have made corrections for emphasis and coherence. This stage of the revision process allows you to check your earlier revisions. The essay should hold together at this point as a coherent argument or explanation presented in a pleasing style. If anything interrupts your reading now, you must go back and see why. The development of the argument, viewpoint, style, and tone should allow the reader to find a set of ideas flowing continuously toward one end. Still, read your essay aloud to ensure that you *hear* what is going on.

■ *What happens if you feel that the essay does not hold together as a whole?* If it is a matter of one or two paragraphs getting in the way of a sense of continuity, simply rework the paragraphs for transitions and coherence, as we discussed in the previous section.

■ If you cannot locate the problem, however, then summarize your essay to locate your main theme and write a brief outline of the essay *as it stands,* not as it ought to be. Don't use your original outline, but make a new one in order to diagnose what you have actually written. In this way, you can check the development of what you have said and spot the inconsistencies more easily. The main point of each paragraph should be part of the summary.

■ *What if the problem is largely one of style?* Say you find a change of style or tone in your writing, as in this exaggerated example wherein the first paragraph is personal and sarcastic and the next one is objective and descriptive:

> I fail to see how ethics enters political decision making when it is plain that our foreign policy is determined by blatantly cynical needs, such as currying favor with those who control the world's oil supplies. Politics and morality make only for a marriage of convenience. How often do we hear warmly sentimental statements from world leaders about democracy and human rights when democracy surely flourishes only where it is convenient for us to allow it to do so. That is, we most clearly make loud noises about human rights and the need for an ethical stance when we think we have something to gain from it.
>
> By viewing democracy simply as a question of political morality, we have blinded ourselves to the fact that, in every country, the system of government is a by-product of the general conditions of life, including, of course, the economic conditions, and that democracy, like any other system, is appropriate for countries where these conditions are suited to it and inappropriate for others with unsuitable conditions, or at least that it is vastly more appropriate for some than for others. Viewed in these terms, there is a strong case for believing that democracy is clearly most appropriate for countries which enjoy an economic surplus and less appropriate for countries where there is an economic insufficiency. In short, economic abundance is conducive to political democracy.
>
> second paragraph from David Potter, **PEOPLE OF PLENTY**

Now you only have to read this aloud to discover that the style changes from the first paragraph to the next. The first paragraph uses informal language and short sentences, and is somewhat cynical in tone. The writer seems to be accusing this country and other democracies of extreme hypocrisy. In the second paragraph, though, the writer presents elaborately subordinated sentences and takes a more formal, studied approach, analyzing the issue with some objectivity. Democracy depends on economics, he says; it is not just a matter of cynical politics but of economic determinism. The style changes from informal to academic, especially in the first long sentence of the second paragraph.

The tone changes, too. The cynicism disappears as the writer becomes more objective and convincing.

You have to watch for changes of tone accompanying changes of style in your writing. These changes usually indicate that you changed your mind or your perspective as you wrote. How can the problem be remedied? Simply by deciding firmly which tone you really want to take and working from that. If you want to write a more ironic essay that pulls no punches and if you think you can do so rationally, then the second paragraph above, for example, could be adjusted to shorter, more informal sentences. The irony of political democracy existing only in places where the economies are good could be pointed out. If you decide to be more scholarly, on the other hand, you could rewrite the first paragraph to match the style of the second.

Considering Your Audience

You have been reading your essay aloud to yourself, which means that you have been your own audience, your own best reader, as it were. But what about the larger audience you have been writing for? In the process of preparing an essay, you should give some thought to your readers and how they might be persuaded. Look hard at your essay once more and ask yourself the following questions:

Have you helped to create the audience of your essay?

Have you been kind to the reader, providing a climate of shared values?

Have you thought of the audience in consistent terms: writing consistently as a friend, say, or an authority, a neutral observer, an equal?

What do you do if you find an inconsistent attitude toward your audience? Any shift in tone and style will reveal this and will disconcert your reader. Thus, the two paragraphs on democracy were written for two different audiences. Or alternatively, the audience was asked to think of the same topic in two different ways without assistance from the writer, who did not forecast that a different approach was being taken (such as "Consider the question of the relation of economics and democracy for a moment . . ."). By adjusting your style to bring about a consistent tone, you treat your audience more kindly. But note too that the attitude *you* take is the attitude you want your audience to take, and it must be one that you can reasonably expect your audience to sympathize with. Being sarcastic, then, rarely works. Chapters 9, 10, and 11 go into more detail about influence and persuasion. But for now, simply keep in mind that whatever the role you want your audience to play, your tone and style must be consistent to achieve your end.

Editing

After you have read for emphasis, coherence, and unity, you need to edit your essay for mechanical errors. This is a most important part of revision which many writers do while they are reading for the development of ideas. The process assumes, however, that you have acquired a knowledge of all the common grammatical errors. So in order to carry out the final stages of the revision process now, review the section on editing in the handbook. Keep the list handy whenever you revise your writing until you can easily recognize common grammatical errors.

The Final Draft

Revision may be time-consuming, but it enables you to accomplish the rethinking and refining that translates your initial draft or drafts into coherent, readable prose that conveys a genuine opinion. Let's look at an example: the corrected version of the first five paragraphs of the gun control essay. Remember to proofread your final draft carefully so that you do not make any old or new errors. (Appendix B outlines a typical manuscript format for a college paper.)

The arguments between pro- and anti-gun con-

trol groups rage on. Why? Because it is both a

genuinely difficult question to answer and one sus-

pects also because there are many special interests

involved. Still it is a question we should all try to

answer because it has implications for everyone.

~~both you and me. Everyone~~ *we all* wants a solution to the

problem of high crime; even anti-guncontrollers *do.*

Its genuinely a constitutional issue. Everyone any-

how acknowledges that there is some connection

between violence and guns, but which one do we

tackle first? The problem is that somehow the guns

and violence connection has become clouded by

political considerations.

This first paragraph strikes you as a weak opening. It is too dense, too compressed in its explanation. You begin by correcting the errors, but then, after reading for unity, you find the paragraph should be rewritten to sort the ideas out more clearly. The second paragraph is affected too. (See the final draft of the essay, pp. 293-299, righthand column, for the rewrite.)

~~So how can we make sense of the problem? We~~

~~have to begin by saying that~~ There is a ~~real~~ stand-

off between the two sides, so the important thing

to do is to take no sides at all amd treat the problem

as an open one, *or* at least as an experiment. There

are difficult legal considerations, so we need to

find a meeting point for the two sides.

Whether we are for or against gun control, we

have to define our terms, *preferably in such a way that both sides might find them acceptable.* For the sake of argument

we will take the phrase "gun control" to refer to

the federal control of the use of handguns, through

licensing or restriction. *Right now some states are considering various forms of gun control legislation,* ~~These are concealed lethal weapons. It doesn't matter what the states do we~~ *but the argument for or against*

291

the issue – if it is to be effective – has to re-
~~have to refer to the national context because we~~
fer to the national context. The argument
~~are arguing the principle of the issue~~
goes beyond the states' rights to invoke the
But why is ⊗ this an issue at all? The question
Constitution
itself.
has boiled down to the main problem of whether

the government has the constitutional rights to ban
for   *There are other questions too:*
handguns ⊗ defense. ~~But then what~~ if we do have
          w ^ *Will law-abiding citizens be*
gun control, Will it control violence effectively?
defenseless against criminals who will still find
~~Will it leave an unarmed public against armed~~
guns?
          gun control
~~criminals? Can~~ ⊗ ~~ever be effective~~ in a country as
large   ^   *Will we just continue in*
~~big~~ as the U.S.? ~~And~~ if we don't have gun control,
a vicious circle? Will the need for guns for self-
~~what happens then as more and more crimes in-~~
defense increase as more crimes involve handguns
~~crease and involve handguns.~~
A at first sight, these questions seem impos-
~~Those questions seem incredible to answer.~~
sible to answer and   *little*   *If*
~~They simply don't~~ have ~~much~~ in common. ~~when~~
you were to take ^ *them isolation, they*
~~you first look at them, and they don't make much~~
would remain difficult to answer. No one knows
~~sense either in isolation.~~ But people do agree on   *for sure if*
          the   *gun control*
something: ~~and that is that we~~ need to control   *would reduce*
          ^   *violence.*
deaths from gun-related crime. ~~somehow. Both~~
                              sidetracked
~~sides agree on that.~~ So instead of getting ~~bogged~~
                              ^ *consider the*
~~down~~ by unanswerable questions, let's ~~see if we~~
following issue:
~~can answer this one.~~ If gun control is a concept

that
~~which~~ makes any sense at all, can it control killings

and burglaries involving handguns, _and_ preserve

our civil rights? ~~Let's see if a compromise is pos-~~ *specifically our right to bear* *arms for defense?* ^ *It may seem as*

~~sible.~~ *though we want to have it both ways by posing* *the question* *in this way,* *but let us* *compromise be-* *tween the* *two sides.*

Now let's look at the full gun control essay in two versions: the first draft (in the left-hand column) and the final draft (in the right-hand column). A careful line-by-line comparison will show you the ways in which revision has clarified and strengthened the essay's organization, style, and tone as well as corrected the various mechanical errors of the first draft.

DRAFT #1

THE QUESTION OF GUN CONTROL

The arguments between pro- and anti-gun control groups rage on. Why? Because it is both a genuinely difficult question to answer and one suspects also because there are many special interests involved. Still it is a question we should all try to answer because it has implications for everyone, both you and me. Everyone wants a solution to the problem of high crime, even anti-guncontrollers. Its genuinely a constitutional issue. Everyone anyhow acknowledges that there is some connection between violence and guns, but which one do we tackle first? The problem is that somehow the guns and violence connection has become clouded by political considerations.

So how can we make sense of the problem? We have to begin by saying that there is a real stand-off

DRAFT #2

THE QUESTION OF GUN CONTROL

There is one thing the sane and the insane, the poor and the rich, the lawful and the lawless have in common in America: the handgun. This has become the symbol of our constitutional right to bear arms _and_ of the high fatality rate in urban crime. Violence and democratic rights have become intimately linked. Yet the question of whether we should _control_ the possession of handguns remains an open one. Is this because we are not sure whether the question is genuinely difficult, or because of special interests and political considerations which stand in the way of solving the issue? It would be naive to assume that special interests and the strength of political lobbies do not play a part in delaying gun control laws. But it would be foolish, too, to assume

between the two sides so the important thing to do is to take no sides at all and treat the problem as an open one at least as an experiment. There are difficult legal considerations, so we need to find a meeting point for the two sides.

Whether we are for or against gun control, we have to define our terms. For the sake of argument we will take the phrase "gun control" to refer to the <u>federal</u> control of the use of handguns, through licensing or restriction. These are concealed lethal weapons. It doesn't matter what the states do we have to refer to the national context because we are arguing the principle of the issue.

But why is all this an issue at all? The question has boiled down to the main problem of whether the government has the constitutional rights to ban handguns in defense. But then what if we do have gun control? Will it control violence effectively? Will it leave an unarmed public against armed criminals? Can it even be effective in a country as big as the U.S.? And if we don't have gun control what happens then as more and more crimes increase and involve handguns.

These questions seem incredible to answer. They simply don't have much in common when you first look at them, and they don't make much sense either in isolation. But people do agree on something and that is that we need to control deaths from gun-

that we automatically ought to have these laws. For the sake of argument, if the issue were to come to a vote now, how could we make sense of it?

There is a stand-off between those for and those against it, with each side claiming to appeal to constitutional rights. One side appeals to the right to bear arms, the other to the need to control arms to preserve our safety. So it would seem that the most important thing to do is not to rehearse the old and by now familiar arguments from each quarter but to consider how the two sides of the argument can be brought together.

Whether we are for or against gun control, we have to define our terms, preferably in such a way that both sides might find them acceptable. For the sake of argument, we will take the phrase "gun control" to refer to the *federal* control of the use of *handguns*, through licensing or restriction. Right now some states are considering various forms of gun control legislation, but the argument for or against the issue—if it is to be effective—has to refer to the national context. The argument goes beyond states' rights to invoke the Constitution itself.

But why *is* it an issue at all? The question has boiled down to the main problem of whether the government has the constitutional right to ban handguns for defense. There are other questions too: If we do have gun control, will it control violence effec-

related crime somehow. Both sides agree on that. So instead of getting bogged down by unanswerable questions, let's see if we can answer this one: If gun control is a concept which makes any sense at all, can it control killings and burglaries involving handguns, and preserve our civil rights? Let's see if a compromise is possible.

If you look at the question closely, it is not hard to see what the rightful context for the issue is. We have constitutional rights and the law and we have social and psychological theory which tries to explain why we have violence. I don't think it matters much if we know that an assassin is insane. We want a practical conclusion. What is more important: theory or protection? Our paradox now is that an individual is guaranteed the right to bear arms but finds herself needing to be protected by those who do carry guns.

The Law alone offers protection, for only the Law has in common the interests of both the gun carrier and the person who won't carry guns. Whatever psychology and sociology have to say about how violence operates in society and why we need handguns must become part of the legal issue. It doesn't matter if we know why handguns are associated with so much crime all that theorizing is irrelevant besides we don't know whether we need gun control or not. Do we need laws against guns or against violence? So is gun control a cause or an effect? What an

tively? Will law-abiding citizens be defenseless against criminals who will still find guns? Can gun control be effective in a country as large as the United States? If we don't have gun control, will we just be continuing a vicious circle? Will the need for guns for self-defense increase as more crimes involve handguns? How do we draw the line between defense and offense?

At first sight, these questions seem impossible to answer and have little in common. If you were to take them in isolation, they would <u>remain</u> difficult to answer. No one knows for sure if gun control would reduce violence. But people do agree on something: the need to control deaths from gun-related crime. So instead of getting sidetracked by unanswerable questions, let's consider the following issue: If gun control is a concept that makes any sense at all, can it control killings and burglaries involving handguns, <u>and</u> preserve our civil rights, specifically our right to bear arms for defense? It may seem as though we want to have it both ways by posing the question in this way, but let's see if we can make a compromise between the two sides.

The rightful context for this issue is not difficult to pin down. On the one hand, we have constitutional rights and the law, on the other, social and psychological theory which tries to explain why we have violence. Let's discount the latter at this point in an obsessive question. Do people kill or do guns? Are handgun killings an effect of social violence or is the availability of guns a cause of social violence? Do you control guns to control violence or violence to control guns or what? Here's a chicken-and-egg argument. I don't think it matters what the answer is, that is whether violence with guns is a cause or an effect. There is a great network of social disorder out there which no simple analysis can solve. The point is that violence <u>with</u> guns is overwhelmingly present and we don't need a sociologist to tell us that. We know it and now we have a legal program which centers on the protection of all of us in our homes and on the streets. Besides you can't assume that gun control is necessarily bad because it blocks our freedom. Should we then have freedom to kill? Is this what is implied? Is freedom an absolute? Surely all laws interfere with someone's freedoms but for the good of the greater number. What we have to do is to make legislation to protect our right to bear arms for defense and control handgun killings. Is it going to be possible to have one with the other?

I don't think that there is going to be a law which satisfies everyone. But a compromize surely seems possible. There could be a gun control law which tightens up alot on present restraints and at the same time leaves the Consitution alone. It should involve the compulsory licensing of all handguns when a police permit would be given for each gun if the

attempt to reach a practical conclusion. It helps little to know, for example, that an assassin is insane. What is more important, after all, theory or protection? Instead we have a legal crisis: we are guaranteed the right to bear arms but find ourselves needing to be protected from those who do. Only the law can offer that protection, for only the law has in common the interests of both the gun carrier and the person who refuses to bear arms. Psychological and sociological explanations of the violence that creates the need for handguns must become part of the <u>legal</u> issue. For even if we can determine why handguns are associated with so much violence, we still have not solved the problem of whether we need gun control.

We will also not solve the issue by becoming obsessed with other often-quoted questions: Do people kill or do guns? Are handgun killings an effect of social violence or is the availability of guns a cause of social violence? Do you control guns to control violence, or the other way round? Clearly this line of questioning rapidly turns into a chicken-and-egg argument: Which comes first? It does not really matter greatly whether violence with guns is a cause or an effect. It is part of a vast network of social disorder which no simple analysis can solve. The point is that violence with guns is overwhelmingly present, and we do not need a sociologist to tell us that. We know it, and now we have a legal problem which centers

owner has no criminal record and is mentally stable and if the owner could give good reasons for owning such a weapon. These are restriced sporting uses and an exceptional need for defense in areas where there is little police patrolling. No one could buy a firearm without a police permit, and the permit should be regularly renewed. Then there would need to be a general amnesty for all gun owners. Also there would be very strict penalties for owning an unlicensed weapon concealed or not, and stricter penalties than at present for committing a crime with the aid of a firearm. All sportsmen and gun owners would be required to take federally sponsored training courses in gun safety.

Of course there will be found loopholes in this argument. And we do know that there is no garantee that this control would stop criminals obtaining black market guns. But we can't go on arguing in circles for ever. Nor should we impose a harsher gun control law than the one I have suggested or else it won't get through Congress at all. We shouldn't avoid the legal issue because gun killings grow greater each year. So why not examine this compromise law for a start. Many guns would be taken out of circulation but the sportsmen could go on using them.

on the protection of all of us in our homes and on the streets.

We also must be careful not to assume that any legislation in favor of gun control is <u>necessarily</u> bad because it impedes our freedom. This is a legal question but one which seems to have been exploited by the anti-gun controllers. Should we then have freedom to kill? Is freedom an absolute? All laws in some way impede freedom, but in the interests of the greater good. The issue really is that of making legislation which both protects our right to bear arms for defense and controls handgun homicide. Is it going to be possible to have one with the other?

Of course no law can satisfy everyone, but a compromise surely seems possible and necessary. There could be a gun control law, for example, which tightens up considerably on present restraints and at the same time preserves the right to bear arms for the purposes of sport or defense. It should involve the compulsory licensing of all handguns. A police permit would be given for each gun if the owner, or prospective owner, has no criminal record and is considered mentally stable (i.e., has no recent history of mental disorder), and if the owner could give good reasons for owning such a weapon. (Restricted sporting use and an exceptional need for defense in areas where there is little police patrolling would be considered good reasons.) No one could buy a firearm without a police permit.

Such a law would be accompanied by a general amnesty for all gun owners, providing they return their weapons to the state, which would buy them back with federal money, no questions asked. Or else the owners could license their guns if they have good enough reason to do so. Accompanying the law would be very strict penalties for owning an unlicensed weapon (concealed or not), or committing a crime with the aid of a firearm. All sportsmen would be required to take federally sponsored training courses in gun safety.

There is no doubt that loopholes can be found in this argument. We do know that there is no guarantee that this control would stop criminals obtaining guns on the black market, or not turning in their guns to begin with. But we should not argue endlessly in circles or impose harsher gun control laws than the one I have proposed, for a harsher law would have even less chance of passing Congress. Nor should we avoid the legal issue while handgun homicides grow greater in number each year. So it would be a good idea to examine the possibilities of a limited control law, based on licensing. Such a law would remove some guns from circulation and preserve the rights of the individual to bear weapons in special cases for defense and sporting purposes. We may have difficulty arguing over the definition of <u>defense</u> but better some compromise version of gun control than no law at all.

Checklist

1. Read your writing aloud.
   Mark passages that do not sound right.
   Mark faulty transitions.
   Mark unclear meanings.
   Mark boring and slow-moving passages.
   Mark wordy and overstated passages.

2. Reread your essay for emphasis, coherence, and unity.

   Emphasis:

   Does the title relate to the thesis or problem?
   Is the topic clearly described and defined early in the essay?
   Are there accurate and forceful main statements about the topic?
   Does the topic have a realistic focus?
   Is there a clear conclusion related to the problem or thesis?
   Does the first paragraph arouse interest and provide a focus?
   Does the closing paragraph show the progress of the argument?
   Do the sentences make clear statements?
   Are there any awkward constructions or roundabout statements?
   Are there any unnecessary repetitions or overqualifications?
   Are there concrete rather than overly abstract references?
   Have you used clichés, jargon, euphemisms, too many intensifiers, or other language that is too colloquial, roundabout, abstract, evasive, unnecessary, overstated, or inappropriate?
   Can you inject more color into your writing?

   Coherence:

   Is there an argument or solution developed from the thesis statement or problem?
   Are there clearly defined relationships and oppositions between facts?

Has a network of accurately established facts been presented?

Do the stages of the argument, explanation, or solution hold together?

If the message involves value judgments, have they been justified?

Does each paragraph have just one major theme?

Is each paragraph made up of coherently related sentences?

Do the paragraphs flow into each other?

Unity:

Are there any passages that stop the flow of the argument?

Is there a consistent point of view?

Is there a consistent and authentic tone of voice?

Does the tone develop from the writer's relationship to the topic?

Is the tone rational and carefully controlled?

Is the style consistent with the tone and appropriate to the topic?

3. Consider your audience.

Have you helped to create the audience of the essay?

Have you been kind to the reader, creating a climate of shared values?

Have you thought of the audience in consistent terms?

4. Edit your text (see Handbook).

Sentence fragments

Run-on sentences

Agreement

Vague pronoun references

Dangling modifiers

Spelling and punctuation

5. Proofread your final draft.

Exercises

1. Revise the essay you have been writing since Chapter 3, referring closely to the revision checklist to make sure you cover all the stages of revision.

2. Revise and, if necessary, rewrite the following paragraphs. Follow the revision checklist, looking for problems with emphasis, coherence, and unity. Correct grammatical and other errors, too.

(a) Although I never played tackle football as an organized event, I would constantly be thrilled at watching the game take place. Especially back home, where I could scream and stamp my feet in support of our local hero's, the Casowary Cavaliers. It was something special to watch your team rout the enemy, and be a part of a huge victory celibration that always followed. These were my warm memories of college football, some of the best thoughts of the past that I hold.

(b) Because of these thoughts, my view of a football team here is slightly prejudice. Nevertheless, a football team here might be just what our students need to bring together a large conglomeration of support for the schools sports program. Of course, a new program might inflict a downfall of attendance at the other sports events now in progress, but I think that the outcome might be just the opposite. The different events could work together, hand in hand. For instance, a good football team should not take away faithful hocky fans, but actually bring a larger attendance, a group of new fans interested in watching sports when a football team is not playing. Football attracts a large number of fans, no matter the weather or the wins, and I'd bet alot on our supportive effort in such a club.

(c) Hamlet's first soliloquy is an emotionally charged speech which summarizes his perspective of life and death. The speech also provides insight into the recent events in Hamlet's life. Specifically, his monologue deals with the recent death of his father and the speedy remarriage of his mother Gertrude to Uncle Claudius.

Furthermore, this soliloquy demonstrates how these incidents have shaped this young prince's attitudes which will continue to influence the rest of the play.

The opening lines of this speech are direct and serious. "O that this too too sullied flesh would melt,/Thaw, and resolve itself into a dew." The immediate mention of suicide by Hamlet testifies to the magnitude of his concerns. Later in the play Hamlet once again toys with the idea of suicide in his famous "To Be or Not to Be" speech. At this moment the laws of the church prevent him from considering suicide as a viable alternative to his miseries. The church laws forbidding suicide are not capable of preventing the suicide of another character, Ophelia, later in the play. Driven the madness and suicide by the recent death of her father and her love for Hamlet, Ophelia throws herself into the river. At her burial site a debate arises between two gravediggers whether or not this young woman should receive a Christian burial and grave, or if a diagonally positioned grave may not be more appropriate. (Because of her social status, Ophelia is allowed a Christian burial by the coroner.) (d) Ever since the evergy crisis in nineteen-seventy-four imported oil has increased in price. I can remember when regular gasoline was eighty-nine cents for one gallon and premium ninety-four cents, that was back in nineteen-seventy-seven, two years after the OPEC nations ended their oil embargo on imports to the U.S. Who would ever think that gasoline prices could cost more than a dollar a gallon. Well it did happen and on an average it increased to a dollar and twenty-four cents for regular and one-thirty-five for premium. Diesel fuel was fifty-six cents a gallon two years ago, but today it is and incredible one-seventeen. Most of these sharp increases were caused by price controls which were lifted by President Reagan and because of the once more high prices; gasoline consumption has fallen in the last month and a half. Engine oil costs has risen in proportion, if compared against gasoline, much faster. Becuase some oil brands like Castrol, Kendall, Oilzum and Elf are basically imported and naturally will cost more. But domestic brands such as Valvoline, Pennzoil, Quaker State and Shell are far less expensive and proven to be superior in quality. To this day Pennsylvania produces some of the best crude in the world.

3. Discuss the general problems of emphasis, coherence, and unity that occur in the following passages. Then rewrite each one in clear, concise, jargon-free English.

a. It is absolutely imperative that the university interface with the context of the business and professional worlds. It must efficiently facilitate its mission to provide substantial assistance to its student population. The university is not only a conduit of higher learning, an edifice of intellectual aspirations, a word processing center in which information transfers itself in vast cybernetic systems, but it must also adequately distribute its products to the public at large. University students are the products of the university environment, and the most meaningful experience we can offer them at this point in time is to create a nonlinear information transferral involving their minds and those of the business and professional sector which must rely on innovative and dynamic thinking. Consequently, the university should become an employment agency.

b. The Great Society is a good thing. Where else would you rather live? I can't think of a better place. Societies come and go, but the Great One is that which we all aspire to. When our government tells us to believe in our inherent greatness and decency and work together to make this a better, more harmonious and mellow place to live in, then I get a warm glow all inside. I think we are great, but of course we can be greater. We don't all work together as we should. Sometimes there aren't enough jobs for all of us to work, but then that's only a temporary setback for the Great Society because everyone knows that inflation will get better, and society can get on the move again.

c. Let's get straight to the point with no fooling around, no double-talk, and no mealy-mouthed pseudo-liberal whining about the poor. I don't believe in welfare. I don't believe we need welfare. All we need is some people to get it into their heads that they have to be innovative and resourceful. There were no jobs waiting for the first settlers to this land when they arrived, no crutch for them to lean on. They had to create them, and create them they did. Their resourcefulness is an inspiration to us all. So where, I ask, is that good old American know-how now? The Japanese humiliate us and we have massive economic deficits all because we have to feed people who won't help themselves. Soon we will all find ourselves second-class citizens. To me the conclusion is clear: take away welfare and restore initiative.

4. Identify the errors in the following sentences, and then rewrite the sentences correctly. Note: there may be more than one error in each sentence.

a. He tried running a campaign and looking after a business at the same time that he found a new wife and delivered several speeches a day. It made it difficult for him to get enough into his day.

b. Most modern art looks like the meandering of an inebriated spider across the web of unfortunate dreams.

c. I don't think that imbibing potent liquors should be allowed within the confines of university housing.

d. Pounding out words on the typewriter, the time seemed to pass awfully fast.

e. There's a good deal of running around involved with the job you must be careful to develop lots of stamina. Since you really want the position.

f. Chess is a game for minds of peculiar skill, it is found in individuals of particular talent.

g. Let's be very clear about this: it's an absolute disgrace that the student union is left partially unfinished in order to start building a useless faculty club.

h. I saw this morning walking to work a man of unusually tall dimensions.

i. So what if the father is 60 and the mother is 39. Older people are learning to do this with more courage now.

j. I know that the trends in modern fashions have reached a stalemate. Because they don't have style any more.

5. Here is an extract from a humorous article called "Talking" by Bruce McCall which appeared in the *New Yorker*. Decide what Ethel Mattice is really saying by picking out all the main statements. Write what she has to say, punctuating it correctly. Then rewrite in plain English what Duane Dix is trying to say. You need not write more than a paragraph or two for each.

ETHEL MATTICE

She's not like most of the other people of America whose stories I've listened to, the soft-spoken folk with voices as faded and anonymous as their lives. Her voice is a bagpipe practicing to be a foghorn. The knickknacks on her mantelpiece jump and dance whenever she talks; I retreat out into the hall and just sort of edge the mike into the parlor doorway. This is what she says:

I started out in the Chin Musicians that was the kids' talking society ages about five to ten and oh goodness I don't think I could have been more than seven myself it was the year of the Columbian Exposition when I entered my first talking bee they had these talking bees out where I grew up in the Dakota Territory put on by the so-called talking societies every little town had its talking society there was let me think the Stephen Douglas and the William Jennings Bryan and of course the Garibaldis that was another one very snooty if you were in the Garibaldis you wore a big red sash and they even used those whatchamacallits those spray things yes atomizers that's the word to moisten their tonsils very la-di-da we used to say and wouldn't you know it one of the Garibaldis went on into the opera. *(Gasps)*

There was just this terrific emphasis on talking not just in my family in every family this came out of those long prairie winters out of the boredom of it being cooped up for months and months in your little sod hut talking was about the only way we knew to beat the blues things really closed in after Buffalo Day now Buffalo Day nobody remembers anymore but it was that day around the end of November when the wind finally got so strong it even blew the buffalo across the prairie I distinctly remember the night the buffalo hit our hut oh my what a commotion it busted Mama's ormolu vase into a million pieces but as I say talking real loud was the only way to drown out the howling of that awful wind. *(Gasps)*

So eventually somebody it was a farmer up Dilemma Falls way who claimed credit on the other hand he also said he invented the dog that man was not altogether reliable if you know what I mean but somebody decided to make it a public competition to buck up the spirits there was talking fastest and of course my specialty talking loudest and longest without taking a breath and then the novelty ones like talking while being tickled and talking with a mouthful of feathers for some reason only the Blackfoot Indians ever did that well and then talking in time with a grandfather clock we called it clocktalk and if you ask me clocktalk was even more boring than silence that was the specialty of a man name of Crowder he called himself the Human Metronome I'll tell you that man never got invited to dinner at the same house twice. *(Gasps)*

My brother Boone he left and went up Athabasca way the first day of spring after I took up the talking he was a patient soul but his nerves couldn't take the noise but my parents they did nothing but encourage me after dinner they'd go stand outside in the snow it got down to thirty below in January mind you just so I could practice what a grand thing it was I got to the All County finals and by age twelve there I was West Dakota Juvenile Champion in my category of talking loudest and longest without taking a breath and guess what I won I won a megaphone imagine that a megaphone. (*Gasps*)

DUANE DIX

He keeps passing in and out of microphone range as he loops and swoops his skateboard around the living room, a figure skater gliding on cut pile. He just misses the coffee table and just misses the sleeping Irish setter. He just misses every object in the room, except the interviewer's casually outflung leg.

There was this one time I remember, this was real feeble, man, it was moron city . . . . . .my buddy Gary, from school? And some other guy from Evanston or someplace, a real konk . . . . .this real sticky gray kind of tape, kind of industrial tape off a truck or something. Real retrograde, man . . . . . . they both go and seal up their whole face and mouth with this stuff, you know, this tape . . . . and they both wrap it around and around their heads like these mummies. It was so ultra-wonk, man . . . double depressing, you know, because . . . . like they couldn't talk or say nothing . . . . but like nobody even noticed and . . . . . hey, man, get out of my . . . . (*Inaudible*)

Readings

Edwin Newman **O Facilitative New World!**

''As the new electronic marvels buzz away furiously, some of what they do will have value. But, as an inevitable accompaniment, they will preserve what ought to be torn up, discarded, cast aside, or should never have been born.''

Robert Crichton **Across the River and into the Prose**

''There is nothing in writing harder to do than start. But in the morning I finish the sentence that has been left unfinished and then I finish the paragraph and all at once I am in the river again.''

O FACILITATIVE NEW WORLD!

Edwin Newman

When I look at the future, I flinch. Many people do, of course, for a variety of reasons. My reason is the expectation, more and more confidently expressed, that the future will be the Age of Information. Already, we are told, an impressive percentage (estimates vary) of those who work no longer grow things or make things or sell things. They engage, instead, in "information transfer." And this, we are assured, is a mere beginning. Which is why I flinch. Much of the information transferred to us now, on paper, is not worth having. Will the world be a better place when, on computer print-outs or flashing word processors, we receive the following?

"It is recommended that the focus, scope and purpose be clearly delineated and understood. Then, with the existing resources, the restructuring of the developmental process will be guided by the central concepts of the previously stated management philosophy. Specific functional and administrative activities, service outputs, and staff capacity development will be defined as real need demands are anticipated or identified. Armed with this real need information, a working management tool can be more accurately designed through the use of the proposed management model."

That paragraph (part of a memorandum that won its author a promotion in the human-resources department of a middle-size state) occupied people, otherwise known as human resources, who might better have been employed doing almost anything else. The Information Age will make it easier to pump out such stuff and circulate it to full-fledged information receivers. Read need knowledge, I imagine it will be called.

Even now, before the Information Age has fully dawned, we may chance upon this:

"For the purpose of communication, some of the dimensions of organization health are listed. The listed dimensions are only a sampling of indicators which can be considered. Each is a job environmental condition created or not created by management which when present indicates with a high degree of predictability that productive work is underway."

O brave new world, that has such information in't! But hold! There is more, the dimensions of organizational health themselves:

"Clarity and acceptability of agency goals by staff.

"Distortion-free vertical and horizontal communication both formal and informal.

"Adequate distribution of influence within the organization through the decentralization of program authority.

"Cohesiveness of staff within and across program boundaries."

Still receiving?

How many Americans on public and private payrolls already spend their time writing—or as they would prefer to say, conceptualizing—this sort of thing, and how many spend time reading it? The nation is drowning in it, in effusions about setting "meaningful, priority-based objectives" and about "the personal and corporate building of physical, psychological and organizational environments that best facilitate the process of innovation and project management." When this gabble appears on paper, the copies can be thrown away. The original, more likely to be saved, at least by its author, may rot. In a computer data bank, it will be with us, such is the magic of "information retrieval" and "electronic memory system," forever.

We have, today, otherwise blameless citizens who will sit at a typewriter and produce this: "I am reluctant to limit myself to specific titles as they tend to limit the parameters that often encompass a number of areas that for one reason or another have a natural interface."

Limited parameters and natural interfaces rub shoulders with linear and non-linear model fitting, negative/positive reinforcement concepts, nonevent feedback mechanisms, cognitive mapping, axial rules and neuro-linguistic programing.

All of this we have, and more. What will we get when cathode-ray-tube keyboards are everywhere, hooked into a mighty network of foolish discourse, and when computers can talk to one another? I don't go as far as Kingsley Amis's Lucky Jim, who decided at an early age that there was no point in acquiring new information because it pushed out an equivalent amount of information he already had, leaving him just where he started. As the new electronic marvels buzz away furiously, some of what they do will have value. But, as an inevitable accompaniment, they will preserve what ought to be torn up, discarded, cast aside or should never have been born.

As a child, my daughter had a ready answer when urged to eat something because it was good for her. "Eat it," she would reply, "your own self." To prophets of the information explosion, I say roughly the same thing. Leave me out of it. Transfer—and receive—that information your own self.

1. Newman is not disturbed by information; he is disturbed by "information transfer." What is this exactly, how does it affect information, and why does it bother Newman?

2. Rewrite the second paragraph in simple English.

3. Write a few paragraphs explaining carefully why you think people write the kind of jargon-ridden prose that Newman is complaining about.

ACROSS THE RIVER AND INTO THE PROSE

Robert Crichton

The only thing I ever wanted to accomplish in life was to write a good novel. I wanted this so much that I came to think of myself as being a novelist even though I had never written one. Despite this little failing I was quite convinced that were I to die right then my obituary would read Crichton, Novelist, Writes Last Chapter because everyone would know how much it meant to me. And it would only be fair; I had all the novels in my head. All that was lacking was the technical formality of transferring them to paper.

This state of affairs went on until I was past thirty. When no novel had appeared, in order to account for the void and save my self-respect, I was driven to conclude that I was a classic example of the pitfalls of Grub Street. I was a free-lance magazine writer then, living from one assignment to the next, always one advance behind, and I saw myself as a victim of the literary sharecropper system, as hopelessly snared in my web of circumstances as those wretched cotton farmers James Agee described in *Let Us Now Praise Famous Men.*

The matter was out of my hands. I was a victim and I was quite happy that way until the spring of 1962 when a magazine publisher named Henry Steeger came back from a lunch he had with some Italian wine growers and told me the story of a small Italian hill town where the people had hidden 1,000,000 bottles of wine from the Germans and how they managed to keep their enormous secret.

"Someone should write that," Mr. Steeger said. "It has the quality of legend and yet it happened in our own time."

I could recognize that much. I was astonished in fact that this fat plum of a story, swelling with possibilities, was still unplucked. By this time, however, I had so perfected my defenses to repel anything that even hinted at the potential of becoming a novel that I was able to tell myself that it actually wasn't a very good story at all. I increasingly found it more desirable to apologize for a book I hadn't written (but which just might be great) than to apologize for one I had written.

Camus has written that ultimately all men are prey to their truths, even in the act of denying them, and Santa Vittoria became one of mine. Even while denying it I knew the story of this town was the basis for a big grab bag of a novel, a *bildungs-roman,* in which, because of the sprawling framework of the story, almost anything goes and anything works. Against my will the story preyed upon me, fermenting in my doughy spirit, fizzing there like a cake of yeast in a wine vat.

I woke one morning in March, there was snow and thunder in the morning, very rare and very strange, with the line "In dreams begin responsibilities" running in my mind. It is a line from Yeats (borrowed, I have since found out, from some obscure Indian poet) that I used to write in all my notebooks when I was in college. It is a line that has been the subject of profound scrutiny and some subtle interpretations have resulted from it. But on this morning the line was very clear to me: If you dream about something all the time you have a responsibility to do something about it. I apologize to William Butler Yeats. I began going around New York that morning trying to raise enough money to take me to Italy. I felt the least I could do was look at this place which had become my responsibility. When I accumulated $800 beyond the cost of a round-trip air fare I set out for Santa Vittoria.

The trip to Italy, which by any other terms than those of a writer would have to be classed as a continuous disaster, I include here because it illustrates something important about the craft, namely, anything that happens to a writer can, with good fortune, be turned into something of value. In a matter of weeks I was run down by a car in Rome, robbed in a country inn, and managed to make a profound fool of myself in Santa Vittoria, and each incident turned out to be more fortunate than the one before it.

The car incident is a good example. I was in a pedestrian crosswalk which guaranteed me the right of way when the car bore down on me. I, an American and a believer in the sanctity of signs, couldn't believe he was going to keep on coming. He couldn't believe I wasn't going to jump out of the way. He must have been a good driver because he only drove halfway over my body before managing to stop. I had my first intimation of the way things were going to go when a man helped me out from under the car.

"You're very lucky," he said. "You didn't dent the fender."

My last intimation, or my first revelation, of truth came in the police station. I was talking about justice and my rights and I could see that they felt I was not well balanced. I didn't get the idea, they assured me. The car was bigger and faster and stronger than me and therefore the car had the right of way. Couldn't I see that much?

So on only my second day in Italy I was privileged to begin to understand the basic fact of Italian life which is that power, the balance of it, the having and not having it, is the key to all life. Survival depends on a respect for it. The possession or lack of it determines the course of a man's existence. Success depends on how well you learn to manipulate it. I was never able to get anyone in Italy to be sympathetic about being run down in a safety zone. They would listen to the story and they would nod and then they would always say: "Yes, but why *didn't* you jump out of the way?"

These people, then, who pass themselves off to the world and to themselves as romantics are the most realistic of people. Two broken fingers and the knees gone from the pants of my one good suit was a small price to pay for such knowledge. I might have spent months in Italy before learning what I did.

The robbery was a very Italian kind of crime. I was headed north to Santa Vittoria, taking all the back roads available so I would have a feel of the country before getting there, and I took a room in a country inn on the second floor with a terrace. Few Italians would have taken that room. It faced away from the inn and not in toward the courtyard. Italians like to be with people. Americans, who have allowed the North European psyche to inflict itself upon our national soul, prefer privacy. Even if he took the room no Italian would have then opened the window on to the terrace. They don't trust the night air and what might come in with it. Americans like to clean the portals of the mind with fresh night air and they like to be trusting and believe in the possibilities for humankind to be good.

It must have looked like a ritual scene from some old Italian *novella*. The thief came up the stone wall at night and onto the terrace and into the room and through my pockets. I should still be angry with him but the thief did one marvelous thing; he left me half of my money. I picture him working swiftly and dangerously in the dark to leave me my share and I warm to him. He was a humanist and a man generous to strangers which is as good a definition of a gentleman as any. So another factor; Life is a matter of power tempered by an incorruptible humanity, which in itself is a kind of power. I was a more tolerant man after that and I was also one long step down toward poverty and my ultimate entry into the Italian lower depths where few outsiders are allowed to go.

In Santa Vittoria, on my first day, I was invited to a luncheon at the winery held for some American wine buyers and I proceeded first to praise and then to rave about one particular wine which I assured those present made all the rest taste like scented toilet water. Certainly someone should have warned me that the wine I was praising was a comparison wine, designed to make the local wines taste good by comparison. It was suggested by a company official after the lunch that I didn't seem to be the right man to tell the story of the great thing they did in Santa Vittoria. I left the town the same day I arrived in it.

And this was fortunate, too. Fearful of attempting a novel I had determined to write a non-fiction book but now I had no alternative. I also thought that I would be able to live off the generosity of the people I was writing about and now I was condemned to live off the land. I headed south, down the spine of the Apennines, in search of my own Santa Vittoria. In all I stayed in twenty hill towns, each one separate in my mind and yet all of them finally merging into one conglomerate city, richer than the sum of its parts. I learned some things of value along the way.

In the beginning I had the belief that people would resent my intrusion and I sat at solitary tables in the cafe in the piazza and sat like Proust at a party, "J'observe, j'observe." It took me time to learn that my discretion only bred suspicion. No one told me anything honest. At last I fell back on the tactic of simple honesty. On arriving in a new town I learned to approach the first person who seemed to command respect and tell him exactly what I was doing in his town. I was an American, a writer, I was planning a book on just such a town as this one, but not this one, and I wanted to know everything good and everything bad about life in a hill town that anyone wanted to tell me. Very often the man would take me to the mayor who would tell me everything good about the town and then the people would come and tell me everything bad about it.

Every day I grew poorer and this was good since it put me into the hands and then the homes of people I couldn't have met otherwise. Toward the end of my stay I was reduced to knocking on stranger's doors and asking if they would like to sell me a plate of peas and rice or some soup and bread and wine for 100 *lire*. They were always happy to do it. Someone could always go without a meal but where could they get an extra 100 *lire?* I learned a great many things with my soup.

The trouble with poverty as a tactic is that you can't fake it. I don't think you can plan to be poor and in this way get to meet what are always referred to as the people. I tried it afterwards in Appalachia and in the coal fields of Scotland and it was no good. Peasants smell the poverty in you. When you pay the 100 *lire* you have to feel the sweat on your forehead as you count the money out. And you have to do sneaky little things to save little sums of money that peasants recognize but which the bourgeoisie never even notice.

There is little to do in hill towns after dark and because of it, the loneliness, I developed a system of information gathering that has proved invaluable to me since. From a simple need to communicate, with no specific purpose in mind, I began to write long rambling letters home, putting down everything that interested me or puzzled me during the day. Months later, when I sat down to start on the first draft of *Santa Vittoria,* it was the letters that turned out to be filled with the kind of information I needed. My notes were mostly useless.

The reason for this, I think, is that a letter is an inclusive thing. Notes tend to be selective and therefore exclusive. When a person is taking notes he generally has some idea of what he is looking for. The haphazard, the irrelevant, the unexpected, since it doesn't fit the pattern is ignored or not even seen. I suppose it is possible to do as well by keeping a diary as writing a letter but most people tend to cheat in diaries. As time passes entries tend to become more terse and cryptic, the diary becomes filled with one-line notations the writer is sure he will be able to re-create later, with all the emotion and sounds and smells. In a letter, since it is going to someone else, the effort to re-create has to be made right then if the letter is going to make any sense at all. It's more interesting to write to someone else than oneself anyway. The only people who write good diaries are people who know their logs will be part of history and egoists who hope theirs will be.

When I returned from Italy I attempted to organize my notes because this is what I felt writers did. The notes were so meagre and pointless, however, I began making notes from the letters. These I put in a large shoebox because I couldn't think of any sensible way to file them. It was sloppy and disorganized and yet the system had an unexpected virtue to it. In order to find out something I was compelled to flip through as many as a hundred notes and while doing this I was reminded of all kinds of facets of Italian life that I wouldn't have remembered if I had been able to go to the source at once. Some of this haphazard extraneous information was bound to seep into the scene I was working on and the scene would be a little richer for it. In time I came to think of the shoebox as my compost pile, a dung heap for potential fertility, and the leaping from note to note as an act of cross-fertilization. Marianne Moore once wrote something close to "Thank God for the privilege of disorganized things" and in this case she is right.

I kept making notes because I was afraid to actually start the book. For the same reason, to avoid starting, I began to read a great deal about Italy, hill towns, wine making, despite the fact that I had been led to believe that it wasn't a good idea for a novelist to read too much about the subject he would be writing about. The idea was that the reading tended to rob the writer of his individuality and that he would be exposed to material similar to his own and would not want to use it although he might actually handle it in quite a different fashion. There is also always the danger of reading something so superlative that the writer will be smothered by it. Who wants to write a novel about the War of 1812 after reading *War and Peace?* In my case, while admittedly stalling, the reading turned out to be enormously rewarding. Everything I read seemed to trigger some kind of creative response in me. It didn't matter very much what the subject was or whether the writing was good or bad, anything at all I read had the potential to give birth to an idea, often one that had no relationship with the reading at all. Some African tribes believe that energy creates energy and it got this way with my reading; every response seemed to create a climate for a heightened response. One of what I will boldly call the more effective scenes in *Santa Vittoria,* a competitive dance in a wine press, was suggested to me by a series of letters from an Edwardian schoolteacher to her class while on vacation in Sicily. She thought the wine pressers were ugly because they looked like hairy pagan goats. One incident, which plays an important part in the book, occurred to me while reading the financial statement of a modern wine company. When the barometer of the creative nature is set for a spell of writing, evidently anything can excite it and in my experience, and to my surprise, reading had the strongest potential of all.

There finally came a time when I could no longer find a believable excuse not to begin. I even announced the fact to my family and friends. "Tomorrow, I begin." I made it easy on myself. I vowed I would write exactly one page and write just one page for a week. This shouldn't frighten anyone and at the end of the week I would be like a colt let out to his first pasture.

But I couldn't do it. All day I sat at my desk and I wrote one word. "If." Toward evening I wrote the word in pencil so that it covered the entire page. The next day I wrote "So now I begin" and never got further than that. The day after that I tried the reliable weather and date technique. "On a cold blustery morning in May, 1943, on the sunless eastern slopes of the Apennines, spring was coming hard. . . ."

After that I quit. I rented an office away from home not to inspire creativity but to hide me from those who could see me doing nothing for hours on end. I gave up the idea of one page; this goal seemed insurmountable. I came under the idea that if I could get one good opening sentence, the keynote, and get it down right, the rest of the book would unravel itself from there. I was very conscious of the fact that I was like the man in Camus' *The Plague* who spends thirty years on *his* opening sentence, honing it, pruning it, polishing it, but it didn't matter. Who was to say if he got his sentence right the rest of his book wouldn't have inevitably followed. It was all I had to hang on to.

"How did it go today?" my wife would ask.

"It's coming; it's coming," followed by several very strong drinks.

One afternoon I realized I was never going to write the sentence and once I understood that I arrived at the idea of disowning art. I had become so self-conscious about style and craft that I had become incapable of reading or hearing words any longer. When I said them they sounded strange and when I put them down on paper they looked strange. I recall writing "This book begins" and then stopping because the word book looked wrong. What kind of word was book. An indefinite word. It could be a checkbook or the Bible. Volume was better. Journal even better. "This journal begins. . . ." Too pompous. But I couldn't go back to book. Novel, that was the real, precise word I wanted. But what kind of novel? The reader had a right to know.

In this way the day went. It was possible to fill a wastebasket in a day and never write over four different words. I always used a clean fresh sheet for a clean fresh start. With every empty sheet there was hope, and failure. On this afternoon, however, I began to write the story of Santa Vittoria in the form and style of a Dick and Jane first reader.

"There is a little town on a hill called Santa Vittoria. It is in Italy. The people in the town grow grapes and make wine. A great thing took place in the town. One day, not too long ago. . . ."

It astonishes me now that I was able to keep this up for several weeks. Because the words didn't count the words poured out. And I was happy about the sound of my typewriter because I had grown embarrassed by the silence from my cubicle.

"What's he do?"

"He's a writer?"

"Oh. What's he write?"

"I don't know. I never heard him write."

I heard that. Now the pages were piling up and I felt good. It was silly, considering the manuscript was one that I would have shot someone over, before allowing him to see it, and yet the feeling was real. In the end I had several hundred pages filled with one-syllable words and while I pretended to disown the pile of paper it meant a great deal to me. It was no good but at last I had *something* which was no good. All kinds of things were missing but now they were missing from something. I was conscious that through Dick and Jane I had outflanked art.

A week later I cut the manuscript down to 125 pages and in the process something strange happened to it. In the starkness of its naked simplicity the book became mysterious in tone. In the cutting the manuscript had become fragmented into a series of pared-to-the-bone pastiches and I was faced with the realization that somehow, inadvertently, I seemed to have written A New Novel. I had the wild thought that Alain Robbe-Grillet would discover me. The book would be published by Grove Press and reviewed by *The New York Review of*

Books, perhaps (who could tell how far it might go) by Susan Sontag, favorably, of course, thereby immortalizing me to my peer group; and then the thought passed. I was a fraud and what could be more fraudulent among the grapes and stones and lives of Santa Vittoria than a novel Alain Robbe-Grillet could approve of? Marienbad, *oui,* Santa Vittoria, *non.*

I had the bones of a book. The problem now was to flesh out the skeleton. I was still afraid to begin but not as much as before. The first act of creation is the terrifying thing and once this is done, it now seems to me, no matter how badly, something menacing has been overcome. I wasn't swimming yet but I was in the water.

I began by putting *place* in the book. I wanted a sense of the town to permeate the book because place plays such an important part in the book. What happened could only happen in an isolated hill town. Whenever there was a change of scene I began to describe in detail what the new place would look like, whether it was a room, the piazza, the entire town itself. In this process of supplying place the absence of people to the place made itself evident. Almost in spite of myself I began to people the places and in this way the book began to get itself written.

I have never had any idea about character. It is one reason I don't think I could teach literature. I only seem to see what people do. I don't recognize an evil man until he does something evil and then I'm not sure that he meant it to be evil. The same goes for good people. There is no good or evil in itself, as Camus has pointed out, but only the consequences of acts. All things are in all people at all times. So I couldn't plot out a character or even conceive of one, they simply happen, and from day to day, capable of a ridiculous, mean action one day and something generous the very next day.

"The character lacks unity." What nonsense. "He wouldn't have done that." What nonsense. He *did* it. Everyone is ultimately capable of almost everything which is after all the fascination and horror of life.

In his book *Individuals,* P. F. Strawson has written that "the primary conceptual scheme must be one that puts people in the world. A conceptual scheme which puts a world in each person must be, at least, a secondary product."

This idea is one of the few dogmas about writing that I am conscious of holding. I didn't want my characters to stand for anything, to explain, to symbolize, to account for anything but simply, in the words of Denis Donaghue when describing what a novel should be, possessed of life to a degree of irrelevance . . . all carelessness and luck, who, when given their first push, would leap on their way.

My final concern was style, although I didn't know it then. I am ashamed to admit that I thought of style as a mannerism, the decor of a book. I learned later that this is a technique, an artifice, not a style. The best description of style I have ever read and one of the most valuable lines about writing is by the same Donaghue who says: Style is the right feeling animating the voice.

I had no voice. I didn't know who was telling the story and why he was telling it. If I chose a Santa Vittorian I would be compelled to accept the limitations of a peasant's vision of life. I could choose to be the author as God, omniscient, wilful, intolerant, irrational, as gods tend to be, but I knew I didn't function well as God. It's not my type. One day I thought of an Italian writing a novel about life in Conway, Arkansas, and I almost fell apart. The opportunities for error were endless. As a result my decision was made for me. I was forced into what might be called a literary cop-out but which became inevitable. To account for my ignorance I invented as narrator an Italian-American airman, a deserter who parachutes from his plane after a pointless bombing of a nearby hill town and who has remained in Santa Vittoria after the war because of his fear of returning and a misguided sense of shame about what he did. He hopes that by telling this story he can earn some money and by explaining why he deserted in one part of the book, in exchange for telling the greater story, perhaps redeem himself.

Was it the proper voice? Does it meet Donaghue's criteria? Probably not. In the long haul the narrator is not truly a voice but a device and not a character (he mercifully almost never appears in the book) but a sound. The worst part of it for me was that I didn't commit the errors that I was certain I would. So I didn't need Robert Abruzzi after all but I didn't know it then and that was important. He served me well but let him know this: If Abruzzi were to come back to Santa Vittoria again I would have him lined up against a wall and edited to death.

When I had written 150 pages through the eyes of Abruzzi I sent what I had done to my publisher, Simon and Schuster, in the hope of getting an advance. Unfinished manuscripts tend to seem more promising to editors, I was told. Also, if the publisher gives an advance he now has a vested interest in the final product. An advance tends to blind an editor's judgement of a manuscript since the house is already committed. Finally the advance is supposed to bolster the unsure writer's confidence.

"They really *want* me. They *believe* in me."

None of it worked this way for me. I did nothing until I got the advance and when I did it had the effect of stopping me altogether. Now there was no way out. I had taken the money and I was the one who was committed. I had a contract. They could take me to court if I didn't produce a novel. But perhaps it was all to the best. I determined not to spend the money, but I did, and it was finally my fear of having to pay the money back, which grew stronger than my fear of failure, which led me to finish the book. It was this version the publisher bought.

I felt they were wrong to buy it. I knew the book was all wrong. I had the place I wanted in the book and the people and the story but each of these elements stood in its own place, one immovable chunk of writing hard by another. The novel seemed to me like a freshly blasted quarry with no one to pick up the pieces. By chance I saw an editor's note about the book that said: "This is really very good you know" and I felt the note was a plant, a kind of editor's waterwings designed to buoy me up for the sea of revisions ahead.

They asked for very few revisions and this I took as a very bad sign. If they were really interested in the book they would want all kinds of changes. I figured they had given up on the book but would go ahead and print it in the hopes of recovering their advance. They gave me two weeks to make the revisions we agreed to. One of them was on page one, a four letter word which wasn't called for but which I had included to show right off that I wasn't afraid to use four letter words. I scratched the word out and the page looked messy and so I retyped it and it came out a line short so I retyped the second page and it came out wrong so I went on to the third page. I began cutting some paragraphs and then an entire scene and to add dialogue and change dialogue and somewhere along the way that morning a new character entered the story. I had meant to work until lunch but when I stopped I was surprised to find that it was five o'clock in the afternoon and I had written 42 pages. I had no sensation of having worked hard. I intended to stop the next day but I didn't. I wrote 35 pages that day, much of it a complete re-working and I knew that evening I was going to do the whole book. There was no question that it was exciting to me and that I knew I was doing something good because, for no reason I could explain, the immovable blocks were beginning to join one another in a way I had never been able to make them do.

The word I have found for the experience was immersion. It is something I intend to work to find again. Previously I had worked on the book and at the book but all at once I was immersed in the book. The book seemed to be carrying me instead of me pushing it. It was a very rare sensation. The book was much more real than anything else in my life then. As I went into the second week I had the sensation of being drawn very fine, as if I could thread myself through a needle. I seemed to have my own sense of the way things were while before I had always been listening over my shoulder to see if I could get a lead on the way things should go. I was out of life, under water, immersed.

I was, of course, making mistakes but they were my own mistakes and because of this they at least had the virtue of a certain consistency about them. I told no one what I was doing for fear of breaking the spell. Physically I must have shown it. In three and a half weeks' immersion I lost 20 pounds. One night my wife said "Bob, you seem so small" but the only physical effect I experienced was the phenomenon of the missing drinks. In the evening I would pour myself a drink and when I looked for it it would be empty. Evidently I was masking fatigue with alcohol and I must have drunk a great deal to sustain myself but I had no conscious desire to do this and never got drunk. At the end of 23 days I finished a manuscript which, when published, occupied 447 reasonably tightly printed pages. The following day, while walking down Madison Avenue, I collapsed in the street. It was, I tried to tell the doctor, a case of the bends, coming up too quick after my immersion, but he didn't understand.

What were the mistakes? I think I know most of them now. Most of them were the products of a lack of self-confidence caused by a lack of experience. Partially they were the results of waiting too long so that the assurance of youth, when one trusts one's judgement even if one has no reason to do so, gave way to the doubts of middle age, which is far more dangerous. I couldn't imagine who would be listening to me and who would want to read anything I wrote. As a consequence I determined to make them hear if I could. I overloaded scenes that were loaded enough as they were. If there was a legitimate chance to grab the reader by the lapels, I took it. I left nothing to trust and I presumed my potential reader was half deaf and half blind. I even worried about Marshall McLuhan and tried to make everything as visual as possible so I couldn't be accused of being a disciple of Gutenberg. The result is that there is too much muscle in the prose. I could see none of this then. When I turned in the book I thought it was thin and reedy and hollow and that wind could blow right through it. I now know that it is actually a rather dense book (in the best sense of that word), too dense, but I didn't know. Now perhaps I will.

Out of the whole experience I developed one tactic about writing that other writers might be able to profit from. I call it across the river and into the prose. During the Second World War a friend of mine serving in the Alaska Scouts noticed that when an American squad came to a river near the end of the day the squad would ford the river so they could build fires and dry their equipment and be dry when starting out in the morning. The squads with Indians always stopped on the near shore. The reason for this was another facet of immersion. In the morning the Americans, comfortable, warm and dry would tend to move very carefully and slowly across the tundra to avoid getting wet. They would detour for miles to avoid crossing a stream. The Indians on the other hand would start the day by fording the river and they didn't give a damn what happened to them after that. The worst had already been done.

I felt this could be applied to writing. There is a desire to finish a paragraph or chapter and enjoy the satisfaction of finishing. It is a good feeling. But in the morning there now is only that empty white blank sheet of paper to be filled. I have wasted days trying to regain a momentum I have lost. Now I don't allow myself the luxury of finishing, or getting dry and comfortable. When I am going good but have worked enough for the day I stop before finishing a paragraph I am anxious to finish and then I stop in the middle of a sentence. It is irritating and frustrating but also effective. There is nothing in writing harder to do than to start. But in the morning I finish the sentence that has been left unfinished and then I finish the paragraph and all at once I am in the river again.

Now I intend to write the book I intended to write all along, the one I used to think I had written, the one they would mention in the first paragraph of the obituary. There is a saying attributed to the French that no man should write his first novel until he is forty. This is the age when most Americans cease writing their last novels. I do hope the French are right.

1. Write a brief summary of this essay, indicating all the good advice you think Crichton offers to any writer, not just writers of novels.
2. How does Crichton turn his experiences getting to Santa Vittoria to good purpose?
3. What is the value of letter writing for Crichton?
4. What stalls Crichton in his writing and why?
5. "Through Dick and Jane I had outflanked art." What is the message here?
6. What does Crichton have to say about revision?

Description

and

Narration

Description

Description aims to give a verbal impression; that is, it tries to say what an event is like. (We'll use the word *event* in this chapter to mean a thing, person, state of mind, action or sequence of actions.) Description is concerned above all with the "when," "where," and "what" of an event, the way it presents itself to the senses: to sight, sound, touch, taste, and smell.

What takes place in the act of description? First, you have to observe closely to see what is happening and you must keep the other senses awake as well. But being sensorily aware is only the start of description; it also calls for analysis and synthesis in that it involves a classification of qualities *and* a sense of how the qualities make up a unified whole. In order to describe anything, then, you need to:

■ *See an event clearly as a whole,* paying attention to its appearance. You may see the event in reality or in your mind's eye if you are writing fiction. Description relies on impressions, on a writer's talent for sensing the tangible presence of an event. It is above all concerned with *form*—color, shape, sound, taste, touch, size, smell, movement, and so on—and the *relationship* between these qualities as they make up a whole event.

■ *Focus on the major qualities of the event.* Choose the dominant qualities that convey essential information or that evoke mood and atmosphere. Although you want your impressions to be coherent and unified and your descriptions to be full, they should be suggestive, not exhaustive. The major qualities may also include dominant relationships between qualities, like color and shape, say.

■ *Compose the scene effectively for a reader.* What do you want the reader to feel? Are you going to be subjective or objective in your description? That is, are you going to deal with highly personal reactions or more impersonal qualities? Whichever you choose, you must reconstruct the scene to convey your sense of the emphasis, coherence, and unity of the event.

So there are three basic activities to description: close observation, focus, and composition. After seeing clearly, you analyze and select from the data, and then offer a coherent synthesis to the reader.

The writer who is describing an event is rather like a painter trying to induce a viewer to imaginatively relive an experience through the use of color, design, and sensation. It is harder to explain the sensation of observing a work of art, perhaps, than it is to comment on a written work.

But the immediacy of art—whether we understand it or not—is a reminder that writing should imitate art in providing tangible sensations. Instead of using paint, the writer colors suggestively with words to represent or invent a *felt* experience. Writing description is not a mechanical act, a matter of copying down what one sees. It is a highly inventive art, for words carry many possible meanings. Descriptive writing requires careful arrangement of detail, for it aims to create a pervasive feeling through appearances that exist not merely for their own sake, but to express a mood and carry a meaning.

So Lawrence Durrell can quite self-consciously imagine himself as a painter aiming for a special effect in words in this passage from his novel *Justine:*

Light filtered through the essence of lemons. An air full of brick-dust—sweet-smelling brick-dust and the odour of hot pavements slaked with water. Light damp clouds, earth-bound, yet seldom bringing rain. Upon this squirt dust-red, dust-green, chalk-mauve and watered crimson-lake. In summer the sea-damp lightly varnished the air. Everything lay under a coat of gum.

Notice that even in this short passage, Durrell mixes different kinds of sense impressions: *sight* ("light filtered," "light damp clouds," "squirt dust-red, dust-green"); *smell* ("sweet-smelling brick-dust," "the odour of hot pavements," "the essence of lemons"); and *touch* ("hot pavements," "sea-damp," "a coat of gum"). The richer the sensory environment in description, the more fully is the reader drawn into the text. In *Justine,* the overall mood is one of an exotic, sultry, humid atmosphere over-whelming the senses. This has been achieved by careful observation, followed by an analysis and then a synthesis of the components of the scene.

Paying Attention

Before you can adequately describe an event, you have to pay attention to it. You have to sense it as fully as you can. If you don't, you will merely be describing incomplete impressions, vague notions, and maybe even preconceived opinions. You have to be *aware* of what is going on. So how can you refine your powers of observation and attention?

Consider this statement by the thinker Krishnamurti: "Awareness is observation without condemnation . . . or identification." An interesting lesson may be learned from this. Usually when we think we are paying attention closely, we are really making judgments in some way: identifying with an event (a film, a person, a sports match, or whatever) in approval or disapproval of what is happening, or perhaps being unaware of why we are involved. There is another state, one of indifferent or befuddled neutrality, in which we have no strong feelings about what is taking place. If pressed for a response, we shrug our shoulders or inform the questioner that we don't have an opinion or that we don't understand.

None of these states necessarily indicates that we are paying close attention; certainly the last one does not, and the others often indicate only that we are confusing what is really happening with what we think is right or wrong about it. Paying attention means that we let an object, person, or action *develop a presence of its own in our imagination*. We must wait for the completion of an action or until we are sure of what is happening before we finish our observation and pass judgment.

No awareness is purely passive, of course. Our consciousness is always doing something; we are always interpreting what is happening. But Krishnamurti's point is suggestive. Awareness is first of all a deliberate attempt to allow impressions to flood in, to let an event take place in its own way and gain a toehold in consciousness. This is only the first stage of the act of describing something, however, for first impressions grow as we think more about an event. Read the following passage, also by Krishnamurti, and note the way the writer has preserved the wonder of that first awareness even as he has clearly interpreted it. He makes a careful attempt to recapture in words the slow accumulation of sensory evidence that leads to the suggestion of significance in the last line:

The clouds were against the hills, hiding them and the mountains beyond. It had been raining all day, a soft drizzle which didn't wash away the earth, and there was in the air the pleasant smell of the jasmine and the rose. The grain was ripening in the fields; among the rocks, where the goats fed, were low bushes, with here and there a gnarled old tree. There was a spring high up on the hillside that was always flowing, summer and winter, and the water made a pleasant sound as it ran down the hill, past a grove of trees, and disappeared among the open fields beyond the village. A small bridge of cut stone was being built over the stream by the villagers, under the supervision of a local engineer. He was a friendly old man, and they worked in a leisurely manner when he was about. But when he was not there, only one or two carried on; the rest of them, putting down their tools and their baskets, sat around and talked.

Along the path by the stream came a villager with a dozen donkeys. They were returning from the nearby town with empty sacks. These donkeys had thin, graceful legs, and they were trotting along quite fast, pausing now and then to nibble the green grass on each side of the path. They were going home, and had not to be driven. All along the path there were little plots of cultivated land, and a gentle breeze was stirring among the young corn. In a small house, a woman with a clear voice was singing; it brought tears to your eyes, not from some nostalgic remembrance, but from the sheer beauty of the sound. You sat under a tree, and the earth and the heavens entered your being. Beyond the song and the red earth was the silence, the total silence in which all life is in movement. There were now fireflies among the trees and bushes, and in the gathering darkness they were bright and clear; the amount of light they gave was surprising. On a dark rock, the soft, flashing light of a single firefly held the light of the world.

Krishnamurti, from **COMMENTARIES**

The title of the passage—"Where There Is Attention, Reality *Is*"—is suggestive. And the message? Without needing to be mysterious, one can repeat that a sense of reality depends on the intensity of awareness, that is, the degree to which we let the world have an impact upon us. You can see from reading this passage that the writer is for the most part a patient and careful receptor of sensory impressions. Clouds, rain, grain, rocks, goats, trees, bridge, old man, villagers, donkeys—all register themselves in his consciousness. He waits and watches, listens, smells, and by and large accepts what goes on around him with all the pleasure that comes from allowing himself to be sensorily stimulated.

Of course, there are many events that one cannot simply stand by and watch with such quiet delight. But here is a simple and effective celebration of a reality that is valuable for the richness of its everyday experience and that crowds in on the attention of the writer, driving him to say in the last line that somehow the beauty of it all, and the happiness that he feels, can be summed up in the "flashing light of a single firefly."

There is nothing mystical about paying attention, even if there is something slightly mystical about Krishnamurti's interpretation of the firefly. Awareness does mean that you eventually interpret an event and that you do not merely lapse into a state of empty-mindedness. It means, again, that you patiently keep all the senses open for the information that is around you, resisting judgment until you are sure you have all the details, allowing the evidence to accumulate and create its own reality without interference.

The most common technique in description, then—the place to start— is to emphasize observation and the visual sense, largely because it allows you to arrive at the *interconnectedness* of things. You can deliberately move the eyes from right to left, top to bottom, near to far, inside to outside, in order to accumulate information and acquire an overview. But do not forget the other senses: try out the sounds, smells, touch, and even the taste of an event. Think of yourself as a fixed viewpoint taking in a moving scene, and then vary that to a moving viewpoint in a fixed scene. Take special note of the relationships among details of color, light, position, sound, touch, odor, and taste.

Focusing

No matter how closely Krishnamurti paid attention, he could not have written the description you have just read without focusing on some highlights of what he saw. A scene is always full of evidence, so full in fact, that one can say that the act of focusing is rather like taking a picture. Confronted by a beautiful scene which you wish to photograph, you must decide whether to use a wide-angle or a telephoto lens, or an intermediate one that reproduces the eye's vision. Where will you point the camera? If you use a telephoto lens, which part of the scene will be in focus and which will not? The art of description begins as the art of *selection* among those qualities you have allowed to flood the senses. So the next stage, once you have paid close attention to what is happening, is to decide which of the qualities you are going to emphasize: Which ones stand out? Where is your *center* of attention? Which qualities seem most influential in creating your attitude?

As you can see from both the Durrell and the Krishnamurti extracts, description creates a *focus* or *perspective* on an event in space and time. This is true of all description. It is through the focus that the writer, and then the reader, organizes the information and evokes a full sense of the event. A focus is a point of concentration, a center of interest, and it can be any aspect, or collection of aspects, of an event.

You can begin by focusing on a part or on the whole—on one dominant quality or a number of related qualities. Either way, though, the aim of any description is a unified experience. It is the relationships among things and qualities that eventually provide a reader the opportunity of reliving the writer's experience.

Durrell deals with the impression of what the Egyptian city Alexandria looks, feels, and smells like on a summer's day. His focus is the sticky sultriness of it all: "Everything lay under a coat of gum." The writer could say more—there is noticeably nothing about the sounds of the city, for example—but he is concerned here with the sensuality of the thick heat and the hazy colors of the city which synthesize his impression. He begins with an "essence of lemons" but ends with the overwhelming feature of the "coat of gum."

Krishnamurti emphasizes the sights, sounds, and smells of the Indian village as a kind of panoramic effect in the first paragraph. In the second paragraph, he concentrates on more "symbolic" events: on the villager with the donkeys which know their own way home "and had not to be driven"; on the beauty of the woman singing, heard but not seen; on the onlooker himself, sitting under a tree amazed by the scene; and on the quiet liveliness of it all summarized by the "flashing light of a single firefly." He moves from whole to part. In the end, the light of the firefly represents a slow narrowing of the focus from the busy scene in daylight, and the viewer becomes increasingly involved in *interpreting* his impressions and guiding the reader to share his sense of awe at the peacefulness of the setting. This is writing that through description takes us to the spirit of a particular place.

Objective and Subjective Description

Once you have paid close attention and have found your focus, you have to decide whether you want to be subjective or objective about your description, or perhaps you want a mixture of both. These are the two basic forms of description, and some decision is necessary before you begin to write. The subjective is sometimes called suggestive or personal, and the objective, technical or scientific. Except for the two extremes of literary writing on the one hand and technical writing on the other (which tends to be subjective and objective, respectively), most writing you will do in college and at work will be a mixture of the two modes:

■ *Objective description* stresses detail in *denotative* language. The reader is given facts with little interpretation or authorial intrusion. If the description is of an action or thing, the subject is divided into clear parts and each part is carefully accounted for. Usually there is an easily followed series of happenings in objective description, as in this piece on a Taoist ritual:

> The Taoist priest stood with his acolytes on stools surrounding a small table. In an earthen pot over a charcoal stove they were concocting an elixir of immortality. This would be applied to paper effigies of the dead woman and of a number of other dead family members whom the costly ritual was meant to benefit. The priest wore elaborate court robes, for he held down a job in the celestial administration. On his head he wore a black Taoist biretta crowned by a flame-shaped pin set with a pearl. This indicated the spirit of the priest tending upwards. He wore wooden shoes that lifted him five or six inches above the ground and nearer Heaven. He made ritual passes over the elixir with a live (Yang) cockerel and a live (Yin) duck. The medication was then fed to the effigies, not, in crude terms, to raise the dead and achieve immortality that way, but to restore them to Yin-Yang harmony and fit them for the rough passage that lay ahead of them. A bubbling elixir might make a very satisfactory Taoist emblem. In the pursuit of immortality, the elixir, what the West might call "the philosopher's stone," the Taoists were China's pioneer alchemists, proto-experimental scientists.

> Ronald Eyre, from **THE LONG SEARCH**

If the description is of a state of affairs—as in a history book—the events are again carefully ordered to give essential details:

> The trend to dictatorship or totalitarianism spread over Europe in the 1930's. By 1939 only ten out of twenty-seven European countries remained demo-cratic, in the sense that different political parties honestly competed for office,

and that citizens within generous limits thought and acted as they pleased. They were Great Britain and France; Holland, Belgium, and Switzerland; Czech- oslovakia and Finland; and the three Scandinavian countries. The Soviet Union still exemplified the dictatorship of the proletariat, and all other European countries possessed more or less dictatorial regimes somewhat vaguely called, with more or less accuracy, "fascist."

R. R. Palmer and Joel Cohen, from A HISTORY OF THE MODERN WORLD

■ *Subjective description* is more impressionistic and interpretive. The language is distinctly *connotative* and personal in its suggestions. The qualities focused on have a special meaning for the writer, who concentrates on their implications and on the tone and atmosphere they create. The description is fueled by the interpretation of the writer, which receives almost as much attention as the event itself. The relationship between the viewer and the viewed is central. The writer's intentions are more complex than in objective description. There may even be some exaggeration in order to make a point, but when you write subjective description, you should be careful not to make state- ments that distort the object described (except for ironic effect). You should try to avoid sentimentality and the *pathetic fallacy,* the tendency to see in nature human qualities ("the drooping tulips wept in the dusk"). On the other hand, you also have to be careful to put enough of yourself in the description, developing a sense of your real feelings about what you are describing. Here is Barbara Harrison writing about Beverly Hills:

> Sunlight in Beverly Hills has an autumnal quality, both harsh and introspec- tive, that is jarringly at odds with the hot-pink, awning-green, terra-cotta, and gold-colored houses that offer themselves for inspection brazenly and nakedly on Sunset Boulevard. If you have grown up among grimy tenements and shuttered and reserved brownstones, there is no way you can understand the smugness and stridency of public architecture on Sunset Boulevard. All houses on Sunset Boulevard are public. They all look as if they had been designed for a giant Monopoly board and set down on their parcels of land for permanent exhibition. There is something chilling in their apparent expansiveness, an air of duplicity prevails: these are houses that are meant to be seen from cars or tourist buses; shelter is the least of their functions. Their blank, supercilious windows, which look out on gravel paths and Mercedes and imported palm trees, seem almost to refute any notion that real people live and move behind them. In this harsh light, objects are clearly defined, and one feels one's own outlines blur in comparison.
>
> I reached the Beverly Hills Hotel—which, on its slight rise, seems to sail over

Sunset Boulevard and Rodeo Drive like a stuccoed pink and white and green ocean liner of cubist design—feeling very blurred indeed. My baggage found its way from the mouth of the long, canopied entrance to my smallish seventy-six-dollar single room without my having to intercede on its behalf. My patio smelled strongly of jasmine and chlorine. At the far corner of the patio was a rustic wooden gate, locked from the outside. I saw the tops of heads as people passed on the other side of the wooden gate, and heard the murmur of voices from behind my walled garden. That gate, suggesting a hint of richer and larger pleasures just out of reach, became symbolic to me of the Beverly Hills Hotel: voyeurism is encouraged and the illusion of privacy is maintained—both in the broader context of exhibitionism.

I fell into a soggy sleep.

Barbara Grizzuti Harrison, from **HOTEL CALIFORNIA**

Composing a Description

Writing description is not a matter of merely listing qualities. Before you begin to write, you should think about the approach you will take.

■ *Determine your dominant tone in terms of the effect you want to achieve.* You have paid close attention to detail and to selecting the dominant qualities, but what is your overall impression? You want your reader to have the same impression, presumably, so how will you convey it? Remember: select vivid and significant detail; express it boldly and precisely; keep your eye moving for details; blend in sensory evidence; focus on qualities that carry the feeling you want to convey.

■ *Decide whether your description is going to be objective or subjective,* or which details will be primarily objective and which will be subjectively treated.

■ *Decide whether you will write in the first, second, or third person.* The third person point of view—*he, she,* or *it*—lends itself well to objective description. It is impersonal and omniscient. The second person—*you*—is slightly less so, and the first person is the voice of either objective or subjective criticism, but more usually the latter.

These decisions can all be made prior to writing, or you can discover which options to take after you have begun writing. But you do have to maintain consistency. Here, then, are a few useful hints about the art of writing sustained description:

Discover the details of the event in the relationship of parts to the whole.

Arrange the details in some kind of emphatic sequence, either working up to or down from a climax. Description needs a sense of development, not merely a cataloguing of facts.

Evoke the mood from the details; don't talk *about* the mood. Suggest, don't state categorically.

Remember that your writing should be reader-centered, that you have to make the reader *aware* of what is going on.

Keep your point of view consistent but dynamic: you can have a consistent point of view but vary its details and the sensory perceptions.

Use concrete details rather than abstractions.

Trust your impressions, and if they create contradictions, examine them closely. Your ambiguous response may be developed into an interesting perspective.

Never forget that description evokes your relationship to some thing or action.

Use comparison and contrast to develop meaning.

Use free adjectival and noun appositive phrases that allow you to build up details to a climax (see Chapter 5, pp. 203–207).

Check through your writing carefully to make sure that all your details are significant, that your point of view and tone are consistent, and that you have left a dominant impression.

Finally, remember that description is a useful strategy in many different kinds of writing. It is one of the most powerful ways of enticing a reader into a text.

■ Even though it is not in itself explanatory, description turns up in *expository writing* to provide the physical setting or the facts about an event or to sharpen an explanation. It appears especially in scientific and technical varieties of expository writing in order to create a context for an explanation.

■ In *argumentative* and *persuasive writing,* description is useful for putting the audience in an event. To describe an event without comment can often be more persuasive than moralizing about it.

■ In *literary writing,* description turns up on almost every page to create mood and atmosphere and to provide essential details about character and place.

Narration

Because it is mainly concerned with qualities and the sequence of actions, description is necessarily linked to *narrative* forms. One rarely finds mere description of qualities sustained for very long for the simple reason that a reader wants to know why those qualities are so interesting. Both description and narration usually go together, as we see in this extract from Vladimir Nabokov's short story "Christmas." Here is a traditional handling of an opening paragraph to a short story, in which the writer moves from pure description of a setting to an action first conveyed in narrative and then in conversation:

The night was smoke-blue and moonlit; thin clouds were scattered about the sky but did not touch the delicate, icy moon. The trees, masses of gray frost, cast dark shadows on the drifts, which scintillated here and there with metallic sparks. In the plush-upholstered, well-heated room of the annex Ivan had placed a two-foot fir tree in a clay pot on the table, and was just attaching a candle to its cruciform tip when Sleptsov returned from the main house, chilled, red-eyed, with gray dust smears on his cheek, carrying a wooden case under his arm. Seeing the Christmas tree on the table, he asked absently:

"What's that?"

Relieving him of the case, Ivan answered in a low, mellow voice:

"There's a holiday coming up tomorrow."

"No, take it away," said Sleptsov with a frown, while thinking, "Can this be Christmas Eve? How could I have forgotten?"

As you can see from this extract, the act of describing is indeed linked to narration. But there remains a difference between these two kinds of writing. Description is concerned with pictures of things, events, and people. Narration, whether it is fictional or nonfictional, is concerned with behavior, with pictures of continuing events.

Aspects of a Narrative

How, then, does a narrative work? In every narrative, we find a point of view, a dominant effect, and a unified action with progress, duration, suspense, and pacing. All these aspects are closely related, but it is useful to think of them separately when you are interpreting a narrative. Read the following extract from John Le Carré's spy thriller, *The Honourable Schoolboy*:

Running out on to the headland, he peered anxiously north and south in search of a patrol boat, but again he saw nothing, and again he blamed the surf and his strained imagination. The junk was nearer, beating in toward the island, her brown batwing sail suddenly tall and terribly conspicuous against the sky. Drake had run to the water's edge and was waving and yelling across the sea.

"Keep your voice down!" Jerry hissed from beside him.

But Jerry had become an irrelevance. Drake's whole life was for Nelson. From the shelter of the near headland, Drake's sampan tottered alongside the rocking junk. The moon came out of hiding and for a moment Jerry forgot his anxiety as a little grey-clad figure, small and sturdy, in stature Drake's antithesis, in a kapok coat and bulging proletarian cap, lowered himself over the side and leapt for the waiting arms of the sampan's crew. Drake gave another cry, the junk filled its sails and slid behind the headland till only the green lights on its masthead remained visible above the rocks, and then vanished. The sampan was making for the beach and Jerry could see Nelson's stocky frame as he stood on the bow waving with both hands and Drake Ko in his beret wild on the beach, dancing like a madman, waving back.

The throb of engines grew steadily louder, but still Jerry couldn't place them. The sea was empty, and when he looked upward he saw only the hammerhead cliff and its peak black against the stars. The brothers met, and embraced, and stayed locked in each other's arms, not moving. Seizing hold of both of them, pummelling them, Jerry cried out for all his life.

"Get back in the boat! Hurry!"

They saw no one but each other. Running back to the water's edge Jerry grabbed the sampan's prow and held it, still calling to them as he saw the sky behind the peak turn yellow, then quickly brighten as the throb of the engines swelled to a roar and three blinding searchlights burst on them from blackened helicopters. The rocks danced to the whirl of landing lights, the sea furrowed and the pebbles bounced and flew around in storms. For a fraction of a second Jerry saw Drake's face turn to him beseeching help: as if, too late, he had recognized where help lay. He mouthed something, but the din drowned it. Jerry hurled himself forward. Not for Nelson's sake, still less for Drake's; but for what linked them, and what linked him to Lizzie. But long before he reached them, a dark swarm closed on the two men, tore them apart and bundled the baggy shape of Nelson into the helicopter's hold. In the mayhem Jerry had drawn his gun and held it in his hand. He was screaming, though he could not hear himself above the hurricanes of war. The helicopter was lifting. A single figure remained in the open doorway, looking down, and perhaps it was Fawn, for he looked dark and mad. Then an orange flash broke from the doorway, then a second and a third and after that Jerry wasn't counting any more. In fury he threw up his hands, his open mouth still calling, his face still silently imploring. Then he fell, and lay there, till there was once more no sound but the surf flopping on the beach and Drake Ko's hopeless, choking grief against the victorious armadas of the West, which had stolen his brother and left their hard-pressed soldier dead at his feet.

■ *Point of view.* Point of view in a narrative is either third person (in which the writer is omniscient, intrusive, or limited) or first person (in which the narrator can be self-conscious, reliable, or unreliable). In general, it is wise to tell a story consistently from one point of view. This does not mean that writers must stand apart from the people mentioned in the text if they adopt either the first or third person viewpoint. A writer may enter any character's consciousness and "see" things from that point of view. In the Le Carré extract, the author takes a third person omniscient viewpoint, which shifts to Jerry's and Drake's perspectives, but largely carries an overview of the whole action. The author's presence is not intrusive because he intends to tell an action story and not interrupt with interpretations. But we sense his control quite clearly nonetheless. Point of view is discussed further in Chapter 12.

■ *Dominant effect.* Every narrative evokes a particular mood that is related to the tone of the piece (see Chapters 2 and 4). We can say that the writer builds up impressions and treats events with a certain attitude in order to create a mood in the reader. This, again, must be consistent and is usually evoked rather than bluntly stated. In his action-packed piece, Le Carré develops a serious tone in order to create suspense. He writes about the action and the characters' feelings as if they are literally involved in life and death matters, thus the mood is suspenseful.

■ *Unified action.* Narratives develop a focus by aiming for a unified effect that depends not only on the mood but on the way the action is developed. Narratives offer a progression, a created order or sequence, which operates over a period of time. They may not always begin at the beginning or end at the end, but effective narratives have to suggest that an action has a unity (a start and a finish) in order for the reader to make sense of it at all. Character relates to action; that is, people *act* in narratives. Progressions develop conflict and usually, at the end, resolution. An action rises and falls, creating the suspense; so in the extract above, we catch the action just as it is building to a climax. It progresses in an exact chronological sequence: first Nelson lands, then he is abducted, then Jerry is killed.

The *pacing* of the action is most important. Narrative development follows certain rhythms, depending on the effect the author is trying to create. The pacing is important because writers help set a mood by the flow of their sentences: the use of long and short sentences and conversational interludes, repetitions, and interruptions. Le Carré, you will note, cleverly varies the length of his sentences in order to cope with complicated and simple actions. And he varies the rhythms with short pieces of conversation.

The *texture* of the language is important, too. The writing is largely carried along by quite dense description, until Le Carré interrupts it with the direct appeal of sentences like "Jerry cried out for all his life." When you examine the texture of writing, look for the choice and juxtaposition of words, the grouping and density of adjectives and nouns, and the handling of verbs. All this has an effect on the pacing of a narrative.

Writing a Narrative

What are you aiming for when you write a narrative? The same thing that matters most in an extended description: the sense of *immediacy*. Again, you have to put a reader in the text, and you can only do that if you indicate that you feel deeply about an event or experience. It does not matter whether you are writing expository or fictional prose, you want your writing to come alive with tangible impressions.

Much of the significance of your impressions is actually discovered in the process of writing, but you still need to prepare and focus. Here is a series of steps you can take to develop a narrative.

■ *Determine the details of the event and why you are writing about it.* It is easy enough to describe an event in great detail, but what is the relevance of the event to *you?* Narrative, too, turns on the significant relationship between you and something else. Do not simply list events; suggest connections. Narratives depend on interpretation, whether you are reacting in awe or disgust, or conveying your emotional response, or suggesting some psychological significance to an event. Of course, your interpretation should not reveal hasty judgments but an honest, carefully considered response. Describe something, recount an action, or examine cause and effect or other relationships between events. On the other hand, *do not strain for effect.* Don't become so deeply personal or private that the narrative serves only as therapy for you. Writing can make you feel better, but it is not a mysterious contemplation of one's own navel. Give the reader adequate details without being unnecessarily mysterious or obvious about them.

■ *Plan your narrative sequence* by deciding on the sequence of events and the point of view you will take. It is not always wise, however, to have this worked out before you start writing. You may simply want to start from a dominant impression and let the point of view emerge in the writing. You will stop and start several times, perhaps, before you decide on the details of your narrative form. Your completed narrative must have structure, though. When in doubt, remember this basic narrative outline, to be found in both fiction and nonfiction:

A scene is set.

An action rises or develops: the plot thickens.

Suspense (or at least interest) is created.

The narrative turns: the plot unravels.

A resolution or climax is reached.

There are any number of variations to this narrative sequence, of course, but it certainly helps a reader if your narrative does have an enticing opening, a sustaining middle, and a climactic end.

Read the following extract from Norman Mailer's *The Armies of the Night,* and consider how Mailer develops a point of view, a dominant effect, a unified action, and a narrative sequence. This is a narrative based on fact: Mailer's arrest while participating in a 1967 anti–Vietnam war march on the Pentagon.

Standing in the truck, a few feet apart from each other, all prisoners regarding one another, the Nazi fixed on Mailer. Their eyes locked like magnets coming into line, and for perhaps twenty seconds they stared at each other. Mailer looked into a pair of yellow eyes so compressed with hate that back of his own eyes he could feel the echo of such hatred ringing. The Nazi was taller than Mailer, well-knit, and with neatly formed features and a shock of blond hair, would have been handsome but for the ferocity of his yellow eyes which were sunk deep in their sockets. Those eyes made him look like an eagle.

Yet Mailer had first advantage in this eye-staring contest. Because he had been prepared for it. He had been getting into such confrontations for years, and rarely lost them, even though he sometimes thought they were costing him eyesight. Still, some developed instinct had made him ready an instant before the Nazi. Every bit of intensity he possessed—with the tremors of the March and the Marshal's arm still pent in him—glared forth into the other's eyes: he was none-theless aghast at what he saw. The American Nazis were all fanatics, yes, poor mad tormented fanatics, their psyches twisted like burning leaves in the fire of their hatreds, yes, indeed! but this man's conviction stood in his eyes as if his soul had been focused to a single point of light. Mailer could feel violence behind violence rocking through his head. If the two of them were ever alone in an alley, one of them might kill the other in a fight—it was not unlike holding an electric wire in the hand. And the worst of it was that he was not even feeling violent himself—whatever violence he possessed had gone to his eyes—by that route had he projected himself on the Nazi.

After the first five seconds of the shock had passed, he realized he might be able to win—the Nazi must have taken too many easy contests, and had been too complacent in the first moment, yes it was like wrestlers throwing themselves on each other: one knuckle of one finger a little better able to be worked on a grip could make the difference—now he could feel the hint of force ebbing in the other's eyes, and could wonder at his own necessity to win. He did not hate the Nazi nearly so much as he was curious about him, yet the thought of losing had

been intolerable as if he had been *obliged* not to lose, as if the duty of his life
at this particular moment must have been to look into that Nazi's eye, and say
with his own, "You claim you have a philosophical system which comprehends
all—you know nothing! My eyes encompass yours. My philosophy contains yours.
You have met the wrong man!" And the Nazi looked away, and was hysterical
with fury on the instant.

"You Jew bastard," he shouted. "Dirty Jew with kinky hair."

They didn't speak that way. It was too corny. Yet he could only answer, "You
filthy Kraut."

"Dirty Jew."

"Kraut pig."

A part of his mind could actually be amused at this choice—he didn't even hate
Germans any more. Indeed Germans fascinated him now. Why they liked his
books more than Americans did. Yet here he could think of nothing better to
return than "Kraut pig." . . .

But now a tall U.S. Marshal who had the body and insane look of a very good
rangy defensive end in professional football—that same hard high-muscled build,
same coiled spring of wrath, same livid conviction that everything opposing the
team must be wrecked, sod, turf, grass, uniforms, helmets, bodies, yes even bite
the football if it will help—now leaped into the truck and jumped between them.
"Shut up," he said, "or I'll wreck both of you." He had a long craggy face
somewhere in the physiognomical land between Steve McQueen and Robert
Mitchum, but he would never have made Hollywood, for his skin was pocked
with the big boiling craters of a red lunar acne, and his eyes in Cinemascope
would have blazed an audience off their seat for such gray-green flame could
only have issued from a blowtorch. Under his white Marshal's helmet, he was
one impressive piece of gathered wrath.

Speaking to the Marshal at this point would have been dangerous. The Marshal's emotions had obviously been marinating for a week in the very special bile
waters American Patriotism reserves for its need. His feelings were now caustic
as a whip—too gentle the simile!—he was in agonies of frustration because the
honor of his profession kept him from battering every prisoner's head to a Communist pulp. Mailer looked him over covertly to see what he could try if the
Marshal went to work on him. All reports: negative. He would not stand a chance
with this Marshal—there seemed no place to hit him where he'd be vulnerable;
stone larynx, leather testicles, ice cubes for eyes. And he had his Marshal's club
in his hand as well. Brother! Bring back the Nazi! . . .

But now the Nazi began to play out the deepest of ceremonies. The truck
standing still, another Marshal at the other end of the van (the one indeed who
had arrested Mailer) and Teague and the Hungarian to different sides, everyone
had their eyes on the Norwegian. He now glared again at Mailer, but then

whipped away his eyes before a second contest could begin, and said, "All right, Jew, come over here if you want a fight."

The Marshal took the Nazi and threw him against the side-wall of the truck. As he bounced off, the Marshal gave him a rap below the collarbone with the butt of his club. "I told you to shut up. Now, just shut up." His rage was intense. The Nazi looked back at him sullenly, leaned on the butt of the club almost defiantly as if the Marshal didn't know what foolish danger he was in to treat the Nazi so, the Nazi had a proud curved hint of a smile, as if he were recording the features of this Marshal forever in the history of his mind, the Nazi's eyes seemed to say to the Marshal, "You are really on my side although you do not admit it—you would like to beat me now because in the future you know you will yet kiss my boots!" And the Marshal traveling a high edge of temper began to slam the Nazi against the wall of the truck with moderate force, but rhythmically, as if he would pacify them both by this act, bang, and bang, step by step. . . .

And the Nazi looked back with a full sullen pouting defiance as if from deep in himself he was all unconsciously saying to the Marshal, "You know I am beautiful, and you are frightened of me. I have a cause and I am ready to die for it, and you are just ready to die for a uniform. Join me where the real war is. Already the strongest and wildest men in America wear our symbol on their motorcycle helmets."

And the Marshal, glaring back at the Nazi, butt of his club transfixing him against the wall of the van, gave a contemptuous look, as if to drop him with the final unspoken word. "Next to strong wild men, you're nothing but a bitch."

Then the truck began to move, and the Marshal calmer now, stood silently between Mailer and the Nazi; and the Nazi also quiet now, stood in place looking neither at the Marshal nor Mailer. Some small storm of hysteria seemed to have worked itself out of the van.

The action in itself is rather limited. Two men, a Nazi and a Jew, taunt each other in a police wagon and confront a Marshal of intimidating proportions. What holds our attention is the account Mailer gives not only of what he saw and did but of what he thought. He manages to get us to live through the narrative with considerable suspense as he touches on that moment of hysteria—to which we are all prone—when extreme anger, fear, guilt, bravery, courage, disgust, and a sense of the pettiness of physical violence all mix together.

Mailer shifts his point of view from himself to the Nazi and to the Marshal, dramatizing each one with his fictionalized thoughts. Mailer is careful to qualify his own role: he can produce tough talk but is somewhat scared of the Nazi and even more so of the Marshal. This is closer to us and even more action-packed than the extract from the adventure novel (of which Le Carré is an acknowledged master). The mood is hysteria, but the tone is one of high seriousness. This is not just Mailer and a small-town American Nazi, but every Jew and every Nazi replayed, with anger and frustration and bewilderment.

Mailer strains a little for effect, it is true; the whole event is somewhat melodramatic. But the strain does not affect the structure of the action. The sequence is clear. The pacing is deliberate and creates a rise and fall of tension; the action rises as Mailer confronts the Nazi, falls when the Marshal cools them down, and rises again as the Marshal roughs up the Nazi. Then the hysteria is dispelled, the eye contact cut, and, ironically, the action ended; ironically, for the Marshal in Mailer's eyes seems no less authoritarian than the young Nazi.

Expressing Yourself

Personal writing—autobiographical sketches, diaries, journals, letters—is usually a mixture of description and narration, explaining your experience and feelings. You tell your story and offer a persuasive presentation of your point of view. Writing letters and keeping journals can be intensely satisfying and can help develop self-understanding. You focus on strong feelings and especially important likes and dislikes. Because you are dealing with intimate matters, you must let your guard down. You write in a relatively uncensored way about problematic events. You write *thera-peutically;* that is, you write because it makes you feel better. You write also because you want someone else to know who you are. You are in fact producing *writer-centered prose* rather than the reader-centered prose we have been discussing so far in this text. That does not mean, however, that you cannot be objective.

What are the important qualities of writing dedicated to self-expression and intimate details? They are many, but the following can be emphasized: *directness, honesty, eloquence, humor, concreteness,* and *self-analysis.* By all means, avoid the narcissistic psychobabble, the interminable self-jus-tification and self-rationalizing that often passes for conversation. You may frequently use *stream of consciousness*—that is, the uninterrupted flow of your thoughts—but you can examine what you are saying as you go along. You want to make a reader interested in what you have to say, even if that reader is only you. At some point, you will come to your journals and diaries, for example, as a reader, not a writer. You will examine your writing critically and may even be embarrassed by it.

You might think that writing any I-narrative—a letter, a journal, a personal description, or an autobiographical piece—is easier than writing in the third person. But sometimes you yourself can be the most difficult of subjects. For it is not always easy to be honest about your feelings: there is a temptation to leave out the aspects of your personality that annoy you. It is easy to overrationalize your motives or overdramatize the importance of what you feel. It is also often difficult to know exactly what you do feel.

Good personal writing should aim to be as direct and honest as possible; that especially includes writing about those feelings that you find paradoxical or hard to pin down.

■ *Avoid clichés about yourself.* Beware of the "typical" view of yourself. When you find yourself lapsing into commonplace and too repetitive descriptions of who you are—that is, when you find yourself rambling on and perhaps even getting tired of the sound of your own voice—then stop. You need to take a new perspective and describe your impressions more concretely. Turn to close observation of events in which you were involved. Describe your feelings carefully, especially your uncertainties. Let paradox and mixed feelings have full play, as you saw in the Mailer passage. Paradoxical feelings actually become the center of interest in personal narratives. If you do analyze how you feel, beware of the glib use of psychological or other theories of human nature or the ego structure.

■ *Think of yourself as a living, changing, growing combination of related and contradictory feelings.* You have a past, a present, and a future—explore them. Subject yourself to the rigors of close description.

■ *Focus on significant details outside yourself* (that is, things *you* find significant). Dramatize yourself in relation to people and events. You too exist in a network of facts, and you can treat yourself, as we did the topic in Chapter 3, in various contexts, even as a "problem."

Autobiographical writing is never particularly easy because it tends to be rather uncompromising in its revelation of things about ourselves that sometimes we would rather not know. Yet it can be one of the most exciting of writing experiences, even when it is painful. An unaffected honesty has its own rewards, not the least of which is a chance to see ourselves clearly, as if for the first time. Read this extract by Oscar Lewis in which a woman, Consuelo, speaks of her childhood:

In school, I liked to be alone all the time. I used to think my classmates were either stuck-up or quarrelsome. I would stay in the classroom, drawing, sewing, or simply looking at the blackboard with the *señorita* sitting at her desk. If I went outside for recreation, I would sit off to one side where there weren't so many girls to take a bite of my roll; or I would go up to the roof to look at my reflection in the water tanks.

I did not think I could ever be pretty. I felt inferior because I was small and thin. My skin was too dark, my eyes slightly slanted, my mouth too large, my teeth too crowded. I searched for some good feature. My nose was straight but big, my hair very thick and dark but would not take a curl. I wished I were lighter-skinned and plump like Marta, with dimples like hers. I dreamed of being blond. Staring at myself in the water I thought, "Consuelo, Consuelo, what a strange name. It doesn't even sound like the name of a person. It sounds very thin, as though it were breaking."

The caretaker usually brought me out of my dreams, taking me by the shoulder and saying, "What are you doing here? Don't you know you can't come up to the roof? Go play or I'll take you to the principal." Blushing with shame, I would go down and sit in the sun in the little garden. When the first bell rang for us to go back to our classrooms, I would wait for the others to get lined up, because otherwise they almost always pushed me. I let them push without protesting; I was afraid of them.

Oscar Lewis, from THE CHILDREN OF SANCHEZ

What makes this interesting to a reader? First, the feeling that the reader is a privileged watcher of something very private, even secret. When you read your own diary, you read yourself in this way. There is a sense of *recognition*. When someone speaks directly and honestly about an experience, you very often recognize moments you too have experienced and have perhaps not wanted to tell others about. You probably admire honesty and recognize the courage to say something that is not easy. Maybe even someone is saying something *for* you.

In this extract, for example, Consuelo speaks of her loneliness in school, of her belief that she was not pretty, of her need to be popular, and of her fear of her classmates. Some aspect of this, surely, we have all felt in adolescence. We realize that the writer/speaker is being self-revealing. Consuelo is not afraid of what she once felt, suggesting that she has learned to cope with the problem or at least has recognized it, and we like that. We also note that Consuelo does not become overly sentimental or make excuses for herself. She relays concrete experiences and settings we can identify with. Her sentences develop through a series of intimately related events, each one logically following from the other. She quite easily tells a good story: setting the scene and letting the action develop to a climax, which in this case is the revelation of her deepest feelings: her narcissm, her lack of self-confidence, her fear of her classmates.

Here is another honest self-revelation by one of the most famous writers of the twentieth century and a great writer of letters, D. H. Lawrence:

Greatham, Pulborough,
Sussex.
Sunday, 30th January, 1915

Dear Lady Cynthia,

We were very glad to hear from you. I wanted to send you a copy of my stories at Christmas, then I didn't know how the war had affected you—I knew Herbert Asquith was joined and I thought you'd rather be left alone, perhaps.

We have no history, since we saw you last. I feel as if I had less than no history—as if I had spent those five months in the tomb. And now, I feel very sick and corpse-cold, too newly risen to share yet with anybody, having the smell of the grave in my nostrils, and a feel of grave clothes about me.

The War finished me: it was the spear through the side of all sorrows and hopes. I had been walking in Westmorland, rather happy, with water-lilies twisted round my hat—big, heavy, white and gold water-lilies that we found in a pool high up—and girls who had come out on a spree and who were having tea in the upper room of an inn, shrieked with laughter. And I remember also we crouched under the loose wall on the moors and the rain flew by in streams, and the wind came rushing through the chinks in the wall behind one's head, and we shouted songs, and I imitated music-hall turns, whilst the other men crouched under the wall and I pranked in the rain on the turf in the gorse, and Koteliansky groaned Hebrew music—Tiranenu Zadikim b'adonai.

It seems like another life—we *were* happy—four men. Then we came down to Barrow-in-Furness, and saw that war was declared. And we all went mad. I can remember soldiers kissing on Barrow station, and a woman shouting defiantly to her sweetheart—"When you get at 'em, Clem, let 'em have it," as the train drew off—and in all the tramcars, "War." Messrs. Vickers-Maxim call in their workmen—and the great notices on Vickers' gateways—and the thousands of men streaming over the bridge. Then I went down the coast a few miles. And I think of the amazing sunsets over flat sands and the smoky sea—then of sailing in a fisherman's boat, running in the wind against a heavy sea—and a French onion boat coming in with her sails set splendidly, in the morning sunshine—and the electric suspense everywhere—and the amazing, vivid, visionary beauty of everything, heightened by the immense pain everywhere. And since then, since I came back, things have not existed for me. I have spoken to no one, I have touched no one, I have seen no one. All the while, I swear, my soul lay in the tomb—not dead, but with a flat stone over it, a corpse, become corpse-cold. And nobody existed, because I did not exist myself. Yet I was not dead—only passed over—trespassed—and all the time I knew I should have to rise again.

Now I am feeble and half alive. On the Downs on Friday I opened my eyes again, and saw it was daytime. And I saw the sea lifting up and shining like a blade with the sun on it. And high up, in the icy wind, an aeroplane flew towards us from the land—and the men ploughing and the boys in the fields on the table-lands, and the shepherds, stood back from their work and lifted their faces. And the aeroplane was small and high, in the thin, ice-cold wind. And the birds became silent and dashed to cover, afraid of the noise. And the aeroplane floated high out of sight. And below, on the level earth away down—were floods and stretches of snow, and I knew I was awake. But as yet my soul is cold and shaky and earthy.

I don't feel so hopeless now I am risen. My heart has been as cold as a lump of dead earth, all this time, because of the War. But now I don't feel so dead. I feel hopeful. I couldn't tell you how fragile and tender this hope is—the new shoot of life. But I feel hopeful now about the War. We should all rise again from this grave—though the killed soldiers will have to wait for the last trump.

There is my autobiography—written because you ask me, and because, being risen from the dead, I know we shall all come through, rise again and walk healed and whole and new in a big inheritance, here on earth.

It sounds preachy, but I don't quite know how to say it.

Viola Meynell has lent us this rather beautiful cottage. We are quite alone. It is at the foot of the Downs. I wish you would come and see us, and stay a day or two. It is quite comfortable—there is hot water and a bathroom, and two spare bedrooms. I don't know when we shall be able to come to London. We are too poor for excursions. But we *should* like to see you, and it *is* nice here.

D. H. Lawrence

What has overwhelmed Lawrence is his feeling of numbness and depression over the war, which leads him to say that he has had "no history," even "less than no history." Nonetheless, he proceeds to write a short autobiography that is a model of conciseness and suggestion. He strings together vivid impressions and close descriptions of the cause of his feelings. The water-lilies and music-hall turns give way to the pain of hearing about the war, and the "electric suspense" and "visionary beauty of everything, heightened by the immense pain everywhere." So he symbolically died—his optimism gone—and his "soul lay in the tomb."

But there is no self-pity here. Lawrence documents how he slowly came back to life and began to have feelings again, but he wanted to do so, he says, without being "preachy." Normally, Lawrence found it difficult to avoid preachiness but here he does so by correlating his emotions with clear events (the sunsets, the seaside scenes, the airplane), which distract him from the cloying nature of his dead "soul." Here is an autobiography that graphs a cycle from life to death to life again. He dramatizes the moments along the way and ends with the optimism of coming through.

I-narratives all depend on the authentic voice: self-revealing but not proclaiming the self too loudly. The reader wants the shock of recognition, not a catalog of self-congratulation. The reader of an I-narrative probably responds most clearly to the human condition of writers honestly and directly coming into consciousness of their feelings through the act of writing. Readers identify with the sense of paradox that is clearly described, honestly accounted for in an interesting narrative, and perhaps finally resolved.

Checklist

1. Description depends on writing reader-centered prose which

    Pays close attention to detail, primarily visual detail, but detail drawn from the other senses too

    Focuses clearly on significant details that carry a dominant impression

    Is mainly objective (technical) or subjective (personal)

    Keeps to a consistent viewpoint

    Arranges detail in emphatic sequence

    Uses concrete rather than abstract terms

    Evokes and suggests feelings rather than blatantly stating them

    Examines a relationship between the writer and the event, including any contradictory detail

    Uses comparison and contrast

    Develops multilevel sentences

2. Narration, either fictional or nonfictional, is a form of description emphasizing sequences of events. Again, this is reader-centered prose which features

    A significant action, or sequence of actions, unified and treated from a consistent point of view and with a dominant effect

    A careful pacing of the progress of the action: the scene is set, the action rises in suspense, the climax occurs

3. Self-expression, or I-centered prose, is a description of one's own feelings and experiences, a narrative of the self which is writer-centered. Aim for

    The direct, honest expression of personal feelings or experiences that develops to some sort of climax or conclusion

The use of concrete and vivid language, avoiding clichés and psychobabble

The exploration of attitudes, memories, desires, and contradictory
feelings: a treatment of the self as a growing combination of complex
and often paradoxically connected feelings

A focus on the self in relationship to others

Exercises

1. Here are two descriptions, one involving a can opener and the other,
work. For each,

a. Explain whether the writing is primarily subjective or objective

b. Explain what you think the writer's purpose is

c. Outline the kinds of sensory evidence the writer uses and note
how else he gains his effects

Then choose any commonplace action (like working, playing, studying)
or item (like a household gadget) and describe it carefully, using
as wide a variety of sensory evidence as possible. Refer to the checklist
on description for pointers.

> Let me describe the instrument. The can-opening device itself is screwed
> to a smooth, grainy-looking wooden handle, about two and a half inches
> around and some five inches long, tapering slightly to its blunt end. The
> opening device consists of a square aluminum case, approximately the size of
> a cigarette lighter, housing on its underside a small metal tooth and a little
> ridged gear; projecting upward from the top side of the case is an inch-long
> shaft to which is attached a smaller wooden handle, about three inches long.
> Placing the can opener horizontally over the edge of the can, you press the
> pointed metal tooth down into the rim, and proceed to open the can by
> holding the longer handle in one hand, and rotating the smaller handle with
> the other; this causes the tooth to travel around the rim until it has severed
> the top of the can from the cylinder. It is a type of can opener that you can
> buy in practically any hardware store for between a dollar and a dollar and
> a quarter. I have priced them since. They are manufactured by the Eglund
> Co., Inc., of Burlington, Vermont—their "No. 5 Junior". I have Maureen's here
> on my desk as I write.
>
> Philip Roth, from **MY LIFE AS A MAN**

> Here are examples of various kinds of work that I observe from the crammed
> tram in which a compassionate woman can always be relied upon to cede
> me her window seat—while trying not to look too closely at me.
> At an intersection the pavement has been torn up next to the track; by

turns, four workmen are pounding an iron stake with mallets; the first one strikes, and the second is already lowering his mallet with a sweeping, accurate swing; the second mallet crashes down and is rising skyward as the third and then the fourth bang down in rhythmical succession. I listen to their unhurried clanging, like four repeated notes of an iron carillon.

A young white-capped baker flashes by on his tricycle; there is something angelic about a lad dusted with flour. A van jingles past with cases on its roof containing rows of emerald-glittering empty bottles, collected from taverns. A long, black larch tree mysteriously travels by in a cart. The tree lies flat; its tip quivers gently, while the earth-covered roots, enveloped in sturdy burlap, form an enormous beige bomblike sphere at its base. A postman, who has placed the mouth of a sack under a cobalt-colored mailbox, fastens it on from below, and secretly, invisibly, with a hurried rustling, the box empties and the postman claps shut the square jaws of the bag, now grown full and heavy. But perhaps fairest of all are the carcasses, chrome yellow, with pink blotches, and arabesques, piled on a truck, and the man in apron and leather hood with a long neck flap who heaves each carcass onto his back and, hunched over, carries it across the sidewalk into the butcher's red shop.

Vladimir Nabokov, from **A GUIDE TO BERLIN**

2. Here are two descriptions of the African spirit of place. Which do you prefer and why? Explain your reasons carefully, basing your judgments on an analysis of the subtlety and range of the descriptions used in each extract.

We penetrated deeper and deeper into the heart of darkness. It was very quiet there. At night sometimes the roll of drums behind the curtain of trees would run up the river and remain sustained faintly, as if hovering in the air high over our heads, till the first break of day. Whether it meant war, peace, or prayer we could not tell. The dawns were heralded by the descent of a chill stillness; the woodcutters slept, their fires burned low; the snapping of a twig would make you start. We were wanderers on prehistoric earth, on an earth that wore the aspect of an unknown planet. We could have fancied ourselves the first of men taking possession of an accursed inheritance, to be subdued at the cost of profound anguish and of excessive toil. But suddenly, as we struggled round a bend, there would be a glimpse of rush walls, of peaked grass roofs, a burst of yells, a whirl of black limbs, a mass of hands clapping, of feet stamping, of bodies swaying, of eyes rolling, under the droop of heavy and motionless foliage. The steamer toiled along slowly on the edge of a black and incomprehensible frenzy. The prehistoric man was cursing us, praying to us, welcoming us—who could tell? We were cut off from the comprehension of our surroundings; we glided past like phantoms, wondering and secretly appalled, as sane men would be before an enthusiastic outbreak in a madhouse. We could not understand because we were too far and could not remember, because we were traveling in the night of first ages, of those ages that are gone, leaving hardly a sign—and no memories.

"The earth seemed unearthly. We are accustomed to look upon the shackled form of a conquered monster, but there—there you could look at a thing monstrous and free. It was unearthly, and the men were—No, they were not inhuman. Well, you know, that was the worst of it—this suspicion of their not being inhuman. It would come slowly to one. They howled and leaped, and spun, and made horrid faces; but what thrilled you was just the thought of their humanity—like yours—the thought of your remote kinship with this wild and passionate uproar. Ugly. Yes, it was ugly enough; but if you were man enough you would admit to yourself that there was in you just the faintest trace of a response to the terrible frankness of that noise, a dim suspicion of there being a meaning in it which you—you so remote from the night of first ages—could comprehend. And why not? The mind of man is capable of anything—because everything is in it, all the past as well as all the future. What was there after all? Joy, fear, sorrow, devotion, valor, rage— who can tell?—but truth—truth stripped of its cloak of time.

Joseph Conrad, from **HEART OF DARKNESS**

When we came to the place where the first antelope had stood up, its bed was still warm with the warmth of its body and the grass spread like a magnetic field around where he had lain. There I suddenly became aware of a familiar, purple glow in the grass, the murmur as it were of a dark purple tide ebbing through the gold of the grass. Irises, the proud, erect flowers of chivalry, were everywhere. We walked from there, I reckoned, through ten square miles of irises. When this heraldic field of gold and purple ended we came to an altitude in which the grass glowed with the orange, red, blue, and gold of wild gladiolus. Most lovely of all, enormous, single, white delphiniums shone like stars on all the darker slopes. In the background on the horizon were those beautiful antelope heads still staring down at us. It was like some fine ancient tapestry suddenly come alive.

At about noon we were right on the top. At last there was no doubt, we were on the true Nyika, high above the low malarial plains, above sleeping sickness, east coast fevers and the paralysing maladies and parasites of the low country. We were so high that the air smarted in our nostrils; it was so keen and cold that we promptly put on our pullovers. But we had reached the summit. There were no more peaks to conquer, no more heart-breaking climbs up one steep valley and the next. We were on a real plateau; far as our eyes could see stretched a gentle, rhythmically-rolling country of grass and flowers. Round the edges other peaks rose out of the shimmering plain, giving us a keen sense of our exalted world; but they were not our concern save as additional ornament to the immense African frame of our view. South

I could see for about fifty miles, then my view was blocked by cloud. But in the whole of the distance between there was nothing but this free, gently rolling country.

I wish I could describe the effect that view had on me, but I will say little more than that it seemed to me miraculous. It was so unlike anything else. It was deep in the heart of Africa and filled with the animals of Africa, and yet it was covered with the grasses, the flowers, and colours of Europe. Yet it was unlike any other colour I have ever seen: I expect, basically, it was a tawny gold, the gold of the leopard's rather than the lion's skin, but this gold was shot through with undertones of a deep blood red and a shadowy purple.

As I looked at it, I understood at once why I had felt below that there was a large, purple cat purring up there behind the clouds. It looked in its colours, its shape, and its isolation, a contented, serene, and deeply fulfilled land. It seemed a place, which, without human interference, had made its own contract with life, struck its own balance with necessity and nature. Beyond that I cannot go.

Laurens van der Post, from **VENTURE TO THE INTERIOR**

Writing Assignment

1. Write two or three paragraphs describing a specific natural setting you know well, indicating in your description the effect the setting has upon you.

2. Write a short narrative, choosing one of the following subjects:

a. Assume that you have been asked to write a short, punchy narrative for your student newspaper, describing and reacting to some everyday or special event that you have found irritating.

b. Attend a committee or group meeting on campus or in the community and write a careful report of the proceedings as if you were taking minutes of the meeting. Then write a short, lively narrative a few paragraphs long in which you tell what really happened.

3. Write about any personal experience that you have found embarrassing or paradoxical. Describe the event clearly and honestly and explore your attitudes then and now, trying to reach some solution and understanding of your embarrassment and confusion.

4. a. For a week at least, keep a daily journal in which you give your honest, directly expressed reactions to the day's events. This may be in either a personal or a larger context; it is *your* responses that are important, however.

    b. Look back on your journal entries at the end of the week and write
a short narrative, ''One week in the life of———'' as if you were a
fictional character. Be sure to examine your reactions closely and explore
any contradictions.

    c. Now which piece of writing do you prefer and why?

Readings

Lyall Watson **GIFTS OF UNKNOWN THINGS**

"If it fits, if it feels good, if it seems appropriate and meaningful, then it doesn't matter how absurd it is in the light of the established explanation of how things work."

Edward Hoagland **THE LAPPING, ITCHY EDGE OF LOVE**

"Young as we were, constituted as we were, and given the jazzy climate of divorce of the period, we did what we did, smashing what we smashed."

Joan Didion **ON GOING HOME**

"Sometimes I think that those of us who are now in our thirties were born into the last generation to carry the burden of 'home', to find in family life the source of all tension and drama."

Nicola Sacco, Bartolomeo Vanzetti, George Jackson **LETTERS**

"If I must die through the injustice of men and circumstances, you may be sure that none of my enemies will be mourned as I am."

"The author of my hunger, the architect of the circumstantial pressures which are the sole cause of my ills will find no peace, in this existence or the next, or the one following that; never, never."

E. B. White **ONCE MORE TO THE LAKE**

"Summertime, oh, summertime, pattern of life indelible, the fade-proof lake, the woods unshatterable, the pasture with the sweetfern and the juniper forever and ever, summer without end...."

Marcel Proust from **SWANN'S WAY**

"The smell and taste of things remain poised a long time, like souls, ready to remind us, waiting and hoping for their moment, amid the ruins of all the rest...."

from GIFTS OF UNKNOWN THINGS

Lyall Watson

On the island of Luzon in the Philippines, healers dramatize their rituals by dressing them up in a way that makes it look as though they were actually going into the body with their bare hands and bringing out all sorts of offending odds and ends. For Filipino patients it is usually sufficient for them to produce banana leaves or bits of coconut husk, objects locally associated with the kind of witchcraft that produces illness. But for foreigners, different productions are obviously necessary. When a Swiss patient was being treated for a stomach complaint, the healer produced a Swiss noodle. Not just any old noodle, but a fresh one of a kind made and eaten only in the canton of Ticino, where the patient lived.

On another occasion, I was traveling up the Amazon in a narrow riverboat with three Brazilian *caboclos* when one of them developed a severe toothache. An abscess beneath a wisdom tooth had become inflamed, and the man had a high fever. I had no appropriate antibiotics, and I battled unsuccessfully to extract the tooth with a pair of the engineer's long-nosed pliers. I was considering calling off the trip and turning back downstream when one of the boatmen mentioned that a healer lived just a few hours up one of the smaller tributaries ahead.

We moved out of the muddy main stream into a quiet pattern of lagoons of clear green water. The mosquitoes and biting flies disappeared, and the air was full of kingfishers and flocks of parakeets. Eventually we reached an area where the forest had been partially cleared to plant a crop of cassava, and pulled in to the bank near a collection of palm-thatched huts.

I went ashore with the patient and saw him seated on a log in a clearing in front of the home of the healer. In a little while the great man himself came out, and he was a terrible disappointment. He was a small, hungry-looking middle-aged man with little hair and fewer clothes. Just a tattered pair of shorts, plastic sandals, and the remnant of a T-shirt which carried the unlikely claim that it belonged not to this strange man but to the State Prison of Louisiana.

A brief conversation took place in Amazonian Portuguese, and the emphasis, as far as I could understand it, was placed not so much on the patient's symptoms as upon the particular circumstances, the exact time and place, in which they had first been noted. Some sort of agreement was reached which seemed to take the blame off poor dental care and place it squarely on a malevolent outside influence, an evil spirit force which, as it happened, the healer knew well.

He returned to his hut for a moment and emerged with a number of unspecified materials tightly rolled into a ball of greasy black cloth. I was dying to see what it contained, but he simply put it on the ground between the feet of the patient and it was never referred to again.

Then the treatment began. Singing softly to himself in an Indian dialect, the healer pushed the patient's head back until his mouth was wide open. Then he put his crooked forefinger into the mouth and stirred around in there. He grunted once or twice, peered in again, and then reached in with thumb and forefinger and picked out the offending molar as though it had been simply lying there loose under the tongue.

We all examined the tooth and peered into the empty socket, which was bleeding only slightly. There was great satisfaction all round, but the healer wasn't finished yet. He said that he must still get rid of the pain. To do this, he massaged the swollen glands on the patient's throat, then made him sit back again with his mouth wide open.

The healer sat cross-legged on the ground opposite him and began to sway to and fro with his eyes closed. I watched very closely, suddenly aware that this was not just a tired little man in rags, but a very impressive person. Then someone in the crowd hissed and pointed at the patient. A trickle of blood was beginning to flow out of the right corner of his mouth and run down his chin. This was not surprising, but what happened next was something that brought a great roar of laughter from all the observers, but made the hair at the back of my neck bristle.

Out of the side of his mouth, following the line of the trickle of blood, came a column of live black army ants. Not a frantic confusion of ants, running in every direction, as they would have been if the healer had dropped some sort of container holding ants into the patient's mouth, but an ordered column of ants. Ants marching two and three abreast, coming from somewhere and going somewhere.

They kept on coming until there were a hundred or more, moving in a stream down the patient's neck, along his bare arm, down onto the log on which he sat. Then he and I and everyone present watched the column as it marched off into the grass at the edge of the clearing and away.

Thinking back on that experience later, I realized that the healer had started off the consultation by concentrating not on the symptoms of his patient, but on the peculiar circumstances connected with them. He was concerned not so much with how he had come to develop the complaint as with why it had happened to him, and why now, just as he was starting on an important trip. He tried, as all Western physicians will, to give the condition an identity separate from the sufferer, to set it up so that it could be treated. But he was not content with a fine-sounding diagnosis. He went beyond treatment of the symptoms to tackle root causes by suggesting that some outside agency, an evil spirit or some personal ritual deficiency perhaps, was responsible. The cause he came up with may not have been the right one, but by recognizing any at all, and by taking obviously appropriate action to deal with it, he was providing, in addition to his efficient dental treatment, psychiatric therapy at no extra charge.

To me that seemed like very good medicine. The patient was simply given the means to make himself well. And this was accomplished by a superbly judged piece of sleight-of-mind.

When the crowd at the healing laughed at the sight of ants crawling out of a man's mouth, it was not the nervous laughter of people in fear or discomfort. It was honest loud laughter over something that struck them as very funny. I didn't see the joke until it was explained to me later. In the local dialect, the same word is used for pain and for the army ant. The healer had promised that the pain would leave, and so it did in the form of an elaborate and extraordinary pun. It walked out.

For that patient, in his culture, with his expectations and beliefs, the treatment was highly effective. He got better very quickly.

For this observer, in his certainty, with his patterns of logic and procedure, the whole affair was shattering. It took me a long time to come to terms with it. It was years before I could even bring myself to talk of it. Whom can a scientist tell about an experience like that?

But I no longer have that problem. Not since I number theoretical physicists amongst my friends. They have taught me that the objective world in space and time does not exist and that we are forced to deal now not in facts, but in possibilities. Nobody in quantum mechanics talks about impossibilities any more. They have developed a kind of statistical mysticism, and physics becomes very hard to distinguish from metaphysics. And that makes things a little easier for a biologist faced with biological absurdities.

Breaking the rules doesn't worry me anymore now that I can see that only one principle really matters. And that is rightness. If it fits, if it feels good, if it seems appropriate and meaningful, then it doesn't matter how absurd it is in the light of the established explanation of how things work. Establishments are no longer as stable as they used to be. They are having to make way for another kind of knowing which is concerned only with harmony, with keeping in touch with Earth's tune.

1. By telling the story about the healers who "tailor" their cures to their patients, Watson is trying to make a point about modern medicine. What is it?

2. Watson admits that he was shattered by the experience on the Amazon. Does he disturb you with his story? Explain your response with reference to the way in which Watson unfolds his narrative. Comment on the arrangement of the sequence, the point of view, and the dominant effect.

3. Do you think that Watson adequately explains the events by the statement in his last paragraph?

THE LAPPING, ITCHY EDGE OF LOVE

Edward Hoagland

My first wife was a mathematician who was living in the Bronx in half of a subway motorman's house. Van Cortlandt Park was close, and Sugar Ray Robinson lived nearby. I was writing a prizefight book, so I watched his house, which was equipped with blinking tree lights and broken pugilists who served as houseboys. I had a motor scooter and combat boots, and when my first wife heard their crunch along the sidewalk she knew that it was either me or a murderer. Mr. Clean, the detergent man, with a ring in one ear and a shaved head, was another neighborhood celebrity. In retrospect the whole courtship has a poignancy because of her earnestness and because of details of this sort, just the kind that old-marrieds recite. She is somebody I'll never meet in anyone else's skin, and when we last talked on the phone I twisted and throbbed and couldn't speak, though I was capricious and domineering as a husband, faithful only in a literal sense. We lived in howling cold tenements because if anybody was living that way in the pomp of New York we wanted to too; I was the radical and she was the idealist. But for half our time together we traveled to Sicily and Spain, needing to lean on each other wherever we were because of being strangers, and hence procrastinating on our central problems. Oddly enough, timid as I was, I was a father in that marriage instead of a son, and while I made some redeeming gestures, my memories of my behavior are mostly of the obstinacies, petty and large. In particular, I wouldn't let her have a child, which is a sore thought in this present gleeful interlude because it bewildered her and made her wretched. It was the sticking point; it was what I withheld. Later I offered her the child, under whatever circumstances, and turned on the waterworks. She was the strong one then, though while we were married it didn't seem she was going to be. To try to describe her—her voice, her dresses, her squirrel's-nest hair, the way she walked and wore her high collars—is fruitless and painful. Later I cried, later I loved, when it was too late. There were reunions and pinpoint depictions of the whole-cake, whole-spirited love that we had hoped in our clearest moments to achieve. Finally we got the divorce, printed in Spanish, which rests in my safe deposit box—that dreary receptacle—along with a yellowing christening certificate, my father's will, and several repudiated contracts and unlucky investments. Young as we were, constituted as we were, and given the jazzy climate of divorce of the period, we did what we did, smashing what we smashed. Although my new marriage casts a wider net and is serene by comparison, this early one remains like a rip in my life.

1. How would you describe the relationship between Hoagland and his first wife?
2. Hoagland is honest and direct about his "obstinacies, petty and large." Do you think he has any regrets about them? Explain.
3. Write a short fictionalized account of an "impossible" relationship you might have with someone whom you know you would eventually be divorced from.

ON GOING HOME

Joan Didion

I am home for my daughter's first birthday. By "home" I do not mean the house in Los Angeles where my husband and I and the baby live, but the place where my family is, in the Central Valley of California. It is a vital although troublesome distinction. My husband likes my family but is uneasy in their house, because once there I fall into their ways, which are difficult, oblique, deliberately inarticulate, not my husband's ways. We live in dusty houses ("D-U-S-T," he once wrote with his finger on surfaces all over the house, but no one noticed it) filled with mementos quite without value to him (what could the Canton dessert plates mean to him? how could he have known about the assay scales, why should he care if he did know?), and we appear to talk exclusively about people we know who have been committed to mental hospitals, about people we know who have been booked on drunk-driving charges, and about property, particularly about property, land, price per acre and C-2 zoning and assessments and freeway access. My brother does not understand my husband's inability to perceive the advantage in the rather common real-estate transaction known as "sale-leaseback," and my husband in turn does not understand why so many of the people he hears about in my father's house have recently been committed to mental hospitals or booked on drunk-driving charges. Nor does he understand that when we talk about sale-leasebacks and right-of-way condemnations we are talking in code about the things we like best, the yellow fields and the cottonwoods and the rivers rising and falling and the mountain roads closing when the heavy snow comes in. We miss each other's points, have another drink and regard the fire. My brother refers to my husband, in his presence, as "Joan's husband." Marriage is the classic betrayal.

Or perhaps it is not any more. Sometimes I think that those of us who are now in our thirties were born into the last generation to carry the burden of "home," to find in family life the source of all tension and drama. I had by all objective accounts a "normal" and a "happy" family situation, and yet I was almost thirty years old before I could talk to my family on the telephone without crying after I had hung up. We did not fight. Nothing was wrong. And yet some nameless anxiety colored the emotional charges between me and the place that I came from. The question of whether or not you could go home again was a very real part of the sentimental and largely literary baggage with which we left home in the fifties; I suspect that it is irrelevant to the children born of the fragmentation after Word War II. A few weeks ago in a San Francisco bar I saw a pretty young girl on crystal take off her clothes and dance for the cash prize in an "amateur-topless" contest. There was no particular sense of moment about this, none of the effect of romantic degradation, of "dark journey," for which my generation strived so assiduously. What sense could that girl possibly make of, say, *Long Day's Journey into Night?* Who is beside the point?

That I am trapped in this particular irrelevancy is never more apparent to me than when I am home. Paralyzed by the neurotic lassitude engendered by meeting one's past at every turn, around every corner, inside every cupboard, I go aimlessly from room to room. I decide to meet it head-on and clean out a drawer, and I spread the contents on the bed. A bathing suit I wore the summer I was seventeen. A letter of rejection from *The Nation,* an aerial photograph of the site for a shopping center my father did not build in 1954. Three teacups hand-painted with cabbage roses and signed "E.M.," my grandmother's initials. There is no final solution for letters of rejection from *The Nation* and teacups hand-painted in 1900. Nor is there any answer to snapshots of one's grandfather as a young man on skis, surveying around Donner Pass in the year 1910. I smooth out the snapshot and look into his face, and do and do not see my own. I close the drawer, and have another cup of coffee with my mother. We get along very well, veterans of a guerrilla war we never understood.

Days pass. I see no one. I come to dread my husband's evening call, not only because he is full of news of what by now seems to me our remote life in Los Angeles, people he has seen, letters which require attention, but because he asks what I have been doing, suggests uneasily that I get out, drive to San Francisco or Berkeley. Instead I drive across the river to a family graveyard. It has been vandalized since my last visit and the monuments are broken, overturned in the dry grass. Because I once saw a rattlesnake in the grass I stay in the car and listen to a country-and-Western station. Later I drive with my father to a ranch he has in the foothills. The man who runs his cattle on it asks us to the roundup, a week from Sunday, and although I know that I will be in Los Angeles I say, in the oblique way my family talks, that I will come. Once home I mention the broken monuments in the graveyard. My mother shrugs.

I go to visit my great-aunts. A few of them think now that I am my cousin, or their daughter who died young. We recall an anecdote about a relative last seen in 1948, and they ask if I still like living in New York City. I have lived in Los Angeles for three years, but I say that I do. The baby is offered a horehound drop, and I am slipped a dollar bill "to buy a treat." Questions trail off, answers are abandoned, the baby plays with the dust motes in a shaft of afternoon sun.

It is time for the baby's birthday party: a white cake, strawberry-marshmallow ice cream, a bottle of champagne saved from another party. In the evening, after she has gone to sleep, I kneel beside the crib and touch her face, where it is pressed against the slats, with mine. She is an open and trusting child, unprepared for and unaccustomed to the ambushes of family life, and perhaps it is just as well that I can offer her little of that life. I would like to give her more. I would like to promise her that she will grow up with a sense of her cousins and of rivers and of her great-grandmother's teacups, would like to pledge her a picnic on a river with fried chicken and her hair uncombed, would like to give her *home* for her birthday, but we live differently now and I can promise her nothing like that. I give her a xylophone and a sundress from Madeira, and promise to tell her a funny story.

1. a. What is the specific evidence that going home is disturbing for Didion?

b. Do you think this is an effective piece of personal writing? Give reasons that refer to the structure and style of the essay. Use the checklist for guidelines.

c. Write a short personal piece about your feelings of a "nameless anxiety" (not necessarily at home, anywhere will do; or maybe it is a person who creates this feeling in you). Examine that nameless anxiety as closely as you can.

LETTERS OF THREE PRISONERS

The following letters were written by three famous prisoners of our time. Nicola Sacco and Bartolomeo Vanzetti were Italian-American anarchists who were executed in August 1927 for a crime they fiercely insisted they never committed, and to which another man confessed. After their execution there was an uproar—including many demonstrations against Americans abroad—and the two have lived on in the minds of many as political martyrs.

George Jackson, while a prisoner at Soledad Prison on a robbery conviction, was accused with two other prisoners of the murder of a white guard. In 1971 he himself was killed at San Quentin Prison; shortly afterwards, the other Soledad brothers were acquitted.

Vanzetti to his father

Dearest father,

I have restrained until this moment the desire to write to you, since I had hoped to be able to give you some good news.

Things have continued to go badly, so I decided to write to you. I know how painful this occurrence in my life must be for all of you, it is this thought that makes me suffer the most. I beg you to be as strong as I am, and to pardon the pain that I am involuntarily causing you. I know that several people have written to you, but I do not know if you are in possession of all the facts, since several letters and collections of newspapers that friends sent to Italy have never been received. This fact forces one to admit that either the Italian or the American authorities are censoring all mail that concerns me. I do, however, know that you have received some letters and are therefore acquainted with the nature and outcome of my trial; it was a true crime against legality. A friend sent me your greetings, your conviction that I am innocent, and the happy news that you are feeling well. These are consolations of incalculable worth. Yes: I am innocent, despite everything I am feeling well, and I do my best to remain in good health. Now they are accusing me of murder. I have never killed or wounded or robbed, but if things go as they did in the other trial they would find even Christ, whom they have already crucified, guilty. I have witnesses that I will call in my defense, and I will fight with all of my energies. The weapons are unequal, and the fighting will be desperate. I will have against me the law with all of its immense resources; the police with its ages of experience in the art of condemning the innocent, a police whose actions are both uncontrolled and uncontrollable. Also arrayed against me are political and racial hate, and the great power that gold has in a country, and in a time, when the depth of human degeneration has been plumbed. The lust for gold has forced certain wretches to tell all sorts of vile lies about me. I have nothing to oppose this formidable coalition of enemies but my popularly acknowledged innocence, and the love and care of a handful of generous souls who love and aid me. The general public proclaims my innocence, demands my liberation. If you knew how much they have done, are doing and will do for me, you would be proud.

I hope that my Italian comrades will not deny me their support. In fact I'm sure they won't.

I have asked for the transcript of my trial. It will be translated into Italian and into other languages, and sent to Italy and to the other European nations.

Take heart therefore and be optimistic. Justice is always triumphant in the end, and so it will be in my case. Do not let this adversity oppress you, let it rather be an incentive to life, to living. Who knows what surprises destiny carries in its breast for us mortals? Who would have thought, a few days before my arrest, in what conditions I would now find myself? Who, therefore, can predict, from the terrible condition in which I now find myself, what tomorrow has in store for me? Let us, therefore, have faith and continue the struggle. . . .

I wish to tell you and all my loved ones one other thing. Do not keep my arrest a secret. Do not be silent, I am innocent and you have nothing to be ashamed of. Do not be silent, broadcast the crime that has been committed against me from the rooftops. Tell the world that an honest man is being sent to jail to restore the reputation of the police, which has been lost in a hundred scandals and a hundred failures. The police have not been able to find one single criminal in all this rising sea of crime. I am being sent to jail because of an old sadist's attachment to his power and his position, and because of his desire to see me deprived of my liberty and my blood. Do not be silent, silence would be shameful.

For the moment I don't need any money. If I should need some I will let you know. The prisons here are much better than in Italy; I say this by intuition and from what I have heard, since I have never been in prison in Italy. We all have our own cells. Our furniture consists of an adequate bed, a closet, a table and a chair. The electric lights are on until nine at night. We are given three meals a day, and a hot drink once or even twice daily. We are allowed to write two letters a month, and an additional letter every third month. The warden allowed me to write several extra letters, this is one of them. There is a library which contains the world's scientific and artistic masterpieces. We work eight hours a day in a healthy atmosphere. We are allowed out into the courtyard every day. The inmates? Except for a few victims of circumstance, who are more to be pitied than censured, they are wretches. I treat everyone as well as I can, but I remain mostly in the company of those few who are able to understand me, know my case and honor and love me. If you have kept the last letters that I sent you, send them back to the address of one of my friends, and insure them at the post office. They may be of great use to me.

I finish on a happy note: it is almost certain that there will be a retrial for the things that I was first accused of.

Be strong, therefore, and encourage my sisters and little brother, as well as all my relatives and friends.

Sacco to his seven-year-old daughter

I would like that you should understand what I am going to say to you, and I wish I could write you so plain, for I long so much to have you hear all the heart-beat eagerness of your father, for I love you so much as you are the dearest little beloved one.

It is quite hard indeed to make you understand in your young age, but I am going to try from the bottom of my heart to make you understand how dear you are to your father's soul. If I cannot succeed in doing that, I know that you will save this letter and read it over in future years to come and you will see and feel the same heart-beat affection as your father feels in writing it to you.

I will bring with me your little and so dearest letter and carry it right under my heart to the last day of my life. When I die, it will be buried with your father who loves you so much, as I do also your brother Dante and holy dear mother.

You don't know Ines, how dear and great your letter was to your father. It is the most golden present that you could have given to me or that I could have wished for in these sad days.

It was the greatest treasure and sweetness in my struggling life that I could have lived with you and your brother Dante and your mother in a neat little farm, and learn all your sincere words and tender affection. Then in the summer-time to be sitting with you in the home nest under the oak tree shade—beginning to teach you of life and how to read and write, to see you running, laughing, crying and singing through the verdant fields picking the wild flowers here and there from one tree to another, and from the clear, vivid stream to your mother's embrace.

The same I have wished to see for other poor girls, and their brothers, happy with their mother and father as I dreamed for us—but it was not so and the nightmare of the lower classes saddened very badly your father's soul.

For the things of beauty and of good in this life, mother nature gave to us all, for the conquest and the joy of liberty. The men of this dying old society, they brutally have pulled me away from the embrace of your brother and your poor mother. But, in spite of all, the free spirit of your father's faith still survives, and I have lived for it and for the dream that some day I would have come back to life, to the embrace of your dear mother, among our friends and comrades again, but woe is me!

I know that you are good and surely you love your mother, Dante and all the beloved ones—and I am sure that you love me also a little, for I love you much and then so much. You do not know Ines, how often I think of you every day. You are in my heart, in my vision, in every angle of this sad walled cell, in the sky and everywhere my gaze rests.

Vanzetti's last letter to his family

I swear to you that I am completely innocent of this or any other crime. Do not be ashamed of me. There will come a day in which my life will be known for what it is, and whoever bears the name of Vanzetti will hold up his head in pride. Everyone who knows me already loves and respects me. I have written my epitaph with twenty years dedicated to justice and liberty for all. If I must die through the injustice of men and circumstances, you may be sure that none of my enemies will be mourned as I am.

I do not want you to cry for me. I want you to be serene and strong, and continue my work for me. I want you to sing of me, rather than cry for me, I want to live in your hearts, which must be whole and strong and happy.

I will fight to the end to win.

Jackson to his mother

Dear Georgia,

For me, the word "soul" has yet to be properly defined. I have seen or felt no evidence of its existence. I have heard the word and listened to the theory connected with it, but it is abstract and academic at best.

The theory of an existing and benevolent god simply doesn't make sense to anyone who is rational. A benevolent and omnipotent god would never allow such imbalances as I see to exist for one second. If by chance I am wrong, however, I must then assume that being born black called for some automatic punishment for sins I know nothing about, and being innocent it behooves me to defy god.

I seriously fail to understand when someone speaks of my soul, but I do know what my body needs. I know what my mind incessantly craves. Gratification of these is what I must pursue. As a woman I can understand your being naturally disposed to servitude. I can understand *your* feelings but what I can't understand is why you would have me feel the same, considering that I am a man. Why have you always attempted to implant womanly ideas into my character. Of course it is your option to do as you please, but please don't feel that I love you less simply because I fail to respond, or feel that I love you any less because I do not have time to explain myself.

Love has never turned aside the boot, blade, or bullet. Neither has it ever satisfied my hunger of body or mind. The author of my hunger, the architect of the circumstantial pressures which are the sole cause of my ills will find no peace, in this existence or the next, or the one following that; never, never. I'll dog his trail to infinity. I hope I never will feel I've love for the thing that causes insufferable pain. What I do feel is the urge to resist, resist, and never stop resisting or even think of stopping my resistance until victory falls to me.

Extreme, perhaps, but involved is my self-determination, and control of the environment upon which my existence depends, and the existence of my father, mother, Delora's and Penny's sons, and all that I feel tied to. We are in an extreme situation.

I didn't create this impasse. I had nothing to do with the arrival of matters at this destructive end, as you infer. Did I colonize, kidnap, make war on myself, destroy my own institutions, enslave myself, use myself, and neglect myself, steal my identity and then, being reduced to nothing, invent a competitive economy knowing that I cannot compete? Sounds very foolish, but this is what you propose when you place the blame on me or on "us." It was a fool who created this monster, one unaccustomed to power and its use, a foolish man grown heady with power and made drunk, dizzy drunk from the hot air that inflates his ego. I am his victim, born innocent, a *total* product of my surroundings. Everything that I am, I *developed* into because of circumstantial and situational pressures. I was born knowing nothing; necessity and environment formed me, and everyone like me. Please accord me at least the social morality that springs from its contorted brain center. I'm through with weakness and cowardice. I've trained it out. Let come what comes. I can never delude myself into thinking that I love my enemies. I can hardly do any worse than I am doing now; if worst comes to worst that's all right, I'll just continue the fight in hell.

George

Sacco and Vanzetti

1. Needless to say, these letters show signs of strain, depression, paradox, and some optimism. Contrast the voices of Sacco and Vanzetti and the ways in which they handle the crisis.

2. For what emotional reasons were these letters written?

3. Describe carefully what you think are the most important elements of the style of these letters.

Jackson

1. Jackson's is an intensely provocative letter over the death of love, a hate-loaded lashing out against mother, God, and society, and even a decision to "continue the fight in hell," all in order to prove what? Explain carefully.

2. Does Jackson consider himself a victim? Explain your answer.

3. Why does Jackson resist his mother's plea?

4. Do you think it is true that the self-revelation here is a gesture of social significance?

ONCE MORE TO THE LAKE

E. B. White

One summer, along about 1904, my father rented a camp on a lake in Maine and took us all there for the month of August. We all got ringworm from some kittens and had to rub Pond's Extract on our arms and legs night and morning, and my father rolled over in a canoe with all his clothes on; but outside of that the vacation was a success and from then on none of us ever thought there was any place in the world like that lake in Maine. We returned summer after summer—always on August 1 for one month. I have since become a salt-water man, but sometimes in summer there are days when the restlessness of the tides and the fearful cold of the sea water and the incessant wind that blows across the after-noon and into the evening make me wish for the placidity of a lake in the woods. A few weeks ago this feeling got so strong I bought myself a couple of bass hooks and a spinner and returned to the lake where we used to go, for a week's fishing and to revisit old haunts.

I took along my son, who had never had any fresh water up his nose and who had seen lily pads only from train windows. On the journey over to the lake I began to wonder what it would be like. I wondered how the time would have marred this unique, this holy spot—the coves and streams, the hills that the sun set behind, the camps and the paths behind the camps. I was sure that the tarred road would have found it out, and I wondered in what other ways it would be desolated. It is strange how much you can remember about places like that once you allow your mind to return into the grooves that lead back. You remember one thing, and that suddenly reminds you of another thing. I guess I remembered clearest of all the early mornings, when the lake was cool and motionless, remembered how the bedroom smelled of the lumber it was made of and of the wet woods whose scent entered through the screen. The partitions in the camp were thin and did not extend clear to the top of the rooms, and as I was always the first up I would dress softly so as not to wake the others, and sneak out into the sweet outdoors and start out in the canoe, keeping close along the shore in the long shadows of the pines. I remembered being very careful never to rub my paddle against the gunwale for fear of disturbing the stillness of the cathedral.

The lake had never been what you would call a wild lake. There were cottages sprinkled around the shores, and it was in farming country although the shores of the lake were quite heavily wooded. Some of the cottages were owned by nearby farmers, and you would live at the shore and eat your meals at the farmhouse. That's what our family did. But although it wasn't wild, it was a fairly large and undisturbed lake and there were places in it that, to a child at least, seemed infinitely remote and primeval.

I was right about the tar: it led to within half a mile of the shore. But when I got back there, with my boy, and we settled into a camp near a farmhouse and into the kind of summertime I had known, I could tell that it was going to be pretty much the same as it had been before—I knew it, lying in bed the first morning, smelling the bedroom and hearing the boy sneak quietly out and go off along the shore in a boat. I began to sustain the illusion that he was I, and therefore, by simple transposition, that I was my father. This sensation persisted, kept cropping up all the time we were there. It was not an entirely new feeling, but in this setting, it grew much stronger. I seemed to be living a dual existence. I would be in the middle of some simple act, I would be picking up a bait box or laying down a table fork, or I would be saying something, and suddenly it would be not I but my father who was saying the words or making the gesture. It gave me a creepy sensation.

We went fishing the first morning. I felt the same damp moss covering the worms in the bait can, and saw the dragonfly alight on the tip of my rod as it hovered a few inches from the surface of the water. It was the arrival of this fly that convinced me beyond any doubt that everything was as it always had been, that the years were a mirage and that there had been no years. The small waves were the same, chucking the rowboat under the chin as we fished at anchor, and the boat was the same boat, the same color green and the ribs broken in the same places, and under the floorboards the same fresh-water leavings and débris—the dead helgramite, the wisps of moss, the rusty discarded fishhook, the dried blood from yesterday's catch. We stared silently at the tips of our rods, at the dragonflies that came and went. I lowered the tip of mine into the water, tentatively, pensively dislodging the fly, which darted two feet away, poised, darted two feet back, and came to rest again a little farther up the rod. There had been no years between the ducking of this dragonfly and the other one— the one that was part of memory. I looked at the boy, who was silently watching his fly, and it was my hands that held his rod, my eyes watching. I felt dizzy and didn't know which rod I was at the end of.

We caught two bass, hauling them in briskly as though they were mackerel, pulling them over the side of the boat in a businesslike manner without any landing net, and stunning them with a blow on the back of the head. When we got back for a swim before lunch, the lake was exactly where we had left it, the same number of inches from the dock, and there was only the merest suggestion of a breeze. This seemed an utterly enchanted sea, this lake you could leave to its own devices for a few hours and come back to, and find that it had not stirred, this constant and trustworthy body of water. In the shallows, the dark, water-soaked sticks and twigs, smooth and old, were undulating in clusters on the bottom against the clean ribbed sand, and the track of the mussel was plain. A school of minnows swam by, each minnow with its small individual shadow, dou-bling the attendance, so clear and sharp in the sunlight. Some of the other campers were in swimming, along the shore, one of them with a cake of soap, and the water felt thin and clear and unsubstantial. Over the years there had been this person with the cake of soap, this cultist, and here he was. There had been no years.

Up to the farmhouse to dinner through the teeming, dusty field, the road under our sneakers was only a two-track road. The middle track was missing, the one with the marks of the hooves and the splotches of dried, flaky manure. There had always been three tracks to choose from in choosing which track to walk in; now the choice was narrowed down to two. For a moment I missed terribly the middle alternative. But the way led past the tennis court, and something about the way it lay there in the sun reassured me; the tape had loosened along the backline, the alleys were green with plantains and other weeds, and the net (installed in June and removed in September) sagged in the dry noon, and the whole place steamed with midday heat and hunger and emptiness. There was a choice of pie for dessert, and one was blueberry and one was apple, and the waitresses were the same country girls, there having been no passage of time, only the illusion of it as in a dropped curtain—the waitresses were still fifteen; their hair had been washed, that was the only difference—they had been to the movies and seen the pretty girls with the clean hair.

Summertime, oh, summertime, pattern of life indelible, the fade-proof lake, the woods unshatterable, the pasture with the sweetfern and the juniper forever and ever, summer without end; this was the background, and the life along the shore was the design, the cottages with their innocent and tranquil design, their tiny docks with the flagpole and the American flag floating against the white clouds in the blue sky, the little paths over the roots of the trees leading from camp to camp and the paths leading back to the outhouses and the can of lime for sprinkling, and at the souvenir counters at the store the miniature birch-bark canoes and the postcards that showed things looking a little better than they looked. This was the American family at play, escaping the city heat, wondering whether the newcomers in the camp at the head of the cove were "common" or "nice," wondering whether it was true that the people who drove up for Sunday dinner at the farmhouse were turned away because there wasn't enough chicken.

It seemed to me, as I kept remembering all this, that those times and those summers had been infinitely precious and worth saving. There had been jollity and peace and goodness. The arriving (at the beginning of August) had been so big a business in itself, at the railway station the farm wagon drawn up, the first smell of the pine-laden air, the first glimpse of the smiling farmer, and the great importance of the trunks and your father's enormous authority in such matters, and the feel of the wagon under you for the long ten-mile haul, and at the top of the last long hill catching the first view of the lake after eleven months of not seeing this cherished body of water. The shouts and cries of the other campers when they saw you, and the trunks to be unpacked, to give up their rich burden. (Arriving was less exciting nowadays, when you sneaked up in your car and parked it under a tree near the camp and took out the bags and in five minutes it was all over, no fuss, no loud wonderful fuss about trunks.)

Peace and goodness and jollity. The only thing that was wrong now, really, was the sound of the place, an unfamiliar nervous sound of the outboard motors. This was the note that jarred, the one thing that would sometimes break the illusion and set the years moving. In those other summertimes all motors were inboard; and when they were at a little distance, the noise they made was a sedative, an ingredient of summer sleep. They were one-cylinder and two-cylinder engines, and some were make-and-break and some were jump-spark, but they all made a sleepy sound across the lake. The one-lungers throbbed and fluttered, and the twin-cylinder ones purred and purred, and that was a quiet sound, too. But now the campers all had outboards. In the daytime, in the hot mornings, these motors made a petulant, irritable sound; at night, in the still evening when the afterglow lit the water, they whined about one's ears like mosquitoes. My boy loved our rented outboard, and his great desire was to achieve single-handed mastery over it, and authority, and he soon learned the trick of choking it a little (but not too much), and the adjustment of the needle valve. Watching him I would remember the things you could do with the one-cylinder engine with the heavy flywheel, how you could have it eating out of your hand if you got really close to it spiritually. Motorboats in those days didn't have clutches, and you would make a landing by shutting off the motor at the proper time and coasting

364

in with a dead rudder. But there was a way of reversing them, if you learned the trick, by cutting the switch and putting it on again exactly on the final dying revolution of the flywheel, so that it would kick back against compression and begin reversing. Approaching a dock in a strong following breeze, it was difficult to slow up sufficiently by the ordinary coasting method, and if a boy felt he had complete mastery over his motor, he was tempted to keep it running beyond its time and then reverse it a few feet from the dock. It took a cool nerve, because if you threw the switch a twentieth of a second too soon you would catch the flywheel when it still had speed enough to go up past center, and the boat would leap ahead, charging bull-fashion at the dock.

We had a good week at the camp. The bass were biting well and the sun shone endlessly, day after day. We would be tired at night and lie down in the accumulated heat of the little bedrooms after the long hot day and the breeze would stir almost imperceptibly outside and the smell of the swamp drift in through the rusty screens. Sleep would come easily and in the morning the red squirrel would be on the roof, tapping out his gay routine. I kept remembering everything, lying in bed in the mornings—the small steamboat that had a long rounded stern like the lip of a Ubangi, and how quietly she ran on the moonlight sails, when the older boys played their mandolins and the girls sang and we ate doughnuts dipped in sugar, and how sweet the music was on the water in the shining night, and what it had felt like to think about girls then. After breakfast we would go up to the store and the things were in the same place—the minnows in a bottle, the plugs and spinners disarranged and pawed over by the youngsters from the boys' camp, the Fig Newtons and the Beeman's gum. Outside, the road was tarred and cars stood in front of the store. Inside, all was just as it had always been, except there was more Coca-Cola and not so much Moxie and root beer and birch beer and sarsaparilla. We would walk out with the bottle of pop apiece and sometimes the pop would backfire up our noses and hurt. We explored the streams, quietly, where the turtles slid off logs and dug their way into the soft bottom; and we lay on the town wharf and fed worms to the tame bass. Everywhere we went I had trouble making out which was I, the one walking at my side, the one walking in my pants.

One afternoon while we were there at the lake a thunderstorm came up. It was like the revival of an old melodrama that I had seen long ago with childish awe. The second-act climax of the drama of the electrical disturbance over a lake in America has not changed in any important respect. This was the big scene, still the big scene. The whole thing was so familiar, the first feeling of oppression and heat and a general air around camp of not wanting to go very far away. In midafternoon (it was all the same) a curious darkening of the sky, and a lull in everything that had made life tick; and then the way the boats suddenly swung the other way at their moorings with the coming of a breeze out of the new quarter, and the premonitory rumble. Then the kettle drum, then the snare, then the bass drum and cymbals, then crackling light against the dark, and the gods grinning and licking their chops in the hills. Afterward the calm, the rain steadily rustling in the calm lake, the return of light and hope and spirits, and the campers running out in joy and relief to go swimming in the rain, their bright cries perpetuating the deathless joke about how they were getting simply drenched, and the children screaming with delight at the new sensation of bathing in the rain, and the joke about getting drenched linking the generations in a strong indestructible chain. And the comedian who waded in carrying an umbrella.

When the others went swimming, my son said he was going in, too. He pulled his dripping trunks from the line where they had hung all through the shower and wrung them out. Languidly, and with no thought of going in, I watched him, his hard little body, skinny and bare, saw him wince slightly as he pulled up around his vitals the small, soggy, icy garment. As he buckled the swollen belt, suddenly my groin felt the chill of death.

1. Explain carefully what you think are White's feelings about
   a. The return to the lake
   b. The passing of time since childhood
   c. "Peace and goodness and jollity"
   d. His relationship to his son
   Back up your responses with close reference to the text.
2. Write a short analysis of White's narrative style explaining why you think it is effective or not.

from SWANN'S WAY

Marcel Proust

Many years had elapsed during which nothing of Combray, save what was comprised in the theatre and the drama of my going to bed there, had any existence for me, when one day in winter, as I came home, my mother, seeing that I was cold, offered me some tea, a thing I did not ordinarily take. I declined at first, and then, for no particular reason, changed my mind. She sent out for one of those short, plump little cakes called "petites madeleines," which look as though they had been moulded in the fluted scallop of a pilgrim's shell. And soon, mechanically, weary after a dull day with the prospect of a depressing morrow, I raised to my lips a spoonful of the tea in which I had soaked a morsel of the cake. No sooner had the warm liquid, and the crumbs with it, touched my palate than a shudder ran through my whole body, and I stopped, intent upon the extraordinary changes that were taking place. An exquisite pleasure had invaded my senses, but individual, detached, with no suggestion of its origin. And at once the vicissitudes of life had become indifferent to me, its disasters innocuous, its brevity illusory—this new sensation having had on me the effect which love has of filling me with a precious essence; or rather this essence was not in me, it was myself. I had ceased now to feel mediocre, accidental, mortal. Whence could it have come to me, this all-powerful joy? I was conscious that it was connected with the taste of tea and cake, but that it infinitely transcended those savours, could not, indeed, be of the same nature as theirs. Whence did it come? What did it signify? How could I seize upon and define it?

I drink a second mouthful, in which I find nothing more than in the first, a third, which gives me rather less than the second. It is time to stop; the potion is losing its magic. It is plain that the object of my quest, the truth, lies not in the cup but in myself. The tea has called up in me, but does not itself understand, and can only repeat indefinitely with a gradual loss of strength, the same testimony; which I, too, cannot interpret, though I hope at least to be able to call upon the tea for it again and to find it there presently, intact and at my disposal, for my final enlightenment. I put down my cup and examine my own mind. It is for it to discover the truth. But how? What an abyss of uncertainty whenever the mind feels that some part of it has strayed beyond its own borders; when it, the seeker, is at once the dark region through which it must go seeking, where all its equipment will avail it nothing. Seek? More than that: create. It is face to face with something which does not so far exist, to which it alone can give reality and substance, which it alone can bring into the light of day.

And I begin again to ask myself what it could have been, this unremembered state which brought with it no logical proof of its existence, but only the sense that it was a happy, that it was a real state in whose presence other states of consciousness melted and vanished. I decide to attempt to make it reappear. I retrace my thoughts to the moment at which I drank the first spoonful of tea. I find again the same state, illumined by no fresh light. I compel my mind to make one further effort, to follow and recapture once again the fleeting sensation. And that nothing may interrupt it in its course I shut out every obstacle, every extraneous idea, I stop my ears and inhibit all attention to the sounds which come from the next room. And then, feeling that my mind is growing fatigued without having any success to report, I compel it for a change to enjoy that distraction which I have just denied it, to think of other things, to rest and refresh itself before the supreme attempt. And then for the second time I clear an empty space in front of it. I place in position before my mind's eye the still recent taste of that first mouthful, and I feel something start within me, something that leaves its resting-place and attempts to rise, something that has been embedded like an anchor at a great depth; I do not know yet what it is, but I can feel it mounting slowly; I can measure the resistance, I can hear the echo of great spaces traversed.

Undoubtedly what is thus palpitating in the depths of my being must be the image, the visual memory which, being linked to that taste, has tried to follow it into my conscious mind. But its struggles are too far off, too much confused; scarcely can I perceive the colourless reflection in which are blended the uncapturable whirling medley of radiant hues, and I cannot distinguish its form, cannot invite it, as the one possible interpreter, to translate to me the evidence of its contemporary, its inseparable paramour, the taste of cake soaked in tea; cannot ask it to inform me what special circumstance is in question, of what period in my past life.

Will it ultimately reach the clear surface of my consciousness, this memory, this old, dead moment which the magnetism of an identical moment has travelled so far to importune, to disturb, to raise up out of the very depths of my being? I cannot tell. Now that I feel nothing, it has stopped, has perhaps gone down again into its darkness, from which who can say whether it will ever rise? Ten times over I must essay the task, must lean down over the abyss. And each time the natural laziness which deters us from every difficult enterprise, every work of importance, has urged me to leave the thing alone, to drink my tea and to think merely of the worries of to-day and of my hopes for to-morrow, which let themselves be pondered over without effort or distress of mind.

And suddenly the memory returns. The taste was that of the little crumb of madeleine which on Sunday mornings at Combray (because on those mornings I did not go out before church-time), when I went to say good day to her in her bedroom, my aunt Léonie used to give me, dipping it first in her own cup of real or of lime-flower tea. The sight of the little madeleine had recalled nothing to my mind before I tasted it; perhaps because I had so often seen such things in the interval, without tasting them, on the trays in pastry-cooks' windows, that their image had dissociated itself from those Combray days to take its place among others more recent; perhaps because of those memories, so long abandoned and put out of mind, nothing now survived, everything was scattered; the forms of things, including that of the little scallop-shell of pastry, so richly sensual under its severe, religious folds, were either obliterated or had been so long dormant as to have lost the power of expansion which would have allowed them to resume their place in my consciousness. But when from a long-distant past nothing subsists, after the people are dead, after the things are broken and scattered, still, alone, more fragile, but with more vitality, more unsubstantial, more persistent, more faithful, the smell and taste of things remain poised a long time, like souls, ready to remind us, waiting and hoping for their moment, amid the ruins of all the rest; and bear unfaltering, in the tiny and almost impalpable drop of their essence, the vast structure of recollection.

And once I had recognized the taste of the crumb of madeleine soaked in her decoction of lime-flowers which my aunt used to give me (although I did not yet know and must long postpone the discovery of why this memory made me so happy) immediately the old grey house upon the street, where her room was, rose up like the scenery of a theatre to attach itself to the little pavilion, opening on to the garden, which had been built out behind it for my parents (the isolated panel which until that moment had been all that I could see); and with the house the town, from morning to night and in all weathers, the Square where I was sent before luncheon, the streets along which I used to run errands, the country roads we took when it was fine. And just as the Japanese amuse themselves by filling a porcelain bowl with water and steeping in it little crumbs of paper which until then are without character or form, but, the moment they become wet, stretch themselves and bend, take on colour and distinctive shape, become flowers or houses or people, permanent and recognisable, so in that moment all the flowers in our garden and in M. Swann's park, and the water-lilies on the Vivonne and the good folk of the village and their little dwellings and the parish church and the whole of Combray and of its surroundings, taking their proper shapes and growing solid, sprang into being, town and gardens alike, from my cup of tea.

1. Briefly outline the sequence of events in this I-centered narrative and explain how Proust describes moving from one step to the next in the play of his memory.

2. There are several pieces in this chapter about memories of things past, not simply as things gone, but things still enigmatically *alive* (Didion, White, Proust). Briefly contrast the efforts of these writers in handling memory in autobiographical narrative.

The Question

of Persuasion

Argument and Persuasion

Argument and persuasion are intimately related. When you argue, you try to persuade someone of something by drawing a connection between evidence and a conclusion: "You should buy this book (conclusion) because it will give you the information you need (evidence)." Sometimes you argue without trying to persuade—"The sun is shining (evidence), so I assume the game will go on (conclusion)"—but most of the time an argument is designed to have an effect on an audience. This pattern of effects is called *persuasion,* and the language event, the writing or speech that tries to bring about the effects, is called an *argument.*

An argument is the process of reasoning whereby a claim is made on the basis of preliminary evidence. When we evaluate an argument, we are concerned with how it gets from the evidence to the claim, that is, with the validity and correctness of the reasoning. As you will see in the next chapter, there are some fairly clear-cut rules and recommendations about the nature of valid and correct arguments.

Persuasion, however, is more difficult to deal with because it is only in part an appeal to reason. We can be persuaded by all sorts of inducements, some of which have nothing to do with a reasoned argument, such as the inducement of wealth or of satisfying a desire or ambition. When we try to persuade someone of something, we are concerned with altering attitudes, values, beliefs, or behavior. In this chapter, we shall concentrate on the broad issue of persuasion itself: the way we are vulnerable to certain kinds of appeals other than that of logical argument. In the next chapter, we'll concentrate on the business of judging arguments according to their validity and correctness (that is, their reasonableness).

How Are You Persuaded?

Read the following speech by William Faulkner which he made in Stockholm on receiving the Nobel Prize for literature.

I feel that this award was not made to me as a man, but to my work—a life's work in all the agony and sweat of the human spirit, not for glory and least of all for profit, but to create out of the materials of the human spirit something which did not exist before. So this award is only mine in trust. It will not be difficult to find a dedication for the money part of it commensurate with the purpose and significance of its origin. But I would like to do the same with the acclaim too, by using this moment as a pinnacle from which I might be listened to by the young men and women already dedicated to the same anguish and travail, among whom is already that one who will some day stand here where I am standing.

Our tragedy today is a general and universal physical fear so long sustained by now that we can even bear it. There are no longer problems of the spirit. There is only the question: "When will I be blown up?" Because of this, the young man or woman writing today has forgotten the problems of the human heart in conflict with itself which alone can make good writing because only that is worth writing about, worth the agony and the sweat.

He must learn them again. He must teach himself that the basest of all things is to be afraid; and, teaching himself that, forget it forever, leaving no room in his workshop for anything but the old verities and truths of the heart, the old universal truths lacking which any story is ephemeral and doomed—love and honor and pity and pride and compassion and sacrifice. Until he does so, he labors under a curse. He writes not of love but of lust, of defeats in which nobody loses anything of value, of victories without hope and, worst of all, without pity or compassion. His griefs grieve on no universal bones, leaving no scars. He writes not of the heart but of the glands.

Until he relearns these things, he will write as though he stood among and watched the end of man. I decline to accept the end of man. It is easy enough to say that man is immortal simply because he will endure; that when the last ding-dong of doom has clanged and faded from the last worthless rock hanging tideless in the last red and dying evening, that even then there will still be one more sound: that of his puny inexhaustible voice, still talking. I refuse to accept this. I believe that man will not merely endure: he will prevail. He is immortal, not because he alone among creatures has an inexhaustible voice, but because he has a soul, a spirit capable of compassion and sacrifice and endurance. The poet's, the writer's, duty is to write about these things. It is his privilege to help man endure by lifting his heart, by reminding him of the courage and honor and hope and pride and compassion and pity and sacrifice which have been the glory of his past. The poet's voice need not merely be the record of man, it can be one of the props, the pillars to help him endure and prevail.

How does this speech influence you? Of course this is a very personal question and the answer will be different for each of us, but were you moved by any of the following?

■ *The authority of the speaker and the occasion.* Faulkner is one of the most important names in twentieth-century literature and certainly one of the two or three best American novelists of our time. The Nobel Prize is the most prestigious of international awards. So you might feel that Faulkner has earned the right to give advice and that you should listen.

■ *The power, optimism, and universality of the sentiments.* Faulkner speaks passionately of the stubbornness and bravery of the human spirit. He refers to universal qualities that no notion of impending doom can eradicate. If we are defined by anything at all, it is most likely by such concepts as love, honor, pity, pride, compassion, sacrifice, and endurance. These qualities alone make us human and can save us or at least dignify our lives. Faulkner refuses to be pessimistic and refers to qualities we can *all* share.

■ *The appeal to fear and the removal of fear.* You might balk a little at Faulkner's question "When will I be blown up?" It seems rather melodramatic, but you might agree with its urgency and decide it is an expression of the fact that, melodramatic or not, we are in some sense caught in a nuclear trap. However *you* define fear, Faulkner is saying that "the basest of all things is to be afraid." He has an antidote for fear: turning back to the "eternal verities," the higher values of the spirit. The writer should give up a preoccupation with violence and lust and start dealing once more with helping "man endure by lifting his heart." It's really an either/or situation that Faulkner is describing: live by turning to "the old universal truths" or give in passively to the nuclear threat. We'll have something to say about this kind of logic in the next chapter, but for now it might be admitted that, oversimplification or not, Faulkner is making an authoritative challenge to contemporary cynicism.

Faulkner's appeal is primarily ethical and emotional: he wants to reach our values and feelings. Now read this extract from a speech by the scholar, critic, and teacher Northrop Frye.

You see, freedom has nothing to do with lack of training; it can only be the product of training. You're not free to move unless you've learned to walk, and not free to play the piano unless you practice. Nobody is capable of free speech unless he knows how to use language, and such knowledge is not a gift: it has to be learned and worked at. The only exceptions, and they are exceptions that prove the rule, are people who, in some crisis, show that they have a social imagination strong and mature enough to stand out against a mob. In the row over desegregation in New Orleans, there was one mother who gave her reasons for sending her children to an integrated school with such dignity and precision that the reporters couldn't understand how a woman who never got past grade six learned to talk like the Declaration of Independence. Such people already have what literature tries to give. For most of us, free speech is cultivated speech, but cultivating speech is not just a skill, like playing chess. You can't cultivate speech, beyond a certain point, unless you have something to say, and the basis of what you have to say is your vision of society. So while free speech may be, at least at present, important only to a very small minority, that very small minority is what makes the difference between living here and living in East Berlin or South Africa.

Northrop Frye, from **THE EDUCATED IMAGINATION**

How are you influenced by Frye? Perhaps by the following:

■ *The simple but clearly reasoned argument.* The argument about free speech unfolds carefully but directly, even addressing the exception that tests the rule. Freedom is usually the product of training, says Frye. There is no free speech until you have *learned* how to to use language or unless you happen to be one of those people who are blessed with articulate speech and a social imagination. But there is no free speech, even if you have learned to use the language, until you have a social conscience, a "vision of society." The argument is powerfully simple and hinges on a definition of terms.

■ *The patriotic and practical appeal.* This is carried by the use of a strong example: the exceptional mother who never got past grade six but who talks with all the eloquence of that most eloquent of statements, the Declaration of Independence.

■ *The hidden warning.* If we do not practice freedom of speech, we will eventually all be living in the equivalent of East Berlin or South Africa. Only a "very small minority" right now combines eloquence with a social conscience. But more of us can do so by *learning* and *working at* the language and gaining a "vision" of society.

An emotional and a rational appeal—with hidden arguments in each—are offered by Faulkner and Frye, respectively. But what about another influence, one that surrounds us constantly in the media, the influence of advertising? Read this advertisement for a perfume. It incorporates a number of appeals advertising often makes.

PERSEPHONE . . . dare a fragrance of underworld love . . . a work of art dedicated to all that lies deep in female beauty . . . a crystal flaçon in the shape of a pomegranate encases the rarest and costliest perfume by Jean-Louis d'Aurévilly . . . a gilded fragrance which beckons you down . . . and out . . . to mysteries as ancient as Eleusis itself . . .

"With PERSEPHONE I have tried to enhance that most enigmatic attraction of every woman: the disturbing, yet innocent paradox of love . . . tender, complex, intimidating, rejuvenating by turn . . . the allure of seductiveness for those women who would weave the world on the loom of love . . ."

Jean-Louis d'Aurévilly

375

From the earth-goddess who walked with Eros . . . PERSEPHONE . . . an attempt to capture your innocence and experience. $480 for ⅛ oz.: flaçon by chemin de fer: d'Aurévilly, Paris.

The appeals of advertising are remarkably close to the appeals of political propagandists, and we shall discuss them in more detail later in this chapter. This particularly cloying piece, however, might be said to appeal to women—and to the men who buy women perfume—by the following:

■ *The offer of instant sexual appeal.* Wear the perfume and you will be desirable.

■ *The exotic suggestions.* References to goddesses, Eros, Persephone, pomegranates, and the mysteries of Eleusis, whether the reader knows their significance or not, are part of the suggestion that all women partake of a mythical allure. Here this is described as a paradoxical mixture of innocence and experience. Of course, the appeal is still sexual—"if you are exotic you will be made even more attractive" is the implication—but there is an inflated attempt to say something important about what women are like. Much perfume advertising aims to give a short course on female psychology and the dynamics of seduction. This one is no exception and pretentiously calls on myth to suggest eternal traits of femininity: the exotic myth of Persephone, goddess of the underworld, who came back for part of the year to live innocently with her mother on earth. She was celebrated in the Greek Eleusinian mysteries as the goddess of rebirth. These matters don't have to be explained, of course, because the attempt is made to influence you by the *hint* of mythical paradox and faraway names. Your imagination takes off with these hints whether you know what they refer to or not.

■ *The offer of control.* In an age in which gender role playing is frequently under attack, many perfume advertisements play it up. They sometimes refer to "passive" women, but here the suggestion is: wear this perfume for enigmatic beauty and sexual *power*. You too can walk with Eros. But the ad further implies that you are not predatory but have an attractive innocence, so in the end you are doing what you and he want.

■ *The appeal to snobbery.* The "work of art," the crystal flaçon (not "flask"), the extravagant price, the imported-from-Paris touch—all these are appeals to your distinctiveness.

Finally, consider *propaganda*. This refers to writing or speech that aims to indoctrinate, to change not only attitudes and behavior but also beliefs. Propaganda reveals national, party, religious, or special interests. Its main

376

arena lies in the exchange between Western versions of democracy and communism—and all the splinter variations of each. It also occurs most obviously in party politics: the rhetoric of the Democrat versus the Republican, Labor vs. Conservative, or Social Democrat vs. Nationalist. Wherever there are strong ideological positions to be expressed, you are likely to find propaganda. But always the ideologies will converge on a central issue: the ideal state of humanity, the universal values implicit in being human, the deepest human desires:

When communist *workmen* associate with one another, theory, propaganda, etc., is their first end. But at the same time, as a result of this association, they acquire a new need—the need for society—and what appears as a means becomes an end. You can observe this practical process in its most splendid result whenever you see French socialist workers together. Such things as smoking, drinking, eating, etc., are no longer means of contact or means that bring together. Company, association, and conversation, which again has society as its end, are enough for them; the brotherhood of man is no mere phrase with them, but a fact of life, and the nobility of man shines upon us from their work-hardened bodies.

Karl Marx, from **ECONOMIC AND PHILOSOPHIC MANUSCRIPTS OF 1884**

This passage does not directly ask the reader to do anything, but the implications are plain: communism is not simply a theory or a propaganda; it is comradeship in action, a satisfaction of our deepest needs for social intercourse. It goes beyond hope to the achievement of essential realities, and hence the author is saying that he too is going beyond mere propaganda (though that term does not have negative implications for Marx) to describe fact and not simply theory. We may not feel the same way about French socialist workers if we saw them, but the point is that Marx is appealing to our shared sense (whether we are communist or not) of the "brotherhood of man," the nobility of work, and the need for comradeship. Westerners, of course, claim the same things for capitalism and add other values besides. It does not matter whether propaganda is Western or Eastern, it will never acknowledge itself as *mere* propaganda. Its main strategy is to elevate itself to the status of essential information and the rightful claim that its message can save. Political propaganda, therefore, always has much in common with religious proselytizing.

We can be influenced by appeals to authority and right reason, by passionately expressed sentiments, by the removal of fear and the offer of transcending the ordinary, by patriotism and practicality, by the chance of instant allure, exoticism, and power, and so on. These are merely a tiny handful of the kinds of bombardments we all undergo from those who would influence us. Let's briefly sum up the range even if it is impossible to account for all the details of how we might be persuaded:

■ *By the appeal to reason:* An argument offers an unavoidable conclusion, as we might feel Faulkner's and Frye's conclusions are. We
appreciate the clarity and inevitability by which a claim follows from
the evidence. Or else an argument appeals to the likelihood of its
conclusions. The argument seems correct and no other alternative
presents itself, so we accept its conclusion.

■ *By an appeal to "universal" values.* These values are anything from
the "big" concerns like God and country, love, honor, pride, and
endurance to "smaller" ones that only each of us knows best, like our
personal feelings about the value of welfare, day care centers, or
psychiatrists.

■ *By having an opinion or belief confirmed.* If we feel that women
should be exotic and "walk with Eros," then we may very well think
that Persephone perfume is for us. Usually we respond well to persuasion that happens to trigger off attitudes, opinions, and beliefs we
already have and that we find now are supported or being encouraged
by others. So our belief in the "old virtues" is reinforced by Faulkner.

■ *By the offer of power or respect of any kind.* This can refer to
popularity, sexual power, money, or any of the offers the advertising
world constantly dangles before us. This kind of appeal, of course,
is not merely media-oriented. Faulkner reminds us of the power the
writer feels in dealing with the time-honored truths. Here is the writer
as prophet. Frye suggests we develop true power of speech. Politicians
constantly offer us the power to choose. Usually the offer of power is
to correct a deficiency—that is, we don't really have the power—so
the remedy. Only some of us have genuine power of speech, suggests
Frye—"a very small minority"—without which we cannot have freedom.

■ *By the pleasurable aesthetic reactions that language can create.* We
are moved by the beautiful: by lyrical language that creates alluring
images or by passionate speech like Faulkner's or simply by words that
for some reason or other "sound good." Some writers have the talent,
too, to be forceful and articulate while speaking very simply in everyday
speech. So Frye gets straight to the point. In short, if we think something or someone is beautiful—like the girl in a suntan ad—we are
often persuaded to accept the message.

■ *By an emotional appeal.* If we are moved to laughter or tears by the
comic or the tragic, we are being influenced. Sometimes we feel we
are being persuaded by the sheer emotional force of an appeal,

especially appeals to mercy and pity. Emotional appeals are often made (like Faulkner's) to our "common humanity."

■ *By recognizing an authority.* We are often moved by the credibility of the person making the appeal. Experts abound, and we are persuaded by authority figures whom we can trust, from the "kindly uncle" who reads the news to the "fathers" of the atomic bomb who now speak out on matters of war and peace.

■ *By the reinforcement of personal images that are part of our identity themes.* Persuaders may not even know what they are doing when they touch on these, but perhaps being paradoxical *is* the most cherished view we have of ourselves, so we run out to try Persephone or buy it for a friend. Or perhaps we have a secret wish to be a writer of the old-fashioned virtues, like Tolstoy or Dickens or Faulkner, and so we find ourself easily persuaded by Faulkner's words. As the early chapters on reading pointed out, we all have intimate identity themes, clusters of images of ourselves, and when these are reinforced we can be easily persuaded.

■ *By conditioning.* This can be direct or indirect and can range from the extreme but unfortunately not extinct form of torture to the media conditioning we all undergo. All environments are part of the conditions for persuasion, from close family and friends to church, college, office, and the media.

How Do You Respond to Persuasion?

You respond in exactly the same way as you respond to any text you read or speech you listen to. As the chapters on reading explained, you read by

Listening to the voices of the text

Interacting with them, adapting experiences to your identity themes

Having your expectations raised and satisfied

Accumulating information through sequences and clusters of related facts

Questioning the text

Reading and rereading to build on your initial experience of the text

All the appeals listed above—to your reason, values, opinions, need for power and respect, sense of beauty, emotions, love of authority, private identity themes, and susceptibility to conditioning—all these appeals are literally "read" by you as you read anything else. Your ability to identify with others and your admiration for them play especially important roles. Your identity themes—those images you have of yourself—determine not only your behavior but also your susceptibility to influence. You will at first stubbornly resist Faulkner if you are impatient with the "old" virtues. You will embrace Frye if you believe in the necessity for learning to handle English well in order to achieve free speech.

You tend to select images that reinforce your attitudes and behavior, which means that you like the literature, films, political speeches, and so on, that are easily assimilated into your own identity themes. You may never be fully aware of the range of those images, but you have *values* embodying the images that are most difficult to change. The *beliefs* you base on those values are not quite so stubborn, but they are hard to budge nonetheless. Would Faulkner's speech alter your opinion that nuclear power is good? Then there are your *attitudes*—your moods, dispositions, feelings—which are based on your self-image, your beliefs, and your values but which, unlike these, can be changed with relative ease. This is where you are most susceptible to influence.

Moods, as we know, swing. We act sometimes for quite impulsive reasons. Politicians and advertisers, for example, will prey heavily on our desires, self-images, values, and beliefs in order to change our attitudes. They rarely try to alter anything more important: they want our vote or they want us to buy; they don't want our souls. They know, for example, that most of us will vote for the most "American" party and that we will agree that we should not buy foreign cars for patriotic reasons. When we do buy foreign cars, it is because they are cheap and economical to drive, or expensive and prestigious: both part of American value systems. Foreign car advertisers emphasize these values and beliefs in order to change our predisposition to buy American, even while they play up the fact that we are doing ourselves a good turn and not really harming the American economy—we're saving gas and money. They leave our patriotic values intact but alter our moods and dispositions. Thus, our attitudes can be changed without changing our value systems, as we shall see in Chapter 11, "Writing Persuasively."

So what is important about your response to persuasion? One thing only: that you must go to the trouble to *interpret* what is placed before you. Follow the advice that Chapter 2 offers about reading for interpretation:

Get the information clear by asking who? what? when? where? how? and why?

Listen carefully to the voices you hear and be aware of conflicting comments.

Examine your personal reactions as closely as you can.

Consider if your expectations have been satisfied.

Check carefully to see which facts relate and which don't.

Do not ignore problem passages, places where the meaning is unclear.

Try to discover the implications of the text.

Examine the relationship between subject and message, diction, tone, style, aims, the writer behind the text, and the implied audience.

In other words, when you are obviously in the presence of persuasive writing, more than ever you need to read critically.

Say you are reading Faulkner's speech and have responded to his words as those of an authority figure. You are moved by the passion of his sentiments, but you are not sure about the appeal he makes to the fear of a nuclear holocaust: "When will I be blown up?" Something jars in you at that point, so you look carefully into the reasons why. Admittedly, the speech was given some years ago, but was the question ever really appropriate? You may think so; if you do, you can be persuaded by his belief that humanity "will prevail" and perhaps accept his reasons for it.

But say you are not sure that the situation is quite so black and white: lust versus love, contemporary writing of "victories without hope and, worst of all, without pity and compassion" versus the "old" literature of "universal truths." You may sense that there is some dramatic oversimplifying going on here, that Faulkner is presenting a rather dubious either/or argument—either embrace the old virtues or wallow in lust. Maybe he is even promoting his own writing, rich in just these universal values.

There is no need for a cynical reading, of course. Faulkner's is still a stirring speech and the call to arms is beautifully made, if somewhat overstated. You may still find your values reinforced; you respond to the images of courage under fire; your belief in the essential optimism of the human spirit remains firm. But you may want to qualify your enthusiasm a little. For certainly, the values Faulkner speaks of are enduring, and certainly, much of literature is about "the human heart in conflict," but does that mean that that is the *only* kind of writing that can counter our malaise? Aren't some of the old virtues like "pride," "honor," and "sacrifice" a little suspect themselves? Might not they, too, have caused some of our problems, been among the causes of war? You need not diminish the grandeur of the prose or the power of the message, but you can still read critically, tempering persuasion with a little careful thought. (At this point it is useful to review the sections in Chapter 2 on interpretation.)

Advertising and Propaganda

It may seem unfair to join advertising and propaganda. Many people feel that advertising is simply a harmless attempt to get us to buy something, an effort kept within bounds by federal regulations. Propaganda is the deviously systematic attempt to promote a doctrine at the expense of other doctrines; it occurs in war time—or cold war time—or during election campaigns. Advertising, or at least specific advertisements, cannot be taken seriously; propaganda could not be more in earnest.

However, we will consider these two modes of persuasion together— with an emphasis on the more common ploys of advertising—for the simple reason that they share the same ways of influencing people. The choices range from products to presidents, but we are persuaded by each in the same way. Even if individual advertisements seem irrelevant in the face of political issues—an amusing diversion perhaps—advertising itself is a highly systematic enterprise no less than propaganda. Both create a climate of need and unsatisfied desire that makes us easy prey to those companies or politics that promise to fulfill our needs. Both work by creating doubt about whether we are doing the best we can: using the best car for the money, getting the best government or the whitest teeth, fighting the just war, or even killing all the roaches. Once a doubt sets in and a range of alternatives is presented, appeals can be made straight to those common human values—Faulkner's "universal virtues"—we hold dear, values ranging from cleanliness to honor.

The Overall Impact

Advertising, as we have noted, works mainly to change attitudes and dispositions. It appeals to values and beliefs but it rarely if ever attacks them. Propaganda works the same way, trying to persuade you to alter your attitude toward the enemy by capitalizing on your beliefs in self-preservation and democratic virtue, in just treatment of the masses and so on. It tries, among other things, to undermine your position by pointing out your side's atrocities, whether they really happened or not. And *we*, of course, do the same thing to the other side, warring in words.

As necessary as it may try to appear, there is something rather sordid about propaganda because we so often associate it with lies: clever lies maybe, but lies nonetheless. There are also those who believe that lying takes place in advertising, that the point about an advertisement is that it gives false information doctored to appear like a most enticing truth. This is too sweeping a generalization perhaps, but advertising and propaganda join together as the art of exaggeration of a single object, person, or political viewpoint to the point that we often do not care whether the truth is told or not, so drawn in are we by the emotional appeals. In fact, many of us resist advertising—or refuse to take it seriously—because we sense that advertising like the language of propaganda is never art but artifice.

This is especially true of television advertising where the medium so manipulates the message that we can scarcely tell them apart. The *way* something is said on television is most clearly *what* is said. You cannot separate the message that Brand X soap powder washes whiter from the testimonials of those aggressively honest housewife-actresses who say it does, or from the way the camera plays carefully on their pained expressions as their favorite brand is taken from them for a week while they experiment with the "opposition," or from the careful editing of scenes, or from some special effect or other. Television delivers the message in its own way, and the message is: come and live for a moment in televisionland—where anything can happen—where clothes, morality, teeth, and politicians are always "pure," and you can receive instant gratification of your desires. In other words, through dramatic oversimplification the commercial claims to see very clearly indeed exactly what the "truth" is.

According to Jonathan Price, whose study *The Best Thing on TV* tries to explain how television advertising works, there are at least twelve ways in which the television commercial creates its message, develops its style and tone, embodies its aim, and manipulates its audience. These methods are, of course, generalized, and all of them are more true of some commercials than others. Commercials, says Price, are dangerous to make, violent to products but not to people, almost obscene, emotional, coldly calculated, carefully written, overdirected, star-studded, extravagantly produced, highly edited, regulated, and censored, and even rated PG. All this in thirty seconds, and still he insists they are the best things on television.

The key feature of a television commercial, we might say in summary, is its remarkably concentrated, calculated, and overproduced effect. Whether the spot is selling a product or a politician, not a moment is wasted. There are few pauses for viewers to interpret, such as we find in real art, for time is quite plainly money. It is not at all unusual for a sponsor to pay up to $1 million for a series of short spots on a major television production like the Oscar presentations. For a limited space of time, then, a message is stripped to bare essentials and a single appeal is made to an audience. The medium is exploited to the full with special effects, melodramatic emotions, and a high-intensity focus on a product or a star, all with split-second precision. In fact, the message nearly always is that something can be quickly and easily done.

The range of emotions and values found in television commercials, therefore, is oversimplified and extreme. The viewer's identity themes scarcely have time to emerge and develop. Most commercials work with anxious haste to spell out a message and bombard the audience with it. Some car and shoe commercials, for example, employ people to jump through hoops, perform high kicks, leap ecstatically around their latest models, and generally emulate or parody production numbers from Broadway shows. At the other extreme, an increasing number of senior citizens appear in commercials, weeping silently with happiness over a phone call from a loved one or quietly knitting four-armed sweaters for mythical creatures that come out at night to make beer. In between come those rare, even perhaps the last, vestiges of wit in commercials as one or two light beer manufacturers allow some of our favorite sportsmen to undercut their macho image and genuinely but affectionately make fools of themselves.

So commercials offer in the main an either/or emotional impact: frenzied anxiety and counterfeited glee, or an unreal and tolerant mellowness which speaks of the calm belief that a product, quietly and efficiently, is all that it is cracked up to be. Neither one of course need be any more convincing than the other, but that is not the point. Rather, we find in television commercials a highly stylized (and increasingly surreal) world in which normal emotions and relationships and simple reason do not exist. Instead we are beckoned into and softened up by a whole environment of startlingly simple opposites which we hardly ever bother to interpret because they *are* so simple and obvious. Individual advertisements rarely work on us because we can reject their message. But we have more trouble rejecting the message of advertising in general. The either/or, switch-hitting world of television commercials takes us on and leaves one or two suggestions dominant in our minds. The rhetoric of advertising infiltrates everyday speech, political claims, and the jargon of all the professions. (It comes complete with myth as Price points out in an extract from his book at the end of this chapter.)

Some of us have been pounded into submission, as Marya Mannes says in her satirical piece about how we are what we eat, drink, wear, drive, pray, and so on (see pp. 25–26). None of us has avoided being influenced at some time, even if it is only by the one, quiet commercial that did not offend or happened to offer a solution to a problem. In fact, the world of advertising—especially on television—provides a *cumulative* effect which spills over into its means of expression and even into our speech and writing. It can be argued that instead of television creating advertising, advertising is now creating television—as melodrama. The soap opera world of morality and overemotional responses—always anxious, short-tempered, and aggressive—begins to take up more and more of our regular programming from news to drama. The moral? Be wary of the environment created by advertising; it affects the way all kinds of information, ranging from the serious to the trivial, are presented.

The Special Appeals of Advertising

So we are conditioned by the environment of advertising in a way that is difficult to escape, except by avoiding television altogether or watching only public broadcasting stations, and discarding radio, newspapers, and magazines. Here is a brief summary of advertising's specific methods of persuasion, following the outline earlier in this chapter.

■ *The appeal to reason.* Some advertisements seem aware that they are dealing with a rational audience. So they provide "evidence": statistics and tests, and graphic depictions of the relative amounts of pain-killer to be found in various aspirin products. Part of the "rational" appeal—and of course, it is only minimally rational, a parody of scientific testing or adequate statistics—involves the use of language that does not make extravagant claims. So one dishwasher powder leaves dishes "virtually" clean, and many products reduce their claim to "most cases" or insert the word *can:* "You too *can* have a cleaner wash with Bleacho." It does not say you *will* have a cleaner wash. These terms are called *weasel words.*

■ *The appeal to "universal" values.* Again, this covers a vast range, but the more usual values referred to are those of family, love, youthfulness, patriotism, naturalness, safety, convenience, and freedom from anxiety. So make your family happy with soft toilet tissue; show your wife you love her with flowers; keep your hands looking soft and lovely with a certain dishwashing liquid; buy an American car; have a whiter wash with new, improved Bleacho; and so on.

■ *The offer of power and prestige.* You can be someone you are not by waving a credit card in the face of local and foreign businesspeople. You can achieve status by buying a German sports car or wearing designer clothes. You can have physical power by exercising in a health club. Power takes many forms in the advertising world from the power of knowledge acquired by buying encyclopedias to social status to sexual power (as we saw from the perfume advertisement) to the power of physical fitness (which is also sexual and psychological).

■ *The appeal to your aesthetic sense. You* can be more beautiful. Furniture, clothing, cars, jewelry—all objects that can be designed, from jeans to cosmetics, to candy, to houses—are presented for their visual appeal (as well as their "name"), usually from their most flattering aspect. Buying these products, furthermore, "improves" your *own* aesthetic appeal.

■ *The appeal to your comic or tragic sense.* Appeals are made to your tragic sense when an organization needs money for famine relief, and to your comic sense in order to sell any number of things from beer to cars. If you find a commercial witty or ironic (like the one with the famous, aggressive baseball manager at a cowboy bar who claims he didn't punch no doggie), you might even think that the manufacturers have some intelligence. You respond favorably to wit and humor: "These people don't take themselves too seriously," you say and are softened up for the message.

■ *The appeal to authority.* This is, of course, one of the most common of all appeals. Rugged individualists and sportsmen drink low-calorie beer, so it isn't sissy. Every star has a testimonial to offer if the price is right. Every housewife or person on the street is, with democratic zeal, an authority on whiteness and stomach acid. Most dentists tend to recommend any number of chewing gums and toothpastes, and most doctors apparently favor two hemorrhoid medications and several pain killers.

■ *The appeal to an identity theme.* This appeal covers all successful advertising. When an advertiser says, "This is you" and you believe it, an identity theme has been reinforced. Hence many identity themes, it would appear, are intimately wrapped up with expensive sports cars and stereo systems. Usually, however, the appeal to your identity themes—since the advertiser can only guess what they are—is generalized. The assumption in some magazine advertising is that we would all like to be rich and wear designer clothes and drive a Maserati. The assumption in television advertising, which tends to be rather less snobbish, is that our identities are tied up with more middle-class values. The assumption everywhere is that desires for what we do not have can be awakened by making a *bandwagon* appeal, that is, an appeal to the presumed fact that "everyone" wants something.

How does advertising go about making these specific appeals? With increasing subtlety. We have briefly discussed the high-intensity appeal of television, but how, for example, does advertising let its focus develop on a theme?

■ *Drama.* This is the most elastic method and can involve any kind of story from a race to paint a fence through highly surreal calisthenics involving designer shoes to enigmatic women seated by swimming pools with lean young men diving in toward them, apparently to get a whiff of a famous perfume. Telling a story or dramatizing an issue makes a point.

■ *Personification.* A product or a nonhuman player in a commercial drama is given human qualities, like the small boy made of dough, the corn sprout that talks, or the cat that provides sardonic commentary on its canned food. By giving a product, or something that will use the product, human qualities, the advertiser offers an audience something ''cute'' to watch, and also leads them to believe that even a nonhuman has feelings, and therefore one can build up rapport with it. One brewery actually personified water, although its advertisements carefully refrained from showing what the water creatures look like—that would have ruined it. Instead, they implied that some nice, naive people really believe they exist.

■ *Testimonials.* This technique has faded somewhat in the years since Watergate when it was ''discovered'' that even our most trusted public figures were not necessarily to be trusted at all. Now the choice of authorities to support a product is very carefully made. Certain film stars blessed with an honest face or a down-home drawl or an ''ideally'' proportioned body are occasionally used in camera and hardware advertisements as well as food and clothing ads.

■ *Demonstrations.* These are always popular, for if you can actually see the flies drop dead or the car hug the corner perfectly on all four wheels at 85 miles per hour, you would seem to have graphic proof that the product really works. In spite of the fact that products can be tampered with and cameras can distort angles and distances, the on-camera demonstration is still a powerful influence.

■ *Songs and jingles.* In the early days of radio advertising, these were perhaps the most popular of all advertising ploys. Thus many listeners still recall a well-known foaming cleanser that wiped the dirt right down the drain to the accompaniment of a bass voice bopping in the background. Jingles and songs set the message to music and quite literally—so the advertisers hope—give you something to sing about which will keep running through your head. Now the jingles are usually more frenzied production numbers with professional choreography.

■ *Argument.* There is a kind of advertisement currently popular with oil, chemical, and engineering companies that aims to appeal through a carefully reasoned argument. This has not in the past been a very popular technique, but now, under fire from ecologists, citizen groups, and politicians, some of our largest companies have felt the need to explain their position clearly. These arguments, however, are not

without their own special ploys. Read, for example, the advertisement
on the next page. The ARCO advertisement appeals, as all arguments
try to do, to reason. The ultimate reasonableness, of course, is to admit
that there are two sides to an argument and to act tolerantly. ARCO
does this, suggesting carefully that its company is *not* one of those
arguing at all. Some say coal is good and others that it is bad, but we
are not on either side, says ARCO, (providing a little humor with the
statement that the coal issue is neither black nor white). Where then,
does ARCO take a position? On the fence? Not exactly, for it ultimately
takes sides with those who think "coal is good." The argument in
favor of large-scale coal development is that coal would provide sufficient resources to solve all our energy problems for three hundred
years and rid us of foreign dependency (the patriotic appeal slips in).
The argument against coal is that coal mining can be an ecological
disaster, cutting up the countryside and creating pollution problems.
ARCO easily counters the latter argument by saying that it is a law-
abiding company that agrees with the new environmental protection
laws. So having demolished the "bad" argument—quite literally in
ARCO's mind—and stated all the advantages of the good, where does
that leave ARCO? Quietly saying that it modestly thinks we should
"reassess our old prejudices" against coal.

The opposition has been labeled as prejudiced (the old device of
name-calling), the company has come out in favor of coal production
but pretended not to, and we are left with "there are no easy answers"
when the whole point of the advertisement has been to show that
there *are* easy answers and they are all on the side of more coal
production. If you can't see that, the advertisement implies, then you
are not very intelligent. ARCO leaves it up to the reader to form the
opinion: here is a good, law-abiding, patriotic, and unprejudiced
company which wants to get on with the business of keeping us in
energy and is willing not to pollute and carve up the countryside
wantonly, so why not let it do it?

Polarizing the question at hand has always been a popular ploy
in advertising and propaganda. When we see opposites, we can
choose. But sometimes opposites are deliberately set up in a prejudiced
way. We call this *stacking the cards,* and ARCO stacks the cards here
with the bold headline: "Some insist coal is good. Some insist coal is
bad." Coal, of course, is neither good nor bad. The moral judgment can
be made only about how it is used. The irony is that even though
ARCO claims it does not want to be part of such a simple-minded
argument and wants to appear the mediator, it nonetheless takes sides,
though, of course, with the "good guys."

Some insist coal is good. Some insist coal is bad.
We insist it's not that black or white.

Those who insist that coal is good point out that we have over 200 billion tons of economically recoverable coal in this country — enough to last us for at least three centuries at current consumption rates.

And, they further point out, that

although this represents 90% of our domestic energy resources, coal currently supplies less than 20% of all our energy production.

It's true, that with greater usage, coal could give us as much as one-half of the new energy we'll need between now and the year 2000 — enough to help loosen the dangerous ties that bind us to expensive and insecure foreign oil.

But those who insist that coal is bad point to abandoned mines which scar the landscape and allow acid water to seep into streams.

And to the fact that coal contains ash and sulfur which, if not removed, can pollute the air when burned.

Still, we believe that these days the advantages of coal outweigh its disadvantages.

Because these days we have extremely tough environmental laws.

Laws that require the restoration of mined lands and the protection of air and water resources. Laws that ensure that coal mine areas are properly restored and that newly constructed or converted power plants remove sulfur and particulates from their stack gases.

Of course, environmental controls are expensive. But because of the current high

price of foreign oil, the cost of using coal is still less than half the cost of using oil.

And when we consider that coal can also be converted into transportation fuels such as gasoline and diesel fuel — reducing even more our dependence on foreign oil — it seems obvious that we ought to reassess our old prejudices against this most abundant of all fossil fuels.

At least Atlantic Richfield thinks so.

There are no easy answers.

ARCO ◆
Atlantic Richfield Company

389

Persuasion and Ethics

Obviously not all persuasion is either logical or good. We will concern ourselves with the logic in the next chapter. Here we will consider briefly the questions of whether it is good or bad for advertising to work the way it does, and whether there is a definable relationship between persuasion and ethics.

Those who believe that advertising and political rhetoric are based on a kind of lying have little trouble in asserting the unethical nature of the two. Lies, as we know, can be amazingly persuasive. Hitler's arguments for race differences between "Aryans" and Jews were illogical to the extreme, but they were frighteningly persuasive for reasons that continue to fascinate researchers and that seem to have had something to do with the social, political, and economic conditions of the time in Germany and Europe. On the other hand, that was a case of persuasion used for demented reasons, and advertising we know is somewhat less consequential even if it creates a pervasive environment. Many think that there is little point in being "moralistic" about advertising, for it is overseen by the Federal Trade Commission and by and large does not get out of control. ARCO may be using some sleight of hand in its argument "from reason," but surely it is not telling lies nor hiding its true position. It is simply being subtle and trying to counter what it interprets to be hostile or at best skeptical public opinion.

It is up to you to decide how seriously you want to take the impact of advertising on your life. Plainly, few people live the Miltown life, and if they did they would rapidly end up in a corner sucking on their Wolfschmidt, as Marya Mannes points out. There have been *just* complaints that advertising employs sexual and race stereotyping, raises prices, tries to dump inferior products on an unsuspecting public, and generally disseminates a banal and boring image of life. But then so do other media events. Short of a rigid aesthetic as well as moral censorship, we have no option but to fall back on the old saying: "buyer beware." Our choices are constantly conditioned by family, religion, education, and the media in general, not just by advertising. The question of influence extends beyond advertising and propaganda and raises the issue of the *personal responsibility we all have not to be led to unethical decisions by poor interpretations.*

Unethical Persuasion

It is much easier to describe unethical than ethical persuasion, but even this is controversial. You may ask why ethics becomes a question at all. "If people are foolish enough to buy this product, then that's their fault," is a statement that is often heard. Well, that is in part true, but it is also

390

true that some of us are more susceptible than others to arguments and need "to be saved from ourselves." Even more important, every statement and claim is a social act. Since the statements are made publicly, whoever makes them must bear responsibility. Whatever is said in public has moral consequences.

So if a persuader *intentionally makes untrue statements,* and *intentionally aims to mislead an audience by not giving all the facts or by presenting them ambiguously,* then the persuasion is *unethical.* Product advertising is regulated for these characteristics. You may remember a recent case when a leading mouthwash manufacturer had to change its advertising and delete the statement that its product "killed germs" because it could not prove that it did. Advertisements, however, still walk the fine line between the ethical and the unethical, *insinuating claims* even if they are unable to prove them. "In *some* cases," runs a familiar ad, "your gas mileage *may* be higher."

You should, of course, interpret very closely every piece of important persuasion you come across. You should always begin your analysis by asking

Are the statements untrue?

Is the persuader trying to mislead me?

If you can answer yes to either of these questions and can substantiate your reaction, you have found a case of unethical persuasion.

Ethical Codes

There is, of course, a large area of ethical judgment that is more personal than public. You may think it unethical for a politician to defend the sale of arms to certain countries that in your opinion will use them to prop up a corrupt government. On the other hand, someone else may say that it is ethical to do so, for that government provides the only stable control in the region and is staving off civil and regional war in which many more people would be killed. What are judgments based on, then? They are based on a code of ethics that may be yours and yours alone but that you want to justify and make as general as possible.

How do you judge ethical codes and questionable persuasive appeals? There are plenty of suggestions available from philosophers, but try these simple questions: Does the code by which you judge appeal to good values? Will it have good effects? This brings us back to the old question: how do we define *good?* That argument is often more philosophical than it need be for everyday terms. In the social arena, we have long associated *good* with the rights of personal freedoms, government for and by the people, and values that represent the greatest happiness for the greatest number. Obviously this casts doubt on any code that asserts that there are no universal standards, that every situation requires individual judgment (situational ethics). It also casts doubt on the notion that all universal standards should free us to pursue our own course of happiness entirely (individual ethics).

Again, you have to decide on the nature of the good, and no discussion as short as this one can possibly hope to provide you with conclusive guidance. For morality is a cumulative, changing set of values defined sometimes by the influence of the few on the many, and sometimes by the many on the few. What is important for you to understand is that persuasion does have ethical implications. Interpretation leads to evaluation, and in your own interests at least, you should be prepared to

Examine the evidence on which claims are made. Is it relevant? True? Unambiguously presented? Choose the best set of standards you know and judge according to it. Do not merely react.

Examine the argument based on the evidence. Is it clear? Does it falsify the evidence? Does it use correct, logical reasoning?

Examine the claim that results from the argument. Is it justified, given the evidence and the argument?

Examine the appeals the argument makes to you. Are they reasonable and fair?

You will notice that discussing persuasion leads us inevitably to ethics, and that in turn leads us to the question of judging arguments, which we shall discuss in the next chapter.

Checklist

1. Argument and persuasion are usually closely linked. Argument is the process of reasoning in words whereby a claim is made on the basis of some evidence. Persuasion is the pattern of effects an argument has on an audience.
2. How are you persuaded?

   By an appeal to reason

   By an appeal to values you hold to closely

   By having an opinion or belief confirmed

   By the offer of power or, at least, respect

   By the pleasurable aesthetic reactions that language can create

   By an emotional appeal

   By recognizing an authority

By the reinforcing of personal images and identity themes

By conditioning

3. Advertising and propaganda

   ■ Create a climate of need based on exaggeration (if not lies) and oversimplified opposites: an either/or world

   ■ Create an environment that is highly stylized, calculated, and overproduced:

   Appeal to reason: weasel words

   Appeal to values: family, love, youthfulness, patriotism, naturalness, newness, revolution, liberation

   Offer of power: status, sex

   Aesthetic appeal: designer image

   Appeal to the comic or tragic: wit and irony especially important

   Appeal to authority: use of testimonials

   Appeal to identity themes: bandwagon

4. Persuasion and ethics

   ■ You have a responsibility to judge efforts to influence you.

   ■ An influence is unethical if the persuader makes intentionally untrue statements or aims to mislead an audience by not giving all the facts or by presenting them ambiguously.

   ■ There is a need to form personal codes of judgment. Does the code by which you judge appeal to good values or have good effects?

   Examine the evidence.

   Examine the argument leading from the evidence to the claim.

   Examine the claim that results from the argument.

   Examine the appeals the argument makes to you.

Exercises

1. Examine the two advertisements on pages 394 and 395 carefully. Write a short interpretation for each one, explaining the specific appeal each makes. Then decide which one is the more effective piece of advertising and explain why.

2. Discuss the ethics of the two advertisements in question 1. Make sure you explain your own code by which you pass judgments.

Managing Chemical Wastes

What the chemical industry is doing to improve waste-disposal methods

America's chemical companies have already invested hundreds of millions of dollars in safer, better waste-disposal methods. We'll spend over *$2 billion* more on waste-disposal facilities in the next two years. Here's how we're advancing the "state of the art":

1. Eliminating wasteful processes

We're redesigning manufacturing processes and improving efficiency. We're adding on-line treatment systems to neutralize, reduce the volume or change the nature of waste by-products. We're also using recovery techniques that let us recycle wastes back into the production process.

2. Building secure landfills

Secure landfills have a barrier that keeps wastes from seeping out into groundwater and keeps groundwater from migrating through the landfill. They may include facilities for recycling liquids, or a wastewater treatment unit to clean up liquids for safe disposal. Landfills—if *properly* designed, operated and monitored—are one of the best ways to dispose of certain kinds of solid wastes.

3. Continuing industry commitment

We were finding ways to manage solid wastes long before the nation recognized the need for better waste-disposal methods. In fact, we already had much of the required waste-disposal technology and remedial strategies in place—or being de-

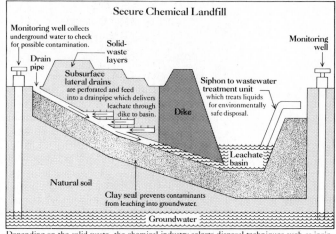

Secure Chemical Landfill

Monitoring well collects underground water to check for possible contamination.

Drain pipe

Solid-waste layers

Subsurface lateral drains are perforated and feed into a drainpipe which delivers leachate through dike to basin.

Dike

Monitoring well

Siphon to wastewater treatment unit which treats liquids for environmentally safe disposal.

Leachate basin

Natural soil

Clay seal prevents contaminants from leaching into groundwater.

Groundwater

Depending on the solid waste, the chemical industry selects disposal techniques such as incineration, by-product recovery, stabilization or secure landfill design to protect the environment.

veloped—when Congress passed the Resource Conservation and Recovery Act of 1976, which sets forth strict waste-disposal guidelines.

4. Sharing knowledge and new technology

As we develop new waste-disposal techniques, we share our knowledge with industry, government and the public. In 1979, the chemical industry began conducting a series of regional seminars that presented current techniques for solid-waste disposal. Individual chemical companies may use videotapes, visual aids or other techniques to train personnel in waste-disposal methods.

5. Encouraging solid-waste exchanges

Sometimes one chemical company's wastes can become another company's raw material. So the chemical industry has encouraged the development of waste-exchange organizations, which develop and distribute lists of available wastes.

For more information, write to: Chemical Manufacturers Assn., Dept. FY-09, Box 363, Beltsville, MD 20705.

America's Chemical Industry

The member companies of the Chemical Manufacturers Association

AS LUXURY SEDANS BECOME MORE EXPENSIVE, THEIR INHERENT WORTH BECOMES MORE CRITICAL.

Due to a variety of economic ills, the day has finally arrived when the price of a luxury automobile can rival that of a small house in the country.

A disturbing trend that has forced many otherwise casual automobile buyers to scrutinize their potential purchases as never before.

At BMW we are not alarmed by this newly enlightened consumer.

For when one examines the features that truly matter in a luxury sedan—performance, craftsmanship and resale value—no other expensive automobile justifies its price quite so thoroughly as the BMW 733i.

Accounting, no doubt, for the fact that last year the demand for the BMW 733i outpaced even our most optimistic predictions.

EVOLUTION IS PREFERABLE TO REVOLUTION.

With a certain predictability, automakers reacted to the realities of the 1980's by bringing forth a plethora of "revolutionary" re-engineered cars.

The 733i, however, is hardly the result of a single year's rush to build an enlightened automobile.

Indeed, decades ago, when luxury car manufacturers were building ever larger cars, reckless in their consumption of fuel, BMW was championing such avant-garde concepts as six-cylinder engines, sensible piston displacements and impressive power-to-weight ratios.

The BMW 733i's 3.2-liter, fuel-injected power plant, for example, is the product of millions of miles of testing and refinement—on and off the great racecourses of the world.

Its double-pivot suspension system has been described by Car and Driver magazine as "...the single most significant breakthrough in front suspension design in this decade."

A five-speed standard transmission (automatic is available) affords one the unique opportunity to pick and choose one's own gears.

ELECTRONIC INNOVATION THAT GOES BEYOND A DIGITAL SPEEDOMETER.

On the BMW 733i, our electronic computerized monitoring system (first installed by BMW in 1975) plays a far more important role than mere decoration:

it actually improves the car's efficiency.

With every engine revolution a computer receives and assesses signals from sensors deep within the 6-cylinder engine. Then instantly determines the precise air/fuel mixture to be injected into the cylinder ports.

Yet the incongruous note here is that BMW efficiency is not achieved at the expense of the sort of exhilarating performance one expects in a BMW—or the power reserves necessary to maneuver safely even under the most demanding conditions.*

LUXURY. NOT SUPERFICIALITY.

It would be difficult to imagine an appointment or an accessory that has been omitted in the BMW 733i.

Yet, all facets have been biomechanically engineered to achieve the perfect integration of man and machine.

Its seats are anatomically correct buckets and covered in wide rolls of supple leather.

All of its vital controls are within easy reach of the driver. Instruments are large, well-marked and totally visible.

So impressive is the total result that one automotive journalist was moved to write of the BMW 733i, "...to drive it is to know all the wonderful things machines can do for man."

To arrange a thorough test drive, we suggest you phone your nearest BMW dealer at your convenience.

THE ULTIMATE DRIVING MACHINE.
BMW MUNICH GERMANY

*The 733i (with manual transmission) delivers 16 EPA estimated mpg, 25 estimated highway mileage and, based on these figures, an estimated mpg range of 360 miles and a highway range of 562 miles. (Actual fuel efficiency figures are for comparison purposes only. Your actual mileage and range may vary, depending on speed, weather and trip length. Your actual highway mileage and highway range will most likely be lower.) © 1981 BMW of North America, Inc. The BMW trademark and logo are registered trademarks of Bayerische Motoren Werke, A.G.

395

3. For each of the following pieces,
   a. Write a short summary of what the piece is about.
   b. Write a short account of how the piece tries to influence you, according to the various kinds of appeals detailed in this chapter. Analyze the extracts carefully, explaining their appeals and how they affect you or not.

I believe I have omitted mentioning that in my first Voyage from Boston, being becalm'd off Block Island, our People set about catching Cod and hawl'd up a great many. Hitherto I had stuck to my Resolution of not eating animal Food; and on this Occasion, I consider'd with my Master Tryon, the taking every Fish as a kind of unprovok'd Murder, since none of them had or ever could do us any injury that might justify the slaughter. All this seemed very reasonable. But I had formerly been a great Lover of Fish, and when this came hot out of the Frying Pan, it smelt admirably well. I balanc'd some time between Principle and Inclination: till I recollected, that when the Fish were opened, I saw smaller Fish taken out of their Stomachs: Then thought I, if you eat one another, I don't see why we mayn't eat you. So I din'd upon Cod very heartily and continu'd to eat with other People, returning only now and then occasionally to a vegetable Diet. So convenient a thing it is to be a *reasonable Creature,* since it enables one to find or make a Reason for every thing one has a mind to do.

Benjamin Franklin, from AUTOBIOGRAPHY

They found a trail. It eventually led to the Dutch Oberkapo. And there, after a search, they found an important stock of arms.

The Oberkapo was arrested immediately. He was tortured for a period of weeks, but in vain. He would not give a single name. He was transferred to Auschwitz. We never heard of him again.

But his little servant had been left behind in the camp in prison. Also put to torture, he too would not speak. Then the SS sentenced him to death, with two other prisoners who had been discovered with arms.

One day when we came back from work, we saw three gallows rearing up in the assembly place, three black crows. Roll call. SS all round us, machine guns trained: the traditional ceremony. Three victims in chains—and one of them, the little servant, the sad-eyed angel.

The SS seemed more preoccupied, more disturbed than usual. To hang a young boy in front of thousands of spectators was no light matter. The head of the camp read the verdict. All eyes were on the child. He was lividly pale, almost calm, biting his lips. The gallows threw its shadow over him.

This time the Lagerkapo refused to act as executioner. Three SS replaced him.

The three victims mounted together onto the chairs.

The three necks were placed at the same moment within the nooses.

"Long live liberty!" cried the two adults.

But the child was silent.

"Where is God? Where is He?" someone behind me asked.

At a sign from the head of the camp, the three chairs tipped over.

Total silence throughout the camp. On the horizon, the sun was setting.

"Bare your heads!" yelled the head of the camp. His voice was raucous. We were weeping.

"Cover your heads!"

Then the march past began. The two adults were no longer alive. Their tongues hung swollen, blue-tinged. But the third rope was still moving; being so light, the child was still alive. . . .

For more than half an hour he stayed there, struggling between life and death, dying in slow agony under our eyes. And we had to look him full in the face. He was still alive when I passed in front of him. His tongue was still red, his eyes were not yet glazed.

Behind me, I heard the same man asking:

"Where is God now?"

And I heard a voice within me answer him:

"Where is He? Here He is—He is hanging here on this gallows. . . ."

That night the soup tasted of corpses.

Elie Wiesel, from NIGHT

Other tax systems do not stimulate investment more than ours but they do act aggressively to hold consumption down. Why does the average American family save 5 percent of its income while the average German family saves 14 percent and the average Japanese family saves 20 percent? Don't foreigners like cars and cameras? Of course they do, but their governments have deliberately structured their tax systems and economies to discourage consumption.

Most of our industrial competitors impose a value added tax (VAT). (Sweden's is now close to 25 percent.) A VAT (a tax based on the "value" any producer adds to the cost of consumer goods) is essentially a national sales tax—a tax on consumption—which you do not have to pay if you don't consume. And if you insist on consuming, government takes a large fraction of your income away from you.

In addition to reducing consumption, the VAT has the advantage of taxing illegal underground activity. Those who earn their living in the underground economy may be able to escape the income tax, but they must pay VATs when they buy goods and services. The larger the underground economy, the more vital a VAT becomes.

The burden of the tax can also be allocated in whatever way one likes with a refundable income tax credit. Suppose a 10 percent VAT were imposed, along with a $1000 refundable credit. A family earning $10,000 and saving nothing would pay $1000 in VATs, but would get it back in the form of an income tax credit. Up the income scale, the $15,000 family would pay $500 ($1500 in taxes minus $1000 in an income tax credit) in net taxes, the $30,000 family $2000, and so on. With such a credit, the VAT can be made progressive (the fraction of income paid in taxes goes up as income goes up).

A 10 percent VAT—lower than that in most of the rest of the industrial world—would yield about $235 billion (10 percent of annual private production of goods and services) in revenue. This would be enough to replace the corporate income tax ($85 billion) and the Social Security tax (about $150 billion).

Both of these taxes should be replaced. The rationale for replacing the Social Security tax is like that for replacing the corporate income tax. If you want to encourage work effort and discourage consumption, you systematically reduce taxes on work and raise taxes on consumption. To lower taxes on savings and investment while raising taxes on work, as we will be doing under the current system for financing Social Security, is perverse. Work effort is probably even more important than investment.

When you shift from a Social Security tax that does not cover investment income, or even all of earnings, to a value added tax, and a progressive value added tax at that, you are making your tax system more, not less, progressive. The very rich who choose to save and invest can avoid taxes, but the big spenders get hit.

Lester C. Thurow, **from GETTING SERIOUS ABOUT TAX REFORM**

4. Find the text of any recent political speech given by an American politician which you think qualifies as propaganda. Analyze the piece carefully, explaining the specific appeals made, and carefully expressing your reaction to the writing.

5. Re-read the section on advertising, and persuasion and ethics in Chapter 9, and read the extract by Jonathan Price attached to the end of this chapter. From your experience of watching TV commercials and reading advertising, do you think the comments you have read are reasonable? Do you agree that there are dangers in advertising or that advertisements have a mythic significance which make them the best thing on TV? Choose any two or three advertisements to analyze and explain your agreements or disagreements with the positions taken.

Readings

Robert Finch **A MOTH IN THE EYE**

"The moths had made me realize that we are like children, like very small children who do not yet understand that the world is not just an extension of ourselves."

Gore Vidal **DRUGS**

"It seems most unlikely that any reasonably sane person will become a drug addict if he knows in advance what addiction is going to be like."

Jonathan Price **AND STILL THE BEST!**

"If, as Americans believe, the new is better than the old, and the hard sell beats the soft, then commercials today are the best myth on TV...."

A MOTH IN THE EYE

Robert Finch

The other evening I was sitting under a lamp doing some research on the migration schedules of our local shorebirds. I was holding in my lap a large book filled with beautiful, soft water-colors of these graceful birds, when rather suddenly several moths began leaping and fluttering across its broad pages—moths with polished, burnished wings, rigid deltoids with elaborate black-and-white filigree on their backs; moths with smooth antennae, curled antennae, feathery antennae; moths with proboscises coiled downward like clock springs or thrown back over their heads like raised elephant trunks; moths with incredibly elastic front legs— all darting, flitting, jumping, all saying, "Look here, look at me," until one flew into my eye and I had to put the book down.

We need to look more at insects, if only to recognize them for what they are. We avoid them so deliberately that I doubt if many adults could give a reasonably accurate, objective description of the commonest garden bugs we spend so much time trying to get rid of. Even in our pesticide ads they are depicted as cartoon characters, anatomically absurd and with faces either childishly monstrous or likeably misguided, but nothing whatsoever like the real things.

Every summer night, attracted by the hall light, a host of moths and other flying insects crowd their pale bodies against the black windows of my front door. The bugs and smaller moths butt and bump softly, silently against the panes, bouncing away again. The mosquitoes flatten their proboscises, or sucking tubes, against the glass, while the larger moths just hang there motionlessly, like dead kites, staring in with their dark, blind eyes.

It is a most gentle siege, a passive threat—hardly something to get anxious about. There is no real aggression in their crowding, of course; if they had serious intentions, they could manage to crawl in around the jamb or under the threshold.

Ordinarily, we see moths only around lights, when they are unnaturally disoriented, inept and awkward in their trapped flight. How does a moth fly in darkness? There is surprisingly little written about the flying equipment of these insects. One source suggests that they navigate using the stars and moon as reference points, and that the brighter, artificial lights throw them off the beam. Whatever the cause of their attraction to lights, moths evolved long ago in prehuman darkness where the disruptive effects of man-made illumination did not exist. Its presence is so recent that the moths have had no time to evolve an adaptation to it. And as we push the darkness further and further back with our lights, moths become increasingly our insect satellites, ringing our fluorescent, incandescent and mercury vapor beacons with their soft, fat, furry, muffling bodies.

They hang and bump and press with the patient indifference of water dripping on stone. It is not so much that they are *trying* to get in that strikes me, but that they *would be everywhere* if they could. They press with a tendency too vague to be resisted, a force too dispersed to be opposed.

One night earlier this summer I came home from a special town meeting, one that lasted long and was full of much heat and sweeping statements—you may know the kind. When I reached the front door, I found the moths there, blocking my way. To avoid letting in a cloud of insects, I had to sneak around the house and come in the unlit back door. When I was inside, the importance and significance of the evening's doings, in which I had been caught up and in which so much seemed to be decided or disposed of, dwindled to nothing. The moths had made me realize that we are like children, like very small children who do not yet understand that the world is not just an extension of ourselves. Caught up in our own concerns, we fail to see the world that is distinct from us—a world with its own lives, aims and desires. Like infants we tend to treat it as though it were actually a part of us, that is, as though its inherent potential were solely to conform to our own desires.

We decree a direction for nature and provoke it with blind reachings out and crude tamperings; and when it does not conform, when it strikes out on its own path, we blame the world's perverseness and redouble our heavy-handed tactics. (Or, like somewhat older children, we blame our fellow nations.)

The difference in the analogy is, of course, that while nature does give each of her children a reasonable chance for survival, she is not a tolerant, indulgent, protective or even constructively disciplinary parent. She doesn't care. It doesn't care. The moths at my door are totally indifferent to me, to town budgets, to proposed golf courses and new police cruisers. They are, in fact, indifferent to their own fate; a moth's existence cannot possibly matter to anyone but a human being.

This is why I think moths and other insects are so important. Their indifference to themselves and to us and both our fates is so complete and total that we dare not see them for what they are. We must caricature them as malicious and designing ("nature on the rampage") so that we do not recognize the terrible impartiality of their existence, their total unawareness of our own. More than any other form of higher life, insects seem at home in an indifferent universe.

As we seek to dominate the earth, we find more and more that we can do so only by destroying it. And as we succeed, we become masters of an increasingly barren world. But it would be a mistake to think that the rest of nature cowers abjectly in ever-shrinking recesses and dark corners of a man-dominated world, waiting there in passive acceptance for us to deliver either the final coup de grâce or a humanitarian reprieve.

Nothing on earth ever accepts defeat in that sense except man. As the woods go and the bulldozers arrive, I know that the woodcocks will continue to rise in starry parabolas on soft spring nights, that box turtles will nudge onward toward slow matings in the deep moist grass beneath the locusts, and that the moths—

the moths will go on bumping ceaselessly, softly, patiently against glowing detours, whose origins or length of duration they cannot care about, until the last human light goes out forever.

1. What appeals does Finch make to you as a reader?
2. What does advertising do to insects, and what is the significance of that?
3. Do you agree that we treat the insect world "as though its inherent potential were solely to conform to our own desires"? Explain.
4. In spite of our efforts to "dominate the earth," Finch is optimistic. Why?
5. Do you find Finch's essay convincing? Explain your response.

DRUGS

Gore Vidal

It is possible to stop most drug addiction in the United States within a very short time. Simply make all drugs available and sell them at cost. Label each drug with a precise description of what effect—good and bad—the drug will have on the taker. This will require heroic honesty. Don't say that marijuana is addictive or dangerous when it is neither, as millions of people know—unlike "speed," which kills most unpleasantly, or heroin, which is addictive and difficult to kick.

For the record, I have tried—once—almost every drug and liked none, disproving the popular Fu Manchu theory that a single whiff of opium will enslave the mind. Nevertheless many drugs are bad for certain people to take and they should be told why in a sensible way.

Along with exhortation and warning, it might be good for our citizens to recall (or learn for the first time) that the United States was the creation of men who believed that each man has the right to do what he wants with his own life as long as he does not interfere with his neighbor's pursuit of happiness (that his neighbor's idea of happiness is persecuting others does confuse matters a bit).

This is a startling notion to the current generation of Americans. They reflect a system of public education which has made the Bill of Rights, literally, unacceptable to a majority of high school graduates (see the annual Purdue reports) who now form the "silent majority"—a phrase which that underestimated wit Richard Nixon took from Homer who used it to describe the dead.

Now one can hear the warning rumble begin: if everyone is allowed to take drugs everyone will and the GNP will decrease, the Commies will stop us from making everyone free, and we shall end up a race of Zombies, passively murmuring "groovie" to one another. Alarming thought. Yet it seems most unlikely that any reasonably sane person will become a drug addict if he knows in advance what addiction is going to be like.

Is everyone reasonably sane? No. Some people will always become drug addicts just as some people will always become alcoholics, and it is just too bad. Every man, however, has the power (and should have the legal right) to kill himself if he chooses. But since most men don't, they won't be mainliners either. Nevertheless, forbidding people things they like or think they might enjoy only makes them want those things all the more. This psychological insight is, for some mysterious reason, perennially denied our governors.

It is a lucky thing for the American moralist that our country has always existed in a kind of time-vacuum: we have no public memory of anything that happened before last Tuesday. No one in Washington today recalls what happened during the years alcohol was forbidden to the people by a Congress that thought it had a divine mission to stamp out Demon Rum—launching, in the process, the greatest crime wave in the country's history, causing thousands of deaths from bad alcohol, and creating a general (and persisting) contempt among the citizenry for the laws of the United States.

The same thing is happening today. But the government has learned nothing from past attempts at prohibition, not to mention repression.

Last year when the supply of Mexican marijuana was slightly curtailed by the Feds, the pushers got the kids hooked on heroin and deaths increased dramatically, particularly in New York. Whose fault? Evil men like the Mafiosi? Permissive Dr. Spock? Wild-eyed Dr. Leary? No.

The Government of the United States was responsible for those deaths. The bureaucratic machine has a vested interest in playing cops and robbers. Both the Bureau of Narcotics and the Mafia want strong laws against the sale and use of drugs because if drugs are sold at cost there would be no money in it for anyone.

If there was no money in it for the Mafia, there would be no friendly playground pushers, and addicts would not commit crimes to pay for the next fix. Finally, if there was no money in it, the Bureau of Narcotics would wither away, something they are not about to do without a struggle.

Will anything sensible be done? Of course not. The American people are as devoted to the idea of sin and its punishment as they are to making money—and fighting drugs is nearly as big a business as pushing them. Since the combination of sin and money is irresistible (particularly to the professional politician), the situation will only grow worse.

1. Identify the sentence(s) in this essay that you think carry the main statement of Vidal's argument. Does he justify the statement? Explain and document.

2. Does Vidal make a fair analogy between drugs and alcohol?

3. ''Since the combination of sin and money is irresistible (particularly to the professional politician), the situation will only grow worse." A fair statement? Explain.

4. Discuss Vidal's "cynical" tone. Do you think it is cynical, or realistic? Explain your answer.

5. Can you take Vidal's proposal seriously? If so, explain his appeal. If not, argue against his appeal and discuss what is wrong with it.

AND STILL THE BEST!

Jonathan Price

Our commercials reveal a very human yearning for experiences so universal, so common, that even without words many American spots can be understood around the world. In this sense, commercials may be the myths of our electronic culture.

Thus, particularly when we are attuned to our own period and its concerns, we may only be aware of the superficial meanings of a commercial (it is about a Japanese car, the car can stand up under pressure), whereas our unconscious may be reveling in the less obvious implications (I can smash it, I can wrap it around toll booths). And we may respond to a commercial in an analytic fashion, either as someone who creates them, or as someone who criticizes them, or in a subjective fashion, simply absorbing them, using them for our own conscious and unconscious purposes. Usually our response mixes both styles of reaction: we try to unmask the commercial's real intention, while at the same time we may get sucked into the story and feel it as if it were a real experience. Hence our mixed feelings about most commercials, and our conviction that we really don't believe them.

Commercials show us the whole mythology of upper-middle-class existence but they don't help us pay for it. If we are poor, we may "buy" that way of thinking without being able to buy the products. As Roland Barthes says of French advertising in *Mythologies,* "The bourgeoisie is constantly absorbing into its ideology a whole section of humanity which does not have its basic status and cannot live up to it except in imagination, that is, at the cost of an immobilization and an impoverishment of consciousness . . . it is as if from the moment when a typist earns sixty dollars a week she recognizes herself in the big wedding of the bourgeoisie." The myth helps her imagine she is rich, even at *le Wimpy.*

Whether aimed at lower classes, or children growing up, commercials sometimes function the way anthropologist Joseph Campbell describes myths operating in primitive cultures:

The aim of education in the primitive, archaic, and Oriental spheres has always been and will no doubt continue to be, for many centuries, not primarily to enlighten the mind concerning the nature of the universe, but to create communities of shared experience for the engagement of the sentiments of the growing individual in the matters of chief concern to the local group. The unsocialized thought and feeling of the very young child are egocentric but not socially dangerous. When the primary urges of the adolescent remain unsocialized, however, they become inevitably a threat to the harmony of the group. The paramount function of all myth and ritual, therefore, has always been, and surely must continue to be, to engage the individual, both emotionally and intellectually, in the local organization. And this aim is best effected—as we have seen—through a solemn conjuring up of intensely shared experiences by virtue of which the whole system of childhood fantasy and spontaneous belief is engaged and fused with the functioning system of the community.

Myths generally justify and motivate some ritual act. And each commercial invites us to participate in at least one ritual: purchase. Through purchase, we are told, we will experience maximum orgasm, see a psychedelic light show, gain the power to wreck whole fleets of trucks at one blow, and clean our filthy home in two seconds.

Commercials, like myths, teach children the important illusions of a culture; they are one way we train our children to read, count, compare (bad versus good, better, best, and jumbo), follow stories, sing along, memorize, and doubt claims. In brief, commercials give children the superficial markings of our nation, the tags of our tribe, the secret handshakes that show we are all middle-class Americans. But underneath this local training, children eventually learn, like their parents, to expect that a gadget will cure them, cheer them up, calm them down, and clean house like magic. And commercials raise children to "participate" in this adult ritual, the economy, by sending in premiums, getting Mom to buy something for them, by quoting from commercials at school. Thus the simplest ritual, that of following along when a commercial comes on, gradually prepares our children for the more complicated lifelong routines that our society demands.

Myths also help us express, and control in a safe way, impulses that could potentially tear our society apart. In primitive cultures, people actually got drunk and made love in night-and-day orgies, and sacrificed human beings, but these activities were carefully limited to a certain phase of the lunar year, and no other. The myths justified this physical expression of the impulses toward sex, craziness, and violence, while also isolating such activity from ordinary life; in a way, hearing the myth at another time served as a substitute for the rites. We are no longer primitive, but our commercials do show numberless visions of the goddess of love unveiling herself, asking us to undress, take it off, let her stroke us, come fly with her, wear nothing at all. She tells us, "I don't wear panties anymore." She urges us, "Do it, come 'doo it." But, of course, there is a screen in the way. And commercials let us imagine blowing up—and reassembling—a camera or a car, tossing cars from planes, from buildings, from waterfalls, smashing watches or shooting locks. Our natural and childish impulses get made into larger-than-life scenes, isolated from real experience by the fact that they are on TV. And the way to reexperience these sensations, at least in our unconscious, is to sacrifice another coin in that basic ritual of America, the buy.

But underneath such locally useful integration of our raucous impulses into society, myths serve a deeper function. They open up awe in us. They remind us of miracles and of wild instincts within ourselves. Primitive myths encouraged ecstatic states, direct communication with the divine, and careful performance of the rituals handed down to people from the god or goddess. Homer's myths made spirits walk the land; in Britain the Druids' tales showed ghosts and witches worked with elves and fairies to protect the wise; but our myths are commercial. The directors and actors, the producers and writers of our commercials may resemble the participants in these primitive rituals in that they often try to believe, want to believe, in the reality of what they do, and, failing that, they make sure we believe. And what do commercials encourage us to believe?

This mythic world is magic. Voices in the air, not attached to bodies, regularly order us around in commercials, take care of us, and give us advice, just like spirits. In this realm we can change the shape of people who have indigestion, make a package of gum as big as a tree, or slice apart a car in an instant. We can fly over golf courses, over the planet, over galaxies; we can drive on water. By mysterious devices, we can make the blind see. We can tame a wild bear to follow us into a bar; we can make a wild deer eat Oreos and go where we want; we can teach koala bears, cats, and elephants to talk, sing, and dance. Commercials resemble the dreams of a primitive hunter or child in their faith in magic.

One central figure dominates many myths—the great Mother, who transforms herself into a thousand forms; sometimes she appears as Mother Nature, sometimes as Mother Earth, sometimes as Lady Fortune, other times as Aphrodite. And in our commercials we see the great Mom go through a hundred transformations in a day, always reappearing with a bottle, a glow, or a rhymed spell to chase the troubles of the suffering representative of humanity. She is the horrid fat harridan checking for dirt in the bathroom, the feathery grandma clutching memories of love, the sprightly WASP woman of fifty abandoning the ancestral home, the chubby fierce huntress forcing a young boy to eat white paste, the stupid but affectionate nurse smothering her child in too many medicinal syrups, Mother Nature making Grand Canyon quake, or a hundred-and-twenty-year-old Soviet yenta eating yogurt. She survives the death of Dad, innumerable times. She makes and pampers the universal baby. And, when the mood strikes, she reaches for another potion, and turns from a gray-haired Mom into a thirtyish swinger who can cut through greasy dirt with another supernatural brew.

Thus, in many ways commercials act as contemporary myths. They awe us, surprising us with trompe l'oeil miracles. They arouse our deepest impulses toward sex, violence, and faith, and they express these instincts while at the same time

406

keeping that expression aesthetic, rather than physical, thus saving our society from the potential chaos of orgies and massacre. Instead of the real thing, we are encouraged to perform a substitute act, a symbolic gesture, in which we put coins on a counter and pick up a magic potion or a symbolic object. And after this ritual we are expected to experience the pleasures hypnotically suggested before: an imaginary ecstasy.

Most programs on TV seem oddly old-fashioned. They imitate films; they take too long; they show people, not just cars, getting hurt; they let lovers get into bed together, rather than just talk about it and kiss; they spend less on convincing and exotic sets; they hardly polish their scenes to the split-second to persuade us and disturb us. They do not demand any ritual follow-up afterward. They lack the glamour, the panache, of commercials.

Commercials work faster, do more magic in less time, arouse more emotions, provoke more real actions in the daily world, keep the economy dizzily spinning. Commercials are not radio news with slides; they are not nineteenth-century novels done up in heavy costumes; they are not even nineteen-forties films redone in color for unsuspecting audiences. In an hour of TV we are likely to see all these aftertraces from several generations of myths—the primitive, the print, the modern film, and the post-modern scene, all jumbled up. Commercials move in fast; tightly edited, quickly paced, their style fits TV better; their contents express contemporary conflicts better, being at once more "primitive" and more highly technological than the programs. If, as Americans believe, the new is better than the old, and the hard sell beats the soft, then commercials today are the best myth on TV.

1. Why do we not believe in commercials, according to Price?
2. How do commercials function as myths?
3. What effects do commercials have on children?
4. How does the image of Mother function in commercials?
5. Why are commercials "the best myth" on television?
6. What can you find in the way Price presents his argument that reminds you of a television commercial?

Judging

Arguments

Your personal reasons for being persuaded, however real to you, do not always make sense to others, nor, for that matter, do their reasons necessarily make sense to you. We have traditionally turned, therefore, to the *reasonableness* of an argument as the most important aspect of its persuasive powers. It will by no means be the only important factor, as we have seen, but reason does at least provide a common reference point to all.

Two Kinds of Argument

An argument is the process of reasoning whereby a conclusion is reached on the basis of some evidence. There are two kinds of argument— one in which the conclusion *necessarily* follows from its evidence:

> All students are people.
>
> Lionel is a student.
>
> Therefore Lionel is a person.

and one in which the conclusion only *probably* follows from its evidence:

> There were many people in line,
>
> so I assumed we would not get tickets.

An argument with a necessary conclusion is called a *deductive* argument; one with at best a probable conclusion is called *inductive. All argument is of one kind or the other,* and knowing how each kind works is a great aid to clear, critical interpretation and writing. There will be times when a deductive argument is made, and then you should know how to judge it, for it is the most powerful of all arguments: swift and irrefutable, even "elegant" as the scientists say of their proofs. But most of the time, of course, we live in a world of inferences that are at best only likely, and this makes it even more important to know how to form hypotheses and draw conclusions as convincingly as possible.

In this chapter, we will discuss ways in which you can interpret and judge the two kinds of argument and check the mixed arguments of extended pieces of persuasive writing. In the next chapter, we will see how those arguments can be made effectively.

Deduction

Syllogisms

All deductive argument is syllogistic. A *syllogism* is an argument made up of three statements: two preliminary statements, or *premises,* that carry

410

the evidence and a final statement that expresses the *conclusion*. The first premise is called the *major,* the second is called the *minor.*

Major premise: All students are people.

Minor premise: Lionel is a student.

Conclusion: Therefore Lionel is a person.

Each of the three statements is a proposition. A *proposition* is the assertion of meaning in a sentence; it is the main statement in which a predicate affirms or denies something about a subject. Note that propositions, however, need not be sentences. In the simple sentence, *The sun shone brightly all day,* the predicate *shone brightly all day* affirms something about the subject *The sun.* As it happens, this proposition *is* one sentence, but often sentences are made up of more than one proposition, as in coordinated and compound sentences. *The sun shone brightly all day and we lay by the pool talking* contains two propositions. Furthermore, different sentences may make the same proposition, a fact that is immediately clear when we compare different languages. *Il pleut* and *pluit* both carry the proposition *It is raining.*

Every valid syllogism contains only three terms: the *major,* the *minor,* and the *middle.* In the argument above, there are three terms: *students, people,* and *Lionel.* The *major* term occurs in both the major premise and the conclusion *(people).* The *minor* term is the subject term of the conclusion which appears in the minor premise *(Lionel).* The *middle* term is the common term in each of the premises *(student).*

There are three kinds of syllogisms, depending on the kind of proposition that is found in the major premise:

■ *Categorical syllogisms* are those in which the major proposition affirms or denies that one class is either wholly or partially included in another. They can be either affirmative or negative. In the syllogism above, for example, the major premise *All students are people* states that the whole class of *students* is included in the class of *people.* It is, therefore, a categorical proposition and the whole syllogism is called a categorical syllogism. All the following propositions are categorical, too:

No students are professors.

Some students are tradespeople.

Some students are not Democrats.

Wherever you find *all, no, nothing, every, everyone, no one,* the categorical propositions are *universal;* that is, they refer to all members of a term's class. The words *some, many, a few,* and so on, indicate that the categorical proposition is *particular;* that is, it refers to particular members of its class. So *Some students are not Democrats* is a particular, negative categorical proposition.

■ *Hypothetical syllogisms* are those in which the major premise contains two statements, the first beginning with *if* (called the *antecedent*), the second beginning with *then* (called the *consequent*). *If Lionel is a student, then he is a person* is a hypothetical proposition with an antecedent *(If Lionel is a student)* and a consequent *(then he is a person)*. Any syllogism that begins with a hypothetical proposition is called a hypothetical syllogism. In such a syllogism, the second premise repeats one of the two statements:

> If Lionel is a student then he is a person.
>
> Lionel is a student.
>
> Therefore Lionel is a person.

■ *Alternative, or disjunctive, syllogisms* are those in which the major premise contains alternatives, that is, two propositions introduced by *either* and *or.* So the proposition, *Either Lionel is a student or Lionel is a professor,* is an alternative, or disjunctive, proposition. Any syllogism that begins with an alternative proposition is called an alternative syllogism. The second premise of such a syllogism asserts the truth of one of the two alternatives:

> Either Lionel is a student, or Lionel is a professor.
>
> Lionel is not a professor.
>
> Therefore Lionel is a student.

The Validity and Truth of Syllogisms

All deductive arguments depend for their effectiveness and value on two things:

The truth of their premises and conclusion

The validity of their form

Unlike any other kind of argument, there are watertight tests for the validity of a deductive argument, but there are no tests that can tell us absolutely whether any proposition is true or not. It is important to remember, therefore, that deductive arguments can be *true but not valid,* and that they can be *valid but not true,* as with this example:

> All rabbits have pigtails.
>
> Alphonse is a rabbit.
>
> Therefore Alphonse has a pigtail.

There is nothing wrong with the *form* of this argument, but the conclusion and the first premise are patently untrue and so the argument is ineffective.

When you evaluate a deductive argument, therefore, you have to ask yourself two questions:

> Are the premises, to the best of my knowledge, true? That is, do they correspond to any verifiable fact? The answer to these questions has nothing to do with formal rules.

> Do the premises necessarily lead to the conclusion? That is, is the argument formally valid? The answer to these questions *is* determined by formal rules.

Remember that deductive reasoning is either valid or invalid. It is *valid* when its conclusion necessarily follows from its premises. It is *invalid* when the conclusion does not follow. Whether a conclusion follows or not depends on the relationship between the *terms* in the propositions that form the premise and the conclusion. Most of the problems with deduction stem from using terms ambiguously or incorrectly, as we shall see.

The following summary of the rules determining validity in deductive reasoning lists certain fallacies. A *fallacy* is an error in reasoning, which, as you will see, is due largely to the way in which terms are distributed. A proposition is said to *distribute* a term if it refers to *all* members of a class. So in the proposition, *all students are people,* the term *all students* is distributed since it refers to all members of the class of students. Similarly if the proposition refers to *no student,* the term *student* is distributed. A proposition is *undistributed* if it refers to particular members of a class *(some, many)* as in the proposition, *some students are tradespeople.* Here *some students* is an undistributed term. Note, too, that in the proposition *all students are people, people* is undistributed even while *all students* is distributed. The proposition does not say that all students are all people. This is important to remember, as you will see below.

Categorical Syllogisms The rules concerning the validity of categorical syllogisms are as follows:

■ *A valid categorical syllogism must contain three terms used with the same meaning throughout.*

> All television sets are adjustable sets.

> All adjustable sets are subject to breakage.

> Therefore all television sets are subject to breakage.

If there are more than three terms in a syllogism or if the terms are used *ambiguously* (that is, a term has two meanings), then the syllogism commits the *fallacy of ambiguity* and is invalid. You cannot make connections between more than three terms in a deductive argument, that is, between the two terms in the conclusion and the one it has in common. A common problem of deductive argument is the use of the common or middle term in more than one sense of its meaning, so that there are in effect *four* terms:

> All animals are inhuman.
>
> Fred was an animal during the fight.
>
> Therefore Fred is inhuman.

The fallacy here is that the middle term *animal* is used literally in the major premise and metaphorically in the minor premise. Sometimes the ambiguity arises from the terms having subtly different meanings that are confused (even deliberately for rhetorical effect):

> All enemies of the United States are un-American.
>
> The Russians are not American.
>
> Therefore the Russians are enemies of the United States.

Un-American does not mean *not American,* so again, there are actually four terms involved.

■ *The middle term must be distributed in at least one premise.* This means that the term must refer to all of a class. So in the syllogism about television sets above, the term *adjustable sets* is distributed in the second, or minor, premise even if it is not in the major premise. Failure to make sure that the middle term is distributed in one of the premises leads to a common fallacy, *the fallacy of the undistributed middle.*

> All rabbits are animals.
>
> All cats are animals.
>
> Therefore all cats are rabbits.

The problem here is that the middle term *animals* is not distributed in either premise; that is, it does not refer to *all animals,* for all animals are plainly not either rabbits or cats.

■ *The conclusion cannot assert more than the premises.* No term can be distributed in the conclusion that is not distributed in the premises. Obviously if I refer to only *some* or even *many* of a term in the premises but claim something about *all* the terms in the conclusion, then I am claiming too much. I can claim that all television sets are subject to breakage only because I made related statements about all of them in the premises. There are two kinds of fallacy that result from a conclusion asserting more than its premises. One is *the fallacy of the illicit major term.*

> All rabbits are animals.
>
> No cats are rabbits.
>
> Therefore no cats are animals.

The major term *animals* is undistributed *in the major premise.* It refers only to particular members of its class, yet it *is* distributed in the conclusion. The second kind of fallacy resulting from a conclusion that asserts more than its premises is *the fallacy of the illicit minor term.*

> All rabbits are animals.
>
> All rabbits are pests.
>
> Therefore all pests are animals.

The minor term *all pests* is not distributed in the minor premise.

■ *No categorical syllogism is valid that has two negative premises.* If there are two negative premises then *the fallacy of the exclusive premises* occurs. The problem here is that no relationship between the minor and major terms can be validly inferred from negative premises since the relationship each has with the middle term is exclusive. For example, in the following syllogism:

> No lizards are rabbits.
>
> No cats are rabbits.
>
> Therefore no lizards are cats.

we have a conclusion that happens to be true, but it has nothing to do with the relationship of lizards to rabbits *or* cats to rabbits. This is one of those occasions when syllogisms can have true propositions but still be invalid. All that can be asserted of the two negative premises is that lizards are wholly or partially excluded from the class of rabbits, and that cats are wholly or partially excluded from the class of rabbits. These conditions exist no matter how lizards and cats are related, so there is no conclusion to be drawn on the basis of the relationship between lizards and cats. Furthermore, if the same form of the syllogism were kept and the argument made as follows:

> No cold-blooded creatures are rabbits.
>
> No lizards are rabbits.
>
> Therefore no lizards are cold-blooded creatures.

the conclusion would be false. Of course, you could say, "But the conclusion *All lizards are cold-blooded* is true." But this syllogism remains invalid, for I have no way of knowing if the conclusion to an argument with negative premises should be positive or negative. (If I were to decide the conclusion to the first example above should be *all lizards are cats,* I would be patently wrong.)

■ *If the premises are universal, the conclusion cannot be particular.* If the premises are universal and the conclusion is particular, the syllogism commits *the existential fallacy.*

> All rabbits are mammals.
>
> No lizards are mammals.
>
> Therefore some lizards are not rabbits.

One cannot infer a particular conclusion from universal premises alone since they do not state the existence of anything in particular.

In sum, then, for a categorical syllogism to be valid, make sure that

It contains three terms only, each used unambiguously.

The middle term is distributed in one of the premises.

Any term distributed in the conclusion is distributed in the premise.

At least one of the premises is positive.

Hypothetical Syllogisms. These are *pure* if both the premises are hypothetical propositions:

> If x, then y
>
> If y, then z
>
> Therefore if x, then z

> If it rains, then the grass will get wet.
>
> If the grass gets wet, then it will grow.
>
> Therefore if it rains, the grass will grow.

Or they can be *mixed,* with the first premise hypothetical and the second categorical:

> If x, then y
>
> x
>
> Therefore y

If it rains, then the grass will get wet.

It is raining.

Therefore the grass will get wet.

Or:

> If x, then y
>
> Not y
>
> Therefore not x

If it rains, the grass will get wet.

The grass is not wet.

Therefore it has not rained.

How do we know when hypothetical syllogisms are valid? There are two simple rules based on whether the syllogism is *pure* or *mixed.*

■ When a hypothetical syllogism is *pure,* it is valid if the first premise and the conclusion have the same antecedent (x), and the second premise and the conclusion have the same consequent (z), and if the consequent of the first premise is the same as the antecedent of the second premise (y).

■ When a hypothetical syllogism is *mixed,* it is valid if the second (or categorical) premise affirms the *antecedent* of the first (or conditional) premise, and the conclusion affirms its consequent; or the second premise denies the consequent and the conclusion denies the antecedent.

These rules for validity may sound complicated, but they have more force if you consider the two common major fallacies that occur with hypothetical arguments. The first is *the fallacy of affirming the consequent.*

> If x, then y
>
> y
>
> Therefore, x

If I jump from the seventh floor, I will break a leg.

I have broken a leg.

Therefore, I have jumped from the seventh floor.

Plainly, I could have broken my leg some other way. The second common fallacy in hypothetical arguments is *the fallacy of denying the antecedent.*

> If x, then y
>
> Not x
>
> Therefore not y

> If I jump from the seventh floor, I will break a leg.
>
> I have not jumped from the seventh floor.
>
> Therefore, I have not broken a leg.

Again, I could have a broken leg from another accident.

Alternative Syllogisms Alternative syllogisms are those that have a major premise containing an *either-or* construction. They are valid only when the second (or categorical) premise affirms (contradicts) one alternative of the first premise and the conclusion denies (affirms) the other.

> Either x, or y
>
> x (not x)
>
> Therefore not y (y)

> Either you are a boy or a girl.
>
> You are a boy. (You are not a boy.)
>
> Therefore you are not a girl. (Therefore you are a girl.)

The Enthymeme Very often deductive reasoning turns up in arguments with a *reduced* number of terms. We may find, for example, only the premise and the conclusion of a syllogism. This is called an *enthymeme* (ĕn-thĭ-mēme), and it is often found in an argument that depends on some kind of common knowledge. If you say *Smith has a B.A. degree, so he has taken some humanities courses,* you would be giving only one premise *(Smith has a B.A. degree)* and the conclusion *(he has taken some humanities courses).* The whole argument would look like this:

> Smith is a person who has a B.A. degree.
>
> Every person who has a B.A. degree is a person who has taken some humanities courses.
>
> Therefore, Smith is a person who has taken some humanities courses.

It would seem long-winded in this argument to go through all the details since it is common knowledge that a number of humanities courses are required for a B.A. degree. Always check enthymemes to make sure that the missing premise can indeed be filled in. The leap from premise to conclusion should not be too large. You would, for example, have problems testing for the validity of this "argument" which commits the *fallacy of non sequitur* (literally, from the Latin, "does not follow"):

> I went to class today.
>
> So the weather will be good tomorrow.

This is not an enthymeme, for the conclusion does not appear to follow from the premise.

Finding Syllogisms in Extended Arguments

Syllogisms need not, of course, appear in standard form. They may be "buried" in discursive prose as short as a newspaper editorial or as long as a book. Again, it is important that the claim is made that a conclusion *must* follow from its premises. In order to understand an argument and test its validity, it is useful, then, to be able to *isolate* the syllogisms. Here is one way you can do that:

- Summarize the piece of writing, following the methods explained in Chapter 2, so that you have an outline of the main details of the argument, especially its *stages* of development.

- Note the logical steps taken in the outline of the argument. Locate the premises and the conclusions and consider their truth value. If the premises seem to be of a general or universal kind, or propose alternatives, it is likely that they will be part of a syllogism. Watch out too for hypothetical syllogisms, though these may be inductive hypotheses in disguise, as you will see later. Much argument in discursive writing is likely to be inductive.

- Reconstruct the outline of the argument in the form of its syllogisms, which may be one or several. If there are several, be sure to note their connections.

- Test the arguments for validity.

For example, the *Denver Post* of February 22, 1982, ran an editorial on the (then major) issue of the federal budget and the proposed cuts in funding for education. The following is a summary of that editorial also printed in the *Post* later in the week:

Slashes in student aid in President Reagan's 1983 budget are a neutron bomb aimed at higher education that will leave the ivy campuses intact but decimate their students. Our economy and defense depend on trained people. Thus, a budget which sacrifices learning to build economic and military strength is like a man who gives up sex because he'd rather have children. Congress should restore the cuts.

Working from this summary, what outline do you think the argument takes? It runs through several stages, but take the conclusions of each first as they are contained in the summary:

Cutbacks in student aid will reduce the number of students at our universities.

This is argued for in the form of an analogy of a neutron bomb that kills people but leaves buildings intact.

Our economy and defense depend on trained people.

Fewer students will result in fewer trained people.

Education cuts will eventually do more harm than good, disturbing our economy and defense.

Expecting effects from education cuts is like wanting children without sex.

Congress should restore the cuts.

Now the argument depends on several analogies, it is true, and that kind of argument we will examine further in this chapter. The analogy with the neutron bomb, for example, seems deliberately rhetorical and perhaps overstated for there is no way of knowing exactly how many students will leave school if government aid is cut. But the analogy in turn depends on deductive reasoning. So examine the premises first for their truth value.

It is reasonable to say that *some students will leave school if government aid is cut,* and it seems equally reasonable to say that *the economy and defense depend on trained people.* Here are two categorical propositions on which the whole argument rests. Are they related? There is a valid hypothetical syllogism implied here:

If government aid is cut, some students will leave.

If some students leave, then there will be fewer trained people.

Therefore, if government aid is cut, there will be fewer trained people.

It is fairly easy to connect this conclusion with the next one about the decline of the economy, without even having to develop an intermediary syllogism showing the connection between the economy and trained people.

If there are fewer trained people, the economy will suffer.

There will be fewer trained people.

Therefore the economy will suffer.

This is a valid deduction with a conclusion that affirms the antecedent. The rest of the argument is based on an analogy that depends on showing that the opposition does not know how to argue validly with hypothetical syllogisms. The writer's argument is that the government's reasoning is similar to that of a man who wants children without sex:

If sex, then children

No sex

Therefore children

This commits the fallacy of denying the antecedent (not to mention the fact that it ignores birth control and the major premise is a non sequitur), and, says the writer, the government's argument is no better:

If a good economy, then cut aid

Cut aid

Therefore a good economy

which commits the fallacy of affirming the consequent.

In conclusion, there is another hypothetical argument that follows logically from the earlier ones offered by the editorial:

If you want a good economy, then restore aid.

You want a good economy.

Therefore restore aid.

which, as you know, is valid since it affirms the antecedent and then the consequent.

The editorial's reasoning, therefore, is both syllogistic and valid. It can be shown that there is a necessary connection between cuts in aid and a shortage of trained people, and the opposition view is muddled by faulty logic.

Induction

We began with deductive logic because it has fixed rules and easily recognized argumentative forms. More common, though, is inductive reasoning. Again, this involves the argument from data to claim—from evidence to conclusion—with varying degrees of probability attached to the claim. Remember that inductive arguments are not valid or invalid, but *correct* or *incorrect*. They can be described as *better* or *worse* than some other inductive argument, or as *efficient* in the development of their claims, based on the various kinds of induction that exist. Above all, we are concerned with the reasoning that connects the evidence and the conclusion. We will cover some of the common fallacies that occur in the transition from data to claim.

Inductive reasoning argues *from evidence, from definition, by comparison and contrast, from analogy, from authority, from cause to effect,* and *from effect to cause.* Here are some examples of each:

■ *From evidence*: Out of a town of five thousand people, over three thousand have come to see this exhibition, so we can say it has been a success.

■ *From definition:* A playboy is ''a wealthy, carefree man devoted to the pleasures of nightclubs, sports, and female company,'' so Fred Bloggs is definitely a playboy.

■ *By comparison and contrast*: When I flew to England last year, Airline A was right on time, but this year Airline B was three hours late, so Airline A is plainly the better one to fly.

■ *From analogy:* You and I are equally strong and fit, so if I can run a mile in five minutes, you can too.

■ *From authority:* The economy will get better; the president said so, and if he doesn't know, who does?

■ *From cause to effect*: If there was a nuclear attack on Denver, over three quarters of the population would be killed.

■ *From effect to cause*: My lawn is dying in spots, and since I know it has received plenty of water in the last few weeks, it must have been burnt by too much fertilizer.

Argument from Evidence

Whenever an argument is made using statistics, reports, or any kind of documentation, the writer is arguing from evidence. The ''proof,'' as far as you know, is contained in the evidence, and you must, like judge and jury, evaluate the conclusion according to the nature of the evidence. It is important, then, to be sure that the evidence presented has the following characteristics:

■ *Relevance.* Check all the details to make sure they relate to the conclusion and that nothing important has been left out.

■ *Accuracy.* Make sure that the writer has presented facts and figures that can be checked if necessary. Are the sources clear?

■ *Clear definition.* The facts should be presented without ambiguity.

■ *Sufficiency.* The statistics and other data present should be adequate to the claim. If you are trying to draw conclusions from statistics, you have to check to ascertain whether the statistics (the sampling procedure) are adequate and the statistical projections are reasonable. It is best not to try to draw conclusions from statistics unless you have had some kind of training in the art of such testing and understand the limits built into the various methods. A sound argument using statistics tries to justify its figures by giving clear percentages and even sometimes explaining in detail its statistical methods. These explanations are not necessary for the presentation of simple statistics.

We could say then that the following argument carries sufficient evidence:

Of the eight thousand students at this university, only fifty are minority students, so there is little doubt that, in spite of our scholarship program, we have not succeeded in attracting many of the five thousand black and Chicano young people in the area who have graduated from high school and are eligible to enter the university. Some three thousand graduating seniors who are black or Chicano were polled this year and over 75 percent gave high tuition costs as the main reason for not attending our university.

The following argument, however, plainly carries insufficient, unclear, and irrelevant evidence:

Of all the students at this university, very few are minority students. Most of them want to have little to do with us because we don't have a good student union. I have asked all my friends in our college what they think and they agree with me.

Argument from Definition

When you come across a definition of a thing, person, institution, value, enterprise, or whatever, you should carefully examine it to see if it is adequate. There are, in traditional logic, several different kinds of definition governed by the writer's intention. Ask yourself which kind the writer seems to be using and the argument demands, and see if the definition serves the purpose:

■ *New definitions.* If a writer is talking about a term or an event that has no previous history, the term has to be defined. *Space shuttle,* referring to the spaceship *Columbia,* had to be carefully described and defined when it first appeared in newspapers because few people knew what a space shuttle could do. A new definition should be adequate and clear.

■ *Dictionary definitions.* A writer can explain clearly a term's meaning by referring to the meanings it already has. The dictionary, of course, is *the* sourcebook for every reader and writer since it lists what those meanings are. If a definition of a term or event does not fall under conventional usage, and there is no attempt made to explain what the new definition is, the argument is suspect. For example, if you were to argue from a definition of *democracy* as the right to do exactly what we want without explaining how that definition can be justified, your argument would be greatly weakened.

■ *Precising definitions.* These are made by a writer who wants to use a term in a way that does not match ordinary usage. If you want to insist that reading *is* interpretation, you would have to offer a precising definition of the term *reading,* as you will find in the first two chapters of this text. Again, check to see that a writer's definition is precise enough for the argument.

■ *Theoretical definitions.* If an argument relies on special information and a vocabulary that is not in everyday use—such as an argument in science, political science, economics, literary criticism, and so on— then a reader can expect a writer to define theoretical and specialized terms unless, of course, the writing is intended for a specialist audience. Thus if a writer of a nonspecialist text uses terms like *the second law of thermodynamics* or *entropy* without defining them, the writer's knowledge and the argument are suspect.

■ *Persuasive definitions.* The reader has to be wary of these. There are as many definitions of *democracy, welfare,* and *communism* as there are politicians, and as many definitions of *love, marriage,* and *happiness* as there are psychologists, social scientists, and guidance counselors. What is more, writers often use special definitions of terms to carry their argument. So *democracy* might be defined as "a noncommunist way of life" by someone arguing against the Marxist line, and "love is a four-letter word" can be a definition used by someone who is trying to persuade by being cute.

Writers argue by using any of the above defining techniques. We shall discuss how you can use definition to develop an argument in the next chapter, but for now you should be aware of some of the common fallacies related to definition:

■ *The fallacy of accident* occurs when an arguer takes an exception to be a general rule, or a general rule to be a universal one. For example, it is generally the case that to kill is a crime. If you argue that it is morally acceptable for the police to kill a homicidal maniac who is holed up in a building sniping at the public and cannot be disarmed, the general principle of the moral evil of killing is not disproved by this "accident" of an exceptional case. So if you insist that the general rule is no longer valid because of the exception, then your "definition" commits the fallacy of accident.

■ *The fallacy of converse accident* is commonly known as the *hasty generalization* and is simply the converse of the fallacy of accident. The fallacy is committed by generalizing on the basis of exceptional particular cases rather than on the basis of typical ones. If you define all roses as being scented because you know some of them are, you would be mistaken and would commit the fallacy of hasty generalization.

■ *The fallacy of begging the question* commits the fallacy of a *circular* definition in which the conclusion of the argument is incorporated into the premise. This argument, for example, begs the question: "Nuclear disarmament is a necessity, and I know this is true because the people who believe in it are decent pacifists." If you want to prove that nuclear disarmament is a necessity, you need more evidence than the word of an avowed pacifist. One has to be careful not to preach to the converted nor to present as evidence the conclusion you want to prove. Here is another circular argument: "Dallas will win the Super Bowl because it has the best team and the best coach and management. I know it has the best team and coach because it will win the Super Bowl. And it will win the Super Bowl because only the best team and the best coach deserve to do so. Besides, it's the outstanding team this year."

■ *The fallacy of the complex question* is not strictly a definition but a question involving a controversial definition that the arguer is taking for granted. One of the best known is the question "Have you stopped beating your wife yet?" This has no simple yes or no answer that will not incriminate the responder. The complex question is similar to the circular argument in that the question asked incorporates a conclusion that has by no means been proved. So it has many popular forms: "When are those pro-abortion advocates going to stop breaking the law?" "Is this another pernicious supply-side economics theory?" "When are we going to stop those foreigners from interfering in the U.S. automobile market?"

■ *The fallacy of composition* occurs when one reasons from the parts of a whole to the whole itself, or from individual members to a group. It is fallacious to argue, for example, that if every chapter in a book is an artistic masterpiece, then the whole book is an artistic masterpiece; or that if every item in a collection is inexpensive, then the whole collection must be too.

■ *The fallacy of division* is the reverse of the fallacy of composition. It is fallacious to argue from the whole to the part. Thus, one should not argue that if a motor car is heavy, all its individual parts must be heavy too.

Argument by Comparison and Contrast

This is perhaps the most common of all arguments found in advertising, for example. Two or three versions of a razor blade or a painkiller are compared in action, and of course, the winner is always the advertisement's sponsor. How convenient it would be if all comparisons could be so easily decided. The writer of an argument knows what the conclusion is going to be; the reader's job is to verify the relevance and correctness of the comparisons that are made.

■ Is the comparison between two items that belong to the same class? You may compare planes and ships as modes of transatlantic transport, but not planes and cars. Comparing events of different classes is called *the fallacy of false comparison.*

■ Has the writer compared enough important qualities of each item? Speed, cost, efficiency, comfort, and so on, make a comparison between planes and ships a useful one if you are planning to travel. The writer dealing with this theme comes to a conclusion about advantages and disadvantages.

■ Has the writer's comparison proved the point? That is, is the comparison relevant to the conclusion?

Argument from Analogy

If you happen to like Brand X motor car, have owned three of them, and are trying to persuade someone to buy one, you would do so on the *analogy* that three of your cars have been great so this one probably will be, too. The argument, of course, has to be made carefully:

If a, b, c, d all have properties x and y

And a, b, c all have property z as well

Then d *probably* has property z.

426

If four models of Brand X motor care are efficient and economical, and three earlier models are powerful as well, the most recent model is likely to be powerful also. The argument from analogy, then, depends on several factors that determine the similarity between two or more things, and not just that a couple of items seem to look alike. For example, if you were arguing that someone should buy the new Brand X on the basis of your having liked the previous three, then the person you were trying to persuade would have every right to know what it was that you liked about the cars and what they had in common *with the new one.*

How do you judge an argument based on analogy for its degree of probability? There are five questions you can ask:

■ *How many things are being compared?* Obviously, the greater the number of instances that are cited as evidence for doing something, the stronger the argument. If in the example above, you had owned only one Brand X car, your argument would be less impressive. Note, however, that this does not mean that the person you are trying to persuade should be three times as impressed—or that the argument is three times stronger!

■ *How many qualities do the items have in common?* It is more convincing if it can be shown that the car's new model has the same or better mileage, power, and styling as the other three than if they are similar in one respect only.

■ *How relevant is the evidence used?* If you were to argue that the latest model of Brand X is as good as the earlier ones because it has the same quality paint work, the same tires, tinted glass, and muffler, then clearly the argument is weaker than a comparison made between the engine capacity, the overall styling, and the mileage figures. It is important that the evidence used be directly related to the conclusion that is reached. Your major consideration in evaluating an argument by analogy is to question the relevance of the informaton cited in the premises.

■ *How strong is the claim of the argument relative to the premises?* Say you argue that the statistics and car reviews show that the new model of Brand X car will definitely win a car-of-the-year award. The claim is based on statistics that are similar to those of previous models of the car, but none of the earlier models won the award. So the claim is not too strong and the argument is weak. But if the mileage of the car and its general performance will be no less than any of the earlier models (of similar capacity and design), and they did win awards, then the argument is considerably strengthened.

■ *How dissimilar are the pieces of evidence used in the premises?* Plainly, you could list many similarities among the three earlier models of the Brand X car. But if it could be shown that the performance of each rated very highly and they were *different* cars in a number of respects (varying engine capacity, strong performance in both automatic and manual drive, and so on), then there would be a very strong argument for the generally high quality of the car. In short, *the more dissimilar the evidence cited, the stronger the argument.*

If any of the above five requirements are not met, then *the Fallacy of faulty analogy* occurs. This is the most common fallacy related to this kind of argument and it occurs when a conclusion is drawn from *irrelevant* premises. There are examples of this listed in each of the five points above.

Argument from Authority

Authority can take different forms, the most usual being well-known people or well-known documentation. In order to effectively argue from authority, the arguer should quote from a source that is genuinely authoritative, relevant, and unprejudiced on the subject. So a military general may be a recognized authority on war tactics but not necessarily an authority on the question of science versus religion. An English teacher may be an authority on language and literature but not necessarily a reliable source on the subject of film.

When you encounter an argument that is based on or even partly refers to an authority—even if the authority is of impeccable credentials and your favorite expert on the subject—you should not simply react, but rather, ask these questions:

■ *Is the argument by authority relevant at all?* Is anyone's opinion relevant when you are deciding which portable radio sounds best to you?

■ *Is the authority really an authority on the subject?* Are all those people offering testimonials for products on television really experts on what they are talking about? Some are, but some are not, and you have to judge the value of the argument accordingly.

■ *Is the authority truly unprejudiced?* Surely people touting products on television stand to gain something for their testimonial.

If you can answer these three questions affirmatively, the argument from authority is indeed convincing. But the problem with arguments that appeal to the weight and reputation of someone's opinion, or even to the "authority" of a common powerful human feeling, is that they often lead to fallacious reasoning. There are a few appeals common in argument that tend to make reasoning ineffective even while they seem to promote the persuasive effect of an argument. Note, though, that some of these appeals tend not to be clear-cut fallacies. We will discuss the pros and cons of each.

■ *The appeal to an irrelevant or prejudiced authority.* This is a fallacy and usually occurs when an argument relies on the good reputation of a well-known figure to promote a cause or provide information that the figure is not an expert on. So a certain golfer advertising a tire because he knows how to drive a golf ball well is irrelevant to the value of the tire.

■ *The appeal to the people.* This is not always a fallacy. You can appeal to popular feelings and patriotism quite reasonably. Various Western leaders raised the spirits of many during the last world war for a reasonable patriotic cause. You always have to ask *why* the appeal is being made, and judge the argument for its effects rather than the logic of its appeal. For sometimes the appeal to the people covers up a motive that is selfish or undemocratic, and it may even involve the *fallacy of name calling.* So we find patriotic appeals being made all over the world in order to sell things, and national flags become emblems of commercial value. This constitutes a fallacy. Also it can be argued fallaciously that it is "un-American" to disagree with the president or "philistine" not to support your local symphony orchestra.

■ *The appeal to pity.* This usually involves the argument that something should or should not take place because of pitiable circumstances. This is the appeal made in law courts when mitigating circumstances are offered. The judgment as to whether the appeal is relevant or not depends of course on the judge in each case, but we can say that in extreme cases the appeal to pity is fallacious because it is irrelevant to the charge. So there is the famous story of the mass murderer who claimed that he came from an unhappy home. Remember, however, that not all appeals to pity are fallacious, for we do rightly temper judgment with mercy.

■ *The appeal to force.* This appeal commits the fallacy of arguing that "might is right," an argument we have all heard when reason breaks down. But it also covers more everyday occurrences. A would-be contributor to a political campaign might use the prospect of a large donation to gain a political favor.

■ *The appeal to fear.* This is used as a cause for action: "You should side with those who want to ban the bomb or else you will surely die." There are more subtle and effective arguments for nuclear disarmament. The appeal to fear is an appeal to self-preservation without any rational inducement.

Argument from Cause to Effect, Effect to Cause

This is perhaps the most difficult kind of argument because it depends on the formulation of a hypothesis about an unknown factor, either cause or effect. You will recall from the discussion of the syllogism that a hypothetical proposition is one that states that *if* something happens, *then* something else will take place. Like many arguments by analogy, the argument from cause or effect predicts that something is or will be the case based on a prior or existing condition. That is, the writer is predicting a *relationship* between two events that is dependent on either an effect or a cause.

There are some obvious cause-effect relationships. If you thrust your hand in a fire, you will get burned. There is, you can assume, a necessary relationship between fire and burning. If you break the law, and you get caught, you can expect to be punished. That is perhaps not quite so highly probable, but there is a likely enough relationship between cause and effect. But most cause-effect relationships are difficult to prove. *You need a sufficient number of conditions in a cause before you can adequately predict what the effects will be.* You need to know, for example, the full theory behind an economic plan in order to guess what effect it will have on inflation. If you know only what the effects are, you can judge the cause only in terms of the necessary relationships between it and the effects. So if you see a heap of ashes, you can very reasonably assume that there has been a fire. But if you see someone driving carelessly all over the road, you are not sure what the cause is without more information.

There are, then, two important rules about cause-and-effect argument:

- You can infer cause from effect only through *necessary* conditions. If there appear to be several possible causes for an effect, you cannot make any reliable inference.

- You can infer effect from cause only through *sufficient* conditions.

So when an argument plainly depends on cause and effect, examine it closely to make sure that the writer has met one of these two conditions.

There are several kinds of fallacious thinking associated with assertions about cause, effect, and the circumstances of an event.

- *The fallacy of false cause.* This mistake occurs when we assume that one event is the cause of another when in fact their relationship is purely coincidental. The fallacy is also committed by oversimplifying a cause, or by choosing one possible cause over several others that would work as well. For example, if you insist that you recovered from a twisted ankle after resting it for a week because you wrapped it in a "miracle bandage," then you are committing the fallacy of false cause. The real cure was more likely the rest period.

- *The fallacy of arguing from ignorance.* This occurs when you assume that because no other cause is known to exist, a proposed cause must be the one. It is fallacious to argue that psychic phenomena cannot exist because they haven't been proven. Arguments that lead to the fallacy of arguing from ignorance usually arise because there is not enough information to argue one way or the other. Note, however, that under our law, an accused person is considered innocent until proven guilty, and if no evidence can be found to convict the accused, then that person goes free. That does not contradict this fallacy.

- *The genetic fallacy.* This fallacy is based on irrelevant statements about a person or thing. It is wrong to argue that Dylan Thomas is a bad poet because he seems to have been an alcoholic, or that a university president is impractical because he has been an academic.

- *The fallacy of the* ad hominem *argument.* (*Ad hominem* comes from the Latin, meaning literally "to the man".) This is a variety of the genetic fallacy and involves an argument to the circumstances of your opponent rather than to the issue itself. So you might argue, fallaciously, that a divorced person can't be an expert on marriage, or that a Frenchman should agree to unlimited imports of Californian wine into his own country because French people are known to like wine.

- *The* reductio ad absurdum (*again from Latin, meaning literally, the "reduction to absurdity"*). In this argument, a possible consequence is described in extreme and oversimplified terms. For example: "The way I see it, Congress is nothing more than a group of businessmen who will lead us further into the murky depths of the capitalism they adhere to. We will eventually be ruled by giant corporations, and the Senate and Congress will be their power playground." It is also worth remembering, however, that some apparently absurd arguments have proven to be uncomfortably close to the truth, such as some predictions of economic decline made a few years ago.

- *Conspiracy theories.* These insist that a cause must always be plural and have perhaps more to do with those uneasily walking the corridors of power than with the average citizen. But again, since the assassination of John F. Kennedy and the conspiracy of Watergate, it has not been unusual to see conspiracies everywhere from the kindergarten lunchroom to the university president's office. Uncovered conspiracies will always remind us that it is naive to assume that people do not gang together for special ends. But it is equally naive to assume that any wrongdoing is *necessarily* the creation of more than one person. Before you claim conspiracy, you should be able to prove your case beyond a reasonable doubt.

As you can imagine, evaluating and avoiding these fallacies is not easy to do. The scientist—who is perhaps our most scrupulous hypothesizer—must do so in order to produce a theory that will earn the respect of fellow-scientists. You do not have to be a scientist, however, to realize that every hypothesis that demands to be taken seriously should meet these conditions. And you do not have to be a scientist to be able to interpret cause-effect arguments.

Checking Extended Arguments

Now that you have surveyed a number of the more common forms of deductive and inductive reasoning, you can apply that knowledge to checking the extended arguments you find in articles and books. Earlier in this chapter, we reconstructed syllogisms "buried" in deductive arguments. It is clear that few extended arguments are *purely* deductive, for there are too many other rhetorical chances to persuade someone of our viewpoint, and too many uncertainties when we try to reach a conclusion. So now, we shall consider a more complete approach to the testing of extended arguments.

■ Read and annotate the text. Summarize it if necessary.

■ Find the conclusion and the premises. There may be more than one conclusion in the argument, so concentrate at first on the major conclusion, the *theme statement.* Is the argument primarily inductive or deductive? Or a mixture of both?

■ Write out an outline of the argument listing all the premises and conclusions and their connections. Identify all the main stages of the argument: analogy, authority, and so on. You can either start from the main conclusion and work back, or follow the natural sequence of the piece of writing.

■ Test the validity of each argument and of the overall argument.

This process is not a difficult one to work through, once you have identified the main conclusion and the preliminary arguments leading up to it. Here is an example of how you might check an extended argument, again in an editorial from the *Denver Post*:

During the 1950s, a joke circulated about efforts of the U.S.A. and the USSR to "psyche" each other. In the "G"-rated version, the Soviets decided to unnerve

the Americans by ordering army bunk beds from a U.S. manufacturer—and spec-
ifying the beds had to be 10 feet long.

As expected, the patriotic bedmaker passed this "intelligence" to the Pentagon,
which bucked it to the president. Recognizing the Soviet ploy, the president
trumped it with an order to "send them the 10-foot bunks—but stamp each one
'medium.' "

These days each side seems determined to convince *itself* that the enemy is 10
feet tall. The Pentagon's recent report, "Soviet Military Power," limned Soviet
strength in worrisome terms. The Soviets parried vigorously. But as Rep. Pat
Schroeder, D-Colo., has been arguing effectively, such "man for man and tank for
tank" comparisons ignore crucial differences in the two nations' political and
strategic situations.

The U.S.A. is only the strongest link in an alliance of free nations. In a showdown,
the combined economic and military power of such friends as Britain, Canada,
France, West Germany, Australia, Israel, Italy, South Korea and many others would
reinforce America.

In contrast, the Soviet Union is an anachronism, the last great imperialist power.
Much of its strength has to be deployed keeping people who detest it in sub-
jugation. As Schroeder notes, much of the reported "gap" in U.S.-Soviet military
spending vanishes when the $100 billion spent by our NATO allies is tallied
against the estimated $30 billion spent by the Soviet Union's Warsaw Pact sat-
ellites. Overall, NATO even has a slight edge in manpower over the pact. The
biggest question of all, of course, is whether Poland, East Germany, Hungary
and Czechoslovakia would side with their oppressors or their liberators in a
final crisis.

Finally, our borders are with Mexico and Canada—good friends. In contrast,
the lands stolen from China by the Russian czars are like Germany's theft of
Alsace-Lorraine from France in 1870—a source of enduring enmity with an unforgiving neighbor.

Of course, the U.S.A. can't be complacent. Our reserve forces, with the exception
of aviation units, have deteriorated badly. Our Navy's sea control capability is
inadequate. The Army is only beginning to scrap the outmoded "Verdun" doctrine
of firepower and attrition and revamp its equipment and tactics around maneuver
principles—the key to victory since Alexander knocked off Darius. All services
need help in retaining trained cadre.

But the proposed military budget seems guided more by what defense contractors want to sell than by any rational assessment of our security needs.

Schroeder has proposed trimming $30 billion, including $13.5 billion in the
upcoming fiscal year. She would slow procurement of the orphaned MX missile
and the Navy's bungled F-A-18, scratch the B-1 bomber and one of two new
nuclear aircraft carriers. Such trims would only slow our defense buildup to a
manageable pace. We disagree with her proposal to slow the Trident missile

submarine, however. Without a new bomber or missile, it's prudent to strengthen the remaining and most crucial leg of the strategic "triad."

But overall, the congresswoman is to be commended for realizing that panic buying spurred by fears of 10-foot-tall Russians is no substitute for measured reforms to revitalize American military power.

"**Ten-foot Russians?**" February 28, 1982

The outline of the argument might look like this:

■ *Opening argument by analogy:* in the 1950s, the U.S. and USSR tried to persuade each other of its military strength; today each is trying to persuade itself of the other's strength. Reasons not given.

■ *Analogy continued:* the U.S. has certain friends, secure borders, $100 billion NATO budget, more manpower in NATO compared with Warsaw Pact countries. In comparison, the USSR has few certain allies, a $30 billion Warsaw Pact budget with less manpower than NATO, and insecure borders with an unfriendly neighbor in China.

■ *Qualification to U.S. superiority:* we cannot afford to be complacent because of military deficiencies.

■ *Cause-effect argument:* the real causes of high defense spending are panic-based because of misassumptions (dispelled by analogy above) and pressure from defense contractors who want to sell their goods.

■ *Schroeder proposal:* trim budget by $30 billion.

■ *Editorial opinion:* agrees with Schroeder but suggests developing Trident missiles, since we would not be building up other defenses. Otherwise, both agree that panic buying is foolish and "measured" defense "reforms" are needed.

Basically, then, the argument is one of *analogy* on which a *hypothesis* is developed.

■ Check the evidence. It seems relevant, clearly defined, and sufficient, but do both sides agree on the statistics?

■ The argument by analogy is adequate. There are a sufficient number of comparisons (U.S. and allies against USSR and allies) and sufficient details in common (defense budget, border conditions, allies, manpower). There is relevant information for the conclusion. Claim is strong in relation to the premises.

■ An advantage of the argument is that it avoids all emotional appeals (especially to force and to the people), but some of its assumptions can be questioned and are unsupported: namely, how friendly our allies would be and how unfriendly the Russian allies would be if a war develops. The analysis of causes of present buying is relatively unworked out. For example, the government presumably does not think it is in a panic or at the mercy of the defense contractors. So we wonder what its reasons are. Similarly, the suggestion of mutual fear leading to panic may make popular psychological sense, but tends to the fallacy of composition (arguing from individual motive to group psychology).

■ The argument from present conditions to the line of action that should be taken is consistent. The hypothesis that we should allow only measured reforms of defense spending depends on the argument by analogy.

In sum, then, the argument is quite consistent and inductively correct except for the analysis of the causes of arms purchases.

Checklist

1. Arguments are either *deductive* or *inductive*. A deductive argument is one in which a conclusion necessarily follows from the premises. An *inductive* argument is one in which a conclusion only probably follows from the premises.
2. All deductive arguments are *syllogistic.* A syllogism comprises three *propositions:* two *premises* (a major and a minor) and a *conclusion.* Every valid syllogism contains only three *terms: a major, a minor,* and a *middle.* There are three kinds of syllogisms: *categorical, hypothetical,* and *alternative,* or *disjunctive,* depending on the nature of the major premise.
3. .All deductive argument is either *valid* or *invalid;* the test for validity is a formal one:
    a. Each valid categorical syllogism must

    Contain only three terms used the same way throughout

    Have a middle term distributed in at least one premise

    Have a conclusion that asserts no more than the premises

    Not have two negative premises

    Not have a particular conclusion if the premises are universal

      ■ In addition, be aware of

        Untrue premises in a valid form of the syllogism

        Fallacy of ambiguity

        Fallacy of the undistributed middle

       Fallacy of the illicit major term

       Fallacy of the illicit minor term

       Fallacy of the exclusive premises

       Existential fallacy

  b. Examples of valid hypothetical syllogisms

          If x, then y

          If y, then z

          Therefore if x, then z

          If x, then y

          x

          Therefore y

- Beware of

       Fallacy of affirming the consequent

       Fallacy of denying the antecedent

  c. Example of valid alternative syllogism

          Either x, or y

          x (not x)

          Therefore not y (y)

  d. The *enthymeme* is an argument in which one premise is missing. It comprises the major premise and a conclusion. Beware of the non sequitur when a conclusion cannot follow from the premise.

4. Finding syllogisms in extended arguments
  a. Summarize the argument.
  b. Isolate premises and conclusion and consider their truth value.
  c. Reconstruct the implied syllogisms.
  d. Test for validity.

5. Induction
  a. The *argument from evidence* must be relevant, accurate, clearly defined, and sufficient.
  b. The *argument from definition* can be a new, dictionary, precising, theoretical, or persuasive definition. Beware of the fallacies of

Accident

Converse accident (hasty generalization)

Begging the question (circular argument)

Complex question

Composition

Division

c. The *argument by comparison and contrast*

d. The *argument from analogy.* Be sure to

Cite as many events as possible in the comparison

Cite as many common qualities as possible

Use evidence only directly related to the conclusion

Make the claim closely dependent on the premises

Cite as much dissimilar evidence as possible

Beware of the fallacy of faulty analogy.

e. The *argument from authority.* The authority should be necessary, relevant, genuinely expert, and unprejudiced. Beware of the following fallacies:

Appeal to irrelevant authority, appeal to the people, appeal to pity, appeal to force

f. The *arguments from cause to effect and effect to cause* are both dependent on the formulation of an hypothesis.

One can argue from a cause to an effect only through necessary conditions.

One can infer effect from cause only through sufficient conditions.

Beware of fallacies of false cause, arguing from ignorance, genetic, *ad hominem, reductio ad absurdum*, and conspiracy.

6. Checking extended arguments

a. Find conclusions and premises, concentrating on the main argument.

b. Write out an outline of the argument, listing all the premises and conclusions and their connections. Identify the kinds of argument.

c. Test the validity of each argument and of the overall argument.

Exercises

A. Deduction

1. Here is a series of syllogistic arguments, some valid, some invalid. With each one, write out the syllogism in standard form, determine whether the syllogism is valid or not, and name and explain any fallacies that occur.

Example:

All nuclear weapons are lethal weapons, but all nuclear weapons are necessary deterrents to nuclear attack. It follows, therefore, that all deterrents to nuclear attack are necessarily lethal.

All nuclear weapons are lethal weapons.
All nuclear weapons are necessary deterrents to nuclear attack. Therefore, all deterrents to nuclear attack are lethal weapons.

This argument is invalid since it commits the fallacy of the illicit minor term. The conclusion expresses more than the premises: "deterrents to nuclear attack" is undistributed in the minor premise but distributed in the conclusion. (Plainly not all deterrents to nuclear attack are nuclear weapons.)

a. All policemen carry guns. Fred Jones is a policeman, so Fred must be carrying a gun.

b. All politicians are human, and all criminals are human. Therefore all politicians are criminals.

c. No roses are growing in this garden, and no roses grow without proper nourishment, so I know that there is no proper nourishment in this garden.

d. This woman has a beautiful face, and since we know that beauty is never just skin deep, we know that she must have a beautiful personality.

e. There isn't a Christian who doesn't believe in God. No Moslem is a Christian. Therefore no Moslem believes in God.

f. All professional football players earn money; all football players are highly trained athletes. So all highly trained athletes like making money.

g. All politicans need the votes of their electorate. No people who need electoral votes are going to stay away from their electorates in Washington all year. So all politicians are not going to stay in Washington all year.

h. All scientists are people who make careful experiments. No scientist is a person who can work without adequate funding. So all careful experiments depend on adequate funding.

i. All men have muscles they've never even used. My boyfriend has muscles he's never even used, so my boyfriend is all man.

j. Rock singers are well-known to the young. Trog Furtive is a rock singer. Therefore Trog is well-known to the young.

k. If you run a small business from your house, then you have to file a special tax return. Since you have to file a special tax return, you must be running a small business from your house.

l. If the lady in the cream dress leaves her seat, you can have it. You can have the seat, therefore, the lady in the cream dress did leave.

m. Whales are dying out, I hear. Well, that animal over there is a whale, so it must be dying out.

n. If I buy your car, I'll have two cars. I do have two cars, so I must have bought yours.

o. All film stars have public lives, but on the other hand, no prisoners do. So it's safe to say that some prisoners are not film stars.

p. If Brown was in New York on November 22, he did not commit the crime. If he did not commit the crime, Smith did. If Smith did, we should indict Jones as well.

q. Some people earn more money than you. I know that I earn more money than some people, so I must earn more money than you.

r. The crime rate is going up in some cities. Murder is a crime, so the murder rate is going up.

s. If I buy your car, I'll have two cars. I didn't buy your car, so I don't have two cars.

t. Either you pay for a lawyer or you will be assigned a public defender. You didn't pay for a lawyer, but that is not to say that you got a public defender either.

2. Here are some enthymemes. Suggest the missing premises, convert the syllogisms, and decide on their validity, naming any fallacies.

a. "And God said, 'Let there be light,' and there was light" (Genesis 1:3).

b. All ice skaters from Czechoslovakia are communists, therefore no ice skaters from America are communists.

c. Animals can't choose their fate, therefore humans can't choose their fate either.

d. You should go on a holiday because it will make you feel better.

e. "Go to the ant, O sluggard; consider her ways, and be wise" (Proverbs 6:6).

f. "When there is peace, the warlike man attacks himself" (F. Nietzsche, *Beyond Good and Evil*).

3. Here are two passages. Read each carefully, and list as many syllogisms as you can that you find "buried" in the argument. These extracts are primarily examples of deductive reasoning, so when you have listed the syllogisms, comment on the validity of the arguments.

For everything there is a season, and a time for every matter under heaven: ²a time to be born, and a time to die; a time to plant, and a time to pluck up what is planted; ³a time to kill, and a time to heal; a time to break down, and a time to build up; ⁴a time to weep, and a time to laugh; a time to mourn, and a time to dance; ⁵a time to cast away stones, and a time to gather stones together; a time to embrace, and a time to refrain from embracing; ⁶a time to seek, and a time to lose; a time to keep, and a time to cast away; ⁷a time to rend, and a time to sew; a time to keep silence, and a time to speak; ⁸a time to love, and a time to hate; a time for war, and a time for peace. ⁹What gain has the worker from his toil? ¹⁰I have seen the business that God has given to the sons of men to be busy with. ¹¹He has made everything beautiful in its time; also he has put eternity into man's mind, yet so that he cannot find out what God has done from the beginning to the end. ¹²I know that there is nothing better for them than to be happy and enjoy themselves as long as they live; ¹³also that it is God's gift to man that every one should eat and drink and take pleasure in all his toil. ¹⁴I know that whatever God does endures for ever; nothing can be added to it, nor anything taken from it; God has made it so, in order that men should fear before him. ¹⁵That which is, already has been; that which is to be, already has been; and God seeks what has been driven away.

¹⁶Moreover I saw under the sun that in the place of justice, even there was wickedness, and in the place of righteousness, even there was wickedness. ¹⁷I said in my heart, God will judge the righteous and the wicked, for he has appointed a time for every matter, and for every work. ¹⁸I said in my heart with regard to the sons of men that God is testing them to show them that they are but beasts. ¹⁹For the fate of the sons of men and the fate of beasts is the same; as one dies, so dies the other. They all have the same breath, and man has no advantage over the beasts; for all is vanity. ²⁰All go to one place; all are from the dust, and all turn to dust again. ²¹Who knows whether the spirit of man goes upward and the spirit of the beast goes down to the earth? ²²So I saw that there is nothing better than that a man should enjoy his work, for that is his lot; who can bring him to see what will be after him?

3.1–15: Man can neither understand nor change the predetermined pattern of his life. Everything happens at the time fixed for it. **11:** Perhaps instead of *eternity* it would be better to translate "obscurity," taking the Hebrew word from a root meaning "conceal." This fits the context. **15:** *Seeks what has been driven away,* causes the past to be repeated.

3.16–4.3: Possible explanations of prevalent evil: (a) God decrees both good and evil, or (b) men are animals and moral distinctions are an illusion. Life is an evil to those who suffer. **16:** *Place,* law court or temple. **18:** *Testing,* literally, "polishing." **19:** *Vanity,* "transience," thus revealing man's insignificance. **21:** Man must be agnostic, for there is no proof of survival; his only good is to enjoy life while he can.

Ecclesiastes 3, from **OXFORD ANNOTATED BIBLE**

What sort of men ought we to be governed by in the coming years? With the high cost of politics and image-making, it is plain that only the very wealthy or those allied with the very wealthy can afford the top prizes. And among the rich, only those who are able to please the people on television are Presidential. With the decline of the religions, the moral sense has become confused, to say the least, and intellectual or political commitments that go beyond the merely expedient are regarded with cheerful contempt not only by the great operators themselves but also by their admirers and, perhaps, by the electorate itself. Also, to be fair, politicians working within a system like ours can never be much more than what the system will allow. Hypocrisy and self-deception are the traditional characteristics of the middle class in any place and time, and the United States today is the paradigmatic middle-class society. Therefore we can hardly blame our political gamesmen for being, literally, representative. Any public man has every right to try and trick us, not only for his own good but, if he is honorable, for ours as well. However, if he himself is not aware of what he is doing or to what end he is playing the game, then to entrust him with the first magistracy of what may be the last empire on earth is to endanger us all. One does not necessarily demand of our leaders passion (Hitler supplied the age with quite enough for this century) or reforming zeal (Mao Tse-tung is incomparable), but one does insist that they possess a sense of community larger than simply personal power for its own sake, being first because it's fun.

Gore Vidal, from "**THE HOLY FAMILY**"

B. Induction

1. Here are a number of inductive arguments. With each, comment on whether the argument is correct or not, giving reasons and naming any fallacies involved:

a. Of course, we have a very fine student body. One of our seniors won a Rhodes Scholarship this year, and we have several honors societies.

b. Undoubtedly the Republican candidate will get the nomination. She's the best qualified and we know that because she said so in her speech. Furthermore, the Republicans are the stronger party this year.

c. You eat the flesh of cows and lambs, don't you? Then don't complain about me because I go hunting.

d. The driver was drunk. I sat next to him at the bar and he had three double bourbons before staggering out to his car with a six-pack. Then later I saw him drinking beer while he drove. At one point, he even threw an empty out of the window.

e. It's insane to think that a small group of people can have any effect on government policy. If we continue to protest, we'll be singled out and carefully eliminated. I know. I've seen what governments can do when they want to.

f. "It's my party and I'll cry if I want to."

g. I don't see how anyone can claim that God really exists since we have no scientific proof.

h. When a famous scientist tells me how the second law of thermodynamics works, I believe him. When a famous author tells me that Shakespeare is our greatest writer, I believe him, too. So when the president tells me that my country wants me to save lots of money, I think it's my reasonable duty to do so. After all, if the president can't be trusted, who can?

i. I know that our football team has not scored a win in five years, but surely it's unfair to disband it when no other school is going to pick up the scholarships for players from a losing team.

j. It is written that thou shalt not covet thy neighbor's wife. Well, my neighbor Frank died last year of a heart attack and I've been seeing a lot of his widow Louise. In fact, we're getting married soon. So I guess that commandment is no longer valid.

k. There is no evidence that the fee raise was decided by the chancellor alone. The athletics' director and the head of the research institute had to have something to do with it, because everyone knows they always want more money in order to siphon off funds to visibly "prestige" causes at the university.

l. The city should definitely fund the new birth-control clinic in the downtown area. There is such a great need for these clinics since many unwanted and illegitimate children are born each year.

m. When Lena got bad tennis elbow, we took her to three doctors who treated her with various support devices. They seemed to work for a while, but then someone told us about this Australian tennis champion who had been cured by soaking in mineral springs in the Rockies. So we took her there and she recovered perfectly after about two weeks.

n. Cruelty to animals is not confined to streets and homes. It goes on in every science laboratory, too.

o. If a, b, c, d, e, and f all have properties p and q, and a, b, c, and d all have property r, and e has property s, then f probably has property r and s, too.

p. Germany lost the First and Second World Wars, so if she goes to war again, she is bound to do badly. We should cultivate other allies in Europe.

q. I have asked my colleagues this question over and over again, and I've yet to hear a reasonable answer: When will the Democrats give up their losing ways in Congress? Never, I say, so long as we refuse to develop a sound economic theory.

r. Cancer research has become the great pioneering enterprise of our day, more so perhaps than space exploration. It is the only hope we have to beat the dread disease, so please give as much as you can to the cancer research fund of your choice.

s. My favorite ice skater is Mary Smith. She has won the world championship twice in a row now, and she said on television the other day that she managed to keep fit on "No-eat" diet candy and little else. So I'm going on the Mary Smith graceful fitness plan, and you should, too.

t. How much longer do we have to spend on this problem? Consider how many people could possibly have taken the money. Only Brown, Jones, and Smith are known to have gone into the locker room. Jones and Smith couldn't have done it because they are both wealthy, which leaves Brown. Let's just confront him with it now.

u. Accept our generous offer of a research grant, and then we won't support your competitors.

v. In 1980, Murdoch produced a four-cylinder sports car called the Mirage. The car had an 1800 cc engine, steel-belted radials, a five-speed transmission, and no air conditioning. It got 16 miles to the gallon in town. In 1981, the car got 18 miles to the gallon with some engine refinements, and in 1982, 20 miles to the gallon by reducing the weight of the body. I understand the 1983 model will increase the number of cylinders and add air conditioning, but that the mileage will be even better than in 1982. With a track record like Murdoch's, how can that not be the case?

w. All you ladies out there will love "Lye-a-wile," the crafty new washing powder from Myrtle Industries. Now washing is truly relaxing for it takes only one teaspoon per washing load in your machine to remove all—yes, *all*—stains from your family's clothes in less than four minutes!

x. We can't avoid losing all the rest of the matches in the women's basketball season. Three of the top players are out with injuries, and the remainder of our matches are away games. So we won't even have the advantages of a home court.

y. The fruit trees in my garden have all given bumper crops in the last two years: big, juicy apples, plums, peaches, and pears. I'm sure they'll all produce as well again this year.

2. Review the section in this chapter on "Checking Extended Arguments", read each of the following excerpts, and

a. Outline the main kinds of argument used, identifying each kind.

b. Test for the validity and correctness of the overall argument.

c. Comment on the effectiveness of the claim. If it's relevant, explain how you can improve on it.

Poverty should be defined in terms of those who are denied the minimal levels of health, housing, food, and education that our present stage of scientific knowledge specifies as necessary for life as it is now lived in the United States.

Poverty should be defined psychologically in terms of those whose place in the society is such that they are internal exiles who, almost inevitably, develop attitudes of defeat and pessimism and who are therefore excluded from taking advantage of new opportunities.

Poverty should be defined absolutely, in terms of what man and society could be. As long as America is less than its potential, the nation as a whole is impoverished by that fact. As long as there is the other America, we are, all of us, poorer because of it.

Michael Harrington, from **THE OTHER AMERICA**

The Trivialization of Personal Relations. Bertrand Russell once predicted that the socialization of reproduction—the supersession of the family by the state—would "make sex love itself more trivial," encourage "a certain triviality in all personal relations," and "make it far more difficult to take an interest in anything after one's own death." At first glance, recent developments appear to have refuted the first part of this prediction. Americans today invest personal relations, particularly the relations between men and women, with undiminished emotional importance. The decline of childrearing as a major preoccupation has freed sex from its bondage to procreation and made it possible for people to value erotic life for its own sake. As the family shrinks to the marital unit, it can be argued that men and women respond more readily to each other's emotional needs, instead of living vicariously through their offspring. The marriage contract having lost its binding character, couples now find it possible, according to many observers, to ground sexual relations in something more solid than legal compulsion. In short, the growing determination to live for the moment, whatever it may have done to the relations between parents and children, appears to have established the preconditions of a new intimacy between men and women.

This appearance is an illusion. The cult of intimacy conceals a growing despair of finding it. Personal relations crumble under the emotional weight with which they are burdened. The inability "to take an interest in anything after one's own death," which gives such urgency to the pursuit of close personal encounters in the present, makes intimacy more elusive than ever. The same developments that have weakened the tie between parents and children have also undermined relations between men and women. Indeed the deterioration of marriage contributes in its own right to the deterioration of care for the young.

This last point is so obvious that only a strenuous propaganda on behalf of "open marriage" and "creative divorce" prevents us from grasping it. It is clear, for example, that the growing incidence of divorce, together with the ever-present possibility that any given marriage will end in collapse, adds to the instability of family life and deprives the child of a measure of emotional security. Enlightened opinion diverts attention from this general fact by insisting that in specific cases, parents may do more harm to their children by holding a marriage together than by dissolving it. It is true that many couples preserve their marriage, in one form or another, at the expense of the child. Sometimes they embark on a life full of distractions that shield them against daily emotional involvements with their offspring. Sometimes one parent acquiesces in the neurosis of the other (as in the family configuration that produces so many schizophrenic patients) for fear of disturbing the precarious peace of the household. More often the husband abandons his children to the wife whose company he finds unbearable, and the wife smothers the children with incessant yet perfunctory attentions. This particular solution to the problem of marital strain has become so common that the absence of the father impresses many observers as the most striking fact about the contemporary family. Under these conditions, a divorce in which the mother retains custody of her children merely ratifies the existing state of affairs—the effective emotional desertion of his family by the father. But the reflection that divorce

445

often does no more damage to children than marriage itself hardly inspires rejoicing.

Christopher Lasch, from THE CULTURE OF NARCISSISM

When one has lived for quite a long time in a particular civilization and has often tried to discover what its origins were and along what path it has developed, one sometimes also feels tempted to take a glance in the other direction and to ask what further fate lies before it and what transformations it is destined to undergo. But one soon finds that the value of such an enquiry is diminished from the outset by several factors, above all, because there are only a few people who can survey human activity in its full compass. Most people have been obliged to restrict themselves to a single, or a few, fields of it. But the less a man knows about the past and the present the more insecure must prove to be his judgement of the future. And there is the further difficulty that precisely in a judgement of this kind the subjective expectations of the individual play a part which it is difficult to assess; and these turn out to be dependent on purely personal factors in his own experience, on the greater or lesser optimism of his attitude to life, as it has been dictated for him by his temperament or by his success or failure. Finally, the curious fact makes itself felt that in general people experience their present naïvely, as it were, without being able to form an estimate of its contents; they have first to put themselves at a distance from it—the present, that is to say, must have become the past—before it can yield points of vantage from which to judge the future.

Thus anyone who gives way to the temptation to deliver an opinion on the probable future of our civilization will do well to remind himself of the difficulties I have just pointed out, as well as of the uncertainty that attaches quite generally to any prophecy. It follows from this, so far as I am concerned, that I shall make a hasty retreat before a task that is too great, and shall promptly seek out the small tract of territory which has claimed my attention hitherto, as soon as I have determined its position in the general scheme of things.

Sigmund Freud, from THE FUTURE OF AN ILLUSION

3. Read the following extract closely. It is about a well-known example of nonvoluntary passive euthanasia, a mercy killing in which the patient does not ask to die. Offer your arguments for or against allowing hopeless patients to be removed from medical support equipment if the family requests it. Identify the *kinds* of argument you are offering.

There have been only two occasions on which *doctors* have been tried for mercy killing in this country. In New Hampshire in 1950, Dr. Herman

Sander gave a patient four intravenous injections of air and then noted on the patient's chart that he had done so. The patient, who had terminal cancer, had asked to be put out of her misery. At the trial, the defense claimed that the patient was already dead at the time of the injections—which was a bit strange, since if the woman was already dead why were the injections given? Anyway, the jury acquitted Dr. Sander. The next such trial of a physician, and the only other one in the United States to date, occurred twenty-four years later in New York. Dr. Vincent Montemareno was charged with giving a lethal injection of potassium chloride to a patient with terminal cancer. At first the prosecutor announced that the case would be tried as a case of mercy killing; Dr. Montemareno, he said, had killed the patient to put her out of misery. But by the time the trial opened, the prosecutor had changed his mind and claimed that the doctor had murdered the patient for his own convenience, so that he would not have to return to the hospital later in the evening. At the conclusion of the trial the jury promptly voted to acquit.

But whatever juries may or may not do, active euthanasia is clearly against the law. The legal status of passive euthanasia is more uncertain. In practice, doctors do allow hopeless patients to die, and as we have seen, the American Medical Association officially endorses this policy when the patient or his family requests it and when "extraordinary" means would be required to keep the patient alive. The legal status of such actions (or nonactions) is uncertain because, although there are laws against "negligent homicide" under which criminal charges could be brought, no such charges have been brought so far. Here district attorneys, and not juries, have exercised their discretion and have not pressed the issue.

It makes an important difference from a legal point of view whether a case of passive euthanasia is voluntary or nonvoluntary. Any patient—except one who has been declared legally "incompetent" to withhold consent—always has the right to refuse medical treatment. By refusing treatment, a patient can bring about his or her own death and the doctor cannot be convicted for "letting the person die." It is *nonvoluntary* passive euthanasia, in which the patient does not request to be allowed to die, that is legally uncertain.

The Case of Karen Ann Quinlan

There has been one famous case in which the question of nonvoluntary passive euthanasia was put before the courts. In April 1975, a 21-year-old woman named Karen Ann Quinlan, for reasons that were never made clear, ceased breathing for at least two fifteen-minute periods. As a result, she suffered severe brain damage, and, in the words of the attending physicians, was reduced to "a chronic persistent vegetative state" in which she "no longer had any cognitive function." Accepting the doctors' judgment that there was no hope of recovery, her parents sought permission from the courts to disconnect the respirator that was keeping her alive in the intensive-care unit of a New Jersey hospital. The Quinlans are Roman Catholics, and they made this request only after consulting with their priest, who assured them that there would be no moral or religious objection if Karen were allowed to die.

Various medical experts testified in support of the Quinlans's request. One doctor described what he called the concept of "judicious neglect," under which a physician will say: "Don't treat this patient anymore . . . It does not serve either the patient, the family, or society in any meaningful way to continue treatment with this patient." This witness also explained the use of the initials 'DNR'—"Do Not Resuscitate"—by which doctors instruct hospital staff to permit death. He said:

> No physician that I know personally is going to try and resuscitate a man riddled with cancer and in agony and he stops breathing. They are not going to put him on a respirator . . . I think that would be the height of misuse of technology.

The trial court, and then the Supreme Court of New Jersey, agreed that the respirator could be removed and Karen Quinlan allowed to die in peace. The respirator was disconnected. However, the nuns in charge of her care in the Catholic hospital opposed this decision, and anticipating it, had begun to wean Karen from the respirator so that by the time it was disconnected she could remain alive without it. (Reviewing these events, one prominent Catholic scholar commented angrily, "Some nuns always were holier than the church.") So Karen did not die; and at this writing she remains in her "persistent vegetative state," emaciated and with deformed limbs and with no hope of ever awakening, but still alive in the biological sense.

It is anticipated that the Quinlan decision will set a precedent for future cases, and that the legal right to terminate treatment in such circumstances will become established. If so, then the law will not have been particularly innovative; it will only have caught up, somewhat belatedly, with medical practice, public opinion, and the best thought of the day concerning passive euthanasia. The question that will then remain is: What about *active* euthanasia? Should *it* be legalized, too?

James Rachels, from **EUTHANASIA**

Readings

Ellen Goodman **ONCE VERBOTEN, NOW CHIC**

"What were these jocks for Jockey doing—aside from earning a lifetime supply of undies? What were they doing wearing hockey gloves and blue-denim bikinis in front of millions of Americans?"

Martin Luther King from **LETTER FROM A BIRMINGHAM JAIL**

"Injustice must be exposed, with all the tension its exposure creates, to the light of human conscience and the air of national opinion before it can be cured."

Florence King **THE NICENESS FACTOR**

"The aloof warmth that makes life so pleasant in socially confident countries is not available to Americans, so we are forced to leap feet-first into instant cloying intimacy whether we like it or not."

ONCE VERBOTEN, NOW CHIC

Ellen Goodman

The whole thing happened in one of those two-story planes they built to make you forget that you're five miles up in the air. I had just settled into a chair and opened a magazine when who should appear but JoJo White, standing half-naked in his little white cotton underpants with a towel wrapped around his neck.

Now, let me explain. I am not the sort of person who even fantasizes about encountering strange men in their underwear on planes, trains, etc. The one time I was sent to interview a houseful of nudists, I broke the *Guinness Book of Records* record for maintaining eye contact. I leave the rest to Erica Jong, who has a less conventional fear of flying than I do.

But Jo Jo was not alone. He was to the right of Denis Potvin and above Pete Rose, happily occupying a page in the middle of a respectable national news-weekly which was not called *Viva.* In short, there were eight male athletes posing in their little nothings for a Jockey ad over the cut-line that read: "Take Away Their Uniforms and Who Are They?"

Well, it seems that Ken Anderson is a Fun Top and Jim Hart is a Slim Guy Boxer. The only one who was fit to be seen in public was Jamaal Wilkes, who looked as if he were merely wearing a uniform of a different color. As for Jim Palmer's teeny-weeny green print bikini, his "Skants" were a scandal. Is it possible that he was not raised under the Eleventh Commandment: Thou Shalt Not Go Out of the House in Unseemly Undergarments Lest Thou Get in an Accident.

What were these jocks for Jockey doing—aside from earning a lifetime supply of undies? What were they doing wearing hockey gloves and blue-denim bikinis in front of millions of Americans?

They were being paid to convince the rest of the male population that it's OK to buy items they wouldn't have been caught dead in at fifteen. At that age, the average American male already had a conditioned response to anything that looked fancy or sexy, or smelled good. That response was to the single word imprinted in the playgrounds of their minds: *sissy.*

At the mere sound of sibilant *s,* strong men pulled their bodies into gray flannel like terrified turtles, shaved their heads to within an inch of their lives and learned how to remove each other's teeth with a single blow.

But over the past handful of years, men have been urged by women and assorted merchants to adopt a variety of products that were once *verboten.* The more questionable the origin of the product, the more they were sold as maler-than-male.

Pocketbooks were not, gasp, pocketbooks, but tote bags and carry-alls designed to look like saddle bags for the Marlboro Man's horse, or tackle boxes for the fisherman. Men wrote articles to each other about how to carry them—carefully—in a distinctively male over-the-shoulder fashion, as opposed to a female over-the-shoulder fashion.

It was obvious that if you wanted to sell men anything even vaguely neuter, you had to inject it with visual and verbal testosterone. Jewelry, for instance, could be sold either in the garrote-chain style or as medallions heavy enough to double as a mace. Rings were popular in the brass-knuckle fashion; bracelets that looked like recycled handcuffs were also all right.

Perfume—forgive me—Male Cologne, was repackaged and rebaptized. It became things like promise-him-anything-but-give-him—Hai Karate. And then came Macho, a perfume in a bottle the shape of which will never appear in this family newspaper.

But nothing has worked quite as well in the fight against sissy stuff as the jock. No one kicks sand in the face of a superstar. Dave Kopay's efforts notwithstanding, an athletic endorsement is as effective in fighting the old conditioned response as an Anita Bryant seal of approval.

Joe Namath sold pantyhose before he turned brute, or should I say, Brut. Pete Rose took to Aqua Velva before he stripped down to his Metre Briefs. (From the look of him in the briefs, I suspect he was drinking the Aqua Velva when he signed the modeling contract.)

The more things change in male décor, the more they stay the same in the ads. The more androgynous the product, the more macho the role-model. So progress inches forward, or downward, to the Tropez Brief. As a trend-watcher might suggest, it's only a matter of time before we have Doctor Julius Erving, the basketball superstar, selling eye-liner under the brand-name "Sado." In the meantime, I wish JoJo White's mother would cover the poor boy up. It must be cold in a Boeing 747 in just a pair of white briefs and a towel over your shoulder.

1. Is Goodman's purpose to amuse the reader, to reveal immodesty on the part of athletes, or to make a serious statement about how the advertising industry defines masculinity? Explain your answer.

2. Do you think Americans consider male athletes to be more masculine than other men? Why or why not?

3. Consider some of the reasons for which television watchers and magazine readers might be persuaded to buy a product because a famous individual has endorsed it. Do you think products that might not otherwise sell well—like jewelry or cologne for men—are really made successful by such endorsements?

4. Can you think of other products or styles—aside from those mentioned by Goodman—that were once forbidden or held in contempt but are now popular? What accounts for such changes?

from LETTER FROM A BIRMINGHAM JAIL

Martin Luther King

I must confess that over the past few years I have been gravely disappointed with the white moderate. I have almost reached the regrettable conclusion that the Negro's great stumbling block in his stride toward freedom is not the White Citizen's Counciler or the Ku Klux Klanner, but the white moderate, who is more devoted to "order" than to justice; who prefers a negative peace which is the absence of tension to a positive peace which is the presence of justice; who constantly says: "I agree with you in the goal you seek, but I cannot agree with your methods of direct action"; who paternalistically believes he can set the timetable for another man's freedom; who lives by a mythical concept of time and who constantly advises the Negro to wait for a "more convenient season." Shallow understanding from people of good will is more frustrating than absolute misunderstanding from people of ill will. Lukewarm acceptance is much more bewildering than outright rejection.

I had hoped that the white moderate would understand that law and order exist for the purpose of establishing justice and that when they fail in this purpose they become the dangerously structured dams that block the flow of social progress. I had hoped that the white moderate would understand that the present tension in the South is a necessary phase of the transition from an obnoxious negative peace, in which the Negro passively accepted his unjust plight, to a substantive and positive peace, in which all men will respect the dignity and worth of human personality. Actually, we who engage in nonviolent direct action are not the creators of tension. We merely bring to the surface the hidden tension that is already alive. We bring it out in the open, where it can be seen and dealt with. Like a boil that can never be cured so long as it is covered up but must be opened with all its ugliness to the natural medicines of air and light, injustice must be exposed, with all the tension its exposure creates, to the light of human conscience and the air of national opinion before it can be cured.

In your statement you assert that our actions, even though peaceful, must be condemned because they precipitate violence. But is this a logical assertion? Isn't this like condemning a robbed man because his possession of money precipitated the evil act of robbery? Isn't this like condemning Socrates because his unswerving commitment to truth and his philosophical inquiries precipitated the act by the misguided populace in which they made him drink hemlock? Isn't this like condemning Jesus because his unique God-consciousness and never-ceasing devotion to God's will precipitated the evil act of crucifixion? We must come to see that, as the federal courts have consistently affirmed, it is wrong to urge an individual to cease his efforts to gain his basic constitutional rights because the quest may precipitate violence. Society must protect the robbed and punish the robber.

I had also hoped that the white moderate would reject the myth concerning time in relation to the struggle for freedom. I have just received a letter from a white brother in Texas. He writes: "All Christians know that the colored people will receive equal rights eventually, but it is possible that you are in too great a religious hurry. It has taken Christianity almost two thousand years to accomplish what it has. The teachings of Christ take time to come to earth." Such an attitude stems from a tragic misconception of time, from the strangely irrational notion that there is something in the very flow of time that will inevitably cure all ills. Actually, time itself is neutral; it can be used either destructively or constructively. More and more I feel that the people of ill will have used time much more effectively than have the people of good will. We will have to repent in this generation not merely for the hateful words and actions of the bad people but for the appalling silence of the good people. Human progress never rolls in on wheels of inevitability; it comes through the tireless efforts of men willing to be co-workers with God, and without this hard work, time itself becomes an ally of the forces of social stagnation. We must use time creatively, in the knowledge that the time is always ripe to do right. Now is the time to make real the promise of democracy and transform our pending national elegy into a creative psalm of brotherhood. Now is the time to lift our national policy from the quicksand of racial injustice to the solid rock of human dignity.

You speak of our activity in Birmingham as extreme. At first I was rather disappointed that fellow clergymen would see my nonviolent efforts as those of an extremist. I began thinking about the fact that I stand in the middle of two opposing forces in the Negro community. One is a force of complacency, made up in part of Negroes who, as a result of long years of oppression, are so drained of self-respect and a sense of "somebodiness" that they have adjusted to segregation; and in part of a few middle-class Negroes who, because of a degree of academic and economic security and because in some ways they profit by segregation, have become insensitive to the problems of the masses. The other force is one of bitterness and hatred, and it comes perilously close to advocating violence. It is expressed in the various black nationalist groups that are springing up across the nation, the largest and best-known being Elijah Muhammad's Muslim movement. Nourished by the Negro's frustration over the continued existence of racial discrimination, this movement is made up of people who have lost faith in America, who have absolutely repudiated Christianity, and who have concluded that the white man is an incorrigible "devil."

I have tried to stand between these two forces, saying that we need emulate neither the "do-nothingism" of the complacent nor the hatred and despair of the black nationalist. For there is the more excellent way of love and nonviolent protest. I am grateful to God that, through the influence of the Negro church, the way of nonviolence became an integral part of our struggle.

If this philosophy had not emerged, by now many streets of the South would, I am convinced, be flowing with blood. And I am further convinced that if our white brothers dismiss as "rabble-rousers" and "outside agitators" those of us who employ nonviolent direct action, and if they refuse to support our nonviolent efforts, millions of Negroes will, out of frustration and despair, seek solace and security in black-nationalist ideologies—a development that would inevitably lead to a frightening racial nightmare.

Oppressed people cannot remain oppressed forever. The yearning for freedom eventually manifests itself, and that is what has happened to the American Negro. Something within has reminded him of his birthright of freedom, and something without has reminded him that it can be gained. Consciously or unconsciously, he has been caught up by the *Zeitgeist,* and with his black brothers of Africa and his brown and yellow brothers of Asia, South America and the Caribbean, the United States Negro is moving with a sense of great urgency toward the promised land of racial justice. If one recognizes this vital urge that has engulfed the Negro community, one should readily understand why public demonstrations are taking place. The Negro has many pent-up resentments and latent frustrations, and he must release them. So let him march; let him make prayer pilgrimages to the city hall; let him go on freedom rides—and try to understand why he must do so. If his repressed emotions are not released in nonviolent ways, they will seek expression through violence; this is not a threat but a fact of history. So I have not said to my people: "Get rid of your discontent." Rather, I have tried to say that this normal and healthy discontent can be channeled into the creative outlet of nonviolent direct action. And now this approach is being termed extremist.

But though I was initially disappointed at being categorized as an extremist, as I continued to think about the matter I gradually gained a measure of satisfaction from the label. Was not Jesus an extremist for love: "Love your enemies, bless them that curse you, do good to them that hate you, and pray for them which despitefully use you, and persecute you." Was not Amos an extremist for justice: "Let justice roll down like waters and righteousness like an ever-flowing stream." Was not Paul an extremist for the Christian gospel: "I bear in my body the marks of the Lord Jesus." Was not Martin Luther an extremist: "Here I stand; I cannot do otherwise, so help me God." And John Bunyan: "I will stay in jail to the end of my days before I make a butchery of my conscience." And Abraham Lincoln: "This nation cannot survive half slave and half free." And Thomas Jefferson: "We hold these truths to be self-evident, that all men are created equal . . ." So the question is not whether we will be extremists, but what kind of extremists we will be. Will we be extremists for hate or for love? Will we be extremists for the preservation of injustice or for the extension of justice? In that dramatic scene on Calvary's hill three men were crucified. We must never forget that all three were crucified for the same crime—the crime of extremism. Two were extremists for immorality, and thus fell below their environment. The other, Jesus Christ, was an extremist for love, truth and goodness, and thereby rose above his environment. Perhaps the South, the nation and the world are in dire need of creative extremists.

I had hoped that the white moderate would see this need. Perhaps I was too optimistic; perhaps I expected too much. I suppose I should have realized that few members of the oppressor race can understand the deep groans and passionate yearnings of the oppressed race, and still fewer have the vision to see that injustice must be rooted out by strong, persistent and determined action. I am thankful, however, that some of our white brothers in the South have grasped the meaning of this social revolution and committed themselves to it. They are still all too few in quantity, but they are big in quality. Some—such as Ralph McGill, Lillian Smith, Harry Golden, James McBride Dabbs, Ann Braden and Sarah Patton Boyle—have written about our struggle in eloquent and prophetic terms. Others have marched with us down nameless streets of the South. They have languished in filthy, roach-infested jails, suffering the abuse and brutality of policemen who view them as "dirty nigger-lovers." Unlike so many of their moderate brothers and sisters, they have recognized the urgency of the moment and sensed the need for powerful "action" antidotes to combat the disease of segregation.

1. Martin Luther King goes to great pains in this letter to respond carefully to his critics—in this case, eight Alabama clergymen who aired their criticism publicly. Describe the tone of his response in this passage, and then what he thinks of his audience. Give evidence.

2. Think of King's justification of his presence in Birmingham as an extended argument with the following conclusion: "The civil rights demonstrations in Birmingham are morally just." Carefully list all the premises King presents that lead to this conclusion.

3. Explain King's justification for the following: (a) nonviolent direct action; (b) extremism; and (c) not waiting for time to bring about desegregation? Can you find any flaws in his argument?

4. King strongly criticizes white moderates. What is his argument against them? How does he justify it?

5. King's letter is a detailed and vivid combination of clear reasoning based on what he sees to be necessary principles for action *and* an imaginative and passionate appeal to win over the skeptical white, religious moderate.

a. Summarize his argument in no more than three connected syllogisms that you think get at the heart of his reasoning.

b. Explain carefully how the imaginative appeal does or does not enhance King's rationalizing.

THE NICENESS FACTOR

Florence King

America had barely become a country when Alexander Hamilton asked himself: "Am I a fool, a romantic Quixote, or is there a constitutional defect in the American mind?'' There is now. Life in America is like life with the governess in *The Turn of the Screw.* There are some good days, but sooner or later something happens to set things off and we're all in the soup again.

If suicide notes can be said to possess nationality, surely the most American is the one left by historian Wilbur J. Cash: ''I can't stand it anymore, and I don't even know what it is.''

I do. According to the laws of logic, *A* is *A*, a thing cannot be other than itself, contradictions cannot exist, and parallel lines cannot meet. Except in America. The movement of Birnam Wood to Dunsinane is an everyday occurrence in the lumberyard of our national psyche. Contradictions haunt us. After a decade of touchy-feely encounter movements we are supposed to take pride in saying ''I'm a very emotional person,'' yet the public stance we admire most, especially in politicians, is ''grace under pressure.'' Which is right? The Wasp or the Latin ideal? The upper-class cool or the lower-class heat? American status seekers, who used to know exactly what to do, are now stymied.

Someone is always getting briefed or debriefed, but no one knows how to behave. The favorite piece of advice for someone in a tense situation is ''Don't try to be a hero''; then the hostages are sprung and hundreds of editorials announce that at last America has the heroes she has been craving.

We are told that it is wicked to stereotype people; then we are called for jury duty and listen in amazement while the defense eliminates Episcopalians who went to college and the prosecution eliminates Catholics who went to trade school, until there is nobody left except twelve people who are incapable of understanding the case. That's the jury.

If, while waiting to be eliminated, we pass the time by reading a magazine, we can find an article on the joys of fathering back-to-back with a Camel cigarette ''Where a Man Belongs'' ad showing a loner, his duffel bag beside him, frantically pumping his way out of town on a railroad handcar. He's smart to get out while he can; discrimination being prohibited on the grounds of race, color, creed, national origin, sex, sexual orientation, political ideology, and age, smokers have become fair game.

The love-it-or-leave-it set will undoubtedly accuse me of being a communist after reading this. For their information, I am more conservative than all of them put together. I am a royalist; I believe in absolute monarchy and the divine right of kings. I would rather live under a capricious tyrant who says ''Off with their heads!'' than be nibbled to death by a bureaucratic duck.

I have thought several times of emigrating, but the only countries in which I would care to live all have strict six-month quarantine laws, so I can't do it. Like Blaise Pascal, ''the more I see of mankind, the more I prefer my dog.''

The Friendly Misanthropes

I was buying groceries at Gulpmart, the Friendly Store, when a woman slithered up to me at the frozen-food bin and whispered, ''I love you. Pass it on.''

She had heard, she explained, about the chain letters of the Thirties and decided that the Eighties needed a chain of love that would reach across America. "When you say it to a little kid, kiss 'em," she recommended. I modestly declined.

I got in the checkout line where, still shaken, I accidentally gave the clerk a penny instead of a dime.

"Trade you this for a dime!" she chirruped.

I couldn't figure out what on earth she meant for a moment, then I realized that this was her friendly way of telling me I had made a mistake. She was, I remembered, the same clerk who invariably said, "What can I do you for?" instead of "What can I do for you?" because inverted wording is warmer.

I went home and turned on the TV. It was a community-service show. The first guest was a thanatologist who spoke on "How to Live with Death," followed by a psychologist engaged in discovering new minority groups, who recommended that midgets be called "persons of reduced stature."

Then came the public-service announcements. "Is someone you know starving him- or herself? Anorexia nervosa CAN be cured if YOU help."

Followed by a paean to the environment by a paper company, featuring a celestial chorus and the slogan THANK A TREE. A smiling little woman, captioning for the hearing-impaired, was enclosed in a lower-left-hand oval like a hysterical genie in a bottle.

I wait for the day when somebody will suggest that the dead be called "non-viable Americans." It's only a matter of time.

America is the Newfoundland puppy of the world. Our obsession with friendliness began when the first settlers wondered, "Are the natives friendly?" and shortly found themselves looking at stoic Indian faces. The natives were friendly for the most part, at least at first, but they didn't *look* it. Unsmiling faces have struck terror in the American heart ever since.

Ask an American traveler what he thinks of a foreign country and he will reply, "The people are friendly." The one country that he cannot bestow this accolade on is that cradle of xenophobia, France. Americans are scared to death of the French. It is quite possible that the French are responsible for our compulsive Good Guyism around the world. The nastier the French get, the nicer we get. In any case, our dread of hostility is so great that it produces a strange form of treason in the American heart. Our desperation to believe that we are not hated personally makes us relax and grow secure whenever a terrorist with five o'clock shadow says, "It's the American government we hate, not the American people."

There are fewer and fewer foreign countries we can snuggle up to, but there's always Canada. When she rescued six of our hostages, our galumphing appreciation left Canadians reeling in shock. Now Algeria's in for it. Anybody who's nice to us can count on being Hallmarked to death.

Meanwhile, here at home, the hysteria builds. The Los Angeles police chief has urged his officers to adopt "a warm and cuddly approach" toward civilians to improve community relations. Our "friendly" banks are robbed constantly because we reject the notion than an ounce of fear is worth a pound of love; all one has to do to get past the security guard is be a member of the human race. The password is "Hi."

Women continue to get into trouble with strange men because they would rather be dead than aloof. Old people are so afraid of fitting the crotchety stereotype of age that they are suckers for bunco schemes that would fail in any other country. Doctors formerly in general practice are now in "family practice," because it sounds warmer. And, incredibly, when a lad of seventeen hijacked a plane at Seattle-Tacoma Airport last summer, a crew member later stated in all seriousness that the boy was "very cooperative, he's been almost a model hijacker."

Why do we behave this way? Politicians are fond of saying that "our diversity is our strength," but in actual fact we are the only people in the world who can experience culture shock without leaving home. There are so many different kinds of people in America, with so many different boiling points, that we don't know how to fight with each other. The set piece that shapes and contains quarrels in homogeneous countries does not exist here. Frenchmen are experts on the precise gradations of the obligatory *"espèce de,"* and Italians know exactly when to introduce the subject of their mothers' graves. But no American can be sure how or when another American will react, so we zap each other with friendliness to neutralize potentially dangerous situations.

The aloof warmth that makes life so pleasant in socially confident countries is not available to Americans, so we are forced to leap feet-first into instant cloying intimacy whether we like it or not. French charwomen call each other *"madame"*; *"gnädige Frau"* makes old ladies easy to respect; and macho Englishmen long ago learned to express intrasex affection with "my dear Smith." But Americans have nothing to call each other by except first names. There is no way to get a stranger's attention without sounding servile ("ma'am," "sir"), and so, committed as we are to equality at any price, we insult him.

Friendliness is especially necessary to a people who live by the maxim, "the country is full of nuts." The chance victim and the innocent bystander have replaced the plucky newsboy and the whore with the heart of gold as the protagonists of American folklore. The paranoid American has no idea "who's out there," as he puts it; Charles Whitman is up on his tower and all's wrong with the world, so smile your way to safety. If you are cool to someone, he might tell the FBI lies about you, or send an anonymous letter to the IRS because he doesn't like your face, so be nice to everybody. Bridges of understanding are good, but walls of friendliness are better.

A Multitude of Virtues

One night while writing this *cri de coeur*, I decided to rest from my labors and listen to the radio. With a drink in one hand, a cigarette in the other, and listening to Rossini, I tried to forget about America for a little while. But nobody can pull off that kind of coup. The music stopped and a voice thick with concern spoke.

"Lung cancer is an equal opportunity disease."

The announcer launched into a history of cigarette smoking, pointing out that when smoking was considered unladylike, most women did not indulge and therefore did not get lung cancer, leading people to think that it was a man's disease from which women were naturally immune. "But now," he continued happily, "women are catching up."

America, in itself a democratic disease, has become the land of the democratic disease. Our obsession with equality has gone so haywire that we go to pieces when a disease discriminates. Read an article on any disease that is widespread and you will come across The Sentence: "Hepatitis [mononucleosis, herpes, the clap] strikes Americans in all occupations and at all income levels, without regard to sex or race."

American blood is so rich with equality that we have come to hate uniqueness of any kind, even the most noble. By having a Tomb of the Unknowns, we really don't have an Unknown Soldier: more than one destroys the concept. In a fit of nostalgia, a reverent "60 Minutes" feature mourned the demise of the Orient Express without grasping the connection between its demise and our compulsion to level. Princess Dragomiroff needs Drawing Room A, and Drawing Room A needs Princess Dragomiroff.

We even condemn the unique hatred. If you hate, say, gays, it stands to reason that you undoubtedly hate blacks, Jews, Chicanos, Orientals, and Indians. To the American mind, it is worse to hate one than to hate them all.

Feminists cannot understand why the ERA has not been ratified by popular demand, since "polls show that a majority of Americans are for it." What the polls actually show is that most Americans would not dare answer no to any question that contains the word *equality*.

It was only to be expected that the Nobel Prize Sperm Bank should have triggered such Lear-like rage. Particularly upset was Mary McGrory, who suggested that breeding reliable home repairmen would benefit society far more. Her reason?

Workmen do not hear unless you scream at them, like police dogs who only respond to a certain high, piercing whistle. It is only when a certain level of frustration has been reached that he is able to judge the sincerity of the consumer and the persistence of his notion that the work may be done. He may oblige if he is persuaded that apoplexy or a lawsuit is not far away.

She begs the question. The attitudes to which she objects are the result of our enshrinement of equality: if everybody is as good as everybody else, why should a plumber pay attention to a syndicated columnist?

Rien que pour pisser

The paradox of women's rights in any era is that egalitarianism, which admits the issue, is also the chief barrier to its fulfillment. Just as despots are the most enthusiastic patrons of the arts, only an aristocracy is secure and eccentric enough to produce the one kind of woman who can bridge the psychological chasm between the sexes: the socially impeccable bawd.

When Whig doyennes like Lady Melbourne and Lady Oxford traded knee-slappers at the Brighton gaming tables, men and women felt comfortable together. Then along came America, where no woman could be a Lady but where all women could be ladies. The result was the terminally middle-class woman who took up "niceness" as a weapon against the frontier, a means of holding the wilderness at bay and maintaining a semblance of civilization. Confronted by her unflagging niceness, the frontier man came to think of women as his social superiors, an attitude that persists today in the American rapist's battle cry, "You think you're too good for me, huh?"

Our niceness factor prohibits the sophisticated intersexual camaraderie enjoyed by the French countess who explained, *"Rien que pour pisser,"* when she asked her male traveling companion—a stranger—to stop the coach by the roadside. An American man would be horrified by such blithe frankness; under his veneer of trendy liberalism he would classify her as a "dirty girl." Unlike the courtly Frenchman, he would refuse to stop the vehicle and would enjoy the countess's physical discomfort and social discomfiture. He could then tell himself that she wasn't so high and mighty after all; that she was, in fact, no better than he.

At first glance, it would seem that we have solved this problem. The American woman is no longer nice, but it's an unniceness without élan. Instead, she has taken on what Henry James called "a certain vague moral dinginess." The more pronounced it is the greater her chances of getting on the "Donahue" show, where everyone will tell her how brave and liberated she is for doing whatever stomach-turning thing she has done. She can do no wrong.

We save our criticism for men. Countless books and articles contain the sentence, "Men commit over 90 percent of all violent crimes," and go on to list murky statistical evidence of the male's apparently inborn evilness.

It is all an updated version of the Victorian hatred for men's "lower nature" and the corresponding reverence for women's moral superiority. There's only one catch: feminism put an end to woman as a creature of innate purity. Technically the sexes are now equal, or at least equally human. Yet men are still somehow worse.

The frontier is still with us. The sexes in America are engaged, not in a sex war, but in a class war.

America, the Hagridden

Under Jimmy Carter America shed its last semblance of manly dignity and started playing Socrates to the world's Xanthippe. For the first time, open aspersions were cast on the masculinity of an American president, and hence on all American men. Pakistan's president, General Zia, advised Carter to "act like the president of a superpower" the way a man in a bar would tell another to stand up to his wife. Our own commentators took up the cudgels and, it would seem, turned to the listings under *feminine* in Roget to describe the Carter personality. George F. Will used "hysteria," "shrillness," and "frenzy." William Safire produced "unrestrained restraint," "self-flagellating," "unprecedented weakness," "acquiescing," and the ubiquitous "caving in." Jack Anderson used "wavering," "waffling," "rhetorical tsk-tsks," "pusillanimous," "obsequious," "hesitancy," "wishy-washy." Robert E. Thompson used all of the above, but outdid everybody after the election when he called Carter "the Mona Lisa."

Of all the words used in print and on the air, the most frequently heard was "impotent." The Iranian crisis was a crisis of American manhood, when everybody suddenly realized what had happened to masculinity in this country. The defeat of Jimmy Carter was less political than sexual, a revulsion against the feminine principle ascendant comparable to what Lamartine called "the revolution of contempt" that occurred in France in 1848, when the Carter-like Louis Philippe was overthrown.

Louis Philippe called himself the "Citizen King." Abhorring symbols of power, he took down the fleur-de-lys from the Palais Royal and walked through the streets of Paris wearing a plain black suit to prove he was no better than anyone else. There was nothing of the man's man about him; he much preferred domesticity. Says historian Priscilla Robertson: "Louis Philippe was one of those kings who distinguish themselves by being good men, and in the nineteenth century that meant being good to his wife and children."

Everybody hates good men, especially women. They move us to lava flows of bitchiness, which explains Rosalyn Carter's mean mouth. The good man is the one who makes a woman scream, "Do something!" We have gotten rid of the good and timid Carter, but have we gotten rid of the feminine principle ascendant?

America shows no signs of relinquishing its gynecologist's-eye-view of life. The obsession with the family that grips Reagan-style God-and-Country conservatives is a feminine obsession. A true conservative operates on the masculine principle expressed in "I could not love thee, dear, so much, loved I not honour more." That would never play in America, where love conquers all, including the armed services. The pseudo-conservatives are so busy trying to Save the American Family they do not see that it is this same family that is destroying America. It is impossible to escape the word. Networks call themselves "the Channel 9 Family," advertisements tell us that products, when not being made for people, are made for families. Touted as our greatest strength, the American family is actually the ultimate Balkanization of an already Balkanized country, the Bosnia-Herzegovina of the body politic.

We have lost the masculine principle and nobody knows it better than foreign countries; like shrewish wives, they present us with demands for weapons and aid in the form of "shopping lists"—surely the most revealing phrase in use today. In the Sixties, men who claimed to be nonviolent often played rough, but even that is gone now; today's young men prefer the candlelight vigil, the classic response of Mother Machree.

Manhood is expressed in silly ways, such as going out in the cold without a coat. The trek from the White House to Blair House is a favorite of hardy capons. Another way is to let it be known that you go without sleep. Diplomatic or union negotiations invariably feature an announcement that everyone involved "went twenty-five hours without sleep."

Try as we might to deny it, men *do* have a need to live dangerously. Homosexuality has become the new French Foreign Legion, the only means men have of escaping the femininity of American life. In an era of women's sexual rights, it is also the only way left to have a normal male orgasm—i.e., a quick one.

But the only completely masculine stance left to American men is a tragic and irreversible one, open to the man who chooses "to advocate and condone violence"—against himself. Gary Gilmore and Jesse Bishop both demanded and got execution for their crimes. Both died bravely: Gilmore with stoicism and Bishop with jauntiness—classic male responses to danger now condemned as sexist. Beau Geste is alive and well—but not for long—on Death Row.

1. What are the main kinds of argument Florence King uses? Are they persuasive?

2. "Why do we behave in this way?" How does King answer her own question?

3. What does King mean by saying that America "has become the land of democratic disease"? What are the symptoms of the disease?

4. Can you find any fallacies in King's argument?

5. What specifically are King's arguments against feminism, the family, and "the feminine principle ascendant"? Do you agree with her? Explain why if you do, and argue back if you don't.

Writing

Persuasively

Knowing how you are persuaded—how writers appeal to your reason, values, emotions, beliefs, and identity themes—is an important step to knowing how you too can be a persuasive writer. That which influences you may very well influence others. As we know from interpreting persuasive writing, the art of persuasion involves

The development of a clear, logical argument

An appeal to a reader

A style that carries a message forcefully

We have already discussed the business of writing persuasively in earlier chapters on the writing process. The basic problem-solving position paper outlined in Chapter 3 has its own built-in persuasive appeal. The reader finds the subject treated from various perspectives: defined in isolation, in contexts, and as a problem or issue. Thus the subject is opened up for discussion and a solution is proposed by resolving opposing viewpoints within each perspective. The art of persuasion begins here, with the development of a clear logical argument that illuminates the subject from more than one point of view.

We shall discuss alternative patterns for organizing an essay in this chapter, patterns that enlarge upon the problem-solution format. The groundwork for this has been laid in the last chapter:

- Writing based on deduction: from evidence to a necessary claim

- Writing based on induction: from evidence to a probable claim
  from definition to claim
  from authority to claim
  from comparison to claim
  from analogy to claim
  from cause to effect
  from effect to cause

A logical argument based on any one of these patterns, however, is not always sufficient to persuade a reader of the value of your position. The writer's presentation of an opinion—its tone and style—plays an important part too. The objective weight of the message is only part of the image building. Attitudes, as Chapter 9 points out, are not changed simply by an appeal to reason. As a writer, you have to take the *whole reader* into account: by appealing to reason, values, opinions, and emotions the reader can have in common with you. Furthermore, the reader must be enticed into the text and find room to move there: to have identity themes reasonably provoked or reinforced by a credible writer. In other words, there is a presentation of the writer and a treatment of the reader in persuasive writing that is common to all kinds of argumentative essays, and that we must examine first.

The Writer's Credibility

In persuasive writing, our feelings often run high on a topic—sometimes too high to allow us to present a lucid, well-argued position. Other times we have no real feelings at all on a topic and are merely going through the motions of presenting an "argument." In both cases, it is important that you not start writing until after you have gone through the initial stages of the writing process: finding a topic, opening up the topic, limiting the topic, and, by playing off opposites, reaching a conclusion about the topic. Only then will too strong or weak feelings be remedied. The question then becomes: *how do you present your case?*

Your basic aim is to present yourself as a writer with as much credibility as possible. You know what kind of writing impresses you: writing in which the writer is talking to *you* and doing so in a way that leads you to trust the writer. So your credibility depends above all on your developing a trustworthy voice, your own voice. Your credibility does not emerge from either showing off or being self-effacing, from refusing to listen to other points of view, or from listing your credentials. It arises from your handling of the topic: your motives and competences, and your values as implied by your relationship to the topic.

There are some general points to remember, and perhaps the most important is that credibility arises from your *being in control of your material.* Let it be known that you know what you want to say and can express it in a qualified and committed tone.

■ You want to appear *rational,* but not overrational. A reasoned justification lies in the direct presentation of the argument, not in long-winded defenses or uncertain repetitions.

■ You might appear genuinely *angry* and *ironic,* but beware of blind rage and sarcasm, for sarcasm is not irony. The persuasive essay is not a slap in the reader's face but an attempt to change attitudes.

■ You want to *express ideas* and show the implications of your topic. You are not mouthing slogans or glibly passing judgments. To the extent that you show a dynamic relationship between facts, you will entice a reader in.

■ You want to *discuss and dramatize a topic,* not merely repeat points about it. The topic is not a list of qualities but, again, a whole network of facts.

■ You want to reveal a genuine, substantiated *opinion,* not a bias. In other words, your point of view must be clear and justified. Your tone should be committed but qualified.

■ You want to show that you have listened well and can understand an opponent's argument, or can think at least of what the arguments of your potential opposition might be.

Read the following passage and think about the writer's credibility as you do so:

And, of course, that raises a very big question. If a good God made the world why has it gone wrong? And for many years I simply wouldn't listen to the Christian answers to this question, because I kept on feeling "whatever you say, and however clever your arguments are, isn't it much simpler and easier to say that the world was *not* made by any intelligent power? Aren't all your arguments simply a complicated attempt to avoid the obvious?" But then that threw me back into those difficulties about atheism which I spoke of a moment ago. And soon I saw another difficulty.

My argument against God was that the universe seemed so cruel and unjust. But how had I got this idea of *just* and *unjust?* A man doesn't call a line crooked unless he has some idea of a straight line. What was I comparing this universe with when I called it unjust? If the whole show was bad and senseless from A to Z, so to speak, why did I, who was supposed to be part of the show, find myself in such violent reaction against it? A man feels wet when he falls into water, because man isn't a water animal: a fish wouldn't feel wet. Of course I could have given up my idea of justice by saying it was nothing but a private idea of my own. But if I did that then my argument against God collapsed too— for the argument depended on saying that the world was really unjust, not that it just didn't happen to please my private fancies. Thus in the very act of trying to prove that God didn't exist—in other words, that the whole of reality was senseless—I found I was forced to assume that one part of reality—namely my idea of justice—was full of sense. Consequently atheism turns out to be too simple. If the whole universe has no meaning, we should never have found out that it has no meaning: just as if there were no light in the universe and therefore no creatures with eyes we should never know it was dark. *Dark* would be a word without meaning.

Very well then, atheism is too simple. And I'll tell you another view that is also too simple. It's the view I call Christianity-and-water, the view that just says there's a good God in Heaven and everything is all right—leaving out all the difficult and terrible doctrines about sin and hell and the devil, and the redemption. Both these are boys' philosophies.

It is no good asking for a simple religion. After all, real things *aren't* simple.

They *look* simple, but they're not. The table I'm sitting at looks simple: but ask a scientist to tell you what it's really made of—all about the atoms and how the light waves rebound from them and hit my eye and what they do to the optic nerve and what it does to my brain—and, of course, you find that what we call "seeing a table" lands you in mysteries and complications which you can hardly get to the end of. A child, saying a child's prayer, looks simple. And if you're content to stop here, well and good. But if you're not—and the modern world usually isn't—if you want to go on and ask what's really happening—then you must be prepared for something difficult. If we ask for something more than simplicity, it's silly then to complain that the something more isn't simple. Another thing I've noticed about reality is that, besides being difficult, it's odd: it isn't neat, it isn't what you expect. I mean, when you've grasped that the earth and the other planets all go round the sun, you'd naturally expect that all the planets were made to match—all at equal distances from each other, say, or distances that regularly increased, or all the same size, or else getting bigger or smaller as you go further from the sun. In fact, you find no rhyme or reason (that we can see) about either the sizes or the distances; and some of them have one moon, one has four, one has two, some have none, and one has a ring.

Reality, in fact, is always something you couldn't have guessed. That's one of the reasons I believe Christianity. It's a religion you couldn't have guessed. If it offered us just the kind of universe we'd always expected, I'd feel we were making it up. But, in fact, it's not the sort of thing anyone would have made up. It has just the queer twist about it that real things have. So let's leave behind all these boys' philosophies—these over-simple answers. The problem isn't simple and the answer isn't going to be simple either.

C. S. Lewis, from **CASE FOR CHRISTIANITY**

Now it does not matter whether you believe in God or not or whether you are a Christian or not—those are not the issues here. The question is: is Lewis convincing? Do you listen to Lewis because he sounds credible? He is at least low-keyed and rational. Unlike so many writers on religion, he does not *rationalize* belief but works via a series of problems and solutions. He points out that a simple religion or a simple opposition to religion will not work. There is no defensiveness in his position. He implies that the enemy to belief lies in part within each of us, in our natural skepticism. So he presents the argument against belief but does so with care, for atheism and skepticism are not necessarily the same thing. Atheism runs into a problem if it claims that the world is unjust and meaningless because even meaninglessness has a meaning: "If the whole universe has no meaning, we should never have found out that it has no meaning."

Not only does Lewis present a strong but quietly stated rational appeal that takes account of the opposite view, but he seems confident in his opinions. He is thinking his way through his argument and not stumbling about. He offers no slogans or strident claims, nor does he glibly pass judgment or pretend to be in possession of the whole truth. Religious belief cannot be simple because it has to contend with a whole network of facts, some of which are unpredictable in their function: like the nature of God as good and the presence of so much unhappiness on earth.

Lewis discusses his topic; he does not simply preach. He wants to reveal a genuine opinion, not a formulated bias. There is no doubt that his tone is committed, but it allows qualification, the major qualification being that religion is not easy. So credibility is built up slowly, modestly, competently, and rationally, with a strong sense of conveying values the writer does believe in. The writer's motive here is not simply to proselytize, but to explain reasonably and persuasively.

Handling Controversy

When you are writing on a topic that is controversial, refuting another argument, or providing a point of view that is not easy to accept, what (beyond ensuring your own credibility) can you do to be persuasive?

First, recognize that whatever you write about a controversial topic is bound to create some conflict between you and the reader, or between readers. But if you follow the writing process outlined in Chapter 3, you will see that the conflict can be dispersed somewhat by your *analysis* of the topic. The reader does not encounter blunt statements but a sense of the complexity of the issue. Assuring your reader that a topic is not being taken lightly by you, that it is seen to exist in relationship to other facts, and that it is worthy of analysis will have a persuasive effect.

Your immediate interest in dealing with a controversial topic is to *avoid conflict,* but this does not mean that you offer immediate compromises. Instead you engage the opposition. When you locate opposing interpretations as you brainstorm your topic, you are locating the arguments that might be made against you. So there is no excuse in a persuasive essay for not anticipating what the opposition might be. Remember the following:

■ State both sides of the question clearly.

■ Show you understand the opposition's argument.

■ Discuss the strengths as well as the weaknesses of the other side.

■ Account for your own weaknesses as well as strengths.

■ Compare opposing interpretations and settle on as many common interests as possible. Aim for *cooperation.*

■ Analyze a potentially hostile or skeptical audience carefully for age, sex, group membership, level of education, level of income, and religious and political affiliations. It is not always possible to do this in detail, of course, but when it is relevant—that is, when you are speaking to a specific audience—your avoidance of unnecessary conflict sometimes depends on your understanding of your opposition's values and beliefs.

■ Explain carefully the *contexts* in which the opposite arguments exist. No argument takes place in a vacuum, and you want to uncover the common influences and even the common fate of your argument and your opponent's. Ask yourself what both your arguments have in common in terms of influence. Does the same set of conditions create both your arguments? You may find that you have a common enemy. You may, for example, be arguing for a day care center in your university and your opponent may want the funds to be used for library books. Both are worthy causes and your common enemy may be an administration official who insists that neither is important and that a new dean of janitorial affairs is needed. Maybe you should join your rival.

■ Try to get your reader to identify with your position by making a careful, reasoned explanation and analysis of the problem underlying the argument—not just your opinion of it.

■ Avoid biased language, name calling, or stacking the cards against your opponent. Build up your credibility by expressing a genuine opinion in a committed but rational argument.

■ Appeal to reason and to common values, justifying your decision as one that is based on a valid code of ethics which your opponent might share. Remember that no argument is without ethical implications.

Consider C. S. Lewis's argument in light of the above. He has stated the atheist position—it was once his own, he says—and he shows he understands the opposition's argument. Of course, in this short section from the whole essay, it is not clear what his answer will be. But the extract does show that he handles the strengths and weaknesses of the other side, though admittedly with an emphasis on its weaknesses. Logically, Lewis points out, it does not follow that because the world is unjust, God cannot exist. For one thing, the fact that the world is unjust does not mean that the concept of justness does not exist. It does, and the world is not entirely meaningless. This does not, of course, necessarily prove that God *does* exist, but it does tend to disprove that particular atheistic argument.

Indeed, Lewis is being rather selective. This is not the only atheistic argument, but it is a common version. Lewis has not disproved, for example, the argument that a just God would at least intervene in the world, but then he may feel that he does not have to do this on the grounds that this argument concerns itself with what God *is like,* not whether God exists or not. The arguments for and against God's existence can go on endlessly. Considering the logic of God's existence is one of the most ancient and mythic of enterprises, carried out by the secular and the religious alike. It is a provoking, challenging question, and Lewis indicates he has been provoked by it. He cleverly turns the atheist argument into his own weakness as well as his opponent's strength, but he manages to do that without being patronizing.

There is evidence that Lewis is concerned about cooperation. He rejects the "good God in heaven" notion as too simple. Then he carefully explains the *common context* of both his own argument and the atheist's. This context falls under the vexing but nonetheless important heading of "the nature of reality." Reality, says Lewis, is anything but simple. Furthermore, reality is odd, it "is always something you couldn't have guessed," and having made that point, which is not difficult to do, he then draws a direct analogy with Christianity as "odd." Again, he has not accounted for all the other things we can say about reality, especially that it is not *merely* difficult and odd, but that it does yield understanding when analyzed. The scientists might make something more of this. But probably no scientist is going to disprove the popular belief that truth is stranger than fiction and that no amount of understanding will disturb our sense of wonder and awe at the way the world works. This is what Lewis is referring to.

The point is that Lewis tries to induce his reader to identify with a common problem: the difficulty of comprehending reality and the danger of simple solutions. He does not name call or stack the cards, but appeals to reason and common values. Whatever one's religious persuasion—and especially if you have no persuasion at all, for the issue here is broadly philosophical—he insists that the matter is worth discussing. He shows this with some credibility by quietly describing his own mental gymnastics in trying to deal with the question.

Using Syllogistic Arguments

There are several ways in which an understanding of deductive logic can help in the construction of arguments. For one thing, you can analyze your opponent's argument if it happens to be syllogistic and point out the strength or weakness of the reasoning. For another, you can use deductive logic to develop your own argument. You may find places where a neat syllogism is most effective. For example, Lewis argues, "If the whole universe has no meaning, we should never have found out that it has no meaning." He claims that if he can show the world is meaningful, the atheist's argument is countered.

We know that the most persuasive of all arguments is the one in which both the premises and the conclusion are accepted by the arguer and the audience, and the conclusion necessarily and validly follows. Of course, human experience is sufficiently complex to make this occurrence rare, but it is worth remembering that an argument that makes absolute claims can be demolished if it happens to be invalid. On the other hand, there are some arguments that you can prove with great strength syllogistically. If you are arguing about moral or any other kind of absolutes—something is definitely good or bad, you say—then consider a syllogistic argument. Any claims that are necessary, any terms that are all-inclusive, can lend themselves to deductive reasoning.

■ Begin with the conclusion you want to prove and work back to the premises to see if a deductive argument is possible.

■ You work back to your premises by checking on the two terms you have in your conclusion while looking for a *middle* term, a term they have in common and that is big enough to include all of one of the terms.

For example, say you want to argue for nuclear disarmament on the grounds that it is a moral good. This is not a difficult argument, but it can take its place in a much more complex discussion of the subject. Your conclusion might be *Nuclear disarmament is a moral good.* (Or, of course, you could be arguing the opposite in exactly the same way.) What premises should you have? Remember, the middle term must be distributed.

You discover your premises by asking yourself what you are basing your conclusion on. In this case, it is the connection between two terms *nuclear disarmament* and *moral good.* What do these two terms have in common? That is, what is morally good *and* involves nuclear disarmament? The choice is up to you, but say you decide to work with *human survival,* because that is a moral good *and* relates to disarmament. You might set up your syllogism this way:

Nuclear disarmament is an event helping human survival.

All events that help human survival are morally good events.

Therefore, nuclear disarmament is a morally good event.

471

Or you could argue another way by ignoring *moral good* altogether and making your two terms *nuclear weapons* and *disarmament,* and your middle term, say, *weapons leading to total destruction.* Then your syllogism becomes:

Nuclear weapons are weapons leading to total destruction.

All weapons leading to total destruction are weapons that should be banned.

Therefore nuclear weapons are weapons that should be banned.

These are simple examples, but sometimes you need a whole string of syllogisms to prove a conclusion. Keep in mind, though, the following points:

■ The most effective syllogistic arguments are those that try to prove the necessity of *all* their terms. For example, it is not enough simply to state that nuclear disarmament is a moral good without showing why, which you do by making a connection between the two terms through a middle term.

■ As you work back from the conclusion to the premises, remember that you are looking for a middle term, for the conclusion already provides the minor and major terms of the syllogism. *It is most important that the middle term be big enough to contain one of the other terms.* So in this case, you would ask what is big enough to contain *nuclear disarmament* and relate to *moral good.* Hence the appropriateness of the middle term *events that help human survival.*

■ If you do claim that your argument is syllogistic, check the truth value of your premises carefully. Remember, an argument may be formally valid but not true.

■ If you are arguing about intangible issues (concepts or things that have not happened yet), remember that hypothetical syllogisms are useful. Similarly, if you are considering a choice of actions, alternative syllogisms can be used. For example: If we have nuclear disarmament, the human race has a good chance of survival. We will have nuclear disarmament. Therefore the human race has a good chance of survival. But remember you cannot argue validly by denying the antecedent. It does *not* follow that if we do not have disarmament, the human race does not have a good chance of survival.

Again, remember that a syllogistic argument is usually hard to construct because most of the conclusions we come to about human experience are at best *likely* and not *necessary.* Nevertheless, there are some issues about which we feel strongly or on which we base beliefs we would rather not do without. These may become appropriate for syllogistic argument if they are no⁺ too complicated.

Persuasion and Inductive Argument

The Basic Outline

The argument variations outlined below simply build on the basic problem-solution outline that was presented in Chapter 3:

Refine your subject to a topic.

Brainstorm your topic, opening up its possibilities by taking three basic perspectives: the topic isolated, the topic in its contexts, the topic as problem.

Limit the topic by considering the connections, oppositions, and resolutions to those oppositions that come from your brainstorming material.

Develop your thesis from the conclusions you reach.

The main question now is: How do you handle your thesis? The first outline we considered was the basic problem-solution outline:

Introduction

Definition of terms: the topic isolated

The topic as problem

The topic in its contexts

Conclusion

Now we can consider some variations to and developments of this outline once the thesis has been formed.

*The Argument
from Evidence*

If you decide to argue for a conclusion from strong evidence, take note of the following ways of handling the evidence.

■ Present the evidence directly with clear unbiased summaries.

■ Show that your evidence is accurate, relevant, and sufficient (see Chapter 10).

■ If possible, substantiate your evidence through a reputable third-party source. That is, use whatever authorities you can to back up your treatment of the evidence.

■ Where possible, use the opposition's evidence—if it is accurate and relevant—and reinterpret it, showing an earlier interpretation to be inadequate.

■ Draw conclusions from your evidence either deductively or inductively, but make sure that you have shown as necessary a connection as you can between the evidence and your conclusion.

■ Beware of unethical uses of evidence: deliberately untrue statements or the slanting of evidence with intent to mislead, such as card stacking, ad hominem arguments, and so on.

Here is a useful outline for the argument from evidence.

Introduction: explaining the relevance of the problem; the connection between the evidence and the conclusion

The evidence defined: what the major contexts are; the relevance and the sufficiency of the evidence; what you hope the evidence will show

The evidence in its contexts: how the evidence relates; the main examples and what they imply; classifying the evidence

The problems with the evidence: contradictions and how they might be resolved

Conclusions based on the evidence

Say you want to write an essay arguing for "The Irresponsibility of Journalists." If you were to argue from evidence alone, you would, of course, have to research major issues covered by the media and see if there is sufficient evidence to prove your point. You would need a few reference cases unless you were arguing for the irresponsibility of journalists in one or two particular cases. The evidence might involve how journalists exaggerate details and create false crises; how journalists do not verify their sources; and instances in which journalists tell only part of the story and ignore some important issues.

In your introduction, you would briefly outline the evidence on which you base your thesis, defining its relevance carefully. Then you would proceed to examine the evidence closely in its contexts. It is most important that you have clear examples that are relevant and that you not take evidence out of context, or else you will be guilty of irresponsible argument. You might then show in a particular incident the specific misuse of information and the problems it raises. You can discuss the problem of reporting the news and making news, and so on. Your conclusion when it is made must follow from some forceful examples that prove your point.

*The Argument
from Definition*

In Chapter 10, we noted that there are five kinds of definition: new, dictionary, precising, theoretical, and persuasive. In Chapter 4, we dealt with denotative and connotative definitions. Go back and review that material. Remember that when you argue from definition, you are setting standards and using them as a measure. If you are arguing for the irresponsibility of journalists, for example, you have to clearly define who you mean by *journalists* and, even more important, what you mean by *irresponsibility.* The definition of that term alone is crucial to your argument. What kind of definition would you use? Probably, you would begin with a dictionary definition of *irresponsibility,* and you might want to follow that up with some details that turn it into a precising definition. Finally, you need to give examples. The kind of definition you choose to write will determine the nature of your argument.

A useful outline for the argument by definition is as follows:

Introduction: the issue and the relevance of the problem.

The problem defined: use one or more of the five kinds of definition.

The definition in its contexts: What other issues does it suggest? What contexts are created by those issues? Broaden your definition (for example, consider irresponsibility not as just a journalist's problem but as a general issue involving many people who directly affect our lives, such as journalists, politicians, and educators).

Consider the main problems created by the definition: Are there alternative definitions opposing yours? What, for example, does a journalist consider to be responsible reporting? Try to reconcile the oppositions or at least describe the stand-off.

The conclusion should be based on the implications of your definition.

So it may very well be that you find your definition sets standards that journalists do not keep to and that you have evidence pointing to that fact. You can also introduce other material here to back up your point. The argument from definition, though, is not just a matter of setting standards; it is also a most important persuasive technique, for it gives reader and writer common ground to engage. For that reason, it is best to make your definition as universal as possible:

Use essential attributes or conventional connotations.

Make sure your definition is not too broad or too narrow (you may find yourself going back over your essay adjusting your definition to fit the evidence).

Your definition should not be circular or in any way obscure and ambiguous (defining removes ambiguity).

The definition should not be negative when it can be affirmative.

The Argument from Authority

It must be admitted that this kind of argument can rarely sustain a whole essay on its own. One man's guru is another man's faker, and in order to argue simply from a single authority, you have to be sure of your audience's sympathy to your cause. So although it may be reasonable to find this argument used frequently in religious communities or among politicians and followers of the same party, it is not reasonable to expect that your audience should worship at the same shrine that you do.

As Chapter 10 makes clear, your authority must indeed be needed, relevant, genuinely an authority, and truly unprejudiced. It is useful to use the argument from authority as part of your *evidence,* or as part of a *definition.* For example, if you want to argue for abolishing the ''cafeteria-style'' college curriculum (for example, taking 160 hours for a bachelor's degree in four-hour courses on a quarter system), you need to define what *education* really means. Is it the acquisition of fragmented general knowledge or of large bodies of knowledge with a specialist emphasis? You may find yourself calling on certain authorities from Plato to Jacques Barzun to define *education* for you, but if you do, you must not take their definitions for granted.

Allow the evidence you use from authorities to fit into your other evidence clearly.

Analyze your authorities' evidence and make clear the relevance and importance of their ideas.

Do not quote from other people without in every instance acknowledging their ideas, even when you do not quote exactly.

Argument by Comparison and Contrast

This is another variety of the argument from evidence, only this time the evidence divides itself into two related but different events that can be compared. This argument is close to the argument by analogy that follows, but it is not quite the same. In analogy, one infers what *might happen* from events that have similar characteristics. In comparison and contrast, equivalent aspects of two things are placed side by side and point by point. You can compare people with computers if both are used as teachers, but not if you are discussing, say, personality.

In order to write an essay based on this argumentative technique, you have to know very clearly what you want to compare. The business of comparison already took place when you brainstormed your topic, at least when you looked at your topic in its contexts. But when you introduce a comparison into the body of your essay, you have to make sure before you start that

The comparison is between two related events, two things that belong to the same class (computers and people in the class of "teachers")

Your comparison is relevant (computers are replacing people as instructors)

You have enough significant qualities of each to compare (all the aspects of learning)

You can prove a point by making the comparison (that people do things computers cannot)

If you have prepared the essay properly during the brainstorming stages, most of the hard work will already have been done. You should be sure that you have established relevance, sufficiency, and significance. If you are comparing responsible and irresponsible journalism, you will already have generated points of contrast (reactions to a crisis, language used, reference to sources, and so on). What remains is for you to plan your essay.

Introduction: the problem, the comparison and contrast, and its relevance.

Definition of the terms of contrast: why they are chosen and their importance.

A point-by-point comparison: the qualities the two events have in common, or if the essay is very short, a description of all of one event compared to a description of all of the other. The former method is recommended when the subject is in any way complex.

Problems created by the comparison: its strengths and weaknesses.

Conclusion.

So you might outline an essay on irresponsible journalism in the following way:

Introduction: why irresponsibility is a problem in journalism; will compare what responsible and irresponsible journalism looks like.

Definition of terms: responsible and irresponsible journalism will be treated under the headings of reaction to crisis, attempts to manipulate audience, use of language, use of sources, creation of the story by the journalist, reactions to the same event; will compare the two kinds point by point with a special emphasis on the comparison of each kind of journalism to the same story.

Problems: some very responsible journalists sometimes lapse into irresponsibility, but strengths of responsible investigative reporting (any examples on "60 Minutes" or "20/20"?).

Conclusion: Censorship? No. Closer editorial control. The media takes risks.

The Argument from Analogy

This is one of the most powerful forms of argument, but it also requires a good deal of careful planning. When you argue from analogy you are again making a comparison, between two or more things, but now you are saying that because something occurs, some other event must too. Because atomic weapons were used in World War II, you might assume that if there is another world war, atomic (or some form of nuclear) weaponry will be used again. Again, you should begin with a discussion of the evidence you are using to build up your argument. If you are arguing for the removal of the "cafeteria-styled" curriculum and the in-stallation of a new "study-block" system, you could argue that the effects of the latter will be superior to those of the former *on the analogy that* knowledge gained by in-depth analysis is more substantial than knowl-edge gained by skimming over the surface, touching on many points so lightly that it becomes hard to relate them.

In the same way that you *judge* arguments by analogy, you must be careful to do the following:

Define the relevance of the analogy.

Set up a comparison between a sufficient number of events.

Note what the events have in common that allows the analogy in the first place.

Set up your claim relative to the evidence of the premises.

Use as many dissimilar pieces of evidence as possible.

With your argument about education, you have to show that it is relevant to set up an analogy between education and the acquisition of knowledge, which of course is not at all difficult to do. There is a direct link between the way our curricula are structured and the way we arrange information that you the student must absorb, for the way the information is arranged affects *how* you absorb it. If information is given to you in fragments over a fairly long period of time, you have to carry in your mind many different pieces of information at once. Each day, say, for a bachelor of arts degree, you have to cover English, a social science, a science, and another humanities course—at least for the first two years. The argument can be made that this fragmenting does not allow for the integration of knowledge, for seeing things whole (or it could be argued that it does). If you wanted to make the argument against fragmentation on the analogy of how the mind works when it acquires knowledge, you would have to present evidence of what happens when people can linger in depth on a subject in relationship to, say, one or two other related subjects. If in that case a network of meaning builds up, you can assume it will do so also in a more integrated study-block system.

So the argument from analogy operates inductively. You do not really know what the outcome will be should you have your own way, but you are trying to persuade people that your conclusion is a likely one. You do know that one event is related to another and they have some common properties, and so you argue for a conclusion *that has not happened yet*. You may want to argue that we are heading for an economic depression on the grounds that the conditions just before the Great Depression were like some of the conditions we have now. You don't know if another depression will occur, but the argument from analogy claims a certain prophetic truth.

A useful outline for an essay based on analogy would be:

Introduction: the analogy stated and defended; its relevance made clear.

The terms in the analogy defined: How many things are being compared? What do they have in common? How dissimilar are the pieces of evidence used?

The analogy developed: the context of your argument, in which you let the analogy run through all its main details.

Strengths and weaknesses of the analogy: How strong is the claim of the argument relative to the premises?

Conclusion: the analogy justified and implications expanded.

Analogies, of course, do not have to be abstract. Use concrete (and even picturesque) analogies in your writing to explain events that may otherwise seem dry or tedious. For example, describing the operations of the human brain can be technical, but many times writers have made the subject interesting by referring to the brain's functions in an analogy with the computer. The analogy still needs to be worked out properly, of course, since computers cannot as yet "think" simultaneously about things the way the human brain can. But it can still be a powerful comparison as a way of making some important statements about information gathering and dissemination.

The Argument from Cause to Effect

You will probably have less occasion to write this kind of essay than the effect-to-cause paper, for this kind of writing, like the argument by analogy, is largely speculative. You work from known causes and predict what the effects will probably be if you have no way of knowing for certain. Or, as in a laboratory report, you work from known causes to discovered effects and explain what they are as a result of experiment.

Writing that makes predictions—for example, that human survival will be threatened if the superpowers continue to stockpile nuclear weapons— tries to assert that if one thing happens, then another will. The argument from cause to effect is basically an argument by analogy and precedent. Something happened earlier that was like what is happening now, so effects can be predicted on the basis of the earlier occurrence. This kind of argument is notoriously difficult to make and yet very popular in political circles. One of the most famous of these arguments is the well-known "domino" theory that was the "explanation" for our presence in Southeast Asia and our continued interest in other parts of the world. If country X falls to the communists, so will all the others in the region. The years since the fall of Vietnam have shown how shaky that reasoning can be, but not necessarily that it is completely wrong.

With all kinds of predictions—except those of psychic origin which are, it seems, untestable for they have no known causes—it is important to ask yourself the following questions:

■ *Are the causes from which you want to predict some effects similar to or different from other causes whose effects you know for a fact?* Compare your causes with earlier known causes and effects and proceed as you would for an argument from analogy. Say you want to argue that nuclear stockpiling will produce World War III. Is there a relationship between the stockpiling of weapons now and the "defensive" preparations of any country before either of the last two world wars?

■ *Are the properties of the causes sufficient for you to assume, again on the basis of analogy, that certain effects will happen?* Examine the properties carefully. Can you infer anything from the nature of nuclear weapons themselves? Or stockpiles?

■ *Have you made sure that you have isolated the appropriate cause for a known effect?* For example, if you argue that the current stockpiling of nuclear weapons will inevitably lead to World War III and the destruction of life as we know it, what exactly are you locating as the causes? The nuclear weapons? Or the people who will want to use them? Be sure to account for all causes if you think there is more than one.

■ *Have you avoided an oversimplified rhetorical appeal?* Such appeals are commonly to fear, a reductio ad absurdum, or a conspiracy theory based on little evidence.

The point is that you are creating a hypothesis: you are making a statement as to what effects will follow once you know what the cause is. No matter what kind of inference you make that involves hypothesizing, there are a few tests you should apply to your hypothesis to see if it is a good one or not.

■ *Is there a probable relationship between the hypothesis and either the cause or the effect it is based on?* If the hypothesis is a cause ("Brown killed the burglar"), the relationship should be a necessary one. If the hypothesis is an effect, it need only be a sufficient one. If you see a car weaving all over the road, can you say with certainty that the driver is drunk? Not unless you have found a necessary relationship between the effects (the erratic driving) and your hypothetical cause (the driver is drunk).

■ *Can you test the hypothesis?* If you say that a car was weaving all over the road because it was driven by a drunken driver, you must have specific evidence.

■ *There should be no confusion between cause and coincidence.* Your hypothesis about the drunken driver could still be based on a coincidence even if you saw him stagger out of a bar before driving away. The driver could be sick or otherwise impaired.

■ *There should be some context for the hypothesis that has been previously established.* That is, the hypothesis should be related to other hypotheses. For example, the hypothesis that a car driven erratically is driven by a drunk driver is a fairly common one because much dangerous driving is drunk driving.

■ *The hypothesis should be as simple as possible but not oversimplified.*

The Argument from Effect to Cause

In writing a paper using this argument, you are involved in *investigative reporting.* You are working from *known effects* to *unknown causes.* What pattern will the effect-to-cause essay take then? There are a series of steps you should follow. Make notes for your essay under each heading.

1. *Understand the effects.* It helps to have clear in your mind the nature of the problem: why the effects pose a problem at all; where the differences of opinion lie; which information is clear and which is unclear; which "facts" are trustworthy and which are merely "opinions"; what the possible consequences are. *Are the effects what they seem?* That is, is the problem *a real one* or blown out of proportion?

2. *Analyze the effects,* isolating specific effects that seem to you to be important. Collect all the information you can with an open mind, noting the way facts group themselves, create oppositions, and make connections. Arrange the causes or effects into groupings that range from reliable facts to hearsay.

3. *Formulate a preliminary hypothesis.* There are four useful ways of arriving at a hypothesis as to a cause for an effect; they also happen to be useful tests for the final argument, as you will see. These are traditional outlines of inductive experiment:

- *The common factor.* Assemble all the effects and find out what property they have in common. That will be a likely cause. For example, the last four winners of the Darwin Grand Prix have all been different drivers driving different cars. Two have in common the use of the same motor oil and three, the same gasoline. But they all have in common the same tire brand and type of tire, so it might be reasonable for the tire company to assume that the tire has had most to do with the winning performances.

- *The significant difference.* Is there a significant difference among the effects that suggests a possible cause? For example, three identical cars are tested for mileage and they are all driven at exactly the same speed over the same distance. They all use the same motor oil and gas except for one that uses a different brand. The one with the different brand has the best mileage, so it is reasonable to assume that the cause of the best performance was this brand of oil and gas.

- *The process of elimination.* If we know, for example, that certain effects happen together, that some of these effects have known causes, and that those causes occur together, then we can establish the missing causes by the process of elimination. Say you visit a beautiful rose garden in which all the beds are in fine shape. You find out from a gardener that four of the five beds have been stocked with bushes from a particular nursery and treated in the same way. It is reasonable to assume, then, that the roses in the other bed have been bought from the same nursery and treated in the same way too. But remember: this is only a probability and by no means certain. It could be the treatment of the roses that is more significant than the source of the bushes, for they may very well have come from another nursery. Supplement the process of elimination by other inductive methods, such as isolating the most significant possible cause if there is more than one.

482

■ *The cause-effect correlation.* Examine the changes that take place in the state of any effect and note if there are any similar changes taking place in any other activity. These two activities may have a cause-effect relationship. For example, if I notice that every summer my lawn is greener when I apply water regularly, and parched when I do not, I can assume that there is a necessary connection between the application of water (cause) and the greenness of my lawn (effect).

4. *Test the hypothesis.* Once you have found which of the above inductive methods yields the best result, try out your hypothesis on the facts.

■ Make sure that the cause you have isolated is the *only* and *necessary* one. If there are several possible causes, you *cannot* make claims for one alone. If you list several causes, discuss the relative merits and likelihood of each.

■ Make sure that you have isolated a cause in relationship to *all* the facts as you know them: are there any possible contradictions?

■ Test the hypothesis, using one or more of the methods outlined above used to formulate the hypothesis (*the common factor, the significant difference,* and so on). You do this by assembling the evidence and showing how the cause-effect relationship works. For example, if you are sure that the one thing all twentieth-century art has in common is that it develops from the Modernist period of, say, 1900 to 1935, then you must list all the major artists and their differing characteristics showing the only common factor is their link to Modernism.

■ *Change your hypothesis if necessary.* If you find information that does not fit your hypothesis, you will have to find another hypothesis.

■ *Come to a conclusion,* but do not do so until you have reached a high degree of probability. It is better to reach no conclusion at all than to leap to one.

(a) *Make sure that the relationships between your effects and their cause are necessary ones and did not occur by chance.* Coincidence is not part of a persuasive inductive argument, so beware of prejudiced conclusions in which cause and coincidence have been confused.

(b) *Avoid the fallacy of the hasty conclusion,* an argument based on only some of the evidence or on oversimplified evidence.

(c) *Beware of the scapegoat fallacy,* pinning the blame on

someone without proper evidence because of the pressure to conform or as a result of sheer prejudice.

(d) *Beware of deciding that an effect is inevitable.* Few predictions can ever hope to carry such certainty.

Mixed Arguments

You can write short essays based on a choice of any of the above methods as most appropriate to a particular topic. But much of your writing in college and after will probably call for *mixed arguments:* that is, arguments that combine several relevant techniques for developing your thesis.

■ A basic position paper will involve some evidence, definitions, authority, and comparison and contrast. These are perhaps the most common and are easily fused into one essay. Your thesis requires evidence, its terms need defining, the support of authorities is useful, and your discussion of an issue will involve some comparison and contrast.

■ Essays arguing from analogy and cause to effect both predict what might happen and are closely related, even frequently found together. They too rely on evidence, definition, and even authority to establish the terms from which you will draw your conclusion.

■ An essay arguing from effect to cause—the investigative paper especially—requires the establishing of evidence.

So you can see, the art of persuasion is a matter of knowing how to reason adequately from evidence to claim, using deduction or any number of inductive techniques. Also, writers must establish credibility and tact in handling controversy and, above all, state the case in a voice that is entirely their own. To adapt a saying from Pascal: "When we see a natural style, we are astonished and delighted for we expected to see an author, and we find a person."

Checklist

1. *A writer's credibility* depends on control of material: rational but not rationalizing, maybe angry and ironic but not enraged, offering ideas and not glib judgments, discussing topics and not listing points, and providing a genuine opinion and not bias.

2. *Refutation and handling controversy:*

State both sides of the question.

Give strengths and weaknesses of both sides.

Show common interests.

Analyze the audience.

Provide contexts for the argument.

Make a reasoned analysis.

Avoid biased language.

Appeal to common values.

3. *Use syllogistic arguments* when dealing with absolute terms: work from conclusion to premises, finding a common middle term.

4. *Inductive arguments:*

From evidence: use when strength of evidence is strong enough to support conclusion; aim for accuracy, relevance, sufficiency, and support.

From definition: use new, dictionary, precising, theoretical, and persuasive definitions.

From authority: use in conjunction with evidence or definition.

By comparison and contrast: use two related events in same class with relevant and significant qualities.

From analogy: use when you want to predict results or argue for an absent cause or effect; relevant comparison between a number of common events; claim is relative to premises.

From cause to effect: predicts an effect based on a known cause; check for other related cause-effect relationships; test the hypothesis.

From effect to cause: investigative paper; understand the problem, analyze the effects, make preliminary hypothesis (common factor, significant difference, elimination, or correlation), test hypothesis, change if needed, and finally, base conclusion on necessary relationships.

Exercises

1. Identify the kinds of argument in the following excerpts—there may be more than one in each piece—and briefly discuss their persuasiveness.

(1) The business about the poor and the black suffering excessively from capital punishment is no argument against capital punishment. It is an argu-

ment against the *administration* of justice, not against the penalty. Any punishment can be unfairly or unjustly applied. Go ahead and reform the processes by which capital punishment is inflicted, if you wish; but don't confuse maladministration with the merits of capital punishment.

(2) The argument that the death penalty is "unusual" is circular. Capital punishment continues on the books of a majority of states, the people continue to sanction the concept of capital punishment, and indeed capital sentences are routinely handed down. What has made capital punishment "unusual" is that the courts and, primarily, governors have intervened in the process so as to collaborate in the frustration of the execution of the law. To argue that capital punishment is unusual, when in fact it has been made unusual by extra-legislative authority, is an argument to expedite, not eliminate, executions.

William F. Buckley, Jr., from **EXECUTION EVE**

"What a beautiful belt you've got on!" Alice suddenly remarked. (They had had quite enough of the subject of age, she thought: and, if they really were to take turns in choosing subjects, it was *her* turn now.) "At least," she corrected herself on second thoughts, "a beautiful cravat, I should have said—no, a belt, I mean—I beg your pardon!" she added in dismay, for Humpty Dumpty looked thoroughly offended, and she began to wish she hadn't chosen that subject. "If only I knew," she thought to herself, "which was neck and which was waist!"

Evidently Humpty Dumpty was very angry, though he said nothing for a minute or two. When he *did* speak again, it was in a deep growl.

"It is a—*most*—*provoking*—thing," he said at last, "when a person doesn't know a cravat from a belt!"

"It's a cravat, child, and a beautiful one, as you say. It's a present from the White King and Queen. There now!"

"It is really?" said Alice, quite pleased to find that she *had* chosen a good subject after all.

"They gave it me," Humpty Dumpty continued thoughtfully as he crossed one knee over the other and clasped his hands round it, "they gave it me—for an un-birthday present."

"I beg your pardon?" Alice said with a puzzled air.

"I'm not offended," said Humpty Dumpty.

"I mean, what *is* an un-birthday present?"

"A present given when it isn't your birthday, of course."

Alice considered a little. "I like birthday presents best," she said at last.

"You don't know what you're talking about!" cried Humpty Dumpty. "How many days are there in a year?"

"Three hundred and sixty-five," said Alice.

"And how many birthdays have you?"

"One."

"And if you take one from three hundred and sixty-five what remains?"

"Three hundred and sixty-four, of course."

Humpty Dumpty looked doubtful. "I'd rather see that done on paper," he said.

Alice couldn't help smiling as she took out her memorandum-book, and worked the sum for him:

$$\begin{array}{r} 365 \\ \underline{1} \\ 364 \end{array}$$

Humpty Dumpty took the book and looked at it carefully. "That seems to be done right—" he began.

"You're holding it upside down!" Alice interrupted.

"To be sure I was!" Humpty Dumpty said gaily as she turned it round for him. "I thought it looked a little queer. As I was saying, that *seems* to be done right—though I haven't time to look it over thoroughly just now—and that shows that there are three hundred and sixty-four days when you might get un-birthday presents—"

"Certainly," said Alice.

"And only *one* for birthday presents, you know. There's glory for you!"

"I don't know what you mean by 'glory,' " Alice said.

Humpty Dumpty smiled contemptuously. "Of course you don't—till I tell you. I meant 'there's a nice knock-down argument for you!' "

"But 'glory' doesn't mean 'a nice knock-down argument,' " Alice objected.

"When I use a word," Humpty Dumpty said, in rather a scornful tone, "it means just what I choose it to mean—neither more nor less."

"The question is," said Alice, "whether you *can* make words mean so many different things."

"The question is," said Humpty Dumpty, "which is to be master—that's all."

Lewis Carroll, from **THROUGH THE LOOKING GLASS**

Man?

A self-balancing, 28-jointed adapter-base biped; an electro-chemical reduction-plant, integral with segregated stowages of special energy extracts in storage batteries, for subsequent actuation of thousands of hydraulic and pneumatic pumps, with motors attached; 62,000 miles of capillaries; millions of warning signals, railroad and conveyor systems; crushers and cranes (of which the arms are magnificent 23-jointed affairs with self-surfacing and lubricating systems, and a universally distributed telephone system needing no service for 70 years if well managed); the whole, extraordinarily complex mechanism guided with exquisite precision from a turret in which are located telescopic and microscopic self-registering and recording range finders, a spectroscope, *et cetera,* the turret control being closely allied with an air conditioning intake-and-exhaust, and a main fuel intake.

R. Buckminster Fuller, from THE PHANTOM CAPTAIN

In the Hasidic tradition it is repeated over and over that if the Zaddick, the wise man, serves only God and not the people, he will descend from whatever "rung of the ladder of perfection" he has ascended to. "If the Zaddick serves God," typically wrote Rabbi Nahman of Bratislav, "but does not take the trouble to teach the multitude, he will descend from his rung."

The great mystics have understood this, and functioned strongly in both worlds. W. R. Inge, a scholar of the subject, has pointed out that "all the great [Western] mystics have been energetic and influential, and their business capacity is specially noted in a curiously large number of cases." The lives of St. John of the Cross, St. Teresa of Avila, Kabir, Vivekananda, and many others show this understanding, concern, and active involvement with the world of multiplicity. In her usual incisive way, St. Teresa once stated the situation clearly. At dinner, a dish of roast partridges had been served, and she was eating with great gusto and enjoyment. Someone reproached her that it was unseemly for a bride of Christ to have such zest for and participation in the mundane aspects of the world. St. Teresa replied, "When it's prayer time, pray: when it's partridge time, partridge!"

L. Le Shan, from THE MEDIUM, THE MYSTIC, AND THE PHYSICIST

Word has somehow got around that a split infinitive is always wrong. This is of a piece with the sentimental and outworn notion that it is always wrong to strike a lady. Everybody will recall at least one woman of his acquaintance whom, at one time, or another, he has had to punch or slap. I have in mind a charming lady who is overcome by the unaccountable desire, at formal dinners with red and white wines, to climb up on the table and lie down. Her dinner companions used at first to pinch her, under cover of the conversation, but she pinched right back or, what is even less defensible, tickled. They finally learned that they could make her hold her seat only by fetching her a smart downward blow on the head. She would then sit quietly through the rest of the dinner, smiling dreamily and nodding at people, and looking altogether charming.

A man who does not know his own strength could, of course, all too easily overshoot the mark and, instead of producing the delightful languor to which I have alluded, knock his companion completely under the table, an awkward situation which should be avoided at all costs because it would leave two men seated next each other. I know of one man who, to avert this *faux pas,* used to punch his dinner companion in the side (she would begin to cry during the red-wine courses), a blow which can be executed, as a rule, with less fuss, but which has the disadvantage of almost always causing the person who is struck to shout. The hostess, in order to put her guest at her ease, must shout too, which is almost certain to arouse one of those nervous, highstrung men, so common at formal dinners, to such a pitch that he will begin throwing things. There is nothing more deplorable than the spectacle of a formal dinner party ending in a brawl. And yet it is surprising how even the most cultured and charming people can go utterly to pieces when something is unexpectedly thrown at table. They instantly have an overwhelming desire to "join in." Everybody has, at one time or another, experienced the urge to throw a plate of jelly or a half grapefruit, an urge comparable to the inclination that suddenly assails one to leap from high places. Usually this tendency passes as quickly as it comes, but it is astounding how rapidly it can be converted into action once the spell of dignity and well-bred reserve is broken by the sight of, say, a green-glass salad plate flying through the air. It is all but impossible to sit quietly by while someone is throwing salad plates. One is stirred to partici-pation not only by the swift progress of the objects and their crash as they hit something, but also by the cries of "Whammy!" and "Whoop!" with which most men accompany the act of hurling plates. In the end someone is bound to be caught over the eye by a badly aimed plate and rendered unconscious.

My contemporary, Mr. Fowler, in a painstaking analysis of the split infinitive, divides the English-speaking world into five classes as regards this construction: those who don't know and don't care, those who don't know and do care, those who know and approve, those who know and condemn, and those who know and discriminate. (The fact that there was no transition at all between the preceding paragraph and this one does not mean that I did not try, in several different ways, to get back to the split infinitive logically. As in a bridge hand, the absence of a re-entry is not always the fault of the man who is playing the hand, but of the way the cards lie in the dummy. To say more would only make it more difficult than it now is, if possible, to get back to Mr Fowler.) Mr. Fowler's point is, of course, that there are good split infinitives and bad ones. For instance, he contends that it is better to say "Our object is to further cement trade relations," thus splitting "to cement," than to say "Our object is further to cement trade relations," because the use of "further" before "to cement" might lead the reader to think it had the weight of "moreover" rather than of "increasingly." My own way out of all this confusion would be simply to say "Our object is to let trade relations ride," that is, give them up, let them go. Some people would regard the abandonment of trade relations, merely for the purpose of avoiding grammatical confusion, as a weakkneed and unpatriotic action. That, it seems to me, is a matter for each person to decide for himself. A man who, like myself, has no knowledge at all of trade relations cannot be expected to take the same interest in cementing them as, say, the statesman or the politician. This is no reflection on trade relations.

James Thurber, "THE SPLIT INFINITIVE"

I lie down. Words come: "honor," "family," "survival," "decadence" ... elegant opium dens with suave, slinky hostesses; bedrooms with mirrored ceilings and black satin sheets on the emperor-sized beds; women in high heels, black stockings, and garter belts; Marlene Dietrich in *The Blue Angel* with Emil Jannings crowing like a rooster; bathrooms with purple or zebra-striped tiling; Tangiers; Pompeii; a Black Mass; Turkish pashas in their play-rooms; *Les Fleurs du mal*; a drag-queen costume ball; a voyeur with expensive binoculars trained on the windows of a girls' boarding-school dormitory; Oscar Wilde and the green carnation; Onassis' yacht with paparazzi snapping pictures from the shore; a Roman orgy with fan-waving Nubian slaves and crimson wine trickling out of the corners of heavy sensual mouths; Regine's; jeweled money belts; fruit-flavored douches and edible panties.

One finds it difficult to believe that such a cluster of images and associations differs too widely in its general import from what would be arrived at by anyone familiar with the history of the word or at least with its current usage. The litany is mostly sexual—or at least open to erotic interpretation—and heavily literary. That is to say, almost none of the images and scenes derive from direct experience of my own, but rather from creations in the realm of culture, that dimension of invented or dramatized existence.

Even such "facts" as opium dens or Tangiers are not truly available to me except through a screen of fiction, of imaginary action, and this would be true even if I were to prowl the streets of that North African city and stumble into a scene of astonishing depravity, or if I were to settle down with a pipeful of hashish on a luxurious sofa in a magenta-colored flock-walled room in Hongkong or Macao. I would respond to or continue to seek for qualities of sensual excitation or fulfillment of which I had first become aware through one or another kind of "tale." This is an important clue, I think. Like so many other categories of the "abnormal," decadence makes itself known to us, at least in the beginning, in the form of a legend.

Richard Gilman, from DECADENCE

2. Here is the beginning of an argument between two people on the familiar topic of abortion. A and B have strongly opposing views. Assume that both parties want to resolve the controversy and reach some kind of agreement without abandoning their deepest beliefs. Is this possible? Write out the rest of the dialogue as you think it might run its course, ending it as closely as you can to an agreement. Each side, of course, is going to have to give some ground, but you are looking for a reasonable statement that might allow legislation to be developed that all but the extremists on both sides will accept. In other words, A and B may start from extreme positions, but you want to find what is necessary to modify them.

a. The main argument for legalizing abortion by licensed medical practitioners lies in the issue of freedom of choice. A woman should not be forced to have an unwanted baby, whether the baby is a child of love or rape, or whether the baby is going to be healthy and live in a comfortable home or not. It is no one else's concern but the mother's, for the child is hers and she must take care of it. The child is part of its mother's body. The state does not legislate what you can do with your arms, legs, and so on, so it has no right to legislate what a woman can do with a fetal child who is not yet of the world. To interfere is to make an unwarranted intrusion upon a woman's freedom.

b. Abortion is murder—nothing less. The fetus is a living human being from its first heartbeat, and to kill a human being is murder. Therefore, anyone who conducts an abortion *and* the mother (and father) who allows it are murderers and should be arrested. You cannot escape the fact that once a fetus is considered medically alive, it is not simply a potential but a real human being. It is therefore protected by the law, and the law does have the right to interfere if it can be proven that a human life is endangered. The law also protects us from the ravages we can inflict on our own bodies. If you attack your own person and mutilate yourself, you can be restrained—and abortion is self-mutilation.

3. Develop what you think are watertight syllogisms (or chains of syllogisms if necessary) to serve as an outline for an argument you might make *in favor of* two of the following: *patriotism, good manners, professional sports, trade unions.*

4. Develop a brief outline for each of four arguments, *or* a mixed argument, involving definition, evidence, authority, and comparison, for or against *one* of the following claims:

Love is a many-splendored thing.

Some day my prince(ss) will come.

Detroit makes the best motors.

5. Develop brief argument outlines—either by analogy, or by cause and effect—or both if possible, for *two* of the following:

Whatever happened to sweetness and light?

Brains are like computers.

Stockpiling oil is good for the economy.

Writing Assignment

Choose any current issue that strikes you as important yet controversial and try to cut through the controversy by creating an argument based on general or absolute truths, matters that you think everyone should be able to agree on. First develop an outline for the argument you will make on the issue without concern for its syllogistic reasoning. Then examine your outline closely for those sections, usually near the beginning, where you can introduce your irrefutable premises and thence develop your necessary conclusion from a deductive argument. Write out those syllogisms clearly as part of your argument. Now write out the argument as an essay.

Readings

George Orwell POLITICS AND THE ENGLISH LANGUAGE

"Political language—and with variations this is true of all political parties, from Conservatives to Anarchists—is designed to make lies sound truthful and murder respectable, and to give an appearance of solidity to pure wind."

Harvey Cox UNDERSTANDING ISLAM

"In the final analysis, given the role our religions play in both our cultures, no real rapport between the Arabs and the West seems possible unless Christians and Moslems make a more serious effort to understand each other."

Kenneth Boulding AFTER CIVILIZATION, WHAT?

"The credit balance of post-civilization is at large. It at least gives us a chance of a modest utopia, in which slavery, poverty, exploitation, gross inequality, war and disease—these prime costs of civilization—will fall to the vanishing point."

POLITICS AND THE ENGLISH LANGUAGE

George Orwell

Most people who bother with the matter at all would admit that the English language is in a bad way, but it is generally assumed that we cannot by conscious action do anything about it. Our civilization is decadent and our language—so the argument runs—must inevitably share in the general collapse. It follows that any struggle against the abuse of language is a sentimental archaism, like preferring candles to electric light or hansom cabs to aeroplanes. Underneath this lies the half-conscious belief that language is a natural growth and not an instrument which we shape for our own purposes.

Now, it is clear that the decline of a language must ultimately have political and economic causes: it is not due simply to the bad influence of this or that individual writer. But an effect can become a cause, reinforcing the original cause and producing the same effect in an intensified form, and so on indefinitely. A man may take to drink because he feels himself to be a failure, and then fail all the more completely because he drinks. It is rather the same thing that is happening to the English language. It becomes ugly and inaccurate because our thoughts are foolish, but the slovenliness of our language makes it easier for us to have foolish thoughts. The point is that the process is reversible. Modern English, especially written English, is full of bad habits which spread by imitation and which can be avoided if one is willing to take the necessary trouble. If one gets rid of these habits one can think more clearly, and to think clearly is a necessary first step towards political regeneration: so that the fight against bad English is not frivolous and is not the exclusive concern of professional writers. I will come back to this presently, and I hope that by that time the meaning of what I have said here will have become clearer. Meanwhile, here are five specimens of the English language as it is now habitually written.

These five passages have not been picked out because they are especially bad—I could have quoted far worse if I had chosen—but because they illustrate various of the mental vices from which we now suffer. They are a little below the average, but are fairly representative samples. I number them so that I can refer back to them when necessary:

"(1) I am not, indeed, sure whether it is not true to say that the Milton who once seemed not unlike a seventeenth-century Shelley had not become, out of an experience ever more bitter in each year, more alien [*sic*] to the founder of that Jesuit sect which nothing could induce him to tolerate."

Professor Harold Laski (Essay in *Freedom of Expression*).

"(2) Above all, we cannot play ducks and drakes with a native battery of idioms which prescribes such egregious collocations of vocables as the Basic *put up with* for *tolerate* or *put at a loss* for *bewilder.''*

Professor Lancelot Hogben (Interglossa).

''(3) On the one side we have the free personality: by definition it is not neurotic, for it has neither conflict nor dream. Its desires, such as they are, are transparent, for they are just what institutional approval keeps in the forefront of consciousness; another institutional pattern would alter their number and intensity; there is little in them that is natural, irreducible, or culturally dangerous. But *on the other side,* the social bond itself is nothing but the mutual reflection of these self-secure integrities. Recall the definition of love. Is not this the very picture of a small academic? Where is there a place in this hall of mirrors for either personality or fraternity?''

Essay on psychology in Politics (New York).

''(4) All the 'best people' from the gentlemen's clubs, and all the frantic fascist captains, united in common hatred of Socialism and bestial horror of the rising tide of the mass revolutionary movement, have turned to acts of provocation, to foul incendiarism, to medieval legends of poisoned wells, to legalize their own destruction of proletarian organizations, and rouse the agitated petty-bourgeoisie to chauvinistic fervour on behalf of the fight against the revolutionary way out of the crisis.''

Communist pamphlet.

''(5) If a new spirit is to be infused into this old country, there is one thorny and contentious reform which must be tackled, and that is the humanization and galvanization of the B.B.C. Timidity here will bespeak cancer and atrophy of the soul. The heart of Britain may be sound and of strong beat, for instance, but the British lion's roar at present is like that of Bottom in Shakespeare's *Midsummer Night's Dream*—as gentle as any sucking dove. A virile new Britain cannot continue indefinitely to be traduced in the eyes or rather ears, of the world by the effete languors of Langham Place, brazenly masquerading as 'standard English.' When the Voice of Britain is heard at nine o'clock, better far and infinitely less ludicrous to hear aitches honestly dropped than the present priggish, inflated, inhibited, school-ma'amish arch braying of blameless bashful mewing maidens!''

Letter in Tribune.

Each of these passages has faults of its own, but, quite apart from avoidable ugliness, two qualities are common to all of them. The first is staleness of imagery: the other is lack of precision. The writer either has a meaning and cannot express it, or he inadvertently says something else, or he is almost indifferent as to whether his words mean anything or not. This mixture of vagueness and sheer incompetence is the most marked characteristic of modern English prose, and especially of any kind of political writing. As soon as certain topics are raised, the concrete melts into the abstract and no one seems able to think of turns of speech that are not hackneyed: prose consists less and less of *words* chosen for the sake of their meaning, and more and more of *phrases* tacked together like the sections of a prefabricated hen-house. I list below, with notes and examples, various of the tricks by means of which the work of prose-construction is habitually dodged:

Dying Metaphors.   A newly invented metaphor assists thought by evoking a visual image, while on the other hand a metaphor which is technically ''dead'' (e.g. *iron resolution*) has in effect reverted to being an ordinary word and can generally be used without loss of vividness. But in between these two classes there is a huge dump of worn-out metaphors which have lost all evocative power and are merely used because they save people the trouble of inventing phrases for themselves. Examples are: *Ring the changes on, take up the cudgels for, toe the line, ride roughshod over, stand shoulder to shoulder with, play into the hands of, no axe to grind, grist to the mill, fishing in troubled waters, on the order of the day, Achilles' heel, swan song, hotbed.* Many of these are used without knowledge of their meaning (what is a ''rift,'' for instance?), and incompatible metaphors are frequently mixed, a sure sign that the writer is not interested in what he is saying. Some metaphors now current have been twisted out of their original meaning without those who use them even being aware of the fact. For example, *toe the line* is sometimes written *tow the line.* Another example is *the hammer and the anvil,* now always used with the implication that the anvil gets the worst of it. In real life it is always the anvil that breaks the hammer, never the other way about: a writer who stopped to think what he was saying would be aware of this, and would avoid perverting the original phrase.

Operators or *verbal false limbs.*   These save the trouble of picking out appropriate verbs and nouns, and at the same time pad each sentence with extra syllables which give it an appearance of symmetry. Characteristic phrases are: *render inoperative, militate against, make contact with, be subjected to, give rise to, give grounds for, have the effect of, play a leading part (role) in, make itself felt, take effect, exhibit a tendency to, serve the purpose of, etc., etc.* The keynote is the elimination of simple verbs. Instead of being a single word, such as *break, stop, spoil, mend, kill,* a verb becomes a *phrase,* made up of a noun or adjective tacked on to some general-purposes verb such as *prove, serve, form, play, render.* In addition, the passive voice is wherever possible used in preference to the active, and noun constructions are used instead of gerunds (*by examination of* instead of *by examining*). The range of verbs is further cut down by means of the *-ize* and *de-* formation, and the banal statements are given an appearance of profundity by means of the *not un-* formation. Simple conjunctions and prepositions are replaced by such phrases as *with respect to, having regard to, the fact that, by dint of, in view of, in the interests of, on the hypothesis that;* and the ends of sentences are saved from anticlimax by such resounding commonplaces *as greatly to be desired, cannot be left out of account, a development to be expected in the near future, deserving of serious consideration, brought to a satisfactory conclusion,* and so on and so forth.

Pretentious diction. Words like *phenomenon, element, individual* (as noun), *objective, categorical, effective, virtual, basic, primary, promote, constitute, exhibit, exploit, utilize, eliminate, liquidate,* are used to dress up simple statement and give an air of scientific impartiality to biased judgments. Adjectives like *epoch-making, epic, historic, unforgettable, triumphant, age-old, inevitable, inexorable, veritable,* are used to dignify the sordid processes of international politics, while writing that aims at glorifying war usually takes on an archaic colour, its characteristic words being: *realm, throne, chariot, mailed fist, trident, sword, shield, buckler, banner, jackboot, clarion.* Foreign words and expressions such as *cul de sac, ancien régime, deus ex machina, mutatis mutandis, status quo, gleich-schaltung, weltanschauung,* are used to give an air of culture and elegance. Except for the useful abbreviations *i.e., e.g.,* and *etc.,* there is no real need for any of the hundreds of foreign phrases now current in English. Bad writers, and especially scientific, political and sociological writers, are nearly always haunted by the notion that Latin or Greek words are grander than Saxon ones, and unnecessary words like *expedite, ameliorate, predict, extraneous, deracinated, clandestine, subaqueous* and hundreds of others constantly gain ground from their Anglo-Saxon opposite numbers.[1] The jargon peculiar to Marxist writing (*hyena, hangman, cannibal, petty bourgeois, these gentry, lacquey, flunkey, mad dog, White Guard,* etc.) consists largely of words and phrases translated from Russian, German or French; but the normal way of coining a new word is to use a Latin or Greek root with the appropriate affix and, where necessary, the *-ize* formation. It is often easier to make up words of this kind (*deregionalize, impermissible, extramarital, non-fragmentatory* and so forth) than to think up the English words that will cover one's meaning. The result, in general, is an increase in slovenliness and vagueness.

Meaningless words. In certain kinds of writing, particularly in art criticism and literary criticism, it is normal to come across long passages which are almost completely lacking in meaning.[2] Words like *romantic, plastic, values, human, dead,*

1. An interesting illustration of this is the way in which the English flower names which were in use till very recently are being ousted by Greek ones, *snapdragon* becoming *antirrhinum, forget-me-not* becoming *myosotis,* etc. It is hard to see any practical reason for this change of fashion: it is probably due to an instinctive turning-away from the more homely word and a vague feeling that the Greek word is scientific.

2. Example: "Comfort's catholicity of perception and image, strangely Whitmanesque in range, almost the exact opposite in aesthetic compulsion, continues to evoke that trembling atmospheric accumulative hinting at a cruel, an inexorably serene timelessness ... Wrey Gardiner scores by aiming at simple bull's-eyes with precision. Only they are not so simple, and through this contented sadness runs more than the surface bitter-sweet of resignation." (*Poetry Quarterly.*)

sentimental, natural, vitality, as used in art criticism, are strictly meaningless in the sense that they not only do not point to any discoverable object, but are hardly ever expected to do so by the reader. When one critic writes, ''The outstanding feature of Mr. X's work is its living quality,'' while another writes, ''The immediately striking thing about Mr. X's work is its peculiar deadness,'' the reader accepts this as a simple difference of opinion. If words like *black* and *white* were involved, instead of the jargon words *dead* and *living,* he would see at once that language was being used in an improper way. Many political words are similarly abused. The word *Fascism* has now no meaning except in so far as it signifies ''something not desirable.'' The words *democracy, socialism, freedom, patriotic, realistic, justice,* have each of them several different meanings which cannot be reconciled with one another. In the case of a word like *democracy,* not only is there no agreed definition, but the attempt to make one is resisted from all sides. It is almost universally felt that when we call a country democratic we are praising it: consequently the defenders of every kind of régime claim that it is a democracy, and fear that they might have to stop using the word if it were tied down to any one meaning. Words of this kind are often used in a consciously dishonest way. That is, the person who uses them has his own private definition, but allows his hearer to think he means something quite different. Statements like *Marshal Pétain was a true patriot, The Soviet Press is the freest in the world, The Catholic church is opposed to persecution,* are almost always made with intent to deceive. Other words used in variable meanings, in most cases more or less dishonestly, are: *class totalitarian, science, progressive, reactionary, bourgeois, equality.*

Now that I have made this catalogue of swindles and perversions, let me give another example of the kind of writing that they lead to. This time it must of its nature be an imaginary one. I am going to translate a passage of good English into modern English of the worst sort. Here is a well-known verse from *Ecclesiastes:*

''I returned and saw under the sun, that the race is not to the swift, nor the battle to the strong, neither yet bread to the wise, nor yet riches to men of understanding, nor yet favour to men of skill; but time and chance happeneth to them all.''

Here it is in modern English:

''Objective considerations of contemporary phenomena compels the conclusion that success or failure in competitive activities exhibits no tendency to be commensurate with innate capacity, but that a considerable element of the unpredictable must invariably be taken into account.''

This is a parody, but not a very gross one. Exhibit (3), above, for instance, contains several patches of the same kind of English. It will be seen that I have not made a full translation. The beginning and ending of the sentence follow the original meaning fairly closely, but in the middle the concrete illustrations—race, battle, bread—dissolve into the vague phrase ''success or failure in competitive activities.'' This had to be so, because no modern writer of the kind I am discussing—no one capable of using phrases like "objective consideration of contemporary phenomena"—would ever tabulate his thoughts in that precise and detailed way. The whole tendency of modern prose is away from concreteness. Now analyze these two sentences a little more closely. The first contains forty-nine words but only sixty syllables, and all its words are those of everyday life. The second contains thirty-eight words of ninety syllables: eighteen of its words are from Latin roots, and one from Greek. The first sentence contains six vivid images, and only one phrase ("time and chance") that could be called vague. The second contains not a single fresh, arresting phrase, and in spite of its ninety syllables it gives only a shortened version of the meaning contained in the first. Yet without a doubt it is the second kind of sentence that is gaining ground in modern English. I do not want to exaggerate. This kind of writing is not yet universal, and outcrops of simplicity will occur here and there in the worst-written page. Still, if you or I were told to write a few lines on the uncertainty of human fortunes, we should probably come much nearer to my imaginary sentence than to the one from *Ecclesiastes.*

As I have tried to show, modern writing at its worst does not consist in picking out words for the sake of their meaning and inventing images in order to make the meaning clearer. It consists in gumming together long strips of words which have already been set in order by someone else, and making the results presentable by sheer humbug. The attraction of this way of writing is that it is easy. It is easier—even quicker, once you have the habit—to say *In my opinion it is a not unjustifiable assumption that* than to say *I think.* If you use ready-made phrases, you not only don't have to hunt about for words; you also don't have to bother with the rhythms of your sentences, since these phrases are generally so arranged as to be more or less euphonious. When you are composing in a hurry—when you are dictating to a stenographer, for instance, or making a public speech—it is natural to fall into a pretentious, Latinized style. Tags like *a consideration which we should do well to bear in mind* or *a conclusion to which all of us would readily assent* will save many a sentence from coming down with a bump. By using stale metaphors, similes and idioms, you save much mental effort, at the cost of leaving your meaning vague, not only for your reader but for yourself. This is the significance of mixed metaphors. The sole aim of a metaphor is to call up a visual image. When these images clash—as in *The Fascist octopus has sung its swan song, the jackboot is thrown into the melting pot*—it can be taken as certain that the writer is not seeing a mental image of the objects he is naming; in other words he is not really thinking. Look again at the examples I gave at the beginning of this essay. Professor Laski (1) uses five negatives in fifty-three words. One of these is superfluous, making nonsense of the whole passage, and in addition there is the slip *alien* for akin, making further nonsense, and several avoidable pieces of clumsiness which increase the general vagueness. Professor Hogben (2) plays ducks and drakes with a battery which is able to write prescriptions, and, while disapproving of the everyday phrase *put up with,* is unwilling to look *egregious* up in the dictionary and see what it means. (3), if one takes an uncharitable attitude towards it, is simply meaningless: probably one could work out its intended meaning by reading the whole of the article in which it occurs. In (4), the writer knows more or less what he wants to say, but an accumulation of stale phrases chokes him like tea leaves blocking a sink. In (5), words and meaning have almost parted company. People who write in this manner usually have a general emotional meaning—they dislike one thing and want to express solidarity with another—but they are not interested in the detail of what they are saying. A scrupulous writer, in every sentence that he writes, will ask himself at least four questions, thus: What am I trying to say? What words will express it? What image or idiom will make it clearer? Is this image fresh enough to have an effect? And he will probably ask himself two more: Could I put it more shortly? Have I said anything that is avoidably ugly? But you are not obliged to go to all this trouble. You can shirk it by simply throwing your mind open and letting the ready-made phrases come crowding in. They will construct your sentences for you—even think your thoughts for you, to a certain extent—and at need they will perform the important service of partially concealing your meaning even from yourself. It is at this point that the special connection between politics and the debasement of language becomes clear.

In our time it is broadly true that political writing is bad writing. Where it is not true, it will generally be found that the writer is some kind of rebel, expressing his private opinions and not a "party line." Orthodoxy, of whatever colour, seems to demand a lifeless, imitative style. The political dialects to be found in pamphlets, leading articles, manifestos, White Papers and the speeches of under-secretaries do, of course, vary from party to party, but they are all alike in that one almost never finds in them a fresh, vivid, home-made turn of speech. When one watches some tired hack on the platform mechanically repeating the familiar phrases—*bestial atrocities, iron heel, bloodstained tyranny, free peoples of the world, stand shoulder to shoulder*—one often has a curious feeling that one is not watching a live human being but some kind of dummy: a feeling which suddenly becomes stronger at moments when the light catches the speaker's spectacles and turns them into blank discs which seem to have no eyes behind them. And this is not altogether fanciful. A speaker who uses that kind of phraseology has gone some distance towards turning himself into a machine. The appropriate noises are coming out of his larynx, but his brain is not involved as it would be if he were choosing his words for himself. If the speech he is making is one that he is accustomed to make over and over again, he may be almost unconscious of what he is saying, as one is when one utters the responses in church. And this reduced state of consciousness, if not indispensable, is at any rate favourable to political conformity.

In our time, political speech and writing are largely the defense of the indefensible. Things like the continuance of British rule in India, the Russian purges and deportations, the dropping of the atom bombs on Japan, can indeed be defended, but only by arguments which are too brutal for most people to face, and which do not square with the professed aims of political parties. Thus political language has to consist largely of euphemism, question-begging and sheer cloudy vagueness. Defenseless villages are bombarded from the air, the inhabitants driven out into the countryside, the cattle machine-gunned, the huts set on fire with incendiary bullets: this is called *pacification*. Millions of peasants are robbed of their farms and sent trudging along the roads with no more than they can carry: this is called *transfer of population* or *rectification of frontiers*. People are imprisoned for years without trial, or shot in the back of the neck or sent to die of scurvy in Arctic lumber camps: this is called *elimination of unreliable elements*. Such phraseology is needed if one wants to name things without calling up mental pictures of them. Consider for instance some comfortable English professor defending Russian totalitarianism. He cannot say outright, "I believe in killing off your opponents when you can get good results by doing so." Probably, therefore, he will say something like this:

"While freely conceding that the Soviet régime exhibits certain features which the humanitarian may be inclined to deplore, we must, I think, agree that a certain curtailment of the right to political opposition is an unavoidable concomitant of transitional periods, and that the rigours which the Russian people have been called upon to undergo have been amply justified in the sphere of concrete achievement."

The inflated style is itself a kind of euphemism. A mass of Latin words falls upon the facts like soft snow, blurring the outlines and covering up all the details. The great enemy of clear language is insincerity. When there is a gap between one's real and one's declared aims, one turns as it were instinctively to long words and exhausted idioms, like a cuttlefish squirting out ink. In our age there is no such thing as "keeping out of politics." All issues are political issues, and politics itself is a mass of lies, evasions, folly, hatred and schizophrenia. When the general atmosphere is bad, language must suffer. I should expect to find—this is a guess which I have not sufficient knowledge to verify—that the German, Russian and Italian languages have all deteriorated in the last ten or fifteen years, as a result of dictatorship.

But if thought corrupts language, language can also corrupt thought. A bad usage can spread by tradition and imitation, even among people who should and do know better. The debased language that I have been discussing is in some ways very convenient. Phrases like *a not justifiable assumption, leaves much to be desired, would serve no good purpose, a consideration which we should do well to bear in mind,* are a continuous temptation, a packet of aspirins always at one's elbow. Look back through this essay, and for certain you will find that I have again and again committed the very faults I am protesting against. By this morning's post I have received a pamphlet dealing with conditions in Germany. The author tells me that he "felt impelled" to write it. I open it at random, and here is almost the first sentence that I see: "(The Allies) have an opportunity not only of achieving a radical transformation of Germany's social and political structure in such a way as to avoid a nationalistic reaction in Germany itself, but at the same time of laying the foundations of a co-operative and unified Europe." You see, he "feels impelled" to write—feels, presumably, that he has something new to say—and yet his words, like cavalry horses answering the bugle, group themselves automatically into the familiar dreary pattern. This invasion of one's mind by ready-made phrases *(lay the foundations, achieve a radical transformation)* can only be prevented if one is constantly on guard against them, and every such phrase anaesthetizes a portion of one's brain.

I said earlier that the decadence of our language is probably curable. Those who deny this would argue, if they produced an argument at all, that language merely reflects existing social conditions, and that we cannot influence its development by any direct tinkering with words and constructions. So far as the general tone or spirit of a language goes, this may be true, but it is not true in detail. Silly words and expressions have often disappeared, not through any evolutionary process but owing to the conscious action of a minority. Two recent examples were *explore every avenue* and *leave no stone unturned,* which were killed by the jeers of a few journalists. There is a long list of flyblown metaphors which could similarly be got rid of if enough people would interest themselves in the job; and it should also be possible to laugh the *not un-* formation out of existence,[1] to reduce the amount of Latin and Greek in the average sentence, to drive out foreign phrases and strayed scientific words, and, in general, to make pretentiousness unfashionable. But all these are minor points. The defense of the English language implies more than this, and perhaps it is best to start by saying what it does not imply.

To begin with it has nothing to do with archaism, with the salvaging of obsolete words and turns of speech, or with the setting up of a "standard English" which must never be departed from. On the contrary, it is especially concerned with the scrapping of every word or idiom which has outworn its usefulness. It has nothing to do with correct grammar and syntax, which are of no importance so long as one makes one's meaning clear, or with the avoidance of Americanisms, or with having what is called a "good prose style." On the other hand it is not concerned with fake simplicity and the attempt to make written English colloquial. Nor does it even imply in every case preferring the Saxon word to the Latin one, though it does imply using the fewest and shortest words that will cover one's meaning. What is above all needed is to let the meaning choose the word, and not the

---

1. One can cure oneself of the *not un* formation by memorizing this sentence: *A not unblack dog was chasing a not unsmall rabbit across a not ungreen field.*

other way about. In prose, the worst thing one can do with words is to surrender to them. When you think of a concrete object, you think wordlessly, and then, if you want to describe the thing you have been visualizing you probably hunt about till you find the exact words that seem to fit. When you think of something abstract you are more inclined to use words from the start, and unless you make a conscious effort to prevent it, the existing dialect will come rushing in and do the job for you, at the expense of blurring or even changing your meaning. Probably it is better to put off using words as long as possible and get one's meaning as clear as one can through pictures or sensations. Afterwards one can choose—not simply *accept*—the phrases that will best cover the meaning, and then switch round and decide what impression one's words are likely to make on another person. This last effort of the mind cuts out all stale or mixed images, all prefabricated phrases, needless repetitions, and humbug and vagueness generally. But one can often be in doubt about the effect of a word or a phrase, and one needs rules that one can rely on when instinct fails. I think the following rules will cover most cases:

(i) Never use a metaphor, simile or other figure of speech which you are used to seeing in print.

(ii) Never use a long word where a short one will do.

(iii) If it is possible to cut a word out, always cut it out.

(iv) Never use the passive where you can use the active.

(v) Never use a foreign phrase, a scientific word or a jargon word if you can think of an everyday English equivalent.

(vi) Break any of these rules sooner than say anything outright barbarous.

These rules sound elementary, and so they are, but they demand a deep change of attitude in anyone who has grown used to writing in the style now fashionable. One could keep all of them and still write bad English, but one could not write the kind of stuff that I quoted in those five specimens at the beginning of this article.

I have not here been considering the literary use of language, but merely language as an instrument for expressing and not for concealing or preventing thought. Stuart Chase and others have come near to claiming that all abstract words are meaningless, and have used this as a pretext for advocating a kind of political quietism. Since you don't know what Fascism is, how can you struggle against Fascism? One need not swallow such absurdities as this, but one ought to recognize that the present political chaos is connected with the decay of language, and that one can probably bring about some improvement by starting at the verbal end. If you simplify your English, you are freed from the worst follies of orthodoxy. You cannot speak any of the necessary dialects, and when you make a stupid remark its stupidity will be obvious, even to yourself. Political language—and with variations this is true of all political parties, from Conservatives to Anarchists—is designed to make lies sound truthful and murder respectable, and to give an appearance of solidity to pure wind. One cannot change this all in a moment, but one can at least change one's own habits, and from time to time one can even, if one jeers loudly enough, send some worn-out and useless phrase—some *jackboot, Achilles' heel, hotbed, melting pot, acid test, veritable inferno* or other lump of verbal refuse—into the dustbin where it belongs.

1. "What is above all needed is to let the meaning choose the word, and not the other way about." Explain carefully what Orwell means by this and its significance in his overall argument.

2. Does Orwell think of language as a cause or an effect of our "decadence"? Or both?

3. Orwell lists a number of now famous attributes of stale, lifeless writing. Assume you are organizing a writing course for yourself and others. How do you think one should go about teaching and learning the avoidance of these problems?

4. Explain carefully Orwell's argument that links together a decline in language and the political use of language.

5. Modern writing is "gumming together long strips of words which have already been set in order by someone else, and making the results presentable by sheer humbug." Find a contemporary example of this—preferably political in nature, but it can be of any kind—and analyze the style briefly.

6. Orwell wrote this essay in 1946, and here we are almost forty years later still thinking that his words are apt and his diagnosis timely. Do you agree? If so, why do you think writing has *not* improved? If not, why do you think writing *has* improved?

UNDERSTANDING ISLAM

Harvey Cox

Odious Western images of Muhammad and of Islam have a long and embarrassingly honorable lineage. Dante places the prophet in that circle of hell reserved for those stained by the sin he calls *seminator di scandalo e di scisma*. As a schismatic, Muhammad's fitting punishment is to be eternally chopped in half from his chin to his anus, spilling entrails and excrement at the door of Satan's stronghold. His loyal disciple Ali, whose sins of division were presumably on a lesser scale, is sliced only "from forelock to chin." There is scandal, too. A few lines later, Dante has Muhammad send a warning to a contemporary priest whose sect was said to advocate the community of goods and who was also suspected of having a mistress. The admonition cautions the errant padre that the same fate awaits him if he does not quickly mend his ways. Already in Dante's classic portrait, we find the image of the Moslem linked with revolting violence, distorted doctrine, a dangerous economic idea, and the tantalizing hint of illicit sensuality.

Nothing much has changed in the 600 years since. Even the current wave of interest in Eastern spirituality among many American Christians has not done much to improve the popular estimate of Islam. It is fashionable now in the West to find something of value in Buddhism or Hinduism, to peruse the *Sutras* or the *Bhagavad Gita,* to attend a lecture by Swami Muktananda or the Dalai Lama, even to try a little yoga or meditation. But Americans in general and Christians in particular seem unable to find much to admire in Islam. As G. H. Hansen observes, with only a modicum of hyperbole, in his book *Militant Islam,* the mental picture most Westerners hold of this faith of 750 million people is one of ''. . . strange bearded men with burning eyes, hieratic figures in robes and turbans, blood dripping from the amputated hands and from the striped backs of male-factors, and piles of stones barely concealing the battered bodies of adulterous couples.'' Lecherous, truculent, irrational, cruel, conniving, excitable, dreaming about lascivious heavens while hypocritically enforcing oppressive legal codes: the stereotype of the Moslem is only partially softened by a Kahlil Gibran who puts it into sentimental doggerel or a Rudolph Valentino who does it with zest and good humor.

There is, of course, one important exception to the West's rejection of the religious value of Islam. This exception's most visible representatives have been Muhammad Ali and the late Malcolm X. Most Americans who seem genuinely drawn to the call of the minaret are blacks. But given the racial myopia that continues to affect almost all American cultural perceptions, this exception has probably deepened the distrust most white Christians feel toward Islam. The dominant image was summed up brilliantly in a Boston newspaper's cartoon showing a Moslem seated in prayer. Over his head the balloon contained one word: ''Hate!''

This captious caricaturing of Moslems and Arabs is not confined to the popular mentality. In his *Orientalism,* Edward Said describes a study published in 1975 of Arabs in American textbooks that demonstrates how prejudices continue to be spread through respectable sources. One textbook, for example, sums up Islam in the following manner:

> The Moslem religion, called Islam, began in the seventh century. It was started by a wealthy businessman of Arabia, called Muhammad. He claimed that he was a prophet. He found followers among the other Arabs. He told them they were picked to rule the world.

This passage is, unfortunately, not atypical. Although phrased with some degree of restraint, it coheres all too well with the popular medieval picture of Muhammad as a sly trickster or the current comic-book depictions of the sated, power-mad Arab. Moreover, Dante's unflattering portrait of the prophet was rooted in traditions that existed long before his time. These primal shadowgraphs have notoriously long half-lives, and they continue to darken our capacity to understand Islam to this day.

Allah works in mysterious ways. Through the stubborn geopolitics of oil, Westerners are being forced, like it or not, to learn more about Islam than they ever thought they would. Inevitably this reappraisal has begun to include a rethinking of the relationship between Islam and Christianity. In the fall of 1979, the World Council of Churches sponsored a conference on the subject in Kenya, and Christian scholars with direct experience of Islam were invited from all over the world. The results were mixed since, ironically, theologians from countries where Islam is a small minority seemed much more eager to enter into dialogue with their Moslem counterparts than did those from countries where Christians form a small minority in an Islamic world. Still, the recent upsurge of Islamic visibility will surely increase enrollments in courses on Islam wherever they are offered, and sales of books on the subject are up.

All such activities are welcome. But what about the shadowgraphs? Conferences and courses will help only if their participants become aware of the deeplying, nearly archetypal images that subvert the whole enterprise from the outset. Along with study and analysis, a kind of cultural archaeology or even a collective psychoanalysis may be necessary if we are to leave Dante's Inferno behind and live in peace with our Moslem neighbors on the planet Earth. The question is, How can Westerners, and Christians in particular, begin to cut through the maze of distorting mirrors and prepare the ground for some genuine encounter with Moslems?

The first thing we probably need to recognize is that the principal source of the acrimony underlying the Christian—Moslem relationship is a historical equivalent of sibling rivalry. Christians somehow hate to admit that in many ways their faith stands closer to Islam than to any other world religion. Indeed, that may be the reason Muhammad was viewed for centuries in the West as a charlatan and an imposter. The truth is, theologically speaking at least, both faiths are the offspring of an earlier revelation through the Law and the Prophets to the people of Israel. Both honor the Virgin Mary and Jesus of Nazareth. Both received an enormous early impetus from an apostle—Paul for Christianity and Muhammad for Islam—who translated a particularistic vision into a universal faith. The word "Allah" (used in the core formula of Islam: "There is no God but Allah and Muhammad is his prophet") is not an exclusively Moslem term at all. It is merely the Arabic word for God, and is used by Arabic Christians when they refer to the God of Christian faith.

There is nothing terribly surprising about these similarities since Muhammad, whose preaching mission did not begin until he reached forty, was subjected to considerable influence from Christianity during his formative years and may have come close—according to some scholars—to becoming an Abyssinian Christian. As Arend van Leeuwen points out in his thoughtful treatment of Islam in *Christianity in World History,* "The truth is that when Islam was still in the initial stages of its development, there was nothing likely to prevent the new movement from being accepted as a peculiar version of Arabian Christianity." Maybe the traditional Christian uneasiness with Islam is that it seems just a little *too* similar. We sense the same aversion we might feel toward a twin brother who looks more like us than we want him to and whose habits remind us of some of the things we like least in ourselves.

The metaphor of a brother, or perhaps a cousin, is entirely germane. Muhammad considered himself to be in a direct line with the great biblical prophets and with Jesus. The title he preferred for himself was *alnabi al-ummi,* the "prophet of the nations" (or of the "gentiles"). He believed he was living proof that the God who had called and used previous prophets such as Abraham and Job, neither of whom was Jewish, could do the same thing again. Later on, Moslem theologians liked to trace the genealogy of Muhammad back to Hagar, the bondwoman spouse of Abraham. The Old Testament story says that Hagar's giving birth to Ishmael stirred up such jealousy between her and Sarah, Abraham's first wife and the mother of Isaac, that Sarah persuaded Abraham to banish the bondwoman and her child into the desert. There Hagar gave up hope and left the child under a shrub to die. But God heard the child's weeping, created a well of water in the desert to save them both, and promised Hagar that from her son also, as from Isaac, He would "create a great nation." According to the symbolism of this old saga, the Jews and the Arabs (and by extension all Moslems) are the common offspring of Abraham (called "Ibrahim" in Arabic). This makes Christians and Moslems cousins, at least by legendary lineage.

The similarity between Christians and Moslems does not stop with religious genealogy. The actual elements of the Koran's message—faith, fasting, alms, prayer, and pilgrimage—all have Christian analogues. Despite its firm refusal to recognize any divine being except God (which is the basis for its rejection of Christ's divinity), Islam appears sometimes to be a pastiche of elements from disparate forms of Christianity molded into a potent unity. Take the Calvinist emphasis on faith in an omnipotent deity, the pietistic cultivation of daily personal prayer, the medieval teaching on charity, the folk-Catholic fascination with pilgrimage, and the monastic practice of fasting, and you have all the essential ingredients of Islam. All, that is, except the confluence of forces which, through the personality of Muhammad and the movement he set off, joined these elements in the white heat of history and fused them into a coherent faith of compelling attractiveness.

Like Paul, who said his apostleship was to both Jews and gentiles, Muhammad believed his mission was twofold. He felt called by God to bring the law and the Gospel to the heretofore neglected peoples of Arabia. But he also felt he had a mission *to* those very peoples—Christians and Jews (whom he called "peoples of the book")—*from* whom the original message of salvation had come. In one important respect, therefore, Muhammad's mission was different from St. Paul's. Since Muhammad carried on his preaching in the early decades of the seventh century, he not only had to deal with a Judaism he considered corrupted (as Paul had too); he also had to face an even more corrupted form of Christianity. Fortunately for St. Paul, since the Christian movement was only a decade or so old when he lived, he had to cope only with a few legalizers and gnostics. The infant Church had not yet tasted the corruption that comes, perhaps inevitably, from power and longevity. From a certain Christian perspective, Muhammad was as much a reformer as an apostle. A prophet of the gentiles, he also saw himself as a purifier of the faith of all the "peoples of the book," Christians and Jews, calling them away from the ornate and decadent versions of the faith they had fallen into and back to its simple essence, at least as he understood it. There is always something of this urge to simplify, to return *ad fontes,* in any reformer. And Muhammad was no exception.

No one should minimize the fact that in any genuine conversation between Christians and Moslems certain real differences in theology and practice will have to be faced, what scholars often call "rival truth claims." But such conflicting assertions can be properly understood only against the flesh-and-blood history that has somehow made them rivals. Religious teachings do not inhabit a realm apart. They mean what they do to people because of the coloration given to them by long historical experience. Therefore a previous question has to be asked. It is this: If Christianity and Islam share such common roots and, despite real differences, some striking similarities, why have they grown so bitter toward each other over the centuries? Why did the average white American feel less sympathetic to Islam than to any other world religion even *before* our current flap with the ayatollahs?

The explanation for this hostility is not a pretty story. Its major lineaments can be indicated with the names of three figures who symbolize its most critical stages. The first is Alexander the Great, whose career corresponds to what might be called the prehistory of Christianity. The second is Constantine the Great, who exemplifies its early period. The third is Pope Urban II, who expresses its classical phase, one of the most formative in the Christian–Moslem interaction.

Christopher Dawson, the late Roman Catholic cultural historian, once remarked that "Muhammad is the Orient's answer to Alexander the Great." At first this sounds like one of those wonderfully sweeping but highly improbable aphorisms. Muhammad, after all, lived and preached a full thousand years after Alexander. The prodigious Macedonian disciple of Aristotle conquered everything between Greece and northern India before he was thirty-three and spread the culture and values of Hellenism wherever his soldiers trod. But a thousand years is not a long time when one is dealing with cultural domination and the backlash it ultimately elicits. This is what Dawson had in mind.

Alexander did more than conquer everything before him. Unlike previous conquerors, who sought mainly booty and tribute, he wanted to convert his colonized peoples into Hellenists. Alexander's conquest mixed military, political, and religious power. It was obviously going to require a comparable fusion of elements to throw off his conquest. After a thousand years that response finally came. It was Islam.

As Albert Memmi writes in his classic book *The Colonizer and the Colonized,* ''. . . the colonized can wait a long time to live. But, regardless of how soon or how violently the colonized rejects his situation, he will one day begin to overthrow his unlivable existence with the whole force of his oppressed personality . . . He attempts to . . . reconquer all the dimensions which the colonization tore away from him.'' When the Islamic response to Roman–Hellenistic domination exploded in the early seventh century, the entire world was stunned by its vitality. In retrospect, however, we can understand its religious ideology in large measure as a reverse mirror image of what it was overthrowing. Take its rejection of the divinity of Christ, for example. Alexander had allowed himself to be viewed as a divine being, a god-emperor, and this ideology persisted through centuries of European culture in one form or another. The Koran's strenuous insistence that there was only one God, and its rejection of all semidivine beings, must be seen at least in part as a rejection of the political use of Christology to sacralize various forms of human rule.

The Moslem rejection of the divinity of Christ is not just simpleminded monotheistic stubbornness. It began as ''political theology.'' For the Arabians, living on what were then the outskirts of the Eastern Empire, it marked a rejection not only of the non-Semitic categories in which the doctrine of Christ's divinity were elaborated in the Church councils (the ''being of one substance with the Father'') but also of the political hierarchy the doctrine helped to sanctify, especially in the Byzantine environment. When the Pantocrator Christ began to sacralize an empire in which the Arabians were the underdogs, their refusal of the doctrine made perfect sense. Alexander the Great had created the cultural imperium for which Christianity eventually supplied the sacred ideology. The Islamic revolt against this system was a revolt not against the Gospel as they understood it but against what Christianity had come to be. Islam's implacable insistence on one God not only freed thousands of people from their fear of the evil jinns and united the feuding tribes of Arabia (and later a vast part of the known world); it also served as a counterideology to the political function that Christian trinitarianism was beginning to serve. No ''rival truth claim'' debate between Christians and Moslems can begin until this history is recognized.

Islam began as a liberation theology, but, like Christianity, which had a comparable beginning, it could not resist the wiles of worldly power. As in the case of most successful liberation movements, Islam incorporated many of the cultural and political characteristics of its enemies. Though Muhammad was hounded out of Mecca by its local power elites, one hundred years after his death a glittering capital for the new Islamic empire was founded at Baghdad, the "Constantinople of Islam." Moslems became imperialists themselves, although in most instances they allowed Christians and Jews to practice their faiths. Forced conversions were rare. Above all, Moslems became the supreme masters and cultivators of the very Greek wisdom that had been imposed on them by Alexander. They became devout disciples of the same Aristotle whose zealous pupil had set out to spread his master's learning in their lands a millennium before. It was the Arabs, after all, who brought Aristotle back to the West and eventually to the cluttered desk of Thomas Aquinas. At its height, Islamic culture vastly outshone that of the Christian West, which most Moslems more or less accurately regarded as a barren outpost. But at the same time, the original liberating impulse of Islam had begun to run out. Today, paradoxically, this very spoiling by success may provide a needed bridge between Christians and Moslems, since Christians have experienced the same sad, familiar story in their own history.

Muhammad's judgment on the Christianity of his day is one of the great ironies of history. This Christianity, which began in the life of a Palestinian Jew who was executed because he was viewed as a threat to the Roman Empire and to the Hellenistically inclined rulers of his colonized nation, was seen a few centuries later by Muhammad, the prophet of another down-trodden nation, as the religious sanction for his own people's domination. What is remarkable about Muhammad is not that he rejected current theories about the divinity of Christ but that he did *not* reject Jesus himself. Rather he tried, from his own vantage point, to bypass the caricature of the Gospel which imperial Christianity had elaborated and to reclaim the faith of a people much like his own who had once looked to Allah for justice and mercy.

Jesus, then, is another vital link between the two faiths. To this day, Jesus holds a central place in Islamic teaching and is sometimes even depicted as a kind of supreme exemplar of what is meant by "submission to God" (the meaning of the word "Islam"). In popular Islamic belief, Jesus often occupies an even more important position. Thus many Moslems believe that when the long awaited "Twelfth Iman," whose name is *al-Mahdi,* finally appears to usher in the reign of justice on earth (*not* in the sky, incidentally), he will either be accompanied by Jesus or will turn out to be the same one whose "coming in Glory" the Christian creeds confess. Obviously there is much to discuss here between these two "Jesus traditions," if the ground can be cleared of spiteful stereotypes and the sibling rivalry can be held at bay.

Both Christianity and Islam began as visions of captive peoples who yearned for deliverance and caught a glimpse of hope in the promise of God. The two can understand each other only when both begin to acknowledge these common roots, step out of the long shadow of Alexander the Great, and try to learn from each other what has gone so terribly wrong over the years of their common history.

Constantine the Great, Roman emperor from 313 to 337 A.D. represents the historical turning point that eventually created the second great obstacle between Christians and Moslems. The Christian movement began not only as a message of hope to a colonized nation but also as the faith of the poor and the brokenhearted. But three centuries later, when Emperor Constantine beheld the cross shining across the sun and later claimed to have won the imperial throne with the help of Jesus Christ, all that changed. Although St. Paul could write to one of his fledgling congregations that there were "not many wise, not many powerful" in their midst, and the common name for Jesus' followers in those earliest days was simply "the poor," Constantine's well-timed and canny conversion totally altered all that for good. It is impossible to understand Muhammad's view of Christianity unless one remembers that he was basing it not on the Gospel accounts but on his observation of how the Church was actually functioning in his world. By their fruits ye shall know them.

Muhammad claimed to be one of the poor, at least when he started, and he never tired of reminding his followers that he was only an illiterate camel driver. He saw his humble origins not as a disgrace but as a wondrous proof that God could raise up from the very stones children unto Abraham. The *al-ummi* with whom Muhammad identified himself has a double sense. The word means not only the "gentiles," or "people without the Law," but also the unlettered, something close to the *am-ha-aretz*, the poor "people of the land" with whom Jesus sided against the learned scribes and Pharisees. The historian H. G. Reisman says that Muhammad was "a leader of the masses against the privileged minorities of wealth and sophistication." This may also explain in part the popular Islamic belief, baffling to many Christians, that every child is a "born Moslem." With growing up and education comes sophistication and corruption. In the Koran, similar to an idea St. Paul defends in the first chapter of his Epistle to the Romans, every person has an inborn, natural awareness of God. We all start out pious but are misled by a fallen civilization and perfidious religions. It is the task of preaching to call us back to what we were, or were intended to be, in the first place.

The Koranic vision of a simple faith by which the poor and the unlettered can withstand manipulation at the hands of the powerful and the better educated makes Christians uncomfortable today, and understandably. It is painfully reminiscent of the "Blessed are the poor" with which Jesus began the Sermon on the Mount and the subsequent "Woe to you rich" with which he made sure he was not misunderstood. The Church has never completely lost its recognition of this aspect of its history. It surfaces repeatedly in such places as Simone Weil's life-shaking discovery that Christianity is essentially a faith of the poor, or in the Latin

American bishops' declaring that the Church's special responsibility is to stand with the jobless and landless. Nor has Islam, despite prodigiously rich oil sheikhs, ever completely lost this central core of its tradition either. Each faith will find it easier to appreciate the other when this special role of the *al-ummi* becomes the major rather than the minor theme of its message. In this respect, Christianity probably has more recovering to do than Islam has.

Pope Urban II, who occupied the throne of Peter from 1088 to 1099, is the third great actor in the tragedy of Christianity's cumulative falling-out with Islam. He was an energetic reformer who became Pope during a period of divisiveness in the Church; his main challenge was to bring it into some semblance of unity. Like many other rulers before him, religious and secular, Urban hit upon a surefire unifying idea. Realizing that nothing unites like an external foe, and inspired by requests from the beleaguered Christians of the East, he preached a holy war against the infidels who were even then holding the Holy Sepulchre and promised the fullest spiritual benefit to those who would take up the cross. Christians and other Americans who criticize the concept of the jihad, or holy war, and decry the taking of hostages and conversion at sword's point are right, of course. But it does not require much reading in this not-so-glorious chapter in Western Christian history to see that Moslems were neither the first nor the only guilty parties in this department. In fact, there is at least one prominent school of historical scholarship that sees the first Moslem expansion not as a jihad but as a large-scale migration similar to the one that had brought the Germanic tribes into the Roman Empire from the other direction. The concept of holy war can be found in more than one Old Testament verse. It did not originate with Islam. To many Arabs it must have seemed the only sensible response to the not entirely pacifist manner in which the Christian empire dealt with its recalcitrant provinces and with those forms of Christianity, such as Nestorianism, that the bishops deemed unacceptable.

Like all wars, holy or unholy, the Crusades produced their quota of atrocity stories on both sides. They also produced countless incidents of generosity and unexpected interfaith respect. The mutual admiration that developed between Richard I of England and the theologically articulate Saladin, celebrated in legend, seems to have had a factual basis. Still, it was the Crusaders and not the Saracens who boasted that when they first took Jerusalem the blood of the infidels, including wives and children, flowed through the streets as deep as the horses' stirrups. Such memories do not die easily, and it is important to recall that although Westerners would sometimes like to reduce the "wars of the cross" to tales of chivalry and late-night movie fare, for many Moslems the Crusades—Christian jihads—remain the most graphic expression of what the cross means. All the more amazing, then, that even the Ayatollah Khomeini, talking to a group of visiting American clergy on Christmas Day, 1979, could ask why, as those who worship the wounded Jesus, Americans were so incapable of understanding a wounded people such as his own. Apparently some feeling for the real meaning of the cross has survived in Islam, despite the Crusades.

If it took Muhammad a thousand years to respond to Alexander the Great, perhaps it should come as no surprise that it has taken the Islamic peoples another 900 years to respond to Pope Urban II, Peter the Hermit, and the hordes of idealists, adventurers, and thugs who in successive waves burned and pillaged their way across Europe toward the Holy Land for nearly 400 years. True, some historians hold that the Crusades might never have occurred had it not been for the previous threat of militant Islam to the West. Still, once the Crusades began, they acquired a lethal momentum of their own. Christian armies started by burning the nearest ghetto, and when their attempts to seize the Holy Sepulchre did not fully succeed, turned their cross-bedecked banners toward the pagan Baltic peoples and the Albigenses of southern France. It is an ugly history. But until the sorry story of Crusade versus jihad is faced frankly and then replaced by a more generous and conciliatory attitude, the hatred and suspicion between Christians and their Moslem cousins can only escalate.

No discussion of the relations of Moslems and Christians can proceed very far without raising the parallel question of the equally long and similarly vexed interaction of Moslems and Jews. The Jewish historian S. D. Goitein is the leading scholar in the study of what he calls the "symbiosis" between Jews and Arabs. Now at the Institute for Advanced Study in Princeton, after having taught at the Hebrew University of Jersusalem, Goitein has spent a lifetime probing Moslem religious literature, the medieval Geniza (documents written in Hebrew characters but in the Arabic language), and the fascinating histories of the so-called Oriental Jewish communities—those of the Arab and Moslem worlds. His *From the Land of Sheba* is an anthology of Yemenite literature. It would be hard to find a more reliable guide to this intricate area.

Goitein believes that Islam is actually far closer to Judaism than to Christianity in its core ideas. In taking this position, he joins a debate that has been going on for years (the other side contending that the similarity with Christianity is more important). Goitein bases his case on the obvious fact that both Islam and Judaism are religions of the Holy Law, and that Moslem law is in many respects similar to the Jewish Halakah, which he calls its "older sister." Both therefore differ, at least in this respect, from Christianity, which, with its emphasis on grace, has always harbored a certain suspicion of religious law (even though Christian theologians have managed to spin out yards of it over the years).

Goitein's "sister" image of the bond between Islam and Judaism should not be surprising when one bears in mind the saying, attributed to Muhammad, "You will follow the traditions of those who preceded you span by span and cubit by cubit—so closely that you will go after them even if they creep into the hole of a lizard.'' This colorful advice takes on even more significance in light of the fact that there were large Jewish settlements in the city of al-Medina, the birthplace of the first Moslem community, and that the biographers of the prophet almost all agree that these communities, far from being an obstacle to the spread of Islam, were in fact wondrous evidence of Allah's merciful and providential preparation of the people for a monotheistic faith. As with Christianity, the early years of Islam seem in retrospect to have promised mostly fraternal—or in this case sororial—congeniality with Judaism. But again, the roiling history of Jewish and Islamic peoples has often turned familial ties into tribal vendettas. Must it always be so?

In his informative book *Jews and Arabs: Their Contacts Through the Ages,* Goitein does what only a seasoned scholar ever dares to do. He compresses eons of history into one volume, risks a few well-grounded generalizations, and even hazards some guesses about the future. He divides the millennia-long give-and-take between these two peoples into four periods. The first, corresponding perhaps to the Alexandrian age of the Christian–Islam story, begins before historical memory and reaches up to the sixth century A.D. and the appearance of Islam. During this early period, a critically formative one for the Jews since it saw the compilation of both the Bible and the Talmud, Goitein believes Jews and Arabs had quite similar social patterns and religious practices. He firmly rejects any notion of a common Semitic race, however, as a modern idea concocted from the misapplication of a term invented by a German scholar in 1781 to denote a group of related languages, not ''races,'' or even peoples. The distinction is an important one. There are several examples of peoples who for a variety of historical reasons now speak a language spoken by other peoples with whom they have no ethnic consanguinity at all. Black Americans are a case in point. Likewise, Jews and Moslem Arabs are related, according to Goitein, but by history and tradition, not by race.

The period from, roughly, 500 A.D. to 1300 A.D. is Goitein's second one. He describes it as one of ''creative symbiosis,'' in which early Islam developed in a largely Jewish environment. Although he agrees that Christian influences, coming especially from monastic groups, played some role in this primal period, he believes that Judaism was even more important, so much so that he is willing to say—with some reservations—that Islam appears to be ''an Arab recast of Israel's religion.'' But the influence was not one-way, and the impact of Islam and the Arabic language on Jewish thought and the Hebrew language was, he adds, at least as considerable. Goitein also reminds his readers that although Jews experienced some legal disqualifications under Moslem rule, they almost always fared better than they did under Christian dominance.

Goitein's third period begins in about 1300, when the previously high-riding Arabs began to ''fade out'' of world history at the same time that the Oriental Jews began to fade out of Jewish history. During this phase, which lasted until about 1900, the Arab nations fell to various conquerors until the entire Arab world had become a colony of the modern West. Meanwhile Jewish religious and intellectual life flourished in Europe, while Jews living in the beleaguered Moslem world, though they nurtured a rich internal culture, shared the suffering and obscurity of their Moslem neighbors.

The present period in Goiten's scheme begins in about 1900 with the coincidental revival of Jewish and Arab cultural and national identities, both influenced by the growing nationalism of nineteenth-century Europe. Since Zionism was an almost exclusively European (and American) movement, however, it was perceived by Arabs and other Moslems more as a new Western intrusion into the East, a pattern going back at least to the Crusades, than as something essentially Jewish, at least at the beginning. But shortly after the founding of the State of Israel, Israelis had to cope with a kind of mirror image of this "intrusion" as Jewish immigrants from Arab countries, the "forgotten Jews" of the previous period, streamed into Israel, making it less "European" with every passing day. The paradox of this apparent double intrusion was illustrated recently when an Oriental Jewish scholar living in Israel complained to a visitor about all the remarks he heard from his European colleagues lamenting the "Levantizing" of Israel. "How, " he asked, "can you 'Levantize' something that is already the Levant?" His comment underscores Goitein's thoughtful prophecy that since the future of Jewish–Moslem relations has everything to do with the relations between Israel and its Arab neighbors, Israel's internal policy toward its Oriental Jews and its Arab citizens will be of decisive importance. Whether or not this turns out to be true, remembering the roller-coaster history of Jewish–Moslem relations helps one not to become too depressed about the steep decline these relations have taken in recent decades. There have been downs before, and ups, and it is not impossible that the tiny minority of Arab-Israeli citizens who are also Christians might eventually be able to play a conciliatory role. Likewise, though it seems far-fetched today, the global Jewish community, with centuries of experience in the Christian and the Moslem worlds, might someday provide an essential bridge between these two faith traditions, both in some ways its offspring. In any case, whatever happens to facilitate the conversation that must go on among Christians, Jews, and Moslems is bound to benefit all three.

Jews may help, but in the final analysis, given the role our religions play in both our cultures, no real rapport between the Arabs and the West seems possible unless Christians and Moslems make a more serious effort to understand each other. Curiously, after being warned for years that our greatest enemies in the world were godless and atheistic, Americans are now faced with a challenge that emanates from profoundly religious sources. Although Islam has never accepted the dichotomy between religion and the civil polity that has arisen in the West, there can be little doubt that the present Islamic renaissance is not a deviation but an authentic expression of the elements that were there at its origin. So we are now told that, instead of atheists, we are dealing with "fanatics," or "Moslem fundamentalists." This language is not very helpful either.

Sometime soon a real conversation must begin. Perhaps the moment has come to set aside Dante, Urban II, and the rest; to remember instead the two children of Father Abraham, from both of whom God promised to make great nations; to recall that Jesus also cast his lot with the wounded and wronged of his time; to stop caricaturing the faith of Arabia's apostle; and to try to help both Christians and Moslems to recover what is common to them in a world that is just too small for any more wars, especially holy ones.

1. What has been the traditional image of the Moslem in the West, and how does Cox account for it?
2. What do Christianity and Islam have in common?
3. How does Cox explain the hostility between Christianity and Islam, and what solution does he propose?
4. What part does the relationship and opposition between Jews and Moslems have to play in Cox's argument?
5. How would you sum up the argumentative techniques Cox uses in this essay? Are they effective?

AFTER CIVILIZATION, WHAT?

Kenneth E. Boulding

We are living in what I call the second great change in the state of man. The first is the change from pre-civilized to civilized societies. The first five hundred thousand years or so of man's existence on earth were relatively uneventful. Compared with his present condition, he puttered along in an astonishingly stationary state. There may have been changes in language and culture which are not reflected in the artifacts, but if there were, these changes are lost to us. The evidence of the artifacts, however, is conclusive. Whatever changes they were, they were almost unbelievably slow. About ten thousand years ago, we begin to perceive an acceleration in the rate of change. This becomes very noticeable five thousand years ago with the development of the first civilization. The details of this first great change are probably beyond our recovery. However, we do know that it depended on two phenomena: the development of agriculture and the development of exploitation. Agriculture, that is the domestication of crops and livestock and the planting of crops in fields, gave man a secure surplus of food from the food producer. In a hunting and fishing economy it seems to take the food producer all his time to produce enough food for himself and his family. The moment we have agriculture, with its superior productivity of this form of employment of human resources, the food producer can produce more food than he and his family can eat. In some societies in these happy conditions, the food producer has simply relaxed and indulged himself with leisure. As soon, however, as we get politics, that is exploitation, we begin to get cities and civilization. Civilization, it is clear from the origin of the word, is what happens in cities, and the city is dependent (in its early stages, at any rate) on the existence of a food surplus from the food producer and some organization which can take it away from him. With this food surplus, the political organization feeds kings, priests, armies, architects, and builders, and the city comes into being. Political science in its earliest form is the knowledge of how to take the food surplus away from the food producer without giving him very much in return.

Now I argue that we are in the middle of the second great change in the state of man, which is as drastic and as dramatic, and certainly as large as, if not larger than, the change from pre-civilized to civilized society. This I call the change from civilization to post-civilization. It is a strange irony that just at the moment when civilization has almost completed the conquest of pre-civilized societies, post-civilization has been treading heavily upon its heels. The student of civilization may soon find himself in the unfortunate position of the anthropologist who studies pre-civilized societies. Both are like the student of ice on a hot day—the subject matter melts away almost before he can study it.

These great changes can be thought of as a change of gear in the evolutionary process, resulting in progressive acceleration of the rate of evolutionary change. Even before the appearance of man on the earth, we can detect earlier evolutionary gear-shiftings. The formation of life obviously represented one such transition, the movement from the water to the land another, the development of the vertebrates another, and so on. Man himself represents a very large acceleration of the evolutionary process. Whether he evolved from pre-existing forms or landed from a space ship and was not able to get back to where he came from, is immaterial. Once he had arrived on earth, the process of evolution could go on within the confines of the human nervous system at a greatly accelerated rate. The human mind is an enormous mutation-selection process. Instead of mutation-selection process being confined, as it were, to the flesh, it can take place within the image, and hence, very rapid changes are possible. Man seems to have been pretty slow to exploit this potentiality, but one suspects that even with primitive man, the rate of change in the biosphere was much larger than it had been before, because of the appearance of what Teilhard de Chardin calls the noosphere, or sphere of knowledge.

Civilization represents a further acceleration of the rate of change, mainly because one of the main products of civilization is history. With the food surplus from agriculture it became possible to feed specialized scribes. With the development of writing, man did not have to depend on the uncertain memories of the aged for his records, and a great process of accumulation of social knowledge began. The past could now communicate, at least in one direction, with the present, and this enormously increased the range and possibility of enlargements of the contents of the human mind.

Out of civilization, however, comes science, which is a superior way of organizing the evolution of knowledge. We trace the first beginnings of science, of course, almost as far back as the beginning of civilization itself. Beginning about 1650, however, we begin to see the organization of science into a community of knowledge, and this leads again to an enormous acceleration of the rate of change. The world of 1650 is more remote to us than the world of ancient Egypt or Samaria would have been to the man of 1650. Already in the United States and Western Europe, in a smaller degree in Russia and in some other parts of the world, we see the beginnings of post-civilized society—a state of man as different from civilization as civilization is from savagery. What we really mean, therefore, by the anemic term "economic development" is the second great transition in the state of man. It is the movement from civilized to post-civilized society. It is nothing short of a major revolution in the human condition, and it does not represent a mere continuance and development of the old patterns of civilization.

As a dramatic illustration of the magnitude of the change, we can contemplate Indonesia. This is a country which has about the same extent, population and per capita income as the Roman Empire at its height. For all I know it is producing a literature and an art at least comparable to that of the Augustan age. It is, therefore, a very good example of a country of high civilization. Because of this fact, it is one of the poorest countries in the world. It is desperately anxious to break out of its present condition. Jakarta is a city about the size of ancient Rome, though perhaps a little less splendid. All this points up the fact that the Roman Empire was a desperately poor and under-developed society. The Roman cities seem to have been always about three weeks away from starvation, and even at its height it is doubtful whether the Roman Empire ever had less than seventy-five to eighty per cent of its population in agriculture.

Civilization, that is, is a state of society in which techniques are so poor that it takes about eighty per cent of the population to feed the hundred per cent. But we do have about twenty per cent of the people who can be spared from food-producing to build Parthenons and cathedrals, to write literature and poetry, and fight wars. By contrast, in the United States today we are rapidly getting to the point where we can produce all our food with only ten per cent of the population and still have large agricultural surpluses. But for the blessings of agricultural policy, we might soon be able to produce all our food with five per cent of the population. It may even be that agriculture is on its way out altogether and that within another generation or so we will produce our food in a totally different way. Perhaps both fields and cows are merely relics of civilization, the vestiges of a vanishing age. This means, however, that even in our society, which is at a very early stage of post-civilization, we can now spare about ninety per cent of the people to produce bathtubs, automobiles, H-bombs and all the other conveniences of life. Western Europe and Japan are coming along behind the United States very fast. The Russians, likewise, are advancing toward post-civilization, although by a very different road. At the moment their ideology is a handicap to them in some places—especially in agriculture, which still occupies forty-five per cent of the people. And, if the Russians ever discover that super-peasants are a good deal more efficient than collective farms, they may cut away some of the ideology that hangs around their neck and move even more rapidly toward post-civilized society.

I'm not at all sure what post-civilization will look like but it will certainly be a world-wide society. Until very recently, each civilized society was a little island in a sea of barbarism which constantly threatened to overwhelm it. Civilization is haunted by the spectre of decline and fall, though it is noteworthy that in spite of the rise and fall of particular civilizations, civilization itself expanded steadily in geographical coverage, from its very beginnings. We must face the fact, however, that post-civilized society will be world-wide, if only because of its ease of communication and transportation. I flew last year from Idlewild to Brussels, and on glimpsing the new Brussels Airport out of the corner of my eye, I thought for a moment that we had come back and landed at Idlewild again.

The characteristic institutions of civilization are, as we have seen, first agriculture, then the city, then war, in the sense of clash of organized armed forces, and finally, inequality, the sharp contrast between the rich and the poor, between the city and the country, between the urbane and the rustic. The state is based very fundamentally on violence and exploitation, and the culture tends to be spiritually monolithic.

In post-civilization all these institutions suffer radical change. Agriculture, as we have seen, diminishes until it is a small proportion of the society; the city, likewise, in the classical sense, disintegrates. Los Angeles is perhaps the first example of the post-civilization, post-urban agglomeration—under no stretch of the imagination could it be called a city. War, likewise, is an institution in process of distintegration. National defense as a social system has quite fundamentally broken down on a world scale. The ICBM and the nuclear warhead have made the nation-state as militarily obsolete as the city-state, for in no country now can the armed forces preserve an area of internal peace by pushing violence to the outskirts. Poverty and inequality, likewise, are tending to disappear, at least on their traditional scale. In civilized societies the king or the emperor could live in a Versailles and the peasant in a hovel. In post-civilized society, it is almost impossible for the rich to consume on a scale which is more, let us say, than ten times that of the poor. There is no sense in having more than ten automobiles!

Another profound change in the passage from civilization to post-civilization is the change in the expectation of life. In civilized society, birth and death rates tend to be about forty per thousand and the expectation of life at birth is twenty-five years. In post-civilized society, the expectation of life at birth rises at least to seventy and perhaps beyond. It may be that we are on the edge of a biological revolution, just as dramatic and far-reaching as the discovery of atomic energy and that we may crack the problem of aging and prolong human life much beyond its present span. Whether or not, however, we go forward to Methuselah, the mere increase of the average age of death to seventy is a startling and far-reaching change. It means, for instance, that in an equilibrium population, the birth and death rate cannot be more than about fourteen per thousand. This unquestionably implies some form of conscious control of births. It means also that a much larger proportion of the population will be in later years.

It is perfectly possible to paint an anti-utopia in which a post-civilized society appears as universally vulgar or dull. On the whole, however, I welcome post-civilization and I have really very little affection for civilization. In most pre-civilized societies the fact that the life of man is for the most part nasty, brutish and short, does not prevent the poets and philosophers from sentimentalizing the noble savage. Similarly, we may expect the same kind of sentimentalizing of the noble Romans and civilized survivals like Winston Churchill. On the whole, though, I will not shed any tears over the grave of civilization any more than I will over pre-civilized society. The credit balance of post-civilization is large. It at least gives us a chance of a modest utopia, in which slavery, poverty, exploitation, gross inequality, war and disease—these prime costs of civilization—will fall to the vanishing point.

What we have at the moment is a chance to make a transition to this modest utopia—a chance which is probably unique in the history of this planet. If we fail, the chance will probably not be repeated in this part of the universe. Whatever experiments may be going on elsewhere, the present moment indeed is unique in the whole four billion years of the history of the planet. In my more pessimistic moments, I think the chance is a slim one, and it may be that man will be written off as an unsuccessful experiment. We must look at the traps which lie along the path of the transition, which might prevent us from making it altogether.

The most urgent trap is, of course, the trap of war. War, as I have suggested, is an institution peculiarly characteristic of civilization. Pre-civilized societies have sporadic feuding and raiding, but they do not generally have permanent organized armed forces, and they do not generally develop conquest and empire; or if they do, they soon pass into a civilized form. An armed force is essentially a mobile city designed to throw things at another mobile or stationary city with presumably evil intent. As far as I know, not more than two or three civilizations have existed without war. The Mayans and the people of Mohenjodaro seem to have lived for fairly long periods without war, but this was an accident of their monopolistic situation and they unquestionably occupied themselves with other kinds of fool-ishness. If pre-civilized society, however, cannot afford war, post-civilized society can afford far too much of it, and hence will be forced to get rid of the institution because it is simply inappropriate to the technological age. The breakdown in the world social system of national defense really dates from about 1949, when the United States lost its monopoly of nuclear weapons. A system of national defense is only feasible if each nation is stronger at home than its enemies, so that it can preserve a relatively large area of peace within its critical boundaries. Such a system is only possible, however, if the range of the deadly missile is short and if the armed forces of each nation lose power rapidly as they move away from home. The technological developments of the twentieth century have destroyed these foundations of national defense, and have replaced it with another social system altogether, which is "deterrence."

"Deterrence" is a social system with properties very different from that of national defense, which it replaced. Under national defense, for instance, it is possible to use the armed forces; under "deterrence" it is not—that is, if the deterring forces are ever used, the system will have broken down. We live in a society with a positive possibility of irretrievable disaster—a probability which grows every year. Herman Kahn recently said: "All we are doing is buying time, and we are doing nothing with the time that we buy." The armed forces of the world are caught in a technological process which not only destroys their own function, but threatens all of us. Even if a few of us do crawl out of the fallout shelters, it is by no means clear that we can put the world back together again. Even if the human race could survive one nuclear war, it is very doubtful that it could survive a second; and as the purpose of the first nuclear war would be to set up a political system which would produce the second, unless there is a radical change in attitude towards national defense, the prospects of the human race seem to be dim. Fortunately, "there is still time, brother" and evolution can still go on in the minds of men. The critical question is whether it can go on rapidly enough. The abolition of national defense, which is what we must face, is going to be a painful process, as we have come to rely on it to preserve many of the values which we hold dear. If the task can be perceived, however, by a sufficient number of people, there is at least a chance that we may avoid this trap before it is too late.

Even if we avoid the war trap, we may still fall into the population trap. Population control is an unsolved problem even for the developed areas of the world, which have moved the furthest towards post-civilization. An equilibrium of population in a stable post-civilized society may represent a fairly radical interference with ancient human institutions and freedoms. In a stable post-civilized society, as I have suggested, the birth and death rates must be of the order of fourteen per thousand, and the average number of children per family cannot much exceed two. There are many social institutions which might accomplish this end. So far, however, the only really sure-fire method of controlling population is starvation and misery.

In many parts of the world—indeed, for most of the human race for the moment—the impact on certain post-civilized techniques of civilized society has produced a crisis of growth, which may easily be fatal. In the tropics especially, with DDT and a few simple public-health measures, it is easy to reduce the death rate to nine or ten per thousand while the birth rate stays at forty per thousand. This means an annual increase of population of three per cent *per annum,* almost all of it concentrated in the lower age groups. We see dramatic examples of this phenomenon in places like the West Indies, Ceylon, and Formosa; but thanks to the activity of the World Health Organization, it is taking place rapidly all over the tropical world. Perhaps the most important key to the transition to post-civilization is heavy investment in human resources—that is, in education. The conquest of disease and infant mortality, however, before the corresponding adjustment to the birth rate, produces enormous numbers of children in societies which do not have the resources to educate them—especially as those in the middle-age groups, who after all must do all the work of a society, come from the much smaller population of the pre-DDT era.

Even in the developed countries, population control presents a very serious problem. The United States, for instance, at the moment is increasing in population even more rapidly than India.* The time when we thought that the mere increase in income would automatically solve the population problem has gone by. In the United States, and certain other societies, in the early stages of post-civilization, the child has become an object of conspicuous domestic consumption. The consumption patterns of the American spending unit seem to follow a certain "gestalt" in which household capital accumulates in a certain order, such as the first car, the first child, the washer and dryer, the second child, the deep freeze, the third child, the second car, the fourth child, and so on. The richer we get, the more children we can afford to have and the more children we do have. We now seem to be able to afford an average of something like four children per family, and as, in a post-civilized society, these four children all survive, the population doubles every generation. A hundred years of this and even the United States is going to find itself uncomfortably crowded. It can be argued, indeed, that from the point of view of the amenities of life we are already well beyond the optimum population.

The third trap on the road to post-civilization is the technological trap. Our present technology is fundamentally suicidal. It is based on the extraction of concentrated deposits of fossil fuels and ores, which in the nature of things are exhaustible. Even at present rates of consumption, they will be exhausted in a time span which is not very long measured against human history and which is infinitesimally small on the geological time scale. If the rest of the world advances to American standards of consumption, these resources will disappear almost overnight. On this view economic development is the process of bringing closer the evil day when everything will be gone—all the oil, the coal, the ores—and

*Not at present—Ed.

522

we will have to go back to primitive agriculture and scratching in the woods.

There are indications, however, that suicidal technology is not absolutely necessary and that a permanent high-level technology is possible. Beginning in the early part of the twentieth century, it is possible to detect an anti-entropic movement in technology. This begins perhaps with the Haber process for the fixation of nitrogen from the air. A development of similar significance is the Dow process for the extraction of magnesium from the sea. Both these processes take the diffuse and concentrate it, instead of taking the concentrated and diffusing it, as do most processes of mining and economic production. These anti-entropic processes foreshadow a technology in which we shall draw all the materials we need from the virtually inexhaustible reservoirs of the sea and the air and draw our energy from controlled fusion—either artificially produced on the earth or from the sun.

This is why I so much resent spending half the world's income on armaments— because the more we do this, the less chance we have of making the transition to a stable, high-level society. The human race is in a precarious position on its planet and it should act accordingly. It has a chance, never to be repeated, of making its great transition, and if it fails, at least one good experiment in intelligence will have gone to waste. I suppose there are similar experiments of this nature going on in other parts of the universe; but I must confess to a hopelessly anthropocentric prejudice in favor of planet earth. It's a nice planet, and I'm in favor of it and I have no desire to see its principal inhabitant blow it up or starve it out.

When we look at the nature of possible remedies for our immediate problems, it seems clear that we all are engulfed in a profound and appallingly dangerous misallocation of our intellectual resources. The misallocation lies in the fact that although all our major problems are in social systems, we persist in regarding them as if they were essentially problems in physical or biological systems. We persist in regarding agricultural problems, for instance, as one of crops, whereas it is clearly fundamentally a problem of farmers. We persist in regarding the flood-control problem as a problem of the river and we even turn it over to army engineers, who treat the river as an enemy. A flood, however, is no problem at all to a river. It is a perfectly normal part of its way of life. The flood, essentially, is a problem of people and of social institutions, of architecture and zoning. Professor Gilbert White, of the University of Chicago, suggests that after spending over four billion dollars on flood control in this country, we are more in danger of major disasters than we were before. What we really mean by flood control is the substitution of a major disaster every fifty or one hundred years for minor inconveniences every five or ten.

In national defense we have fallen into exactly the same trap. We regard this as a problem in physical systems and in hardware, whereas it is essentially a problem in social systems. Here again, we are building into our societies the eventual certainty of total disaster. In face of the fact that war and peace is the major problem of our age, we are putting practically nothing into peace research; even when we do put money into arms control and disarmament research we spend sixty million dollars for Project Vela, which deals wholly with physical systems, and one hundred and fifty thousand on Project Vulcan, which deals with social systems and with unanswerable questions at that. When we look at biological and medical research, and still more, research into population, the disparity is just as striking. We persist in regarding disease as a biological problem, whereas it is fundamentally a bio-social system. Yet the number of sociologists in our medical schools can be counted almost on the fingers of one hand.

Nevertheless, in spite of the dangers, it is a wonderful age to live in, and I would not wish to be born in any other time. The wonderful and precious thing about the present moment is that there is still time—the Bomb hasn't gone off, the population explosion may be caught, the technological problem can, perhaps, be solved. If the human race is to survive, however, it will have to change more in its ways of thinking in the next twenty-five years than it has done in the last twenty-five thousand. There is hope, however, in the fact that we are very far from having exhausted the capacity of this extraordinary organism that we call man. I once calculated the capacity of the human nervous system in terms of the number of different states it might assume, which is a very rough measure. This comes to two to the ten billionth power, assuming that each of our ten billion neurons is capable of only two states. This is a very large number. It would take you ninety years to write it down at the rate of one digit a second. If you want a standard of comparison, the total number of neutrinos, which are the smallest known particles, which could be packed into the known astronomical universe (this is the largest physical number I could think of) could easily be written down in three minutes. I find it hard to believe, therefore, that the capacity of the human organism has been exhausted.

What we have to do now, however, is to develop almost a new form of learning. We have to learn from rapidly changing systems. Ordinarily we learn from stable systems. It is because the world repeats itself that we catch on to the law of repetition. Learning from changing systems is perhaps another step in the acceleration of evolution that we have to take. I have been haunted by a remark which Norman Meier, the psychologist, made in a seminar a few months ago, when he said that a cat who jumps on a hot stove never jumps on a cold one. This seems precisely to describe the state we may be in today. We have jumped on a lot of hot stoves and now perhaps the cold stove is the only place on which to jump. In the rapidly changing system it is desperately easy to learn things which are no longer true. Perhaps the greatest task of applied social science at the moment is to study the conditions under which we learn from rapidly changing systems. If we can answer this question, there may still be hope for the human race.

1. Contrast the civilized and post-civilized societies. Which would you rather live in?

2. What are the four major "traps" we face in post-civilized society? Explain them carefully, and say which one you think is the worst.

3. How does Boulding build up his argument?

4. What is the significance of the saying that "a cat who jumps on a hot stove never jumps on a cold one"?

5. Do you find Boulding's optimism persuasive? Explain your response carefully.

Reading and

Writing About

Literature

Literature and Expository Writing

What is literature? No one since the time of the ancient Greeks has found a satisfactory answer to this question, or at least an answer that satisfies everyone. It remains as enigmatic as ever and will doubtless continue to do so. Why? Because literature can *do* so many things and *is* so many things. It is not unusual to find song lyrics, film scripts, letters, and essays described as literature, alongside poetry, novels, short stories, and plays. One scholar has gone so far as to suggest that "literature includes any text worthy to be taught to students by teachers of literature,"[1] which is one way of being diplomatic. If anything that is in writing can qualify as "literature," the practical question becomes, what do we have to know about reading and writing about literature that is different from reading and writing about any other kind of discourse?

This question will keep us close to the business of reading and interpretation that we dealt with in the first two chapters. There we concentrated on language that is primarily referential; that is, the writing refers *out* to something beyond the text that is in some way verifiable. The writer has a practical intention that is available to the reader. Interpreting this kind of writing proceeds by annotating, summarizing, and judging the text's emphasis, coherence, unity, and significance. When we read any kind of expository writing, we are expected to be able to complete the meaning by reconstructing a writer's statements in our own words.

Is literary writing any different from this? Not in terms of the basic process of reading. In the reading of literature, as in the reading of any other kind of writing, you cannot understand an event unless it in some way relates to or enlarges upon your experience. The experience in the text may be far removed from you, but there must be some moment of identification, recognition, or development of your knowledge for understanding to take place. Knowledge never exists in a vacuum, but builds on what you already know.

So literary writing has to some extent to refer *out* to personal experience or to personal fantasies (which are also part of your experience). Literature, however, is more self-contained than expository writing. No event is ever totally absurd. No matter how strange they are, events can relate to each other in a literary *context*. Even if someone mentions together two or three apparently unconnected words—say, spinach, shipbuilding, paper— you can eventually make connections between them, for your imagination *wants* to make a context for them. That is the way the imagination works. It is never passive, and can be defined only as an activity.

1. E. D. Hirsch, Jr., "What Isn't Literature?" in *What Is Literature?*, ed. Paul Hernadi (Bloomington: Indiana University Press, 1978).

Metaphor, Symbol, and Irony

Metaphor

One special way in which the imagination works in literature is to re-create the real world in the form of metaphor. No other kind of writing employs metaphor so consistently, though metaphor is very common and turns up everywhere from advertisements to business reports. You will recall from Chapter 4 that a metaphor is a statement in which one thing is used to explain another. A poetic metaphor: "The death of hope and despair, / This is the death of air" (T. S. Eliot, *Four Quartets*). How can air die? It can't. Nor can hope and despair. An everyday metaphor: money. Dollar bills stand as symbols of exchange: this car = $6000. In a metaphor, a description is offered in the form of an equation as if some thing *is* another, even though we know it actually is not.

Be careful not to confuse metaphor with simile. "Smith fought like a lion on the ERA issue" is a simile: one thing is *like* another. The imagination need not be stretched too far. But the metaphor "Smith is a lion among politicians" is more emphatic. It is a genuine equation, whereas the simile is more restrained. Smith obviously isn't literally a lion, but the writer wants to speak more strongly than in a simile.

Metaphors state an imaginary identity. They claim that fictions are, in a symbolic way, unusual truths. They claim that certain events are symbolic, and this raises the question, what is a symbol?

Symbol

In the first place, all words are symbolic; that is, they stand for something. The word *cat* stands for the animal that the dictionary defines as "a carnivorous mammal, *Felis catus*" (*American Heritage Dictionary*). But sometimes we use words so that they imply a broader range of meaning than their strict denotation. Words used connotatively tend to be symbolic. So "She was catty about her friend's success" employs the term *cat* in a way that adapts a literal meaning to a symbolic use.

In literature, however, writers take the process of symbolization inherent in language one step further. Through language, they can suggest that events are of such importance and raise the possibility of so many connections to other events that they become symbols. That is, an event can suggest a range of possible meanings beyond itself. It is in this way that literature becomes full of symbolic possibilities which seem to multiply themselves. Literature makes highly imaginative, even surreal and "absurd" suggestions that are given great importance, even though we may not at first know why. Melville's white whale in *Moby Dick* is obviously something more than just a white whale. Hester's letter *A* in *The Scarlet Letter* is no mere letter of the alphabet nor does it simply imply "adulteress." The bullfight in Hemingway's *The Sun Also Rises* is not simply a sport.

But a word of caution here. Even though literature relies heavily on metaphor and symbols, this does not license indiscriminate symbol hunting. Every symbol, or event that a reader thinks is symbolic, must be seen *only in the context from which its suggestions spring*, namely, the text. You should be very wary of interpretations that talk only of single symbolic meanings or that introduce information plainly not implied by the text. Good literature is most often a complex metaphor, and metaphor, remember, is always a connection between things in a text and in a context. When something has a dominant presence in a piece of fiction and you think it is a symbol, do not isolate it and take it out of the text. The white whale as symbol makes little sense without Captain Ahab and his search. The letter *A* refers in part to Hester's relationships to Dimmesdale and Chillingworth in all their complexity within the context of the novel. The same is true of the bullfight as a battle between man and nature, or fate.

Irony

Writers rarely use symbols predictably or conventionally; they use them ironically. The whale, the letter *A*, and the bullfight are events with more than one meaning. They set off a chain of associations in the mind of the reader who reads closely. The text broadens in scope and suggestiveness through the use of symbols. In short, irony in literature is cosmic (as well as verbal, dramatic, or satiric, as we learned in Chapter 1), because there is usually more than one meaning to a text, and events are open to interpretation. Whereas the expository writer often aims to *limit* meaning, the literary writer uses language at its most suggestive.

Irony is the staple of literary writing, for literature does not deal with experience that can be so easily summed up that a paraphrase is enough. The *ambiguity, uncertainty*, and *complexity* of experience is part of the literary emphasis. Writers most often write because they don't know for sure what the meaning of experience is, but they want to find out. If Hawthorne had been absolutely sure that the letter *A* simply stood for adulteress and gave Hester a neat, all-encompassing label, it is unlikely that he would have written such a complex novel as *The Scarlet Letter*. In fact, it's unlikely that he would have written a novel at all. A simple statement about the problems of adultery would have been enough. So the world of Hawthorne's fiction is not black and white. Like most great writers, he lives in grey areas of uncertainty: lingering questions, paradoxes, and ever-emerging human values by which he can illuminate experience for us as he dramatizes a whole set of relationships among his people.

530

Thinking Metaphorically

If the nature of literature is to be metaphoric, symbolic, and ironic, how do we read it? By *thinking metaphorically*. This is something we cannot avoid doing when we make an interpretation. It amounts to letting a writer's metaphors develop in the imagination to the point that we make sense of something by creating connections or developing insights. You, the reader, are forced to play imaginatively in interpreting literature in order to make any meaning at all. There is no model for reading a literary text accurately, but we can safely generalize and say that literary inter-pretation is basically a *problem-solving process* which operates by de-veloping suggestions and trying to find common factors and identifications between contradictory or apparently contradictory events. This is best explained by a reading:

THE STILLNESS

Basho

So still:
  into rocks it pierces—
    the locust-shrill.

I begin by finding the emphatic events: the stillness and the locust-shrill piercing into the rocks. Is the subject "stillness"? Or "rocks"? Or "locust-shrill"? The poem is entitled "Stillness," which is a help, and I should accept the clue, but the locust-shrill is part of the action too. The message? It elaborates on the subject. I could say: things are so still that the shrill voice of the locust (really the rubbing of parts of the body) pierces into the rock or rather seems to pierce into the rock. I need to pause for a moment to consider my options.

What can I say of the writer's intention, for example? Apart from the fact that he is writing in a recognized poetic form, the haiku, he is trying to make a point, to deliver a message, in as few words as possible. But why? The poet is fascinated by a single event—the locust screech—which he has presumably meditated on or at least been acutely aware of, and he is describing that happening in order to encourage me, the reader, to re-create the event. How does he entice me in? By carefully arranging his words in order to direct my attention. (There is no need to know anything about the haiku form or to go into technical details to carry out this basic interpretation because I am reading an English translation which does not retain the same seventeen-syllable stress of the original.)

There is a description of stillness followed by an event that contradicts it. The language is both denotative—I can imagine a locust on or near a rock—and highly suggestive: the shrill pierces the rock. How can I imagine stillness? Or a screech piercing a rock? Now I must be careful of irony. Is Basho saying one thing and meaning another? In an interesting way, yes. Irony is the art of contrast, and at the center of the poem is the contrast between stillness and the screech, between sound and no-sound, between the imaginable and sensory and the unimaginable. *The emphasis is on contrast*, and the contrast is puzzling. Why the stillness and locust-shrill together? The poet does not tell me, so perhaps he is assuming that I will play with the poem and make up my own mind. *Stillness* and *shrill*—and then the *pierced rock*. If I play with those three items, I can find something in common. So piercing and shrill is the locust screech that it does not disturb the stillness. It *is* the stillness: perfect, elongated, balanced, vibrating, controlled—like a long note on a violin string. So fine and powerful, it seems to pierce even the rock.

I think now that I have found a resolution, and I can go on to say that I find in this poem the poet's admiration for moments of perfect order in nature. The stillness suggests not a vacuum, but times of harmony in nature, when looking at it is indeed an aesthetic response, when the order to be found there has a beauty all its own. It also suggests an idea. There is in the contrast of the poem almost a philosophical point to be made. There is no stillness without noise, no sound without its counterpoint calm. Balance: a controlled but powerful energy in the locust and in nature.

You may like the poem for its careful suggestiveness in so few words, or you may be frustrated by its indirectness or plain bored by its simplicity. But remember from Chapters 1 and 2 that reading is an active process of constant questioning in order to fill in the gaps in the text.

Imagination and Magic

We have said that metaphorical thinking does not imply that you take vast leaps beyond the text to another world and draw connections between things that are plainly not in the text. To think metaphorically is to let the imagination play at solving the problems in the text itself, following the arrangement of events the writer makes.

Consider Ezra Pound's famous two-line poem "In a Station of the Metro":

> The apparition of these faces in the crowd;
> Petals on a wet, black bough.

Clearly this is not a poem about milking cows, although, believe it or not, that suggestion has been made. It is a poem about a connection between the rows of faces in a crowd the poet saw in a metro station in Paris and rows of leaves "on a wet, black bough." The word *apparition* is suggestive, but it would be an exaggeration to assume that the poem is a ghost story or a wildly occult intuition, because there is no evidence to back that up. It would be more reasonable to assume that somehow the likeness of colors and shapes of the faces relate to those of petals on a bough to give off a "ghostly" effect. Pound himself said he thought those faces were "beautiful." The ghosts are not occult but the haunting memories of the incident he is recalling. The poem offers a perception valued for its complex suggestiveness. How often faces hang before us, elusive and fascinating, yet we do not know why we are fascinated.

One could sum up the business of thinking metaphorically by saying that it soon reveals that the imagination has a magic all its own, a point that can be explained by this short tale, "The Prince and the Magician," from John Fowles's novel, *The Magus*:

Once upon a time there was a young prince, who believed in all things but three. He did not believe in princesses, he did not believe in islands, he did not believe in God. His father, the king, told him that such things did not exist. As there were no princesses or islands in his father's domains, and no sign of God, the young prince believed his father.

But then, one day, the prince ran away from his palace. He came to the next land. There, to his astonishment, from every coast he saw islands, and on these islands, strange and troubling creatures whom he dared not name. As he was searching for a boat, a man in full evening dress approached him along the shore.

"Are those real islands?" asked the young prince.

"Of course they are real islands," said the man in the evening dress.

"And those strange and troubling creatures?"

"They are all genuine and authentic princesses."

"Then God also must exist!" cried the prince.

"I am God," replied the man in full evening dress, with a bow.

The young prince returned home as quickly as he could.

"So you are back," said his father, the king.

"I have seen islands, I have seen princesses, I have seen God," said the prince reproachfully.

The king was unmoved.

"Neither real islands, nor real princesses, nor a real God, exist."

"I saw them!"

"Tell me how God was dressed."

"God was in full evening dress."

"Were the sleeves of his coat rolled back?"

The prince remembered that they had been. The king smiled.

"That is the uniform of a magician. You have been deceived."

At this, the prince returned to the next land, and went to the same shore, where once again he came upon the man in full evening dress.

"My father the king has told me who you are," said the young prince indignantly. "You deceived me last time, but not again. Now I know that those are not real islands and real princesses, because you are a magician."

The man on the shore smiled.

"It is you who are deceived, my boy. In your father's kingdom there are many islands and many princesses. But you are under your father's spell, so you cannot see them."

The prince returned pensively home. When he saw his father, he looked him in the eyes.

"Father, is it true that you are not a real king, but only a magician?"

The king smiled, and rolled back his sleeves.

"Yes, my son, I am only a magician."

"Then the man on the shore was God."

"The man on the shore was another magician."

"I must know the real truth, the truth beyond magic."

"There is no truth beyond magic," said the king.

The prince was full of sadness.

He said, "I will kill myself."

The king by magic caused death to appear. Death stood in the door and beckoned to the prince. The prince shuddered. He remembered the beautiful but unreal islands and the unreal but beautiful princesses.

"Very well," he said. "I can bear it."

"You see, my son," said the king, "you too now begin to be a magician."

First, get the characters and the events of the plot clear in your mind. A king tells his son that princesses, islands, and God do not exist. The son is told by a magician in another land that they do exist and that the king is a magician too, keeping the truth from his son. The king admits this and the son wants to kill himself because he can never know the truth; he changes his mind when the king, truly the magician, makes death appear. He remembers the islands and princesses and, his father says, learns to become a magician himself when he says that he can bear the fact that "there is no truth beyond magic."

The most important statement in this story seems to be the king's comment that "there is no truth beyond magic," and its most emphatic event is perhaps the moment when the son decides to accept this as truth and believe his father. Why does he do this?

Consider the problems, paradoxes, and questions raised by the events. Either the prince lives and accepts the necessity of magic, never knowing for sure what is real or unreal, or he dies. The story seems to pose some serious questions that go beyond the realm of mere character and plot in the fairy tale: Is what we see only an illusion? What is the difference between illusion and reality? Can we ever know if God exists? Is God just the master magician? Is life merely a puzzle that can never be solved? Is there no truth beyond the magic of the imagination?

Our interest in the characters and events in this tale depends largely on the extent to which they handle these impossible-to-answer questions. Every character seems to act consistently, as if they were all part of the magician's plot, except for the prince. Impetuously, he wants to kill himself when he finds out that there is no truth beyond magic, no God beyond the magician who says he is God. But he changes his mind upon meeting death, presumably because he is unwilling to give up the beauty of either the islands or the princesses he has seen, even though he thinks they are unreal. The prince accepts the resolution to the problem—he accepts the world as constantly changing before his eyes—but we have to decide whether this is a satisfactory choice.

Rather than taking up these questions in terms of a serious philosophical discussion (which has been carried out so many times before), Fowles tells a story that *opens up the questions to various answers*: that is what metaphorical thinking does. After all, would death provide him with a greater reality, when even it is governed by the magician/king? As Fowles himself points out later in the novel, there is little point in reducing life fanatically to a "detective story." Nor is life an either/or proposition—accept the magic or die—but a necessary compromise with never knowing the whole truth about the nature of reality. So what can we do but accept the magic and the uncertainty and *think metaphorically*? The prince never explains his actions, and Fowles deliberately structures the story so that the resolution must be made by the reader. But the prince does not have to explain his actions. In a nice parody of coming-of-age tales, the prince learns to join the *adult* world of "magic," in which we have to choose to accept the mystery of the imagination and make marvelous connections. Our adult magic is part of the world of literature, religion, philosophy, and the play of desire, for surely the prince desires those princesses, however unreal they are. If desire is not imaginative, it dies.

But is this resolution to the tale quite satisfactory? It may occur to us that we could judge this story to be whimsical and wise, simply and eloquently told, *or* we could decide that it is indeed a cynical tale. The prince is forced to become a magician and to give up his search for God. The magician is a manipulator, and we have no option but to see ourselves as puppets of some larger, unknowable fate. Which interpretation would you take: that which speaks for the optimistic play of the imagination making connections, or that which says we can never know all, so all is lost?

No matter which interpretation you make, the irony is that you must read imaginatively in order to understand the tale at all. You must think metaphorically as you read or write. But beware of finally deciding on the author's supposed view of life. There is enough irony here in this tale to require a good deal of caution. Be prepared for the imagination to raise uncertain questions and for fictions to be open-ended. You have to stand back from it and ask: Why tell this story? What does it imply? And then you will find that literary writing has a marvelous ability to *continue working in the imagination* even after a poem or story has ended.

Literature and Reality

In the main, literature is writing that emphasizes an imaginative treatment of reality and experience for both the writer and the reader. The relationships created in a text are sometimes not very obvious, but in good literature they are subtle and revealing. *Literature is a way of making sense of reality* which often deals with the complexity and ambiguity of experience, re-creating it in metaphors that many readers have found offer order amid the disorder of things. So an important aspect of the literary experience for the reader is the discovery of new ways of seeing. Your play has serious consequences. Experience can be more intense and better understood after reading literature. Writing may offer a single marvelous insight or a sharp sense of irony, or it can offer entire systems of moral, political, social, and psychological meaning. Whatever distinguishes it, a literary text has to be imaginative, it has to create an alternative world to the one we live in that justifies its existence. Read this short story by the famous South American writer Julio Cortázar:

He had begun to read the novel a few days before. He had put it down because of some urgent business conferences, opened it again on his way back to the estate by train; he permitted himself a slowly growing interest in the plot, in the characterizations. That afternoon, after writing a letter giving his power of attorney and discussing a matter of joint ownership with the manager of his estate, he returned to the book in the tranquillity of his study which looked out upon the park with its oaks. Sprawled in his favorite armchair, its back toward the door—

even the possibility of an intrusion would have irritated him, had he thought of it—he let his left hand caress repeatedly the green velvet upholstery and set to reading the final chapters. He remembered effortlessly the names and his mental image of the characters; the novel spread its glamour over him almost at once. He tasted the almost perverse pleasure of disengaging himself line by line from the things around him, and at the same time feeling his head rest comfortably on the green velvet of the chair with its high back, sensing that the cigarettes rested within reach of his hand, that beyond the great windows the air of afternoon danced under the oak trees in the park. Word by word, licked up by the sordid dilemma of the hero and heroine, letting himself be absorbed to the point where the images settled down and took on color and movement, he was witness to the final encounter in the mountain cabin. The woman arrived first, apprehensive; now the lover came in, his face cut by the backlash of a branch. Admirably, she stanched the blood with her kisses, but he rebuffed her caresses, he had not come to perform again the ceremonies of a secret passion, protected by a world of dry leaves and furtive paths through the forest. The dagger warmed itself against his chest, and underneath liberty pounded, hidden close. A lustful, panting dialogue raced down the pages like a rivulet of snakes, and one felt it had all been decided from eternity. Even to those caresses which writhed about the lover's body, as though wishing to keep him there, to dissuade him from it; they sketched abominably the frame of that other body it was necessary to destroy. Nothing had been forgotten: alibis, unforeseen hazards, possible mistakes. From this hour on, each instant had its use minutely assigned. The cold-blooded, twice-gone-over re-examination of the details was barely broken off so that a hand could caress a cheek. It was beginning to get dark.

Not looking at one another now, rigidly fixed upon the task which awaited them, they separated at the cabin door. She was to follow the trail that led north. On the path leading in the opposite direction, he turned for a moment to watch her running, her hair loosened and flying. He ran in turn, crouching among the trees and hedges until, in the yellowish fog of dusk, he could distinguish the avenue of trees which led up to the house. The dogs were not supposed to bark, they did not bark. The estate manager would not be there at this hour, and he was not there. He went up the three porch steps and entered. The woman's words reached him over the thudding of blood in his ears: first a blue chamber, then a hall, then a carpeted stairway. At the top, two doors. No one in the first room, no one in the second. The door of the salon, and then, the knife in hand, the light from the great windows, the high back of an armchair covered in green velvet, the head of the man in the chair reading a novel.

Julio Cortázar, "**CONTINUITY OF PARKS**"

This is a witty and ironic parable about the experience of reading. The moral might be: beware of the text, for reading can be dangerous for your health. The reader in the story is so involved in the fiction that, quite literally, he becomes a part of it. The boundary line between fiction and reality is crossed both in his imagination and in real life. "Word by word," he is "absorbed to the point where the images settled down and took on color and movement," ironically not knowing, of course, that he himself is the victim of the plot. You might say that this short story is an unusually strong exploitation of dramatic irony.

The reader has just returned from writing a letter giving his power of attorney (presumably to his lawyer) and "discussing a matter of joint ownership with the manager of his estate." This is rather obscure, but perhaps it has something to do with his wife and her lover who, unknown to him but according to the novel he is reading, are planning to kill him. There seems to be a sense of urgency about their plot which may relate to the matter of joint ownership, presumably with the estate manager. Is part of the irony the possibility that the lover may be the estate manager? Or is it the joint ownership that makes the wife unhappy? She wants the husband dead before it becomes legal; otherwise, the estate will revert to the estate manager if her husband dies. (In that case, the estate manager would not be her lover.) Or is it none of the above? Perhaps the wife and lover are simply motivated by the heat of their passion and don't know that these other things are going on. You, the reader, must fill in the gaps. Whatever the answer, the murder has become a matter of some urgent seriousness, ironically as intense as the protagonist's reading!

A continuation of experience between life and the world of literature is humorously evoked here, but it is a serious connection nonetheless. This is a story about the experience of reading, which thrives on precisely the same intense involvement and dramatic revelation that the reader in the story experiences. Your reading of the story, in turn, entails your following the same plot the armchair reader reads and finding that the business of reading is what the plot is about. Like our fated reader, you are engrossed by the steamy details of the little melodrama enacted by the two lovers. But you are also implicated in the drama of reading. The irony here is that the reader in the text does not realize the continuity between reality and fiction nor does any other reader who is really involved in a text. With tongue in cheek, Cortázar warns us therefore of the problems of reading and of the fate of those who finally will not see the connections between art and life, as well as those who cannot separate art and life. Both kinds of readers are satirized here.

So what is the moral of this tale? Perhaps that art and life are in a paradoxical relationship: *one spills over into the other* (truth, as you have no doubt heard, can be stranger than fiction) but we must be careful not to confuse them. Art refers to life but is not life, though it may very well be, in Picasso's famous statement, the *truth* about life. Literature is nothing if it does not relate to some experience—and it can hardly avoid doing that—but it is an imaginative version of that experience, *a necessary fiction*, which in its intensity can appear uncommonly real.

We'll continue a reading of this story through our discussion of the parts of a literary text.

The Parts of a Literary Text

In Chapter 2, we saw that the environment of nonfictional writing is made up of various aspects of the text: the subject, message, style, tone, use of language, motive or aim, writer, and reader. The environment of the literary text is really no different. All these components still play a part, but they function now a little differently.

*The Subject and
the Message*

The Subject Literary works are about things, people, ideas, societies, states of mind, and so on. But finding the subject in a literary text can be complicated, for its title does not always suggest a precise reference and the range of options offered by the text is usually wider since it aims to be imaginatively suggestive. The title of the Cortázar story, "Continuity of Parks," is not at first helpful in locating the subject of the piece, but as you read and reread the story, you come to see its relevance. The park in the novel that the man in the armchair is reading is the same park on which his house stands. So the title points toward the subject of the story, which has something to do with the relationship of literature and life. That, you might say, is the real subject, because it is the most specific, suggestive theme. It is not just a matter of "x reading a novel and finding out that he is in it," although that is a helpful explanation of the subject also.

Message What about the message? For Cortázar's story, we might say it is the paradoxical relationship of literature and life. The message of a literary text, however, is rarely summed up so briefly. One can hardly declare merely that *Moby Dick* is about whaling and revenge or that *Huckleberry Finn* is about growing up on the Mississippi. The message of a literary work is complex and involves the connections that are made between ideas and events in the text and between the text and the reader. Finally, the message is what the text means to *you*. A poem may contain only one or two connections or a single highly suggestive insight, as does the poem by Basho. In a novel, the connection usually involves a whole series of events and people; in a short story or play, there may be fewer, but relationships among characters and action exist nonetheless.

You have to play with these connections. Let's briefly compare the ways in which messages are carried in fiction and poetry.

The Message in Fiction and Poetry The experience of reading fiction is the experience of reading *an extended development of character and event in narrative.* Plot and character are the staples of fiction. Even if plot is often replaced in the novel by long meditations offered by characters or the narrator, fiction still centers on what happens to people. As you read fiction, you become involved with locating beginnings, middles, and ends of events. The novel is unavoidably linear; it must have direction to develop its sense of meaning. It may, however, jump about in its time scheme for special effects because it is making a subtle point about plot reversals or strange associations in human memory. It will sometimes take you into the past or the future rather than the present. But you the reader begin to understand the novel only when you have some idea of how the plot has developed. It is important that something happen, even if it happens enigmatically, because the novel works on arousing your expectations over an extended period of time.

On the other hand, the most intensely imaginative of all literary writing is often said to be poetry. There is no simple description of poetry because it turns up everywhere: in prose, musical lyrics, and media uses of language. One could define poetry as writing in verse, but that would be weak and prohibitive, since it cannot account for what we also recognize to be the poetic nature of prose. It is perhaps better to think of poetry as poetic writing, and of poetic writing in turn as writing that most intensely reveals the connotative value of words. The real message of poetry is the dramatic *suggestiveness* of ideas, feelings, and events as they form relationships. Fiction moves deliberately, with time on its hands. Poetry tends to be more intense, to take imaginative leaps, to carry a message by squeezing words together to create new and unusual meanings.

Diction, or the Use of Language

Literary uses of language are not entirely connotative. You'll notice that Cortázar is mainly denotative as he explains who the novelist is and what actions are taking place in the armchair reader's life. But when he describes the novel he is reading and his immersion in that imaginative world, the language shifts to more suggestive terms. The lovers are, or are not, involved in ''ceremonies of a secret passion, protected by a world of dry leaves and furtive paths through the forest. The dagger warmed itself against his chest, and underneath liberty pounded.'' This is highly connotative. Then, as the lover leaves the novel and re-enters the world of the reader, the language again becomes more strictly referential.

In reading literature, it is relevant to decide whether the use of language is primarily suggestive or referential. But the fact that we know we are dealing with a *fiction* (in poetry or prose), an imaginary event, whether it is based on "real life" or not, is also very important. The language of any writing that treats a subject imaginatively will be more suggestive than factual in the end, but we need denotation and connotation to set a scene. We need events we can relate to as well as the symbolic implications carried by connotative language.

Tone

Tone is very important in literary writing. Again it reveals the attitude of the writer to the work, but it also reveals the writer's attitude to the reader. We would miss the point of Cortázar's short story if we didn't realize how ironic he is being. The suggestiveness of any piece of writing is dependent on tone. Writers can be deadpan and flat in a piece of fiction, merely offering a list of events, and they can still be making a point. And, of course, tone varies enormously from one character to the next, as we see clearly in drama, where tonal subtleties are exploited by actors. Writers, too, can change tone even within a single piece of writing, depending on their attitudes toward their characters. If you read a Dickens novel—say *Oliver Twist*—you will find that Dickens treats his hero, in this case Oliver, with rather more affection than he does the villain, Bill Sikes. Writers change tone to influence readers, and that tone is part of the meaning of the text.

The Writer

When we notice the tone of a text, we usually notice the writer. We discover some version of who the writer is: the author's presence lies somewhere behind all the goings-on in a text or all the clever insights of a poem, and we want to reach it. Often we can get to the poet faster than we can to the novelist, short story writer, or playwright, for the last three have more opportunities for dramatizing different perspectives at once and we cannot be sure exactly who the writer is taking sides with. Many writers, of course, sympathize with all their characters, merely observing the whole scene. But they too have an attitude, and discovering that attitude is an essential part of learning how to make meaning out of a literary work.

The writer not only reveals an attitude through tone, but also has a *point of view*. Point of view usually may be of two kinds:

■ *Third person*, in which *he*, *she*, *it*, or *they* is the subject of the narrative. We say the writer is omniscient and sees all. Sometimes the writer intrudes and tells us something about the characters; sometimes the writer limits the focus to only one character.

First person, in which *I* is the subject of the narrative. Narrators can be self-conscious, telling a story that is their own, that is, an exploration of their lives and states of mind. The first person narrator can know a lot or a little, can be central to the action or outside much of it, having to rely on other information. In short, narrators can be *reliable* (we know they have the information) or *unreliable* (their interpretations are not to be trusted). In general, beware of rushing to a conclusion about the *I* narrator.

Both the tone and the point of view give a writer a *presence* in a text, and we as readers always want to know what the writer is like. Reading a book or a poem, or watching a play, is after all a way of getting to know someone else's way of seeing things, and it is inevitable that we try to find the man or woman behind the text. Many writers use some kind of persona or mask in a work; they hide behind a character or use a character to provide their commentary.

If you have read enough of the author's work to feel confident that you know what he or she sounds like, go ahead and argue for the author as a particular character. But in general, it is better to be very careful with judgments as to who an author is in a text. Beware especially of the *I* in a text and the ironic voice. Do you think, for example, that we can tell exactly what Cortázar is thinking in "Continuity of Parks"? It is likely that he has an ironic view of the function of reading and the nature of the text in its relationship to the real, but one wouldn't want to hazard too many judgments about his opinions beyond that. The next time you read a Cortázar story, however, you will be on the lookout for his irony.

Style

As you will recall from Chapter 2, style is the way a writer conveys a message. It refers to the structure of the sentences and paragraphs and the use of language as they convey a particular tone. Again, we look in our reading for the kind of stylistic effect a writer is reaching for: is the writing serious and tragic, ornate and analytical, simple and direct, sober and dull? There are so many styles in literature it would be foolish to generalize about them here except to say that they sometimes are associated with particular periods of writing as they are in music or art (like baroque, classical, modern) and that they are generally seen as falling into broad categories of high, low, everyday (informal), and mixed styles, as we discussed earlier.

It is probably safe to say that most literary writing is mixed, especially in its fictional modes, and that writers aim for varied effects. Poems tend, however, to keep to a single style within each poem. Cortázar mixes his style, moving from an everyday, or informal, style at the opening to the melodramatic high style of a rather second-rate romance in the middle and back to the everyday at the end.

The Aim or Motive

The four basic rhetorical modes of explanation, persuasion, narration, and description are all mixed in literary writing. Authors *describe* in order

542

to set scenes in poetry and prose. They *narrate*, or tell stories, mainly in prose but also in poetry. They sometimes have to *explain* what is going on in some detail, and they have also been known frequently to want to make a moral point and therefore *persuade* us of something. The aims of literary texts are so varied that, again, they defy generalization, except to say that usually the rhetorical play of a text, the mixing of motives, is in the service of making some kind of connection between things and of establishing the validity of the imaginary world. The primary aim, that is, of any literary text is first of all to justify itself and then to establish its link to the real world. If the text does not have a well-made world of its own, you the reader have nowhere to go.

Remember that, as the Cortázar story reveals, the world of literature relies on life, gets its themes from life, and cannot fail to be a human document since humans produce it. But literature is first of all about itself. Only when you get deeply involved with it do you find that the outside world begins to creep up behind you, paradoxically, even when you don't know why and just when you thought you had left it behind.

The Reader

As this chapter has been emphasizing, the reader of the literary text, probably more than any other kind of reader, helps make the meaning. The reader *is* the man in the armchair, and as intimidating as that position might be, the reader has no choice but to get involved with the ideas, characters, and actions. But in all kinds of writing, the reader has some assistance in that the text implies how the reader should regard it. Thus, the reader who overlooks Cortázar's irony will miss the point and think that the story is sheer nonsense. The tone, style, use of language, and so on, are the signposts that create an implied reader, as we saw in Chapter 2. They make demands that only a reader reading in a certain way can satisfy. If the writer writes ironically, the reader must read ironically. But the implied reader is only a partial creation, for no writer knows what you the reader are like and what you will do. You find the clues and you start the process of interpretation from there, developing possible meanings from among your options as you saw in the commentary on Basho's haiku.

Writing an Interpretation of a Literary Text

We can adapt the reading and interpretation process outlined in the first two chapters to the interpretation of literature. Again, remember that your writing about literature begins with your reactions; then you put your reactions into words as quickly as possible.

Annotation and Summary

These have a place in literary interpretation, especially if you are dealing with fiction. You can mark significant passages in the margin, paraphrasing or writing summary points that call attention to important passages, that is, passages that recount a significant event, comment on a character's motive, make some kind of judgment, or convey something uncertain. If you are reading a poem, you can annotate by underlining words or sentences that strike you as significant. The first thing to do is to read and reread the text enough times to get a sense of its emphatic words or comments.

Spring is like a perhaps hand
(which comes carefully
out of Nowhere) arranging
a window, into which people look (while
people stare
arranging and changing placing
carefully there a strange
thing and a known thing here) and

changing everything carefully

spring is like a perhaps
Hand in a window
(carefully to
and fro moving New and
Old things, while
people stare carefully
moving a perhaps
fraction of flower here placing
and inch of air there) and

without breaking anything.

e. e. cummings

Say you have underlined the significant parts of the poem as they occur to you. In this case, you have looked for whatever direct statements you can find: actions, who is carrying them out, and who or what is affected. You have also underlined problem passages. If this were a piece of prose, you would now try out a summary of the action or plot. But a summary is not usually appropriate for a poem because there is no plot and your interpretation itself is needed for the summary. We are often not sure what a poem is saying until we have gone through most of the interpretation process because a poem is usually very compressed in meaning. Of course, you may not be sure what a piece of fiction means either until you have analyzed it, but usually there is a sequence of events or some characters related to actions that are more readily accessible.

Questioning the Text

Having underlined the essentials, you go on to question the text. You still have all the options listed in Chapter 2, from following a key idea through a text to asking about the voices of the text. The journalist's questions (who? what? why? when? and where?) are perhaps not likely to yield much information about a poem, but they can be useful when thinking about a novel or any fiction filled with information that may be difficult to keep in mind.

Here is a useful set of questions you can ask yourself about your re-actions to a text. They are based on the questions and perspectives dis-cussed in Chapter 2, adapted for literary readings. They relate to the parts of the literary text we have just discussed and to thinking metaphorically. Understand, this is not meant to be a prescriptive sequence; your ideas may tumble out in any order. You may find other more relevant questions to ask as you develop your talent for thinking metaphorically. Use the list as a starting point for your own approach to reading literature. As you did before, jot down rough notes and comments in response to the ques-tions; organize your thoughts in whatever order they occur under these headings. The questions work as well for prose as they do for poetry, but for the sake of example, we will refer here to e. e. cummings's poem "Spring is like a perhaps hand." You should review a whole text in the light of each question.

■ *Which emphatic voices do you hear in the text?* What are they saying? Are there any conflicting voices? What is their tone? In what sequence do they offer information? Begin answering this question at the start of the poem and work your way through, emphasizing the parts you understand.

Cummings writes with a meticulous hand ... carefully describes the growths of spring as if they were new items arranged in a window ... strange rhythms that go fast and slow, stop and start ... seems to be no irony in his voice and no conflict.

■ *What puzzles you most about the text? What are the problem pas-sages?* In other words, as you work your way through the text, what stands in the way of coherence? Have your expectations been raised and not met? At this point, an interesting thing happens in your reading. You have so far been concentrating on what you get out of a text, what you think you know about it. Now your reading is directed as much by what you don't know as by what you do.

*Why is spring a "perhaps hand"? Why are Nowhere and New and Old capital-
ized? Why is there an emphasis on everything changing "carefully"? Why do
"people stare"? What can "an inch of air " be? Why is nothing broken? Why
is the poet writing about all this at all? What is so special about spring that
attracts his interest? Why the strange syntax and parentheses?*

■ *Can you make connections between events in the text?* This is where
you really begin thinking metaphorically. You want at this stage to
make some preliminary decisions about the message of the work. Which
events group together? Which events seem stubbornly to stand apart
from the others? Have any oppositions formed? Even if you can find
distinct differences between facts, you have made progress. You have
also reached a crucial time in your reading in which you face the
problems of the text head on. The temptation at this point may be to
back off from the text, wondering if it is worth it, or to dawdle with it.
But remember the process of thinking aloud with a poem—as we did
with the Basho poem—and accept the challenge of the text. You now
literally play with the possibilities the text has to offer. Try out different
perspectives if necessary. If it is fiction, put yourself in different characters' shoes. Consider how the ideas in the text fit together. Look for
the common factors in events.

*I do know that the poem is about spring and that the poem works through the
simile that spring is like a "perhaps hand" which comes out of "Nowhere"?
... there is a clue in that it's like a window-dresser's hand in a window ... so
is spring like the hand of a window-dresser, appearing from the side of the display
or the top? ... and just the hand ... very carefully adjusting the display, putting
something new in the window and trying carefully not to disturb anything else
... things begin to make sense now that this central simile seems to control the
whole poem ... the poem is about the way flowers appear very carefully at the
beginning of spring: bulbs poking up in odd places next to still dormant plants
(the New and Old things) ... cummings capitalizes the words to emphasize their
importance: it is amazing that spring comes at all without any apparent reason
from Nowhere, like the disembodied hand in the window, creating the New next
to the Old.*

■ *Are the language, tone, and style appropriate to the message?* What
do they tell you about the writer and his relationship to his subject?
You are considering the writer's use of language, tone, and style to
determine whether there is any information to be had from the way in
which the writer says what he has to say. You may be inclined not to
take this question too seriously if you think you have solved the
problem of what things "mean" in the text after answering the last
question. But be careful. Finding out how things fit together in a plot

or a poem is only part of the business of interpretation. The meaning
lies as much in *how* something is said as in *what* is said. And besides,
you still have to account for your reactions more fully.

*Cummings's style seems quite lyrical ... he actually seems to be arranging the
words in his poem just the way a window-dresser arranges wares or spring, its
flowers—carefully, but with a "strange thing" here and a "known thing" there
... the style and format, the arrangement of the words, actually bears out his
theme ... the last lines of each verse seem left hanging in the air, as if the bloom
has just arrived: the pause after the careful movement ... a lovely irony that the
poet works like spring, too ... poetry then is about the careful placement of words
"without breaking anything."*

■ *What do you think the writer thinks of the reader?* Here you begin
to concentrate on how the writer helps create the reader's interpretation, and how you may go along with this or resist it.

*No doubt that cummings forces the reader through his rhythms and line arrange-
ments to see his point. This is most effective and carefully done ... the reader is
lured into the meaning carefully, nudged along by the poet's hand ... I enjoyed
this for the care of the craftsmanship, the subtlety of the understatement, and the
possibilities of meaning which seem to multiply from such a simple poem ...
nothing pretentious about this but a delicate wit tantalizing the reader.*

■ *Do you have a strong, unified impression of the text?* In the end, do
you think that the text holds together? Be critical. If you do not find
coherence, it is unlikely you will find unity, but even with coherence a
text sometimes leaves you wondering if it is a finished whole. You
are looking here as much for the unity of your response as you are for
the formal unity of the text. You are also going over the text again
and trying out *your* interpretation for unity and further ideas.

*Yes, cummings's poem is in one piece ... it seems repetitive ... for example, what
does the second section say that the first doesn't? ... a change of emphasis mainly
... but it carries careful variations within its one central theme (the arrival of
spring) ... the poem talks about spring, the window-dresser, and the poet, but
now I also see that it involves the reader and onlooker too ... in the first section,
the second set of parentheses contains the implication that the people looking
into the window change their places carefully too, something that is repeated in
the next section ... furthermore, the implication is that the people are engrossed
in the window-dresser (and in spring) moving objects with a mysterious arm
... the people wonder what is going to happen next, anticipating things, in awe
of the "fractional" movements that leave everything intact as spring flowers
emerging in unlikely places leave everything intact ... so the poem is unified
around the theme of spring and its miraculous and careful arrival, together with*

the themes of the window-dresser, the poet, and the viewer/reader, all of whom take part in the event: the reader must read in this way too.

■ *What are the implications of the text?* In rather inelegant terms, this question could be rephrased "so what?" You should always ask that question. Here is where you try to sum up the text's significance: its impact on you, the suggestions it makes, its range of reference. Does it provide valuable or moving commentary on something significant? What happens to the meaning when you let it play in your imagination beyond the boundaries of the text?

Although cummings has not chosen to treat his theme as if it were a profound one, he has offered us a poet's perspective which speaks in some ways louder than theory . . . he has shown us spring's first flowers and a window-dresser and how the imagination works—just like the hand of spring, carefully arranging things . . . this is really a poem about thinking metaphorically . . . we relate to his way of seeing in this poem, and that seems to be an important function of poetry . . . he centers the first section on "Nowhere" and the second on "New and Old": "big" concepts which have no explanation and cummings without pretension does not try one . . . instead the poetry is in awe of spring and is a humble but effective imitation of spring's careful beginnings.

Writing the Interpretation

In Chapter 2 we described a further stage in the process of writing an interpretation which involved reorganizing the information gained from questioning. You were asked to subject the information to judgments as to the text's emphasis, coherence, unity, and significance. We will use the same process here, but note first that there are two related aspects of literary interpretation that should appear in any essay you write about a literary work.

■ *The experience of reading the text.* When you write about literature you are describing the interpretation process, that is, the progress you make as you come to grips with the text. This is what you were doing when you responded to the questions above.

■ *Making judgments about the text.* Your description of how you read a text is not open-ended, however. You tend to arrive at conclusions about the value of the text or its impact on you or its general significance—you pass judgment on it. In doing so, try to unify your responses and make them emphatic and coherent. The most important point to remember is that your reading must not be reductive; it must leave the literary work alive for others after they have read your interpretation.

At this point, then, you want to develop an outline for your interpretive essay that accommodates both your experience of reading and the business of making judgments about the text. You are letting a reader know that you have opinions and, equally important, how you reached them. Remember that you are reorganizing your notes at this point and rewriting them to form a fresh sequence that focuses on the emphasis, coherence, unity, and significance of the text and your response to it. (Remember, too, to keep your original notes handy for extra comments you may not list.) Here are suggestions for making each judgment with examples of how they might be applied to the e. e. cummings poem.

Judging Emphasis Consider the writer's focus, listing the emphatic points. Work from your summary; the voices in the text; the relationships between facts; your findings on language, style, and tone; and the implications of the text. Find your most important points.

A poem about spring which develops the meaning through the simile of window-dressing and develops that further to take in the art of poetry (the poem is carefully arranged in a form that mimics the "window-dressing") and reading (the viewers at the window) . . . that is, form mimics content.

Judging Coherence Turn to your notes on the relationship and non-relationship of facts and to your comments on style and tone. The main questions are: Is the argument coherent and integrated? Are the problem passages resolved? Do the characters and plot relate carefully? Do the themes relate? Are the poet's metaphors consistent and appropriate? Here you describe the development of the plot or poetic argument.

Initial uncertainties about the poem—the strange syntax, capitalizations, and so on—dissolve when the theme of spring is seen to relate all the parts of the poem to each other . . . coherence through this theme .. the careful balance of "No-where" and "New and Old," spring's hand with the people watching, the poet with the reader . . . and the style and syntax bear out the theme with the added touch of each last line of each section left carefully hanging: "without breaking anything" beautifully reinforces "changing everything carefully" . . . the poetry itself is a careful arrangement of words.

Judging Unity Now you are concerned with the overall unity and impression of the text. Does a consistent attitude or theme hold everything together? Are there conflicting voices? Is the message complete? Are your reactions consistent? Do you have any unsatisfied expectations?

With subtle repetitions, the poem is unified around the theme of spring and its miraculous handling of things. (You could use the rest of your notes answering the question "Do you have a strong unified impression of the text?")

Judging Significance Now you turn to the large implications of the text and even your most personal reactions, explaining why you think the text is good or bad, effective or ineffective, in terms of what it tries to do. Turn to your notes on the poem's implications, and review all your other notes for value judgments. Develop an overall opinion.

Cummings may not have said anything of shattering philosophical importance, but he has done something very important: he has shown us how the imagination works with its careful arrangements, and allowed us to see how the reader can relate to the poem like the window-viewers to the window-dressing and all of us to spring . . . a poem that imitates what it describes . . . it captures our attention through its connection of form to content.

Again, the outline you have arrived at is not fixed. But the exercise should lead you to organize your ideas, however random they appear to be, and test the emphasis, coherence, unity, and significance of *your own* interpretation. You may begin your essay with your discussion of the poem's emphasis or its significance, or you may evoke the coherence and unity of the argument first. Here is a short example of what a literary interpretation based on the sequence created by the judgments looks like.

e. e. cummings's "Spring"

Emphasis

Here is a poem in which form—the arrangement of words—cleverly and suggestively mimics the content. Cummings has written a poem about spring that works through a simple yet most effective simile. The flowers appear in spring in the same way that a window-dresser makes an adjustment to a window-dressing: carefully and deliberately arranging the new with the old.

Coherence

The poet, too, arranges his words carefully in his poem: his is a hand out of "Nowhere" like the disembodied hand appearing from the side of a window setting or the "perhaps hand" of spring. He sets the words delicately on a page. So the form of the poem imitates the art of spring, and, in the poet's witty analogy, the art of window-dressing. The syntax and its rhythms suggest careful, deliberate, fractional moves. The people watching the window-dresser, themselves carefully arranging and staring, are like the readers of the poem, fascinated by the moves and wondering if they will succeed or if something will be disturbed. All are like the viewers of spring flowers in a garden, wondering at their talent for springing up in the most unlikely places, flowers from bulbs of long-forgotten plantings.

Unity

This simile of spring-is-like-window-dressing-is-like-poetry is beautifully consistent and thought through, controlling the whole poem and making its repetitions seem like reinforcements, not merely repetitions. The first section carefully highlights "Nowhere," the second "New and Old." Neither is meant to carry inflated meanings; both are humorously overstated to create the whimsical tone. Two lines are balanced—"changing everything carefully" and "without breaking anything"—which are close in meaning yet subtly different in their emphases. The latter is an effective and emphatic ending: the poet asserts that the hand has moved with precision. The former is only slightly less emphatic in calling our attention to the care of spring, the dresser, and the poet. Both lines are carefully poised after "and," each left hanging like a new bloom. Poetry too is the careful arrangement of words "without breaking anything," ushering in a fresh meaning.

Significance

With its subtle repetitions, then, the poem is unified around the theme of spring, carefully guiding the reader to re-enact the whole process of watching the poetry-dressing take place, in awe of the fractional movements that leave everything intact in the way that spring flowers leave everything intact as they emerge in unlikely places next to still dormant plants. Cummings may not have said anything of shattering philosophical importance, but he has done something that we might appreciate very much in poetry. He has shown us how the imagination can work like the perhaps hand of spring, subtly imitating its movements.

551

Checklist

1. Literary writing is often more self-contained than expository writing, creating meaning within its own context. The reader matches the imaginative intensity of the text with reading as imaginative play.

2. Literature is a way of making sense of reality. Literature—like all art—offers a *necessary* fiction. Literature and life are in a paradoxical relationship, one spilling over into the other, which can raise problems of reader confusion if we do not understand the irony of the reader's position.

3. Literary writing re-creates the real world as metaphor: an imaginary identity between things, not to be confused with the simile in which one thing is *like* another.

4. All language is symbolic, even in denotation, but sometimes words in literary writing are used to suggest a range of references that extend beyond the term itself. Symbols always exist in contexts.

5. Irony is a staple of literary writing because the ambiguity, uncertainty, and complexity of experience is part of the literary emphasis.

6. The parts of the literary text are its subject and message, diction, tone, style, aims, writer, and implied reader.

7. Reading literature is a matter of thinking metaphorically, of finding relationships between events.

8. Writing a literary interpretation begins with the process of annotation and summary and then moves on to the questioning process: Which emphatic voices do you hear in the text? What puzzles you most about the text? Can you make connections between events in the text? Are the language, tone, and style appropriate to the message? What do you think the writer thinks of the reader? Do you have a strong, unified impression of the text? What are the implications of the text?

9. Writing the interpretation involves organizing the information gained from your questioning. Judge your notes according to information about the text's emphases, coherence, unity, and significance.

Exercise

In a metaphor, a description is offered in the form of an equation as if some thing *is* another, even though we know it actually is not. A metaphor states an imaginary identity that expresses a specially strong meaning the writer wants to convey. Here are three short poems, each of which turns on a strong metaphor. For each one:

1. State what the metaphor is and paraphrase it in your own words.
2. Interpret the writer's unusual connection, explaining what you think it means, its appropriateness, and its effects.

THERE IS A GARDEN IN HER FACE

Thomas Campion

There is a garden in her face,
Where roses and white lilies grow,
A heavenly paradise is that place,
Wherein all pleasant fruits do flow.
There cherries grow, which none may buy
Till "Cherry ripe!"[1] themselves do cry.

Those cherries fairly do enclose
Of orient pearl a double row;
Which when her lovely laughter shows,
They look like rosebuds filled with snow.

Yet them nor peer nor prince can buy.
Till "Cherry ripe!" themselves do cry.

Her eyes like angels watch them still;
Her brows like bended bows do stand,
Threatening with piercing frowns to kill
All that attempt with eye or hand
Those sacred cherries to come nigh,
Till "Cherry ripe!" themselves do cry.

THE GARDEN OF LOVE

William Blake

I went to the Garden of Love,
And saw what I never had seen:
A Chapel was built in the midst,
Where I used to play on the green.

And the gates of this Chapel were shut,
And "Thou shalt not" writ over the door;

---

1. The cry of a London street vendor.

So I turn'd to the Garden of Love,
That so many sweet flowers bore,

And I saw it was filled with graves,
And tomb-stones where flowers should be:
And Priests in black gowns were walking their rounds,
And binding with briars my joys & desires.

PERMANENTLY

Kenneth Koch

One day the Nouns were clustered in the street.
An Adjective walked by, with her dark beauty.
The Nouns were struck, moved, changed.
The next day a Verb drove up, and created the Sentence.

Each Sentence says one thing—for example, "Although it was a dark rainy
    day when the Adjective walked by, I shall remember the pure and
    sweet expression on her face until the day I perish from the green,
    effective earth."
Or, "Will you please close the window, Andrew?"
Or, for example, "Thank you, the pink pot of flowers on the window sill
    has changed color recently to a light yellow, due to the heat from the
    boiler factory which exists nearby."

In the springtime the Sentences and the Nouns lay silently on the grass.
A lonely Conjunction here and there would call, "And! But!"
But the Adjective did not emerge.

As the adjective is lost in the sentence,
So I am lost in your eyes, ears, nose, and throat—
You have enchanted me with a single kiss
Which can never be undone
Until the destruction of language.

Writing Assignment

Read the following poem by William Carlos Williams and write a short
essay "thinking aloud" the stages of imaginative play you pass through
in order to open up the poem. (Review the commentary on Basho's
"Stillness.")

THE GREAT FIGURE

Among the rain
and lights
I saw the figure 5
in gold
on a red
firetruck
moving
tense
unheeded
to gong clangs
siren howls
and wheels rumbling
through the dark city.

Readings

Donald Barthelme   **THE KING OF JAZZ**

Joseph Heller   **SNOWDEN**

Michael Herr   from **DISPATCHES**

Ursula K. Le Guin   **THE ONES WHO WALK AWAY FROM OMELAS**

D. H. Lawrence   **THE SNAKE**

T. S. Eliot   **PRELUDES**

Elizabeth Bishop   **THE FISH**

James Joyce   **ARABY**

THE KING OF JAZZ

Donald Barthelme

Well I'm the king of jazz now, thought Hokie Mokie to himself as he oiled the slide on his trombone. Hasn't been a 'bone man been king of jazz for many years. But now that Spicy MacLammermoor, the old king, is dead, I guess I'm it. Maybe I better play a few notes out of this window here, to reassure myself.

"Wow!" said somebody standing on the sidewalk. "Did you hear that?"

"I did," said his companion.

"Can you distinguish our great home-made American jazz performers, each from the other?"

"Used to could."

"Then who was that playing?"

"Sounds like Hokie Mokie to me. Those few but perfectly selected notes have the real epiphanic glow."

"The what?"

"The real epiphanic glow, such as is obtained only by artists of the caliber of Hokie Mokie, who's from Pass Christian, Mississippi. He's the king of jazz, now that Spicy MacLammermoor is gone."

Hokie Mokie put his trombone in its trombone case and went to a gig. At the gig everyone fell back before him, bowing.

"Hi Bucky! Hi Boot! Hi Freddie! Hi George! Hi Thad! Hi Roy! Hi Dexter! Hi Jo! Hi Willie! Hi Greens!"

"What we gonna play, Hokie? You the king of jazz now, you gotta decide."

"How 'bout 'Smoke'?"

"Wow!" everybody said. "Did you hear that? Hokie Mokie can just knock a fella out, just the way he pronounces a word. What a intonation on that boy! God Almight!"

"I don't want to play 'Smoke,' " somebody said.

"Would you repeat that, stranger?"

"I don't want to play 'Smoke,' 'Smoke' is dull. I don't like the changes. I refuse to play 'Smoke.' "

"He refuses to play 'Smoke'! But Hokie Mokie is the king of jazz and he says 'Smoke'!"

"Man, you from outa town or something? What do you mean you refuse to play 'Smoke'? How'd you get on this gig anyhow? Who hired you?"

"I am Hideo Yamaguchi, from Tokyo, Japan."

"Oh you're one of those Japanese cats, eh?"

"Yes I'm the top trombone man in all of Japan."

"Well you're welcome here until we hear you play. Tell me, is the Tennessee Tea Room still the top jazz place in Tokyo?"

"No, the top jazz place in Tokyo is the Square Box now."

"That's nice. O.K., now we gonna play 'Smoke' just like Hokie said. You ready, Hokie? O.K., give you four for nothin'. One! Two! Three! Four!"

The two men who had been standing under Hokie's window had followed him to the club. Now they said:

"Good God!"

"Yes, that's Hokie's famous 'English sunrise' way of playing. Playing with lots of rays coming out of it, some red rays, some blue rays, some green rays, some green stemming from a violet center, some olive stemming from a tan center—"

"That young Japanese fellow is pretty good, too."

"Yes, he is pretty good. And he holds his horn in a peculiar way. That's frequently the mark of a superior player."

"Bent over like that with his head between his knees—good God, he's sensational!"

He's sensational, Hokie thought. Maybe I ought to kill him.

But at that moment somebody came in the door pushing in front of him a four-and-one-half-octave marimba. Yes, it was Fat Man Jones, and he began to play even before he was fully in the door.

"What're we playing?"

" 'Billie's Bounce.' "

"That's what I thought it was. What're we in?"

"F."

"That's what I thought we were in. Didn't you use to play with Maynard?"

"Yeah I was on that band for a while until I was in the hospital."

"What for?"

"I was tired."

"What can we add to Hokie's fantastic playing?"

"How 'bout some rain or stars?"

"Maybe that's presumptuous?"

"Ask him if he'd mind."

"You ask him, I'm scared. You don't fool around with the king of jazz. That young Japanese guy's pretty good, too."

"He's sensational."

"You think he's playing in Japanese?"

"Well I don't think it's English."

This trombone's been makin' my neck green for thirty-five years, Hokie thought. How come I got to stand up to yet another challenge, this late in life?

"Well, Hideo—"

"Yes, Mr. Mokie?"

"You did well on both 'Smoke' and 'Billie's Bounce.' You're just about as good as me, I regret to say. In fact, I've decided you're *better* than me. It's a hideous thing to contemplate, but there it is. I have only been the king of jazz for twenty-four hours, but the unforgiving logic of this art demands we bow to Truth, when we hear it."

"Maybe you're mistaken?"

"No, I got ears. I'm not mistaken. Hideo Yamaguchi is the new king of jazz."

"You want to be king emeritus?"

"No, I'm just going to fold up my horn and steal away. This gig is yours, Hideo. You can pick the next tune."

"How 'bout 'Cream'?"

"O.K., you heard what Hideo said, it's 'Cream.' You ready, Hideo?"

"Hokie, you don't have to leave. You can play too. Just move a little over to the side there—"

"Thank you, Hideo, that's very gracious of you. I guess I will play a little, since I'm still here. Sotto voce, of course."

"Hideo is wonderful on 'Cream'!"

"Yes, I imagine it's his best tune."

"What's that sound coming in from the side there?"

"Which side?"

"The left."

"You mean that sound that sounds like the cutting edge of life? That sounds like polar bears crossing Arctic ice pans? That sounds like a herd of musk ox in full flight? That sounds like male walruses diving to the bottom of the sea? That sounds like fumaroles smoking on the slopes of Mt. Katmai? That sounds like the wild turkey walking through the deep, soft forest? That sounds like beavers chewing trees in an Appalachian marsh? That sounds like an oyster fungus growing on an aspen trunk? That sounds like a mule deer wandering a montane of the Sierra Nevada? That sounds like prairie dogs kissing? That sounds like witchgrass tumbling or a river meandering? That sounds like manatees munching seaweed at Cape Sable? That sounds like coatimundis moving in packs across the face of Arkansas? That sounds like—"

"Good God, it's Hokie! Even with a cup mute on, he's blowing Hideo right off the stand!"

"Hideo's playing on his knees now! Good God, he's reaching into his belt for a large steel sword—Stop him!"

"Wow! That was the most exciting 'Cream' ever played! Is Hideo all right?"

"Yes, somebody is getting him a glass of water."

"You're my man, Hokie! That was the dadblangedest thing I ever saw!"

"You're the king of jazz once again!"

"Hokie Mokie is the most happening thing there is!"

"Yes, Mr. Hokie sir, I have to admit it, you blew me right off the stand. I see I have many years of work and study before me still."

"That's O.K., son. Don't think a thing about it. It happens to the best of us.

Or it almost happens to the best of us. Now I want everybody to have a good time because we're gonna play 'Flats.' 'Flats' is next.''

"With your permission, sir, I will return to my hotel and pack. I am most grateful for everything I have learned here."

"That's O.K., Hideo. Have a nice day. He-he. Now, 'Flats.' ''

1. What do you think this showdown between the two fastest trombones in the west is really about? That is, explain the real theme of this piece.

2. Explain Barthelme's irony.

3. How does Barthelme treat the public's attitude toward reputation, especially the need to have a "No. 1" or a "King" of music, football, news broadcasters, whatever?

4. What is familiar about the pattern of the two "meetings" between Hokie and Hideo? Explain what you think Barthelme might be satirizing here.

5. How does Barthelme get his comic effects?

SNOWDEN

Joseph Heller

"Cut," said a doctor.

"You cut," said another.

"No cuts," said Yossarian with a thick, unwieldy tongue.

"Now look who's butting in," complained one of the doctors. "Another county heard from. Are we going to operate or aren't we?"

"He doesn't need an operation," complained the other. "It's a small wound. All we have to do is stop the bleeding, clean it out and put a few stitches in."

"But I've never had a chance to operate before. Which one is the scalpel? Is this one the scalpel?"

"No, the other one is the scalpel. Well, go ahead and cut already if you're going to. Make the incision."

"Like this?"

"Not there, you dope!"

"No incisions," Yossarian said, perceiving through the lifting fog of insensibility that two strangers were ready to begin cutting him.

"Another county heard from," complained the first doctor sarcastically. "Is he going to keep talking that way while I operate on him?"

"You can't operate on him until I admit him," said a clerk.

"You can't admit him until I clear him," said a fat, gruff colonel with a mustache and an enormous pink face that pressed down very close to Yossarian and radiated scorching heat like the bottom of a huge frying pan. "Where were you born?"

The fat, gruff colonel reminded Yossarian of the fat, gruff colonel who had interrogated the chaplain and found him guilty. Yossarian stared up at him through a glassy film. The cloying scents of formaldehyde and alcohol sweetened the air.

"On a battlefield," he answered.

"No, no. In what state were you born?"

"In a state of innocence."

"No, no, you don't understand."

"Let me handle him," urged a hatchet-faced man with sunken acrimonious eyes and a thin, malevolent mouth. "Are you a smart aleck or something?" he asked Yossarian.

"He's delirious," one of the doctors said. "Why don't you let us take him back inside and treat him?"

"Leave him right here if he's delirious. He might say something incriminating."

"But he's still bleeding profusely. Can't you see? He might even die."

"*Good* for him!"

"It would serve the finky bastard right," said the fat, gruff colonel. "All right, John, let's speak out. We want to get to the truth."

"Everyone calls me Yo-Yo."

"We want you to co-operate with us, Yo-Yo. We're your friends and we want you to trust us. We're here to help you. We're not going to hurt you."

"Let's jab our thumbs down inside his wound and gouge it," suggested the hatchet-faced man.

Yossarian let his eyes fall closed and hoped they would think he was unconscious.

"He's fainted," he heard a doctor say. "Can't we treat him now before it's too late? He really might die."

"All right, take him. I hope the bastard does die."

"You can't treat him until I admit him," the clerk said.

Yossarian played dead with his eyes shut while the clerk admitted him by shuffling some papers, and then he was rolled away slowly into a stuffy, dark room with searing spotlights overhead in which the cloying smell of formaldehyde and sweet alcohol was even stronger. The pleasant, permeating stink was intoxicating. He smelled ether too and heard glass tinkling. He listened with secret, egotistical mirth to the husky breathing of the two doctors. It delighted him that they thought he was unconscious and did not know he was listening. It all seemed very silly to him until one of the doctors said,

"Well, do you think we should save his life? They might be sore at us if we do."

"Let's operate," said the other doctor. "Let's cut him open and get to the inside of things once and for all. He keeps complaining about his liver. His liver looks pretty small on this X ray."

"That's his pancreas, you dope. This is his liver."

"No it isn't. That's his heart. I'll bet you a nickel this is his liver. I'm going to operate and find out. Should I wash my hands first?"

"No operations," Yossarian said, opening his eyes and trying to sit up.

"Another county heard from," scoffed one of the doctors indignantly. "Can't we make him shut up?"

"We could give him a total. The ether's right here."

"No totals," said Yossarian.

"Another county heard from," said a doctor.

"Let's give him a total and knock him out. Then we can do what we want with him."

They gave Yossarian total anesthesia and knocked him out. He woke up thirsty in a private room, drowning in ether fumes. Colonel Korn was there at his bedside, waiting calmly in a chair in his baggy, wool, olive-drab shirt and trousers. A bland, phlegmatic smile hung on his brown face with its heavy-bearded cheeks, and he was buffing the facets of his bald head gently with the palms of both hands. He bent forward chuckling when Yossarian awoke, and assured him in the friendliest tones that the deal they had made was still on if Yossarian didn't die. Yossarian vomited, and Colonel Korn shot to his feet at the first cough and fled in disgust, so it seemed indeed that there was a silver lining to every cloud, Yossarian reflected, as he drifted back into a suffocating daze. A hand with sharp fingers shook him awake roughly. He turned and opened his eyes and saw a strange man with a mean face who curled his lip at him in a spiteful scowl and bragged,

"We've got your pal, buddy. We've got your pal."

Yossarian turned cold and faint and broke into a sweat.

"Who's my pal?" he asked when he saw the chaplain sitting where Colonel Korn had been sitting.

"Maybe I'm your pal," the chaplain answered.

But Yossarian couldn't hear him and closed his eyes. Someone gave him water to sip and tiptoed away. He slept and woke up feeling great until he turned his head to smile at the chaplain and saw Aarfy there instead. Yossarian moaned instinctively and screwed his face up with excruciating irritability when Aarfy chortled and asked how he was feeling. Aarfy looked puzzled when Yossarian inquired why he was not in jail. Yossarian shut his eyes to make him go away. When he opened them, Aarfy was gone and the chaplain was there. Yossarian broke into laughter when he spied the chaplain's cheerful grin and asked him what in the hell he was so happy about.

"I'm happy about you," the chaplain replied with excited candor and joy. "I heard at Group that you were very seriously injured and that you would have to be sent home if you lived. Colonel Korn said your condition was critical. But I've just learned from one of the doctors that your wound is really a very slight one and that you'll probably be able to leave in a day or two. You're in no danger. It isn't bad at all."

Yossarian listened to the chaplain's news with enormous relief. "That's good."

"Yes," said the chaplain, a pink flush of impish pleasure creeping into his cheeks. "Yes, that is good."

Yossarian laughed, recalling his first conversation with the chaplain. "You know, the first time I met you was in the hospital. And now I'm in the hospital again. Just about the only time I see you lately is in the hospital. Where've you been keeping yourself?"

The chaplain shrugged. "I've been praying a lot," he confessed. "I try to stay in my tent as much as I can, and I pray every time Sergeant Whitcomb leaves the area, so that he won't catch me."

"Does it do any good?"

"It takes my mind off my troubles," the chaplain answered with another shrug. "And it gives me something to do."

"Well, that's good, then, isn't it?"

"Yes," agreed the chaplain enthusiastically, as though the idea had not occurred to him before. "Yes, I guess that is good." He bent forward impulsively with awkward solicitude. "Yossarian, is there anything I can do for you while you're here, anything I can get you?"

Yossarian teased him jovially. "Like toys, or candy, or chewing gum?"

The chaplain blushed again, grinning self-consciously, and then turned very respectful. "Like books, perhaps, or anything at all. I wish there was something I could do to make you happy. You know, Yossarian, we're all very proud of you."

"Proud?"

"Yes, of course. For risking your life to stop that Nazi assassin. It was a very noble thing to do."

"What Nazi assassin?"

"The one that came here to murder Colonel Cathcart and Colonel Korn. And you saved them. He might have stabbed you to death as you grappled with him on the balcony. It's a lucky thing you're alive."

Yossarian snickered sardonically when he understood. "That was no Nazi assassin."

"Certainly it was. Colonel Korn said it was."

"That was Nately's girl friend. And she was after me, not Colonel Cathcart and Colonel Korn. She's been trying to kill me ever since I broke the news to her that Nately was dead."

"But how could that be?" the chaplain protested in livid and resentful confusion. "Colonel Cathcart and Colonel Korn both saw him as he ran away. The official report says you stopped a Nazi assassin from killing them."

"Don't believe the official report," Yossarian advised dryly. "It's part of the deal."

"What deal?"

"The deal I made with Colonel Cathcart and Colonel Korn. They'll let me go home a big hero if I say nice things about them to everybody and never criticize them to anyone for making the rest of the men fly more missions.''

The chaplain was appalled and rose halfway out of his chair. He bristled with bellicose dismay. ''But that's terrible! That's a shameful, scandalous deal, isn't it?''

''Odious,'' Yossarian answered, staring up woodenly at the ceiling with just the back of his head resting on the pillow. ''I think 'odious' is the word we decided on.''

''Then how could you agree to it?''

''It's that or a court-martial, Chaplain.''

''Oh,'' the chaplain exclaimed with a look of stark remorse, the back of his hand covering his mouth. He lowered himself into his chair uneasily. ''I shouldn't have said anything.''

''They'd lock me in prison with a bunch of criminals.''

''Of course. You must do whatever you think is right, then.'' The chaplain nodded to himself as though deciding the argument and lapsed into embarrassed silence.

''Don't worry,'' Yossarian said with a sorrowful laugh after several moments had passed. ''I'm not going to do it.''

''But you must do it,'' the chaplain insisted, bending forward with concern. ''Really, you must. I had no right to influence you. I really had no right to say anything.''

''You didn't influence me.'' Yossarian hauled himself over onto his side and shook his head in solemn mockery. ''Christ, Chaplain! Can you imagine that for a sin? Saving Colonel Cathcart's life! That's one crime I don't want on my record.''

The chaplain returned to the subject with caution. ''What will you do instead? You can't let them put you in prison.''

''I'll fly more missions. Or maybe I really will desert and let them catch me. They probably would.''

''And they'd put you in prison. You don't want to go to prison.''

''Then I'll just keep flying missions until the war ends, I guess. Some of us have to survive.''

''But you might get killed.''

''Then I guess I won't fly any more missions.''

''What will you do?''

''I don't know.''

''Will you let them send you home?''

''I don't know. Is it hot out? It's very warm in here.''

''It's very cold out,'' the chaplain said.

''You know,'' Yossarian remembered, ''a very funny thing happened—maybe I dreamed it. I think a strange man came in here before and told me he's got my pal. I wonder if I imagined it.''

"I don't think you did," the chaplain informed him. "You started to tell me about him when I dropped in earlier."

"Then he really did say it. 'We've got your pal, buddy,' he said. 'We've got your pal.' He had the most malignant manner I ever saw. I wonder who my pal is."

"I like to think that I'm your pal, Yossarian," the chaplain said with humble sincerity. "And they certainly have got me. They've got my number and they've got me under surveillance, and they've got me right where they want me. That's what they told me at my interrogation."

"No, I don't think it's you he meant," Yossarian decided. "I think it must be someone like Nately or Dunbar. You know, someone who was killed in the war, like Clevinger, Orr, Dobbs, Kid Sampson or McWatt." Yossarian emitted a startled gasp and shook his head. "I just realized it," he exclaimed. "They've got all my pals, haven't they? The only ones left are me and Hungry Joe." He tingled with dread as he saw the chaplain's face go pale. "Chaplain, what is it?"

"Hungry Joe was killed."

"God, no! On a mission?"

"He died in his sleep while having a dream. They found a cat on his face."

"Poor bastard," Yossarian said, and began to cry, hiding his tears in the crook of his shoulder. The chaplain left without saying good-bye. Yossarian ate something and went to sleep. A hand shook him awake in the middle of the night. He opened his eyes and saw a thin, mean man in a patient's bathrobe and pajamas who looked at him with a nasty smirk and jeered,

"We've got your pal, buddy. We've got your pal."

Yossarian was unnerved. "What the *hell* are you talking about?" he pleaded in incipient panic.

"You'll find out, buddy. You'll find out."

Yossarian lunged for his tormentor's throat with one hand, but the man glided out of reach effortlessly and vanished into the corridor with a malicious laugh. Yossarian lay there trembling with a pounding pulse. He was bathed in icy sweat. He wondered who his pal was. It was dark in the hospital and perfectly quiet. He had no watch to tell him the time. He was wide-awake, and he knew he was a prisoner in one of those sleepless, bedridden nights that would take an eternity to dissolve into dawn. A throbbing chill oozed up his legs. He was cold, and he thought of Snowden, who had never been his pal but was a vaguely familiar kid who was badly wounded and freezing to death in the puddle of harsh yellow sunlight splashing into his face through the side gunport when Yossarian crawled into the rear section of the plane over the bomb bay after Dobbs had beseeched him on the intercom to help the gunner, please help the gunner. Yossarian's stomach turned over when his eyes first beheld the macabre scene; he was absolutely revolted, and he paused in fright a few moments before descending, crouched on his hands and knees in the narrow tunnel over the bomb bay beside the sealed corrugated carton containing the first-aid kit. Snowden was lying on his back on the floor with his legs stretched out, still burdened cumbersomely by his flak suit, his flak helmet, his parachute harness and his Mae West. Not far away on the floor lay the small tail gunner in a dead faint. The wound Yossarian saw was in the outside of Snowden's thigh, as large and deep as a football, it seemed. It was impossible to tell where the shreds of his saturated coveralls ended and the ragged flesh began.

There was no morphine in the first-aid kit, no protection for Snowden against pain but the numbing shock of the gaping wound itself. The twelve syrettes of morphine had been stolen from their case and replaced by a cleanly lettered note that said: "What's good for M & M Enterprises is good for the country. Milo Minderbinder." Yossarian swore at Milo and held two aspirins out to ashen lips unable to receive them. But first he hastily drew a tourniquet around Snowden's thigh because he could not think what else to do in those first tumultuous moments when his senses were in turmoil, when he knew he must act competently at once and feared he might go to pieces completely. Snowden watched him steadily, saying nothing. No artery was spurting, but Yossarian pretended to absorb himself entirely into the fashioning of a tourniquet, because applying a tourniquet was something he did know how to do. He worked with simulated skill and composure, feeling Snowden's lackluster gaze resting upon him. He recovered possession of himself before the tourniquet was finished and loosened it immediately to lessen the danger of gangrene. His mind was clear now, and he knew how to proceed. He rummaged through the first-aid kit for scissors.

"I'm cold," Snowden said softly. "I'm cold."

"You're going to be all right, kid," Yossarian reassured him with a grin. "You're going to be all right."

"I'm cold," Snowden said again in a frail, childlike voice. "I'm cold."

"There, there," Yossarian said, because he did not know what else to say. "There, there."

"I'm cold," Snowden whimpered. "I'm cold."

"There, there. There, there."

Yossarian was frightened and moved more swiftly. He found a pair of scissors at last and began cutting carefully through Snowden's coveralls high up above the wound, just below the groin. He cut through the heavy gabardine cloth all the way around the thigh in a straight line. The tiny tail gunner woke up while Yossarian was cutting with the scissors, saw him, and fainted again. Snowden rolled his head to the other side of his neck in order to stare at Yossarian more directly. A dim, sunken light glowed in his weak and listless eyes. Yossarian, puzzled, tried not to look at him. He began cutting downward through the coveralls along the inside seam. The yawning wound—was that a tube of slimy bone he saw running deep inside the gory scarlet flow behind the twitching, startling fibers of weird muscle?—was dripping blood in several trickles, like snow

567

melting on eaves, but viscous and red, already thickening as it dropped. Yossarian kept cutting through the coveralls to the bottom and peeled open the severed leg of the garment. It fell to the floor with a plop, exposing the hem of khaki undershorts that were soaking up blotches of blood on one side as though in thirst. Yossarian was stunned at how waxen and ghastly Snowden's bare leg looked, how loathsome, how lifeless and esoteric the downy, fine, curled blond hairs on his odd, white shin and calf. The wound, he saw now, was not nearly as large as a football, but as long and wide as his hand, and too raw and deep to see into clearly. The raw muscles inside twitched like live hamburger meat. A long sigh of relief escaped slowly through Yossarian's mouth when he saw that Snowden was not in danger of dying. The blood was already coagulating inside the wound, and it was simply a matter of bandaging him up and keeping him calm until the plane landed. He removed some packets of sulfanilamide from the first-aid kit. Snowden quivered when Yossarian pressed against him gently to turn him up slightly on his side.

"Did I hurt you?"

"I'm cold," Snowden whimpered. "I'm cold."

"There, there," Yossarian said. "There, there."

"I'm cold. I'm cold."

"There, there. There, there."

"It's starting to hurt me," Snowden cried out suddenly with a plaintive, urgent wince.

Yossarian scrambled frantically through the first-aid kit in search of morphine again and found only Milo's note and a bottle of aspirin. He cursed Milo and held two aspirin tablets out to Snowden. He had no water to offer. Snowden rejected the aspirin with an almost imperceptible shake of his head. His face was pale and pasty. Yossarian removed Snowden's flak helmet and lowered his head to the floor.

"I'm cold," Snowden moaned with half-closed eyes. "I'm cold."

The edges of his mouth were turning blue. Yossarian was petrified. He wondered whether to pull the rip cord of Snowden's parachute and cover him with the nylon folds. It was very warm in the plane. Glancing up unexpectedly, Snowden gave him a wan, cooperative smile and shifted the position of his hips a bit so that Yossarian could begin salting the wound with sulfanilamide. Yossarian worked with renewed confidence and optimism. The plane bounced hard inside an air pocket, and he remembered with a start that he had left his own parachute up front in the nose. There was nothing to be done about that. He poured envelope after envelope of the white crystalline powder into the bloody oval wound until nothing red could be seen and then drew a deep, apprehensive breath, steeling himself with gritted teeth as he touched his bare hand to the dangling shreds of drying flesh to tuck them up inside the wound. Quickly he covered the whole wound with a large cotton compress and jerked his hand away. He smiled nervously when his brief ordeal had ended. The actual contact with the dead flesh had not been nearly as repulsive as he had anticipated, and he found excuse to caress the wound with his fingers again and again to convince himself of his own courage.

Next he began binding the compress in place with a role of gauze. The second time around Snowden's thigh with the bandage, he spotted the small hole on the inside through which the piece of flak had entered, a round, crinkled wound the size of a quarter with blue edges and a black core inside where the blood had crusted. Yossarian sprinkled this one with sulfanilamide too and continued unwinding the gauze around Snowden's leg until the compress was secure. Then he snipped off the roll with the scissors and slit the end down the center. He made the whole thing fast with a tidy square knot. It was a good bandage, he knew, and he sat back on his heels with pride, wiping the perspiration from his brow, and grinned at Snowden with spontaneous friendliness.

"I'm cold," Snowden moaned. "I'm cold."

"You're going to be all right, kid," Yossarian assured him, patting his arm comfortingly. "Everything's under control."

Snowden shook his head feebly. "I'm cold," he repeated, with eyes as dull and blind as stone. "I'm cold."

"There, there," said Yossarian, with growing doubt and trepidation. "There, there. In a little while we'll be back on the ground and Doc Daneeka will take care of you."

But Snowden kept shaking his head and pointed at last, with just the barest movement of his chin, down toward his armpit. Yossarian bent forward to peer and saw a strangely colored stain seeping through the coveralls just above the armhole of Snowden's flak suit. Yossarian felt his heart stop, then pound so violently he found it difficult to breathe. Snowden was wounded inside his flak suit. Yossarian ripped open the snaps of Snowden's flak suit and heard himself scream wildly as Snowden's insides slithered down to the floor in a soggy pile and just kept dripping out. A chunk of flak more than three inches big had shot into his other side just underneath the arm and blasted all the way through, drawing whole mottled quarts of Snowden along with it through the gigantic hole in his ribs it made as it blasted out. Yossarian screamed a second time and squeezed both hands over his eyes. His teeth were chattering in horror. He forced himself to look again. Here was God's plenty, all right, he thought bitterly as he stared—liver, lungs, kidneys, ribs, stomach and bits of the stewed tomatoes Snowden had eaten that day for lunch. Yossarian hated stewed tomatoes and turned away dizzily and began to vomit, clutching his burning throat. The tail gunner woke up while Yossarian was vomiting, saw him, and fainted again. Yossarian was limp with exhaustion, pain and despair when he finished. He turned back weakly to Snowden, whose breath had grown softer and more rapid, and whose face had grown paler. He wondered how in the world to begin to save him.

"I'm cold," Snowden whimpered. "I'm cold."

"There, there," Yossarian mumbled mechanically in a voice too low to be heard. "There, there."

Yossarian was cold, too, and shivering uncontrollably. He felt goose pimples clacking all over him as he gazed down despondently at the grim secret Snowden had spilled all over the messy floor. It was easy to read the message in his entrails. Man was matter, that was Snowden's secret. Drop him out a window and he'll fall. Set fire to him and he'll burn. Bury him and he'll rot, like other kinds of garbage. The spirit gone, man is garbage. That was Snowden's secret. Ripeness was all.

"I'm cold," Snowden said. "I'm cold."

"There, there," said Yossarian. "There, there." He pulled the rip cord of Snowden's parachute and covered his body with the white nylon sheets.

"I'm cold."

"There, there."

from DISPATCHES

Michael Herr

You could watch mortar bursts, orange and gray-smoking, over the tops of trees three and four kilometers away, and the heavier shelling from support bases further east along the DMZ, from Camp Carrol and the Rockpile, directed against suspected troop movements or NVA rocket and mortar positions. Once in a while—I guess I saw it happen three or four times in all—there would be a secondary explosion, a direct hit on a supply of NVA ammunition. And at night it was beautiful. Even the incoming was beautiful at night, beautiful and deeply dreadful.

I remembered the way a Phantom pilot had talked about how beautiful the surface-to-air missiles looked as they drifted up toward his plane to kill him, and remembered myself how lovely .50-caliber tracers could be, coming at you as you flew at night in a helicopter, how slow and graceful, arching up easily, a dream, so remote from anything that could harm you. It could make you feel a total serenity, an elevation that put you above death, but that never lasted very long. One hit anywhere in the chopper would bring you back, bitten lips, white knuckles and all, and then you knew where you were. It was different with the incoming at Khe Sanh. You didn't get to watch the shells very often. You knew if you heard one, the first one, that you were safe, or at least saved. If you were still standing up and looking after that, you deserved anything that happened to you.

Nights were when the air and artillery strikes were heaviest, because that was when we knew that the NVA was above ground and moving. At night you could lie out on some sandbags and watch the C-47's mounted with Vulcans doing their work. The C-47 was a standard prop flareship, but many of them carried .20- and .762-mm. guns on their doors, Mike-Mikes that could fire out 300 rounds per second, Gatling style, "a round in every square inch of a football field in less than a minute," as the handouts said. They used to call it Puff the Magic Dragon, but the Marines knew better: they named it Spooky. Every fifth round was a tracer, and when Spooky was working, everything stopped while that solid stream of violent red poured down out of the black sky. If you watched from a great distance, the stream would seem to dry up between bursts, vanishing slowly from air to ground like a comet tail, the sound of the guns disappearing too, a few seconds later. If you watched at close range, you couldn't believe that anyone would have the courage to deal with that night after night, week after week, and you cultivated a respect for the Viet Cong and NVA who had crouched under it every night now for months. It was awesome, worse than anything the Lord had ever put down on Egypt, and at night, you'd hear the Marines talking, watching it, yelling, "Get some!" until they grew quiet and someone would say, "Spooky understands." The nights were very beautiful. Night was when you really had the least to fear and feared the most. You could go through some very bad numbers at night.

1. Two ways of treating the terror of war are offered here: one through black humor and confronting the reader with graphic details of a mutilated body ("Snowden"), the other through the frightening aesthetics of war, the enticing beauty seen from a distance which leaves the viewer in awe (*Dispatches*).

    a. Contrast these approaches, outlining the strong and weak points (if any) of each treatment, referring to the subject, the message, the style, and the tone.

    b. Discuss the impact each one had on you.

    c. Which do you think is the more powerful statement and why?

2. Fear is a dominant emotion of war. It can be covered up with bleak laughter or exclamations of how unusually "beautiful" it all is, but it remains *fear*. Contrast the treatment of fear in each extract.

3. "Snowden" really takes place in two parts: Yossarian in the hospital and Yossarian in the plane with Snowden. How do the *events* and the *tone* of each part relate?

4. In Herr's passage, why do you think "someone would say, 'Spooky understands' "?

5. Contrast the treatment of violence in the two passages.

THE ONES WHO WALK AWAY FROM OMELAS

Ursula K. Le Guin

(Variations on a theme by William James)

With a clamor of bells that set the swallows soaring, the Festival of Summer came to the city Omelas, bright-towered by the sea. The rigging of the boats in harbor sparkled with flags. In the streets between houses with red roofs and painted walls, between old moss-grown gardens and under avenues of trees, past great parks and public buildings, processions moved. Some were decorous: old people in long stiff robes of mauve and grey, grave master workmen, quiet, merry women carrying their babies, and chatting as they walked. In other streets the music beat faster, a shimmering of gong and tambourine, and the people went dancing, the procession was a dance. Children dodged in and out, their high calls rising like the swallows' crossing flights over the music and the singing. All the processions wound towards the north side of the city, where on the great water-meadow called the Green Fields boys and girls, naked in the bright air, with mud-stained feet and ankles and long, lithe arms, exercised their restive horses before the race. The horses wore no gear at all but a halter without bit. Their manes were braided with streamers of silver, gold, and green. They flared their nostrils and pranced and boasted to one another; they were vastly excited, the horse being the only animal who has adopted our ceremonies as his own. Far off to the north and west the mountains stood up half encircling Omelas on her bay. The air of morning was so clear that the snow still crowning the Eighteen Peaks burned with white-gold fire across the miles of sunlit air, under the dark blue of the sky. There was just enough wind to make the banners that marked the racecourse snap and flutter now and then. In the silence of the broad green meadows one could hear the music winding through the city streets, farther and nearer and ever approaching, a cheerful faint sweetness of the air that from time to time trembled and gathered together and broke out into the great joyous clanging of the bells.

Joyous! How is one to tell about joy? How describe the citizens of Omelas?

They were not simple folk, you see, though they were happy. But we do not say the words of cheer much any more. All smiles have become archaic. Given a description such as this one tends to make certain assumptions. Given a description such as this one tends to look next for the King, mounted on a splendid stallion and surrounded by his noble knights, or perhaps in a golden litter borne by great-muscled slaves. But there was no king. They did not use swords, or keep slaves. They were not barbarians. I do not know the rules and laws of their society, but I suspect that they were singularly few. As they did without monarchy and slavery, so they also got on without the stock exchange, the advertisement, the secret police, and the bomb. Yet I repeat that these were not simple folk, not dulcet shepherds, noble savages, bland utopians. They were not less complex than us. The trouble is that we have a bad habit, encouraged by pedants and sophisticates, of considering happiness as something rather stupid. Only pain is intellectual, only evil interesting. This is the treason of the artist: a refusal to admit the banality of evil and the terrible boredom of pain. If you can't lick 'em, join 'em. If it hurts, repeat it. But to praise despair is to condemn delight, to embrace violence is to lose hold of everything else. We have almost lost hold; we can no longer describe a happy man, nor make any celebration of joy. How can I tell you about the people of Omelas? They were not naïve and happy children—though their children were, in fact, happy. They were mature, intelligent, passionate adults whose lives were not wretched. O miracle! but I wish I could describe it better. I wish I could convince you. Omelas sounds in my words like a city in a fairy tale, long ago and far away, once upon a time. Perhaps it would be best if you imagined it as your own fancy bids, assuming it will rise to the occasion, for certainly I cannot suit you all. For instance, how about technology? I think that there would be no cars or helicopters in and above the streets; this follows from the fact that the people of Omelas are happy people. Happiness is based on a just discrimination of what is necessary, what is neither necessary nor destructive, and what is destructive. In the middle category, however—that of the unnecessary but undestructive, that of comfort, luxury, exuberance, etc.—they could perfectly well have central heating, subway trains, washing machines, and all kinds of marvelous devices not yet invented here, floating light-sources, fuelless power, a cure for the common cold. Or they could have none of that: it doesn't matter. As you like it. I incline to think that people from towns up and down the coast have been coming in to Omelas during the last days before the Festival on very fast little trains and double-decked trams, and that the train station of Omelas is actually the handsomest building in town, though plainer than the magnificent Farmers' Market. But even granted trains, I fear that Omelas so far strikes some of you as goody-goody. Smiles, bells, parades, horses, bleh. If so, please add an orgy. If an orgy would help, don't hesitate. Let us not, however, have temples from which issue beautiful nude priests and priestesses already half in ecstasy and ready to copulate with any man or woman, lover or stranger, who desires union with the deep godhead of the blood, although that was my first idea. But really it would be better not to have any temples in Omelas—at least, not manned temples. Religion yes, clergy no. Surely the beautiful nudes can just wander about, offering themselves like divine soufflés to the hunger of the needy and the rapture of the flesh. Let them join the processions. Let tambourines be struck above the copulations, and the glory of desire be proclaimed upon the gongs, and (a not unimportant point) let the offspring of these delightful rituals be beloved and looked after by all. One thing I know there is none of in Omelas is guilt. But what else should there be? I thought at first there were no drugs, but that is puritanical. For those who like it, the faint insistent sweetness of *drooz* may perfume the ways of the city, *drooz* which first brings a great lightness and brilliance to the mind and limbs, and then after some hours a dreamy languor, and wonderful visions at last of the very arcana and inmost secrets of the Universe, as well as exciting the pleasure of sex beyond all belief; and it is not habit-forming. For more modest tastes I think there ought to be beer. What else, what else belongs in the joyous city? The sense of victory, surely, the celebration of courage. But as we did without clergy, let us do without soldiers. The joy built upon successful slaughter is not the right kind of joy; it will not do; it is fearful and it is trivial. A boundless and generous contentment, a magnanimous triumph felt not against some outer enemy but in communion with the finest and fairest in the souls of all men everywhere and the splendor of the world's summer: this is what swells the hearts of the people of Omelas, and the victory they celebrate is that of life. I really don't think many of them need to take *drooz*.

Most of the processions have reached the Green Fields by now. A marvelous smell of cooking goes forth from the red and blue tents of the provisioners. The faces of small children are amiably sticky; in the benign grey beard of a man a couple of crumbs of rich pastry are entangled. The youths and girls have mounted their horses and are beginning to group around the starting line of the course. An old woman, small, fat, and laughing, is passing out flowers from a basket, and tall young men wear her flowers in their shining hair. A child of nine or ten sits at the edge of the crowd, alone, playing on a wooden flute. People pause to listen, and they smile, but they do not speak to him, for he never ceases playing and never sees them, his dark eyes wholly rapt in the sweet, thin magic of the tune.

He finishes, and slowly lowers his hands holding the wooden flute.

As if that little private silence were the signal, all at once a trumpet sounds from the pavilion near the starting line: imperious, melancholy, piercing. The horses rear on their slender legs, and some of them neigh in answer. Sober-faced, the young riders stroke the horses' necks and soothe them, whispering, "Quiet, quiet, there my beauty, my hope...." They begin to form in rank along the starting line. The crowds along the racecourse are like a field of grass and flowers in the wind. The Festival of Summer has begun.

Do you believe? Do you accept the festival, the city, the joy? No? Then let me describe one more thing.

In a basement under one of the beautiful public buildings of Omelas, or perhaps in the cellar of one of its spacious private homes, there is a room. It has one locked door, and no window. A little light seeps in dustily between cracks in the boards, secondhand from a cobwebbed window somewhere across the cellar. In one corner of the little room a couple of mops, with stiff, clotted, foul-smelling heads, stand near a rusty bucket. The floor is dirt, a little damp to the touch, as cellar dirt usually is. The room is about three paces long and two wide: a mere broom closet or disused tool room. In the room a child is sitting. It could be a boy or a girl. It looks about six, but actually is nearly ten. It is feeble-minded. Perhaps it was born defective, or perhaps it has become imbecile through fear, malnutrition, and neglect. It picks its nose and occasionally fumbles vaguely with its toes or genitals, as it sits hunched in the corner farthest from the bucket and the two mops. It is afraid of the mops. It finds them horrible. It shuts its eyes, but it knows the mops are still standing there; and the door is locked; and nobody will come. The door is always locked; and nobody ever comes, except that sometimes—the child has no understanding of time or interval—sometimes the door rattles terribly and opens, and a person, or several people, are there. One of them may come in and kick the child to make it stand up. The others never come close, but peer in at it with frightened, disgusted eyes. The food bowl and the water jug are hastily filled, the door is locked, the eyes disappear. The people at the door never say anything, but the child, who has not always lived in the tool room, and can remember sunlight and its mother's voice, sometimes speaks. "I will be good," it says. "Please let me out. I will be good!" They never answer. The child used to scream for help at night, and cry a good deal, but now it only makes a kind of whining, "eh-haa, eh-haa," and it speaks less and less often. It is so thin there are no calves to its legs; its belly protrudes; it lives on a half-bowl of corn meal and grease a day. It is naked. Its buttocks and thighs are a mass of festered sores, as it sits in its own excrement continually.

They all know it is there, all the people of Omelas. Some of them have come to see it, others are content merely to know it is there. They all know that it has to be there. Some of them understand why, and some do not, but they all understand that their happiness, the beauty of their city, the tenderness of their friendships, the health of their children, the wisdom of their scholars, the skill of their makers, even the abundance of their harvest and the kindly weathers of their skies, depend wholly on this child's abominable misery.

This is usually explained to children when they are between eight and twelve, whenever they seem capable of understanding; and most of those who come to see the child are young people, though often enough an adult comes, or comes back, to see the child. No matter how well the matter has been explained to them, these young spectators are always shocked and sickened at the sight. They feel disgust, which they had thought themselves superior to. They feel anger, outrage, impotence, despite all the explanations. They would like to do something for the child. But there is nothing they can do. If the child were brought up into the sunlight out of that vile place, if it were cleaned and fed and comforted, that would be a good thing, indeed; but if it were done, in that day and hour all the prosperity and beauty and delight of Omelas would wither and be destroyed. Those are the terms. To exchange all the goodness and grace of every life in Omelas for that single, small improvement: to throw away the happiness of thousands for the chance of the happiness of one; that would be to let guilt within the walls indeed.

The terms are strict and absolute; there may not even be a kind word spoken to the child.

Often the young people go home in tears, or in a tearless rage, when they have seen the child and faced this terrible paradox. They may brood over it for weeks or years. But as time goes on they begin to realize that even if the child could be released, it would not get much good of its freedom: a little vague pleasure of warmth and food, no doubt, but little more. It is too degraded and imbecile to know any real joy. It has been afraid too long even to be free of fear. Its habits are too uncouth for it to respond to humane treatment. Indeed, after so long it would probably be wretched without walls about it to protect it, and darkness for its eyes, and its own excrement to sit in. Their tears at the bitter injustice dry when they begin to perceive the terrible justice of reality, and to accept it. Yet it is their tears and anger, the trying of their generosity and the acceptance of their helplessness, which are perhaps the true source of the splendor of their lives. Theirs is no vapid, irresponsible happiness. They know that they, like the child, are not free. They know compassion. It is the existence of the child, and their knowledge of its existence, that makes possible the nobility of their architecture, and poignancy of their music, the profundity of their science. It is because of the child that they are so gentle with children. They know that if the wretched one were not there snivelling in the dark, the other one, the flute-player, could make no joyful music as the young riders line up in their beauty for the race in the sunlight of the first morning of summer.

Now do you believe in them? Are they not more credible? But there is one more thing to tell, and this is quite incredible.

At times one of the adolescent girls or boys who go to see the child does not go home to weep or rage, does not, in fact, go home at all. Sometimes also a man or woman much older falls silent for a day or two, and then leaves home. These people go out into the street, and walk down the street alone. They keep walking, and walk straight out of the city of Omelas, through the beautiful gates. They keep walking across the farmlands of Omelas. Each one goes alone, youth or girl, man or woman. Night falls; the traveler must pass down village streets, between the houses with yellow-lit windows, and on out into the darkness of the fields. Each alone, they go west or north, towards the mountains. They go on. They leave Omelas, they walk ahead into the darkness, and they do not come back. The place they go towards is a place even less imaginable to most of us than the city of happiness. I cannot describe it at all. It is possible that it does not exist.

But they seem to know where they are going, the ones who walk away from Omelas.

1. What role, exactly, does the child in the cellar play for the people of Omelas? How is its misery justified? Why does everything depend on its misery?

2. Why do most of the people of Omelas accept the "terrible justice of reality"? Why are they so credulous? Where do those who don't accept Omelas go?

3. Why do we apparently think happiness is stupid? Explain the definition of happiness offered in the middle of the third paragraph. What is the real source of happiness in Omelas?

4. This story is based on a paradox. Explain the paradox as carefully as you can, together with its relevance to us.

5. Discuss the way in which Le Guin tells her tale, explaining
   a. The relevance of her style and tone
   b. Why she wants to talk to the reader directly (for example, in statements like "I wish I could convince you" and "If an orgy would help, don't hesitate")

SNAKE

D. H. Lawrence

A snake came to my water-trough
On a hot, hot day, and I in pyjamas for the heat,
To drink there.

In the deep, strange-scented shade of the great dark carob-tree
I came down the steps with my pitcher

And must wait, must stand and wait, for there he was at the trough
   before me.

He reached down from a fissure in the earth-wall in the gloom
And trailed his yellow-brown slackness soft-bellied down, over the
   edge of the stone trough
And rested his throat upon the stone bottom,
And where the water had dripped from the tap, in a small clearness,
He sipped with his straight mouth,
Softly drank through his straight gums, into his slack long body,
Silently.

577

Someone was before me at my water-trough,
And I, like a second comer, waiting.

He lifted his head from his drinking, as cattle do,
And looked at me vaguely, as drinking cattle do,
And flickered his two-forked tongue from his lips, and mused a
    moment,
And stooped and drank a little more,
Being earth-brown, earth-golden from the burning bowels of the
    earth
On the day of Sicilian July, with Etna smoking.

The voice of my education said to me
He must be killed,
For in Sicily the black, black snakes are innocent, the gold are
    venomous.

And voices in me said, If you were a man
You would take a stick and break him now, and finish him off.

But must I confess how I liked him,
How glad I was he had come like a guest in quiet, to drink at my
    water-trough
And depart peaceful, pacified, and thankless,
Into the burning bowels of this earth?

Was it cowardice, that I dared not kill him?
Was it perversity, that I longed to talk to him?
Was it humility, to feel so honoured?
I felt so honoured.

And yet those voices:
If you were not afraid, you would kill him!

And truly I was afraid, I was most afraid,
But even so, honoured still more
That he should seek my hospitality
From out the dark door of the secret earth.

He drank enough
And lifted his head, dreamily, as one who has drunken,
And flickered his tongue like a forked night on the air, so black;
Seeming to lick his lips,

And looked around like a god, unseeing, into the air,
And slowly turned his head,
And slowly, very slowly, as if thrice adream,

Proceeded to draw his slow length curving round
And climb again the broken bank of my wall-face.

And as he put his head into that dreadful hole,
And as he slowly drew up, snake-easing his shoulders, and entered
    farther,
A sort of horror, a sort of protest against his withdrawing into that
    horrid black hole,
Deliberately going into the blackness, and slowly drawing himself
    after,
Overcame me now his back was turned.

I looked round, I put down my pitcher,
I picked up a clumsy log
And threw it at the water-trough with a clatter.

I think it did not hit him,
But suddenly that part of him that was left behind convulsed in
    undignified haste,
Writhed like lightning, and was gone
Into the black hole, the earth-lipped fissure in the wall-front,
At which, in the intense still noon, I stared with fascination.

And immediately I regretted it.
I thought how paltry, how vulgar, what a mean act!
I despised myself and the voices of my accursed human education.

And I thought of the albatross,
And I wished he would come back, my snake.

For he seemed to me again like a king,
Like a king in exile, uncrowned in the underworld,
Now due to be crowned again.

And so, I missed my chance with one of the lords
Of life.
And I have something to expiate;
A pettiness.

1. Write two or three paragraphs describing the feelings of the speaker on being confronted by the snake. In your answer, refer to the following questions:
    a. Why is the speaker a "second-comer"?
    b. What are the voices he hears and what are they saying?
    c. Why is the speaker afraid of the snake and yet admires it?
2. The snake is given a life of its own in this poem. Consider the snake and answer the following questions:

a. What is the snake's reaction to the speaker?

b. Why is the snake "like a god," "like a king in exile, uncrowned in the underworld," and "one of the lords of life"?

c. Why does the poet emphasize the "horrid black hole" the snake withdraws into?

3. What do you think is the major effect for the reader of this dramatic tension between snake and man?

4. Why does the speaker say he has "something to expiate; / A pettiness"?

5. Discuss the appropriateness of Lawrence's language and style to what he is saying about the confrontation of man and snake.

PRELUDES

T. S. Eliot

I

The winter evening settles down
With smell of steaks in passageways.
Six o'clock.
The burnt-out ends of smoky days.
And now a gusty shower wraps
The grimy scraps
Of withered leaves about your feet
And newspapers from vacant lots;
The showers beat
On broken blinds and chimney-pots,
And at the corner of the street
A lonely cab-horse steams and stamps.

And then the lighting of the lamps.

II

The morning comes to consciousness
Of faint stale smells of beer
From the sawdust-trampled street
With all its muddy feet that press
To early coffee-stands.

With the other masquerades
That time resumes,
One thinks of all the hands
That are raising dingy shades
In a thousand furnished rooms.

III

You tossed a blanket from the bed,
You lay upon your back, and waited;
You dozed, and watched the night revealing
The thousand sordid images
Of which your soul was constituted;
They flickered against the ceiling.
And when all the world came back
And the light crept up between the shutters
And you heard the sparrows in the gutters,
You had such a vision of the street
As the street hardly understands;
Sitting along the bed's edge, where
You curled the papers from your hair,
Or clasped the yellow soles of feet
In the palms of both soiled hands.

IV

His soul stretched tight across the skies
That fade behind a city block,
Or trampled by insistent feet
At four and five and six o'clock;
And short square fingers stuffing pipes,
And evening newspapers, and eyes
Assured of certain certainties,
The conscience of a blackened street
Impatient to assume the world.

I am moved by fancies that are curled
Around these images, and cling:

The notion of some infinitely gentle
Infinitely suffering thing.

Wipe your hand across your mouth, and laugh;
The worlds revolve like ancient women
Gathering fuel in vacant lots.

1. Why do you think the poem is called "Preludes"?
2. How are each of the sections related?
3. Why is the speaker "moved by fancies that are curled / Around these images, and cling"?
4. What do the last three lines of the poem suggest to you?
5. Explain Eliot's tone carefully, noting your answers to the last two questions, and then discuss how the style conveys the tone.

There follows a poem, Elizabeth Bishop's "The Fish," and "Araby," a short story by James Joyce. Write an interpretation for each, going through all the stages outlined in this chapter from annotation to the final draft and, of course, reading as imaginatively and metaphorically as you can.

THE FISH

Elizabeth Bishop

I caught a tremendous fish
and held him beside the boat
half out of water, with my hook
fast in a corner of his mouth.
He didn't fight.
He hadn't fought at all.
He hung a grunting weight,
battered and venerable
and homely. Here and there
his brown skin hung in strips
like ancient wallpaper,
and its pattern of darker brown
was like wallpaper:
shapes like full-blown roses
stained and lost through age.
He was speckled with barnacles,
fine rosettes of lime,
and infested
with tiny white sea-lice,
and underneath two or three
rags of green weed hung down.
While his gills were breathing in

the terrible oxygen
—the frightening gills,
fresh and crisp with blood,
that can cut so badly—
I thought of the coarse white flesh
packed in like feathers,
the big bones and the little bones,
the dramatic reds and blacks

of his shiny entrails,
and the pink swim-bladder
like a big peony.
I looked into his eyes
which were far larger than mine
but shallower, and yellowed,
the irises backed and packed
with tarnished tinfoil
seen through the lenses
of old scratched isinglass.
They shifted a little, but not
to return my stare.
—It was more like the tipping
of an object toward the light.
I admired his sullen face,
the mechanism of his jaw,
and then I saw
that from his lower lip
—if you could call it a lip—
grim, wet, and weaponlike,
hung five old pieces of fish-line,
or four and a wire leader
with the swivel still attached,
with all their five big hooks
grown firmly in his mouth.
A green line, frayed at the end
where he broke it, two heavier lines,
and a fine black thread
still crimped from the strain and snap
when it broke and he got away.
Like medals with their ribbons
frayed and wavering,
a five-haired beard of wisdom
trailing from his aching jaw.
I stared and stared
and victory filled up
the little rented boat,
from the pool of bilge
where oil had spread a rainbow
around the rusted engine
to the bailer rusted orange,
the sun-cracked thwarts,

the oarlocks on their strings,
the gunnels—until everything

was rainbow, rainbow, rainbow!
And I let the fish go.

ARABY

James Joyce

North Richmond Street, being blind, was a quiet street except at the hour when the Christian Brothers' School set the boys free. An uninhabited house of two stories stood at the blind end, detached from its neighbours in a square ground. The other houses of the street, conscious of decent lives within them, gazed at one another with brown imperturbable faces.

The former tenant of our house, a priest, had died in the back drawing-room. Air, musty from having been long enclosed, hung in all the rooms, and the waste-room behind the kitchen was littered with old useless papers. Among these I found a few paper-covered books, the pages of which were curled and damp: *The Abbot,* by Walter Scott, *The Devout Communicant,* and *The Memoirs of Vidocq.* I liked the last best because its leaves were yellow. The wild garden behind the house contained a central apple tree and a few straggling bushes under one of which I found the late tenant's rusty bicycle pump. He had been a very charitable priest; in his will he had left all his money to institutions and the furniture of his house to his sister.

When the short days of winter came dusk fell before we had well eaten our dinners. When we met in the street the houses had grown sombre. The space of sky above us was the colour of ever-changing violet and towards it the lamps of the street lifted their feeble lanterns. The cold air stung us and we played till our bodies glowed. Our shouts echoed in the silent street. The career of our play brought us through the dark muddy lanes behind the houses where we ran the gauntlet of the rough tribes from the cottages, to the back doors of the dark dripping gardens where odours arose from the ash-pits, to the dark odorous stables where a coachman smoothed and combed the horse or shook music from the buckled harness. When we returned to the street, light from the kitchen windows had filled the areas. If my uncle was seen turning the corner we hid in the shadow until we had seen him safely housed. Or if Mangan's sister came out on the doorstep to call her brother in to his tea we watched her from our shadow peer up and down the street. We waited to see whether she would remain or go in and, if she remained, we left our shadow and walked up to Mangan's steps resignedly. She was waiting for us, her figure defined by the light from the half-opened door. Her brother always teased her before he obeyed and I stood by the railings looking at her. Her dress swung as she moved her body and the soft rope of her hair tossed from side to side.

Every morning I lay on the floor in the front parlor watching her door. The blind was pulled down to within an inch of the sash so that I could not be seen. When she came out on the doorstep my heart leaped. I ran to the hall, seized my books and followed her. I kept her brown figure always in my eye and, when we came near the point at which our ways diverged, I quickened my pace and passed her. This happened morning after morning. I had never spoken to her, except for a few casual words, and yet her name was like a summons to all my foolish blood.

Her image accompanied me even in places the most hostile to romance. On Saturday evenings when my aunt went marketing I had to go to carry some of the parcels. We walked through the flaring streets, jostled by drunken men and bargaining women, amid the curses of labourers, the shrill litanies of shop boys who stood on guard by the barrels of pigs' cheeks, the nasal chanting of street singers, who sang a *come-all-you* about O'Donavan Rossa, or a ballad about the troubles in our native land. These noises converged in a single sensation of life for me: I imagined that I bore my chalice safely through a throng of foes. Her name sprang to my lips at moments in strange prayers and praises which I myself did not understand. My eyes were often full of tears (I could not tell why) and at times a flood from my heart seemed to pour itself out into my bosom. I thought little of the future. I did not know whether I would ever speak to her or not or, if I spoke to her, how I could tell her of my confused adoration. But my body was like a harp and her words and gestures were like fingers running upon the wires.

One evening I went into the back drawing-room in which the priest had died. It was a dark rainy evening and there was no sound in the house. Through one of the broken panes I heard the rain impinge upon the earth, the fine incessant needles of water playing in the sodden beds. Some distant lamp or lighted window gleamed below me. I was thankful that I could see so little. All my senses seemed to desire to veil themselves and, feeling that I was about to slip from them, I pressed the palms of my hands together until they trembled, murmuring: "O love! O love!" many times.

At last she spoke to me. When she addressed the first words to me I was so confused that I did not know what to answer. She asked me was I going to *Araby.* I forgot whether I answered yes or no. It would be a splendid bazaar, she said; she would love to go.

"And why can't you?" I asked.

While she spoke she turned a silver bracelet round and round her wrist. She could not go, she said, because there would be a retreat that week in her convent. Her brother and two other boys were fighting for their caps and I was alone at the railings. She held one of the spikes, bowing her head towards me. The light from the lamp opposite our door caught the white curve of her neck, lit up her hair that rested there and, falling, lit up the hand upon the railing. It fell over one side of her dress and caught the white border of a petticoat, just visible as she stood at ease.

"It's well for you," she said.

"If I go," I said, "I will bring you something."

What innumerable follies laid waste my waking and sleeping thoughts after that evening! I wished to annihilate the tedious intervening days. I chafed against the work of school. At night in my bedroom and by day in the classroom her image came between me and the page I strove to read. The syllables of the word *Araby* were called to me through the silence in which my soul luxuriated and cast an Eastern enchantment over me. I asked for leave to go to the bazaar on Saturday night. My aunt was surprised and hoped it was not some Freemason affair. I answered few questions in class. I watched my master's face pass from amiability to sternness; he hoped I was not beginning to idle. I could not call my wandering thoughts together. I had hardly any patience with the serious work of life which, now that it stood between me and my desire, seemed to me child's play, ugly monotonous child's play.

On Saturday morning I reminded my uncle that I wished to go to the bazaar in the evening. He was fussing at the hall-stand, looking for the hat brush, and answered me curtly:

"Yes, boy, I know."

As he was in the hall I could not go into the front parlour and lie at the window. I left the house in bad humour and walked slowly towards the school. The air was pitilessly raw and already my heart misgave me.

When I came home to dinner my uncle had not yet been home. Still it was early. I sat staring at the clock for some time and, when its ticking began to irritate me, I left the room. I mounted the staircase and gained the upper part of the house. The high cold empty gloomy rooms liberated me and I went from room to room singing. From the front window I saw my companions playing below in the street. Their cries reached me weakened and indistinct and, leaning my forehead against the cool glass, I looked over at the dark house where she lived. I may have stood there for an hour, seeing nothing but the brown-clad figure cast by my imagination, touched discreetly by the lamplight at the curved neck, at the hand upon the railings and at the border below the dress.

When I came downstairs again I found Mrs. Mercer sitting at the fire. She was an old garrulous woman, a pawnbroker's widow, who collected used stamps for some pious purpose. I had to endure the gossip of the tea table. The meal was prolonged beyond an hour and still my uncle did not come. Mrs. Mercer stood up to go: she was sorry she couldn't wait any longer, but it was after eight o'clock and she did not like to be out late, as the night air was bad for her. When she had gone I began to walk up and down the room, clenching my fists. My aunt said:

"I'm afraid you may put off your bazaar for this night of Our Lord."

At nine o'clock I heard my uncle's latchkey in the hall door. I heard him talking to himself and heard the hall-stand rocking when it had received the weight of his overcoat. I could interpret these signs. When he was midway through his dinner I asked him to give me the money to go to the bazaar. He had forgotten.

"The people are in bed and after their first sleep now," he said.

I did not smile. My aunt said to him energetically:

"Can't you give him the money and let him go? You've kept him late enough as it is."

My uncle said he was very sorry he had forgotten. He said he believed in the old saying: "All work and no play makes Jack a dull boy." He asked me where I was going and, when I told him a second time he asked me did I know *The Arab's Farewell to His Steed.* When I left the kitchen he was about to recite the opening lines of the piece to my aunt.

I held a florin tightly in my hand as I strode down Buckingham Street towards the station. The sight of the streets thronged with buyers and glaring with gas recalled to me the purpose of my journey. I took my seat in a third-class carriage of a deserted train. After an intolerable delay the train moved out of the station slowly. It crept onward among ruinous houses and over the twinkling river. At Westland Row Station a crowd of people pressed to the carriage doors; but the porters moved them back, saying that it was a special train for the bazaar. I remained alone in the bare carriage. In a few minutes the train drew up beside an improvised wooden platform. I passed out on to the road and saw by the lighted dial of a clock that it was ten minutes to ten. In front of me was a large building which displayed the magical name.

I could not find any sixpenny entrance and, fearing that the bazaar would be closed, I passed in quickly through a turnstile, handing a shilling to a weary-looking man. I found myself in a big hall girdled at half its height by a gallery. Nearly all the stalls were closed and the greater part of the hall was in darkness. I recognised a silence like that which pervades a church after a service. I walked into the center of the bazaar timidly. A few people were gathered about the stalls which were still open. Before a curtain, over which the words *Café Chantant* were written in coloured lamps, two men were counting money on a salver. I listened to the fall of the coins.

Remembering with difficulty why I had come I went over to one of the stalls and examined porcelain vases and flowered teasets. At the door of the stall a young lady was talking and laughing with two young gentlemen. I remarked their English accents and listened vaguely to their conversation.

"O, I never said such a thing!"

"O, but you did!"

"O, but I didn't!"

"Didn't she say that?"

"Yes, I heard her."

"O, there's a . . . fib!"

Observing me, the young lady came over and asked me did I wish to buy anything. The tone of her voice was not encouraging; she seemed to have spoken to me out of a sense of duty. I looked humbly at the great jars that stood like the eastern guards at either side of the dark entrance to the stall and murmured:

"No, thank you."

The young lady changed the position of one of the vases and went back to the two young men. They began to talk of the same subject. Once or twice the young lady glanced at me over her shoulder.

I lingered before her stall, though I knew my stay was useless, to make my interest in her wares seem the more real. Then I turned away slowly and walked down the middle of the bazaar. I allowed the two pennies to fall against the sixpence in my pocket. I heard a voice call from one end of the gallery that the light was out. The upper part of the hall was now completely dark.

Gazing up into the darkness I saw myself as a creature driven and derided by vanity; and my eyes burned with anguish and anger.

Appendix A

The Research Paper

Research papers are written to analyze and synthesize source material that you have researched on a topic. If you are writing on a topic that requires a search for information, then you visit your college library and read up on the subject. Your findings are then transformed into a research paper. This paper is an important variant on the basic position paper covered in Chapters 3–7. Where the procedures overlap, you will be referred to those chapters.

However, there is one major difference between the two kinds of papers. Instead of mainly brainstorming ideas on a topic, the writer of the research paper draws on written and other sources to find most of the seed ideas—the raw material of *facts,* especially—that will help form the thesis. Of course, position papers may make some reference to sources outside the writer's imagination, and every research paper requires the writer to make some kind of original arrangement and provide a critical interpretation of the sources. The writer of the research paper should never be taken over by the sources and merely list facts clinically. But in the research paper the writer is basically dealing with topics that *require* research because they are too complex or too dependent on historical data to be handled adequately in a position paper. Here, then, are some recommended procedures for writing the research paper. They are discussed in the following pages.

■ Choose a subject and narrow it down to a manageable topic.

■ Open up the topic by obtaining information from library sources.

■ Evaluate the sources, choosing the most important ones.

■ Prepare a preliminary bibliography on small index cards.

■ Take notes from your source materials, choosing important quotations. Use large index cards.

■ Read and organize your notes, selecting important themes from the assembled information. Note contradictions and questions. Limit your topic. Fill in research gaps.

- Make a preliminary outline working from the major themes of your sources.

- Develop a thesis from the preliminary outline.

- Prepare a final outline, choosing final quotations and coming to a conclusion.

- Decide on the audience, tone, and style.

- Write the first draft, revising as you write. This draft will include footnotes.

- Make a final revision for emphasis, coherence, and unity.

- Type up the final draft following the recommended format. Prepare your endnotes and bibliography.

- Proofread.

Choose a Topic

See Chapter 3 for full details. In brief: choose a subject that interests you and is likely to yield interesting information, one that you think you can reasonably handle. Free associate on the subject to create ideas from which you can choose your topic. It is also a good idea to check the *subject card index* in your library to see what aspects of the subject have proved interesting to other writers. Browsing through recently published full treatments of the subject can also help.

It is wise not to simply borrow a specific topic from another source. Such borrowing can quickly lead to your reliance on that major source and to copying someone else's work, which is a serious offense. The more original your topic, the more interesting and valuable your research paper will be. Use your browsing through the subject index and reference books to stimulate ideas only. Write down the ideas and then select your topic from among them.

The topic should not be so broad as to require massive research, nor so narrow as to leave you with only one or two sources. It should be a topic general enough to interest most readers and one that you can realistically write about. Usually, the most interesting topics are open for discussion—that is, they can evoke divergent reactions from readers. Remember that the topic is usually a narrowing down of your subject. For example:

Social issues → The law → Problems with the law → Miscarriages of justice → Famous trials → Sacco and Vanzetti

Open up the Topic: Find the Relevant Sources

The next step is to find the relevant sources for your topic. The major location for these will be your college library. All college libraries are designed for reference and research, and you should familiarize yourself with the layout of your library. Most libraries have orientation tours—often arranged by your English instructor—and librarians are always on hand to answer questions, so only the development of the research paper itself will be covered here.

The Card Catalog

The card catalog remains the most widely used alphabetical index of all books in the library. The same information may also be found in some libraries on microfilm, microfiche, or computers. The card catalog is usually in three parts comprising an author index, a title index, and a subject index. Check to see how they are arranged in your library. Many libraries include the author and title cards together and keep the subject cards in separate files.

Learn to interpret the information on the three different kinds of cards. The cards offer you three ways of finding the same information depending on what you know about the book: the author, the title, or only the broad subject.

```
 ⎧ Ref
 ⎨ Z              Adler, Bill
 ⎪ 278                Inside publishing / Bill Adler. --
 ⎩ .A3            Indianapolis : Bobbs-Merrill Co., 1982.
                      p. cm.




                 ⎧ 1. Publishers and publishing.
                 ⎨ 2. Book industries and trade.   I. Title


         23 JUL 82      7978020   HMCCat      81-17978
```

Inside publishing

Ref.
Z
278
.A3

Adler, Bill.
    Inside publishing / Bill Adler. --
Indianapolis : Bobbs-Merrill Co., 1982.
    p. cm.

    1. Publishers and publishing.
2. Book industries and trade.   I. Title

23 JUL 82   7978020   HMCCat   81–17978

PUBLISHERS AND PUBLISHING.

Ref.
Z
278
.A3

Adler, Bill.
    Inside publishing / Bill Adler. --
Indianapolis : Bobbs-Merrill Co., 1982.
    p. cm.

    1. Publishers and publishing.
2. Book industries and trade.   I. Title

23 JUL 82   7978020   HMCCAT   81–17978

General Idexes

There are many specialized reference books in the library; most likely one or two at least will be relevant to your topic. In order to find them, you need to consult several basic source areas that will direct you to specialized references.

For Book References

Sheehy, Eugene P. *Guide to Reference Books.* 9th ed. Chicago: American Library Association, 1976. A supplement to the 9th edition was published in 1980.

Books in Print. New York: R. R. Bowker, 1948 to present.

Cumulative Book Index. New York: H. W. Wilson, 1898 to present.

Book Review Digest. New York: H. W. Wilson, 1905 to present. Contains indexes and excerpts of reviews of books of general interest.

Book Review Index. Detroit: Gale, 1965 to present. More complete than *Book Review Digest.*

Index to Book Reviews in the Humanities. Williamstown, Michigan: Thomson, 1960 to present.

Essay and General Literature Index. New York: H. W. Wilson, 1900 to present. Indexes essays and articles found in books.

For Magazine and Periodical References

Readers' Guide to Periodical Literature. New York: H. W. Wilson, 1900 to present.

Magazines for Libraries. 3rd ed. New York: R. R. Bowker, 1978.

Union List of Serials in Libraries of the United States and Canada. 3rd ed. 5 vols. New York: H. W. Wilson, 1965. Contains a list of over 150,000 titles and the libraries that hold them.

British Humanities Index. London: Library Association, 1962 to present. Indexes British periodicals in the humanities.

Humanities Index. New York: H. W. Wilson, 1974 to the present.

Social Sciences Index. New York: H. W. Wilson, 1974 to the present.

General Science Index. New York: H. W. Wilson, 1978 to the present.

The following is a selection of major specialist indexes.

Business Periodicals Index. New York: H. W. Wilson, 1958 to the present.

Dow Jones-Irwin. *Dow Jones Business Almanac.* Homewood, Illinois, 1977 to present.

Amstutz, Mark R. *Economics and Foreign Policy: A Guide to Information Sources.* Detroit: Gale, 1977.

Field, Barry C., and Cleve E. Willis, eds. *Environmental Economics: A Guide to Information Sources.* Detroit: Gale, 1979.

Current Index to Journals in Education. New York: Macmillan, 1969 to the present.

Education Index. New York: H. W. Wilson, 1929 to the present.

Resources in Education (ERIC). Washington, D.C.: U.S. Government Printing Office, 1966 to present.

Standard Education Almanac. Los Angeles: Academic Media, 1968 to the present.

MLA International Bibliography of Books and Articles on Modern Language and Literature. New York: Modern Language Association of America, 1921 to the present.

ABC Pol. Sci. Santa Barbara, California: ABC-Clio, 1969 to the present.

Pfaltzgraff, Robert L. *The Study of International Relations: A Guide to Information Sources.* Detroit: Gale, 1977.

Vose, Clement E. *A Guide to Library Sources in Political Science: American Government.* Washington, D.C.: American Political Science Association, 1975.

Psychological Abstracts. Lancaster, Pennsylvania: American Psychological Association, 1927 to the present.

Cumulative Subject Index to Psychological Abstracts, 1927–1960. 2 vols. Boston: G. K. Hall, 1966.

Religion Index One: Periodicals. Chicago: American Theological Library Association, 1977 to the present.

Applied Science and Technology Index. New York: H. W. Wilson, 1913 to the present.

Sociological Abstracts. New York: Sociological Abstracts, 1952 to the present.

For Newspaper References

The New York Times Index. New York: The New York Times Book Co., 1913 to the present.

Newspaper Index. Wooster Ohio: Bell and Howell, 1972 to the present. Indexes the *Washington Post, Chicago Tribune, Los Angeles Times,* and *New Orleans Times-Picayune.*

The Times Index. London: The Times, 1906 to the present.

For U.S. Government Information

Jackson, Ellen. *Subject Guide to Major United States Government Publications.* Chicago: American Library Association, 1968.

Monthly Catalog of United States Government Publications. Washington, D.C.: Government Printing Office, 1895 to the present.

General Reference Books

The following list covers books that can give you a general overview of your topic and help you to define its terms.

General Encyclopedias

Collier's Encyclopedia. 24 vols. New York: Macmillan, 1977.

Encyclopedia Americana. 30 vols. New York: Americana Corporation, 1977.

The New Columbia Encyclopedia. 1 vol. New York: Columbia University Press, 1975.

The New Encyclopaedia Britannica. 15th ed. 30 vols. Chicago: Encyclopaedia Britannica, 1979.

Random House Encyclopedia. 1 vol. New York: Random House.

Dictionaries

The American Heritage Dictionary of the English Language. Boston: Houghton Mifflin, 1978.

The Oxford English Dictionary. 13 vols. with supplements. New York: Oxford University Press, 1933–77.

The Random House Dictionary of the English Language. New York: Random House, 1973.

Webster's Third New International Dictionary of the English Language. Springfield, Massachusetts: G. & C. Merriam, 1976.

Special Dictionaries

Copperud, Roy H. *American Usage: The Consensus.* New York: Van Nostrand Reinhold, 1970.

Follett, Wilson, *Modern American Usage.* Ed. Jacques Barzun. New York: Hill and Wang, 1966.

Fowler, Henry W. *Dictionary of Modern English Usage.* Englewood Cliffs, N.J.: Prentice-Hall, 1974.

Oxford Dictionary of Quotations. 2nd ed. London and New York: Oxford University Press, 1953.

Partridge, Eric. *Dictionary of Slang and Unconventional English.* 7th ed. New York: Macmillan, 1970.

Partridge, Eric. *Origins: A Short Etymological Dictionary of Modern English.* 4th ed. New York: Macmillan, 1966.

Pei, Mario A., and Salvatore Ramondino. *Dictionary of Foreign Terms.* New York: Delacorte Press, 1974.

Roget's International Thesaurus. 3rd ed. New York: Crowell, 1962.

Webster's Synonyms, Antonyms, and Homonyms. New York: Barnes & Noble, 1974.

Biographical Reference Works

Current Biography. New York: H. W. Wilson, 1940 to the present.

Dictionary of American Biography. 16 vols. and index. New York: Scribner's, 1927–80 with supplements.

Dictionary of National Biography (British). 21 vols. London: Oxford University Press, 1938.

International Who's Who. London: Europa Publications, 1935 to the present.

The New York Times Biographical Service. New York: Arno Press, 1970 to the present.

Who's Who in America. Chicago: A. N. Marquis, 1899 to the present.

Almanacs and Yearbooks

Britannica Book of the Year. Chicago: Encyclopaedia Britannica, 1938 to the present.

Facts on File. New York: Facts on File, 1940 to the present.

Information Please Almanac. New York: Viking Press, 1947 to the present.

U. S. Bureau of the Census. *Statistical Abstract of the United States.* Washington, D.C.: GPO, 1878 to the present.

World Almanac and Book of Facts. New York: World-Telegram, 1868 to the present.

Atlases and Gazetteers

Atlas of the Universe. Chicago: Rand McNally, 1970.

Britannica Atlas: Geography Edition. Chicago: Encyclopaedia
Britannica, 1974.

National Geographic Atlas of the World. 4th ed. Washington, D. C.
National Geographic Society, 1975.

The Times Atlas of the World. Boston: Houghton Mifflin, 1975.

Evaluate the Sources

Working from the library catalogs, indexes, and other general bibliographies you can soon find a range of references that may very well provide the kind of information you need. But how do you know which to choose? If you take into account articles as well as books, and if your subject is a fairly general one, then you may very well have so many possible references that you do not know where to start. To help you to decide which references to pursue, here are a few hints:

■ Begin with known classics in the field, or those books written by respected scholars. You can get advice on this from any instructor in the specialized discipline.

■ Concentrate on the most recently published works that survey thinking in the field and contain comprehensive bibliographies. That is, consider first the most recent comprehensive works you can find.

■ Note titles of books and articles that are especially relevant to your topic. Check the list of chapter headings in books (scan table of contents). A quick survey of the index, too, will tell you whether a book makes an important enough reference to your topic.

Don't assume from the above advice that only recently published works are worth reading. That is not always the case. In recent and comprehensive studies, however, you are likely to find not only the most up-to-date facts and perspectives, but also reference to the established "classics" in the field, which you can then go back and check.

Prepare a Preliminary Bibliography

When you have chosen your relevant sources, and before you take notes from them, prepare a bibliography which you can finalize and update later, depending on whether you find the material useful or not. A bibliography is a list of all sources (books and articles) you consult in order to write any kind of essay. That is, bibliographies should be attached to all kinds of essays whether you think of them as "research papers" or not.

It is probably a good idea at this time to check on the correct format for listing books and articles in bibliographies. This is found in Appendix B, Manuscript Format, pages 617–620.

Keep full information of all your sources in the form of your own card index, using small (3" x 5") cards which can then be arranged quickly in alphabetical order. Here are sample bibliography cards for books and articles:

Your bibliography card should contain all the information you will need later to enable you to find the book quickly again if you return it, and to set up your footnotes or endnotes and compile your final bibliography.
1. The call number of the book, for easy reference.
2. The author's name, last name first.
3. The full title of the book.
4. The place of publication.
5. The publisher's name.
6. The date of publication.

Kuhns, Richard.[1] "The Beautiful and the Sublime."[2] *New Literary History*[3], Vol. XIII (Winter 1982), No. 2[4], pp. 287-307.[5]

1. The author of the article, last name first.
2. The title of the article in full.
3. The journal in which the article is found.
4. The volume number and date of the journal.
5. The page numbers of the article.

Take Notes from the Sources

As you read your source materials, take careful notes. Again, you will have to be selective in your reading, but you must still be as thorough as possible. Remember that the art of note-taking can involve *annotation and summary* (see Chapter 2), but if you are going to read a number of sources, you will have to work through this process as quickly and efficiently as possible. Here, as a supplement to the commentary in Chapter 2, are some hints for handling note-taking from multiple research sources:

■ Be selective in your reading, not only in choosing the sources you will explore, but in dealing with the sources themselves. Use the book indexes to help you.

■ Read quickly, concentrating on material directly on your topic. Resist the temptation to summarize book length arguments unless they are *directly* relevant to your topic, no matter how interesting they may seem in their own right.

■ Read to accumulate information about particular points and not merely to collect a mass of unrelated details. You are reading for the relationship between facts, so every now and then stop and query the relevance of what you are reading.

■ Read critically, trying to get as full a picture of the writer's position as you can. Try not to be reductive. See Chapter 2 on *interpretation.*

■ Read in context. Don't pull out specific arguments or statements from the source without being sure that those comments are consistent with the writer's general position.

■ As you read list major ideas or facts with concise notes about them on large index cards (4 x 6 inches or 5 x 7 inches). Be sure to indicate clearly on the cards the author, work, and page number where the facts and ideas are to be found in the source. Write no more than *one* major idea or fact on each card and label it clearly.

You will probably develop your own shorthand for preparing note cards. The most important thing to remember is that the cards must contain accurate *summaries* (see Chapter 2) and references which you can understand later if you take a rest away from your cards. There is no need to write down the full title of the work since you already have a bibliography card, but if there is more than one work by an author, remember to identify clearly each reference on your note cards.

■ Some researchers like to use note paper as opposed to cards. Decide for yourself. A useful technique, in fact, is to use both, especially if you are taking notes from a fairly long source. On the note paper list your annotations and comments and then write your *summary* and references on the note cards. Remember, your note taking is summary-making.

■ Copy down on note cards those quotations that you think you will want to use. *Quote sparingly.* No one will think of your writing as original if it is peppered with quotations. A research paper is not a string of quotes with your transitions provided. Also, *quote accurately.* Copy down exactly what is on the page, mistakes and all. If there is an error simply put [sic]—the Latin for "thus"—after it. (For example: "He came from Nieuw York [sic].") Use brackets and ellipsis dots where necessary (see Handbook, 650, 652–653), and make sure your quotation marks are used accurately. (For quotation punctuation, see the Handbook p. 652.) Check each quotation carefully after you have copied it, for your card will be your reference when you come to write your paper.

The Ballistics Tests   Feuerlicht, p. 421

"The key question still is whether Weller and Fury were testing Sacco's gun barrel and bullet III. Since there is no proof and much doubt that the bullet is authentic, there is no point to testing it. If the bullet was substituted by the prosecution and the barrel is Sacco's, they will match. What is needed are not more ballistics tests but unimpeachable evidence that what is being tested is the fatal bullet."

A Note on Plagiarism

Plagiarism is the use of another writer's or speaker's words and/or ideas without crediting the other person by proper documentation. It is most important, therefore, that you document all influences on your writing, whether you are copying *any* portion of the source, or paraphrasing or summarizing an argument or idea. You should acknowledge sources of important facts and statistics too. The usual method of acknowledging source material in the body of the essay is to place all copied material within quotation marks and footnote the reference clearly. All paraphrases and summaries that rely on a specific source should also be footnoted. The process of footnoting is explained in Appendix B.

Organize Your Notes

Like the position paper, the research paper must develop from ideas, facts, opinions, and interpretations. So you must now *interpret* your research findings. How would you arrange the information? What conclusion can you draw from it?

The simplest place to begin is with the basic divisions suggested by your note card headings (see above). Read through your cards so that you have an idea of the range of information you have collected, then lay them out on a large flat surface so that the titles of the cards show. Rearrange them into groups of related major themes.

Say you were researching the story of Sacco and Vanzetti. You might decide on the following headings and the grouping of cards beneath them:

The Crime	*The Trials*	*The Appeals*	*The Contexts*	*The Significance*
Who? Where?	Plymouth trial	Basis	Italian anarchists	Public outcry
When? Why?	Dedham trial	Judges'	Attitude to Reds	Miscarriage of justice
	Witnesses &	reactions	Economic	or not?
	evidence	Why they failed	problems	What have we
	The judge & jury		Racism	learned?

(See Chapter 3 for further detail about seeing a topic in perspective.)

When you have arranged your cards into relevant groupings, read through the information in each group separately for continuity and coherence. There are two important questions you should ask yourself at this point:

Are there any information gaps that need further research?

Are there any contradictions or questions to be resolved?

You must fill in gaps and answer questions before you can go any further, so you may very well find yourself back in the library at this stage of the process. Remember that this is primarily a time for assembling your main

fact and ideas. You are not simply collecting quotes; you are explaining
the *relationships between events* and maybe even setting up questions
that need further exploration. Your headings should not be left to form
a mere list of events. "The Crime" is plainly related to "The Trials" and
"The Trials" to "The Significance" and so on. In fact, in this case (and in
most other cases), all the headings relate to one another. So experiment
with their relationships to find the strongest way you can develop the
information.

Prepare a Preliminary Outline

Working from your arrangement of note cards, write out a preliminary
outline of the essay. Research papers usually begin with an introductory
paragraph that sets up the topic and how it will be treated, and states
the thesis. Then the paper develops a series of related main ideas and
their supporting ideas with examples of each. It helps to know that the
final outline should look like the following:

Introduction
  I. Main Idea or Event
    A. Supporting or Constituent Idea or Event
      1. Example or Detail
      2. Example or Detail
    B. Supporting or Constituent Idea or Event, with Example(s)
  II. Main Idea or Event
    A. Supporting or Constituent Idea or Event
      1. Example or Detail
      2. Example or Detail
    B. Supporting or Constituent Idea or Event, with Example(s)
And so on, for as many *Main Ideas* and their *Supporting Ideas* and *Ex-
amples* as you need, followed by a *Conclusion.*

The preliminary outline should be based on this format, even if you are
not sure of all the details. Certainly you do not have to have a conclusion
or even a thesis before you make up the preliminary outline. This, again,
is an *organizational* stage.

So you may arrange the material as follows for the Sacco and Vanzetti
paper:
Introduction: Why write about this trial?
  I. The Crime
    A. The alleged circumstances & people involved
      1. etc. Details

    B. The Arrest of Sacco and Vanzetti
      1. etc. Details
II. The Trials
    A. The Plymouth trial
    B. The Dedham trial
    C. Witnesses and evidence
    D. Judge and jury
III. The Appeals
    A. Basis
    B. Judges' reactions
    C. Why they failed
IV. The Context of the Accusation and Trial
    A. Italians in America around 1920
    B. Economic issues
    C. Fear of the Reds
    D. Italian anarchism
    E. Racism
V. The Significance of the Trial
    A. Reactions in the U.S. and abroad
    B. Miscarriage of justice?
    C. What have we learned?

Develop a Thesis or Working Question

It is hard to write a coherent research paper without a thesis or a working question which your research responds to. After all, you are not trying merely to list facts but to make a point. In your preliminary outline you have a topic with various perspectives on it. You do not yet have a firm thesis, but it is most likely that various possibilities are forming themselves in your imagination as you have been reading and assembling your material.

The thesis in a research paper is the organizational principle of the essay as is any question that guides your research. Each summarizes your treatment of the topic. So if your topic is "The Draft," then your thesis might be "The Draft will not produce as efficient an army as that created on a high-incentive volunteer basis," or "The draft is unavoidable in time of war."

The thesis reflects an opinion you have formed from dealing with the information. It may be one that confirms a predisposition you had to your topic. That is, you may have begun with the opinion only to find it justified by the information. It may be an opinion that has formed itself slowly in the process of research. Either way, the thesis must be supported by your findings, and it becomes the focus of your paper.

A working question does not necessarily reflect an opinion but it sets a problem that you think is important to solve. It effectively organizes your thinking as you read and as you assemble information. With a topic like Sacco and Vanzetti you could develop either a thesis or a working question. You could decide from your arrangement of material that you will address the question "Did Sacco and Vanzetti get a fair trial?" or "Why the Injustice to Sacco and Vanzetti?" Or you could state your response to the research directly and make that your thesis: "The injustice of the Sacco and Vanzetti case."

Prepare a Final Outline

With your thesis as your focus, go back to your preliminary outline and your note cards, and revise your original outline so that it develops your thesis or working question in a logical sequence. For example, if your thesis is "The Injustice of the Sacco and Vanzetti Case," would you deal with the context of the accusation and trial *after* the information of the trial (as in the preliminary outline), or would you begin with that material? There are two clear options here, each with its own advantages.

Your final outline should, again, list the *Main Ideas* or *Events* in sequence with their *Supporting Ideas* and *Details.* Instructors often require that the final outline be handed in with the paper. In fact, for any kind of submission, required or not, the final outline functions as a useful table of contents for the reader, so it is a good idea to include it.

As you go over your material, decide on the quotations you will use and keep those cards handy. Set aside the quotations you don't want to use. You will also need to think about the conclusion of the essay. This need only be tentative because in the business of writing you may very well find your ideas changing. The conclusion depends on and must be closely related to the nature of the evidence you have assembled. If you have organized your material around a working question, then your conclusion will be the answer to that question. If you have taken a thesis as your focal point, then the conclusion must in part repeat that thesis and add to it, expanding its terms. So if you were writing about Sacco and Vanzetti and used the working question "Did Sacco and Vanzetti get a fair trial?" your conclusion must involve the answer "yes" or "no" with an explanation. If you were operating with the thesis "The injustice of the Sacco and Vanzetti case," then your conclusion must present a *summary* of the evidence.

Decide on Audience, Tone, and Style

See Chapter 4 for a full discussion of these matters. In general, the reader of the research paper wants a sharp focus on an interesting topic, a clear thesis or probing question to organize the material, and an orderly assemblage of information with a relevant, well-supported conclusion. Everything should be clearly explained in a neutral, factual tone and an easy informative style. However, you should try to avoid being dully factual: merely listing or cataloging ideas or events. Remember that a research paper offers *your* perspective on the facts and not just the information itself.

Write the First Draft

Again, see Chapter 4 for full details on translating an outline into a first draft. Remember to revise as you write. In addition, here are some further points to keep in mind:

■ Write a clear introduction that declares what your topic is, how you will treat it, and what the focus of your treatment will be. See Chapter 6 for opening paragraphs.

■ Describe and explain the relationships between your facts and ideas and make sure that all your statements and generalizations refer clearly to those relationships. (You are referring to the organization of your notes; see above.)

■ Pause occasionally if you are handling a number of facts or a survey of events and summarize what you have been saying.

■ Insert quotations sparingly and carefully. You need not copy them out in the first draft, but key the quotation cards to your first draft so that you can read through the quotations in their context.

Revise the First Draft

See Chapter 7 for full details of the revision process. Remember that, as always, you are revising for emphasis, coherence, and unity. Keep your

outline close at hand and check that you have maintained a logical sequence of information and that your introduction and conclusion are both
adequate.

Prepare the Final Draft

As you type up your revised version, you will now insert in full all
quotations and carefully footnote those and all other references. In addition you will prepare your final bibliography. Appendix B, Manuscript
Format, contains all the relevant information, whether you are writing a
research paper or any other kind of paper that involves citing works in
the text and reading resource material. Remember after you have prepared
your final draft to *proofread* your manuscript carefully and to check all
footnotes and bibliographical entries.

Appendix B

Manuscript Format

This format applies to all papers you will prepare in college, not simply research papers. Details of the format follow the recommendations of the widely accepted *MLA Handbook for Writers of Research Papers, Theses, and Dissertations* (New York: Modern Language Association of America, 1977). Consult the *MLA Handbook* for details not covered in this appendix. Your instructor will let you know of any acceptable variations.

General Manuscript Presentation

- *Paper and Typing.* If your instructor requires you to type your papers, then use the standard white, twenty-pound, *non*-erasable bond measuring 8½″ × 11″. Type with a fresh ribbon and a plain pica or elite type, avoiding unusual prints. Type *all* the paper double-spaced, including block quotations and notes.

- *The Title.* On the first page of the paper in the upper right hand corner type your name one inch from the top and against a one-inch margin on the right-hand side of the page. One double-space beneath your name, type the name of your professor, followed, a further double space beneath by your class number, and then the date. A double space beneath the date and in the center of the page, type the title. Do not put the title in quotation marks or underline it or capitalize all the letters.

- *Margins and Spacing.* Begin the body of the essay *two* double spaces beneath the title. You should keep to a one-inch margin on both sides of the page and at the top and bottom. Begin each new paragraph five spaces in from the margin.

- *Pagination.* Type page numbers consecutively in the upper right-hand corner of all pages except the first page of the manuscript (where the page number is omitted), the first page of the endnotes, and the first page of the bibliography. It is a good idea also to type your last name under each page number. There is no need to add any punctuation to the numbers.

- *Corrections* can be made while you type by using the various kinds of liquid and other correction papers. A very few handwritten corrections are usually permissible, written in ink above the line with a clear indication of where the words fit. You should always retype a page marred by several corrections.

1"

Martha Klondike
Professor Pennyweather ◄1"►
Eng. 101 A
February 6, 1982

Myths about Oedipus

Quadruple space

5 space indentation ➤ Perhaps the most familiar of all versions of the Oedipus myth is

that which Freud has made famous. . . .

Handling Quotations

Prose

If a quotation comes to about four full lines or less of your type, then place the quotation in the body of your text within quotation marks. (See punctuation of quotations, Handbook, p. 652.)

James Baldwin writes short, sharp, staccato sentences in "Sonny's Blues":

"I read about Sonny's trouble in the spring. Little Grace died in the fall.

She was a beautiful little girl."

When the quotation comes to over four lines then set it off from your commentary. Begin typing it a triple space beneath the last line of text and ten spaces from either margin. Type all quotations double-spaced. Do not indent the first line of the quote if one paragraph only is quoted. But if two or more paragraphs are used, then indent *each* fully quoted paragraph three spaces. The quotation is usually introduced by a colon:

Eudora Welty has a wonderful talent for expressing the rhythms of speech. There is high humor in her realistic talk:

> I says, "Oh, Papa-Daddy," I says, "I didn't
> say any such of a thing, I never dreamed it was
> a bird's nest, I have always been grateful
> though this is the next to smallest P.O. in the
> state of Mississippi, and I do not enjoy being
> referred to as a hussy by my own grandfather."
> But Stella-Rondo says, "Yes, you did say it
> too. Anybody in the world could of heard you,
> that had ears."
> "Stop right there," says Mama, looking at *me*.

Poetry

Quotations of up to three lines may be incorporated in the text with lines separated by a slash (/):

In "The Sick Rose" William Blake speaks of an "invisible worm, / That flies in the night."

Quotations of more than three lines should be begun triple-spaced below the text following a colon. The verse line should begin ten spaces (or less if the lines are long) from the left hand margin, keeping as closely as possible to the original format of the poem:

The first stanza of Wordsworth's "Immortality Ode," speaks of a time when the poet could see reality with a "freshness" and vitality which is somehow missing now:

> There was a time when meadow, grove and stream,
> The earth, and every common sight,
> To me did seem

Apparelled in celestial light,

The glory and the freshness of a dream.

Citing Sources and References

You can make reference to works and sources in three places in the text: in the body of the text, in footnotes or endnotes, and in the bibliography. Since the simplest and most efficient way of annotating notes is at the end of a paper—a practice recommended by the *MLA Handbook*—we shall only consider endnote format here along with citations in the text and in the bibliography.

Citing a Source Within a Text

a. The following titles should be underlined in the text: titles of published books, plays, long poems, periodicals, pamphlets, films, art works, musical pieces, and radio and television programs.

War and Peace   Hamlet   The Winged Victory of Samothrace

Time   Citizen Kane   Madame Butterfly   Hill Street Blues

b. The following titles should be placed in quotation marks: titles of essays, articles, short stories, poems, songs, book chapters, speeches, unpublished works, and lectures.

"A Rose for Emily"   "Birches"   "The Beautiful and the Sublime"   "The Gettysburg Address"   "The Black Humor of James Joyce" (an unpublished Ph.D dissertation)

Do *not* underline or place within quotation marks the titles of any sacred writings (including the Bible) or any series.

Endnotes

a. When you cite a source in the text *for the first time,* and when you want to acknowledge the source of a quotation, use *note numbers* and explain the full reference in an endnote. Note numbers should be placed after all punctuation, preferably at the end of the sentence in which the reference appears:

In *Justice Crucified,* Feuerlicht argues for the injustice done to Sacco and
Vanzetti.[1]

For subsequent references, place the author's name and the page number
in parentheses after the reference, or simply the page number if the author's name is already mentioned.

b. List your notes consecutively at *the end of your essay.* Avoid notes at
the foot of the page. Start your endnotes on a clean sheet. Here is the
endnote page layout:

Use the heading "Notes" typed center page and two inches from
the top of the page.

Quadruple space between "Notes" and the first note.

Begin each note with the note number raised slightly, five spaces in
from a one-inch margin on the left side of the sheet.

Leave one space after the number before starting the note.

Double space within notes and between them.

Leave a one-inch margin on the right side of the sheet and at the
bottom of the page.

2"

Notes

single space *Quadruple space* *5 space indentation* *1"* *double space*

[1] Roberta Strauss Feuerlicht, Justice Crucified: The Story of Sacco
and Vanzetti (New York: McGraw Hill, 1977), pp. 31–35.

[2] Marion Frankfurter and Gardner Jackson, eds., The Letters of Sacco

and Vanzetti (New York: Dutton, 1960), p. 65.

Endnote Format

- List authors' names in their normal order, first names first.
- Underline titles of books. Use quotation marks for articles.
- If a work is translated, edited, or compiled and it has an original

author, place the name of the editor (etc.) after the title preceded by "ed.," "trans.," or "comp."

¹ Rudolf Otto, <u>The Idea of the Holy</u>, trans. J. W. Harvey (London: Penguin, 1959), p. 32.

If the work is edited and you are concentrating on the editor's contribution, then place the editor's name first followed by "ed." as in note 2 in the figure above.

■ If you use a book which is not a first edition, then note the number of the edition after the title.

² Herbert Read, <u>A Concise History of Modern Painting</u>, 3rd ed., (New York: Praeger, 1975), p. 67.

■ If you are using a book in a series, then note the name of the series without underlining it:

³ Carl Jung, <u>The Collected Works of Carl Jung</u>, eds. G. Adler, M. Fordham, and H. Read, trans. R. F. C. Hull (Princeton: Princeton University Press; Bollingen Series XXX; 1959, 1969), p. 98.

■ State the place of publication, the publisher, and the date of publication all within parentheses. Follow the place by a colon and the publisher by a comma, as in any of the notes above. When citing university presses write out the full name of the publisher (University of California Press). Commercial houses may be abbreviated: for example, E. P. Dutton & Co., Inc. becomes Dutton.

■ State the page reference numbers after the parentheses, following a comma. Use *p.* for a single page reference (p. 68) and *pp.* for a spread of pages (pp. 56–78), as in all the notes above.

Endnote Format for Various Kinds of Authors

■ *A book with one author*

⁴ T. S. Eliot, <u>Collected Poems 1909–1962</u> (New York: Harcourt, 1970), p. 123.

■ *A book with two or more authors*

State the names of the authors in the order they appear on the title page:

⁵ Burton Feldman and Robert Richardson, <u>The Rise of Modern Mythology 1680–1860</u> (Bloomington: Indiana University Press, 1972), p. 94.

If there are more than three authors, use the first name followed by *et
al.*:

⁶ Carl A. Raschke et al., <u>Deconstruction and Theology</u> (New York:
Crossroad, 1982), p. 126.

■ *A book with a corporate author*

⁷ Equal Rights Amendment Project, <u>The Equal Rights Amendment: A
Bibliographical Study</u> (Westport, Conn.: Greenwood Press, 1976), p. 76.

⁸ <u>Annual Review of Information Science and Technology</u> (Washington,
D.C.: American Society for Information Service, 1966), p. 105.

Endnote Format for Various Kinds of Works

■ *A work in several volumes*

Use a roman numeral to designate the volume number and omit the *pp.*
before the page numbers.

⁹ H. J. Eysenck et al., <u>Encyclopedia of Psychology</u> (New York: Herder
and Herder, 1972), II, 99–103.

■ *A work in a book containing contributions by the same author*

¹⁰ D. H. Lawrence, "The Novel," in <u>Phoenix II</u>, ed. and intro. W. Roberts
and H. T. Moore (London: Heinemann, 1968), p. 416.

■ *A work in a book containing contributions by different authors*

¹¹ Alfred Appel, Jr., "Nabokov's Puppet Show," in <u>The Single Voice</u>, ed.
Jerome Charyn (New York: Collier, 1969), pp. 76–95.

Articles in reference works are quoted as works in collections but without
in before the name of the encyclopedia or reference work title, and without
the editor's name:

¹² John Hick, "Evil, The Problem of," <u>The Encyclopedia of Philosophy</u>,
1967.

Endnote Format for Articles

■ *An article in a journal with continuous pagination*

[13] Lionel Grossman, "Literature and Education," New Literary History, XIII (1982), 345–347.

■ *An article in a journal without continuous pagination*

[14] Shahram Chubin, "U.S. Security Interests in Persian Gulf in the 1980s," Daedalus, 109, No. 4 (Fall 1980), 51.

Note that if a volume number is cited, *p.* and *pp.* are not used. Do not precede the volume number with "Vol." Follow the sequence of author, title of article, name of journal, volume number, year of issue in parentheses, and page numbers.

■ *An article from a monthly magazine*

[15] Anthony Brandt, "Rite of Passage," Atlantic, February 1981, p. 40.

■ *An article from a newspaper*

[16] Willard O. Eddy, "Is Mediocrity the Standard in Higher Education?" Denver Post, 30 May 1982, p. 5D, col. 3.

■ *A review article*

[17] Joseph Carroll, "The Secret Life of Empedocles," rev. of Matthew Arnold: A Life, by Park Honan, Denver Quarterly, 17, No. 1 (Spring 1982), 113.

Repeated References to a Book or Periodical

■ You only need to quote a reference in full once. When it is repeated, simply include the author and the page. So notes 4 and 16 above would appear as follows:

[18] Eliot, p. 99.

[19] Eddy, col. 5.

■ If there is more than one work cited by the same writer, then use a brief version of the title:

[20] Lawrence, "The Novel," p. 417.

[21] Carroll, "Empedocles," p. 114.

■ If you are continually quoting from a single work, such as a literary text, then you can add to the first note the sentence "All further references to this work appear in the text."

[22] Eldridge Cleaver, <u>Soul on Ice</u>, intro. Maxwell Geismar, (New York: Delta, 1968), p. 83. All further references to this work appear in the text.

Then simply place the page number in parentheses after the quotation in the text, making sure, of course, that it is clear who the author is:

In his essay "Lazarus, Come Forth" Cleaver has this to say about boxing:

"The boxing ring is the ultimate focus of masculinity in America" (p. 84).

Note that when the quotation is part of the text, place the period outside the parenthesis. When the quotation is set off from the text, then place the period before the parenthesis:

> . . . all of our mass spectator sports give play to the basic cultural ethic, harnessed and sublimated into national-communal pagan rituals. (p. 85)

The Bibliography

At the end of your essay, after the note page(s), you must provide a list of all the works—books, articles, etc—that you consulted and *found in any way useful* for your paper. It is not necessary to list every book you looked at merely to present an "impressive" and inflated bibliography. But if a text is in any way relevant to your research paper then you must cite it. All books cited in footnotes or endnotes must appear in the bibliography as well as the notes.

Bibliography Page Layout

■ Use the heading "Bibliography" typed center page and two inches from the top of the page.

■ Quadruple space between the heading and the first note.

■ Begin each note by the left hand margin, one inch from the edge of the page.

■ Subsequent lines for each entry are indented five spaces.

■ Keep a one-inch margin on the right-hand margin and from the bottom.

■ Double space both within and between notes.

■ Two or more works by the same author are listed without repeating the author's name. Instead of the name, type ten hyphens followed by a period and two spaces.

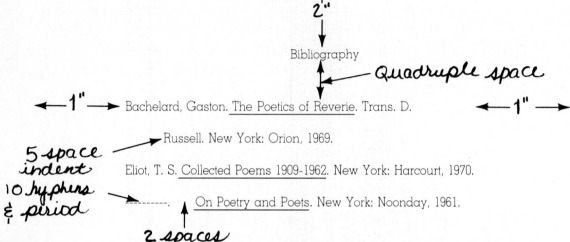

2"

Bibliography

Quadruple space

←—1"—→ Bachelard, Gaston. The Poetics of Reverie. Trans. D.

5 space indent

Russell. New York: Orion, 1969.

Eliot, T. S. Collected Poems 1909-1962. New York: Harcourt, 1970.

10 hyphens & period

----------. On Poetry and Poets. New York: Noonday, 1961.

2 spaces

←—1"—→

Bibliography Format

Note some important differences between the format of entries in the endnotes and in the bibliography.

■ The author's name is reversed (last name first) for the alphabetical index. If more than one author is involved, then reverse only the first name.

■ The title is again underlined.

■ The publication information is not surrounded by parentheses, but again the publication place is separated from the publisher by a colon, and the publisher from the date by a comma.

■ The translator and editor are placed after the title.

■ Each fragment of information is followed by a period and not commas as in the endnotes.

Bibliography Format for Various Kinds of Authors

■ *A book with one author*

Burke, Kenneth. Language as Symbolic Action. Berkeley: University of

California Press, 1968.

■ *A book with two or more authors*

Feldman, Burton, and Robert Richardson. <u>The Rise of Modern Mythol-</u>
<u>ogy 1680–1860</u>. Bloomington: Indiana University Press, 1972.

■ *A book with a corporate author*

<u>The Equal Rights Amendment: A Bibliographical Study</u>. By the Equal
Rights Amendment Project. Westport, Conn.: Greenwood Press,
1976.

Bibliography Format for Various Kinds of Works

■ *A work in several volumes*

<u>The Encyclopedia of Philosophy</u>. New York: Macmillan, 1967. Vol. III.

This indicates that only volume three has been used. The volume
information is therefore placed after the publication information. If all
the volumes have been used, then place the information before the
publication information:

<u>The Encyclopedia of Philosophy</u>. 8 vols. New York: Macmillan, 1967.

■ *A work in a book containing contributions by the same author*

Lawrence, D. H. "The Novel." In <u>Phoenix II</u>. Ed. and intro. W. Roberts
and H. T. Moore. London: Heinemann, 1968, pp. 416–420.

■ *A work in a book containing contributions by different authors*

Appel, Alfred. "Nabokov's Puppet Show." In <u>The Single Voice</u>. Ed.
Jerome Charyn. New York: Collier, 1969, pp. 76–95.

Bibliography Format for Articles

This follows the format for books, but remember to give the full extent
of pagination.

■ *An article in a journal with continuous pagination*

Grossman, Lionel. "Literature and Education." <u>New Literary History</u>,
XIII (1982), 345–347.

Again, do not use *pp.* when the volume number is cited.

■ *An article in a journal without continuous pagination*

Chubin, Shahram. "U.S. Security Interests in the Persian Gulf in the
    1980s." <u>Daedalus</u>, 109, No. 4 (Fall 1980), 31–65.

Again, the full date of the issue must be included.

■ *An article from a monthly magazine*

Brandt, Anthony. "Rite of Passage." <u>Atlantic</u>, February 1981, pp. 40–43.

■ *An article from a newspaper*

Eddy, William O. "Is Mediocrity the Standard in Higher Education?"
    <u>Denver Post</u>, 30 May 1982, p. 5D, col. 1–5.

■ *A review article*

Carroll, Joseph. "The Secret Life of Empedocles." Rev. of <u>Matthew Ar-
    nold: A Life</u>, by Park Honan. <u>Denver Quarterly</u>, 17, No. 1 (Spring
    1982), 112–114.

Handbook of

Grammar and

Mechanics

Grammar

Grammar describes the way words function and relate together in sentences according to the conventions of usage. Grammar is a description of *sentence structure,* of the way in which words fit together in sentences to create meaning.

PS The Parts of Speech

The parts of speech describe the function of words as they refer to events, things, qualities, time, and place.

PS-1 **Nouns** are words that name or refer to things *(dogs, cats, Peter).* They are of several kinds:

- *Common nouns* refer to members of a general class *(musician, a woman, a camel).*
- *Proper nouns* refer to specific names of particular people, places, and things. Proper nouns are capitalized *(Giles, New York, Casablanca).*
- *Collective nouns* refer to groups *(family, team, air force).*
- *Concrete nouns* refer to tangible things *(sofa, cabbage, ankle).*
- *Abstract nouns* refer to ideas, concepts, beliefs, or qualities *(love, democracy, bravery).*

PS-2 **Adjectives** are words that usually describe the qualities of things *(gray, round).* They modify nouns or pronouns. There are several different kinds of adjectives:

- *Predicate adjectives* follow the verb and modify the subject of the sentence:

    The roses are *blooming.*

- *Proper adjectives* carry heavy emphasis and are usually capitalized (a *Tahitian* lagoon, *Welsh* singing).
- *Possessive adjectives (your, her, his, its, our, their).*
- *Demonstrative adjectives (this* horse, *that* horse, *these* horses, *those* horses).
- *Indefinite adjectives (each, every, any, some* horses).

622

PS-3 **Pronouns** are words that usually stand for nouns *(he, she, it, they)* or function as nouns of such broad reference that no specific noun can be pinned down *(something, anything, someone, none)*. There are several kinds of pronouns:

■ *Personal pronouns* refer to a person or a thing: *I, you, he, she, it, we, you, they (We'll* meet again.)

■ *Reflexive pronouns* refer to an action the subject carries out on itself (Jean hurt *herself* cutting vegetables.)

■ *Interrogative pronouns* are used to ask questions: *who, whom, which* (*Who* came first?)

■ *Relative pronouns* are used to introduce adjectival or noun clauses: *who, which, that, whoever, whom, whomever, what, whose* (I came for the letter *which* you found today.)

■ *Demonstrative pronouns* point out or make specific reference: *this, that, these, those* (Here are three apples, but *those* over there are better.)

■ *Indefinite pronouns* refer to a person or thing generally, not specifically: *any, each, everyone, everybody, anyone, anybody, one, neither, some (Anyone* can climb this hill.)

■ *Intensive pronouns* end in *-self* or *-selves* and are used to emphasize a word that comes before it in a sentence (The teacher *himself* was bored by the class.)

■ *Reciprocal pronouns* are compounds which refer to a mutual action or relationship: *one another, each other* (Learn to live with *each other.*)

PS-4 **Verbs** are words that convey actions, states of being, or occurrences (The committee *meets* twice a week.).

■ Verbs are either *transitive* or *intransitive.* A transitive verb is one that takes an object to complete its meaning; an intransitive verb does not need an object to complete its meaning. The same verb may be transitive in one context and intransitive in another:

Trans.: Jim *runs* a country store. (object: *country store*)

Intrans.: Jim *runs* fast.

■ A verb used with a main verb to help complete its meaning is called an *auxiliary verb: be, have, do:*

You *have been* running too many enterprises at once.

Did you go to the fair?

I *have* come to see my friend.

Some verbs express a state of affairs or a condition rather than an action, and these are known as *linking verbs.* The most common is the verb *to be;* others are *appear, become, seem, feel, look, taste, smell, sound:*

I *feel* like a million dollars this morning.

It *seems* like spring.

This cat *is* my friend.

PS-5   **Adverbs** are words that mainly describe or modify actions (she ran *quickly* through the woods), but adverbs can modify adjectives and other adverbs as well as verbs:

This is a *very* slow train. (modifying the adjective *slow*)

She was *impressively* quick. (modifying the adjective *quick*)

This train runs *very* slowly. (modifying the adverb *slowly*)

Sometimes an adverb can be used to modify a whole phrase, clause, or sentence:

Certainly, we'll come to your party.

Some adverbs—known as *conjunctive adverbs*—function as conjunctions:

I like my relatives; *moreover,* I even give them presents.

(See p. 648 for punctuation with conjunctive adverbs.)
Common conjunctive adverbs are: *also, consequently, finally, furthermore, however, instead, meanwhile, moreover, nevertheless, next, nonetheless, still, then, therefore,* and *thus.*

PS-6   **Prepositions** are words that indicate place or time and are always accompanied by a noun. They connect a noun or pronoun to another word in the sentence: *in, upon, under, through, before, after, from, to, of, with, without, among, at, against, behind, below, along with, in spite of.*

The tracks come *through* the trees *by* the river.

The preposition introduces a *prepositional phrase,* a group of words used as an adjective or an adverb containing the preposition and its object:

through the trees, by the river

PS-7   **Conjunctions** connect words, phrases, clauses, and sentences. Conjunctions are of three main kinds:

■ *Coordinating conjunctions* connect words or groups of words that are of equal rank: *and, but, or, nor, for, so, yet.*

I have called my parrots Lionel *and* Giles.

Owning a business *and* running for office are quite a strain, *but* I plan on dropping one of these soon.

■ *Subordinating conjunctions* introduce a subordinate or dependent element of a sentence, such as a phrase or a clause. The most common subordinating conjunctions are *when, after, as, as if, because, since, unless, while, if, where:*

I am giving up politics *because* of a conflict of interest.

When the wind howls, my dog imitates the noise.

■ *Correlative conjunctions*—sometimes just called correlatives—are used in pairs. Common examples are *both . . . and, either . . . or, not only . . . but also:*

We had *both* hail *and* snow this week.

PS-8 **Interjections** are words that exclaim or express strong emotion on their own. They can be set off or be a part of a sentence:

Oh no!

Wow, what a beautiful horse!

PS-9 **Articles** are indicator words immediately preceding nouns that can also be classified as adjectives: *the, a, an. The* is the *definite* article; *a* and *an* are *indefinite* articles:

The man took *a* walk on *the* footpath.

V   Verbals

Verbals are verb forms that cannot function on their own as verbs but take the place of other parts of speech, especially nouns, adjectives, and adverbs.

V-1 **Gerunds** are *-ing* forms of the verb that can be used as *nouns.* A gerund may take an object, a complement, or a modifier. Gerunds are *verbal nouns:*

Winning is most pleasant. (gerund as subject)

Winning lots of money is my aim. (gerund phrase—the gerund *winning* and its object *lots of money*—as subject)

I became rich by *winning lots of money*. (The gerund *winning* is the object of the preposition *by* and itself takes an object *lots of money*.)

V-2   **Participles** are a form of the verb that usually function as *adjectives* but may also appear as *verb phrases* or as verbs with an *adverbial* function. Participles may take objects, complements, and modifiers.

- *Present participles* end in *-ing.* (*running, walking*)

- *Past participles* usually end in *-d* or *-ed.* (*exhausted, trimmed*)

- *Perfect participles* are formed by *having* or *having been* and the past participle. (*having finished*)

Be careful not to confuse gerunds and participles:

There is *running* water in every room. (present participle as adjective)

He was *running* down the road when he fell. (present participle as part of a verb phrase)

He came *running* towards us. (present participle with an adverbial function)

Tired of the noise, she moved to another dorm. (Past participle *tired* takes an object *noise* and the whole participial phrase modifies *she*.)

Having lost the battle, the enemy retreated. (Perfect participle *having lost* takes an object *battle* and modifies *enemy*.)

V-3   **Infinitives** are verbals that begin with *to.* They may be used as *nouns, adjectives,* or *adverbs.* Infinitives may have subjects, objects, complements, or modifiers:

She did not want *to move* house just yet. (The infinitive *to move* takes an object *house* and is modified by *just yet.* The whole infinitive phrase *to move house just yet* is the object of *want.*)

You have no one *to love*. (The infinitive *to love* is used adjectivally to modify *no one.*)

Note that sometimes infinitives contain *be, have,* and *have been* with a past participle: *to be completed, to have run, to have been completed.*

SE   Sentence Elements

SE-1   All sentences contain a **subject** and a **predicate.** The subject (S) is a noun or pronoun which carries out the action of the verb, or is described, or has something done to it. The predicate (P) is that word or group of words that is affected by the verb and either affirms or denies something about the subject. The most basic kind of sentence involves a *simple subject* and a *simple predicate:* that is, a single word subject (or implied subject) and a single word predicate.

```
    S      P
```
Orwell writes.

```
    S         P
```
(You) Watch out!

A *complete subject* is the group of words containing the simple subject and its modifiers. The *complete predicate* is the simple predicate and its modifiers and complements:

```
         S                    P
```
The novelist Orwell wrote several novels.

A *compound subject* is made up of two or more subjects linked together. A *compound predicate* is made up of two or more verbs linked together:

```
    S     S    P          P
```
Jones and I organized and paid for all the entertainment.

SE-2 The **direct object** (DO) is a noun or pronoun that is directly affected by the action of the verb. The **indirect object** (IO) is a noun or pronoun that is indirectly affected by the verb. The indirect object is one *for whom* or *for which* or *to whom* or *to which* something is done:

```
              DO
```
Orwell writes *a book.*

```
          IO      DO
```
Orwell bought *his friend a book.*

Note that when a preposition is expressed, the word that follows is an *object of the preposition* and not of the verb, as in this sentence where, strictly speaking, there is no indirect object:

Orwell bought *a book for his friend.* (*A book* is a direct object; *his friend* is an object of the preposition *for.*)

SE-3 **Complements** of the verb (C) are nouns, pronouns, or adjectives that can be a *subject complement* (SC) or an *object complement* (OC). A complement is a word or group of words in the predicate that completes or complements the subject or the object. The subject complement follows a linking verb such as the verb *to be*:

      S   SC
Orwell is a good writer.

      S   DO   OC
Orwell called his novel *1984.*

The subject complement is either a *predicate adjective* (PA) or a *predicate noun* (PN):

      S   SC-PA
Orwell is very political.

            SC-PN
Orwell is a political thinker.

SE-4 **Modifiers** are adjectives, adverbs, articles, and possessive pronouns that modify the subject, object, or verb. The term *modifier* is used to cover all the possible ways in which nouns and verbs can be limited. All the words italicized below are modifiers:

Good critics have *often* called Orwell *a brilliant political* satirist. (All the italicized words are adjectives except for the adverb *often.*)

SE-5 **Appositives** are nouns or noun substitutes that stand beside other nouns or their substitutes and identify, describe, or explain them. Appositives are often, but not always, set apart from the noun by commas:

Orwell, *the political satirist,* sold many books.
Orwell *the novelist* is well known.

SE-6 A **phrase** is a group of words that does not have a subject and a predicate. Phrases function as *nouns, adjectives,* or *adverbs.* Their function has been described in Chapter 5, ("Sentences") but for easy reference here are the main kinds of phrases:

Noun phrases: groups of words that include modified nouns:

> Paris, *my favorite city,* was our next stop.
>
> I longed for *the country life* again.

Verb phrases: the main verb and its auxiliary verbs:

> We *had travelled* for three weeks.
>
> *Will* you *be coming* home next week?

Verbal phrases: gerund, participial, or infinitive phrases.

- A *gerund phrase* is made up of the gerund and its object:

> *Playing for time* was our only hope.
>
> *Running a business* can be fun.

- A *participial phrase* always acts as an adjective:

> The ship *straining at its moorings* is ours.
>
> The dancers *wearing green* are Irish.

- An *infinitive phrase:*

> We hope you want *to work well.*
>
> *To love badly* is better than never *to love* at all.

Prepositional phrases: prepositions together with their objects functioning as nouns, adjectives, and adverbs:

> *Within three weeks* you will be finished.
>
> The horsemen came *from beyond the hills.*

Absolute phrases are always made up of a noun and a participle and stand unrelated to the rest of the sentence:

> *The dishes having been washed,* our hosts retired.
>
> *The ship having docked,* the crowd went home.

SE-7   A **clause** is a group of words that contains both a subject and a predicate. There are two main kinds of clauses: *main* (or *independent*) and *subordinate* (or *dependent*).

- A *main clause* (MC) can stand on its own like a complete sentence or it may be joined with other main clauses by a *coordinating conjunction* or modified in some way by subordinate clauses:

> MC
> The crowd went wild.

MC   MC

The crowd went wild and cheered its favorites throughout the match.

- *Subordinate clauses* all begin with either a *relative pronoun* or a *subordinating conjunction* (like *after, although, as, because, if, since, when, where, in order that*). All subordinate clauses function as nouns, adjectives, or adverbs.

- *Noun clauses* can be subjects or objects:

  I never believed *that you would come without an invitation.* (object)

  That you would come without an invitation was never my belief. (subject)

- *Adjectival clauses:*

  All the films *that were shown yesterday* will rerun next week. (The relative clause modifies *films.*)

- *Adverbial clauses:*

  You will receive a degree *when you have completed the course.* (The adverbial clause modifies the verb *receive.*)

ST Sentence Types

There are four basic kinds of sentences in English depending on the nature and relationship of clauses.

ST-1   A **simple sentence** has no subordinate clauses, only one independent main clause: one subject and one predicate:

Computers are essential to scientific research.

ST-2   A **compound sentence** contains at least two main clauses:

Computers are essential to scientific research and we must have one. (two main clauses)

ST-3   A **complex sentence** contains one main clause with one or more subordinate clauses:

Because computers are essential to scientific research, we must have one. (adverb clause + main clause)

ST-4   A **compound-complex sentence** contains at least two main clauses and at least one subordinate clause:

Because computers are essential to scientific research, we must have one;

therefore we must raise money fast. (adverb clause + main clause; main clause)

C Case

Case refers to the form that nouns or pronouns take dependent on their use in a sentence. In English there are only three cases.

C-1 The **subjective case** is used when a word is the subject or subject complement, or is an appositive describing the subject. The subjective pronouns are *I, we, you, he, she, it, they, who, whoever*:

> *You* and *I* will meet in the spring. (subjects of the verb)
>
> The winners of the competition were *you* and *I.* (subject complements)
>
> The players—*he* and *she*—were both fit. (in apposition)

C-2 The **objective case** is used when a word is the object (direct or indirect) of a verb, preposition, or verbal, or is in apposition to the object of the verb. Pronouns in the objective case are *me, him, her, it, us, you, them, whom, whomever*:

> Everyone likes *Harvey* and *you.* (direct object of the verb)
>
> He sends *her* his love. (indirect object)
>
> He sends his love to *her.* (object of the preposition)
>
> For *whom* the bell tolls. (object of the preposition)
>
> Please send it to both of us, *me and him.* (in apposition)
>
> Some of *us* teachers get paid well. (not *we* teachers)
>
> Let me try to entertain *you.* (object of the verbal)

C-3 The **possessive case** is used to express possession of an object or responsibility for an action. The possessive case is used before a gerund. Pronouns in the possessive (or genitive) case are *my, mine, his, hers, its, ours, yours, theirs, whose.* Note: there are no apostrophes used with possessive pronouns: *it's* means *it is.*

> *My* test scores are better than *yours,* but *your* essay grades are better than *mine.*
>
> *My* arriving early was a good idea. (before a gerund)

C-4 After **than** or **as** beginning an incomplete clause, use the same case of a pronoun as you would if the clause were complete:

> He really does it better than *I* (do).

Anyone can do it better than *he* (does).

He loved no one as much as (he loved) *himself.*

C-5 **A noun before a gerund** *may* be objective as well as possessive, though in most cases it is the latter. When it would be awkward to use a possessive, use the objective case:

x   I did not like his family lawyer's interrupting all the time.

√   I did not like his family lawyer interrupting all the time.

Or restructure the sentence when the possessive of an abstract or inanimate object is used:

x   I fear time's endless passing.

√   I fear the endless passing of time.

C-6 Always use the subjective case for the **complement of the verb *to be:***

It's *I* who must run the longest.

The person who will win will be either you or *he.*

C-7 *Who/Whom/Whoever.* The case of the interrogative or relative pronoun is determined by its function in its own clause.

■ When *who/whoever* is the subject of the clause:

Who was the first man on the moon?

I will give a prize to *whoever* solves this puzzle. (*Whoever* is the subject of *solves.* The whole clause *whoever solves this puzzle* is the object of the preposition *to.*)

■ When words come between the pronoun and the verb then either *who* or *whom* may be appropriate. When the intervening words are *I think, he says, she thinks, we believe, we know* and so on, make sure that you understand the function of *who* or *whom* in its own clause:

The car will pick up those *whom* we know. (*whom* is the object of *we know*)

The car will pick up those *who* we know are late. (*who* is the subject of *are late*)

As well as asking whether the relative pronoun is the subject or object of the verb in its own clause, you can also test to see if the intervening words can be omitted altogether, as *we know* can in the second example above.

■ When in doubt, and certainly when you are writing formally, use *whom* for all objects:

Whom will you be seeing tomorrow? (object of the verb *seeing*)

I don't know *whom* to ask. (object of the infinitive to ask)

I asked you *whom* you will call. (object of the verb *call* in the adjectival clause)

VSA   Verb-Subject Agreement

Verbs agree in number with their subjects. Singular subjects take singular verbs; plural subjects take plural verbs:

This text *needs* a colorful design. (singular)

These texts *need* colorful designs. (plural)

There are a number of rules for agreement that refer to special cases.

VSA-1   Compound subjects joined by *and* take a plural verb:

My dog and cat *are* well taken care of.

Britain and France *are* in the Common Market.

There are exceptions to this rule:

■ If the compound subject refers to the same person, idea, or thing it takes a singular verb:

My tutor and friend *is* Arnold Smith.

■ *Every* and *each* take a singular verb when they refer to singular subjects:

Every comma, period, and semicolon *is* important.

■ *Each* following a compound subject may take a singular or plural verb:

The comma and the semicolon each *have (has)* their (its) own rules.

VSA-2   Compound subjects joined by *or, either . . . or* or *neither . . . nor* take either a singular or a plural verb depending on the number of the nearest subject:

Either Michael or Helen *is* responsible.

Neither the scientists nor the President *is* willing to answer the question.

Neither the President nor the scientists *are* willing to answer the question.

VSA-3 The addition of nouns, pronouns, or phrases between the subject and the verb does not affect the number of the verb. Typical **intervening phrases** are *along with, together with,* and *as well as:*

> *Gone With the Wind,* along with numerous other Hollywood epics, *has* had an impact on how we view the Civil War in America.

VSA-4 **Collective nouns** take a singular verb when they refer to the subject as a whole and a plural verb when they refer to individual members of the subject:

> Patton's army *swept* through Europe.
>
> The minority *is* unhappy with the vote.
>
> A minority of us *are* unhappy with the vote.
>
> Three-quarters of these soldiers *have been wounded.*

VSA-5 **Indefinite pronouns** such as *each, everyone, neither, one, no one, nobody, somebody* take a singular verb:

> Nobody *wants* to go to the lecture.
>
> Neither runner *is* fast enough.
>
> Everyone *is* susceptible to flattery.

VSA-6 **Words denoting amount**, such as *none, some, part, all,* and all fractions take a singular or plural verb depending on the context of the noun or pronoun that follows:

> Some of these roses *are* dead. (plural because *roses* is plural)
>
> Some of this plant *is* alive. (singular because *plant* is singular)
>
> None of these lettuces *are* edible. (plural because *lettuces* is plural)
>
> None of this carrot *is* edible. (singular because carrot is singular)

VSA-7 The words **there** or **here** beginning a sentence take a verb of the same number as the subject:

> There *is* no truth in this claim.
>
> There *are* no certainties in life.
>
> Here *lie* many victims of the earthquake.

Similarly, sentence inversions should not distract you from basic verb + subject agreement:

> Lying close to the table *is* an Indian carpet.

VSA-8 The verb in a **relative clause** has the same number as the antecedent to the **relative pronoun**, which is used as a subject. A relative clause is an adjectual clause that begins with *who, which,* or *that.*

> He was the one who *was* sick.
>
> We who live in the suburbs *complain* about taxes.

VSA-9 **Plural nouns** that have a singular meaning usually take singular verbs. Such nouns include *news, economics, physics, electronics:*

> Electronics *is* a fast-growing science.

Trousers and *scissors* are plural (except *a pair of trousers* or *a pair of scissors*), and *athletics* and *politics* can be plural when they refer to organized activities and singular when they refer to a body of knowledge or a collective event:

> Politics *makes* fools of us all.
>
> In this primitive tribe, there *were* no politics.

VSA-10 A **linking verb** agrees with its subject and not with its subjective complement (or predicate noun):

> Her deepest love *is* classical music.
>
> What you find *are* many mistakes.

PRA Pronoun-Reference Agreement

Pronouns agree in number with their antecedents (that is, with the preceding nouns they refer to). Singular antecedents take singular pronouns; plural antecedents take plural pronouns:

> This *text* has *its* own designer. (singular)
>
> These *texts* have *their* own designer. (plural)

There are a number of rules for agreement that refer to special cases.

PRA-1 A **compound subject joined by** *and* takes a plural pronoun reference:

> Jane and Louise were fond of *their* music teacher.

PRA-2 A **compound subject with** *either . . . or, neither . . . nor, or,* **or** *not only . . . but also* takes a pronoun that agrees in number with the nearer antecedent:

> Neither Jane nor Louise lost *her* purse.
>
> Either the cello or the violins *were* at fault.

Not only the President but the entire Senate *refuses* to act.

PRA-3 *Each, either, neither, one, anyone* take a singular pronoun:

> Each mother loves *her* child.
>
> Neither camel in the zoo has *its* freedom.

PRA-4 **Collective nouns** take a singular pronoun when they are considered as a whole or unit and a plural pronoun when they are used in a plural sense:

> Politics has *its* own rewards.
>
> The army needs *its* way paid by Congress.
>
> The group of lawyers posed on the steps for *their* photograph.

PRA-5 *Who/Which/That. Who* is used mainly in reference to people or to *named* animals and things. *Which* is used only in reference to things and animals. *That* also mainly refers to animals and things but can refer to people when it has an impersonal reference, such as to a profession:

> The cat *which (that)* sat on the mat fell asleep.
>
> The boy *who* owned the cat woke it up.
>
> The plumber *that (who)* fixed this pipe did a good job.

PRA-6 **Pronouns referring to antecedents of unknown or unspecified gender** create a special problem. Traditionally writers have treated the problem with little thought and used *he, him,* or *his* as the basic pronoun reference:

> The student ate *his* lunch quickly.
>
> Everyone has *his* cross to bear.

This practice is now considered sexist by many readers and writers of both sexes. Thus it is no longer appropriate to use either *he* or *she* with reference to an antecedent of *unspecified* gender if it can at all be avoided. You cannot be certain that a specific gender alone fills a certain role in society: nurses, astronauts, train drivers, doctors, soldiers, pilots, and firefighters and many others can now be either men or women.

What can you do to avoid sexist pronoun references? The easiest method is to make all general antecedents *plural:*

> Train drivers like *their* work.
>
> Psychiatrists have to spend a long time at *their* studies.

But what do you do when the antecedent must remain singular because of a specific reference (still of unknown gender)?

The pilot bailed out of *his* plane but had trouble opening *his* parachute.

It is possible to avoid pronoun references altogether in many cases either by leaving them out or by replacing them with the definite article *(the)* or the indefinite article *(a* or *an)*:

The pilot bailed out of *the* plane, but had trouble opening *the* parachute.

The student ate lunch quickly.

Everyone has *a* cross to bear.

VF Verb Forms

If you look up a verb in a dictionary to check its meaning and use, you will find at least three forms of the verb listed after the initial entry:

drive (drīv) v. drove (drōv) or *archaic* drave (drāv), driven (drivən), driving, drives.

These forms of the verb are the *principal parts* and from these parts you can see how the verb is used in all its forms. The parts most usually quoted are *the infinitive (to drive,* with the *to* dropped), *the past tense (drove), the past participle (driven), the present participle (driving),* and the *present tense (drives).* In some dictionaries you find only three basic principal parts: the infinitive, the past participle, and the past tense.

Along with the principal parts, it is useful to know if a verb is *regular* or *irregular.* Regular verbs form the past tense and the past participle by adding *-d* or *-ed* or, more rarely, *-t; walk, walked, walked,* and *burn, burnt, burnt.* Irregular verbs, on the other hand, tend to form their past tense and past participle by some internal vowel change. Following is a list of some commonly misused irregular verbs giving the present and past tenses and the past participle.

VF-1 Here are some **commonly misused irregular verbs:**

Present	Past	Past Participle
awake	awoke, awaked	awoke, awaked, awoken
be	was/were	been
bear (bring forth)	bore	born, borne
bear (carry)	bore	borne
become	became	become

Present	Past	Past Participle
begin	began	begun
bend	bent	bent
bid (command)	bade	bid, bidden
bid (offer to pay)	bid	bid
bite	bit	bitten
blow	blew	blown
break	broke	broken
bring	brought	brought
build	built	built
burn	burned, burnt	burned, burnt
buy	bought	bought
catch	caught	caught
choose	chose	chosen
cling	clung	clung
come	came	come
creep	crept	crept
deal	dealt	dealt
dig	dug	dug
dive	dived, dove	dived
do	did	done
draw	drew	drawn
drink	drank	drunk, drunken
drive	drove	driven
eat	ate	eaten
fall	fell	fallen
feed	fed	fed
feel	felt	felt
fight	fought	fought
find	found	found
fling	flung	flung
fly	flew	flown
forbid	forbade, forbad	forbidden, forbid
forget	forgot	forgotten, forgot

Present	Past	Past Participle
forgive	forgave	forgiven
freeze	froze	frozen
get	got	got, gotten
give	gave	given
go	went	gone
grow	grew	grown
hang (to execute)	hanged	hanged
hang (to suspend)	hung	hung
hide	hid	hidden, hid
hold	held	held
keep	kept	kept
kneel	knelt, kneeled	knelt, kneeled
know	knew	known
lay	laid	laid
lead	led	led
lean	leaned, leant	leaned, leant
leap	leaped, leapt	leaped, leapt
learn	learned, learnt	learned, learnt
leave	left	left
lend	lent	lent
lie (recline)	lay	lain
lie (tell a falsehood)	lied	lied
light	lighted, lit	lighted, lit
mean	meant	meant
mow	mowed	mowed, mown
pay	paid	paid
prove	proved	proved, proven
ride	rode	ridden
ring	rang	rung
rise	rose	risen
run	ran	run
saw	sawed	sawed, sawn
see	saw	seen

Present	Past	Past Participle
seek	sought	sought
send	sent	sent
sew	sewed	sewed, sewn
shake	shook	shaken
shave	shaved	shaved, shaven
show	showed	shown, showed
shrink	shrank, shrunk	shrunk, shrunken
sing	sang	sung
sink	sank, sunk	sunk, sunken
slay	slew	slain
sleep	slept	slept
slide	slid	slid
sling	slung	slung
smell	smelled, smelt	smelled, smelt
sow	sowed	sown, sowed
speak	spoke	spoken
speed	sped, speeded	sped, speeded
spin	spun, span	spun
spoil	spoiled, spoilt	spoiled, spoilt
spread	spread	spread
spring	sprang	sprung
steal	stole	stolen
stick	stuck	stuck
stink	stank, stunk	stunk
stride	strode	stridden
strike	struck	struck, stricken
string	strung	strung
strive	strove	striven
swear	swore	sworn
sweat	sweat, sweated	sweat, sweated
sweep	swept	swept
swim	swam	swum

Present	Past	Past Participle
swing	swung	swung
take	took	taken
tear	tore	torn
throw	threw	thrown
tread	trod	trodden, trod
wake	woke, waked	woke, waked, woken
wear	wore	worn
wed	wed, wedded	wed, wedded
weep	wept	wept
wind	wound	wound
wring	wrung	wrung
write	wrote	written

VF-2 All verbs have **tense,** which is the form of the verb that indicates the time that an action is taking place. There are six tenses that cover present, past, and future time.

	Regular Verb	Irregular Verb
Simple Tenses		
Present	I work	I draw
Past	I worked	I drew
Future	I shall (will) work	I shall (will) draw
Perfect Tenses		
Present perfect	I have worked	I have drawn
Past perfect	I had worked	I had drawn
Future perfect	I shall (will) have worked	I shall (will) have worked
Simple Progressive Tenses		
Present progressive	I am working	I am drawing
Past progressive	I was working	I was drawing
Future progressive	I shall (will) be working	I shall (will) be working
Perfect Progressive Tenses		
Present perfect progressive	I have been working	I have been drawing

| Past perfect progressive | I had been working | I had been drawing |
| Future perfect | I shall (will) have been working | I shall (will) have been drawing |

VF-3 Note the following **tense uses:**

■ The *simple present tense* indicates not only that an action is going on at the time of writing or speaking, but that an event occurs

habitually: He *walks* to work every day.

as a general truth: Truth *is* stranger than fiction.

in the historical present: In 1945, World War II *ends*.

in a certain future time: Next year *is* my fortieth birthday.

in a literary text: In *Moby Dick* the great white whale *seems to win*.

■ The *present progressive tense* indicates that an action is in progress either at the time of speaking or writing or that it is still relevant as a general truth:

Life *is becoming* more pleasant now that I have a degree.

Fewer people *are getting* married early these days.

■ The *present perfect tense* indicates that a past action is somehow still relevant to the present:

I *have travelled* many miles across America.

I *have just seen* that movie for the first time.

■ The *present perfect progressive tense* indicates that an action has not only continued from the past into the present but that there is every likelihood it will go on in the future:

The levels of pollution in our cities *have been rising* steadily for years now.

■ The *simple past tense* indicates an action completed in the past:

Last year I *went* to Hong Kong.

The choir *sang* beautifully in Beethoven's Ninth Symphony.

■ The *past progressive tense* indicates that a past action was continuing when another event occurred:

Leila *was working* hard when her pen broke.

■ The *past perfect tense* indicates that an action was completed by a specific time in the past or by the time another action occurred:

Leila *had completed* her assignments by the time her friend called.

The past perfect is also used to indicate a hope or plan that is unfulfilled:

Leila *had hoped* to complete her assignments before her friend called.

■ The *past perfect progressive tense* indicates that one action went on until a second action took place:

The flowers *had been growing* very well until the frost came.

■ The *simple future tense* indicates that something will occur in the future:

I *will watch* the hockey match tomorrow.

Prices *will rise* next year.

The simple future can have an emphatic effect:

I *will be* there regardless of what you say.

Or it can indicate what will happen following certain conditions:

If you buy this house, you *will not be able* to meet the payments.

■ The *future progressive tense* indicates that the action will be going on for some time in the future, or will take place at a certain time:

I *will be studying* tax law next year.

■ The *future perfect tense* indicates that an event will be completed by a certain time in the future, or by the time something else happens:

You *will have finished* your supplies by the time you get there.

■ The *future perfect progressive tense* indicates that an action will go on in the future until a certain time:

You *will have been running* for an hour by the time I get up.

VF-4 The **sequence of tenses** should be consistent throughout. Make sure you have the sequence of actions in the right order:

x   He came with many thoughts which will trouble him.
√   He came with many thoughts that troubled him.

x   I shall go if I will have had the time.
√   I shall go if I have the time.

x   I had wanted to have played basketball.
✓   I had wanted to play basketball.

x   I was working hard when the bell had rung.
✓   I was working hard when the bell rang.

VF-5   **Voice** affects transitive verbs only. These can be either *active* or *passive*. A verb is active when the subject carries out the action and passive when the subject is acted upon:

> The satellite sent back strong signals to earth. (Active)

> Strong signals were sent back to earth by the satellite. (Passive)

VF-6   **Mood.** The mood of a verb indicates the writer's attitude to the statement being made. There are three moods in English: *indicative, imperative, subjunctive.*

■ The *indicative mood* is the mood of factual or probable statements and of questions:

> Will it be fine tomorrow?

> The stars were brightly shining.

■ The *imperative mood* carries commands and requests:

> Get out at once!

> Would you please tidy your room right now!

■ The *subjunctive mood* is used to express statements that convey wishes (as opposed to strong requests or commands), conditions, hypotheses, suggestions, statements contrary to fact, and recommendations:

> If I *were* you, I *would resign.*

> *May* you *rest* in peace.

> *Would* you *reply* at your earliest convenience?

> They recommended that we *exercise* more often.

Punctuation and

Mechanics

P The Period

P-1 Use the period to end sentences that are statements, polite commands, or indirect questions:

> The river ran over a cliff and into the sea.
>
> Please turn the tap off.
>
> He asked whether we would be attending the party.

P-2 Use the period after most abbbreviations:

> Mrs. Mr. B.A. Ph.D. No. 56 6:30 p.m. etc. Ms.

Do not use periods after short forms or titles:

> math 11th 2nd gym lab *The Last of the Mohicans*

Do not use periods for abbreviations of national and international agencies:

> NATO UNESCO VISTA AFL-CIO

Follow abbreviations with commas, question marks, and exclamation points but not with an extra period:

> As soon as you have finished your B.A., don't you think you should go on for an M.A.**?**

Q The Question Mark

Q-1 Question marks are used after direct questions:

> Why did you come home early**?**
>
> You say you went to Bangkok**?**

Question marks are never combined with periods or commas:

> x She asked her friend, "Why are you leaving home?**.**"
>
> √ She asked her friend, "Why are you leaving home**?**"

Q-2   Question marks can be used in a series after each item, followed by a capital:

> So how much do you think it's worth? Ten dollars? Twenty? Thirty?

EXC   The Exclamation Point

The exclamation point should be used sparingly after emphatic statements: words, phrases, or sentences that express surprise, disbelief, or some other strong emotion:

> How can you say that!
>
> Get out of here!
>
> Wow! I really did win!

COM   The Comma

Probably more mistakes in grammar and style are made with commas than with any other item of punctuation. Commas are generally used to mark pauses or to separate elements within sentences. The misuse or omission of a comma can alter the meaning of a sentence:

> I suggested he leave without any use of force.
>
> I suggested he leave, without any use of force.

COM-1   Use a comma before a conjunction that links two main clauses:

> There is no reason for you to come tomorrow, nor should you come any time in the near future.

Remember: use a comma before *and, but, or, nor, for, so, yet* when these conjunctions join two main clauses, unless the comma can be omitted to make reading smoother (usually when the two main clauses are short).

> Do come tomorrow and bring a friend.

There is another important exception to this rule. If the two main clauses are long or if the clauses already contain commas, then use a semicolon before the conjunction to join the two clauses:

> There's no question the music was played beautifully and with sharp attention to detail; but, however grand the performance, I'm not sure it was all worth $50 a ticket.

COM-2   Use a comma to set off introductory material:

> Before the sun sets, you must come to our house.
>
> On the other hand, the sale was a great success.
>
> Yes, of course you should come.

Adverbial clauses, long introductory phrases, or transitional expressions should be set off by a comma. Do *not* use a comma after an introductory conjunction:

> But the weather was still good.

And note that common usage does allow no punctuation after short introductory phrases:

> In a day or two I'll join you.

COM-3   Use a comma between words, phrases, or clauses in a series:

> Lionel ran three miles, swam fifty laps, and then played an hour of basketball.
>
> Italy, Austria, Switzerland, and France all took part in competition.

COM-4   Use a comma between coordinate adjectives but not between an accumulation of adjectives that modify each other as well as the noun.

Coordinating adjectives:

> They seemed so young, innocent, and unprepared for war.

Cumulative adjectives which, unlike coordinating adjectives, are not reversible in their order:

> He wore a large brown felt hat.

COM-5   Use commas to set off nonrestrictive modifying elements such as a phrase or a clause that does not restrict the meaning of the subject:

> Michael, *panting furiously*, came in last.
>
> Martha, *whose hair was long and golden*, was chosen for the role.
>
> The Chinese, *for example*, discovered gunpowder.

Note, however, that phrases and clauses can be used restrictively; that is, they follow and limit the meaning of the words they modify. Restrictive elements are not set off by commas:

> The girl *whose hair was long and golden* was chosen for the role.
>
> My friend *Michael* is a runner.
>
> The experience *that I dread most* is a visit to the dentist.

COM-6 Use commas to set off contrasted and absolute phrases:

> What I really want is affection, not pity.
>
> Glaring furiously, he stalked off.

COM-7 Use commas with abbreviations after names, places, letter greetings, and in dates and addresses:

> After next week you will be Fred Simpson, B.A., and not just plain old Fred.
>
> The exhibition will be held in Fort Collins, Colorado, and then move to Laramie, Wyoming.
>
> Dear Lionel,
>
> With best wishes,
>
> The graduation ceremony is on Friday, June 4, 1982.

Note that commas need not be used in dates when the day of the month is left out or when the day of the month comes before the name of the month (June 1982; 4 June 1982). Do not use a comma between the number of a house and the street name or before a zip code (432 West St; CO 80208).

SEM The Semicolon

SEM-1 Use a semicolon between two main clauses not linked by a conjunction. The two elements must be closely related in meaning. Do not use a semicolon unless they are related:

> Painting gives me a thrill; sculpture bores me to death.
>
> You can't come tomorrow; you can only come next week.

SEM-2 Use a semicolon to join two main clauses when the second clause begins with a conjunctive adverb:

> You may not care for sculpture; *nevertheless,* its history is part of the course.
>
> The wheat crop appears to be good this year; *in fact,* it's going to be one of the best this century, the experts say.

SEM-3 Use a semicolon between items in a series that contains commas:

> The following people have been elected to the national committee: Bill Smith from Medford, Oregon; Anne Clark from Medanales, New Mexico; and Cynthia Brown from Santa Cruz, California.

COL The Colon

COL-1   Use a colon as an introduction to a list, an explanation, or a quotation:

> There is no end of flowers we can plant: peonies, dahlias, petunias, roses, irises, and so on.

> This is what I think happened: you panicked and against your better judgment told a lie.

> Remember what Shakespeare had to say about time: "The end crowns all, and some day that old common arbitrator time will end it."

COL-2   Use a colon between titles and subtitles and between hours and minutes:

> Dancing on the Head of a Pin: A Study of the Development of Theology
> 9:15 a.m.

D The Dash

D-1   Use a dash to mark an interruption in a sentence; indicating a shift in thought or expression, or an uncertain moment:

> He wanted to play ball—to play ball, mind you—with a broken wrist.
> I'll come next week for sure—at least if I can get off.

D-2   Use a dash to set off an explanation or example that summarizes other parts of the sentence:

> Paris, Amsterdam, Brussels, Luxembourg—we saw them all from the bus window.

PN Parentheses

PN-1   Use parentheses to close off an explanatory comment in a sentence such as an example or a point of clarification:

> I chose that suit over there (the one with the pin stripes) because it was such an unusual shade of gray.

If a whole sentence is placed in parentheses, then remember to put the period *inside* the parentheses:

> One of my favorite pastimes is walking the dog in the park. (That is, I walk him when I can get off work.)

PN-2   Use parentheses to set off numbers and letters that introduce items in a list:

> There are several things to do: (a) feed the cat, (b) clean the kitchen, and (c) mow the lawn.

Also use parentheses to enclose numbers that represent amounts spelled out in words:

> You can have the car for two thousand dollars ($2000).

BR   Brackets

BR-1   When you need to use parentheses within parentheses, use brackets for the inner set:

> His first novel (*Titanic* [New York: Scriptor]) was a best seller.

BR-2   Use brackets when you want to insert a comment in a passage written by someone else:

> "There are so many books and articles on D. H. Lawrence [over 2000, in fact] that we can easily forget what the author himself has to say."

AP   The Apostrophe

AP-1   Use an apostrophe to mark the possessive case of nouns and indefinite pronouns:

> Fred's hat   girls' cars   someone's umbrella   one's own house

Here are the general rules for using the possessive apostrophe:

- With a singular noun add the apostrophe and *s*:

  Michael**'s** essay

- If the singular noun ends in *s*, then the possessive may be indicated by the apostrophe alone or by adding the apostrophe and *s*:

  Hans's boat

- With plural nouns ending in *s*, add only the apostrophe:

  ships' bows   boys' pants

- With plural nouns not ending in *s*, add the apostrophe and *s*:

  men**'s** hats   women**'s** rights

- With compounds, add the apostrophe and *s* to the last word:

  mother-in-law**'s** feelings

  the President of America**'s** address

- To denote joint ownership, add the apostrophe and *s* to the last name:

  Linda and Mary**'s** books

- To denote individual ownership, add the apostrophe and *s* to each name:

  The professor**'s** and the student**'s** books were stolen.

AP-2 Use an apostrophe to mark letters left out in contracted words and numerals:

    she'll   they'll   o'clock   battle of '44

AP-3 Apostrophes may be used to mark the plural of figures and letters. This is optional:

    the 1800's *or* the 1800s   six y's *or* six ys

AP-4 Remember *not* to use an apostrophe with possessive pronouns: *its, his, hers, theirs, ours, whose. It's* means *it is* and is a contraction, not a possessive.

QUO Quotation Marks

QUO-1 Use double quotation marks to enclose direct quotations from speech or written material:

> The philosopher Fichte is reputed to have said, "I positively owe every man absolute frankness and truthfulness."

QUO-2 Use single quotation marks to enclose quotations within quotations:

> The teacher said "The philosopher Fichte is reputed to have said, 'I positively owe every man absolute frankness and truthfulness.' "

Note that in long quotations set off from the text, quotation marks are not used. (See Appendix B.)

QUO-3 Use double quotation marks *sparingly* around words you are not sure of or want to be ironic about:

He said that if we went to the study session we would have a "good time." Now here's a "tasty" hamburger.

QUO-4 Use double quotation marks for certain titles. See Appendix B. Use single quotation marks when the title falls within a quotation:

"I told you that Wordsworth's poem 'Tintern Abbey' is worth reading," he said.

QUO-5 When punctuating quotations:

■ The period and the comma fall within quotation marks:

"The stars," he assured us, "were shining brightly."

When a quotation is followed by information within parentheses, then the period follows the last parenthesis:

"Act according to your conscience" (p. 45).

■ Colons and semicolons fall outside quotation marks:

He wrote an article called "Freedom and Duty"; however, he also loved, as he said, "dabbling in paint and creating happenings on the walls of town buildings": the police station, the bank, and the post office.

■ When question marks, dashes, and exclamation marks are part of a quotation, they fall within quotation marks; otherwise, they fall outside:

"Are you going for a swim?" she asked.

Did she ask "Are you going for a swim"?

ELL Ellipsis

ELL-1 Ellipsis dots . . . (three spaced dots) are used to mark the omission of words in a quotation or to suggest uncertainty:

"Fichte's moral philosophy emphasized . . . the dutiful will, in utter devotion to ideal ends."

"Would you . . . I don't know how to ask this . . . would you lend me a hundred dollars?"

ELL-2 Four spaced dots are used at the end of a quotation when words have been left out:

"Fichte's moral philosophy emphasized . . . the dutiful will. . . ."

Four spaced dots are also used within quotations to show that at least one whole sentence has been omitted.

ELL-3   A whole line of spaced dots is used to show that one or more lines of poetry have been left out:

> When my love swears that she is made of truth
> I do believe her, though I know she lies
> That she might think me some untutored youth,
>
> . . . .
> Thus vainly thinking that she thinks me young . . .
>
> Shakespeare

SL The Slash

The slash / is used to indicate alternatives and typed fractions, and to mark off lines of poetry quoted in your text (see Appendix B):

mine/yours   5 9/10

HYP The Hyphen

HYP-1   Use a hyphen to form a compound unit from several words:

"mackerel-crowded seas" (W. B. Yeats)

a voyage-through-space movie

HYP-2   Use a hyphen to break up a word at the end of a line. This is not a recommended practice—better to begin the word on a new line—but if you do hyphenate, make sure that you break the word at the end of a syllable. Consult a dictionary if in doubt.

HYP-3   Use a hyphen to join a prefix to a capitalized word but not to an uncapitalized one:

pro-American

anticlimax

HYP-4   Numbers below one hundred that are written out are hyphenated:

fifty-six

CAP   Capitalization

CAP-1   Capitalize proper names and words used with proper names:

Lenore Smythe	Martin Chuzzlewit
The United States	The Bible
Hardy Brothers Manufacturing	
Company	
November	Paris
Jews	Christians
Pacific Ocean	San Francisco

CAP-2   Abbreviations are capitalized:

M.A.   UNESCO   R. Q. Knowles

CAP-3   Capitalize the first word of every sentence and the first word of every quoted sentence:

He stood by the well and heard her say, ''I wonder how deep it is?''

CAP-4   Always capitalize the pronoun *I*:

I came, I saw, I ran.

ITAL   Underlining for Italics

ITAL-1   Titles of books, magazines, plays, films, television programs, newspapers, musical works, and long poems are underlined. (In print they are italicized.) See Appendix B.

ITAL-2   All foreign words or phrases should be underlined, unless they are a regular part of English vocabulary (like *pizza*). A dictionary will indicate whether a word is foreign:

Must you always be so au courant?

ITAL-3   You can underline words, letters, or phrases to give them emphasis, but do so sparingly:

You want me to come tonight?

654

AB Abbreviations

AB-1 Abbreviate titles that accompany a name, except when referring to religious, military, and government leaders:

Mr. Arthur Jones   **Mrs.** Peter Smith

Ms. Kaplow   **Dr.** Helen Curtis

General Westmoreland   the **Reverend** Billy Graham

Senator Ted Kennedy

AB-2 Abbreviate words used with dates and figures; the District of Columbia, the United States, the United Kingdom; names of organizations; and some often-used Latin expressions:

1268 **A.D.**   600 **B.C.**   9:30 **a.m.**

Washington, **D.C.**   **U.S.-U.K.** relations

CIA   NATO   USMC   FBI   ERA

cf. [compare]

e.g. [for example]

i.e. [that is]

etc. [and so on]

vs. [versus]

In ordinary and more formal writing, however, it is usual to spell out the following:

days of the week

measurements

names of states

names of countries

words like *street, company, avenue, road*

NU Numbers

NU-1 Use numerals for times of day, addresses, dates, identification numbers, pages, decimals and percentages, and when spelling out a number would require more than two words:

9:56 p.m.   **25** December, **1976**

Highway **5**   page **47**

8.6 percent   **102; 756; 98,073**

NU-2   Write out a number when it begins a sentence. If that means using more than two words, reorder the sentence:

> **Ninety-three** would-be players assembled for the camp.
>
> The army released 976 men.

Write out numbers given as round figures:

> If you come by **twelve** you can be gone by **two.**
>
> The wage is a **hundred** dollars a day.

Editing Checklist

The following checklist covers the major common errors in sentence structure, diction, style, and organization. Use the checklist as a diagnostic guide for checking your own work. As a summary of common writing problems, the material is worth knowing for its own sake in order to avoid similar problems in your own writing.

COMMON ERRORS IN SENTENCE STRUCTURE

FRAG Sentence Fragments

A *sentence fragment* is a phrase or dependent clause that plays the role of a sentence.

- It can be a *participial phrase:*

  x   Fred ran a grocery store in Boise.
      Having left the army in 1975.
  √   Having left the army in 1975, Fred ran a grocery store in Boise.

- Or an *infinitive phrase:*

  x   Fred left the army in 1975. *To run a grocery store in Boise.*
  √   Fred left the army in 1975 to run a grocery store in Boise.

- Fragments can also be *absolute phrases and prepositional phrases.*

- *Dependent clauses* can appear as fragments, as with this *adverbial clause:*

  x   Fred went to manage a grocery store in Boise. *Because he left the army.*
  √   Fred went to manage a grocery store in Boise because he left the army.

- Or this *adjectival clause:*

  x   Fred went to manage a grocery store. *That is in Boise.*
  √   Fred went to manage a grocery store that is in Boise.

- Dependent *noun clauses,* too, often turn up as fragments. But note that it is acceptable to use fragments when writing out conversation, or as strong statements in response to questions:

  And then we can ask: What do we do next? *Run? Hide out in the mountains?*

Sentence fragments are the result of mispunctuation. They are easily corrected by either linking the fragment to the sentence before or after (as in all the examples above) or by making a complete sentence out of the fragment itself:

x   Fred left the army in 1975. *To run a grocery store in Boise.*

√   Fred left the army in 1975. He then opened a grocery store in Boise.

COM/S   Comma Splice

A comma splice occurs when two independent clauses are joined together by only a comma when a conjunction or a semicolon should be used:

x   Louise ran for the student senate, she was tired of her friend's apathy.

√   Louise ran for the student senate *because* she was tired of her friend's apathy.

Note that you can only use a semicolon to join two clauses of equal rank. This gives a balanced effect:

x   She ran the business, I did the housework.

√   She ran the business; I did the housework.

A very common comma splice occurs when speech is being quoted:

x   "Come and sail this boat with me," he said, "you need the exercise."

√   "Come and sail this boat with me," he said. "You need the exercise."

RUN/ON   Run-On Sentence

A run-on sentence occurs when two or more clauses are run together without any punctuation at all:

x   Louise ran for the student senate tired of her friends' apathy and sure that she could get lots of support if she had a good platform and didn't promise the impossible.

√   Tired of her friends' apathy, Louise ran for the student senate, sure she could get lots of support if she had a good platform and didn't promise the impossible.

Again, comma splices and run-on sentences are punctuation problems, but they are easily corrected by carefully subordinating elements (see Chapter 5) and by using coordinating conjunctions (see pp. 620–621) and correct punctuation (see pp. 646–648).

FA Faulty Agreement

See pp. 633–636. The most common errors involve

■ plural nouns that happen to take a singular verb:

x   Gymnastics are tough.
√   Gymnastics *is* tough.

■ unit quantities, which take a singular verb:

x   Fifty pounds of rock are all I can carry.
√   Fifty pounds of rock *is* all I can carry.

■ *either . . . or, or/nor, neither . . . nor,* which take verbs governed by the *last* subject:

x   Either the pie crust, or the fillings, or the whipped cream are rotten.
√   Either the pie crust, or the fillings, or the whipped cream *is* rotten.

TS Tense Shifts

Verbs should be used in their appropriate tenses and follow a logical sequence. See pp. 642–644. The present tense is most appropriate:

■ When expressing a general or continuing condition, or truth, whether in the past or present:

The moon *has* an effect on the tides.

The Victorians believed that the earth *is* round.

■ When writing about a book, or a film, or an art work:

James Bond *is* a man who loves his work.

But for earlier action described in a story, use the past and future tenses as you would in reported speech:

Bond then *reports* that he *had* evaded capture in his trick car.

Here are some frequent problems with tense sequence:

■ If the first verb in a sentence is in the *past* and the action of the second verb is yet to be completed, use *would have:*

Bond idled up to the beautiful agent knowing he *would have* to find out who she worked for.

659

■ If the first verb is in the *present* and the second refers to an act yet to be completed, use the *future perfect:*

Bond idles up to the beautiful agent, knowing he *will have* to find out who she works for.

■ If the first verb is in the *past* tense and the second verb refers to a time *before* it, then use the *past perfect* tense:

Bond *stayed* because he *had seen* that all exits were blocked.

■ Use *present participles* and *gerunds* to refer to action at the same time as the action of the main verb:

Running away was not Bond's style. (gerund)

While *running* away, Bond tripped and fell. (present participle)

And use *past participles* to refer to action *earlier* than that of the action of the main verb:

Having lost his martini in the pool, Bond was not in good humor.

CP   Clumsy Predication

Errors in predication often occur in overelaborate or overqualified statements:

x   What is going on is something which I don't like.
√   I don't like what is going on.

x   The book deals with Paolo's love affair with Francesca.
√   The meaning of the book *is that* Paolo loves Francesca.

x   The reason for Louise's running for the senate is because of student apathy.
√   Louise is running for the senate because of student apathy.

VPR   Vague Pronoun References

See pp. 635–637. Be sure that your pronouns refer to *specific* antecedents and not just to a general reference. Beware of *this* and *which* used ambiguously or with no clear reference:

Fred stayed in the army a long time and travelled throughout Europe. He enjoyed *this* very much.

Enjoyed what? The army? The travel? Replace *this* by the full reference:

Fred is a better poet than Bob, but I prefer *his* fiction.

Whose fiction? Probably Bob's, but why put the reader in doubt? Replace *his* with Bob's:

Fred was a veteran and had saved $5000 before he opened his grocery store. *This* allowed him to get a government loan.

What did? Being a veteran or saving the money? Replace *this* with *Being a veteran* or *Saving money*:

They say he is a good writer.

Who says? Rewrite: *He has a reputation for being a good writer:*

x   In this book, it says that grammar is fun.

√   This book says that grammar is fun.

FPC   Faulty Pronoun Case

For use of pronouns after *than* or *as*, see pp. 631–632.

■ *Fred is as tall as me* may be acceptable in colloquial speech, but it is often considered incorrect in writing. Revise to

Fred is as tall as I.

Always try to complete the sentence, adding the verb even if you do not actually use it:

Fred is as tall as I (am).

■ Beware of possible confusion with the use of pronouns after *than*: *Fred liked the store more than me* actually means that Fred liked the store more than he liked me. So if you mean *Fred liked the store more than I (did),* then say so.

■ Use of pronoun complement: See p. 632. Which is correct: *I am sorry, it was me* or *I am sorry, it was I?* The argument has gone on for a long time about that one. Either one is acceptable, the former especially in speech, the latter in formal, written language. Try avoiding the problem where you can and say *Sorry, I did it.*

■ The over-formal pronoun appositive: remember that pronouns always keep the same case as the noun, but this can sound overformal:

Two people, Fred and I, wanted the grocery store.

Simplify the subject:

> Fred and I wanted the grocery store.

Similarly, revise

> The owner wanted to sell to both of us, Fred and me.

to

> The owner wanted to sell to Fred and me together.

FPA   Faulty Pronoun Agreement

See p. 635.

> x   If one (a person) eats, *they* will get fat.
> √   If one eats too much, *he* (or *she*) will get too fat.

WW   Use of *Who* and *Whom*

See p. 632. This is another case where the formal and informal uses tend to be blurred. A good rule is to stick to the formal—*who* is the subject of a verb, *whom* is the object—but try to avoid over-formal uses where possible:

> *I ran into Fred who was managing a grocery store* is correct, as is *I ran into Fred whom I knew in the army.*

But then there is *Whom was Fred with last night?* which is strictly correct but rather over-formal. You might want to change it to *Who was that person you saw with Fred last night?*

It is important to remember to keep *who/whom* with the verb it goes with.

> I ran into Fred *who* Marge thought had left Idaho.

Who is correct here because it is the subject of *had left.*

DANG   Dangling Modifiers

A dangling modifier occurs when the subject that is being described, or modified in some way, is absent:

> Leaving the army, the grocery store business seemed the best future to him.

662

It seems as if the grocery store business left the army, for it is grammatically the only subject available. Always make sure your subject and its modification are clearly together:

> Leaving the army, Fred felt that the grocery store business was the best future for him.

MIS Misplaced Modifiers

When a modifier is placed some distance from the word it is modifying, then clumsiness or confusion can result. The problem frequently occurs with phrases used adjectivally or adverbially and is easily corrected by moving the misplaced modifier close to what it modifies:

x The plane trip was to Argentina which cost $500.
√ The plane trip which cost $500 was to Argentina.

x She told me how to climb the mountain on the boat.
√ She told me on the boat how to climb the mountain.

SPLIT Split Infinitives

The *split infinitive* is controversial. It is not a serious error (if it is an error at all) to put an adverb between *to* and the verb. *To clearly state,* for example, is a common expression and needs no change. But the trouble occurs when not one adverb but a whole string of them (and adverbial phrases, too) are squeezed in between *to* and the verb:

> Fred decided to *carefully and with great preparation* open a grocery store in Boise.

Avoid such constructions, placing the adverb phrase before or after the verb:

> Fred decided with great care and preparation to open a grocery store in Boise.

PAR Faulty Parallelisms

■ With *both . . . and, either . . . or, neither . . . nor, not only . . . but also,* and related constructions, verbs should be matched with verbs, nouns with nouns, adjectives with adjectives, clauses with clauses. Do not mix these elements:

x   Louise was both a good student and played sport well.

✓   Louise was both a good student and a good sportswoman.

x   Fred wanted not only to leave the army but he also wanted to open a grocery store.

✓   Fred wanted not only to leave the army but to open a grocery store.

Keep the parallelisms as spare and carefully balanced as possible.

■ Do not mix gerunds and infinitives in a series:

Priscilla liked to jump off high dive boards, to float on her back, and dog-paddling.

Dog-paddling is not an infinitive in keeping with the rest of the series. So replace *dog-paddling* with *to dog-paddle.*

■ Consistently repeat prepositions and possessive pronouns that you have started to use:

x   Louise excelled at classwork, at sport, and music.

✓   Louise excelled at classwork, sport, and music.

✓   Louise excelled at classwork, at sport, and at music.

PUNC Faulty Punctuation

(See pp. 645–656.) The most glaring punctuation errors involve sentence fragments, comma splices, and run-on sentences. Remember, do not use a comma alone to join two independent clauses. Here are some other common problems:

■ If a sentence ends with an abbreviation, do not add another period:

In spring I will have my B. A.

■ Do not use a period or a comma after a question mark:

"You want to buy this car?" he asked.

■ Do not use a comma between a subject and its predicate even if the subject appears quite long:

x   The knights in shining armor and waving plumes, rode across the dunes.

■ Do not use a semi-colon between a main clause and a subordinate clause:

x   Please visit me in the summer; when we are at the beach house.

■ Do not use a colon to introduce a list which follows *of* or any form of the verb *to be:*

   x   The material I want is: roofing nails, a length of guttering, and some siding.

■ Do not overuse quotation marks for effect. Say what you mean:

   x   This really is a "good" film, one we can all "enjoy."

■ When you end a quote with an ellipsis make sure you have *four* spaced dots:

   "Life and Death are two locked caskets. . . ."

■ Beware of *it's* which is not a possessive *(its)* but *it is:*

   The dog liked its kennel.
   It's late.

■ Do not use an apostrophe with nouns that refer to inanimate things:

   x   nuclear apocalypse**'s** dire consequences
      the dire consequences of nuclear apocalypse
   x   the fence**'s** white pickets
      the white pickets of the fence

■ Spell out a number that can be written in one or two words:

   six   seventy-five

but use numerals for numbers that take more than two words:

   367   19,760

SPELL Spelling

Readers accept no excuses for misspelled words. If you are unsure of a word, then look it up in a dictionary. You should keep a list of all words you find yourself frequently misspelling and tack it up where you can see it. Looking at the correct spelling over and over again does help. Everyone has a few problem words to think over before spelling, so don't delay in making up your own list as soon as possible. Here are some common problem areas:

■ *Homonyms* are words that sound alike but are spelled differently such as *there, their,* and *they're,* and *gorilla, guerilla.* Be careful with these words. Often when we are writing quickly we misspell words that sound like others. It is very common to substitute *there* for *their*. This is one important reason why it is essential to proofread.

■ *Plurals* can be tricky. If you are unsure of a plural, then check it in the dictionary. The general rules are

Add *s* to the singular: *girls, tables*

Add *es* to nouns ending in *ch, sh, x* or *s*: *churches, boxes, wishes*

Add *es* to nouns ending in *y* and preceded by a vowel once you have changed the *y* to *i*: *monies, companies*

■ Know the difference between *ei* and *ie*. The old jingle will help you remember it:

Put *i* before *e*

Except after *c*

When the sound is *ee*

So: *achieve,* but *deceive*

■ *Prefixes* such as *mis-, re-,* and *un-* change the meaning of a word when they are added to a root *(mis + placed)*. They can also create spelling problems. The simple rule to remember is that you do not double the last letter of the prefix when it is different from the first letter of the root:

re + constitute → reconstitute

un + holy → unholy

Nor do you drop a letter when you add the prefix to a root that begins with the same letter:

mis + spell → misspell

re + enter → reenter

■ *Suffixes* are letters added to the end of a word that help form a new word, like *-ness, -ed, -ful*:

kind + ness → kindness

love + ing → loving

There are three basic rules to remember.

a. Drop a silent *e* before a suffix beginning with a vowel:

care + ing → caring

desire + able + desirable

But do *not* drop the silent *e* before a suffix beginning with a consonant:

care + ful → careful

desire + less → desireless

There are some exceptions: for example, *mileage, hoeing,* and the silent *e* which follows after *c* or *g* before *-able* or *-ous* (*peaceable, changeable, noticeable*).

b. When a word ends in a single consonant, double the consonant before a suffix which begins with a vowel:

trowel + ing → trowelling

regret + able → regrettable

c. Change the final *y* to *i* if the *y* follows a consonant, but keep *y* before *-ing*:

happy + ily → happily

mediocrity + es → mediocrities

But pays → paid

SPELL-1 Here are some **commonly misspelled words:**

absence	affect	apparatus
accessible	aggravate	apparent
accidentally	aggression	appearance
accommodate	aisles	appreciate
accuracy	alcohol	appropriate
accustomed	all right	approximately
achievement	almost	arguing
acquainted	already	argument
acquire	altogether	arrest
acreage	a lot of	aspirin
address	amateur	assassination
admission	ancestry	assistance
adolescent	annihilate	associate
advice	annual	atheist
advised	answer	athletic
aerial	apiece	attendance

Commonly misspelled words (continued)

authentic	chocolate	crowd
author	chosen	cruelty
average	commitment	curiosity
awful	committed	dealt
balloon	committee	deceive
barbarous	competition	decision
bargain	complement	decorate
belief	completely	definitely
believed	conceited	degree
beneficial	conceivable	descend
benefited	concentration	description
biggest	condemn	desirable
boundary	confident	despair
breath	connoisseur	desperate
breathe	conquer	destroy
bulletin	conscience	develop
bureaucracy	conscientious	device
business	consensus	devise
cafeteria	consistency	different
calculator	consistent	disagree
calendar	continuous	disappear
capital	contradict	disappoint
carrying	controlled	disapprove
category	controversial	disastrous
cede	convenience	discipline
cemetery	coolly	discussion
census	corporal	disease
certain	corroborate	dispel
changeable	council	dissatisfaction
changing	courses	distinct
channel	courteous	disturb
characteristic	criticism	divide
chief	criticize	divine

Commonly misspelled words (continued)

doctor	extremely	height
dormitory	familiar	heroes
drunkenness	fascinate	hideous
easily	favorite	hindrance
ecstasy	February	holiday
effect	finally	hoping
efficient	financial	humane
eighth	fluorine	humorous
embarrass	foreign	hurriedly
emphasize	foresee	hypocrisy
empty	foretell	hypocrite
enemy	formerly	ideally
engineer	forty	idiosyncrasy
entirely	forward	ignorant
environment	friend	illogical
equipment	frightening	imaginary
equipped	fulfill	immediately
escape	gardener	immensely
especially	gauge	immigrant
everything	generally	incalculable
evidently	government	incidentally
exaggerate	governor	increase
excel	grammar	incredible
excellent	grievous	independent
except	group	indispensable
exceptional	gruesome	influential
exercise	guaranteed	initiative
exhaust	guard	inoculate
existence	guerrilla	innocuous
expense	guidance	insurance
experience	happened	intelligent
experiment	happily	interference
explanation	harass	interrupt

Commonly misspelled words (continued)

irrelevant	miniature	opportunity
irresistible	minutes	opposite
irritated	mirror	oppression
island	mischievous	optimistic
jealousy	missile	ordinarily
jewelry	misspelling	originally
judgment	morale	oscillate
kindergarten	mortgage	paid
knowledge	muscle	panicky
laboratory	mysterious	parallel
led	naturally	paralleled
leisure	necessary	particle
length	nevertheless	particularly
lenient	newsstand	pastime
library	nickel	peaceable
license	niece	peculiar
lightning	nineteen	perceive
likelihood	ninety	permanent
liveliest	ninth	permissible
loose	noticeable	persuade
lose	nowadays	phase
luxury	nuclear	physical
lying	nuisance	piece
magazine	occasion	pigeon
maintenance	occasionally	pitiful
manageable	occurred	planned
maneuver	occurrence	playwright
marriage	occurring	pleasure
material	official	poison
mathematics	omission	politician
meanness	omit	pollute
meant	omitted	possession
medicine	omitting	practical

Commonly misspelled words (continued)

practically	rarity	saxophone
precede	realize	scarcity
preferred	really	scenery
prejudice	rebellion	schedule
prepare	recede	secede
preparation	receipt	secretary
presence	receive	seize
prevail	recession	senseless
prevalent	recipe	separate
principle	recognize	sergeant
prisoner	recommend	several
privilege	referring	sheriff
probably	rehearsal	shrubbery
procedure	relief	significant
proceed	relieve	similarly
processes	religious	sincerely
professor	remembrance	skiing
pronunciation	reminisce	sophomore
propaganda	repetition	source
propeller	representative	souvenir
prophecy	resemblance	specimen
prophesy	resistance	sponsor
psychology	resources	statistics
publicly	restaurant	stayed
pumpkin	review	stopped
pursue	rhythm	straight
pursuing	ridiculous	strategy
quandary	roommate	strength
quantity	sacrifice	strenuous
quarter	sacrilegious	stretch
questionnaire	safety	stubbornness
quiet	sandwich	studying
quizzes	satellite	suburban

Commonly misspelled words (continued)

succeed	through	vengeance
succession	till	view
superintendent	tobacco	villain
supersede	tomorrow	violence
suppose	tragedy	vitamins
suppress	transferred	warring
susceptible	truly	weather
syllable	twelfth	Wednesday
tariff	typical	weird
technical	tyranny	whereabouts
technique	unanimous	wherever
temperament	unconscious	whichever
temperature	undoubtedly	wholly
temporary	unnecessary	without
tendency	until	women
their	usage	wretched
therefore	usually	writing
they're	vacuum	written
thorough	valuable	yield
though	vegetable	

Common Errors in Diction and Style

These errors are explained in the text. See chapter and page references.

EMP *Weak Emphasis on Nouns and Verbs.*   See Chapter 5, pp. 192–193, 196. Remember to emphasize verbs over nouns.

IND *Indirect Form of the Verb.*   See Chapter 5, p. 196.
Avoid the passive voice unless it is necessary.

■ *Unnecessary inversion or indirect statement:* See Chapter 5, pp. 196, 197. Let simple, direct statements carry the weight of your message.

■ *Weak Use of "To Be," "Do," "Got," "It Is," "There Are,"* etc. See Chapter 5, p. 196.

■ *Use of the Negative When the Positive is More Effective.* See Chapter 5, p. 197.

VAR   *Poor Sentence Variety.*

■ *Too many bound phrases or clauses.* See Chapter 5, pp. 203–212. Remember that free elements are essential for a lively style.

■ *Insufficient Pauses.* See Chapter 5, p. 212.

SUB   *Insufficient Subordination.*   See Chapter 5, pp. 201–202. Excessive coordination leads to choppy sentences.

PAR   *Poor Paragraph Structure.* See Chapter 6, pp. 232–255.

PAR-1   *Poor Opening or Closing Paragraph.*   See Chapter 6, pp. 248–255.

PAR-2   *Poor Sentence Transition Within Paragraph.*   See Chapter 6, pp. 243–256.

PAR-3   *Poor Transition Between Paragraphs.*   See Chapter 6, pp. 246-247.

DIC   *Problems with Diction.*   See Chapter 4, pp. 154–160.

DIC-1   *Wordiness, Overwriting, Needless Repetition.*   See Chapter 4, pp. 157–159.

DIC-2   *Imprecise Adjective or Adverb.*   See Chapter 4, pp. 157–158.

DIC-3   *Jargon or Slang.*   See Chapter 4, pp. 156–157.

DIC-4   *Mixed Metaphor.*   See Chapter 4, p. 160.

DIC-5   *Euphemism.*   See Chapter 4, p. 157.

DIC-6   *Overly Abstract Language.*   See Chapter 4, p. 156.

Common Organizational Errors

These, too, have been fully covered in the text. See references.

THES   *Unclear Thesis.*   See Chapter 3, pp. 120–122.

IV   *Inconsistent Viewpoint: Lack of Coherence.* See Chapter 3, pp. 107–118; Chapter 7, pp. 278–289.

LF *Lack of Focus.* See Chapter 3, pp. 107–118; Chapter 7, pp. 278–289.

IT *Inconsistent Tone.* See Chapter 4, pp. 154–156; Chapter 7, p. 289.

MS *Unclear Main Statement in Paragraph.* See Chapter 6, pp. 233–236; Chapter 7, pp. 281–282.

UI *Unrelated Ideas.* See Chapter 3, pp. 112–113.

Acknowledgments continued

BUCKLEY, WILLIAM F., JR. Excerpt reprinted by permission of G. P. Putnam Sons from *Execution Eve and Other Contemporary Ballads* by William F. Buckley, Jr. Copyright © 1972–1975 by William F. Buckley, Jr.

CASTENADA, CARLOS Extract from *The Teachings of Don Juan: A Yaqui Way of Knowledge,* © 1968 by The Regents of the University of California. Reprinted by permission of the University of California Press.

CLARK, KENNETH Extract from *The Nude: A Study in Ideal Form,* Princeton University Press. Copyright © 1956 by the Trustees of the National Gallery of Art. Reprinted by permission of Princeton University Press.

COCKBURN, ALEXANDER excerpt from "Blood & Ink," copyright © 1980 by Harper's Magazine. All rights reserved. Reprinted from the February 1981 issue by special permission.

COLETTE "From *The Pure and the Impure*" from *The Pure and the Impure* by Colette, translated by Herma Briffault. Copyright © 1966, 1967 by Farrar, Straus and Giroux, Inc. Reprinted by permission of Farrar, Straus and Giroux, Inc.

CONCORD WATCH Advertisement, pp. 171–172, prepared for Concord Watch Corporation by Harry Viola Advertising, Inc. Used by permission.

COX, HARVEY "Understanding Islam" reprinted by permission of The Sterling Lord Agency, from the January 1981 *Atlantic Monthly.* Copyright © 1981 by Harvey Cox.

CORTAZAR, JULIO "Continuity of Parks" from *End of the Game and Other Stories,* by Julio Cortazar, translated by Paul Blackburn. Copyright © 1967 by Random House, Inc. Reprinted by permission of Pantheon Books, a Division of Random House, Inc.

CUMMINGS, E. E. "Spring is like a perhaps hand" reprinted from TULIPS & CHIMNEYS by E. E. Cummings, by permission of Liveright Publishing Corporation. Copyright 1923, 1925, and renewed 1951, 1953 by E. E. Cummings. Copyright © 1973, 1976 by the Trustees for the E. E. Cummings Trust. Copyright © 1973, 1976 by George James Firmage.

Denver Post Staff, "Ten-Foot Russians?" February 28, 1982; editorial, February 22, 1982.

DIDION, JOAN "On Going Home" from *Slouching Towards Bethlehem* by Joan Didion. Copyright © 1967, 1968 by Joan Didion. Reprinted by permission of Farrar, Straus and Giroux, Inc.

DILLARD, ANNIE From pp. 104–107 in *Pilgrim at Tinker Creek* by Annie Dillard. Copyright © 1974 by Annie Dillard. Reprinted by permission of Harper & Row, Publishers, Inc.

Ecclesiastes 3 From the Revised Standard Version of the Bible, copyrighted 1976, 1952 © 1971, 1973. Permission is granted by the National Council of the Churches of Christ.

EISELEY, LOREN Loren Eiseley, "Brown Wasps," in *The Night Country.* Copyright © 1971 by Loren Eiseley. Reprinted with the permission of Charles Scribner's Sons.

ELIOT, T. S. "Preludes" from *Collected Poems 1909–1962* by T. S. Eliot, copyright 1936 by Harcourt Brace Jovanovich, Inc.; copyright © 1963, 1964 by T. S. Eliot. Reprinted by permission of the publisher and Faber & Faber.

FALLOWS, JAMES Excerpts from "The Civilization of the Army," copyright © 1981 by James Fallows. Reprinted by permission of the Julian Bach Literary Agency. Originally published in the *Atlantic Monthly.*

FAULKNER, WILLIAM Extract from "Nobel Prize Address" from *The Faulkner Reader* by William Faulkner. Reprinted by permission of Random House, Inc.

FEUERLICHT, ROBERTA S. Excerpts from *Justice Crucified* by Roberta S. Feuerlicht. Copyright © 1977 by Roberta S. Feuerlicht. Used with the permission of McGraw-Hill Book Company.

FINCH, ROBERT "A Moth in the Eye" from *Common Ground: A Naturalist's Cape Cod* by Robert Finch. Copyright © 1981 by Robert Finch. Reprinted by permission of David R. Godine, Publisher, Inc.

FISHER, M. F. K. "Let the Sky Rain Potatoes" reprinted with permission of Macmillan Publishing Co., Inc. from *The Art of Eating* by M. F. K. Fisher. Copyright 1937, 1954 by M. F. K. Fisher.

FOWLES, JOHN Excerpt from *The Magus: A Revised Version* by John Fowles. Copyright © 1965, 1977 by J. R. Fowles Ltd. By permission of Little, Brown and Company.

FREUD, SIGMUND Excerpt reprinted from THE FUTURE OF AN ILLUSION by Sigmund Freud. Translated and Edited by James Strachey, copyright © 1961 by James Strachey. Used by permission of W. W. Norton & Company, Inc. and The Hogarth Press.

GILMAN, RICHARD "From *Decadence*" is from *Decadence* by Richard Gilman. Copyright © 1975, 1979 by Richard Gilman. Reprinted by permission of Farrar, Straus and Giroux, Inc.

GOLDING, WILLIAM "Thinking as a Hobby" copyright © 1961 by William Golding. First published in *Holiday* Magazine. All rights reserved. Reprinted by permission of Curtis Brown Ltd.

GOODMAN, ELLEN "Once Verboten, Now Chic" from *Close to Home* reprinted by permission of The Washington Post Company.

GREGORY, DICK Excerpt from *The Shadow That Scares Me* by Dick Gregory. Copyright © 1968 by Dick Gregory. Reprinted by permission of Doubleday & Company, Inc.

HALL, EDWARD Excerpt from *The Silent Language* by Edward T. Hall. Copyright © 1959 by Edward T. Hall. Reprinted by permission of Doubleday & Company, Inc.

HARRISON, BARBARA GRIZZUTI Excerpt from "Hotel California" reprinted by permission of the author from *Harper's* Magazine, February 1981, copyright © 1981 by Barbara Grizzuti Harrison.

HAWKES, JOHN Excerpt from pp. 11–12 in *The Passion Artist* by John Hawkes. Copyright © 1978, 1979 by John Hawkes. Reprinted by permission of Harper & Row, Publishers, Inc.

HELLER, JOSEPH "Snowden" from *Catch 22,* Copyright © 1955, 1961 by Joseph Heller. Reprinted by permission of Simon & Schuster, a Division of Gulf & Western Corporation.

HERR, MICHAEL Excerpt from *Dispatches,* by Michael Herr. Copyright © 1977 by Michael Herr. Reprinted by permission of Alfred A. Knopf, Inc.

HOAGLAND, EDWARD "The Lapping, Itchy Edge of Love," from *The Courage of Turtles,* by Edward Hoagland. Copyright © 1970 by Edward Hoagland. Reprinted by permission of Random House, Inc.

JACKSON, GEORGE From *Soledad Brother: The Prison Letters of George Jackson.* Copyright © 1970 by World Entertainers Limited. By permission of Bantam Books, Inc. All rights reserved.

JOYCE, JAMES "Araby" from *Dubliners* by James Joyce. Originally published in 1916 by B. W. Huebsch. Definitive Text © 1967 by the Estate of James Joyce. Reprinted by permission of Viking Penguin Inc.

KELLER, HELEN "Three Days to See," from the *Atlantic Monthly,* 1933, reprinted by permission of The American Foundation for the Blind, Inc.

KING, FLORENCE "The Niceness Factor" reprinted by permission from the author. Originally appeared in *Harper's* Magazine, August 28, 1981.

KING, MARTIN LUTHER, JR. "I Have A Dream" reprinted by permission of Joan Daves. Copyright © 1963 by Martin Luther King, Jr. Excerpt from pp. 87–93 in "Letter from Birmingham Jail—April 16, 1963" from *Why We Can't Wait* by Martin Luther King, Jr. Copyright © 1963 by Martin Luther King, Jr. Reprinted by permission of Harper & Row, Publishers, Inc.

KOCH, KENNETH "Permanently" reprinted by permission of the author. Copyright 1962 by Kenneth Koch.

KRISHNAMURTI, J. Extract from *Commentaries,* Third Series, pages 142–143, published with the permission of K & R Foundation, Ojai, CA.

676

LASCH, CHRISTOPHER   Extract reprinted from THE CULTURE OF NARCISSISM by Christopher Lasch, by permission of W. W. Norton & Company, Inc. Copyright © 1979 by W. W. Norton & Company, Inc.

LAWRENCE, BARBARA   Extract from "—— Isn't A Dirty Word," © 1973 by The New York Times Company. Reprinted by permission.

LAWRENCE, D. H.   Letter from D. H. Lawrence to Lady Cynthia Asquith, from *The Collected Letters of D. H. Lawrence,* edited by Harry T. Moore. Copyright 1932 by the Estate of D. H. Lawrence, copyright 1934 by Frieda Lawrence, copyright 1933, 1948, 1953, 1954, and each year 1956 through 1962 by Angelo Ravagli and C. Montegue Weekley, Executors of the Estate of Frieda Lawrence Ravagli. "Snake" by D. H. Lawrence from *The Complete Poems of D. H. Lawrence,* edited by Vivian de Sola Pinto and F. Warren Roberts. Copyright © 1964, 1971 by Angelo Ravagli and C. M. Westley, Executors of the Estate of Frieda Lawrence Ravagli. Both reprinted by permission of Viking Penguin Inc.

LECARRE, JOHN   Excerpt from *The Honorable Schoolboy,* by John LeCarre. Copyright © 1977 by Authors Workshop AG. Reprinted by permission of Alfred A. Knopf, Inc.

LE GUIN, URSULA   "The Ones Who Walk Away from Omelas," Copyright © 1973, 1975 by Ursula K. Le Guin; reprinted by permission of the author and the author's agent, Virginia Kidd.

LEWIS, C. S.   Extract reprinted with permission of Macmillan Publishing Co., Inc. and Collins Publishers from "What Christians Believe" in *The Case for Christianity.* Copyright 1943, 1945, 1952 by Macmillan Publishing Co., Inc. Copyrights renewed. Collins Publishers title, *Mere Christianity.*

LEWIS, OSCAR   Excerpt from *Children of Sanchez,* by Oscar Lewis. Copyright © 1961 by Oscar Lewis. Reprinted by permission of Random House, Inc.

MCCALL, BRUCE   Excerpt from "Talking" by Bruce McCall; © The New Yorker Magazine. Reprinted by permission.

MAILER, NORMAN   Excerpt from *Armies of the Night* by Norman Mailer. Copyright © 1968 by Norman Mailer. Reprinted by arrangement with The New American Library, Inc., New York, New York.

MANNES, MARYA   Excerpt from "Miltown Place, or Life with Sponsors," from *The Reporter,* December 1956.

MUFSON, STEVE   "Anatomy of Continuing Pipeline Controversy," *The Wall Street Journal,* August 31, 1982, reprinted by permission of *The Wall Street Journal,* © Dow Jones & Company, Inc. 1982. All Rights Reserved.

NABOKOV, VLADIMIR   Excerpt from *Details of a Sunset and Other Stories* by Vladimir Nabokov. © 1976 by McGraw-Hill International Inc. Reprinted by permission of McGraw-Hill Book Company.

NEWMAN, EDWIN   "O Facilitative New World!" from *Newsweek,* October 5, 1981. Copyright 1981 by Newsweek, Inc. All Rights Reserved. Reprinted by Permission.

New Yorker Staff   "Tableware" from *The Talk of the Town;* © 1981 The New Yorker Magazine, Inc. Reprinted by permission.

ORWELL, GEORGE   Excerpt from "Politics and the English Language," from *The Collected Essays, Journalism and Letters of George Orwell,* Volume 4, copyright © 1968 by Sonia Brownell Orwell. Excerpt from "Why I Write" from *The Collected Essays, Journalism and Letters of George Orwell,* Volume I, copyright © 1968 by Sonia Brownell Orwell. Both reprinted by permission of Harcourt Brace Jovanovich and A. M. Heath & Company Ltd., the Estate of the Late Sonia Brownell Orwell, and Martin Secker & Warburg Ltd.

POIRIER, RICHARD   Excerpt from *The Performing Self: Compositions and Decompositions in the Languages of Contemporary Life* by Richard Poirier. Copyright © 1971 by Oxford University Press, Inc. Reprinted by permission.

PORTER, KATHERINE ANNE   "The Necessary Enemy" from the book *The Collected Essays and Occasional Writings of Katherine Anne Porter.* Copyright © 1948 by Katherine Anne Porter.

Originally published in *Mademoiselle* as "Love and Hate." Reprinted by permission of Delacorte Press/Seymour Lawrence.

POUND, EZRA "In a Station of the Metro," Ezra Pound, *Personae*. Copyright 1926 by Ezra Pound. Reprinted by permission of New Directions Publishing Corporation.

PRICE, JONATHAN "And Still the Best" from *The Best Thing on TV* by Jonathan Price. Copyright © 1978 by Jonathan Price. Reprinted by permission of Viking Penguin Inc.

REGAN, TOM Excerpt from *Matters of Life and Death,* edited by Tom Regan. Copyright © 1980 by Random House, Inc. Reprinted by permission of the publisher.

ROSZAK, THEODORE Excerpt from *The Making of A Counter Culture* by Theodore Roszak. Copyright © 1969 by Theodore Roszak. Reprinted by permission of Doubleday & Company, Inc.

PROUST, MARCEL Excerpt from *Remembrance of Things Past,* Volume 1, by Marcel Proust, translated by C. K. Scott Moncrieff. Copyright 1928 and renewed 1956 by The Modern Library, Inc. Reprinted by permission of Random House, Inc.

SERVAN-SCHREIBER, J. J. J. J. Servan-Schreiber, from *The American Challenge*. English translation copyright © 1968 by Atheneum House, Inc. Reprinted with the permission of Atheneum Publishers.

SCHLESINGER, ARTHUR, JR. Excerpt from *The Bitter Heritage* by Arthur M. Schlesinger, Jr. Copyright © 1966 by Arthur M. Schlesinger, Jr. Reprinted by permission of Houghton Mifflin Company.

SMITH, ADAM "Zen and the Cross-Court Backhand" from *Powers of Mind,* by Adam Smith. Copyright © 1977 by Adam Smith. Reprinted by permission of Random House, Inc.

SONTAG, SUSAN "From *On Photography*" from *On Photography* by Susan Sontag. Copyright ©1973, 1974, 1977 by Susan Sontag.

THOMAS, LEWIS "Debating the Unknowable" reprinted by permission of Harold Ober Associates Incorporated. Copyright © 1981 by Lewis Thomas.

THURBER, JAMES "There's An Owl in My Room" copyright © 1935 by James Thurber. Copyright © 1963 by Helen W. Thurber and Rosemary T. Sauers. From *The Middle-Aged Man on the Flying Trapeze,* published by Harper & Row. "The Split Infinitive" copyright © 1931, 1959 by James Thurber. From *The Owl in the Attic,* published by Harper & Row. Both used by permission of Mrs. James Thurber.

THUROW, LESTER Excerpt from "Getting Serious About Tax Reform" from *The Atlantic,* March 1981, copyright © 1981, by The Atlantic Monthly Company, Boston, Mass. Reprinted with permission of the author.

TILLICH, PAUL "The Lost Dimension in Religion" reprinted from *The Saturday Evening Post*. © 1958 The Curtis Publishing Company. Reprinted by permission.

UPDIKE, JOHN "Beer Can," copyright © 1964 by John Updike. Reprinted from *Assorted Prose,* by John Updike, by permission of Alfred A. Knopf, Inc. Originally appeared in *The New Yorker.*

VAN DER POST, LAURENS Excerpt from pp. 244–246 in *Venture to the Interior* by Laurens van der Post. Copyright 1951 by Laurens van der Post. By permission of William Morrow & Company.

VIDAL, GORE "Drugs" and "Tarzan Revisited," copyright © 1972 by Gore Vidal. Reprinted from *Homage to Daniel Shays: Collected Essays 1952–1972,* by Gore Vidal, by permission of Random House, Inc. Excerpt from "The Holy Family" from *Reflections Upon a Sinking Ship* by Gore Vidal. Copyright © 1967, 1968 by Gore Vidal. By permission of Little, Brown and Company.

WARDWELL, ALLEN Allen Wardwell, "The Sculpture of Polynesia," The Art Institute of Chicago, 1967, p. 9. Reprinted by permission.

WATSON, LYALL Excerpt from *Gifts of Unknown Things*. Copyright © 1976 by Lyall Watson. Reprinted by permission of Simon & Schuster, a Division of Gulf & Western Corporation, and Hodder & Stoughton Limited.

678

Acknowledgments

WEINER, HERBERT   Excerpt from *9½ Mystics* by Herbert Weiner. Copyright © 1969 by Herbert Weiner. Reprinted by permission of Holt, Rinehart and Winston, Publishers.

WHITE, E. B.   "Once More to the Lake" from *Essays of E. B. White* by E. B. White. Copyright 1941 by E. B. White. Reprinted by permission of Harper & Row, Publishers, Inc.

WIESEL, ELIE   Reprinted by permission of Hill and Wang, a division of Farrar, Straus and Giroux, Inc. "From *Night*" from *Night* by Elie Wiesel, translated from the French by Stella Rodway. © Les Editions de Minuit, 1958. English translation © Mac Gibbon & Kee, 1960.

WILLIAMS, WILLIAM CARLOS   "The Great Figure" by William Carlos Williams, *Collected Earlier Poems of William Carlos Williams.* Copyright 1938 by New Directions Publishing Corporation. Reprinted by permission of New Directions Publishing Corporation.

WILSON, EDMUND   "Indian Corn Dance" is from *The American Earthquake* by Edmund Wilson. Copyright © 1958 by Edmund Wilson. Reprinted by permission of Farrar, Straus and Giroux, Inc.

WOLFE, TOM   "The Ringleader" reprinted from *Harper's* Magazine, January 1981, by permission of the author.

WOOD, MICHAEL   Excerpt from *America in the Movies* by Michael Wood, © 1975 by Basic Books, Inc., Publishers, New York. Reprinted by permission.

WOOLF, VIRGINIA   "Professions for Women" and "The Death of the Moth" from *The Death of the Moth and Other Essays* by Virginia Woolf, copyright 1942 by Harcourt Brace Jovanovich, Inc.; renewed 1970 by Marjorie T. Parsons, Executrix. Reprinted by permission of the publisher and The Hogarth Press.

Illustrations: page 389, used by permission of Needham, Harper, and Steers Advertising, Inc.; page 394, contributed by the Chemical Manufacturers Association; page 395, BMW of North America, Inc.

Index

Index

Index

Index of
Readings
For Exercises

Index of Readings for Exercises

Handbook References

GRAMMAR